WEMBLEY H

AS Level and A Level
Applied ICT
Brian Sargent and Graham Brown

CAMBRIDGE
UNIVERSITY PRESS

CAMBRIDGE UNIVERSITY PRESS

Cambridge, New York, Melbourne, Madrid, Cape Town, Singapore,
São Paulo, Delhi

Cambridge University Press
The Edinburgh Building, Cambridge CB2 8RU, UK

www.cambridge.org
Information on this title: www.cambridge.org/9780521717649

First published 2008
Reprinted 2008

Printed in the United Kingdom at the University Press, Cambridge

A catalogue record for this publication is available from the British Library

ISBN   978-0-521-71764-9 paperback

ACKNOWLEDGEMENTS
Cover image: © Dennis Hallinan/Alamy

Every effort has been made to reach copyright holders of material in this book
previously published elsewhere. The publisher would be pleased to hear from
anyone whose rights they have unwittingly infringed.

Contents

Acknowledgements

Thanks to the following for assistance, patience, understanding and proofreading: Janine Sargent, Catherine Sargent, Elizabeth Sargent, Tracy Brown, Philippa Brown, Laura Brown, Jenna Brown, Karla Brown, John Reeves, Stuart Morris, Robert Ross, Chris Scott, Udoka Ogbue, Dave Watson, Keith Chandler, Dan Bray and Kate Gentles.

Letters used with page numbers: b, *bottom of the page;* l, *left-hand side of the page;* c, *centre of the page;* r, *right-hand side of the page;* t, *top of the page. These letters are also used in combination.*

Cover: Dennis Hallinan/Alamy; p. 1(*l*) German Ariel Berra/Shutterstock; p. 1(*r*) www.theworldofstuff.com; p. 2(*tl*) InstinctDesign/Shutterstock; p. 2(*bl*) Cambium Learning Technologies; p. 2(*tr*) David Brimm/Shutterstock; p. 2(*br*) Bet Noire/Shutterstock; p. 3(*l*) Adam Borowski/Shutterstock; p. 3(*r*) © Kensington Computer Products Group; p. 4(*tl*) Komplett; p. 4(*bl*) silver-john/Shutterstock; p. 4(*r*) Craig Berhorst/Shutterstock; p. 5(*tl*) David R. Frazier/Science Photo Library; p. 5(*bl*) Cambridge University Press; p. 5(*r*) Petr Rehor/Shutterstock; p. 6(*l*), 52 David Pearson/Alamy; p. 6(*r*) Michael Ransburg/Shutterstock; p. 7(*l*) 0833379753/Shutterstock; p. 7(*r*) Tommy Ingberg/Shutterstock; p. 8 Martyn F. Chillmaid/Science Photo Library; p. 9(*tl*) Musikhaus Thomann; p. 9(*bl*) Wacom Technology Corporation; p. 9(*r*) © MagTek Inc.; p. 10(*tl*) Sekonic Corporation; p. 10(*bl*) Access IS; p. 10(*tr*) Voznikervich Konstantine/Shutterstock; p. 10(*cr*) Pastushenko Taras/Shutterstock; p. 10(*bc*) Motorola Inc.; p. 10(*br*) Wikipedia; p. 11(*tl*) Joanna Zopoth-Lipiejko/Shutterstock; p. 11(*bl*) Dimitar Janevski/Shutterstock; p. 11(*r*) Feng Yu/Shutterstock; p. 12(*l*) Dmitry Rukhlenko/Shutterstock; p. 12(*tr*) Helene Rogers/Alamy; p. 12(*br*) Tom Kinsbergen/Science Photo Library; p. 13 Helene Rogers/Alamy; p. 14(*tl*) Utemov Alexey/Shutterstock; p. 14(*bl*) CRD Devices/Hiwin; p. 14(*tr, br*) Andrew Lambert Photography/Science Photo Library; p. 15(*tl*) Leslie Garland Picture Library/Alamy; p. 15(*bl*) Alibaba Inc.; p. 15(*tr*) In-Finity/Shutterstock; p. 15(*br*) Stefan Glebowski/Shutterstock; p. 16(*l*) 869047242/Shutterstock; p. 16(*r*) Vankina/Shutterstock; pp. 17, 18(*tl*) Imation; p. 18(*bl*) R. Mackay Photography/Shutterstock; p. 18(*r*) Pchemyan Georgiy/Shutterstock; p. 19(*l*) Popovici Ioan/Shutterstock; p. 19(*r*) alysta/Shutterstock; p. 20(*l*) Nelson Hale/Shutterstock; p. 20(*r*) 7505811966/Shutterstock; p. 21(*l*) Yevgen Timashov/Shutterstock; p. 21(*r*) Szymon Apanowicz/Shutterstock; p. 24 Pascal Goetgheluck/Science Photo Library; p.25 www.osha.gov; p. 27 Ian Shaw/Alamy; p. 29(*t*) WiredRed UK Ltd; p. 29(*b*) Ace Stock Limited/Alamy; p. 30 Randall Schwanke/Shutterstock; p. 31 howstuffworks.com website; p. 35 International Paper Knowledge Centre http//:glossary.ippaper.com; pp. 41, 68, 69(*b*) Moneysoft Ltd; pp. 45, 127(*bl, r*) © Crown copyright www.direct.gov.uk; pp. 47(*l*), 102 images courtesy of Tesco Stores Ltd, Cheshunt, Herts.; p. 47(*r*), 48 © 2007 Amazon.com Inc. and its affiliates. All rights reserved; pp. 49, 50 © HSBC Holding plc (2008); p. 51(*l*) Adam Lubroth/Getty Images; p. 51(*r*) Peter Menzel/Science Photo Library; p. 56 Cordelia Molloy/Science Photo Library; p. 59 © Open Ergonomics Ltd; p. 83 © Crown copyright 2008 The Met Office; p. 87 source: Hamburg educational server, modified by Elmar Uherek for the ACCENT Global Change Magazine; p. 88(*l*) image courtesy of Evans & Sutherland, Salt Lake City, UT. All rights reserved. Used by permission; p. 88(*r*) NADS, University of Iowa, photo by Shawn Allen; p. 99(*l*) © Crown copyright www.nhsdirect.nhs.uk; p. 99(*r*) Simon Frazer/Science Photo Library; p. 101(*l*) Disability Access In Action; p. 101(*r*) www.microsoft.com; p. 104 Legalhelpers Ltd; p. 106 Deschutes County Government; p. 109 Symantec Corporation;

p. 110(*t*) Neo Edmund/Shutterstock; p. 110(*bl*) Martin Muransky/Shutterstock; p. 110 (*bc*) Grin Maria/Shutterstock; p. 110(*br*) Dmitry Pistrov/Shutterstock; p. 111(*l*) Tom Uhlenberg/Shutterstock; p. 111(*c*) pandapaw/Shutterstock; p. 111(*r*) Francoise Sauze/Science Photo Library; p. 115 eBay; pp. 116, 117 EgyptAir; p. 119 Radiant Systems; p. 122(*t*) University of Cambridge; p. 122(*b*) University of Manchester; p. 123(*l*) Friends of the Earth (England, Wales and Northern Ireland); p. 123(*r*) © Crown copyright www.hmrc.gov.uk; p. 124(*tl, bl*) Gujarat Chamber of Commerce & Industry; p. 124(*r*) Waltham Forest Council; p. 126(*l*) © Crown copyright www.ips.gov.uk; pp.126(*r*), 127(*tl*) www.nadra.gov.pk; p. 133 Chepko Danil Vitalevich/Shutterstock; p. 134(*l*) AdventNet Inc.; p. 134(*r*) dwphotos/Shutterstock; p. 135(*bl*) Wayne Johnson/Shutterstock; p. 135(*tl*) Georgios Alexandris/Shutterstock; p. 135(*tc*) Giphotostock/Science Photo Library; p. 135(*tr*) Hugh Threlfall/Alamy; p. 135(*br*) Psycho/Shutterstock; p. 136(*l*) Marc Dietrich/ Shutterstock; p. 136(*tr*) Omega; pp. 136(*br*), 137 Florida Centre for Instructional Technology, University of Southern Florida; p. 140(*bl*) Intel Corporation; p. 140(*bc*) Rob Bouwman/Shutterstock; p. 140(*tr, cr*) Natalia Siverina/Shutterstock; p. 140(*br*) Bob Ainsworth/Shuttestock; pp. 160, 161 Google.

Examination questions in Chapters 1–7 reproduced by permission of the University of Cambridge Local Examinations Syndicate.

Microsoft product screenshots reprinted with permission from Microsoft Corporation.

Copyright images used in source-data files: Boarder.jpg – Jenna Brown; JetSki.jpg – Tracy Brown; Large.jpg – Philippa Brown; Small.jpg – Philippa Brown; Power.jpg – Tracy Brown; Yacht.jpg – Chris Scott.

Introduction

Aims

This book has been written to provide the knowledge, understanding and practical skills that you need for the Cambridge International Examinations Advanced Level and Advanced Subsidiary Level in Applied Information and Communication Technology. In particular, the book, together with the accompanying CD provides:

- practice examination questions for the theory elements of the A Level course
- practice tasks which offer guidance on how to answer questions for the practical elements of the A Level course
- activities which allow students practice in answering questions for the practical elements of the A Level course
- practice source data files for the tasks and activities
- hints and tips for the written and practical examination papers
- teacher's notes, suggesting possible teaching methods.

Although it has been written with the CIE syllabus in mind, it can also be used as a useful reference text for other practical Applied ICT qualifications at AS Level, A Level and other equivalent Level 3 courses.

Using the book

The text is in 16 chapters. Although it is possible that some elements of the practical chapters may be examined in the theory question papers, and vice versa, the sections for the AS Level examinations are:

- Chapters **1–4** cover the theory work
- Chapters **8–14** cover the practical work.

For the A2 Level examinations:

- Chapters **1–7** cover the theory work
- Chapters **8–17** cover the practical work.

Symbols used

Throughout the book there are a number of elements. These are described below, in the style in which they are presented in the text, if appropriate.

Examination questions

These are examination-style questions at the end of each theory chapter for students to answer. Model answers are available in portable document format (.pdf) on the CD. These answers also include a detailed breakdown of the mark scheme, in a similar format to that used for the AS and A Level examinations.

 Hint These give hints, tips, shortcuts and advice on examination techniques.

Tasks

These are examination-style questions in the practical section (which often include the use of source files from the CD for the practical tasks) that are answered within the chapter. The text demonstrates the techniques used to solve the task and gives some example answers. These provide easy-to-follow step-by-step instructions, so that practical skills are developed alongside the knowledge and understanding.

Activities

Text colours

Some words or phrases within the text are printed in red. Definitions of these terms can be found in the glossary.

In the practical section, other words may appear in blue to indicate an action or location found within the software package, for example 'Select the File menu from the toolbar.'

Words found in green have different meanings, depending on whether the chapter is dealing with databases or spreadsheets:

- In chapters on databases, they are used for the names of fields or the fieldname and the table name, for example the PayNumber field in the Employees table, or the field Employees.PayNumber.
- In chapters on spreadsheets, they are used to show the functions or formulae entered into the cell of a spreadsheet, for example a cell may contain the function =CONCATENATE(B2,C2).

Hardware and software used

The practical elements of the examinations can be undertaken on any hardware platform and using any appropriate software packages. For the purposes of this book, we have needed to choose specific software packages, but the functionality of many other packages is very similar. Many of the skills demonstrated in Chapters **8** to **17** are transferable and can be easily adapted for other hardware and software platforms.

All the tasks and activities within the practical chapters have therefore been created using a PC platform with *Microsoft Windows XP* operating system and include the use of *Windows Paint* and *Notepad*. Independent packages used for the practical sections include packages from *Microsoft Office Professional Edition 2003*, including *Word*, *Excel*, *Access*, *PowerPoint*, *Publisher* and *Visual Basic for Applications*. *Internet Explorer* has been used as the web browser and *Microsoft Hotmail* as a web-based e-mail editor.

Using source files

Source files can be found on the CD and will need to be copied onto your local machine or network drive in order to use them with read/write access. This is essential to ensure that you can use some of the file types included on the CD. For example, you cannot create queries or reports in *Access* when working from the CD. The CD will contain all source files in a series of sub-folders.

PC users

Open **My Computer** and locate the CD drive, which may be called drive D: or E:, and so on. For the purposes of this section, we will assume that it is called drive D:. If your machine has a different drive for the CD letter, adapt these instructions accordingly. Locate the source_files folder, which can be found at D:\ICT\source_files. To locate an individual file, such as the image Boarder.jpg used in Chapter 10, use the path D:\ICT\source_files\chapter_10\Boarder.jpg.

It may be better to copy the contents of this folder into a new folder on your local machine or network drive. Open each file as you wish to use it and use the File menu followed by Save As... to save a new copy with an amended filename. You may need to change the file permissions of these files to read/write to enable you work on them; however, check with your network administrator before attempting to make these changes.

MAC users

Double click on the CD icon on the desktop. Use *Finder* to navigate to the location for the new folder, then create a new folder (Apple+<Shift>+N). With *Finder*, choose the CD and select all files (Apple+A) and copy them (Apple+C). Go to new folder using *Finder* and paste the files (Apple+V).

Changing the source files to match your regional settings

The source .csv (comma separated value) files supplied on the CD have commas as separators between fields and full stops within currency values. If your regional settings for these values are different to these (for example, if you use commas within currency values rather than full stops and your software settings require you to use semicolons for separators between fields) then the source-data files will need to be edited for use with the regional settings for your software. This process may be required to convert the source data files before the start of the practical examinations. There are two easy methods of converting these files, using *Word* and *Excel*. Before attempting to use these methods, make sure that you have a backup of the source files.

```
BoatID, Title, Forename, Surname, Add 1, Add 2, Add 3, Postcode, Make, Type
2, Mr, Shahad, Sharreif, 12 Brain Lane, Pompey, Rustic, PO14 7QT, Sealine 218,
Power
7, Mr, Li, Kwong, The Cricketers, Saffron Lane, Bilsby, BR11 7EE, Kawasaki Zxi
1100, Jet Ski
14, Mr, Abisayo, Akinlade, Heaths End, Stir Lane, Bromsford, BR3 8YT, Seeker 31,
Yacht
15, Miss, Philippa, Brown, 15 Tree Tops, Hills Road, Bromsford, BR6 8TD,
Macwester Rowan Crown, Yacht
23, Mrs, Mei Mei, Han, The Jays, Tall Trees, Skipley, BR20 1LL, Jaguar 25, Yacht
30, Mrs, Jenny, Kwong, 14 The Close, Hills Road, Bromsford, BR6 8UL, Ta Yang,
Yacht
42, Mr, Jeremy, Smith, Pintsize, Bent Lane, Bromsford, BR6 8KH, Contessa 32,
Yacht
43, Mr, Ian, McGregor, Fairview, Tall Trees, Skipley, BR20 1LT, Bavaria 32,
Yacht
50, Mr, Kapil, Patel, 13 Acacia Avenue, Shrub End, Havering, TT7 8TT, Sealine
218, Power
```

```
BoatID; Title; Forename; Surname; Add 1; Add 2; Add 3; Postcode; Make; Type
2; Mr; Shahad; Sharreif; 12 Brain Lane; Pompey; Rustic; PO14 7QT; Sealine 218;
Power
7; Mr; Li; Kwong; The Cricketers; Saffron Lane; Bilsby; BR11 7EE; Kawasaki Zxi
1100; Jet Ski
14; Mr; Abisayo; Akinlade; Heaths End; Stir Lane; Bromsford; BR3 8YT; Seeker 31;
Yacht
15; Miss; Philippa; Brown; 15 Tree Tops; Hills Road; Bromsford; BR6 8TD;
Macwester Rowan Crown; Yacht
23; Mrs; Mei Mei; Han; The Jays; Tall Trees; Skipley; BR20 1LL; Jaguar 25; Yacht
30; Mrs; Jenny; Kwong; 14 The Close; Hills Road; Bromsford; BR6 8UL; Ta Yang;
Yacht
42; Mr; Jeremy; Smith; Pintsize; Bent Lane; Bromsford; BR6 8KH; Contessa 32;
Yacht
43; Mr; Ian; McGregor; Fairview; Tall Trees; Skipley; BR20 1LT; Bavaria 32;
Yacht
50; Mr; Kapil; Patel; 13 Acacia Avenue; Shrub End; Havering; TT7 8TT; Sealine
218; Power
```

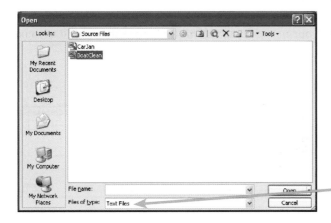

Converting .csv files using Word

1 Open the .csv file in *Word* using File and Open.
2 Make sure that the Files of type: box displays All Files so that the csv files will be visible within the list of available files.

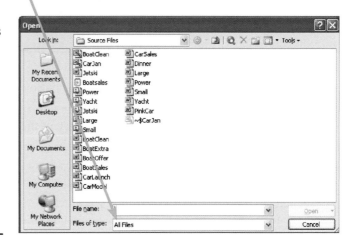

3 Select the .csv file that you wish to convert; for this example, choose the file BoatClean and then click on [Open ▾]. This will open the file, which will look similar to this.
4 Select the Edit menu, then Replace….
5 Enter a , (comma) into the Find what: area.

6 Enter a ; (semicolon) into the Replace with: area.
7 Click on [Replace All].
8 Repeat Steps 4 to 7, replacing a . (full stop) with a , (comma). All the characters will have been replaced within the file like this.
9 Save the file with the same file name using File, then Save, or using the 🖫 button from the standard toolbar. This will ensure that the file is saved in .csv format.

Converting .csv files using Excel

1 Open the .csv file in *Excel* using File, then Open….
2 Make sure that the Files of type: box displays Text Files so that the .csv files will be visible within the list of available files.

3 Select the .csv file that you wish to convert; for this example choose the file BoatClean and then select 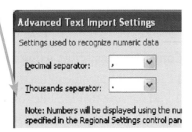 Open ▾. As the file opens, because the file format does not match the regional settings all of the data will appear in column A.

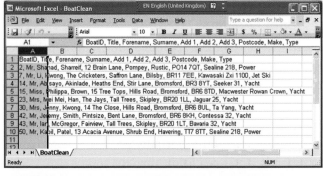

4 Select column A by clicking the left mouse button here. ———————————————→

5 Select the **Data** menu, then **Text to Columns….** This opens the **Convert Text to Columns Wizard**.

6 In the **Original data type** section, click on the radio button for **Delimited**. ———

7 Click on **Next >** to move to the next step of the wizard.

8 The file structure for .csv uses commas as the separators (delimiters), so you must change the **Delimiters** section from the default **Tab** setting (by removing the tick) to a **Comma** setting (by adding a tick to the tick box).

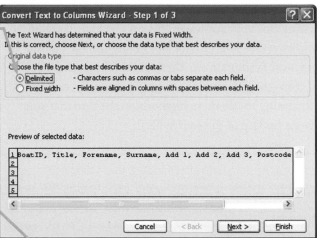

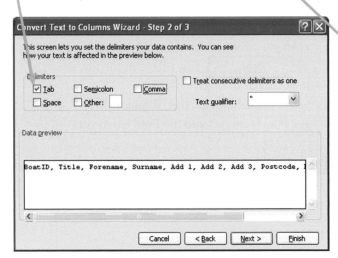

9 The vertical lines have replaced the commas to show that these are now separate columns within the spreadsheet. Click on **Next >** .

10 Click on the **Advanced…** button to change the settings for the numeric data, especially the decimal separator and separator for the thousands in larger numbers. The settings can be changed by using the drop-down lists. In this example, the settings are correct for the regional setting on this machine which is set to Spanish (Argentina).

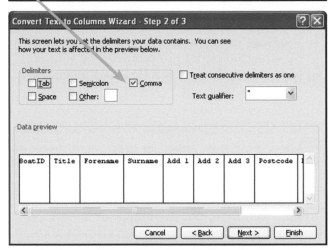

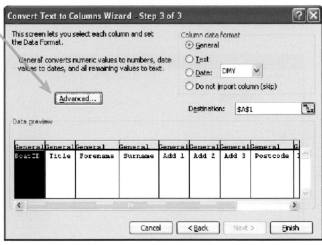

11 Click on **OK**, then **Finish**. All the characters will have been replaced within the file like this. ────────▶

12 Save the file with the same filename using File, then Save, or using the 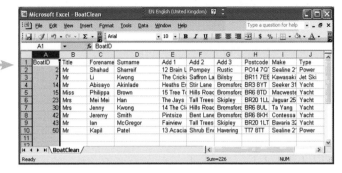 icon from the standard toolbar. This will ensure that the file is saved in .csv format. This window will appear. ────

13 Select **Yes** to save the file.

Microsoft Excel

BoatClean.csv may contain features that are not compatible with CSV (Comma delimited). Do you want to keep the workbook in this format?

• To keep this format, which leaves out any incompatible features, click Yes.
• To preserve the features, click No. Then save a copy in the latest Excel format.
• To see what might be lost, click Help.

[Yes] [No] [Help]

	BoatID	Title	Forename	Surname	Add 1	Add 2	Add 3	Postcode	Make	Type
1	BoatID	Title	Forename	Surname	Add 1	Add 2	Add 3	Postcode	Make	Type
2	2	Mr	Shahad	Sharreif	12 Brain L	Pompey	Rustic	PO14 7Q'	Sealine 2'	Power
3	7	Mr	Li	Kwong	The Crick	Saffron La	Bilsby	BR11 7EE	Kawasaki	Jet Ski
4	14	Mr	Abisayo	Akinlade	Heaths E	Stir Lane	Bromsforc	BR3 8YT	Seeker 31	Yacht
5	15	Miss	Philippa	Brown	15 Tree T	Hills Road	Bromsforc	BR6 8TD	Macweste	Yacht
6	23	Mrs	Mei Mei	Han	The Jays	Tall Trees	Skipley	BR20 1LL	Jaguar 25	Yacht
7	30	Mrs	Jenny	Kwong	14 The Cl	Hills Road	Bromsforc	BR6 8UL	Ta Yang	Yacht
8	42	Mr	Jeremy	Smith	Pintsize	Bent Lane	Bromsforc	BR6 8KH	Contessa	Yacht
9	43	Mr	Ian	McGregor	Fairview	Tall Trees	Skipley	BR20 1LT	Bavaria 3	Yacht
10	50	Mr	Kapil	Patel	13 Acacia	Shrub En	Havering	TT7 8TT	Sealine 2'	Power
11										

1 ICT systems

You already understand the terms:

➤ hardware and software
➤ input and output
➤ storage.

In this chapter you will learn how to identify:

➤ a range of input devices and their features
➤ suitable uses of the input devices, stating the advantages and disadvantages of each
➤ a range of output devices and their features
➤ suitable uses of the output devices, stating the advantages and disadvantages of each
➤ a range of storage devices and their features
➤ suitable uses of the storage devices, stating the advantages and disadvantages of each
➤ a range of portable communication devices and their features
➤ suitable uses of the portable communication devices, stating the advantages and disadvantages of each.

1.1 Input devices

These are devices that are used to input data into the computer. There is a variety of such devices, from the common mouse and keyboard to the more specialised devices such as barcode readers and magnetic ink character readers, as well as the type of input devices used in computer control. These will all be described in this section.

Computer keyboards

The computer keyboard is the most common input device. It is used for inputting text and instructions using a number of software applications. As well as text, numbers, punctuation marks and symbols that are entered using the keyboard, there are some very important keys such as the Control (Ctrl), Alt, Shift, Tab, Enter, Function and cursor arrow keys. You will see more of their use in the practical chapters (Chapters **8–17**).

The QWERTY keyboard pictured above (so-called because these are the first letters along the top line of letter keys) is the most common keyboard but it is not the easiest to use. Because the earliest keyboards were designed for use in mechanical typewriters the most frequently used keys were deliberately kept apart so that the keys would not jam. A much more efficient layout is seen in the DVORAK keyboard, named after its inventor. It is much easier to use than the QWERTY version but because the vast majority of computer users are used to using the QWERTY keyboard the DVORAK is unlikely to increase in use.

Ergonomic keyboards, sometimes called ergonometric keyboards, are a recent invention. Because more and more people are

becoming frequent users of computers an increase in repetitive strain injury (RSI) has become apparent. These keyboards are shaped so that the user is less likely to suffer from RSI.

Another type of keyboard is the overlay or concept keyboard. This usually consists of an A4-sized tray that can have an overlay sheet in it. The overlay sheet can consist of boxes with phrases in, letters of the alphabet, numbers or other symbols. It is used by people who may have disabilities, as it is easier to press a large symbol than to press the key on the keyboard.

Uses

- Keyboards are used to input text, for example into a word-processed document. There are other devices used for copying text, so keyboards tend to be used where the text concerned is original and is entered directly by the author of the document. Examples of such documents are letters, business documents, user guides etc.
- Keyboards are also used to type commands into a computer, for example pressing the control (Ctrl) key at the same time as pressing X (to cut selected text) or C (to copy the selected text) or V (to paste the selected text).
- They are also used to type in unusual selections of characters, such as passwords.

Advantages:
- They allow accurate entry of data, in combination with a monitor to check accuracy.
- They allow quick entry of original text.
- They are robust devices.
- Concept keyboards are helpful to people with disabilities.

Disadvantages:
- Conventional keyboards can be difficult for people with disabilities to use.
- They are not very quick for inputting data compared with direct data entry devices such as barcode readers, and magnetic ink character recognition (MICR) and optical mark recognition (OMR) devices.
- They take up more space than other input devices.

Numeric keypads

A numeric keypad is used specifically to enter numbers, although alphabetic characters can be entered by using the function key.

Uses

They are used in situations where only digits have to be entered, for example:

- at electronic point of sale (EPOS) terminals, where they are very useful when a barcode is damaged; when this happens, the checkout operator can key in the number using the numeric keypad
- with automated teller machines (ATMs)
- on mobile phones
- when delegates at a conference need to record their responses to questions
- when inserting personal identification numbers (PINs), such as for chip and PIN credit/debit cards.

Advantages:
- They are small and compact and can be carried easily.
- Many devices can be connected to the same computer at conventions.
- They are easy to cover up when entering a PIN.

Disadvantages:
- It is difficult to enter text.
- They can be too small for the numbers to be used effectively.

Mice

A mouse is a pointing device. It is moved by the user in order to control the position of a pointer on the computer screen. It consists of a small plastic case, held under the user's hands, and normally has two buttons, although Apple® computers use a one-button mouse. Inside the case can be a ball, which allows the mouse to glide over the desk surface it is being used on. However, an increasingly popular type of mouse is the optical mouse, which relies on movement being detected using reflected light, rather than by using the movement of a ball. It has no moving parts, which means less damage through regular use, unlike mechanical mice, which can fail due to dirt getting inside the mouse. Mechanical mice also require a special surface, such as a mouse pad, which optical mice do not. A further development has been the introduction of cordless mice, which need a transmitter and a receiver. The transmitter is based in the mouse, while the receiver is usually a separate device that is sometimes similar in appearance to a memory stick and fits into a universal serial bus (USB) port on the computer. Most mice also have scroll buttons so that documents can be moved through quickly.

Uses

- Mice are used to move the pointer on the screen as well as for selecting items such as check boxes, radio buttons and options from a drop-down menu.
- They can be used to draw objects in drawing and art packages.

Advantages:

- They allow faster entry of the chosen option, compared with typing on a keyboard.
- They allow fast navigation through slideshows/ websites.
- They are smaller and more compact than keyboards.

Disadvantages:

- They can be difficult to use for people with disabilities.
- They can be damaged fairly easily.
- They can be difficult to use for entering data other than choices on a menu, radio buttons or by means of hyperlinks.

Touchpads

A touchpad is incorporated into most laptops and is meant to simulate the use of the mouse. It usually has two buttons close to it, similar to a mouse, but these tend to be sunk below the level of the touchpad itself. The user touches the touchpad with a finger and by gently tapping it can make choices on menus, and so on. By keeping the finger in contact with the touchpad and moving the finger around, the user can control the pointer on the screen.

Uses

On a laptop a touchpad can be used in much the same way as a mouse is with a desktop computer. It can be used to move the pointer on the screen as well as for selecting items such as check boxes, radio buttons and options from a drop-down menu.

Advantages:

- They allow faster entry of the chosen option compared with typing on a keyboard.
- They allow fast navigation through slideshows/ websites.
- They are integrated within the laptop computer and don't have to be plugged in.

Disadvantages:

- People with disabilities can find them difficult to use.
- Many users find them difficult to control compared to a mouse.
- They can be difficult to use for entering data other than menu choices, radio buttons or by means of hyperlinks.

Tracker balls

A tracker ball is an upside-down mouse-like device. It has been designed for users who have limited ability regarding movement of their fingers or hands. The key feature is the large ball in the middle of the device that is controlled by using the palm of the hand and enables the user to control the pointer on a screen. There are also a number of buttons, depending on the application. There are usually three, with two tending to be used in the same way as the left-and right-click buttons on a mouse, while the third button is usually used instead of a double click. As it is stationary, it is useful where the user has limited motor skills or where there is a lack of space.

Uses

- They can used for any application by people with disabilities or RSI where the use of a mouse would be too difficult.
- They are used in control applications where objects on a screen are used to control a process.
- Pilots on fast ferry ships and air traffic controllers use them to control the appearance of radar screens and their contents.

Advantages:

- They do not require the fine control that a mouse does.
- They are easier for people with disabilities or RSI to use.
- They can be more accurate when positioning the pointer on a screen.
- They are fixed, so they cannot be knocked accidentally (for example, onto the floor, where a disabled person could have problems retrieving them).

Disadvantages:

- It is difficult to enter data that the button has not been programmed for.
- They can be slower for selecting options compared with using a mouse.

Video digitisers

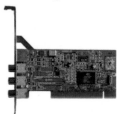

A video digitiser is used to input video to a computer from a television or video camera. In order for the computer to be able to handle the resulting images the video has to be converted from analogue to digital using the digitiser. Video digitisers are usually video cards that are fitted into your computer.

Remote controls

A remote control is used to control other devices remotely by emitting an infrared signal to the external device. Buttons are pressed to choose different options such as selecting channels on the television or radio, changing the sound volume, setting times for recordings, and much more. Remote controls are small, so that they can be held in the hand, and wireless, communicating with the device by means of infrared signals.

Uses

They are mainly used with home-entertainment devices such as televisions, satellite boxes, video / digital versatile disk (DVD) recorders and stereo systems.

Advantages:

- They can be any distance from the device and still operate it.
- People who have difficulty walking find it easier to control devices.

Disadvantages:

- People with disabilities or RSI can find it difficult to use.
- If somebody or an object comes between the remote control and the device, the device can no longer be controlled remotely.

Joysticks

A joystick carries out similar functions to the mouse and tracker ball. It consists of a stick that is gripped by the hand and moved around and buttons that can be used to select options. The stick is used to control the cursor, pointer or other objects on the screen. Generally, the stick is used to move people or other objects around a screen and the buttons for firing weapons or increasing/decreasing speed.

Uses

- They are used with video/computer games.
- They are used in the training of airline pilots to control various aspects of flying an aircraft.

Advantages:

- They allow faster entry of the chosen option compared with typing on a keyboard.
- They can be used to control objects in three dimensions.

Disadvantages:

- They can be difficult to use for entering data other than menu choices, radio buttons or by means of hyperlinks.
- It is more difficult to control the pointer than other windows, icons, menu and pointer (WIMP) input devices.

Touch screens

Despite their appearance, these are input devices. The user can choose from options on the screen simply by pressing the option on the screen with a finger or a stylus. There are normally icons on the screen representing buttons as well as arrows to move backwards and forwards through screens.

Uses

They are used in many applications, including:

- ATMs by bank customers
- EPOS terminals in cafes and other retail outlets, with buttons on the screen representing prices for products
- tourist-information kiosks and for public-transport enquiries
- personal digital assistants (PDAs), for choosing options and handwriting recognition
- interactive whiteboards in education.

Advantages:

- They allow faster entry of the chosen option compared with typing on a keyboard.
- It is easier to select options than by using a mouse.
- People with disabilities can find them easier to use.
- There is less likelihood of selecting a wrong option.

Disadvantages:

- It can be difficult to enter data other than from a list/set of options.
- The screen is fairly firm, so RSI could result from continual use of a finger to select options.

Magnetic strip readers

As the name implies, a magnetic strip (or stripe) reader is used to read information from magnetic strips found on plastic cards. The strip normally has three tracks containing information, although track 3 is often unused. The information stored in a track depends on the card's use. In banking, the second track contains the account details such as account number, sort code, expiry date and issue number or start date.

Uses

- They can be used anywhere a payment is made using a bank or credit card, such as:
  - ◇ in bank ATMs
  - ◇ as part of electronic funds transfer at point of sale (EFTPOS) terminals in supermarkets and other types of shops and restaurants.
- In security, they are used to prevent unauthorised access to restricted buildings or hotel rooms.

Advantages:

- They allow faster entry of data compared with typing on a keyboard.
- Data entry is more accurate than with a keyboard.
- Data entry is more secure than with a keyboard.
- Their use prevents entry to restricted areas without a card.

Disadvantages:

- If the strip is damaged, data has to be entered manually, resulting in loss of speed at EFTPOS terminals.
- If the strip is damaged or the card is lost, the holder cannot gain access to the building or hotel room.

Smart card readers

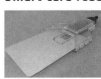

Smart cards are often referred to as chip cards. They are similar in appearance to a magnetic strip card, but information is stored on a chip on the card. This can be used for storing a PIN and/or other personal data. The chip can be updated and so, in the case of a payment card, can be used to store the amount of money left on the card. Debit and credit cards do not store the amount of money left on the card as they can be used without a reader (e.g. paying in a telephone transaction); in this case, the money in the account would not match the amount stored in the chip. Other types of smart card serve as loyalty cards, with the number of loyalty points being updated on the chip when a customer uses the loyalty card to buy goods at a shop.

These cards have greater memory storage and security of data than a magnetic strip card. They can also process data on the card.

Uses

- Smart cards are used as payment cards (e.g. phone cards), loyalty cards, identification cards and public transport tickets.

- They are used with satellite broadcasters to decode television programmes.
- They are used with subscriber identification modules (SIMs) in mobile telephones.
- They are used as electronic passports and in driving licences.

Advantages:

- They allow immediate updating, thereby preventing fraud.
- The cards do not need to be in immediate contact with the reader and so receive less damage through regular use.
- Data entry is more secure than using a magnetic strip.
- Their use prevents entry to restricted areas without a card.

Disadvantages:

- If the card is lost the owner loses a proportion, if not all of the money value of the card.
- There is a lot of information on some cards – if the card is stolen, hackers can use it for fraudulent purposes and identity theft.

Chip and PIN readers

These are a type of smart card reader, but tend to be used only at EFTPOS terminals. There are a number of versions of these readers.

For example, the combined PIN pad and chip reader does not have a magnetic strip reader. This device has a slot for inserting the chip card manually, a keypad for entering the PIN and a small display to show instructions and indicate progress of the transaction.

Some chip and PIN readers have a separate magnetic strip reader slot, either down one side or across the top or bottom of the reader. The data on the chip contains much the same information as is to be found in the strip on a magnetic strip card. It contains account information, but, more importantly, contains the PIN (personal identification number). The card cannot be used unless the person knows the PIN.

Uses

Chip and PIN readers are used wherever a payment needs to be made; for example, in restaurants, supermarkets, shops of all descriptions, travel agents and banks.

Advantages:

- They allow secure transactions to take place, as without the PIN the transaction cannot proceed.
- They save time in the transaction compared with using cash or cheques.
- Chips are more robust than magnetic strips.

Disadvantages:

- If the customer forgets their PIN, the transaction has to be cancelled.
- The card holder needs to be very careful to protect their PIN when using their card.

Scanners

Scanners are used to enter hard-copy images into a computer. The most common type is the flatbed scanner, where the user places the document flat on a glass panel and closes the lid. An array of sensors and a light source move underneath the document, producing a scanned image that can then be manipulated using drawing packages. If the document being scanned is text, the scanner can also be used with optical character recognition (OCR) software. This produces text suitable for use in other software packages such as word processors, desktop-publishing and presentation software, and spreadsheet and database packages. Another type of flatbed scanner is that used in supermarkets for reading barcodes. There are also handheld scanners, but other than being used as relatively portable barcode readers they are not used greatly.

Uses

- Scanners are used to scan documents that can be converted into text-based documents using OCR software.
- They are used to scan old documents for keeping records; for example, birth, death and wedding certificates.
- They are used to scan images that can be transferred as faxes.

- Photographers use scanners to obtain digital images of photographs. Not all photographers use digital cameras and even those that do, still have many photographs in their collection which were produced using a traditional form of camera.
- They are used as barcode readers.

Advantages:

- Scanners allow images to be stored for further editing.
- Using OCR on printed documents saves time compared with typing the text in again.
- Using a barcode scanner is quicker than typing in the barcode.

Disadvantages:

- The accuracy of reproduction is limited.

Digital cameras

Digital cameras are now being used far more frequently than traditional cameras. They are used in exactly the same way, i.e. by pointing the camera at the subject and clicking when the settings are satisfactory. Photographs can be deleted if they are not quite what was wanted and the photograph can then be retaken. The major difference is that the camera can be connected directly to a computer and photographs uploaded to a photo library on the user's computer. Alternatively, software packages such as photo-editing packages are used to manipulate the photographs; for example, cropping, resizing or recolouring them. Many digital cameras can also be connected directly to photo printers for immediate printing. Most cameras have the capacity to store many photos and the number can be increased by adding an additional memory card, which can then be temporarily removed from the camera and inserted directly into a PC. Digital cameras can also take short videos.

Uses

- They are used by professional photographers in their work and by amateur photographers for personal use.
- They are used to insert photographs directly into all types of software, including presentation software, word processors, desktop-publishing software and database software.

Advantages:

- Digital cameras produce better quality photographs than a traditional camera.
- It is quicker to upload a number of images than to scan them in.
- It is quicker to upload images than to have a film developed.
- A memory card can hold more images than a roll of film.

Disadvantages:

- They are more expensive than traditional cameras.
- Batteries need changing more often than with traditional cameras.

Microphones

Microphones can be connected directly to the computer. They are used to input sounds, which can then be stored and manipulated. The sound input to the microphone is converted into an analogue electrical signal, which has to be converted in turn into a digital signal so that the computer can process it. This is usually done by the computer's sound card, which acts as an analogue-to-digital converter.

Uses

- Microphones are used most often to input speech for incorporation as a voiceover in slide shows or in web pages.
- They are used to input dictated text for use with voice recognition software. The software is used to convert the speech into text so that it can be used with other software packages such as word processors.

Advantages:

- Changes to the sound/voice can be done in real time rather than recording it and inputting the recording.
- It is quicker to input text by speaking into the microphone rather than typing it in.

Disadvantages:

- When inputting a voiceover, the computer cannot be used for any other purpose at that time.
- Voice recognition software is not as accurate as using a keyboard.

Sensors

Most examination questions referring to the use of sensors are actually referring to analogue sensors. As a result, this book concentrates on these and makes little mention of digital sensors.

A sensor is a device used to input data about physical changes in an environment that is being monitored (measured) or controlled. The most commonly used sensors are temperature, pressure, light, sound and humidity sensors. Because physical variables are analogue in nature, i.e. they are continually changing, the data transmitted by the sensor has to be converted into digital (discrete) data, otherwise the computer would not be able to process it. The device used to convert analogue data from the sensor into digital data is called, naturally enough, an analogue-to-digital converter. When used in monitoring and measuring applications, the data can be input from the sensor to the computer and transferred to a spreadsheet package for use in data logging, scientific experiments and environmental monitoring.

Uses

- **Temperature sensors** are used in automatic washing machines. The temperature is input to the microprocessor, which compares it with a preset value. If the reading is lower than the preset value, the microprocessor switches on the heater. If the temperature is higher than the preset value, it switches off the heater unless the heater is already off, in which case the microprocessor takes no action. This process is continuous until the washing cycle has finished. Temperature sensors are also used in a similar fashion with automatic cookers, central heating controllers and computer-controlled greenhouses.
- **Pressure sensors** can be used with burglar alarms, normally under carpets by doors and windows. The microprocessor is programmed with a preset value, normally low, although it cannot be zero – otherwise, if a piece of paper, for example, fell on the sensor, the alarm would sound. The microprocessor monitors the readings, continuously checking that the preset value has not been exceeded. If it is, then a siren or loud noise is triggered by the microprocessor. They are also used in automatic washing machines to check that the weight of the clothes is not higher than the preset value, otherwise it triggers a warning

light or sound. In addition, they are used as part of a robotic arm that grips objects and also in production-line control.

- **Light sensors** are used in computer-controlled greenhouses, with preset values input to the microprocessor. Unlike with most other sensors, there are at least two preset values: one is for a cloudy day, the other for night-time. The microprocessor continuously monitors the readings from the sensors. If the reading falls below the lower value, it must be night-time, so the microprocessor switches off the light (or if it is already off does nothing). If it is higher than this value but lower than the higher value, it switches on the light. If it is higher than the higher value the microprocessor switches off the light (or if it is already off does nothing). Light sensors are also used in burglar-alarm systems to see if a light beam has been broken by a burglar. It can be used in automatic washing machines where the amount of light passing through the water can be detected; if it is low, then the water is cloudy and the cycle should finish. They are also used as part of robotic arms and in production-line control. They can be used in street lights, where the microprocessor switches them on if the readings from the light sensor indicate that it is getting dark.
- **Sound sensors** can be used in a microphone. They can also be used in burglar-alarm systems whereby if the preset value is exceeded the microprocessor switches on the alarm.
- **Humidity sensors** are sometimes referred to as moisture sensors and are used to detect the amount of moisture present. They are used in computer-controlled greenhouses, where the microprocessor compares the readings of the sensor with a preset value. If it is lower than this value, the microprocessor switches on water sprinklers. These sensors are also used in washing machines to enable the microprocessor to determine whether there is sufficient water in the drum or not.

Advantages of using sensors:

- The readings are more accurate than those taken by humans.
- Readings are taken continuously and so the microprocessor can take immediate action.
- They facilitate automatic processes so that humans can do other tasks.

Disadvantages of using sensors:

- If there is a power cut, readings cannot be taken.

MIDI instruments

These are musical instruments connected to a computer using a musical instrument digital interface (MIDI). This can either be separate to the instrument or be an integral part of it. The interface converts the output signals from the instrument into a digital form understood by the computer.

Uses

- A performance can be directly recorded onto a computer and stored as a MIDI file.
- MIDI files can in turn be used to supplement other instruments. For example, if a group of musicians are lacking a particular instrument, they can use a pre-recorded MIDI file.

Advantages:

- They allow files to be produced that can be manipulated.
- Any errors in performance can be removed.

Disadvantages:

- The music produced can sound manufactured rather than spontaneous.

Graphics tablets

Graphics tablets are used together with a stylus or puck to trace round maps or hand-drawn images. As they are traced round, the resulting images appear on the computer screen. They can then be stored for further use.

Uses

- Graphics tablets are often used to create computer graphics.
- In East Asia, graphics tablets are widely used to write Chinese, Japanese and other language characters, as users find it easier than typing these characters on a keyboard.

- Tablets are used to produce technical drawings and in computer-aided design (CAD).
- In some situations, users prefer to use a graphics tablet rather than a mouse as a pointing device.

Advantages:

- They allow alterations to occur as the drawings are input, rather than later, as happens with a scanned image.
- They are a more accurate way of drawing than using a mouse.

Disadvantages:

- They are more expensive than mice.
- They can be difficult to use in choosing menu selections.

MICR devices

Magnetic ink character recognition (MICR) is the system used in the processing of bank cheques. Information, such as bank sort code and customer account number, is printed in a special font at the foot of the cheque. Before the cheque is processed, the value of the cheque is printed on to it using the same special magnetic font. The cheques are then collected together in a batch for input and processing (usually overnight when the computer system is not so busy).

Uses

They are used in banking applications for the processing of cheques. The customer accounts are updated after processing.

Advantages:

- They are more secure than OCR as they cannot be tampered with.
- It is a more accurate method than OCR or manually inputting the information.
- Cheques can be read even if they have been overwritten.

Disadvantages:

- There is a limit to the character set that can be used.
- It is an expensive method of data entry.

OMR devices

Optical mark recognition (OMR) is the use of a reader to input data from pencil or pen marks on a form. The computer stores the position of the mark as an item of data.

Uses

◆ They are used for the processing of many types of form; for example, registers and examination responses.
◆ A form of OMR is used to input barcodes.

Advantages:

◆ It is a quick method of data entry.
◆ These devices produce greater accuracy of input than using OCR.
◆ It is easy for the user to fill in the form or paper to be processed.

Disadvantages:

◆ Compared with manual methods of marking, it is an inaccurate method. Forms sometimes need to be manually checked prior to input.
◆ Forms have to be carefully designed, and this can be expensive.

OCR readers

Optical character recognition (OCR) is the software used after documents have been scanned and saved into the computer, converting the image into understandable text. The resulting text can then be processed by other software packages such as word processors and spreadsheet and database packages. Purpose-built OCR readers can be used to scan documents.

Uses

OCR is used with purpose-built readers such as multiple line OCR readers to process passports and identity (ID) cards and to sort mail.

Advantages:

◆ It is a faster method of data entry compared with manually typing in the document.

◆ It is an easier method of entering data for people with disabilities.

Disadvantages:

◆ A lot of errors are produced.
◆ They cannot read handwriting very well.

Barcode readers

Barcodes are used to represent information about products. A barcode is normally a pattern of thick and thin, dark and light lines. A form of scanner called a barcode reader is used to read them. Some are handheld and some are built into the EPOS terminal. The different thicknesses of lines are converted by the computer into a number.

Uses

◆ They are used in all kinds of shops, wherever the details of products represented by code numbers need to be input.
◆ In libraries, they are used to input the book number and library-card number.

Advantages:

◆ They are faster than typing the number in using a keypad.
◆ It is a more accurate method of data entry compared with typing the number in.

Disadvantages:

◆ They can be expensive.

RFID readers

Radio frequency identification (RFID) tags are attached to objects so that the object can be identified through the use of radio waves. The tag consists of two parts: an integrated circuit storing information about the object, and a miniature aerial for transmitting and receiving radio signals. The reader is used to transmit a radio signal in order to communicate with the RFID tag. It then uses the data it receives to identify the object. Some are handheld and some – called portals – are used at doors to detect objects passing through the doorway or entrance or exit to a building.

Uses

- ◆ They are used in passports in a number of countries.
- ◆ They are used by companies to track movements of their products and for stock taking.
- ◆ They are used in pet identification.
- ◆ In some libraries, they are replacing the use of barcodes on books.

Advantages:

- ◆ Unlike barcode readers, they can cope with objects between the tag and the reader.
- ◆ They can be read from and written to.
- ◆ They are more difficult to copy than a barcode.
- ◆ Tags are very robust.

Disadvantages:

- ◆ They are more expensive than other methods of input.
- ◆ When used to hold personal data, people's movements can be tracked easily, leading to lack of privacy.

Video cameras

Video cameras are used to take moving pictures. These can then be input to a computer using a video digitiser. The resulting files are stored using a variety of media. From there, they can be incorporated into a slide show or web page.

Uses

- ◆ They are used by both professional film-makers and by people making home movies.
- ◆ They are used for security purposes in closed circuit television (CCTV).
- ◆ They are also found in mobile phones.

Webcams

Webcams are similar to video cameras but are connected directly to the computer. They have no storage capability but instead transmit directly to the computer. Another major difference is that they tend not to be used as portable devices. They are, in effect, miniature video cameras

with no storage facility other than that provided by the computer.

Uses

High-quality webcams are used by businesses in videoconferencing to input moving pictures from a fixed position into a computer.

Advantages:

- ◆ They can be online constantly.
- ◆ They provide elderly or disabled people with the opportunity to stay in touch visually with friends and relatives without leaving their home.

Disadvantages:

- ◆ A webcam has very limited features, for example no zoom facility.
- ◆ They are not portable, as they must be connected to a computer.

- ◆ The software is fairly limited, often failing to include video-editing facilities.

1.2 Output devices

These are devices that are used to obtain output from the computer. Some of these devices hold temporary output (e.g. monitors and speakers), while others produce hard copy (e.g. printers and plotters). There is also the type of output device used in computer control. These will all be described in this section.

CRT monitors

Cathode ray tube (CRT) monitors are the cheapest type of monitor but are gradually becoming less popular because of their bulk. They work by an electron gun firing against phosphor particles. Monitors come in different  sizes, usually starting at 14 inch (36 cm) and going up to usually 24 inch (61 cm). This is the length of the screen measured diagonally from corner to corner. Larger size monitors, which are needed for higher resolutions, are more expensive than smaller ones.

Uses

- ◆ They are used in environments where space is not a problem.

- They are used when more than one user may need to view the screen simultaneously such as in design use, for example when several designers may need to offer suggestions on a prototype.

Advantages:

- They are cheaper than thin film transistor (TFT) monitors.
- They produce better quality images than TFT monitors, in terms of colour display and refresh time.
- The screen display can be viewed from a number of angles.

Disadvantages:

- They are difficult to lift and manoeuvre.
- They emit harmful radiation in very small quantities.
- They can have a flickering screen, so prolonged use can cause headaches and eyesight problems.

TFT monitors

TFT or LCD monitors can be used in applications where space is limited, such as small offices. They are, however, becoming more and more popular for normal use, as prices fall. The screen contains thousands of miniature transistors that are activated by the processor. Each pixel is formed by three separate colour transistors: red, green and blue.

Uses

- They are often used when only one person needs to view the screen at a time.
- A TFT screen is an integral part of a laptop.

Advantages:

- They are easy to carry and manoeuvre.
- They produce less glare than CRT monitors.
- They emit less radiation than CRT monitors.

Disadvantages:

- The angle at which they can be viewed is limited.
- There is an inconsistency of colour tones when viewed from different angles.
- Videos can have slight blurring.
- They are more expensive than CRT monitors.

Laser printers

This type of printer produces very high-quality hard copy. It consists of a drum that is electrically charged.

A laser is used to change the charge on the drum for each dot of the output to be produced. Electrically charged toner is then attracted to the oppositely charged dots. The paper presses against the toner-coated drum and is output with the pattern of dots required. The page cannot be printed until the whole document has been stored in a large buffer.

Uses

- They are used in applications where low noise is essential, for example most networked systems.
- They are essential in applications which require fast, high-quality, high-volume output, for example in most offices and schools.

Advantages:

- Fast output is achieved.
- Running costs are cheaper than for inkjet printers.
- Large printout jobs can be carried out quickly.
- The quality tends to be higher than other printers.
- Toner cartridges last much longer than inkjet cartridges and so laser printers can be used on longer print runs than inkjet printers.

Disadvantages:

- They are limited in the paper size that they can take.
- Initial costs are high as they are expensive.
- The first page can be slow to print.

Inkjet printers

Microscopic droplets of ink are forced out of a nozzle directly onto the paper. Inkjet printers tend to weigh less than laser or dot matrix printers. Signals are sent from the computer to the printer and the printout is produced little by little. There can often be pauses in the printing process as the printer doesn't have a buffer capable of storing a whole page at a time in the way that a laser printer does.

Uses

- They are used where there are low output volumes; the need to change cartridges at regular intervals renders them unsuitable for high-volume output processes. They therefore tend to be used in small offices and stand-alone systems.

- They are very good when applications require very high-quality output and where speed is not an issue, for example digital camera applications.
- Inkjet printers are being developed that will create three-dimensional models. Successive layers of plaster or resin are placed on top of each other using the inkjet nozzle. Layers of adhesive may be 'printed' on top of each layer to fix them together. The result is a three-dimensional model representation using computer-aided design (CAD) software.

Advantages:

- They produce high-quality output.
- They are fast for printing one-page documents.
- They are cheaper to buy than other printers.
- They are easier to move than other printers.

Disadvantages:

- They are slow to print more than one page.
- They are more expensive to run because inkjet cartridges do not last as long as toner cartridges.
- In very long print jobs, the printing could stop due to the need to change an ink cartridge.

Dot matrix printers

These are impact printers. They work by a printhead comprising several pins (usually a matrix of 24 by 24) pressing against a carbon ribbon onto paper. The ink from the ribbon then appears on the paper. Impact printers were developed as the result of the need to replace the typewriter in the early days of computing. It is particularly suited to applications that involve the use of multi-part or continuous stationery and when carbon copies are required.

Uses

They are used in noisy industrial environments, such as garages and car servicing, car sales and car repair services.

Advantages:

- They can work in environments which would cause problems for laser and inkjet printers, as dirt and oil in the atmosphere do not affect their performance.

- They produce carbon copies.
- Running costs are low.
- Continuous printjobs using pre-printed stationery are more easily managed.

Disadvantages:

- They are very noisy and so unsuitable for most office environments.
- They are now more expensive than inkjet printers.
- They are much the slowest type of printer.

Plotters

A plotter is a device that can produce hard copy like a printer can. However, it is not limited to paper size. There are three types of plotter, but all basically place ink on a roll of paper rather than individual sheets. The most common used to be a pen plotter, which prints to paper using a number of different colour pens. The other two types that are commonly used are electrostatic and inkjet plotters (using the same technology as in laser and inkjet printers, respectively). The pen plotter relies on the computer controlling the movement of the pens and also the movement of the paper. The paper can be moved forwards and backwards to achieve the required output and means that plotters can draw continuous curves. Plotters are often called graph plotters as this was their main function in the early days of the technology.

Uses

- Plotters are still used to produce printouts of graphs, but are more frequently used to produce blueprints, such as plans for the construction of a building, since these can be very large. They are also used in other technical drawing and CAD applications.
- They are sometimes used to produce billboards and signs by replacing the pen with a cutter and using special vinyl film on paper. This type of plotter can also be used to cut garments to order.

Advantages:

- Extremely large printouts can be produced.
- The graphic output is of very high quality.

Disadvantages:

- They are very slow to produce output.
- Filled areas of colour are difficult to produce using pen plotters.
- They are very expensive.

Speakers

Speakers can be either connected directly to the computer or inbuilt into the monitor. They output sounds that are produced by, or have been stored on, the computer. The digital data from the computer is converted into analogue signals by a digital-to-analogue converter, and are then amplified and output using the speakers.

Uses

- Speakers are required to play sound files attached to multimedia presentations and websites.
- Computers and MP3 players are used to play music from CDs and DVDs.
- Speakers are an integral part of home entertainment systems.

1.3   Control output devices

This section of the book examines a limited number of output devices associated with computer control.

Actuators

Actuators are used to convert computer signals into movement. Some devices such as motors are considered to be actuators in their own right. Others, such as light bulbs and heaters, are passive even when attached to a computer unless an intermediary actuator is included. In these cases the actuator would convert a computer signal into movement to cause the light bulb or the heater to come on. Some examples, together with their uses, are given below.

Motors

Instructions are input to the computer. After processing these, the computer sends electrical signals to the motor to cause it to operate.

The most common form of motor used with computers is the stepper motor. As its name implies, it moves in steps that can be very tiny, enabling precise control because of these small steps.

Uses

Motors are used in many computer control applications.

- In the home they are used in automatic washing machines to make the drum go round. They are used in automatic cookers to switch on the heating fans. They cause water pumps to come on in central heating systems. They are also used in computer-controlled greenhouses to open the windows and switch on fans. They cause dishes that are being cooked to go round in a microwave.
- In industry they are used to move robot arms and on production lines they cause the conveyor belt to go round. They are also used to cause component parts to be picked up and placed accurately where they should go.
- In computers themselves they are used to cause moving parts to work in disk drives, both optical and magnetic, as well as in scanners, printers and plotters.

Buzzers

An actuator is connected from the computer to the buzzer. The actuator is set to switch the buzzer either on or off.

Uses

- Buzzers are used in automatic cookers and microwaves to tell you when the cooking process has been completed.
- They are used in mobile phones designed specifically for young people. If someone feels threatened they can hold down the # key on the phone and it actives an extremely loud buzzer.

Lights

An actuator is connected from the computer to the light bulb and set to switch the light either on or off.

Uses

- Lights are used in computer-controlled greenhouses to increase the amount of light for the plants.
- Many forms of lights are used in computer control, including dimmers inside the home and bright security lamps as part of an outside security system.

Heaters

An actuator is connected from the computer to the heater and set to switch the heater either on or off.

Uses

- Heating elements are needed in automatic washing machines to heat the water to the required temperature.
- In automatic cookers they are needed to heat the hotplates and the oven.
- They are an integral part of central heating systems as they are needed to heat the water before it is pumped to the radiators.
- They are required in computer-controlled greenhouses to increase the temperature of the greenhouse.

1.4 Backing storage media and devices

All computer systems require some form of backing storage. When a computer user is typing in data, the data is temporarily stored in random access memory (RAM). When the computer is switched off the data disappears. However, it is important that the data is saved permanently. This is why backing storage is needed. In this section we will look at a variety of storage media and their associated devices. Memory is measured in bytes. A byte represents one character. 1 MB is a million bytes and 1 GB is a billion bytes.

Magnetic tapes

Magnetic tapes are very thin strips of plastic that are coated with a magnetic layer and are fed through a read/write head mechanism. Data, as with any magnetic

medium, is stored on the tape in the form of magnetised bits. The data is stored sequentially, i.e. record by record, file by file, and so is a relatively slow method of retrieving data. You cannot go straight to the data you want; all the data before the item you want has to be read in sequence.

Uses

They are used in any application that requires an extremely large storage capacity and where the speed of accessing data is not an overriding requirement, such as:

- batch-processing situations, for example updating bank accounts with cheques
- utility billing systems, where all customer bills are produced at the same time and every customer record has to be processed
- payroll applications, because all records have to be read in sequence, so direct access has no advantage in this case
- making backups, as this is also an application where every item of data has to be read.

Advantages:

- They are cheaper bit for bit than using disks.
- They are very robust as they are encased in a cartridge.
- They are easier to remove and keep away from the computer than equivalent-sized disks.
- The data transfer rate is fast.

Disadvantages:

- Access is slow, so uses are limited.
- Updating files requires a new tape to be created.

Fixed hard disks

This is the industry standard for storing data on any computer. A hard disk drive in a PC usually consists of one fixed disk, although in commercial applications there may be several disks. They are mounted on a spindle which is operated by a motor to spin the disk very quickly. There is usually one read/write head for each disk surface being used – normally one with PCs. These write data to the disk as well as reading data from it. The disks are used in PCs to store the disk operating system as well as software programs and data files. Any application that requires very fast access to data for both reading from and writing to will require a hard disk drive system.

Uses

Fixed hard disks are essential in any system that requires fast data access times and fast data transfer rates.

- They are used in real-time system such as robotics, rocket launching, etc.
- They are essential in any online system such as booking systems, EPOS stock control and electronic funds transfer.
- They are used in file servers in computer networks.

Advantages:

- The data transfer rate is fast.
- Data access times are fast.
- They have a very large capacity.

Disadvantages:

- They are easily damaged.

Portable hard disks

These are used to store data in exactly the same way as a fixed hard disk but, as their name suggests, they can be easily disconnected from a computer. They are used to transfer large files from one computer to another. They often have a capacity in excess of 100 GB and so can store much larger files than an optical disk.

Uses

They are used as backup media and for transferring large files from one computer to another. They are particularly useful for transferring server software from one network to another.

Advantages:

- Data access times are fast.
- The data transfer rate is fast.
- They have a large capacity.

Disadvantages:

- If dropped, they are easily damaged.
- The transfer rates are not as fast as with fixed drives.
- They are more expensive than other forms of removable media, such as CDs or DVDs.

Optical backing storage media such as CDs and DVDs

The next few devices all rely on the use of optical devices to read them.

All optical devices operate using a laser beam. The laser, a beam of focused light radiation, reads from and writes to the disk. The disk is polycarbonate plastic covered in a very fine layer of reflective metal. This is etched into using the laser beam and microscopic 'pits' are formed on the surface. These pits are then read and converted into data.

CD ROMs/DVD ROMs

This form of optical disk is read only memory (ROM), which means it can only be read from. It cannot be recorded over. The main difference between CDs and DVDs are their capacity. DVDs can hold up to ten times the amount of data that a CD can store; DVD writers use a shorter wavelength of laser light than CD writers do, so the pit on the disk surface is a lot smaller and more can be stored in the same space. Both forms of the media are portable and most CDs can be read using a DVD drive but not vice versa.

Uses

They are used for applications which require the prevention of deletion of data, accidental or otherwise.

- CD ROMs are used to store music albums and to provide audio output in home entertainment systems. They are also used to store software, computer games and reference books such as encyclopedias.
- DVD ROMs are mainly used for storing films, but are increasingly being used for data storage.

Advantages:

- DVDs hold more data than a CD.
- CDs are cheaper to buy than a DVD.
- Both hold much more data than a floppy disk.
- Both are cheaper than hard disks.
- Both are more robust than hard disks.

Disadvantages:

- Data transfer rates for both CDs and DVDs are slower than hard disks.
- Data access times are longer than for hard disks.

CD Rs / DVD Rs

The 'R' in their names stands for recordable. They can only be written to once, and then they become CD and DVD ROMs. The feature that enables them to be recorded over is the use of a very thin layer of organic dye. There are no pits formed on the surface. Instead, the laser beam causes spots on the dye cover to be heated up and the reading process distinguishes between the heated and unheated spots. As for CD and DVD ROMs, the DVD recorder uses a shorter wavelength of light than the CD recorder, which enables smaller spots to be heated and hence more data to be stored. A different dye has to be used with a DVD because of the shorter wavelength.

Uses

- They are used for home recordings of music on CD and films on DVD.
- They are both used for storing and transferring data from one machine to another.

Advantages:

- They are cheaper than CD/DVD RWs.
- Once burned they cannot be accidentally written over.

Disadvantages:

- They can only be recorded on once. If a mistake is made, then the disk needs to be thrown away.
- If several versions of a file are written to the disk, there is less space available than on CD/DVD RWs.
- Not all CD players will read CD Rs.

CD RWs / DVD RWs

These are rewritable (RW) optical disks and can be written over several times. Unlike CD/DVD Rs they do not become CD/DVD ROMs after being written to once. The recording surface of CD/DVD RWs is a metallic alloy layer. The alloy is a phase change alloy that can exist in an amorphous state or a crystalline state. The power of the laser changes spots on the surface from one phase to the other by causing it to melt or freeze. The surface appears to be pitted like a CD/DVD ROM but this is just an optical effect.

Uses

DVD RWs are frequently used for recording a television programme that would otherwise be missed. This recording can then be erased after viewing, ready for recording another programme.

Advantages:

- They can be used more than once.
- Different versions of files can be overwritten, thereby virtually increasing capacity.

Disadvantages:

- Their cost makes them impractical for use as permanent backup media, unlike CD/DVD Rs.
- Files can be overwritten accidentally, unlike with CD/DVD Rs/ROMs.

DVD RAMs

The digital versatile disk random access memory (DVD RAM) is a newer technology. The recording surface is an alloy coating, as with DVD RWs. However, the data is stored in concentric tracks like  magnetic media, unlike the single spiral of a single track that is used in other optical media. They usually come in cases that have to be loaded into the DVD RAM drive. They have the same properties as DVD RW but have quicker access times. Writing and reading can occur simultaneously, so it is possible to record one programme whilst watching another. They are much longer lasting than other forms of optical media and can be rewritten approximately 100 times more than a DVD RW. Writing to disk is more reliable because the drive has an inbuilt data check to ensure data is written to the disk accurately.

Uses

- DVD RAMs are used for general data storage.
- They are used for archiving, as they are longer lasting than other media.
- In some camcorders, they are used for recording video.

Advantages:

- They have a greater capacity than CD/DVDs.
- They are more durable than DVDs, in that they can be overwritten more times.

Disadvantages:

- They are not compatible with most DVD players.
- They are more expensive than other types of DVD media.

Blu-ray disks

These have the largest capacity of all optical disks: 25 Gb, 50 Gb and 100 Gb. The increased capacity is due to the fact that it uses a shorter wavelength for its laser beam, using light that is close to the blue/violet spectra (hence its name) rather than the red light used by other optical devices. They are coated in a protective lacquer to prevent damage to the surface but operate in a similar fashion to other optical disks. They are used for storing films (movies): 25 Gb equates to 2 hours high definition (HD) television, 13 hours standard definition television. It is possible to play back video on a disk while simultaneously recording high definition video.

Uses

- Their main use is in home video game consoles.
- Devices have been developed to facilitate the playing and recording of videos.
- PCs and laptops are being developed that use blu-ray disk drives for data storage as well as playing videos.
- They are used in many camcorders.

Advantages:

- They store more than other optical media.
- Data transfer rates are high.
- Access speeds are higher with blu-ray players than with other optical devices.

Disadvantages:

- They are very expensive compared with other data storage media.
- There have been problems with the encryption techniques used to prevent piracy.

Minidisks

This is a form of hybrid media, that is to say it uses both magnetic and optical methods to record data. A laser is used to heat one side of the disk which makes it easy for the disk to be magnetised. A magnetic head is used to magnetise spots on the other side of the disk to record data. The data is read using only the laser. Disks can be recorded over several times. The disk is permanently housed in a cartridge. Although extremely popular in Japan, it has not enjoyed as much success elsewhere.

Uses

They are used in portable music players, but have been superseded by MP3 players, iPods, and so on.

Advantages:

- Minidisks can be recorded over more times than other media.
- They are more robust than other optical media.

Disadvantages:

- Minidisks have slower transfer rates than other disks.
- They hold less data than other music players.
- They are more expensive than other portable players.

Solid state backing storage

We now move away from optical media and move on to other types, which are not necessarily optical or magnetic. Solid state backing storage is basically a silicon chip consisting of a grid of columns and rows of cells, each cell comprising two transistors separated by a thin oxide layer. The cell has a value of 1 or 0 depending on its charge. They have no moving parts and so are less likely to break down. They are used as removable storage in flash memory, in the form of either memory cards or memory sticks, as described below.

Memory sticks / pen drives

These can store up to several Gbytes. In order that the data stored on a memory stick can be used, the memory stick must be connected to a computer, achieved by means of a USB connector. In order to work, the memory stick draws power from the computer via the USB interface.

Uses

- They are used to transport files and backup data from computer to computer.
- They are used by system and network administrators for carrying software fixes.

Advantages:

- They are more compact than equivalent optical or magnetic media.

- They are more robust than other forms of memory, even surviving being 'washed'.
- They do not need software drivers to operate.

Disadvantages:
- They are more expensive per Gbyte than hard disk drives.
- The drives cannot be write protected.

Flash memory cards

Flash memory is a form of electrically erasable programmable read-only memory (EEPROM). It is solid state memory.

Uses

- They are used for storing photographs in digital cameras.
- They are used in mobile phones to store phone numbers, photographs, etc.
- They are used in MP3 players to store music.
- They are used as backing storage in many handheld computers.

Advantages:
- They are more compact than equivalent optical or magnetic media.

Disadvantages:
- They are more expensive per Gbyte than hard disk drives.
- They can only be used for a particular number of read/write operations.
- They have lower storage capacity than hard disk drives.

1.5   Portable communication devices

These are devices that can be carried on one's person. For the purpose of this section, we have included devices that communicate with us and not just devices that we use to communicate with other people.

Mobile phones

Mobile phones work using the transmission of electromagnetic radio waves. They have a transceiver that is only powerful enough to transmit or receive data from the nearest mobile phone mast or tower. This must be usually within 10 kilometres of the phone.

They are used primarily for making phone calls for personal and business use. However, most phones have other features as well, such as Internet access, a personal digital assistant (PDA) interface, games and e-mail and text facilities. They are used to store information about personal contacts. They are also used to watch television and can be used to record video or still photographs.

Uses

- They are mainly used to make business and personal phone calls.
- They are particularly useful in remote areas with satellite dishes if a landline is unavailable.
- They are a convenient method of sending and receiving urgent messages for business purposes without necessarily interrupting conferences.

Advantages

- They can be used while travelling if a public phone is unavailable.
- They can be used to send photographs/video footage.

Disadvantages

- They cost more to use than a landline.
- The quality of photographs/video can be poor.
- They can lose connection if travelling through a 'blindspot'.
- Displays are still small compared to other devices.
- They have a limited battery life.

Portable DVD players

These work in exactly the same way as conventional DVD players but come equipped with a built-in screen. The size of the player is smaller, as is the screen, so making them easy to carry.

Uses

They are mainly for personal use rather than business. They are used in cars for passengers to watch while on a long journey.

Advantages:
- They are small and compact.
- They can play music from CDs.

Disadvantages:

- ◆ The screen is low resolution and the quality of viewing can be poor.
- ◆ The screen is small, making it difficult to view.

Portable media players

These can be basic devices for storing music for playback using earphones. There are also more advanced devices, with screens that are capable of playing back video or can be used for video games. They

can be connected to speakers to enhance the quality of the output. Although the batteries have to be recharged from time to time, they can be connected to home computers that can charge the battery while allowing the user to listen to the music. Connecting the player to the computer also enables the downloading of music and data files as well as Internet data. Various methods of data storage are used, depending on the manufacturer, including small hard disks, microdrives and flash memory.

Uses

- ◆ They can be used for downloading music and radio/television programmes.
- ◆ They can be used for downloading data from the Internet or the movement of large amounts of data from one computer to another in a similar way to memory sticks.

Advantages:

- ◆ They are compact.
- ◆ They can hold up to 100 GB of data.

Disadvantages:

- ◆ They have very small screens.
- ◆ The earphones that come with the player are low quality.

Global positioning systems

Global positioning systems (GPS) work by making use of satellites that orbit the earth. There are a number of these satellites, such that at least four are visible in the sky to any point on the Earth's surface. Receivers are used in navigation (see below) and for drawing maps as well as for military purposes. The exact position of the receiver can be determined by carrying out calculations based on the position of the satellites and the time

taken for the signals to get to the receiver. Three satellites would normally be enough for this purpose but the use of four makes it a very accurate system.

Uses

- ◆ GPS can be used by runners to pinpoint their position, distance travelled and speed.
- ◆ They are also used by surveyors.

Advantages:

- ◆ Positioning and distance travelled can be achieved regardless of the surrounding terrain, tall trees or buildings.
- ◆ Greater accuracy for measuring distances than using cars or bicycles.

Disadvantages

- ◆ Transmission of data can be a little slow at times, leading to slight inaccuracies.
- ◆ They are expensive devices.

Satellite navigation systems

Using GPS and stored data the system can be used to quickly calculate a route. The GPS calculates the position of the driver and the stored data consists of data about all roads in the country in the form of map coordinates. Up-to-date information about traffic congestion or accidents are also fed to the device using radio waves.

Uses

These are used by drivers to produce a route for their cars or lorries, including alternative routes in the case of a traffic jam.

Advantages:

- ◆ They are quicker to use than a normal road map.
- ◆ They receive up-to-date traffic conditions.

Disadvantages:

- ◆ The display is very small.
- ◆ Unsuitable roads can be recommended.

Handheld computers, including PDAs

These refer to any type of small computer that can be carried in one hand. They have small screens and keyboards. They are used mainly in areas where the power supply cannot be relied upon. They are also very useful for studying the environment and also as data loggers, due to their portability. Mobile phones are considered to be handheld computers, as are PDAs.

PDAs are a particular kind of handheld computer that come with many of the modern technologies. They are fitted with a touch screen that is activated by using a detachable stylus. Text is entered by pressing a keyboard which appears on the screen. They have several features including basic database, word-processing and spreadsheet software. They have the facility to be used as phones, to connect to larger computers using Bluetooth technology, to access the Internet and to use GPS. Some PDAs that are used primarily as phones may not have a touch screen but use a basic keyboard instead.

Uses

- They are used by professionals whose job requires them to be travelling some or much of the time, for example:
  ◇ doctors who are on call can keep track of patient records
  ◇ computer engineers who move from installation to installation can use them to keep records of their day, as well as scheduling appointments and carrying any software 'fixes' that need to be used on systems.
- They are used to store addresses, phone numbers and e-mail addresses as well as keeping track of appointments.

Advantages:

- They can be used remote from the place of work.
- They are easier to carry than laptops.

Disadvantages:

- It is difficult to enter much text.
- They are about as expensive as laptops.

- They have a limited operating system.
- They have limited application software.

Bluetooth

Bluetooth was developed by a Scandinavian company and was named after King Harald Batan of Denmark, whose nickname was Bluetooth. It uses radio waves to connect devices such as a headset and a mobile phone. The maximum distance over which two devices can communicate is usually 10 metres, although greater distances are possible with a power boost. The data transfer rate is usually lower than 1 Mbit per second.

Wireless fidelity (WiFi) is an alternative to Bluetooth and is used for all but the smallest of wireless communication areas.

Uses

- It is used for communication between a mobile phone and a headset so that drivers can concentrate on driving.
- A mouse, keyboard and printer can be connected wirelessly to a PC using Bluetooth.
- Data can be transferred between devices such as photographs from one mobile phone to another.
- Games consoles use Bluetooth to connect to their wireless controllers.

Advantages:

- It can be used for a variety of applications, whereas WiFi is only used in local area networks (LANs) where cables would otherwise be used.
- It has cheaper hardware requirements than WiFi.
- It consumes less power than WiFi.

Disadvantages:

- The data transfer rate is slower than with WiFi.
- It covers smaller distances than WiFi.

2 How organisations use ICT 1

You already know how ICT is used in applications such as:

➤ control
➤ communication
➤ data handling
➤ modelling
➤ measuring
➤ simple stock control.

In this chapter you will learn about ICT systems and how organisations use them. In particular, you will learn about the use of ICT in a wider range of applications:

➤ control systems
➤ working practices
➤ advertising
➤ teaching and learning
➤ publishing
➤ time management
➤ data management
➤ payroll applications
➤ technical and customer support
➤ art and design work.

2.1 Control systems

A control system is one that uses microprocessors or computers to control certain physical conditions, either keeping them the same over a period of time or varying them according to pre-defined values and lengths of time. Physical conditions or variables that are controlled by computer and microprocessors include temperature, pressure, humidity, light and moisture.

Examples of control systems that have to maintain one or more of these variables are:

◆ air-conditioning systems
◆ refrigeration
◆ central-heating systems
◆ car manufacture
◆ medical applications
◆ process control.

Air-conditioning systems

An air conditioner is a closed system of copper tubes in the form of coils containing a chemical liquid (called the refrigerant) that can easily be converted to a gas and back to liquid again. One set of coils (the condensing unit or condenser) is outside the building and the other set (the evaporating unit) is inside. The compressor compresses cool low-pressure gas into hot high-pressure gas. As the gas then moves through the condenser outside the building, it cools down into a liquid. This liquid flows through the piping and passes through an expansion valve, causing it to evaporate into a cold low-pressure gas. As the liquid changes to gas and evaporates, it absorbs heat from the inside of the building. A fan blows air across metal fins that have been chilled as a result of the heat being absorbed. This causes the room to cool down. The gas then continues to the compressor to continue the cycle.

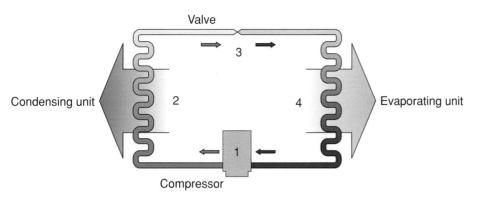

There are many sophisticated systems that have sensors built into the air-conditioning unit itself. There are usually two temperature sensors that monitor the temperature of the refrigerant, allowing the system to control the amount of heat being let out of the system. There can also be a pressure sensor that monitors the pressure of the refrigerant so that the valve can be controlled to reduce or increase the flow of refrigerant.

Most systems also have a temperature sensor in each of the rooms where the system operates. These systems control the heat loss from individual rooms by altering the speed of the fans or merely by switching them on or off. The person in the room uses a touch screen to input the temperature. The temperature in each room is monitored and if it is above the pre-set value, the fans for that room are switched on by the microprocessor (or their speed increased); if it is below the value, the fans remain off.

Refrigeration

The refrigeration process works on much the same principle as air conditioning. The condensing unit is at the rear of the refrigerator and the evaporating unit is inside the refrigerator.

The main inputs are a temperature sensor to monitor the temperature inside the refrigerator, a contact switch or pressure sensor for the door and a number pad or similar device to input the required temperature. The microprocessor compares the data from the sensor (after it has been converted to digital by an analogue-to-digital convertor (ADC)) with the pre-set value input by the user. If the temperature is higher than this value, the microprocessor activates an actuator to switch the compressor on. If it is not, then the microprocessor switches the compressor off. Other outputs from the system can include light-emitting diodes (LEDs) indicating the current temperature of the inside of the refrigerator and a warning buzzer if the door is left open.

Freezers work on the same principle, but obviously the required temperatures are much lower.

Central-heating systems

Most modern central-heating systems use water as the medium to get heat from the central source (the boiler) to all of the areas to be heated. The main parts of a central-heating system consist of a boiler, a hot-water cylinder, a pump and some radiators. The boiler is used to heat the water in the system, although, despite its name, it does not boil the water. The water from the boiler flows into a hot-water cylinder and the pump then causes the heated water from the cylinder to flow round the system to the radiators. The radiators are metal panels that are fixed to the wall in the rooms that need heating.

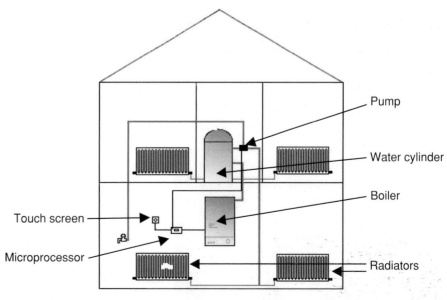

In a microprocessor-controlled central-heating system, users press the touch screen to select the temperature they want. The microprocessor reads the data from a temperature sensor on the wall and compares it with the value the user has requested. If it is lower, then the microprocessor switches the boiler and the pump on. If it is higher, the microprocessor switches both off. In order for the microprocessor to 'understand' the data from the temperature sensor (which is an analogue variable sensor), it uses an ADC to convert this data to a digital form that it can process. The microprocessor controls separate actuators: one opens the gas valves in the boiler and the other switches the pump on.

The microprocessor usually has the capacity to control the times at which the system switches itself on and off. For example, users can set the system to come on an hour before they wake up in the morning, so that the house is warm to get up to and set it to switch off 30 minutes before they go out to work. It can be set to switch on one hour before they return from work, and so on. When the system is off, the microprocessor ignores all readings.

Car manufacture

Computer-controlled robots are used in various manufacturing industries, including the manufacture of cars.

Most robots are controlled by the use of actuators in the form of electric motors. A direct current (DC) motor spins quickly if an electric current is applied to it, and it spins in the reverse direction if the current is made to flow in the other direction. A more popular type of motor for robotic use is a stepper motor. This does not spin freely like a DC motor, but moves in minute steps and so is easier to control by a computer. The industrial robots used in car manufacture are generally robot arms rather than a complete robot. The most common type

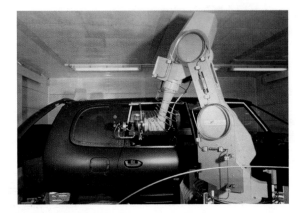

of robot arm consists of seven metallic sections with six joints, each joint being controlled by a separate stepper motor.

The computer controls the movement of the arm so that, using different end effectors, a variety of jobs can be carried out. End effectors are the devices attached to the end of a robot arm. A common one is a 'gripper', which acts like a hand; for example, it can be used to hold (grip) a part of the car body, so that the robot arm can move it to somewhere else. The types of end effector used in car manufacture are:

- cameras to inspect work
- welding guns to weld parts of the car body together
- grippers to pick up parts and place them somewhere else – grippers often have built-in pressure sensors that tell the computer how hard the robot is gripping a particular object, so that the robot does not drop or break whatever it is carrying
- vacuum cups to pick up parts without obstructing the sides or bottom, for example windscreens or small complex car parts
- drills to make holes in the car body
- screwdrivers/spanners/riveters to place and tighten screws, nuts, bolts and rivets
- spray guns to paint the car body
- sanders/polishers/finishers to produce a shiny finish after painting.

A robot arm can have any of the above attachments, but if the end effector is changed then the programming also has to be changed. It is not possible to replace a gripper with a screwdriver head, for example, and expect it to work without changing the programming of the robot controller.

Industrial robots are designed to perform exactly the same operation over and over again. For example, as a car passes along the production line the robot arm tightens the nuts on the car wheels in exactly the same position and with exactly the same pressure.

A robot arm carries out the following tasks on a car production line:

- painting car bodies
- putting on car wheels
- drilling the holes in car bodies
- fixing rivets to car bodies
- tightening bolts
- assembling the electric circuits in cars
- inserting car engines.

In order that the robot knows how to do its job, the programmer guides the arm through each step, either by physically holding the arm (and having sensors attached to their arm to allow data to be transmitted back to the computer) or by using a remote control. The computer stores the exact sequence of movements as a program in its memory. The robot arm is therefore able to do it again and again every time a new unit comes down the assembly line.

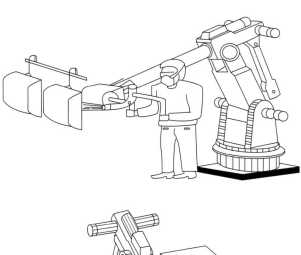

Methods are being developed whereby a programmer can program the arm offline, although they still have to refine the instructions by using one of the two methods above.

Robots are used rather than human beings because:

◆ a robotic arm has greater accuracy than a human
◆ the running costs are lower compared with paying a person
◆ robotic arms do not get tired, so work is of a consistent standard

◆ the whole process can be continuous, without having to stop at shift changeovers.

Medical applications

Computer control is used in two major medical applications – intensive care and surgery – but both still require human intervention.

Intensive care

Patients in intensive care are monitored through the use of sensors. The sensors feed back a variety of body functions to the computer such as:

◆ blood pressure
◆ pulse rate
◆ body temperature.

The computer is pre-set with the normal range of values and is constantly comparing the data fed back by the sensors to these pre-set values. If any of the body function data falls outside the pre-set range the computer sounds an alarm. However, such a system is not a computer control system as we understand it, since there has to be human intervention.

The use of sensors and computers makes the process more accurate and the computer can monitor the health of several patients simultaneously, thus enabling nurses to carry out other tasks.

Surgery

Robotic surgery is an extension of keyhole surgery that involves using robotic arms and cameras inside the patient's body. The robotic arms and cameras are a lot smaller than normal. The end effector is usually a scalpel.

The surgeon wears goggles connected to the computer and is able to see inside the patient. They control the robotic arms and cameras by putting their hands in a console. When they move their hands, the robot arms and cameras respond exactly to the movements they make.

The benefits are that the work is more accurate, but the surgeon is in complete control. The procedures replace large-scale, invasive surgery, meaning that patients recover more quickly and do not occupy hospital beds for as long.

Process control

Process control is the use of computers or microprocessors to control a process. Process control is used in oil refining, chemical processing, car manufacture and temperature control, as well as the food and beverage industries. Process control makes extensive use of analogue-to-digital and digital-to-analogue conversion.

There are three types of process control.

◆ **Batch process control.** This is used in processes where specific amounts of raw materials are combined together and mixed for a certain length of time. An example is the manufacturing of food products such as pre-packed meals. The ingredients are measured into a large vessel and mixed together for a certain amount of time. They are then heated to cook them. The amount of each ingredient that is added is controlled by computer, as is the length of time for each stage and the temperature. Batch processes are generally used to produce relatively small amounts of a product per year.

◆ **Continuous process control.** This refers to processes that appear to be unending, for example the maintaining of temperature in confined surroundings. A refrigeration plant where it is necessary to maintain a constant low temperature uses continuous process control. Other examples are a refining process for petroleum and a paper machine with continuous output of paper onto rolls. These manufacturing processes are used to produce very large quantities of product per year.

◆ **Discrete process control.** This is when specific items are produced. It is likened to an on/off or stop/start process. One example is the manufacture of cars. The computer control involved in fitting the wheels, for example, is discrete in so far as a wheel is fitted; then the next car comes along, and the same robot fits a wheel to that car in the same position. In between waiting for cars to arrive the robot stops.

Most process control is not overseen by a computer as such but by a **programmable logic controller (PLC)**. This is a type of computer or microcomputer that is used for a single purpose. It is able to accept analogue and digital inputs, and a set of logic statements is used to compare the input with a pre-set value. Depending on the result, it activates the output devices. It is most often found in industrial processes and is normally programmed to operate a machine or system using just one program. There is rarely any input to it from the user once it has been programmed. It is not really used in systems such as domestic central heating, as here the pre-set temperature

might change to suit the conditions. However, it is used in situations where the pre-set value is a constant such as in a large industrial refrigeration system.

One system for programming a PLC is a **proportional-integral-derivative (PID)** algorithm. These are used with closed-loop control systems. A closed-loop system is one in which a physical variable, such as temperature, is being continuously monitored using a sensor connected to the PLC and the outputs from the controller affect the input, i.e. the temperature. It is a continuous process, the purpose of the PLC being to make the input value equal to the pre-set one. PID is the best way of accomplishing this and is found in many versions of **control software**.

In its simplest form, PID calculates the difference between the input value and the pre-set value. It then causes the PLC to make proportional changes to the output so that the pre-set temperature is eventually reached. In other words, if the temperature in some form of heating system is lower than the required temperature it calculates the difference. Instead of just switching the heater on until the pre-set value is reached the PLC switches it on for a short time and checks the difference again. If, as is likely, there is still a difference, it switches the heater on for another small burst. This is repeated until the required temperature is reached.

EWT

Embedded web technology (EWT) is a technology developed by NASA so that experiments in outer space could be conducted by authorised personnel anywhere in the world, providing they had access to a computer and the Internet. The technology combines the Internet, the worldwide web and real-time systems into one technology for controlling embedded systems.

An embedded system is an integration of microprocessors, input sensors, output actuators and the software needed to control them. They can be built into any real-time control system.

For example, ovens have been developed that allow users to control them remotely. The embedded software enables the user to adjust and control oven temperatures using a mobile phone, PDA, laptop computer – basically, any device that can connect to the worldwide web.

2.2 Working practices

This section covers the use of ICT and how it has changed patterns of working. We will look at how various jobs have changed from the traditional office-based approach to employment, and also how the use of particular ICT applications have enabled this to happen.

Home working or teleworking

Teleworking is another name for working from home. When a person 'teleworks', it means that some or all of the work they do is done at home using modern technology. Developments in ICT devices and systems have made it easier for jobs that used to be done in an office to be carried out at home. The number of people working from home using ICT systems is increasing year by year. In 2005, 11% of the working population in Europe was working at home using ICT. This varied from Finland with 29% to France and Spain, which both had 5% of the workforce working from home. (empirica, 8 March 2006)

In this section, we are going to look at what is involved in teleworking. The benefits and disadvantages will be discussed in some detail in Chapter **3**.

New technology developments such as portable communication devices as well as home computer systems and networks have enabled people to become less tied to an office to do their work. The ability to communicate with colleagues from a distance has led to employees working away from their offices for substantial periods of time. Teleworkers can stay in contact with the office using a broadband connection or a virtual private network (VPN). Many use portable communication devices when going away for business purposes: a mobile phone and either a laptop with wireless network capability or a personal digital assistant (PDA) with similar features.

In order to work from home, a teleworker needs:

- a PC with Internet access
- access to e-mail
- a fax machine
- a landline phone
- a mobile phone
- a printer/photocopier (either laser or inkjet).

Some also need videoconferencing equipment and there may be need for a scanner if the work involves, for example, putting together artwork. In addition, workers will need to have appropriate software.

Some jobs are better suited to teleworking than others. Most managers needing to make the decision as to whether an employee should be allowed to work from home consider the following types of employment to be very suitable:

- professional services such as tax advice, legal advice and financial advice
- writing
- book editing
- proofreading of documents and books
- translation of documents
- technical and customer support
- telesales and marketing.

Workers involved in any of these will need to have word-processing and web-browsing software. Tax advisers would need to have spreadsheet and database software.

Most of the above jobs are suitable because they tend to be done on an individual basis. There is often little immediate need for liaising with managers or colleagues. However, managers need to consider other issues when looking to see if teleworking is appropriate. The decision may well not just depend on the type of work but also the specific employee. The manager may well want answers to questions like: What type of person are they? Could they work well on their own? The employee would have to:

- be able to manage their time well
- be well motivated
- have good communication skills
- have good self-discipline
- have good time management skills.

One decision that managers need to make is how frequently the employee needs to be in contact with the office and how that contact would take place. Many managers may feel that the employee needs to make personal contact with the office at least once a week, while others consider that it is necessary for the employee to e-mail their daily progress.

Other important decisions that managers may need to take are based on the provision of support and the technology involved. Good managers want to include their teleworkers in various activities that their office-based colleagues experience, such as:

- training sessions at head office
- staff meetings
- company outings.

All these help them to feel part of the team.

The managers would also probably wish workers to use time management and project management software, which are both discussed later in this chapter.

Remote working

Teleworking or home working is a major aspect of remote working, but there is another type. This is when people work at a distance from the main office, for example travelling salesmen, employees working in a temporary office, doctors on call and engineers working on site.

Employees can use any of the following technologies to carry out their work and communicate with the main office:

- PDAs or other handheld computers with wireless networking capability
- mobile telephones
- laptops with wireless networking capability.

Engineers on site can use a PDA to e-mail their reports. They are able to view technical manuals relevant to their field of work and use quite sophisticated database and word-processing software.

Doctors can use laptops with wireless network capability connected to a high-security VPN. They are able to access patient records, X-rays, and so on. whilst visiting patients in their home.

Travelling salesmen who have to work away from their office can take advantage of wireless hot-spots with their laptop or PDA. They can use their mobile phones to talk to other salesmen. They can also connect to their main office using wireless connectivity through the hotel they are staying at.

For any of these groups of workers, remote access services (RAS) are available. These allow them to access the desktop on their own PC when they are away from home or the office.

Office-based working

Despite the tendency for the number of teleworkers to increase there are a number of reasons why many companies retain their offices. Some are based on what is best for the company and some are at the request of the workers. A number of the companies' reasons are not well founded. Many companies still think that if they allowed their employees to work at home, many workers would spend the day watching television or taking part in other non-productive activities. There is also the feeling that data is not safe or confidential if it is being transmitted outside the company. As far as employees are concerned, many fear the prospect of isolation. They look forward to chatting with their colleagues during their breaks. A number are also fearful for their jobs, feeling that if they are out of the normal daily office routine they might be easier to lay off when the company is looking to make redundancies.

The equipment that needs to be in an office is, by its very nature, fairly fixed:

- desktop computers connected to a local area network (LAN) and/or a wide area network (WAN)
- Internet and e-mail facilities
- networked printers.

Videoconferencing

A videoconference is the electronic equivalent to a conventional conference usually held in a conference suite, sometimes called a face-to-face conference. The essential components of a videoconference are:

- a standard PC with mouse and keyboard
- a monitor
- speakers
- a network connection (a broadband speed of at least a few hundred Mbits per second is essential to ensure that the quality of the transmission is sufficient)
- a webcam
- a microphone
- videoconferencing software.

Members of the conference need to log on to the system or Internet and when the software is running they can normally see and hear all the delegates involved. They communicate by speaking into the microphone and looking at the webcam, which is normally fixed to the top of the monitor. Conference members are able to examine documents using normal software, discuss modifications or additions to the documents and physically make the amendments.

Videoconferencing is used in a wide variety of applications. In education, schools quite commonly use it to communicate with other schools, particularly in remote locations. In medical applications, nurses and doctors can discuss cases even though they might be a long way away from each other. Businesses use it quite often instead of face-to-face conferences, and also for teleworkers to communicate with their base office.

When videoconferencing was first introduced, a problem was the poor quality of transmission. However, this has improved due to the relatively low cost of fast Internet connections through the use of broadband. There have also been major increases in the quality of hardware available.

There are two main types of videoconferences: each person has individual access to the conference; or groups are involved rather than individuals.

Phone conferencing

This is the linking together of several people on a phone line so that they can have a collective conversation. It is possible to hold these conferences using mobile telephones, landline telephones or voice over the Internet protocol (VOIP – the use of phones connected through computers to the Internet) but each participant must have a touchtone phone. VOIP is described in more detail in Chapter 7.

In order for a phone conference to take place, at least three people must be involved (two people would just be having a normal phone conversation). Each participant has a personal identification number (PIN) that they key into the phone after they have dialled the phone number for the conference. This gives them access to the conference and they can join in with the conversation and discussions already taking place. Before the conference can take place everyone must agree a time and date, then the organiser will book the conference with the phone company.

The person who is organising the conference is given two PINs by the phone company. One is their personal PIN and the other is the participants' PIN. The organiser then contacts all the people who are going to be involved in the conference and tells them the participant PIN and the agreed time and date of the conference. Just before the conference the organiser dials the phone number and keys in the special PIN. This is the start of the conference and the participants can now phone the same number and join the conference by typing in the participant PIN.

Instant messaging

Instant messaging is the exchange of text messages between two or more people logged into a particular instant messaging (IM) service. It is an interactive service, as people can reply immediately to others logged into the same system. It requires a user name (often an e-mail address) and a password. When someone logs on for the first time they have to make a list of people they want to contact – these individuals need to agree to be contacts. Then they select the individual they want to talk to and send a message. If the contact happens to be online at the same time they can reply, leading to a conversation. It is better than e-mail because messages are sent immediately, whereas e-mail messages can be stored on a mail server for seconds or even minutes. However, the screen display is very basic and does not contain all the options available with e-mail. This topic is discussed in more detail in Chapter 7.

Faxing

Fax is short for facsimile transmission. A fax machine is connected to a phone line. A document is scanned and then transmitted through phone lines to another fax machine that then prints it out. It requires the use of a modem and so the speed of transmission tends to be slow. It is used when exact copies of originals are required, although the quality of the copy is sometimes not very good.

Many organisations tend not to use fax machines as such but prefer to have 'all-in-one' printers. These are inkjet printers which have scanning and faxing facilities built in to them.

Although many uses of fax are being replaced by the use of e-mail and other Internet services the fax is still used in a number of ways. In the UK, signed documents are not considered to be legally acceptable when sent by e-mail but they are acceptable when sent by fax. In the USA, weather maps are distributed by government bodies using fax. Many newspapers are prepared at a central location and then printed at a number of printing plants. The publishers send copies of their newspapers by fax to these plants using fax via satellite.

Electronic faxing

Since the introduction of manual faxing a number of electronic systems have been developed.

For example, there are systems that use the Internet for faxing. Instead of printing out a document and faxing it using a fax machine, the user 'prints' the document directly to fax software, which uses the modem or broadband to send the fax. The receiver either receives it on their fax machine or uses the same type of software to convert it into a document for storage.

Electronic faxing has the following advantages over traditional, manual faxing:

- ◆ It saves the time of going to the fax machine to retrieve or send faxes.
- ◆ Equipment costs are lower as there is no need for a fax machine.

- ◆ Running costs are lower as there is no need for a dedicated fax line.
- ◆ Confidential faxes are secure. On a manual fax, any worker might pick up a fax sent to someone else.
- ◆ It is not necessary to be in the office to receive faxes as they can be downloaded remotely.

2.3   Use of ICT in advertising

Advertising is used by many companies and organisations to promote their products or services. They have to pay a lot of money to advertising companies for the service. A variety of media are used for advertising, including billboards, cinema advertising, flyers, magazines, newspapers, posters, radio, the sides of buses, television programmes, video games and the worldwide web. Many of these can be considered to be ICT media. Even those that are not considered to be directly ICT media such as magazines and newspapers also have versions available on the Internet and in that sense can be considered to be ICT media. Others such as flyers and posters are produced using ICT.

Types of advertising
Product advertising

This is the advertising of a specific product. Product advertising is all about advertising one item: it might be a specific model of car, but not the whole range of cars the company sells.

Whether the product is a soft drink, a chocolate bar, a computer or a car, the principles are the same. The target audience is identified and an advertising campaign that will appeal to that type of audience is created. The media is decided upon. This can be one medium such as newspaper advertising or a mixture of, say, television, newspaper and Internet advertising.

For example, if a new soft drink is being produced and it is felt that the drink will appeal more to younger children than teenagers or adults, the approach becomes clear: advertising in children's comics and on children's television channels.

Business advertising

In order for a business to become well known so that it can make money it needs to advertise itself. Unlike product advertising, where only a single item is being advertised, business advertising seeks to make the company name familiar. As for product advertising, the company needs to identify the type of customer that it wants to attract. For example, if it sells shoes that are mainly aimed at the wealthy, then it will want to advertise itself as an upmarket company. It will therefore advertise in magazines and newspapers read by the richer end of society.

Service advertising

The service industry involves, as its name implies, services rather than goods being provided to the customer. Examples of service industries are:

- insurance
- government
- tourism
- banking
- education
- social services.

The approach to advertising services is much the same as advertising businesses. However, some profit-making organisations will be prepared to spend a lot of money on advertising in order to increase their profits. In contrast, government, social services and some aspects of education are not profit-making and may spend just sufficient money on advertising so that people are aware of their existence. These public services tend to advertise on the television if they need to reach the whole population, whereas profit-making service providers tend to use a variety of advertising media.

Methods of advertising

All aspects of the above types of advertising require the use of some or all of the following methods.

Websites

Advertising on the Internet is a recent development. It tends to be a cheap form of advertising and allows organisations to advertise nationally and internationally at much cheaper rates than other forms of advertising.

One way of advertising is for an organisation to have its own website. Web designers are employed who will produce a website to the organisation's specification using a web authoring package. The designers will use a variety of devices to create the website:

- scanners to input hard copy pictures such as photographs
- microphones to input voiceovers (somebody speaking over some video, for example)
- speakers so that they can check the sound input has been successful and is of sufficient quality
- video cameras to upload videos
- digital cameras to upload photographs.

Many factors have to be considered at this point. Cost is a limiting factor as designers tend to charge a large fee. The actual website has to have many features. It may need to have the whole range of multimedia, including sound, video and/or animation, as well as text and images. It must be easy for the user to navigate. In order to do this, hyperlinks to other pages or sites will need to be provided. The name of the organisation as well as the products or services it offers must be obvious to the user, as must the contact details. When the website is created it is essential that an organisation is aware of the power of search engines. They need to find out why certain websites appear in the first ten hits after a potential customer types in their search criteria. It is necessary also to find out ways of getting to the top of this list of matching websites when searches are made.

Advertising on other people's websites

A cheaper alternative may be to advertise on existing websites. In this example, T-Mobile is advertising on the howstuffworks website.

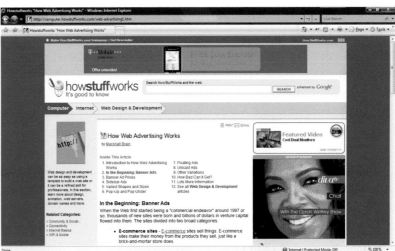

Many websites allow other organisations to advertise on their site. One method is to simply add a banner to the top of the screen advertising the organisation, its products or services. Another method is **pop-up** advertising where little windows suddenly appear on top of the web page when a user accesses it. The advantage to the advertiser is that a pop-up instantly grabs the attention of the consumer. However, a disadvantage is that a discontented consumer, who didn't request that information, may make a conscious decision to avoid that organisation in future. Another disadvantage is that many computer users now have pop-up blocking software that stops them from appearing. An alternative is the use of 'pop-unders'. These are small windows that are placed underneath the web page being accessed. They don't appear to users until they close the page they are working on. The advantage to the advertiser is that they are not removed by pop-up blocking and also the consumer regards pop-unders as less of a hindrance than pop-ups. Pop-ups and pop-unders can both be linked to the organisation's own website.

Getting into an online directory

Organisations can advertise their name by getting it included in an online directory. These are directories for businesses and service providers. Not only is the name placed alphabetically in the directory but it is also placed in the correct business/service section.

For this and the use of website advertising, the business is relying on the customer having all the necessary equipment such as a PC, including speakers, with modem or Internet connection. If they do not, they will not be aware of the advertisements.

Multimedia presentations

Although these are an integral part of some websites, many multimedia presentations can also be used on purpose-built display monitors placed in strategic locations. The presentation is produced using presentation software and makes use of the normal features of multimedia:

- sound/music
- video
- animation
- text
- images
- hyperlinks.

There are other features that can also be included, such as slide transition effects, special text effects, image transition, and so on.

Many retail outlets make use of these. They vary from being displayed on an extremely large screen placed in a central position in the outlet to small screens attached to the shelves in supermarkets. The larger screens can also be found in shopping malls. One advantage of this type of advertising is that it is on all the time that the mall, shop or store is open. Another advantage is that the user cannot switch it off with the remote control or click it off with a mouse button. Furthermore, they are quicker and easier to update than an Internet site or television commercial, for example.

Advertising companies see these as a major revenue earner, as more and more businesses request them.

Flyers

A flyer is usually a single-page leaflet. It can be used to advertise a restaurant, an event or a service. Flyers tend to be used by individuals or small businesses. They are generally used to advertise in the local community and as such have a limited impact. Many are produced by the individual or small business using their own PCs and printers, although for larger print runs it may be easier to take a copy to the printers and pay to have them run off.

A flyer doesn't take very long to produce using basic desktop-publishing software. This allows the accurate placing of images and text and also incorporates a number of text-enhancing facilities such as distorted character shapes as well as a variety of patterns and colours inside individual characters. Desktop-publishing packages also come with a library of clipart.

Posters

A poster is a large printed piece of paper used to advertise products or services. They are normally A1 size, although billboard posters are much larger. Due to their size, they have to be printed by professional printers. Posters can be produced using word-processing, desktop-publishing or presentation software. Presentation software is quite often the choice made as it has the ability to use paper sizes in excess of those available in the other packages, most of which are limited to A3 size. Images and text are combined together in a way to make the poster appeal to the target audience. Posters can be produced to advertise a local event or can be used by larger national organisations to advertise a product or service.

2.4 Use of ICT in teaching and learning

Schools, universities and colleges make use of what is collectively called learning technology, e-learning or sometimes educational technology.

Learning technology includes the use of computers, multimedia materials and networks and communications systems to support learning. Learning technology covers all aspects of the use of computers or ICT in teaching and learning, including:

- CAI – computer-aided instruction
- CAL – computer-aided learning
- CBL – computer-based learning
- CBT – computer-based training
- CMC – computer-mediated communications
- CAA – computer-aided assessment.

Many practitioners have great difficulty in defining each of these terms. For the purpose of this course, we shall group CAL and CBL together and CAI with CBT. Record keeping will be treated separately.

Computer-aided instruction

Generally, CAI is the same as CBT, although in the USA it appears to have a different meaning where it can apply to any aspect of education involving the use of computers. In the UK and other countries, there are different interpretations of the use of computers in education. With CAI, computer software tends to replace the teacher or indeed the current learning environment. It involves the use of the computer as the main method of delivering subject knowledge, with little consideration for other methods of learning. In contrast, CAL is considered to be the use of software to support existing methods of teaching and learning.

With CAI, the computer takes over the whole learning process. It is usual, at the outset, for the student to undergo a pre-test on the computer to see what level they should start work at. A good CAI package will make carrying out this assessment straightforward. The materials then make it easy for the student to navigate from page to page and section to section. Use is made of repetition of skills to reinforce the student's knowledge. There are usually built-in games and quizzes to make the whole experience more enjoyable. The software will also be capable of assessing the student's progress with tests and will keep a record of the scores achieved in these tests.

Computer-aided learning

CAL or CBL are the methods by which the computer and associated software do not replace a lecture or lesson, but are introduced into the course as a learning resource in much the same way as a textbook or television programme. CAL should be considered to be an integrated approach to teaching where learning technology is part of the whole approach. The teacher is in total control of the learning experience, not the computer. It should only be introduced after assessment of the current teaching methods and it must be integrated with textbooks, worksheets and other media. It is not necessarily the use of games or the Internet, where often learning can be achieved despite the use of ICT, rather than because of it. However, the Internet is an important component in CAL, allowing students to investigate ideas and perform research as part of the lesson. Some aspects of Internet usage could be considered to be CAI, however, as specific learning programmes are available which the student can log on to and which replace any teacher input. When used as a resource, with the teacher still taking responsibility for where the learning will go, it remains CAL.

There are a number of ICT devices and media used by teachers to help them to deliver their lessons and are considered to be integral parts of the CAL learning experience. These include:

- computers
- DVD players
- interactive whiteboards
- multimedia projectors
- overhead projectors
- televisions.

Students are able to access CAL software through their PCs, which will sometimes have overlay keyboards attached especially for students with special needs. Specially written overlay keyboard software allows key presses to be converted for interpretation by the CAL software.

Computer-mediated communications

CMC consists of e-mail, instant messaging and chat rooms. E-mail can be used for the sending of completed tasks to the teacher or tutor, whether these be class work or home work assignments. E-mail can also be used by the teacher to send tasks to all their students in a class.

Computer-aided assessment

As well as schools, universities and colleges, examination boards also make use of computer-aided assessment. Computers are being used a lot more to test students and to determine the progress they are making. The type of assessment can be either formative or summative. Summative assessment is asking questions and recording responses. A total mark is given and the teacher and student are informed of the scores. No suggestions for improvement are forthcoming. Formative assessment is the use of the results of answers to specific questions to form a judgement on specific progress. The program normally outputs areas for improvement.

An attempt to use computers for summative assessment was made by the Qualifications and Curriculum Authority in testing students in ICT at the age of 14 in the UK. Pupils took two 50-minute tests where they were asked a variety of questions and had to perform a series of tasks. These were assessed, but there were several problems with the software and often the level produced was not deemed to be an accurate assessment of their ability.

Recently, examination boards in the UK have been using online marking software. This is a process whereby candidates' scripts are scanned into a computer system and then examiners log on to the system and mark the scripts on screen. There have been very few problems with the system, which is proving to be an accurate approach to marking.

Even with manual marking, examination boards often enter candidate marks through the use of a special optical mark recognition (OMR) form, where the marks are recorded using a pencil. These forms are then read by a scanner. A number of boards, however, are moving over to examiners entering marks online.

Record keeping

Spreadsheets can be used to store test and examination marks, predicted grades, targets and attendance records of students. The scores can be plotted in graphs and used to demonstrate progress, or otherwise. Statistics such as percentage attendance, or the difference between target grades and actual performance can be used. Conditional formatting is a feature that many teachers use to indicate progress or lack of it. The spreadsheet can be programmed to format cells as red for students who are scoring much lower than they should or green if they are performing as expected.

Separate sheets can be used to store information about different classes and these statistics can be used for comparison.

2.5 Use of ICT in publishing

This section will look at how the use of computers and ICT has influenced the way that publishers produce a variety of publications.

The first stage in the production of a newspaper is that correspondents send their stories into the editorial office from the location of the story. This is usually by e-mail. The journalists will have typed up their story using word-processing software and possibly taken photographs using a digital camera and uploaded these onto their laptop. If they are dealing with a local story, they can send their story in using their home Internet connection or may go into the newspaper offices and hand their story over. If they are further from home and office, they will have to e-mail their stories and photographs by using their mobile phone and laptop or by logging in at an Internet hotspot or perhaps their hotel. These are transmitted to the editorial staff, who collect and edit the stories sent in by the newspaper's journalists and are located at the main office. They have PCs with Internet and e-mail capability. The articles are edited by the editorial staff and the page layout of the newspaper is created. It is only complete after it has been edited to remove mistakes and then proofread for accuracy.

The production of a magazine is very similar, with contributors sending in their articles to the editorial staff, who then edit and lay out the articles to create that issue of the magazine. Book publishing varies mainly in the length of the material being sent and the longer period of time taken to produce the final product.

CD and DVD covers are produced in a similar fashion, but generally there is a less complex process. There is liaison between the graphics designer and a graphics director prior to it being printed.

The rest of this section will focus on the use of ICT in the various stages of producing a newspaper, but the same principles apply to magazines and books.

Typesetting

This is the setting of the layout of the typed page. There are many features of typesetting which have to be addressed. The layout of the page has to be created so that it is easy to read. This means that the correct font and size have to be chosen. There are other features such as kerning – this is the space between individual letters in a word: certain letters can be close together like a and v, but others have to be further apart such as r and y. The leading (the space between lines on the page, pronounced 'ledding') also has to be accurately defined to give the correct appearance. The length of each line (the number of characters on a line) is important to the appearance. There are also issues such as the size of the body text font when compared to that of the headings on a page. If a story is too long to fit in the available space it may need to be edited to make it shorter.

Before computers, people were employed specifically to manually set the typed page out so that all the stories were included but also the page was still easy to read. They used individual letter blocks which were inked up and then pressed to the paper for printing.

Despite the use of computers, typesetting is still a very difficult job. Although all the necessary features are included in the common desktop-publishing packages, the difference between an amateur attempt and that of graphic designers (who are usually employed to do this) is normally quite considerable.

Once the page has been set out to the editor's requirements, it can be sent for plate making.

Transmitting completed pages

After the editor has accepted the layout of a page in the newspaper and is happy that it can be printed exactly as it is, they need to send the page to the printing plant. There are two main ways of doing this:

- The page is printed and the image of the page is then burned onto light-sensitive film. The film of the page is placed in a large fax machine that is used to transfer the image to the print plant.
- Some publishers have several printing plants and the complete newspaper, in digital form or in fax form, is sent up to a satellite and then transmitted by the satellite to the various outlying printing plants simultaneously.

An alternative for smaller publishers is to burn a CD or transmit the newspaper in digital format using a WAN.

Computerised plate making

Images from the negatives are transferred to printing plates in much the same way as photographs are developed. Ultraviolet light is allowed to pass through the film negatives to expose the printing plate. When the plates are exposed to light, a chemical reaction occurs that allows the light-sensitive coating on the aluminium to develop the image.

Printing

The aluminium plate now has to be fixed to the actual printing press. The press consists of three rollers or cylinders. The aluminium plate is flexible so can be bent to fit around the plate cylinder. The most common method of printing newspapers is called web offset lithography. The 'offset' refers to the fact that the plate does not actually touch the paper being printed on. The roller with the plate attached has ink directed onto it and it then rotates against the blanket cylinder which is rubberised and this roller forms an image from the plate roller. As it rotates the blanket roller presses against the paper (which is being continuously fed into the press) causing the image to printed. The third cylinder is just there to press the paper against the blanket cylinder.

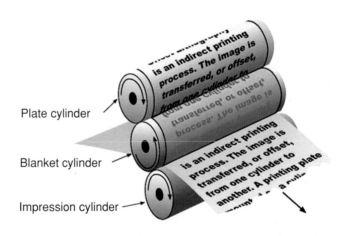

The large sheets containing the copies of the newspaper are cut into separate versions of the newspaper and these are stacked into bundles. These bundles are then loaded onto delivery trucks for distribution.

2.6 Use of ICT in time management

The ability to manage the time people spend on tasks or projects is probably the most important part of achieving success in work. It has become very important to many organisations that their workers manage their time effectively. There are certain skills which people can develop so that they are able to achieve success with their work even when they are under a great deal of pressure. The ability to master these skills enables them to manage their workload more efficiently.

Some people find it easy to manage their time. It tends to come naturally to them, but many people do not have good time management skills and this leads to them wasting time. Wasted time cannot be replaced and therefore is probably the most difficult aspect of our daily lives to manage.

Time management is finding and using the most efficient way of completing tasks or projects in the most acceptable period of time but with the highest quality. It applies to the most simple of tasks that could be done in a few minutes right up to complex projects that can take months or even years. The 'most acceptable period of time' does not necessarily refer to the shortest time possible. Time management applies to all aspects of business, for example the manufacture of products, writing documents, providing services and making decisions.

Approaches to good time management

Organisations often feel it necessary to keep up to date with good time management techniques. The better application of time management makes an organisation more profitable. There are different approaches an organisation can take. Outside experts can be brought in or the organisation can employ people full time as workers in a specialised department. They themselves could possibly examine existing good practice as well as attending courses and gaining qualifications in this area.

The next step is to put into practice the features of time management:

- identifying short- and long-term targets – organisations, whilst appreciating the need to identify the end point of a project, are also mindful of the need to identify the steps needed to be taken to get there; these short-term targets can in themselves prove to be very motivational when achieved
- prioritising – in order that the project can be completed successfully in the time allowed, it is important when setting targets, which are independent of each other, to decide on the relative importance of each target and devoting the appropriate resources to achieving that target
- planning – organisations find that much time is saved in the actual production of an item if time has been spent planning the steps needed to produce it

- decision making – whole books have been written on this subject; it is sufficient to say that making the correct decisions is important at all stages of a project and will affect the time taken at each stage
- use of ICT – organisations benefit through the use of software and communication devices such as faxes, telephones and even express delivery of conventional mail.

Use of software packages in time management

There are several software companies competing to gain business based on their time management software. There are also a number of packages that come built in with most computers that can help with various time management tasks.

Organising meeting times

Organiser packages that come with most computers have features such as organising e-mails, contacts, tasks and a calendar function. The calendar function enables users to keep a record of their appointments and meeting times. A public calendar can be created so that many workers in an office can have access to it over a network, allowing them to see when there would be a suitable time for a meeting (i.e. when they are free and when others are free). This public calendar is separate to the user's own calendar (which might contain information private to them) and also advises them of any clashes, i.e. meetings scheduled for the same time and date.

Arranging workload

There are a number of software products that act as a stopwatch device. They allow users to click on a specific task and the computer periodically reminds the user how long they have been working on that task. Users can change tasks whenever they want and the computer will inform them how long they have spent on each task. It is then easy to see how much emphasis is being paced on each task. It can allow the manager to allocate extra resources to a task if too much time is being spent on it by one person. The software can also be used as a predictor. If the manager is accurate in predicting the time that will need to be spent on a task, resources can be allocated appropriately. Such an approach helps with daily and weekly planning as well as ensuring an equitable workload for all workers.

	01/12/2008	02/12/2008	03/12/2008	04/12/2008	05/12/2008
Assembling of car body					
Assembling of car engine					
Assembling of car seats					
Fitting of car engine					
Fitting of steering wheel					
Fitting of car seats					

Research and development projects

Business software helps to support these projects with calendars, timescales, Gantt charts, and so on.

Gantt charts are used in many aspects of research and development. They help to plan out the tasks that are involved in a process. Let us consider the manufacture of a new car.

There are two main types of activity: sequential and parallel. Some activities cannot take place until others have happened. These are called sequential. For example, you cannot put an engine into a car body until the car body has been made. Others are independent of each other. For example, while some workers are assembling the car engine, other workers can be putting the car seats together. These are called parallel activities. To plan the whole process, a Gantt chart can be created. A simplified Gantt chart for this set of tasks is shown above.

Notice how the tasks are arranged so that the parallel tasks finish (not start) at the same time. Notice that obviously the car steering wheel cannot be fitted until the engine is fitted but that the seats can be fitted at the same time as the engine.

If we look at this Gantt chart we can see that the whole set of tasks can be finished in five days. A manager might want to change one or two things so that if they took longer no time would be lost. It might be better to start the assembling of the car engine a day earlier so that if it took a day longer to actually assemble it could still be fitted on 4 December.

Construction project management

Construction project management is not just specific to the construction of buildings. This method of project management is now applied to different types of project. It involves a critical path method of finding the optimum time to be spent on individual tasks. The critical path is the order in which tasks must be completed so that the entire project is completed on time.

Because of the nature of the construction industry, which often involves vast projects, many of the

techniques developed are used in all forms of project management.

The software developed to go with this approach to project management helps to identify the progress being made with specific sub-projects and also helps with daily and weekly planning. By identifying progress, or lack of it, this contributes to planning future tasks.

Project management is disscussed in Chapter **5**.

2.7 Use of ICT in data management

A database or database system is a collection of related data. In its simplest form a database consists of a collection of records and fields. Each record contains the same set of fields, each of which contains one piece of information.

A database management system (DBMS) is, as its name suggests, the software used to manage a database system. It manages:

- ◆ the structure of the individual data files
- ◆ the relationships between data items and between data files
- ◆ how the data is interrogated (i.e. how you get information from the database)
- ◆ the properties of the database, i.e. ensuring that all queries, updating and amendments to structure are processed reliably.

Databases are discussed in some detail in Chapter **11**. For the purposes of this part of the course we will concentrate on file systems and how data within them is organised and retrieved.

Sequential files

In a sequential file, records are stored one after the other, in the order in which they were added to the storage medium, usually magnetic tape. To read data from or write data to tape, sequential files must be used.

There are two ways that records can be arranged in a sequential file. One way is to have the records in some sort of order using a key field. A key field is one

Ordered file

ID	Customer name	Country
1	Jose Carreras	Brasil
2	Julia Fernandez	Brasil
3	Joseph Pinkerton	USA
4	Nabil Mohammed	Brasil
5	Luis Nova	Venezuela
6	Egídio Leitão	Chile
7	Andreza Bistene	USA
8	James Brand	USA
9	Alexandre Hoffman Reis	Chile
10	Tyler Moncrieff	USA

Unordered file

ID	Customer name	Country
7	Andreza Bistene	Brasil
3	Joseph Pinkerton	Brasil
8	James Brand	USA
10	Tyler Moncrieff	Brasil
6	Egídio Leitão	Venezuela
4	Nabil Mohammed	Chile
5	Luis Nova	USA
9	Alexandre Hoffman Reis	USA
1	Jose Carreras	Chile
2	Julia Fernandez	USA

which is unique to every record, i.e. every record has a different value in that field. This is called ordered sequential. Alternatively, the records might be arranged with no thought given to their order so they appear to be unordered. Whether the file is ordered or unordered affects the way in which the data is processed as well as the type of processing that can be used. An unordered sequential file is often referred to as a serial file, as the only method for retrieving information is to go through each record one by one.

In an ordered file, the records are put in order of a key field such as customer ID, as shown above (this is part of a file you will meet in much more detail in Chapter **16**). In an unordered file, the records are not in any particular order.

There are a number of disadvantages to using sequential files. For example, the only way to add new records to a sequential file is to store them at the end of the file. A record can only be replaced if the new record is exactly the same length as the original. Records can only be updated if the data item used to replace the existing data is exactly the same length.

The processing of records in a sequential file is slower than with other types of file. In order to process a particular record all the records before the one you want have to be read in sequence until you get to the one you want. The use of sequential files is recommended only for those types of application where most or all the records have to be processed at one time.

Adding records to the end of the file is fairly straightforward. However, amending or deleting records is not so easy. If the file is an unordered sequential file, then it cannot be easily done. If it is an ordered sequential file, then the changes can be made relatively easily providing the transaction file – which contains the actions to be carried out on the records – has been sorted into the same order as the master file, using the key field. Below are a master file and a transaction file.

The letter in the Trans. column is the type of transaction. D is a deletion of, C is a change to and A is an addition of a record.

The computer reads the first record in the transaction file and the first record in the old master file. If the ID doesn't match, the computer writes the master file record to the new master file. The next record of the old master file is read and if it matches, as it does in this example, the computer carries out the transaction.

Master file

ID	Customer name	Country
1	Jose Carreras	Brasil
2	Julia Fernandez	Brasil
3	Joseph Pinkerton	USA
4	Nabil Mohammed	Brasil
5	Luis Nova	Venezuela
6	Egídio Leitão	Chile
7	Andreza Bistene	USA
8	James Brand	USA
9	Alexandre Hoffman Reis	Chile
10	Tyler Moncrieff	USA

Transaction file

ID	Trans.	Customer name	Country
2	D	Julia Fernandez	Brasil
5	C	Luis Nova	Chile
9	D	Alexandre Hoffman Reis	Chile
11	A	Chuck Winter	USA

In this case the record has to be deleted, so instead of writing this old master file record to the new master file the computer ignores it and reads the next old master file record and the next transaction record. We are now on the second record of the transaction file and the third record of the old master file. If they don't match, the old master file record is written to the new master file and the next record (the fourth) of the old master file is read. This carries on until the next old master file record is found which matches the transaction file record. In this case, the fifth old master file record ID matches the second transaction record. This requires a change, so data in the transaction file is written to the new master file (not the old master file record). This whole procedure carries on until the transaction type 'A' is met. After this, all the remaining records of the old master file are written unchanged to the new master file and then the remaining records of the transaction file are added to the master file.

Indexed sequential and random access files

Indexed sequential files are stored in order. Ordinary sequential or serial files can be stored on tape. An indexed sequential file is stored on disk to enable some form of direct access. Each record consists of fixed length fields. This is a leftover from the use of magnetic tapes where records had to be stored in the order they were written to the file. The use of ordering facilitated a greater speed of access.

With an indexed sequential system the records are in some form of order, for example by Surname for a record of employees. The index is a pointer to whereabouts on the disk the record is stored. In simple terms, the table might be numbered 1 to 26 (A to Z) and the whereabouts on the tape that all the As can be found, all the Bs, and so on, is stored in this index. This means that when a name beginning with S is required the part of the file containing all the As to Rs can be ignored and the disk is accessed where the Ss begin. All the records beginning with S still have to be read one by one until the appropriate record is found, but it does mean that not every record from A onwards has to be read. Banks use sequential access systems for batch processing cheques. This system would have to be at least indexed sequential for faster access to records for online banking. Indexed sequential files are used with hybrid batch-processing systems, such as employee records. The index will allow for direct access when individual records are required for human resource/personnel use. The records will be held sequentially to allow for serial access when producing a payroll, since all records will be processed one after the other.

Random access is the quickest form of access. It does not matter whereabouts in the file the desired record is; it will take the same amount of time to access any particular record. Each record is fixed length and each has a key. The computer looks up the key and goes to the appropriate place on the disk to access it.

Hierarchical database management systems

Hierarchical DBMS are no longer used as a form of file management to any extent, as they suffer from the problem of one-way relationships. Hierarchical DBMS use a tree-like structure similar to a family tree system. There are few records or files at the top of the structure but many below it. If you think of family tree structure you can see that a woman can have many children but the children can only have one mother. Its main use is in file organisation within computer directory structures. Folders can have several folders below them in a *Windows* system, for example, but only one folder at the level one above their level. For example, the folder Users in a typical *Windows* system can have several users within it and they in turn can have several documents stored within each user. It enables fast access to data, however, as large amounts of data are bypassed as you go down the levels.

Network database management systems

Network DBMS were developed to overcome a lot of the faults of the hierarchical type. Although the technology is outdated, many existing databases still rely on this form of DBMS. Many are distributed database systems. Parts of the database are usually stored on a number of computers that are linked through a WAN or LANs. Many of the parts of the database are duplicated so that it is unlikely that any data is lost. Despite this, it appears to each user to be a single system. The duplication also enables faster processing. The system caters for very complex searches or filters but does not necessarily carry out the processing at the site where the user is.

Another type of network database is stored on one device but can be accessed from a number of network locations through either a LAN or a WAN. Users of the database can access the system simultaneously without affecting the speed of accessing data. Examples of this type are the Police National Computer (PNC) and the Driver and Vehicle Licensing Authority (DVLA) in the UK. Both of these can be accessed by police officers from their cars.

Relational database systems

These are demonstrated in detail in Chapter **11**. A relational database consists of a number of separate tables that are related in some way. Each table has a key field that is a field in at least one other table. Data from one table can then be combined with data from another table when producing reports. It is possible to select different fields from each table for output, using the key field as a reference point. For example, relational tables could be used to represent data from a payroll application and from a human resources application. The key field could be the works number. Fields of personal data from the human resources table could be combined with fields from the payroll in a report.

The standard programming language in large applications to deal with relational tables is the structured query language (SQL), which is used for queries and producing reports.

An advantage of relational databases is that data is not repeated and therefore doesn't waste valuable storage capacity. In contrast, the problem with flat file databases is that they repeat data. A payroll file may have the name and contact details of a worker and this would be duplicated in a human resources file. In a relational database, these would be in separate tables connected by the key field – worker number. This leads to another advantage, that data retrieval is quicker. Furthermore, duplicated data can mean that hackers have easier access to personal data that might be repeated across different files, so relational databases reduce this risk. Another advantage of relational databases is the room for expansion that is allowed. It is a straightforward exercise to extend the database with other data or tables.

2.8 Payroll applications

Payroll systems normally involve the use of batch processing. This usually means that the files that are needed are stored on separate magnetic tapes. There are two data files involved. The first is called the master file and this holds all the data about the workers. This data includes the employee number,

their name, their contact details, their rate of pay and the pay they have received so far this year as well as the taxes and insurance they have paid so far this year. The employee number is used as the key field and the file is sorted in that order. There is less data on the second file – the transaction file. This is a temporary file as it contains some data which can change from week to week or month to month. It contains details of the number of hours worked and any overtime with, of course, the employee number. The transaction file also has details of any new workers or workers who have left the company or any worker whose details have changed.

At the end of the week or month, depending on how often the workers are paid, the master file is processed using the transaction file. Before processing, the transaction file has to be sorted into the same order as the master file, i.e. records in order of employee number.

The computer calculates the pay of each worker using the number of hours worked contained in the transaction file and the rate per hour from the master file. Payslips are then printed, together with reports showing overall statistics as well as error reports. The records from the old master file are read and updated using these calculations and any deletions, additions or amendments are made. These records are written to a new tape which becomes the new master file.

This process can be seen in the following diagram.

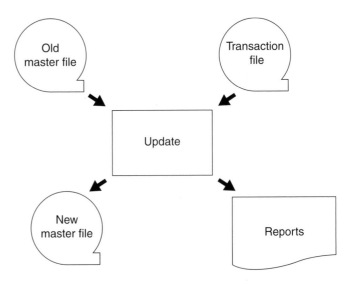

The reports consist of financial reports, error reports and, of course, payslips.

The old master file contains the data that was up to date at the end of the previous week/month. The update

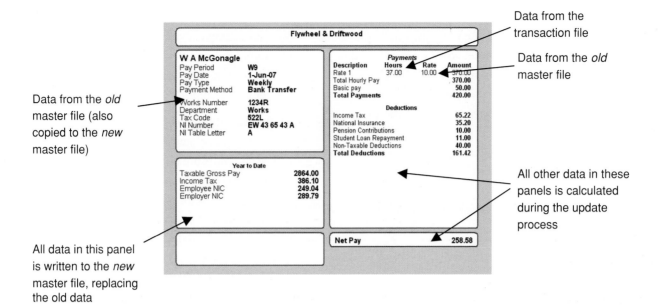

Data from the transaction file

Data from the *old* master file

Data from the *old* master file (also copied to the *new* master file)

All other data in these panels is calculated during the update process

All data in this panel is written to the *new* master file, replacing the old data

process involves the calculation of the employee's wage for this week/month using the hours worked from the transaction file. The wages are calculated together with any National Insurance payments and tax payments. These values are used to bring the year-to-date totals up to date so that they can be written to the new master file. The following week the new master file becomes the old master file and is used with a new transaction file to produce new payslips.

Payslips

The payslip contains information that can be found on the new master file and also information from the transaction file.

The master file provides information such as the employee number, the department worked in, the pay rate per hour, the tax code, National Insurance number, year-to-date values etc. To create the payslip, the above information is linked to the transaction file containing the employee number and the hours worked.

Above is an example of a UK payslip.

Financial reports

Most payroll software has a report generator facility. This provides detailed payroll listings and exception reporting. Examples of typical reports are as follows:

- information about all employees of the company
- information about employees in a given department
- information about the salaries of all employees
- National Insurance contributions for all employees
- the total amount of National Insurance contributions paid to the tax authorities

- the income tax that each employee has paid
- the total amount of income tax paid to the tax authorities
- the amount of money paid to each bank that employees have an account with
- all the earnings and deductions of employees
- the earnings and deductions of each employee by department
- a summary of all the totals of the earnings and deductions of each department.

Exception reports – reports of certain validation rules being broken – are also produced from the system. Examples might be:

- an employee earning an unusually large amount of money
- an employee who has been on an emergency tax code for a long period of time
- two employees having the same National Insurance number.

2.9 Technical and customer support

Many companies that offer customer support do so through the use of call centres. A large office space, housing as many as 100 operators, is used for the purpose of taking calls and responding to requests for help. Each operator sits at a desktop computer that is connected via a dedicated telephony server to the company's phone line. Each computer has a headset (integrated headphones and microphone) connected to it.

The operator's computer must be fitted with computer telephony cards and each computer is linked to a telephony communications switch. As there is a need for many operators to be accessing the same line at the same time, sophisticated computer software is required. Computer telephony integration (CTI) software is used to integrate all aspects of the system together. It sends commands from the operator's computer to the telephony server. The operator's computer has no direct connection to the phone, but any computer in the network has the potential to control any phone in the telephone system.

The way the system works is that phone calls are processed using interactive voice response (IVR) software. This is software that does not require a human response. Automatic services such as giving account information can be accessed by the caller who connects to the system database via the IVR software.

CTI allows the computers to direct the phone call to either the appropriate operator or another solution. As well being able to queue calls, the system needs to be able to transfer calls to a person with the appropriate expertise.

Some of the features of CTI software are as follows:

♦ It combines the data and voice input to the system.
♦ It displays the caller's number, number dialled, etc.
♦ There are multiple dialling techniques: fast dial, preview and predictive dial.

CTI software takes two forms. First-party call control works by allowing the operator to have a direct connection between their computer and the phone set. This means that the operator's computer can control the functions of the operator's phone. This type of software is unsuitable for any but the smallest of call centres. Third-party call control is the software used by large call centres, but requires a dedicated telephony server to connect the telephone network and the computer network. It works by the operator's phone communicating directly with the server; this allows the server to control all the phones. The operator's computer is not connected directly to the phone set in the virtual sense, although it may be physically. Any computer in the system can be used to control any phone. This allows supervisors, for example, to intervene if the call proves too complex for the operator to handle.

Examples of businesses that use call centres include the following:

♦ Utility companies, such as electricity, gas and water companies, make use of call centres where operators give customer support. These operators are able to help when customers want to pay their bills, for example, or change details of their account. Operators can also deal with any reports of poor service or lack of supply. In addition, the automated service carries reports on any known problems.

♦ Mail order catalogue firms offer customers help in the form of payments and account information. Call centre operators are also used to accept orders or enquiries about orders.

♦ Computer hardware and software suppliers and manufacturers offer technical support. These are operators who have technical expertise and are able to help customers whose computers are not operating as they should.

Many call centres are sited abroad, as UK companies, for example, find this more profitable. They pay lower wages to their workers than they would if they had to operate a centre in the UK. The cost of buying or renting premises is also lower. It also means that many of the UK calls, which are in the evening, occur at a more sociable time than in the UK. Consequently, the company does not have to pay higher wages for unsociable hours.

Many customers, however, do not like this as the operators sometimes have difficulty understanding UK regional dialects and vice versa. There are also problems with understanding the UK culture. Furthermore, workers abroad can be less flexible in their approach and are more inclined to stick to their 'script'. The script is generated by software, separate to the telephony software, and appears on the operator's screen. The operator asks questions on the script that are relevant to the query. The script will also contain examples of possible advice, which can be given depending on the reply. In addition, the operator will have access to online technical help if they are unable to answer the question because it is not on the script. The system should have a link to the customer's file on the system.

2.10   Art and design work

ICT is used in a wide range of activities when producing art and design work. We have already briefly looked at how CD and DVD covers, posters, books and magazines are published. Now we need to look at some of the hardware and software that is involved when ICT is used to produce artwork.

Most companies that deal with this type of work use computers with large storage capacities. Many have to have appropriate graphics software installed. This is often referred to as image-editing software, as it is used to alter the appearance of images that have been imported into the software using input devices such as digital cameras and scanners. This type of software often has features such as the ability to:

- crop (i.e. remove a portion of) an image
- rotate an image
- flip an image
- fill parts of the image with colour
- look at three-dimensional views
- remove scratches from photos
- draw lines and other geometric shapes
- add text in a variety of fonts.

The software will also have access to a lot of clipart and photo galleries. In addition, it will have the facility to store libraries of designs so that the same basis for a design can be used over and over again.

The devices used to manipulate these images are either a mouse or a tracker ball.

Examination questions

In South Africa, a car engine manufacturing company has just started manufacturing complete cars. They are looking to sell cars throughout Africa. The factory is in East London and they have a main office in Johannesburg, where the manager, Simphiwe, organises the day to day running of the business. The main office employs a lot of workers to produce the company payroll for all the workers in East London and for those in Johannesburg. There is also a human resources department in the main office in Johannesburg which keeps all the files on each worker.

Simphiwe has asked Capetown Publicists, an advertising company, to publicise the business on a large scale. The publicist company employs four people including the manager Mosola. They need to have regular meetings to discuss their progress with various jobs. This is difficult as they are very rarely in the office together as they all do a lot of their work at home.

1 (a) The company uses robotic arms to control a number of processes. Give two reasons why they use these robotic arms. [2]
    You will need to make two points.

(b) Describe how robotic arms are used in **two** of these processes. [4]
    You will need to make two points for each process.

(c) Describe how the movements of the robotic arm were originally programmed into the computer. [5]
    You will need to make five points.

2 (a) Mosola decides he needs to get in touch with his fellow executives. This has to be done as soon as possible. Describe at least **two** methods by which they could exchange ideas without having to travel into work. Include in your answer the additional hardware they would need to add to their home computers and printers. [4]
    You will need to make four points.

(b) Mosola has considered a number of ways in which ICT could be used to advertise the company but has decided on a web page. Discuss the reasons for his choice when compared with the other ICT alternatives. [6]
    You will need to make six points.

3 Simphiwe has decided it might be a good idea to computerise the payroll system and also the human resource department records. He has asked a systems analyst to investigate the current system and to suggest a replacement system.

(a) One of the recommendations of the systems analyst will probably be to create a database of information about the workers. The information will contain details about both the payroll and personnel information. Explain how the data will be organised on the database including details of how they will be retrieved. [4]
    You will need to make four points.

(b) The workers in East London are hourly paid. The number of hours of workers in East London are sent, via the company network, to the main office. Describe how a payroll system would take in this data and produce their payslips. [4]
    You will need to make four points.

Mr Devlin is the principal of a college of education. He has decided to upgrade the computer network. He wants to have a new system which will allow the college to keep student personal records and test marks. He also wants to have a system which will let the students have the opportunity to use computers to improve their learning. He has invited Sara Lopez, a systems analyst, to design and create the new system.

4   Describe the types of input devices and software that she could recommend so that students will benefit from the use of CAL and CBL.   [6]
    You will need to make six points.

5   Companies, such as banks, are setting up Call Centres in the Far East to provide support to customers in the West.
    Describe how a computer-based system, such as a bank enquiry help desk, can support a telephone call centre operator when dealing with a customer's telephone call.   [4]
    You will need to make four points.

The impact of ICT on society 1

In this chapter you will learn about:

➤ online services such as:
  ➢ online transactions
  ➢ online shopping
  ➢ online banking
➤ the effects of the use of online services on society in terms of:
  ➢ employment issues
  ➢ increased leisure time
  ➢ changing working patterns
  ➢ security and privacy of data
  ➢ health and safety issues.

3.1 Online services

We can use the Internet in many ways. It is very useful for finding out information about a number of different topics. It can also be used by companies to provide services for users of the Internet. There are different types of online services, but these can be broken down into three main areas:

◆ people can pay online for services provided by particular organisations
◆ people can do their shopping online
◆ bank customers can use online banking.

In order to carry out these activities, Internet users need some basic hardware and software. In terms of hardware, they need to have a personal computer with a modem, preferably a broadband type. The only software they need is an Internet browser. However, word-processing or text-editing software is very useful for copying confirmation of orders and dispatch details for future reference. It is therefore often useful to have a printer so that these details can be printed out.

Online transactions and other services

These are now available in many ways. For example, at local government level in the UK, people can pay

their council tax, parking fines and many more items. There are other services which can be paid for at national level, such as car tax. Here is a page from a UK government website that lists all the transactions which can be carried out.

Home | Directories | Guide to Govt | Do it online | Newsroom

Do it online

Motoring
Transactions, services, interactive tools, forms and leaflets.

Transactions and services

▸ Apply online for a first provisional driving licence
▸ Apply for your tax disc online
▸ Blue Badge parking map – find disabled parking bays across the UK
▸ Book a theory or practical test online (opens new window)
▸ Check an MOT record (opens new window)
▸ CO2 emissions and the vehicle excise duty calculator (opens new window)
▸ DVLA form ordering service (opens new window)
▸ DVLA personalised registrations (opens new window)
▸ Order your official DSA learning to drive books, DVD etc online (opens new window)
▸ Report an unlicensed vehicle online (opens new window)
▸ Take an official practice theory test (opens new window)
▸ Tell DVLA your vehicle is off road (SORN) (opens new window)
▸ Vehicle details enquiry (opens new window)
▸ Vehicle recalls database (opens new window)
▸ View your online driver licence applications

Some of these services require payment online, such as:

◆ applying online for a first provisional driving licence
◆ applying for a tax disc online
◆ booking a theory or practical test online
◆ ordering official learn-to-drive books, DVDs, etc. online.

Many banking services called card payment gateway systems are now available. These make it possible for companies and businesses to accept credit card payments online. Electronic payment – also known as e-payment – is very convenient. Modern businesses and companies find it essential to accept electronic payments. This is particularly the case as business and commerce is increasingly done globally and so a faster and easier way to make payments is important.

Other services are just for information and are not, therefore, transactions, for example:

- finding the location of disabled parking bays
- checking a certificate of roadworthiness record
- using an online calculator to calculate CO_2 emissions and vehicle excise duty
- finding a personalised registration plate.

There are many other examples of online services that would not be called transactions, such as:

- customers arranging for packages to be picked up and delivered to a destination of their choice – for a fee
- people filling in their tax returns and making tax payments
- reserving and renewing library books.

Online shopping

It is important at this stage to explain the distinction between the Internet and the worldwide web. The Internet is often defined as being a network of computer networks connected together by routers, and can be thought of as the cabling and connectors as well as the computers themselves. The worldwide web is just one aspect of the Internet, along with e-mail, file transfer and so on. It is a collection of hypertext documents, menus etc., often in HTML format. It is an information retrieval system that needs a web browser to access it. The worldwide web was invented by Tim Berners-Lee, an Englishman, in 1989 while he was working at CERN, a scientific research centre in Switzerland. The first website built was at http://info.cern.ch/ and was put online on 6 August 1991.

The first instance of companies allowing their customers to purchase products using the Internet happened in 1994, when Pizza Hut offered customers the opportunity to order pizzas on its web page. Amazon was founded as an online bookshop in 1995 and now operates separate online shopping sites in Canada, China, France, Germany, Japan, the UK and the USA. According to a recent Amazon statement, the company currently ships items to 217 countries.

An online shop can be called by other names such as Internet shop, web shop or online store. It is an electronic commerce (e-commerce) application that businesses can use with each other or they can offer services or goods directly to the customer. Online shopping has become very popular for many reasons:

- Items are usually cheaper online because warehouse and staff costs are lower, and because shops that only operate online want to attract and keep customers.
- Some shops allow customers to get products at the cheaper online price by ordering online, reserving the product and then collecting and paying at the shop.
- Customers can compare products and prices at their leisure.
- Customers can shop at a convenient time for them.
- Customers can shop at their favourite shop even when they are miles away.
- Food shops can remember the customer's shopping list and favourite brands, and deliver at a time to suit them.
- Customers can shop around without having to spend time and money travelling around different shops.
- The Internet allows customers to look at a wide range of shops all around the world.
- There is a greater choice of manufacturers. Many main street shops can only stock items from a few manufacturers because of space and cost constraints.

Although it saves customers the cost of travelling to the shops, online shops tend to charge delivery or postage costs, which reduce, or even remove, the advantages of not having any travelling costs.

The purchase of goods from a foreign country can also be problematic. The monetary exchange rate between two countries can rise, so what may appear to be a good bargain when the goods were purchased may turn out to be more expensive when the payment is actually made. However, the rate could also fall so it could prove to be more of a bargain than was first thought. Either way, this is a consideration which must be taken into account. Another problem is that the country where the customer lives may impose some sort of tax on the goods when they are shipped into the country, resulting in the customer paying even more. This is a particular problem in the UK for customers buying goods from US sites, for example.

Let us now look at how an online shop operates.

Purchasing goods

There are a number of steps which customers may go through when buying online.

1 Deciding which online shop to use

It is possible to use price comparison services. These are sites that show you the cheapest price for a particular item. These sites generally do not accept liability for any transaction resulting from the use of their sites. Having decided on the shop offering the goods at the cheapest price and that the shop is a reputable one, the customer goes to its website.

2 Browsing product categories

Most online shops have a number of categories on their home page. These can be represented by icons which are clicked on to go to a category of products that they sell. Frequently, such sites use tabs at the top of the page which link to a different web page on the site for each category. Customers are invited to choose the category they require by clicking on it and then they can look through (or browse) the individual products to get to the one they want.

3 Using the virtual shopping basket

Having decided which product the customer wants, they place it in their shopping basket.

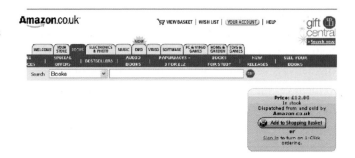

As in a real shop, the contents of the basket can be added to, removed or changed. When the customer has decided that they have finished shopping and they want to pay, they go to the checkout.

4 Going to the checkout

Here is an example of the sequence of events leading up to payment. Note, however, that the actual sequence of events may differ from site to site.

If the customer has never used this shop's site before they may need to register by choosing a username and a password. Customers then enter their personal data, which usually includes the following:

- the billing address – where the bill will be sent
- a shipping address – where the goods will be sent to; this might be different to the billing address
- the customer's phone number
- an e-mail address – this is nearly always needed, as most sites want to be able to send the customer notification that they have received the order; using e-mail, shops can tell the customer when the order has been dispatched.

However, customers who have already registered with the shop on a previous visit just need to log on using their username and password, rather than entering the above data.

Another step is to choose the method of payment. There are several alternatives, but the most popular is to pay by credit card or debit card. Cheques can be used but this usually means that the delivery time will be longer, as the shop has to wait for the cheque to clear. It is sometimes also possible to pay on delivery, but this is not so common as the other methods.

Another step is for the customer to choose how quickly the goods should be delivered as well as the method of delivery. Some shops, particularly supermarkets and hypermarkets, have their own delivery vans. Generally, however, the options are to have a fast method of delivery such as a courier or next-day delivery by post. Customers can choose to pay less for the delivery as long as they are prepared to wait longer. Whichever method is used, the customer usually has to pay a delivery charge in addition to the price of the goods.

Choose your delivery options

Delivery Details: (Learn more)
Choose a delivery preference:
◉ Group my items into as few deliveries as possible.
○ I want my items sooner. Dispatch them as soon as they become available. (at additional cost)
Choose a delivery option:
○ FREE Super Saver Delivery
◉ First Class
○ Express Delivery

The final steps are to confirm the order and to log off. All online shops will ask you to confirm the order you want to place. This will be the last opportunity for the customer to change their mind and not go through with the order.

Click the "Place your order" button to complete your order.   ▶ Place your order

Finally, after confirming the order, or not, the customer must log off from the system.

Security issues

If the customer's personal data and payment details were intercepted by a hacker they could be used by the hacker to defraud both the shop and the customer.

The data could be used to log on to the shop's computer system and order a large number of products which can be dispatched to another address other than the credit owner's. For this reason, some online shops will only dispatch to the billing address. The hacker now has possession of these goods which they can sell on and the shop and the customer are left to dispute who is responsible and who should pay the bill. Once the hacker has the credit card details, they can also be used to make purchases at a number of other shops. This is just a small part of identity fraud.

In order to protect customers, personal data and payment details are encrypted when they are transferred over the Internet. This means that data is encoded so that anybody who intercepts the data, such as a hacker, is unable to decipher the meaning of the data. The data can only be decoded if the receiving network server has the correct encryption key.

However, banks have spent a lot of money guarding against hackers gaining access to customers' personal data, and so hacking is less likely these days. It is now more common for fraudsters to use methods such as phishing, pharming or attaching spyware in order to obtain customer data. These are described in Section **3.5**.

Customers should be aware that:

◆ if their credit or debit card is used fraudulently, in many countries the card company must refund them
◆ they should keep a copy (printout) of what they've ordered, in addition to a copy of the supplier's confirmation message
◆ their consumer rights (e.g. refunds for faulty goods) apply online
◆ they should only use reputable sites.

Selling goods

There are many reasons why companies sell their goods online. They can save a lot of money; for example, they do not need to pay shop assistants or rent buildings on expensive main streets, nor do they need to answer a lot customer questions before the sale of goods. They can compete with larger businesses by reaching a much wider audience, possibly worldwide, and being open 24 hours a day, seven days a week, giving them the opportunity to increase sales. Costs associated with processing orders are lower due to customer orders automatically coming straight into the company's orders database from the website. Companies also receive payments more quickly because payment is made online. Finally, companies can keep track of purchases and see which are the most or least popular products.

Before a shop goes online, it has to have a website with an easy-to-remember domain name that is related to the business. The domain name or website address will also be used for e-mail. The company needs a high-specification web server that will operate 24 hours per day.

To operate online, the shop needs to have a method of accepting payments. It will also need a secure server, shopping cart software and software to keep track of stock and orders. The shop will need to incorporate into its website a database of product names, descriptions, pricing and photos.

The online shopping system must allow the administration staff to add, edit and delete categories, products, manufacturers, customers and reviews. Usernames and passwords are essential to make the system secure. These staff must be able to contact customers directly via e-mail. They must also be able to back up and restore the database easily. They will need to have access to statistics for products and customers, as well as being able to select what to display, and in what order, in the product list page.

The online shopping system must allow customers to make use of the orders stored in a database, finding them quickly and easily as well as seeing their order history and being able to maintain their own accounts. Prospective customers should be able to use a temporary shopping basket if they are a 'guest' or a permanent shopping basket if they are returning customers. There will need to be a friendly user interface so that searches and advanced searches can be carried out easily and allow customers to progress smoothly to the checkout. Finally, customers should be confident that all transactions are secure.

Online banking

Opening and maintaining bank accounts

Many customers are using online banking because of the convenience of banking at any time of day (or night) and the reduced amount of time and fuel costs incurred when travelling to and from the bank. Security and fraud are issues that are considered in some detail in Section **3.5**.

Online banking usually offers such features as:

◆ up-to-date bank statements
◆ bill payment
◆ transfer of funds between the customer's different accounts
◆ loan applications
◆ higher interest rates for savers because of lower costs.

There are a number of steps that customers go through when banking online. The details of different banks' websites differ, but they all use a similar procedure.

1 Customers have to log on

In order to log on to some banks, customers go to the website's online banking page. They are asked to type in their user ID, or username.

After they have done this they may be taken to another page before being asked for security information.

2 Security information

All sites require customers to type in a password. Some will ask for additional information such as a favourite place or their mother's maiden name or, as in this case, their date of birth.

Alternatively, they may ask for a number of characters from a character string specified by the customer.

3 Account information and services available

The next page will have a list of the customer's accounts and account numbers, together with links to the customer's personal details. There is also a list of the different services that the customer can apply for.

4 Account details

When the customer selects a particular account, all the recent transactions are listed. A number of services are now available, although these differ from bank to bank.

In this example, the customer can:

- order a bank statement
- go to a summary of the customer's bank charges
- pay a bill
- transfer money between accounts
- get account details
- change or create standing orders and direct debits
- stop a cheque
- get a new PIN sent to them.

Security issues

An example of possible identity fraud runs like this. Sadiq gets a loan from the bank by pretending to be somebody else, say Rajvinder. Sadiq uses personal information about Rajvinder, such as address, birth date and bank account number that he has obtained by hacking into a database. He manages to convince the bank that he is Rajvinder. Sadiq does not pay back the loan and the bank thinks it is Rajvinder who has taken out the loan. They expect Rajvinder to pay the loan back. When he can't or won't, this causes him to have a poor credit rating so that he cannot borrow money himself.

Advantages to banks using online banking

- They don't have to rent so many main street premises, which can be very expensive.
- They can employ fewer staff, which means that they pay less in staff wages. They also have lower costs, as they don't have to pay running costs of the branches for electricity, heating and lighting.
- Because of their lower costs, they can offer higher rates of interest for savers and lower rates of interest for borrowers, thus attracting more customers.
- There is less likelihood of the bank being robbed.
- Less money is spent on security staff.

Advantages to customers using online banking

- There is no need to spend money on transport going to and from the local branch.
- People with disabilities find it easier than going to the local branch.
- Customers can bank at any time of day or night.
- They can ask for a loan over the Internet without being embarrassed about asking a cashier.
- Interest rates on savings accounts are higher.
- They don't have to worry about whether the mail will get their bill payments to companies on time.
- There is less likelihood of robbery and no likelihood of violence.

Disadvantages to banks using online banking

- There is a less personal touch and so it is harder to sell other services that may be available.
- There is potential for fraud and interception of account information by hackers, resulting in the banks losing money.
- There are still costs involved in running the business, such as having to pay website developers.
- There are initial costs, such as buying the hardware when starting up.
- They need to retrain staff, which is costly.

Disadvantages to customers using online banking

- They may lose contact with their friends as they may not go out of the house as much.
- Customers must have a computer, Internet access, basic computer skills and a reliable electricity supply.
- There is a small risk that hackers may intercept data and take money from the customer's account.
- Customers may not like the fact that the bank is not providing the 'personal touch'.
- Customers may mismanage accounts now that it is so easy to transfer money from one account to another.
- Because customers must use the phone line to carry out online banking, their phone bills can increase.
- If customers don't have broadband, other family members will not be able to use the phone at the same time as one person is using online banking.
- Customers are unable to make cash deposits or withdraw cash without physically going to the bank or to an ATM.
- Customers may receive e-mails that claim to be from the bank but are fraudulent, asking them to

give out bank details, including passwords. This is called phishing.

3.2 Online services and employment

The introduction of online services has had two effects on employment. Some staff have lost their jobs because the use of ICT has replaced the need for some types of worker, for example shop assistants and bank clerks. However, the other effect has been an increase in the need for workers in more technical aspects of work.

General unemployment

Before looking at the specific effect of online services on unemployment, it is useful to consider a few examples of how other aspects of ICT have affected unemployment.

There are many areas where the use of ICT in the fields of business and commerce has generally caused unemployment. Many car workers have lost their jobs when car manufacturing companies have introduced the use of robots into factories. Jobs that used to be done by clerical workers have been replaced by computers; for example, the calculation of payroll, the issuing of invoices and requests for payment and receipts of payment, to name but a few. Most car parks are now automated and there is less need for car park attendants.

The main reason for these changes has been cost, although there have been other factors. These are discussed below, before considering those workers who have been most affected by the introduction of online services.

Repetitiveness and accuracy

Robots are used because certain tasks must be performed in the same way and with the same degree of accuracy every time. Many jobs such as car assembly have

little need for feedback and so do not require human judgement and reactions, for which computers and robots are difficult to program.

Similarly, there are aspects of shopping and banking which must be performed the same way and with the same degree of accuracy every time.

Industrial robots can be small and compact or can be very large depending on what they are required for: fine, detailed tasks or those that need very heavy objects to be lifted. Robots can also be used in situations that are unpleasant or dangerous for humans to work in, such as bomb disposal, working in space, underwater, in sewers (as in the photo at the top of this page), in mines and working with toxic waste.

Time and automation

Office jobs have been replaced or have changed due to the introduction of computers in the work place. One such office application is the production of the workers' payroll. Many payroll systems required a great deal of paperwork. The number of hours people worked and their rate of pay used to be written down manually and their wages would be worked out using calculators. The results of the calculations would then be typed out manually. Now, computers are used to carry out the whole process. The only need for any manual input is to have somebody type in details of the workers. Even here, the manual entry of weekly data such as hours worked tends to have been replaced by computers using direct data entry methods (e.g. magnetic cards). In the same way, online services can use many automated services to reduce the amount of time and paperwork required for each transaction.

Bank workers

The introduction of online banking has seen a reduction in the need for certain types of worker. Bank cashiers are now no longer needed in the numbers that used to be required. Both the use of ATM machines by many customers and the increase in online banking have led to fewer cashiers being needed.

Furthermore, the number of cheques being processed is estimated to be dropping by 3% per year. This is due to online banking allowing bills or other outgoings to be paid directly from one account to another without the need for writing cheques. As a result, more and more cheque-processing centres are closing, so fewer jobs are available to workers involved in cheque processing.

Shop workers

The use of online shopping has also led to fewer workers being required, so the number of shop assistants has fallen dramatically. For example, in Europe the number of shop workers who are unemployed form the second highest group of unemployed workers in the region. In addition, fewer staff are required to organise stock control, due to the introduction of electronic point of sales (EPOS) terminals. These use barcode readers to input product data and are often linked to automated stock control systems.

New employment opportunities

With the introduction of online services and the use of ICT in the business sector generally, there have been new jobs created. Furthermore, most jobs in any aspect of industry, business and commerce now require some ICT skills, leading to an increase in the need for skilled workers.

As new ICT systems are introduced and updated, systems analysts are in great demand. Systems analysts analyse existing systems and recommend the design and implementation of new systems. In addition to systems analysts, computer programmers are needed to write code for the new systems. Many new systems require the creation of a website for the organisation concerned, which involves the services of website designers and authors. Computer technicians are required to install and service the computer hardware. All these people are needed by online service providers to create and maintain systems.

The need for help desk or support staff has developed. When people have problems with the system, be it online shopping or banking, they need to be able to contact somebody for help.

In addition, call centres have created fresh opportunities, particularly for women in developed countries and for men and women in developing countries.

3.3 Online services and leisure time

The effect of the use of online services is to allow the possibility of workers working fewer hours. As has been mentioned above, the use of online services has caused an increase in the unemployment rate in many work areas. The alternative for companies who do not wish to make too many of their workers unemployed is to reduce the number of hours employees work, rather than reducing the number of workers.

Many people think that the increased use of online services has caused a reduction in the number of hours employees are required to work. However, there is evidence to suggest that the use of ICT has not provided more leisure time. People who have studied the work–life balance of many workers are suggesting that for many people new technology has had the opposite effect. Rather than decreasing the average employee's workload, the expectation by employers is that people should take work home. Often employees are phoned at weekends or after hours to do something. Most people have computers at home. This means that, instead of reducing the number of hours they work, they just take the work home with them and do it there.

Another factor to take into consideration is the level of pay of many workers. It is possible, and many governments have passed laws to make sure it happens, for workers to reduce the number of hours they work. However, fewer hours worked means less money. Most workers want to earn as much money as they did before this cut in hours. Many workers, therefore, volunteer to work longer hours than the government says they have to. This is legal provided the employer agrees. Employers cannot make them work this long but workers may choose to do so. The effect of this is that the number of hours a worker actually works has not changed, despite the introduction of online services.

It can be argued that the introduction of online services has affected more people than just the employees. Because so many activities, such as shopping and banking, can be performed online, most people now have more leisure time as they don't spend so much time going to shops or banks.

3.4 Online services and working patterns

ICT developments, including the increased use of online services, has increased the amount of flexible working that organisations can offer their workers. Flexible working is any working pattern that can be decided by the employee and is not the normal '9 to 5' routine.

In this section we will be looking at different types of flexible working such as:

- part-time working
- job sharing
- flexible working hours (sometimes referred to as flexitime)
- working from home
- compressed hours
- moving from branch to branch.

Part-time working

This is when people only work a limited number of hours. The use of online services means that there are fewer jobs available but an advantage is that workers can work less than the normal full-time hours. The number of hours worked can vary from a few hours a week to just less than full time. One of the benefits to employers is that these workers can be used at the busier times for a business. Another is that it can help to retain and attract staff. Also, where fully trained staff are retained, this means that the company or business will not have to spend money on training new people how to do the work. Online services also need call centres or help lines that need to be available in the evening. Most full-time employees do not like working at these times, so shops and banks have to employ part-time workers.

Unfortunately, there are some possible problems for employers. There can be extra costs on those occasions when training has to be provided. This is because there are more staff, even though they are working fewer hours. However, employers often say that the higher productivity, lower absenteeism (workers having time off from work due to ill health or family commitments) and fewer changes in personnel more than compensate for the extra costs. As well as the higher costs associated with training, there can be problems with organising training. This is because the dates for training have to fit in with when the part-time workers are actually at work.

One of the benefits for workers is that they can organise their life outside work more easily. Another is that workers can continue in the job they have been used to doing. If they had to change jobs they might lose their skills and self-confidence.

There are some problems for workers, however. Part-time workers are less likely to receive in-work training than their full-time colleagues. Those working part time earn considerably less per hour than full-time workers. The difference is greatest for women working part time, who earn just over half the rate per hour that male full-time workers earn. Part-time jobs are still more common in the lower paid occupations. It is sometimes very difficult for part-time workers to become part of a company's pension scheme.

Job sharing

Job sharing is where two people share a job that would normally be done by one person. Each person is paid on a part-time basis but together they do a full-time job. This can be achieved by one person working specific days, mornings or afternoons and the other person working the days, mornings and afternoons when the other doesn't, although there may be times when the employer wants them to work certain times together.

There are benefits for employers. The two workers can have different skills, knowledge and experience. The employer can be said to be getting the skills of two workers for the price of one. As with any part-time worker, because they are working fewer hours they may be fresher and more creative. When the business is particularly busy the employer can get the two workers to work together. For particular types of job, it doesn't matter that at less busy times neither is working. Obviously, this does not apply to jobs like customer help, where somebody must always be available. If one worker is ill or on holiday, part of the job still gets done. Using a job-share arrangement may mean that workers stay with the business, whereas they might leave if they had to work full time. As with part-time working, there is no need to spend money on training a new person.

A possible problem for employers is that money may need to be spent on providing an extra desk or additional equipment. As when employing part-time workers, there may be extra training costs associated with training both workers and trying to arrange training times to suit all workers may be difficult.

The benefits for workers are much the same as with part-time working. Additionally, job sharing can give greater enjoyment at work as problems can be shared with someone else.

However, there are some problems for employees. Managers may not want certain jobs to be shared. Workers may not get as much job satisfaction if what was considered to be 'their' job now has to be shared with someone else. A further issue is that those who job share have to be extremely organised in terms of the handover between them; it can also help if they think in a similar way.

Flexible working hours

Flexible working hours, or flexitime as it is sometimes called, give workers some choice about what times of day they work. They can vary them from day to day. They work the same number of hours each week, but they can choose when to do these hours, providing it fits in with other workers' requirements and also the employer's needs.

One benefit for employers is that it can enable businesses to be open for longer during the day. This is very useful when the business has call centres and wants the phones to operate from say, eight in the morning until ten at night. Employers are able to match working hours with busy and not-so-busy times. It is also easier to allow for employees' personal needs, leading in turn to a reduction in absenteeism and improved punctuality. Because flexitime appeals to many workers, it can help recruitment and reduce the number of staff leaving for another job. As far as workers are concerned, flexitime is one of the most popular types of flexible working. This leads to greater productivity because employees work harder when they are at work. Where teams of workers

are allowed to organise work rotas this can lead to a better working atmosphere and greater productivity.

However, there are some problems for employers. It may take managers longer to organise the system. It may not be possible with some areas of work. Employers have to make sure that essential working times are always covered. There is a danger of lower productivity, as some workers may work unsupervised during early or late times, and when left alone they might not work as hard.

There are a number of benefits for workers. Flexitime allows workers to organise their working lives to suit their personal needs. Travelling to work can be easier and cheaper if it happens outside peak times. If workers stay late to finish a job, they can take time off at a later date. If the job requires great concentration, it can be done at quiet times of day.

There are, however, some problems for employees. It can put extra pressure on some workers if they are required to work when other workers are not prepared to work.

Working from home

Working from home, sometimes called teleworking, involves employees spending all or some of their working week at home, using their home as an office. More and more employees are being allowed to work at home from time to time in order to work without interruption.

One benefit for employers is that less money has to be spent on renting or buying offices. Some workers have commitments which make it difficult for them to leave their home, for example having young families, looking after elderly relatives or having disabilities. When employers allow these people to work from home it means that the company doesn't lose the services of staff who might otherwise leave.

One problem for employers is that they must make sure that workers are on task and not wasting time. In general, it is a case of employing strategies that are effective in an office-based situation, such as setting and monitoring targets and being available to answer any questions and to provide support. An essential part of managing people working from home is to ensure that there is technical support available to the teleworker. Without fully functioning equipment, the teleworker will be unable to meet targets. Maintaining contact, through weekly meetings, regular phone calls and e-mails, is essential if the worker is to feel valued.

There are obviously benefits for workers. They can manage their work and home life more easily. It is no longer essential for them to live close to their work. They save on transport costs and travelling time. They can work hours which suit them.

There are also disadvantages:

- Some people find it difficult to work without having contact with other people.
- They do not see their manager as regularly. This means that they are less able to impress him or her, and this can affect career prospects.
- It is not always easy to find an office space in the home.
- Sometimes it is difficult to concentrate on work when distracted by what is going on at home:
  ◇ Friends or relatives may drop in for a chat, making it difficult to work.
  ◇ Young children at pre-school age demand attention.
  ◇ Pets can cause distractions, such as dogs needing to be taken for a walk.
- Keeping work documents confidential and secure while travelling from work to home and vice versa can be hard.

Compressed hours

Compressed hours working involves employees working the same number of hours but over a shorter number of days. It usually involves working four or four and a half days in a week, or nine days out of ten in a period of two weeks.

One benefit for employers is that by giving extra time off it helps to keep employees who might otherwise leave for the same reasons as with flexitime. Because some workers work longer it means that the company can operate longer hours. Also, absenteeism is less of a problem because employees have more time off.

Workers benefit because they earn the same amount of money but work fewer days. They can also have 'long weekends' if they complete all their working hours by early Friday. A problem for workers is that by working longer days they can get very tired and not be able to enjoy their extra free time.

Ability to move from branch to branch

With many companies having centralised computer systems, it is not as important which office workers operate from. They will still be able to access their work. This means that employers can organise it so that they can move employees from a branch that is less busy to one that is busier at certain times of the week.

3.5 Online services and security and privacy of data

Need to protect confidentiality of data

When we talk about the confidentiality of personal data we mean that information should only be seen by those people who are authorised to see it. Keeping data confidential is an essential part of information security. Encryption is the main ICT technique used to ensure the confidentiality of data in online systems. Ordinary data is converted into a secret code, so anybody illegally accessing data will not be able to understand it. They can still do malicious things like deleting the data but they cannot gain any information from it. To read an encrypted file requires a secret key or password that enables the person to decrypt it. Unencrypted data is called plain text; encrypted data is referred to as cipher text.

Shop security

User and payment data are encrypted when they are transferred using the Internet. You will not need to go into much detail for the AS part of the course but you need to understand that there are public encryption keys and private encryption keys. Encryption is explained in more detail in Chapter 7 for A2 students. Individuals have a public key which they can tell everybody about. They also have a private key which only they know. Provided you know an individual's public key, you can use it to encrypt a message to send to them. Only that individual, however, is able to decrypt it using their private key. Public-key systems are used to encrypt information that is transmitted using the Internet for payment purposes. These systems are extremely secure and relatively simple to use. When paying using the Internet, individuals do not need to worry about the public/private key as the browser manages this task itself by asking the remote server for its public key.

Online banking

Many banking systems do not consider that the use of a single password provides sufficient protection against the interception of data by hackers. Online banking uses secure sites and all data transferred using the Internet, including the password, are encrypted. This makes it very difficult for an unauthorised person to get any meaningful information after it has been sent. However, encryption alone does not prevent hackers or fraudsters from gaining access to your PC at home. Using key-logging software, they can detect the keys you are pressing on the keyboard. There is also the slight possibility that they can discover your password or even somebody could steal your password if you are careless enough to write it down.

Many online banking services therefore use additional methods of security.

One method is to use what are called transaction numbers (TANs). These are basically passwords which are used once only. They are sent to you by your bank either through the post or a more recent development is you request one on the Internet and the bank sends the TAN to your mobile phone. It is only valid for a few minutes, thereby reducing the time available for a hacker to intercept and use it.

Another method is to ask the user to type in only part of their password, such as the second, third and fifth characters. Every time the user logs in they are asked for a different combination. This way, a hacker can only get to know part of the password, which is not very useful to them. What is the point of knowing the second, third and fifth characters if when they log on the system asks them for the first, fourth and sixth?

A third method involves providing customers with a handheld chip and PIN device which is capable of generating single-use passwords (this is called 'two-factor authentication' or '2FA'). To access their account a customer would need their debit card, its PIN number, their online security number and the chip and PIN device itself. Once the customer has inserted their card into the device and entered their PIN number, they will be issued with an eight-digit code. This is the password they use to log in to pay somebody and it changes each time the information is entered.

Online shopping

The same encryption techniques are used for data transmission as are used by banks.

In addition most sites use the 'https' secure prefix to their URL rather than the more common 'http'.

The onus is, however, on the customer to ensure that they are using a reputable, secure online store. In addition, to show that data is being transmitted using either the secure socket layer (SSL) or transport layer security (TLS) protocols, there should be a padlock at the bottom of the site. Both are protocols used in the encryption of messages between a client computer and a server, although TLS is now taking over from SSL. You will not need to know about these in detail for your final AS exam, just that they exist. They are explained more in Chapter 7 for A2 students.

It is important that the customer checks the contact details and details of the company to make sure of its reliability. It is equally important that the store has a privacy policy and that the customer reads this. If there isn't one or it is too difficult to understand, the customer should go to another store. It is important to know what exactly they are agreeing to buy. Both the description and what to do in the event that they are not satisfied should be clear. Most transactions, if paid for by credit card, are protected by bank legislation so they should always use a credit card. Customers should always print out details of the transaction in case of future disputes.

Data protection legislation

Data protection acts exist in most countries. These set down rules for keeping data private as well as confidential. Most countries have similar sets of data protection rules. As an example, here is a summary of what the UK Data Protection Act states:

- Personal data shall be processed fairly and lawfully.
- Personal data shall be obtained only for a lawful purpose (or purposes), and shall not be used for anything other than that purpose (or purposes).
- Personal data shall be adequate, relevant and not excessive in relation to the purpose (or purposes) for which they are processed.
- Personal data shall be accurate and, where necessary, kept up to date.
- Personal data processed for any purpose (or purposes) shall not be kept for longer than is necessary for that purpose (or purposes).

- Personal data shall be processed in accordance with the rights of data subjects.
- Appropriate measures shall be taken against unauthorised or unlawful processing of personal data and against accidental loss or destruction of, or damage to, personal data.
- Personal data shall not be transferred to a country outside the European Economic Area unless that country guarantees the same level of data protection.

The Act also allows you to find out, on payment of a nominal fee, what information is being held about you by an organisation.

Punishment for breaking any of the above principles is a very large fine.

Social and ethical implications of access to personal information

A number of employees in large organisations have to look at the personal data of other individuals. They are trusted to keep the nature of their work confidential and not share any of this data with people outside (and some inside) that organisation. It is important that they are aware of their duties in this work.

Duty of confidence

Employees who handle confidential information about individuals have a personal duty of confidence both to the individuals and to their employer. This means that they must not tell anybody or use the information for any reason except with the permission of the person who told them. Should they attempt to do so the person who told them can take out a legal injunction preventing them.

Examples of confidential information are trade secrets, business secrets, personal information such as diaries and photographs and professional information.

In order for a duty of confidence to exist, the employee must be asked to treat the information as confidential or it must be obvious to them that the information is given in confidence. The best way to do that is for the employer to ask the employee to sign a confidentiality agreement.

Duty of fidelity

A duty of confidence is often confused with an employee's duty of fidelity. An employee must be loyal to their employer for so long as they work for them. That means that they must not tell any rival companies about their work. This does not mean that the information is confidential. Once an employee leaves a company they are free to use the skills and knowledge they got with that company when they go to work for another one.

Responsibility for passing on information

Organisations are accountable for their decisions to pass on information. When they pass on information about an individual they have to make sure that only the least amount of information that could identify the individual should be used. Online services, particularly online banking and shopping, allow organisations to have access to the most private of data such as names, addresses, phone numbers, financial situation etc. It is essential that such information is not passed on from organisation to organisation without authorisation from the individual.

Anonymised information

Information about individuals without mentioning the person by name is called anonymised information. Where anonymised information would be sufficient for a particular purpose, organisations should always omit personal details wherever possible.

Aggregated information

Aggregated information is where personal details of individuals are combined to provide information without naming those individuals. However, this may not always safeguard details adequately. An example could be a hospital which statistically analyses all of its patients (without using their names) who suffer from a particular illness or disease and produces information about those patients, for example the number of patients who suffer from a specific disease whose income is below a certain level. As this covers all the patients, no one patient is identifiable. The problem is that there may be only one patient suffering from a particular disease and so it is obvious who the hospital is referring to.

Breaches of confidence

As was mentioned above, organisations should include a duty of confidence clause in employment contracts. Individuals who feel that their confidential data has been made public (i.e. their confidentiality has been breached) should complain to the organisation.

Need for security

Under the Data Protection Act, security measures must be in place within an organisation to protect computerised information. As has been explained earlier in this section, under 'Online banking', many methods are used and are being developed to ensure security of personal information.

Some customers do not use online banking because they think that they could be open to somebody defrauding them. We have already seen what measures banks take to prevent this but such systems can never be totally foolproof. However, the actual risk of fraud is very tiny. Currently, more people still use conventional banking rather than online banking, and they are more likely to be defrauded than those who go online.

Identity theft

Credit card fraud and identity theft occur more often with conventional banking than with online banking. Many people today are concerned about identity theft, which usually occurs in the form of stolen credit card data.

When a purchase is made in some restaurants, shops or petrol stations some customers let the waiter or cashier take the credit card out of their sight. The waiter might use the excuse that the card reader is in the back of the building. The card is then skimmed on a special reader and all the details are copied from the card. Sometimes, to try and avoid suspicion, the 'skimming' machine can be just below the cash till and the customer hardly notices that it has been skimmed as well as swiped for the transaction. With all these details, numerous Internet transactions can be carried out.

A rarer method, but it still happens, is when retail outlets' databases are hacked into and all customer data is copied for illegal use.

Call-line centres for banks have had employees copy data to pass on to criminals, who then use the data to make illegal transactions.

Online transactions tend to be more secure. However, even though the data is encrypted, at some point it has to be decrypted in order to process it. At this point, it becomes vulnerable to theft.

Phishing

Phishing is when details of credit cards, debit cards or bank accounts are given out by customers to people they think are representatives of banking organisations. It can be as simple as an e-mail that might ask for a customer's details and appear to be from the bank they normally use. The e-mail may say that the bank needs the information so that its systems can be updated or that it is checking that it has the correct e-mail address. It asks the customer for their password, card or account number and other security details. Most banks overcome this by making it clear that they would never ask for the full password, just a number of characters from it (usually three). Phishers often include a website address for the customer to go to which, looks just like the actual bank's website. It is actually a fake website they have set up purely to get customer details.

Pharming is a variation of phishing. The fraudster can redirect a genuine website's traffic to their own website. The customer thinks they are dealing with their bank (the site is the normal site they would log on to) but are actually sending their details to the fraudster's website.

Spyware

Spyware is software which customers unwittingly download. This usually happens when computer users download certain software. They do not realise that the fraudster or hacker has attached spyware to it to gather personal details of the user, often by means of detecting key presses on the keyboard when the user logs on to their bank accout or goes online shopping.

Online auction or shopping fraud

This is when somebody uses a genuine site such as an auction site, puts expensive items up for sale and either just does not deliver them or sends cheap imitations in their place. Some people set up complete online shopping sites which seem to be genuine, but then they take the money and never deliver the goods.

3.6   Online services and health and safety

Health

Increase in repetitive strain injury

It is felt that the increased use of online services may have an effect on the degree of repetitive strain injury (RSI) that computer users will experience. This is more likely to be the case with telephone operators at call centres than with other users.

The two most common RSI ailments experienced by computer users are:

- **Carpal tunnel syndrome**, the name given to a condition causing pain in the forearm and wrist. The number of cases has increased since the 1980s, due to the increased use of computers in offices. It affects women more than men.
- **Cubital tunnel syndrome**, a similar condition which affects the elbow. It is sometimes referred to as 'cell phone elbow', caused by keeping the elbow bent in order to make and take calls on a mobile phone.

RSI is often caused by computer users having their arms and wrists at awkward angles when working at the computer. This picture illustrates the ideal arm and hand positions for computer work.

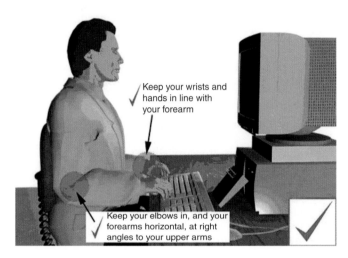

Keep your wrists and hands in line with your forearm

Keep your elbows in, and your forearms horizontal, at right angles to your upper arms

Vision and posture problems

Upper back and neck problems are often caused by bad positioning of a computer screen or bad lighting. Typical symptoms include neck pain, shoulder pain, weakness of the arm and hand muscles and headaches. Lower back pain can be caused by prolonged sitting or standing. Visual problems such as eye irritation and eye strain are also quite common among long-term computer users. This can be caused by glare from the screen, poor positioning of the screen and poor lighting. Most call centres are designed to reduce these and times should be set aside for the operators to be able to get up and walk around.

To prevent these problems, companies and workers must follow health and safety guidance regarding the height, position and distance of monitors and keyboards from operators when working. If operators are going to be seated for extended periods, they must be provided with good-quality seating that supports the back. Seating should be height adjustable, so that monitors and keyboards are correctly positioned and operators do not have to look up or down at the monitor for prolonged periods. This picture illustrates the ideal sitting position for computer work.

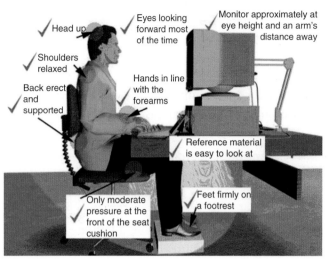

Head up

Eyes looking forward most of the time

Monitor approximately at eye height and an arm's distance away

Shoulders relaxed

Hands in line with the forearms

Back erect and supported

Reference material is easy to look at

Only moderate pressure at the front of the seat cushion

Feet firmly on a footrest

Safety

Many safety problems are caused by the use of a large number of computers close to each other, as is particularly the case at online centres. This leads to a need for increased safety measures, against electrocution, fire and other dangers.

Electrocution

This is a rare occurrence but can occur wherever there are lots of computers, electrical cables and sockets.

Safety measures include the following:
- Electrical sockets should not be overloaded. The use of automatic fuse trips means that when there is an overload the circuit trips out.
- All electrical installations must be carried out by a qualified electrician.
- All equipment must be of a reliable standard and should be checked annually by qualified electricians.
- All electrical equipment must be located away from water supplies and workers must have a sound knowledge of electrical safety.
- Workers must not take drinks to tables where they are working with electrical equipment

Fire

When computers overheat or wires fray, this can lead to fire.

Safety measures include the following:

- There must always be plenty of CO_2 fire extinguishers.
- Fire exits must be kept clear at all times and not blocked by equipment.
- All electrical equipment must be located away from water supplies and operators must have a sound knowledge of electrical safety.

Tripping hazards

When electricity or computer wires, cables or leads are left lying around, people can easily trip over them.

Safety measures include the following:

- Cabling must not trail on the floor.
- Additional equipment must be situated where it will not result in trailing cables.

Danger caused by heavy equipment falling

All sorts of personal injuries can be caused by computer equipment falling off a workstation or by a workstation collapsing.

Safety measures include the following:

- Benching must be sturdy enough to withstand the weight of the hardware and additional equipment stored on it.
- No equipment, no matter how small, must overhang the workstation. Even something as small as a mouse is connected to the computer and if the computer or monitor is not stable it may topple over if the mouse is pulled away.

Examination questions

Questions 1 and 2 relate to the car engine manufacturing company in South Africa, described in the Examination questions on page **43**.

1   The company has to follow government data protection rules when it comes to storing data about the workers. One of these rules is that the company has to keep the data secure. Describe three other rules which the company must obey.   [3]
    You will need to make three points.

2   Explain why it is necessary to have data protection rules.   [6]
    You will need to make six points.

After many successful years of trading, Shazad supermarkets are extending their services to include a home shopping service. Customers will log on to the service using their home computers, choose the products they wish to buy and then these will be delivered to their home for a small extra charge. The local supermarket will have workers who will go round the store collecting the goods together so that home delivery can take place.

3   Describe the minimum hardware and software requirements of the home computer which will be used in this system and why they are needed.   [3]
    You will need to make three points.

4   Describe what effect the introduction of the system will have on the working opportunities and practices for the supermarket employees.   [5]
    You will need to make five points.

5   Some customers are worried that they will have to pay using a credit card. Discuss why you think this will be a problem or not.   [5]
    You will need to make five points.

6   A number of staff will be needed to update the website on a regular basis. They will be required to use computers for long periods of time. Describe the health and safety issues arising from this.   [3]
    You will need to make three points.

7   Companies such as banks are setting up call centres in the Far East to provide support to customers in the West.
    Describe some of the effects on the individual and society of a company having call centres in the Far East.   [4]
    You will need to look at Chapter **2** for part of your answer.
    You will need to make four points.

The systems life cycle

You already have some basic knowledge of the stages in the systems life cycle:

➤ feasibility study
➤ analysis
➤ design
➤ development and testing
➤ implementation
➤ documentation
➤ evaluation.

In this chapter you will learn about ICT systems and how they are created and developed. You will also be introduced to the scenario-based examination papers that are used by CIE. You will learn, in more detail, about:

➤ the stages of the systems life cycle
➤ the different methods of researching a situation
➤ the steps involved in designing a new ICT system
➤ developing and testing a new ICT system
➤ implementing a new ICT system
➤ the development of the documentation of a new ICT system
➤ evaluating a new ICT system.

In the early days of computing, most existing work-based systems were manual. There were very few computers around. It was important therefore to see if it was desirable to replace the manual system with a computerised one. The first stage in looking at an existing system and seeing whether a new computer system is needed is the feasibility study. Once this has been completed and the decision to proceed with or to abandon the examination of the system has been made, the feasibility study is finished. All subsequent stages in the systems life cycle tend to be repeated.

Stages of the systems life cycle

With modern day computing it is more likely that there is one of two possible situations. One is where a system is computerised but may be out of date and need

replacing. The other is where a small company has a computer system in place but it is very limited and could be improved upon to allow many more aspects of the business to become computerised.

The examination papers for this course are based on scenarios – 'scenario' is just another name for situation – that are developed specifically for the examination. Because the subject is Applied ICT we look at how ICT is applied in real situations rather than just studying the theory of it. We are going to use the scenario approach to look at the systems life cycle.

We are going to look at a building supply company scenario and consider the need for an improved ICT system. Let us consider a fictional company called Biashara Street Building Supplies in Nairobi, Kenya. The company buys in bricks, cement, gravel, sand and roof tiles from big companies and then sells them in smaller quantities to local house builders. The company is run by two directors called Peter Kimanthi and Irene Kibaki. It employs two secretaries, three sales people and two truck drivers. It has a computer, but this is mainly used for creating word-processed letters and sending emails to customers. Its only other use is to keep records of the company's customers on a database. One secretary, Josephine, deals with the workers' personal information and is also in charge of keeping customer details. The other secretary, Mary, keeps information about the hours worked by the workers and also processes orders from customers. Irene is in charge of the paying of the workers.

Peter and Irene feel that they could make better use of their computer system and need a systems analyst to look at how the computer is used, and to advise them whether or not their business would improve if they made increased use of the computer. They have invited Daniel Mathuru to perform this role.

Let us look at how Daniel will approach the situation.

The systems life cycle is so named because it is a circular process (see diagram). There is no real start and finish point, because after a new system has been evaluated this leads to further improvements being needed and so the whole process starts over again.

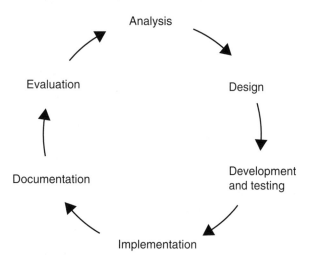

The purpose of analysing the existing system is to see how data flows around the system. If you think of the system as being the company itself, in simple terms analysis is to see what data comes in to the company, how it is processed and what outputs they produce. Only after this has been determined will the analyst decide on what sort of computer system should be implemented.

4.1 Systems analysis

Systems analysis involves examining the existing system in detail, in particular:

- collecting information on how the existing system works
- establishing its inputs, outputs and processing
- recording information, for example in the form of data flow diagrams
- identifying problems.

Having carried out these stages, the systems analyst then needs to:

- identify suitable hardware and software for a new system
- identify user and information requirements.

Collecting information

The first stage of systems analysis is collecting information about the current system. There are four methods of doing this:

- examination of documents
- interviews
- observation
- questionnaires.

Examination of documents

All documents that are used within a system need to be examined. The documents may be, for example, bills, invoices, letters, order forms, payslips etc. If, after the analysis, it is considered necessary, they will be replaced with ones produced by the computer system.

An example of a document:

Invoice
From:
Biashara Street Building Supplies 20 Biashara Street PO Box 13579 Nairobi Phone: (020) 254637 Fax: (020) 254698
20 tons sand@5 000 Ksh = 100 000 Ksh
Tax 15 000 Ksh
Total 115 000 Ksh
To: Kenya Airways Airport Road PO Box19142 Nairobi

This method of collecting information will help the systems analyst to identify the inputs and outputs of the system as it operates at the moment. He can then assess the **processing** that the computer system will need to carry out. Using the payslip as an example:

- the new variable each week is the number of hours worked – this is the input
- the outputs are all the figures that appear on the payslip
- the processing is the use of the input and other, stored figures to perform calculations to produce the outputs.

The other use the systems analyst will make of these documents is to calculate the number of documents that are processed and the volume of data on all the documents. This is simply the amount of data on one document multiplied by the number of documents of that type. This would be calculated for each type of document. The systems analyst would use this information to decide on the size of memory as well as the types of input and output devices needed to cope with this volume of data.

Questionnaires

This is perhaps the most common form of collecting information. The way questions are phrased is very important, as the way a question is asked can influence people's answers in the questionnaire. For example, Daniel may want to know what information Peter and Irene would like to see on a computer-produced payslip. A question along the lines of:

What details of the workers and their pay would you like to see on your workers' payslips?

is less likely to help the systems analyst to produce a payslip design than if the question was asked in this way:

Which of the following information would you like to see on a worker's payslip:
- ◇ worker's name
- ◇ worker's number
- ◇ rate of pay
- ◇ hours worked
- ◇ income tax rate
- ◇ income tax paid
- ◇ any other information?

This would tend to produce more precise information for the systems analyst than trying to get Peter and Irene to produce a list which might include information that is not really relevant. This is where the systems analyst's previous experience of designing documents such as invoices and payslips will help the directors.

An advantage of questionnaires is that although it takes a lot of time to produce an effective one, once it is produced as many copies as you want can be given out. For example, Peter and Irene might decide at the last minute that the workers ought to be asked what information they would like to see on their payslip. With any other method it would take a lot of organising to get the information, whereas with a questionnaire it is just a matter of producing extra copies and distributing them.

A disadvantage of questionnaires is that, because they are impersonal and can be anonymous, workers might exaggerate their answers as they know there is no comeback. In our scenario, however, because there are so few workers involved, they would be fairly easily identified.

Interviews

This method is used in every situation, but because of its nature it has a very limited format. Because it takes time to complete an interview it is not possible to interview every worker. Instead, interviewing is a technique that is used with key personnel and representatives of the other workers.

An advantage with interviews is that they are flexible. With questionnaires it is very difficult to ask further questions based on the response to another question. With interviews this is straightforward. The interviewer can move away from their 'script' and ask a more in-depth question if a particular response is given. A questionnaire cannot be adapted like this without a great deal more time being spent on altering and redistributing it.

As with questionnaires, a lot of time is spent on producing the most appropriate set of questions. It also takes a lot of time to organise an interview. The workers or directors have to be available at the time the systems analyst wants to interview them. This is not always possible and compromises often have to be reached. The systems analyst has to be very flexible in all this and must try to accommodate the busy working schedule of the people who are to be interviewed.

There are other drawbacks with interviews. There is a temptation for certain interviewees to give not very accurate answers. They may try and provide answers that they think the interviewer wants to hear rather than giving accurate responses. In contrast, as a questionnaire can be anonymous answers tend to be, on the whole, more accurate.

Another drawback with interviews is the time taken to complete interviews with many people. This compares unfavourably with questionnaires, where everyone can complete the questionnaire in the same amount of time instead of one after the other.

Observation

There are many situations where the three methods described above do not provide the full picture that the systems analyst requires. All the other methods give information about an individual's role within the business but do not really provide information about how separate tasks overlap and how workers interact, or even if the methods being used are efficient.

Observation involves the systems analyst just watching all the activities going on in the office. For example, it may be necessary to see how the data comes in about a customer and how that is processed and used to produce an invoice. A number of tasks performed by individual workers may involve the inputs to the system, such as recording new sales to customers, while another worker may be involved in processing that data so that an invoice can be created.

Observation will enable the systems analyst to see the process as a whole. From this, a data flow diagram can be produced that will enable the analyst to determine the inputs, outputs and processing which exist in the current system.

One drawback of observation is the 'Hawthorne effect'. This is when some people who know they are being observed change the way they work. They may start to work more efficiently than normal, which could lead to misleading statistics being collected by the analyst.

Choice of method

The choice of method for collecting data about the existing system depends on the type of information being collected and also the practicality of using the method in the situation presented to the analyst. If, for example, there were hundreds of employees it would take too long to personally interview each one. This would also be the case where employees are spread over a number of areas, for example with companies such as banks that

have separate branches in different towns. In this case, questionnaires might be a better method of collecting information from the workers.

In our scenario, there are very few employees and so, in addition to examining the documentation of the company, any of the other three methods might be appropriate. However, in reality different methods would be used for different employees:

- ◆ Peter and Irene would need to be interviewed as the owners of the company, so that their specific needs could be established. These needs might be difficult to discover in any other way.
- ◆ The two secretaries may need to be observed, as their roles involve different aspects of the work. Asking them questions may make it difficult to discover their precise roles, but these would be fairly easily seen using observation.
- ◆ The sales people are very busy all day as their job entails speaking to customers most of the time. It might be easier to give them questionnaires and collect their responses at a later date. This would mean that they had enough time to complete them, rather than having a possibly rushed interview.
- ◆ The van drivers would rarely be in the office as they spend most of their time driving between customers delivering the building materials. Again, questionnaires might be the most appropriate method for them.

It is sometimes a good idea when collecting information about an existing system to use more than one method with each type of worker, although this particular scenario does not necessarily call for such an approach. However, the very nature of the business involves the production of many orders and invoices as well as a regular, although small, need for production of payslips. Because of this, as with the majority of, if not all, companies, it would be essential to examine the paperwork and documents used in the system.

Establishing the inputs, outputs and processing in the existing system

After the systems analyst has finished collecting information about the current system he needs to identify all the inputs, outputs and processing in the existing system. By examining all the documents used in the current system it can be established which relate to information coming into the system and which relate to information going out. This will then enable the analyst to produce documentation of the system, as opposed to the company's documents that the analyst has been looking at so far. Quite often this stage is done whilst producing a data flow diagram.

Each section of the system will need to be examined to see what specific inputs, outputs and processing are required. For the payroll system, for example, the input would be the details of the workers, the processing would be the calculation of the payrolls and the output would be the payslips. Each part of the system will be examined and broken down into these three elements.

Recording information about the current system

Whilst carrying out the fact-finding methods, the systems analyst needs to record all the results in order to establish all the relevant features of the existing system. It is always important to keep accurate records of systems analysis since the system will continually evolve and other systems analysts and programmers will need to develop the system even further. There are a number of ways of formally recording the flow of data, but the use of data flow diagrams is the most popular. Data flow diagrams are a graphical method of recording the inputs, outputs and processing that have been identified.

A data flow diagram consists of four components: terminators, processes, flow arrows and stores. Look at the very basic data flow diagram below showing how Peter and Irene deal with customer orders. It shows that the customer sends in an order to the company. It is checked to see if it has all the information required such as customer name and address and an order for an existing product. If does not, it is rejected and sent back to the customer. If it does the order is processed and the order information is printed and filed. In addition, an invoice is generated and filed ready to send to the customer.

The order has come from the customer; customers are not part of the process order system and so are placed in a **terminator**. When data flows from or to somebody or somewhere outside the system, that somebody or somewhere is called a terminator. Here we are using a rectangular box with curved corners for a terminator.

The data from the customers are the orders. This information is processed to produce the invoices. The process order is put in a **process box**, shown with a circle.

The actual data output from the system, such as the individual invoices and the printed orders, are recorded for future use. Although this is not kept on computer, the data can still be viewed as being stored. Such data is therefore called a **store** and placed inside a rectangle with no vertical sides.

The last component is the **data flow**. These are the arrows. It is important that the direction of data flow is accurately recorded and that each arrow is labelled to show what data is flowing at that point in the diagram.

There are different levels of data flow diagram. The context level or level 0 data flow diagram is basically a diagram showing a very generalised diagram with the terminators linked to the current system as a whole. A very basic one might look like this.

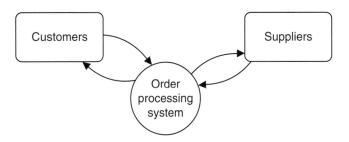

The next level is level 1. It would have many more processes, with more detail about all aspects of the system. It would have the process boxes for receiving orders and also for producing invoices. The next level would be level 2 – there would be many of these, each showing parts of the level 1 diagram in much more detail.

Another way of representing the data flow diagram for processing customer orders (shown above) is by using a **system flowchart** as in the diagram below. This, however, is generally a method of designing a systems solution and so is not found very frequently in the analysis stage. Notice that the orders that are considered to be a store in the data flow diagram have to be represented as being stored on a storage medium in a computerised system. The invoices, which will actually be sent to the customers, are now considered to be output documents. This is because the system flowchart is designed to represent the new computerised system, whereas the data flow diagram represents the old, mainly manual system. In a manual system, keeping information filed on paper is equivalent to storing the data on a computerised system.

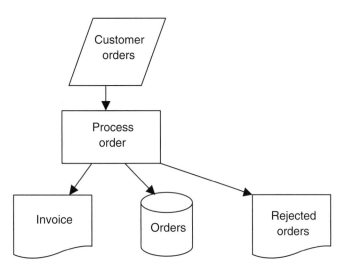

The shapes of boxes used are:

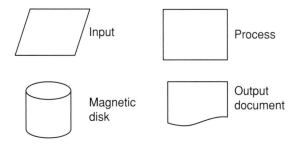

Identifying problems with the current system

Another use of data flow diagrams is to help the systems analyst to identify problems with the current system. By examining the system in great detail, many weaknesses can be identified. In the payroll example above, it might seem unnecessary to have both secretaries involved in entering data into the payroll process. In a new system, these two files of information would need to be linked to make processing easier. By showing the stages of a process in great detail it is easier to see where there is job duplication or unnecessary time wasted in gathering data. After the data flow diagrams have been produced, they are examined together with the other results of analysis such as interview transcripts and questionnaire

analysis to identify the problems with the current system.

Identifying suitable hardware and software for a new system

The actual hardware and software will not be recommended at this early stage in the systems analysis. However, having decided upon the required outputs, storage and processing requirements of the system using the data flow diagrams, the systems analyst will be able to make generalised recommendations for the software and hardware.

Daniel will know the volume of data being input to the system from the terminators and flow arrows in the data flow diagram. This will allow him to determine an appropriate method of input to the system. He will have looked at all the processes that occur and this will give him an idea about the size and speed of the processor required. The stores in the data flow diagram will give him an idea of how much data needs to be stored and this will help him recommend the size and number of storage devices. The terminators and flow arrows coming out of the system will also indicate the quantity and format of the output.

Identifying the user and information requirements

When the new system is developed it will be essential to involve all workers in the process of design. The new system must meet the needs of the people who will be using it.

The process of collecting information about the existing system will have been very important to see exactly what job each worker is doing. Daniel will have interviewed Peter and Irene to discover their requirements for the new system. In addition, he will have recorded his observations and used the data flow diagram to come to a conclusion about the user requirements in general. From this, he will have produced a requirements specification. This will be a list of the features of the system that are required. It will contain general requirements such as what the user wants the overall system to do, i.e. produce the payroll, deal with orders, file customer information, and so on. It will also include specific requirements such as, 'I want the system to find me the details of an individual customer quickly' or, 'I want the system to produce the payroll overnight so I can just set it to print at the end of one day and it's there for me the next morning.'

4.2 Design

Having analysed the existing system, the next stage is to design the new system. The systems analyst, Daniel, may involve the use of a **programmer** (or programmers) at this stage. A programmer is a person who will actually write the software, if new software has to be written. Daniel, together with the programmer, if needed, will have to design:

- the inputs to the system
- the outputs from the system
- the files and/or databases needed to store the data
- the processing required to produce the outputs
- any validation checks that will be needed
- the data needed to test the system.

In addition, the analyst will need to specify the hardware and software needed to form the system.

Designing data collection forms and screen layouts

Great care must be taken in producing **data collection forms** and **screen layouts**. Data collection forms can be either hard copy or screen based. In our example, the drivers have rarely needed to use the computers. It might therefore be best, if data is to be collected about them for entry to the personnel file, that they complete hard copy data collection forms.

When designing a data collection form, the analyst must make it easy both for the worker to fill in and for the secretary to read the information. One of the most common methods for ensuring this is to put boxes in each section to be completed. The rule is to put one box for every character of required input. The use of these boxes will mean that the worker is likely to make fewer errors when filling in the form. Also, as the form will be easier for the secretary to read, errors are less likely when typing the data in. The requirements for completing the form should be clear to workers, so that they know which sections to complete. An example of a basic form is shown below.

The design of these forms will depend on the user requirements as well as output required from system and file structures.

When designing **input screens**, the systems analyst or programmer must consider a number of factors. Each screen will need to be set out in such a fashion that it is easy to use. It will need to be attractive to look at and also it will need to limit the possibility of inaccurate data being entered. In our scenario, Daniel will need to make sure that Mary and Josephine are not distracted by an over-elaborate screen design. The use of lots of different colours and fonts should be avoided, otherwise they will find it difficult to focus on their work and this may lead to them making mistakes.

The screen designs must contain guidelines to workers on how to fill in any data entry forms as well as allowing them to navigate from one screen to another without any difficulty.

The choice of input design will influence the choice of **input devices**. For example, it might be decided that each type of building material should be given a barcode. This would mean that one of the input devices would be a scanner or other hardware capable of inputting a barcode. Decisions regarding the type of input devices may well be taken at this stage.

Designing report layouts and screen displays

When designing **report layouts** and **screen displays**, the systems analyst and programmer will be heavily influenced by the views of the users and what the systems analyst has agreed are the users' requirements. Daniel will decide on what outputs are required by looking at existing documents and examining the results of the interviews that he carried out.

Many of the features of input designs have to be included in output designs, such as being attractive to look at and not being over-elaborate. Screen displays should have instructions on how to move from screen to screen.

The two main aspects of the way output is designed are the format of the output and the medium it is to

Please complete by filling in one letter in each box using a black pen.																			
First name							Family name												
Address 1																			
Address 2																			
Address 3																			

be produced on. The formats are likely to be one or more of:

- graphs
- lists of records
- reports
- tables.

The medium that will be used will be one or more of:

- paper
- screen display
- sound.

Daniel will have spoken with Peter and Irene about their requirements. This and the examination of existing documents will have probably suggested to him that the invoices and payslips could be produced using existing database software to produce reports. For other parts of the system, there will need to be other types and forms of output.

For the layout of the documents, the systems analyst needs to consider who will see them. There will also need to be consultation with the owner(s) of the company. Peter and Irene in our scenario will want their customers to gain a good impression of the company. They will want to see that they advertise the company favourably and contain all the required information in an orderly, easy-to-read format. Furthermore, when designing invoices Peter will know that the style and content of the invoice will have to match the needs of the customer as well as the company.

It is normal for systems analysts to produce three or four different designs of an item of output. When designing these, the analyst is fully aware of what the proposed system is capable of producing. The users of the system will also be asked for their views.

As far as screen output is concerned, the usual rule is to keep it as simple as possible. The users of this system will be the secretaries and sales people and they will not need to have the company advertised to them. It is not necessary for screen output to contain any extra material other than that required. Each screen of output

must have a consistent theme so that the user does not get confused by changing appearances. Instructions on how to navigate between screens should be included on the screen. As stated above, there are different available formats, and these need to be relevant to the output produced and what the user is comfortable with.

Designing the required data/file structures and processing

Although the steps outlined above are in order of how they should happen in theory, in practice the design of the processing would probably occur at the same time as designing the files and databases.

In order to produce a data structure, the systems analyst will have to produce a systems flowchart or similar. The programmer will break then down parts of the systems flowchart into algorithms or program flowcharts.

If we look at a typical UK payslip, we can see that the processing is fairly straightforward.

The type of payslip we will be looking at in this section is shown below, although the payslip for our scenario is simpler than this.

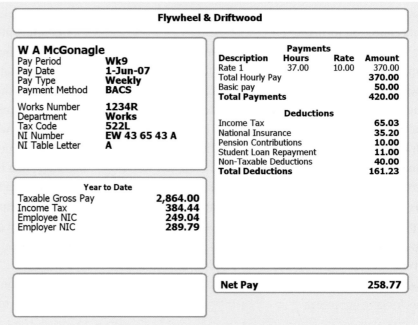

The systems analyst will have to design a structure that will have two files. One will be the **master file** containing data that does not change often, such as name, works number, department, hourly rate, and so on. The other will be a **transaction file** containing the data that changes each week, such as hours worked. These two files will be processed together to produce the payroll.

Before the transaction file is used in combination with the master file, it will need to be checked for errors and sorted in the same order as the master file (as discussed in Chapter **2**). Magnetic disks are now used much more than magnetic tapes, which tend only to be used for backing up systems. The transaction file will therefore be stored on disk, even though it holds data in sequential order. A system flowchart showing the processing in a little more detail than we discussed in Chapter **2** is shown to the right.

Having decided on the need for these files, the systems analyst will then decide on individual file structure and whether any programming is required. He will need to look at the following attributes of the master file:

- ◆ field names
- ◆ field types
- ◆ field lengths
- ◆ validation rules
- ◆ field descriptions
- ◆ selection of key field.

The analyst will also want to design a test plan: the files will need to be tested, as you will see in the development section.

Designing validation routines

When using a computer system, data entry is probably the most time-consuming process compared with processing, storing or outputting data. It is therefore important to try and ensure that the number of errors, which will lead to retyping some of the data, is very small. This can be done by using validation.

In order to ensure that data input to the system is valid it is essential to incorporate as many validation routines as possible into the system. The number and types of routines or checks will obviously depend on the form of input and also the file structures that are being used in the system. Not every field can have a validation check. For example, there are so many variations of peoples' names that this would be very difficult to validate. Some fields will be calculated fields and so will not require a validation check that has not already been built into the calculation. We will only be looking at validation checks which can be used on single items of data individually.

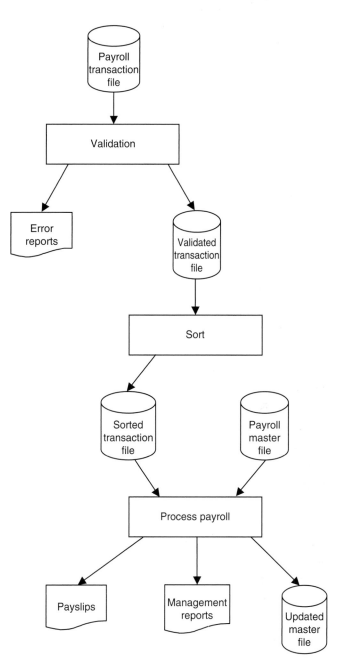

Below are some of the fields on a typical payslip, with examples of data. Many will be stored on the master file but when the master file was set up the input data would have had to be validated and any new records would also require validation.

Fields which contain numeric data tend to have range checks designed for them. Using the payslip below, we can see that Total Payments are £420.00. It is unlikely that any worker will receive more than £1 000. The range

Pay Type	Weekly
Payment Method	BACS
Works Number	1234R
Department	Works
Tax Code	522L
NI Number	EW 43 65 43 A

Total Hourly Pay		370.00
Basic pay		50.00
Total Payments		**420.00**
Deductions		
Income Tax		65.03
National Insurance		35.20

check we could put on this field is that Total Payments must be less than or equal to £1000. Text fields can have length checks put on them. The Works Number has five characters and cannot be more or less than this. There are other validation checks which can be used such as a format or picture check. This would be used to check that the Works Number has four numbers followed by a letter.

The possible validation checks are shown in the table below:

Field name	Validation check
Pay Type	Must be 'Weekly' or 'Monthly'
Payment Method	Must be 'Bank Transfer' or 'Cheque'
Works Number	Length check: must be five characters Format/picture check: must be four digits followed by a letter
Department	Must be 'Works'
Tax Code	Length check: must be more than three and less than six characters Format/picture check: must be three or four digits followed by 'L' or 'H'
NI Number	Length check: must be 13 characters (including spaces) Format check: must be two alphabetic characters (letters), then a space, two digits, a space, two digits, a space, two digits, a space, an alphabetic character
Total Payments	Range check: must be >= 0 and <= 1 000

In our scenario it will be simpler as there will be no fields such as Works Number, Department, etc., and there are many fewer deductions in terms of pension contributions, and so on.

Other validation checks that could be used in other scenarios are:

◆ invalid character check, when the input is checked to make sure it is all digits or all text, depending on the requirements of the field
◆ check digit, when a calculation is performed on a long series or string of digits to produce an extra digit; this is then added to the end of the string; the computer re-calculates when data is entered to check whether it gives the same result.

Other ways of reducing errors when inputting data

The programmer or systems analyst will need to consider ways of reducing errors in addition to designing validation checks.

Another way of reducing errors is to reduce the volume of data that has to be input. For example, the use of coding can help in reducing the number of errors made when entering data. Many students get confused over the use of the word 'coding'. It should not be used in the sense of 'encoding' as in encryption, where 'encoding' is the correct term. It is often used in the sense of programming code. However, the interpretation of the word, in this instance, is totally to do with input and storage of *data*. Students should understand that what is meant by coding data is reducing the number of letters in a word, such as 'Y' instead of 'yes' and 'M' instead of 'male'. When data is shortened in this way, less data is entered and fewer mistakes are made. You are less likely to make spelling mistakes by typing in the letter 'F' than if you typed in the whole word 'female'. It also means that simpler and shorter validation routines can be used.

Another way of reducing errors is to use direct data entry methods such as barcode reading and optical mark reading. These lead to a reduction in the number of errors when compared with manual typing.

Specifying the required hardware and software

The final stage in the design of the new system will be to decide upon the required hardware and software. Now that Daniel has completed the analysis stage of the cycle, he needs to specify exactly what hardware and software is to be purchased. A supplier will be chosen based on cost, reliability and the after-sales support that can be offered. In the analysis stage of the systems design cycle the systems analyst would have made general recommendations regarding the size and type of hardware as well as suggesting some software requirements. Now, he will need to be specific. He will already have made a record of the existing software and hardware being used by the company.

We have already seen in Section **4.1** that the volume of data will determine the choice of output devices. If there is a heavy volume of data then it would mean that an inkjet printer, for example, would not be as suitable as a large volume output device such as a fairly large laser printer. The order that data will be output in will affect the choice of storage devices. If the data is to be stored

Software type	Advantages	Disadvantages
Off-the-shelf	◆ Cheaper as it is mass produced ◆ Available straight away ◆ Testing rigorously carried out by the developers ◆ Helplines with operators who have had to deal with a wide range of problems	◆ May be difficult to adapt to the particular use ◆ May have several distracting extra features unsuitable for the use ◆ May not necessarily match up with the existing system and software use
Purpose-built	◆ Designed specifically for the task ◆ Does not have to be adapted for use ◆ Programmers can make any changes required	◆ Costs more to pay programmers to write code specifically for the task ◆ Testing limited to the perception of use by the programmer ◆ Support limited to the team of programmers ◆ Can take a long time to develop

in an indexed sequential fashion, because the workers' payroll data may need to be accessed directly as well as sequentially, then a hard disk drive will be recommended rather than a magnetic tape drive.

The systems analyst must also choose the software. In our scenario, Daniel may decide that the existing software will be sufficient and that it only needs to be adapted to provide the solution to all the system requirements. Because of the small size of the company, it might be appropriate for Daniel to adopt this strategy. It is likely that other companies dealing with more customers and employing more workers might need to have software written especially for them. However, he will need to be sure that the existing software is capable of producing word-processed documents that can be mail merged and that the various aspects of payroll and invoice production can be completed successfully using the existing database software.

For a larger organisation, it may be necessary for them to employ a programmer to write software specific to their use. There is number of reasons why a company would want to have software specially written for their own purposes: for example, they may need web pages designed which require specialist programming skills; or their database needs may be more complex than that of small companies.

Generally, therefore, there are two choices:

◆ off-the-shelf software, which is already written and available
◆ purpose-built software, which has to be specially written to solve the problem.

There are many big software houses that produce off-the-shelf software, for example database software, invoicing software, accounting software, payroll software and many more types of, predominantly, business-oriented software. The table above gives the advantages and disadvantages of each type of software.

4.3 Development and testing

Having designed the system required, the next three stages are:

◆ creating the system
◆ testing the system
◆ improving the system.

Each time the system is changed as a result of test results, it will need testing again, so the second and third of these stages may be repeated several times, until the system is completed.

Creating data structures and program modules

After the data structures have been designed, they will need to be created using the software or programming language recommended by the systems analyst. The programmer will produce the program code needed to solve the problem. The nature of the problem will determine the amount of programming that is required. Some small organisations such as Peter and Irene's may require very little as it may be possible to adapt existing software in order to produce the outputs required. For example, if the main requirement is the production of invoices and payslips this could be done using a basic database package, a spreadsheet package and a word processor.

However, some organisations and companies are so large that this may not be practical. Instead, their requirements may be so complex that they need to have software written especially for them.

In our scenario, Daniel will need to create file structures for customers, their orders and the payroll. He will have already designed these and selected the software and so, unless he needs to employ a programmer, he will now use the software to create these files.

Testing strategies

In order to make sure that the system works as it is intended the system has to be tested. It is important that the systems analyst produces a test plan. The test plan will consist of a list of test data together with the results expected to be produced by the system (expected results). The systems analyst will then make a note of the results which the system in fact produced when this data was used (actual results). There will also be a note made by the analyst of any comments if there are differences between the actual results and the expected results.

The two main ways of testing a system are by using test data and live data, both of which will need to be carried out.

Test data

First of all, let us look at the three types of test data:

- ◆ normal data
- ◆ extreme data
- ◆ abnormal data.

Normal data is data that is acceptable or valid to the system. This is data which should not produce error messages from the system. For example, if we look at the payslip example we would not have anybody working more than 65 hours in a week and the lowest number of hours would be 0 in the event that somebody was ill all week. Normal data

to test this part of the system would therefore be any number between 0 and 65, including 0 and 65. If data such as this is entered and error messages are produced then there is a problem with the system.

Extreme data is only used where a range of data is input. For names and addresses, for example, there would be no extreme data. Where a range is used, extreme data are the values at either end of the acceptable range. For our payslip example, extreme data would be 0 and 65 only.

Abnormal data is data which is not acceptable or valid. For example, in a numeric field in a database we would not expect alphabetic characters to be entered. Where a range of data is used, numbers outside the range would be considered abnormal. In our payslip example, any negative number or any number greater than 65 or any item of text would be considered abnormal data. Examples of abnormal data here would be −1, 66, 140, 'Akhbar'.

Every aspect of the new system will need to be tested with different types of test data.

A test plan used for the above data might look something like the table below.

If the entry of 65 had produced an error message then the validation check would need to be looked at again. The validation check may have been written as <65 instead of < = 65. Extreme test data is very important as it helps to identify this sort of mistake.

Live data

This is data that has been used in the existing system. It will be used because the outputs are already known. In our example, Daniel will use the hours worked by the workers in past weeks. Because there will be records of the payslips produced from these figures, it will be

Test	Test data	Expected results	Actual results	Comment
Input hours worked	−1	Rejected	Error message	Abnormal data – the system works as expected
	65	Accepted	Wages calculated	Extreme data – the system works as expected
	0	Accepted	Wages calculated but result was 0	Extreme data – the system works as expected
	40	Accepted	Wages calculated	Normal data – the system works as expected
	140	Rejected	Error message	Abnormal data – the system works as expected
	Akhbar	Rejected	Error message	Abnormal data – the system works as expected

easy for him to see that the correct output has been produced.

He will select a week in the year where there may have been special circumstances such as a public holiday. He will also choose another week where it was quite an average week. He will then run these sets of data on the new system and compare the results with the payslips already in existence for those two weeks.

If there are differences between the results, using the new system and the existing payslips, amendments will need to be made to the system.

Improvements that could be needed as a result of testing

The next step is to correct any mistakes. Before the system is implemented, the analyst will correct any faults that were identified as a result of testing. If we look at the example for hours worked being 65, it might be necessary to change the validation check as suggested. Checking the data validation, calculations and file structures should be reasonably straightforward as the test plan will show where there are differences between the expected and actual results of the system.

However, the output from the system may still not have been exactly as expected when live data was used. The next step will be to see where and when the differences occurred. This can be achieved by a process called single stepping. Certain software allows you to run the system one step at a time so that the exact point where the differences occurred can be clearly seen in the programming code. That section of code can then be amended to produce the correct result.

4.4 Implementation

After the system has been developed the systems analyst will want to get the system up and running. His next step will be to choose a method of implementing the new system. There are four methods to choose from: parallel running, direct changeover, phased implementation and pilot running. They all have their own advantages and disadvantages.

Parallel running

Parallel running is running the new system while the old system is still running. This means that the results from the new system can be checked against those of the existing system. When the new system is consistently producing the same results as the existing system, the existing system can then be stopped and replaced by the new system.

Advantages:

- Workers can be trained to use the new system gradually while it is being implemented.
- If there are any problems with the new system and it has to be stopped, there is still the old system as a backup.

Disadvantages:

- Two sets of workers have to be paid to keep both systems working.
- It takes a lot longer to fully implement than any other method.

Direct changeover

In direct changeover, the existing system is replaced by the new one instantly. The existing system is stopped and the new system starts running immediately. This method can only be used when the new system has been thoroughly tested. There are risks associated with this method, as once the old system is closed down it cannot be reintroduced.

Advantages:

- The cost is less than parallel running as only one set of workers needs to be paid.
- It is a very quick method of fully implementing a new system.

Disadvantages:

- If there are problems, there is no backup system.
- It can be difficult to make improvements to the new system and keep it working.

Phased implementation

Phased implementation involves the introduction of the new system one part at a time. It could be that the production of invoices is done by the new system whilst other aspects like the payroll and processing of orders carries on as before. Any problems with the new method can be overcome and when the system is working perfectly another aspect can be moved onto the new system such as processing orders. This approach continues until all aspects have been transferred to the new system.

Advantages:

- If the new system does not work as intended with one aspect, the other aspects of the work can carry on as normal.
- Workers have time to get used to the new system.

Disadvantages:

- It is a slow method of implementation compared with direct changeover.
- If the new system doesn't work properly, it is not possible to fall back on the old system

Pilot running

Pilot running is the method adopted by large organisations. The new system is implemented in one branch of the organisation whilst the other branches continue with their existing system. Workers from other branches can be taught on the new system before it is introduced to their branch.

Advantages:

- If the system does not work properly, not all branches are affected.
- The later branches benefit by learning from the mistakes made in earlier branches.

Disadvantages:

- It is a slow method of implementation.

4.5   Documentation

When a system is ready to be implemented, documentation has to be produced for the new system. This documentation will take one of two forms: technical or user.

Technical documentation is produced specifically for systems analysts and programmers. It is meant to help when the system needs further development or upgrading. It also very helpful should any errors occur in the system and they need to amend the system to get rid of these errors.

User documentation is provided to help users operate the new system. It can take the form of a tutorial that helps users work their way through the system.

Developing elements of technical documentation

Technical documentation consists of systems documentation and program documentation. Together, these will relate to information about the structure of any data files, document templates and spreadsheet workbooks.

The systems documentation provides a detailed overview of the whole system and includes:

- test plans and test results so that systems analysts can see the results of these – this means that when they find an error in the system they will be able to use this data again to check if they have successfully removed the errors
- the results of the systems analysis, including elements like data flow diagrams – this should help anybody who wants to develop the system
- what is expected of the system
- overall design decisions such as the choice of hardware and software as well as file, input and output structures.

Program documentation also needs to be produced for those pieces of program code that have been written. It includes:

- a description and the purpose of the software – this will explain what the software does and its features, as well as the reasons for choosing those pieces of existing software that were used instead of the programmer having to write code
- the input and output data formats that have been used
- the program flowcharts that were produced at the design stage
- the program listing – this will be a complete copy of the code used as well as annotations explaining what each module of code does
- notes that will help any future programmer to make modifications to the system.

Designing and developing elements of user documentation

User documentation has a different function. It is provided to help the user actually use the system. There are a number of reasons why the systems analyst needs to produce this. Firstly, the users of the system will not be at all familiar with the system and so will need help with various parts of the system until they are familiar with it. It will also save the analyst time in the long term, as if the documentation is effective they will not be contacted on a regular basis to show users how to do certain things. The user documentation will include:

- screenshots, as well as descriptions of how to use the software to save a file, perform a search, sort data, print data, add records, delete records and edit records
- the purpose of the system
- the input and output formats
- the hardware and software needed to run the system
- examples of sample runs of the system so that the user can tell if they are using the system in the correct way
- what to do when errors occur
- a troubleshooting guide or a list of Frequently Asked Questions.

4.6 Evaluation

After the system has been developed, tested and implemented, it must be evaluated. There are a number of stages in the evaluation process.

A system is usually evaluated against a set of criteria:

- Is the system reliable and robust?
- Does the system do what it was intended to do?
- Is the system easy to use?
- Is the new system efficient?
- Is the solution appropriate?

A system needs to be evaluated in terms of the efficiency, ease of use and appropriateness of the solution. The evaluation process involves using test results, obtaining feedback from users, identifying limitations of the system and assessing the benefits of proposed improvements.

Using test results to evaluate the solution

As we have seen above, the test results will help the systems analyst to make judgements. In our example, Daniel will have recorded the results of his testing in the form of a table from which an excerpt was shown above. Comparisons will have been made of the actual results with the expected results. If the results are not as expected, Daniel would use the comparisons and comments to make any refinements which may be needed. For example, if a worker's wage should be $300 for a particular week but the output wage was $30, Daniel would need to check the relevant calculation and see if the formula used had the decimal point in the correct place. Other comments in the comparison table would also help in this process.

Obtaining feedback from users

In order to see if the system is working as it should, users must be consulted over the new system. The way users' responses are recorded may differ from one evaluation to another.

First of all, the systems analyst could observe users performing set tasks and record their progress using video recording. For example, Daniel could record Josephine and Mary working on the new system.

Alternatively, he could get a user to perform a task and measure the time it takes them to carry out the task compared to the old method. Daniel could time Irene over the running of the payroll system and compare it with the original method. He would then be in a position to make his conclusions based on the time it took Irene to produce the required output and consequently make a report on the efficiency of the new system.

Another method is for the systems analyst to interview users to gather their responses about what they thought of the system and how easy it was to use. The systems analyst could use their findings to see whether the system needs changing. This might be an appropriate method for Daniel to use with Peter.

Finally, the systems analyst could hand out questionnaires to all the workers to ask them about their thoughts on the new system with regard to how easy they found it to use. These results could be analysed statistically.

Identifying limitations of the system

The systems analyst will have discussed how successful the new system has been in meeting the original objectives as specified in the requirements specification. He will have gained information about how easy the system is to use. He will have seen if the users have accepted it and are happy to work with the new system. He will also have recorded any extensions to the system that users have said they would like. This will have given him a fair idea of any limitations in the system. These could vary from the minor, such as the colours used on the input screen distracting the user, to major limitations such as not being able to produce connected output, for example the past records of the customer together with the current orders of the customer.

Making improvements to the system

In order to make improvements, the systems analyst evaluates the results of testing against the requirement specification. He also needs to evaluate the results of user testing. Users are interviewed for their opinions on the limitations there are with the new system. They will also be asked about any extensions to the system they would like to see. In order to do this, the analyst identifies users who are typical of the workforce and the tasks that they might perform. They are then interviewed as a result of performing these tasks.

Having identified the limitations, the systems analyst must decide with the users whether the good points of the system compensate for these. They will need to decide whether any extensions to the system that the users have identified should be included. It may be that the system needs to be improved in view of the limitations that have been identified. After the improvements have been made, the system will need to be developed, tested and evaluated again.

Examination questions

In South Africa, a car engine manufacturing company, has just started manufacturing complete cars. They are looking to sell cars throughout Africa. The factory is in East London and they have a main office in Johannesburg, where the manager, Simphiwe, organises the day to day running of the business. The main office employs a lot of workers to produce the company payroll for all the workers in East London and for those in Johannesburg.

There is also a human resources department in the main office in Johannesburg which keeps all the files on each worker.

1   Simphiwe has decided it might be a good idea to computerise the payroll system and also the human resource department records. He has asked a systems analyst to investigate the current system and to suggest a replacement system.
    Discuss the different methods of researching the current system and suggest an appropriate method the systems analyst could use.   [6]
    You will need to make six points.

Mr Devlin is the principal of a college of education. He has decided to upgrade the computer network. He wants to have a new system which will allow the college to keep student personal records and test marks. He also wants to have a system which will let the students have the opportunity to use computers to improve their learning. He has invited Sara Lopez, a systems analyst, to design and create the new system.

2   When Sara is designing the new system she will produce a number of recommendations. She will need to choose input devices and software for use with the system. Explain some of the other choices she will have to make at this stage and what factors will affect these choices.   [4]
    You will need to make four points.

How organisations use ICT 2

You already know how ICT is used in applications such as:

➤ control systems
➤ working practices
➤ advertising
➤ teaching and learning
➤ publishing
➤ time management
➤ data management
➤ payroll applications
➤ technical and customer support.

In this chapter you will learn about:

➤ expert systems
➤ monitoring and measurement
➤ project management
➤ modelling
➤ market research
➤ research applications
➤ online applications
➤ stock control.

5.1 Expert systems

Expert systems are computer-based systems that make use of a wide range of human knowledge on a specific topic to solve various problems. They are different to other problem-solving software as they use reasoning to produce the solution. Such a system stores data inside the computer, which represents the knowledge, and uses a set of rules, which is a form of reasoning. One way of approaching this section is to think of encyclopedias. They contain a huge amount of information, otherwise known as knowledge. This knowledge is used to solve a problem by the system asking a series of questions. The answers to these questions are used to produce possible solutions. The user then considers these before making a decision on the most appropriate solution.

It should be remembered that expert systems can only operate in fields where there are already human experts in existence. They can only be used in areas where there are clearly defined rules and established facts. They cannot be used in areas where there are gaps in the available facts or where rules are open to different interpretations.

Expert systems are not like most problem-solving programs. Problem-solving programs are produced to solve particular problems – such a program can only produce solutions to that particular problem and the knowledge required to solve the problem is embedded within the program instructions. If the knowledge changes then the whole program may need to be re-written. In contrast, expert systems are used to gather the knowledge of experts to form a knowledge base.

A **rules base** is a set of rules which an **inference engine** uses, together with the data or facts in the knowledge base, to reason through a problem. Consequently, a different problem can be solved with the same expert system using the knowledge that is appropriate.

In addition, the system explains the logical reasoning that it has used to come to its conclusions.

In order to create an expert system it is necessary to employ a **knowledge engineer**. The engineer collects information and knowledge from the subject specialists (experts), based on the experts' experience in the field concerned, as well as finding out their requirements for the system. The engineer also gathers data from databases that may exist for the topic. This process is often referred to as data mining, so called because it can be thought of as extracting relevant and accurate information and knowledge whilst sifting out what can be thought of as the impurities, i.e. the irrelevant data.

The knowledge engineer must then design the knowledge base and the rules base. These often come as two interrelated parts of the system rather than as separate entities. The knowledge base can be considered to be the data related to the problem and the rules. These rules are usually of the form IF...THEN, which is used in many forms of programming. Another aspect of the expert system that has to be designed and created is the inference engine, which is the reasoning part of the system. A good inference engine is independent of the subject. For example, it may be specific to a particular aspect of the use of expert systems, such as diagnosis – of illnesses or engine faults.

The other important feature of an expert system is the **user interface**. This is how the computer interacts with the user. It displays questions and information on a screen and enables the user to type in answers to the questions, thereby enabling the inference engine to find appropriate solutions or even further questions. There are a number of validation checks imposed within the user interface in order to prevent the input of invalid responses to the system.

Here is a schematic view of an expert system. As you can see, many of the components are represented diagrammatically as being part of a **shell**. The shell

often includes knowledge base editing software that enables the knowledge engineer to edit rules and facts within the knowledge base.

The inference engine is able to find solutions by using a form of reasoning. This reasoning involves **forward chaining**, **backward chaining** or a combination of both.

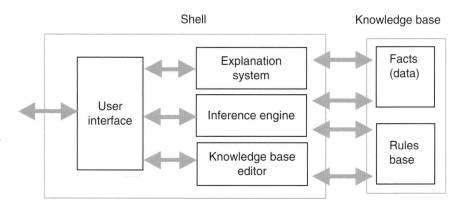

Forward chaining allows an expert system to add facts to its knowledge base. If we have some rules such as:

1 If a student is 16, they are taking GCSEs.
2 If a student is 16, they wear school uniform but do not wear a tie.
3 If a student is taking GCSEs, they will take AS levels next year.

Suppose you now tell the system that Ahmed is 16.

A forward-chaining system would see that Rules 1 and 2 are both obeyed and would add the new facts:

New fact 1:　Ahmed is taking GCSEs.
New fact 2:　Ahmed wears school uniform but does not wear a tie.

This first new fact causes Rule 3 to be obeyed so a third new fact is added:

New fact 3:　Ahmed will take AS levels next year.

The second new fact does not cause any rule to be obeyed. This means that no new fact arises from it.

Forward chaining leads to new facts being added to the knowledge base all the time.

Backward chaining is different. Referring to the three rules listed above and using backward chaining, if we input that Ahmed is 16 to the system, it will do nothing at all. If, however, we ask the system if there is anybody who will be taking AS levels next year, the following happens:

Rules and facts are checked to see if anybody is taking AS levels next year. The only rule which helps is Rule 3. The system then checks *backwards* and sees that Rule 1 is linked to Rule 3. As it has been informed that Ahmed is 16, it can make the correct inference that Ahmed is taking GCSEs and therefore will be taking AS levels next year. Rule 2 is ignored as being irrelevant to the question and, in addition, no new facts are added to the system as a result of the process.

Most applications use a combination of both these approaches.

The use of expert systems to gain facts and generate rules from the 'experts' means that when experts or advisers leave a company, it still has the benefit of their experience. It also means that staff who are not as highly trained or have not got a great deal of experience can make decisions with help from the expert system.

Having outlined the basic elements of an expert system, we will now consider a number of specific applications.

Mineral prospecting

This is the exploration of geological sites with a view to discovering the likelihood of a particular ore being present. This type of expert system can gather inputs directly from sensors sited in a particular location or use satellite data from such sensors. Alternatively, the data could be input by an expert. The system is used to calculate the probability of minerals being found in that location. This is done by comparing the input values with models of similar areas, stored in the form of a knowledge base that represents the knowledge and reasoning processes of geological experts. This type of system is used by an exploration geologist investigating a possible drilling site.

The information required by the system is data such as the geological make-up of the area and the types of rocks and minerals present, as well as those which are required. The system compares the inputs with its knowledge base of stored models of the make-up of sites where those particular ore deposits are to be found. The inference engine is used to determine the similarities and differences between the models and the site under investigation.

Investment analysis

A number of major investors use expert systems for a number of purposes. They are used to monitor stock markets by looking at how prices of the various stocks vary. They can also be used to sell shares automatically if that is what the rules in the knowledge base suggest.

Huge knowledge bases containing facts about the prices of a multitude of stocks over years are kept and the expert system can suggest possible trends. They are not foolproof, since the human experts contributing to their knowledge bases are not, but using such sytems in combination with human experts can result in some profitable decisions being made.

They are also used by investment companies to select the companies that their investors should put their money into. The questions asked by the expert system are much the same as those that an expert financial adviser would ask, for example:

- Does the investor mind investing in risky companies with a possible high return or are they happy to have a lower return on their investment but with a 'safe' company?
- Has the investor got specific areas that they want to invest in (e.g. oil, gold or other commodities)?
- Are there specific companies the investor wants to avoid (e.g. companies that contribute to global warming)?

The expert system uses the answers to previous questions to decide on the next question to be asked. In order to come to a conclusion about the stocks to be recommended to the investor, the expert system uses its extremely large store of facts. Several possible scenarios are created by the system and the investor, with the guidance of a financial adviser, chooses one of the options.

Financial planning

Expert systems are used by individuals for their own personal situation or by companies on a large scale. They can be used to assess what actions to take in a given situation or to set out a financial plan for an individual. Such a plan would include suggestions as to how someone can manage their debts, reduce the amount of income tax they pay and organise investments, as well as suggesting the amount of insurance they should have and how to plan for their retirement. In addition, short-term personal saving plans could be recommended.

The user enters the individual's personal and financial information and the expert system then devises personal financial plans.

Credit analysis

Banks often use expert systems to help them decide on the creditworthiness of potential customers, both companies and individuals. The speed with which the bank can respond to requests is much faster if it uses an expert system, rather than relying on human advisers to make the necessary calculations and judgements. It has also led to a marked reduction in the number of bad debts which have had to be written off.

Experts are presented with requests from companies for loans. The facts they request and the rules that they apply in deciding on such requests are added to the expert system's knowledge base. In addition, the balance sheets (the records of income and expenditure) of all the companies who have requested loans in the past are added.

For companies, users have to respond to questions asking about the sector the company works in and detailed balance sheet information, as well as the more technical details of how they manage their accounts.

Requests for loans or credit cards from individuals are dealt with by an expert system asking questions relating to how much the individual earns, what their outgoings are and other loans and credit cards they might have already.

As with all expert systems, only recommendations are made. They do not take over the decision process. That is left to the user, taking into account the expert systems' suggestions.

Tax systems

Expert systems are quite frequently used in connection with tax calculations. Many countries require their citizens to complete their own tax form, which determines how much income tax they have to pay. The system asks questions about:

- ◆ their income
- ◆ the number of children they have (some countries allow tax relief for children)
- ◆ savings they have (most countries make people pay tax on any interest they earn)
- ◆ pension contributions they make (some countries allow tax relief on these)
- ◆ how old they are (people of a certain age pay less tax in some countries)
- ◆ whether they are a resident (some countries allow non-residents to pay a different level of tax).

It then calculates the tax payable. As with any expert system, the way a question is framed (worded) will depend on the responses to the previous question.

Systems dealing with other forms of tax, such as sales tax (VAT, called GST in a number of countries and TVA in France) are available, as well as company tax systems.

Insurance planning

These engines, quite often based on the worldwide web, take certain details from a user and search through the database to find the best deal for that user for, say, car or life insurance. This subsection discusses the example of life insurance but the same approach is used in insurance generally.

No parent would knowingly leave their children with debts to pay should the parent die. To safeguard against this, many parents take out life insurance. They pay the insurance company a certain amount of money every month and should they die the insurance company pays the dependents an agreed amount of money. The longer a person lives the more profitable it is for the insurance company as they can invest the money the individual is paying them. Some policies are only for a fixed number of years and so if the individual dies after this time the insurance company does not have to pay out.

The insurance company must work out how many policies it may have to pay out on compared with how many policies it will not. This will help it to work out the likely profitability of approving a particular life insurance policy.

Insurance advisers are able to decide whether an individual should be offered a policy and, if so, how much they should pay each month. By interviewing these experts a set of rules can be set up, providing guidance on whether individual applications should be accepted. In addition, if all the existing policies of an insurance company are examined, a much broader range of facts and rules can emerge.

When somebody applies for a life insurance policy, the expert system asks the individual questions about their age, whether they smoke, about their health record and so on. Based on the responses, it will make recommendations as to whether the policy should be issued, for what length and at what cost.

Car engine fault diagnosis

Most car drivers are not very knowledgeable when it comes to understanding how their cars work. When something goes wrong with a car an experienced mechanic is needed to identify what is wrong. As experienced or expert mechanics are not as widespread as we would like, expert systems have been created. The necessary rules and data have been collected from mechanics and knowledge bases have been developed.

There are two forms of such a system. One is the usual question-and-answer session, where the system asks the mechanic questions about what is wrong with the car and then suggests possible causes. The mechanic can then decide which of the suggestions are most likely. This choice can be fed into the expert system so that it has extra rules and facts on which to base future diagnoses.

The second system is an expert fault diagnosis system of the type fitted to many modern cars and connected to the engine management system. When the car owner sees a particular symbol light up on the dashboard this is a warning that there is a possible fault with the engine. The car is then driven to the garage where a mechanic inserts a connector from the portable expert system into a special socket. This enables the portable computer system to interrogate the engine management system. From this the system is able to suggest probable faults. An experienced mechanic is able to select the most likely fault and suggest corrective treatment.

Medical diagnosis

This type of expert system is used by doctors. Some systems allow the patient to type in their symptoms and then generate possible illnesses. However, most require a doctor to input the symptoms for a particular patient and the system outputs the possible illnesses that the patient might be suffering from. The doctor then considers the alternatives and, using their own expert knowledge and experience, makes a diagnosis. Many people think that the expert system replaces the doctor but this is not the case. Rather, it acts in a consultative and supporting role.

A medical diagnosis expert system is probably the largest of all expert systems. There is an incredible number of facts or data and the rules are varied and quite intricate. It has to take into account that simple symptoms like stomach ache can have a large number of potential causes. Therefore, it is important that in such a system, which frames successive questions on previous responses, that responses are entered accurately and unambiguously.

Route scheduling for delivery vehicles

This type of expert system calculates the most efficient route for delivery vehicles. The towns or areas to be visited are input to the system and it then outputs the shortest route for the vehicle to enable it to visit all the delivery points. This enables the delivery company to make the deliveries in the cheapest way. Typical users are postal service delivery vehicles, courier companies and travelling sales people.

The inputs required are details about:

◆ the number of drop-off points
◆ the distance between each point
◆ the type and speed of the vehicle being used
◆ the total available time
◆ the layout of the area being delivered to, for example whether it is mountainous or flat.

Some systems also allow for the price of fuel at the various locations to be entered, so that the most economical route can be produced.

The manager of the transport system will be able to take suggestions from the expert system and decide on the number of vehicles and drivers needed and the total time to be taken.

Plant and animal identification

The user is asked questions about the features of the species of the plant or animal. From the responses to the questions, the expert system can suggest the likely plant or animal. For example, the system might ask the following questions about an animal:

◆ Does it eat meat?
◆ Does it have a long neck?
◆ Does it have four long legs?

If the answer to the first question is 'no' and the answers to the other two questions are both 'yes', then the system might suggest giraffe. Alternatively, if the answer was 'no' to the last question, it might suggest ostrich.

Both these systems use forward chaining as they are required to expand the extent of their knowledge. They are created by using reference books about plants and animals as well as by gathering data from experts in the field.

Advantages and disadvantages

Advantages of the use of expert systems:

◆ It reduces the time taken to solve a problem (e.g. for a technician to find a fault or a doctor to make a diagnosis).
◆ As it is based on the knowledge of many experts, it is more accurate than a single expert.

- It improves customer/patient service and the standing of the expert (e.g. technician or doctor).
- It can predict future problems as well as current ones.
- It saves companies money due to faster service time.
- In some areas such as car fault diagnosis, it can mean that a less skilled work force is required, therefore resulting in a lower wage bill.

Disadvantages of the use of expert systems:

- Expert systems cost a lot to set up.
- The users (mechanics/patients/doctors) will need training in how to use it, which takes time and money.
- It will need continually updating, which can take it temporarily out of use.
- In a company or doctors' practice, there will need to be one in every garage/branch/surgery.

5.2 Monitoring and measurement

This involves the use of a computer or microprocessor-based device to monitor or measure physical variables over a period of time. For this course you will need to know which sensors would be appropriate in a given scenario to measure physical variables such as temperature, pressure, humidity, moisture, light, sound, blood pressure and pH (acidity).

In Chapter **1**, we saw that a sensor is a device that is used to input data about physical changes in an environment that is being monitored. For example, a temperature sensor could be used to feed data back to the computer about the temperature in a weather station. Monitoring and measuring systems are not like control systems, which use the data to take actions that modify the environment, such as in a central heating system. They only record data for the purpose of enabling users to identify trends in the patterns of changing data.

The computer is continually monitoring the sensors. Sensors send data continually, not just when a certain event happens, such as a sudden increase in temperature. The data sent to the computer or microprocessor is in an analogue form. As the computer can only process digital data the analogue data must be converted to digital using an analogue-to-digital converter, which can be built into an interface box that the sensor plugs into and is itself plugged into a computer.

Depending on the output from the system, the results will be shown on a monitor, printed on a printer or even output through speakers if the output is sound.

The software used in such systems to record the results and interpret them is generically termed measuring software or data logging software. These systems are therefore often referred to as data logging systems. They are used in a variety of applications, some of which we will look at now.

Medical applications

Patient monitoring systems are used in intensive care units in hospitals. Sensors are connected to the patient and then the computer. Many variables are fed back to the computer, including pulse rate, rate of breathing, blood pressure, body temperature and the amount of oxygen in the blood. For each patient there is a computer monitor networked to a central display for the nurses to observe.

These patient monitoring systems are fitted with alarms. The computer is constantly comparing the physical variables to a range of pre-set values. This range is the limit of acceptability. Above or below these values signifies that the patient is in danger. The alarm sounds when any of the patient's readings fall outside the acceptable range.

This type of system is not to be confused with a control system, which would actually take action to restore the status quo.

Weather monitoring

Sensors are used in weather stations, where the main function of the computer is to collect data. The variables quite commonly measured are:

- wind speed, using the rotation of a rotor to generate pulses that are proportional to the wind speed
- wind direction, using an angle sensor
- temperature, using a temperature sensor
- barometric pressure, using a form of pressure sensor
- rainfall, using a tipping mechanism – when a certain depth is reached (typically 0.025 cm) it closes a normally open circuit, generating a pulse to a counter which is recorded
- humidity, using a humidity sensor
- sunshine, using a light sensor.

The data is collected and input to a database or spreadsheet. Weather statistics can be collected over long periods of time. This data can be used to observe trends, particularly in global warming. It is also used by weather centres to input to their modelling software to help them forecast the weather.

Climate monitoring

This is an extension of the use of ICT in weather monitoring. Climate is measured over a much longer time scale.

The data collected over many decades can be used to plot graphs of the different variables over time. The examples here show the graphs of temperature over the last 150 years for the northern and southern hemispheres, together with the overall global trend.

Monitoring the environment

This is the use of monitoring to warn the public or authorities of very high levels of pollutants. For example, the air quality in cities is monitored with regard to the level of nitrogen dioxide, sulphur dioxide, ozone and particulates. Noise levels are also monitored in some cities. Rivers are monitored, measuring different variables such as stream temperature, pH, dissolved oxygen, turbidity and water level. (Turbidity is the cloudiness of a liquid caused by individual particles usually invisible to the naked eye. These particles have a similar effect in water as smoke has in air.)

Scientific experiments

There are many scientific experiments involving the use of computers and sensors. Many of these relate to chemical experiments, which can take place for a short duration or over a long period of time. Using sensors provides greater accuracy and enables automatic or immediate processing. The data collected

from a science experiment can be imported into a spreadsheet and so used to produce graphs. The table of values and the graphs can then be imported into word-processing or desktop-publishing software for inclusion in a text report on the findings.

5.3 Project management

A project is a relatively short-term undertaking, whereby a problem or series of problems are solved. Projects are not to be confused with the normal day-to-day way a business operates. The management skills and approach required to bring a project to a satisfactory conclusion

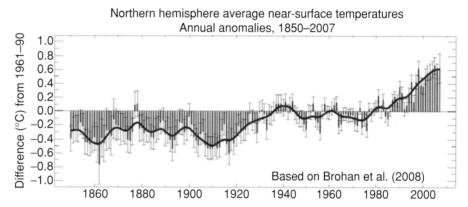

Northern hemisphere average near-surface temperatures
Annual anomalies, 1850–2007

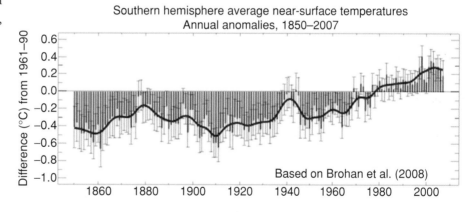

Southern hemisphere average near-surface temperatures
Annual anomalies, 1850–2007

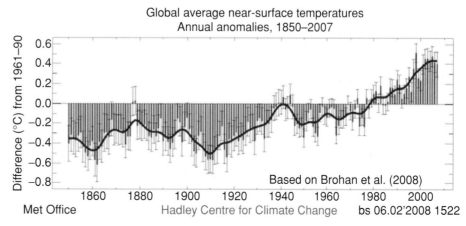

Global average near-surface temperatures
Annual anomalies, 1850–2007

Met Office   Hadley Centre for Climate Change   bs 06.02'2008 1522

are quite different to those required for the normal running of a business. Project management has to ensure that the project is completed within the timescale and monetary budget allowed by the business.

Project management is an essential part of successful project completion for large projects involving large teams. For smaller projects, involving only a few people, project management in its technical sense is not so important. The objectives and the schedule of work can be agreed without formal meetings.

Using project management, each project has a number of resources allocated to it in the form of money, manpower and materials. The number of resources or lack of them will be a factor contributing to the successful completion of the project.

There are a number of tools used in project management. These include Gantt charts (which you met in Chapter 2), Pert charts and event chain diagrams, as well as general project management software. There are many software packages that specialise in producing any or all of these, thus saving the user time. In addition, special timeline software allows the drawing of many parallel timelines so that the progress of projects can be monitored. All of these can be used on a basic PC.

In large projects, where a number of teams work together to a planned schedule, the project is divided into small units to make it more manageable. The tasks are linked to come together at the end of the project. It is important to understand that some tasks have to start before others can begin but that it is possible, and even likely, that other tasks will run in parallel. In other words, tasks that are unrelated will run alongside each other, providing they don't require the same team of people.

A major method of project management is called 'Projects in Controlled Environments' or PRINCE for short. This was first developed by the UK government in 1989 and came to be the standard used by central government. Since then, PRINCE has been developed so that it can be used in the management of all types of projects. Its successor, PRINCE2, has become the standard approach to project management both at government level and in private industry in the UK. It is now used widely around the world. It divides the project into a number of processes, saying who should be responsible for each and when they should be put into operation. It limits the number of meetings that are needed. Too many approaches to project management encourage regular meetings, which can cause projects to

be delayed. PRINCE also makes use of language common to users, suppliers and customers.

Here we will discuss two examples of project management: software development and building construction. Both benefit from the use of ICT in helping to organise the project. There are many software writers that help users create Pert charts, as well as there being a variety of construction project management software packages (including PRINCE software) in what is now a very competitive market.

Software development

When a new piece of software has to be produced to solve a particular problem it is often broken down into modules. Teams of programmers will be involved in writing the code, each team being allocated a module or a number of modules. The modules will then be combined before undergoing testing as set out in Chapter 4. Many of the modules will be written in parallel, although some will have to be written in sequence, for example processing modules would normally be written after input modules. The sequence would tend to be Input $\rightarrow$ Processing $\rightarrow$ Output.

Opposite is a Pert chart representing the implementation of a simple information system.

Each rectangle represents a stage in the progress of the project. Each arrowed line represents the action that needs to be taken to get to that stage. Where lines split up (for example into Stages 4, 5 and 6) these actions can be undertaken independently of each other. The dotted lines show where stages that are initially independent of each other must be combined to proceed to the next stage.

Building construction

The first stage in construction project management is to define the project objectives. Next plans are drawn that include the setting out of the scope of the project, the budget allowed, the timetable and the team of people who are going to be involved. The scope of the project has to be defined so that the required aspects of the project are included – but *only* the required aspects.

The schedule will dictate the stages at which groups of workers who will be involved in the different stages of the construction will be employed and for how long. This ensures that workers are not engaged for any period of time longer than necessary. The timing of the purchase of materials and equipment is included in the plans, so that

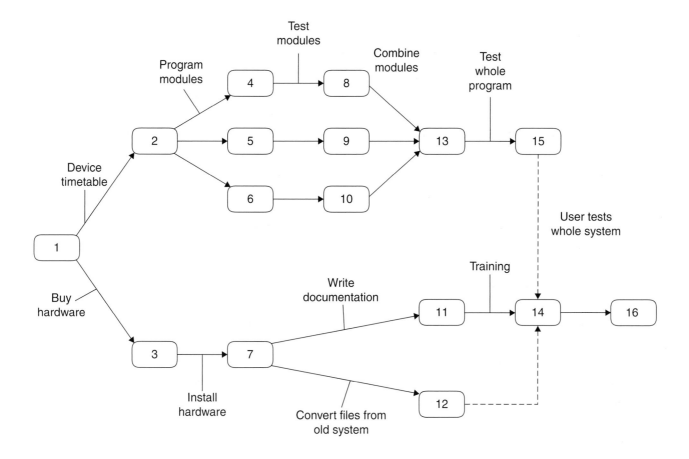

they do not take up unnecessary storage space. The final stages will be the actual implementation and testing of the construction.

A large project such as building a bridge or an aeroplane needs lots of materials, equipment and workers to make sure that it is built on time. Taking the bridge as an example, the work must progress in a logical order or the bridge will fail. Project management is essential. The stages in such a project could be:

- designing the bridge
- testing a prototype (see Section **5.4**)
- hiring workers to prepare the groundworks
- preparing groundworks and access to building site
- building foundations
- hiring construction workers
- starting construction of main towers
- making the different sections of the bridge
- having sections of bridge delivered just in time for fitting
- live testing
- completion of project.

Here it is possible to have a number of tasks running at the same time. The different sections of the bridge could be made separately before being delivered. At the same time the groundworks could be prepared, followed by the foundations.

5.4 Modelling

This is the use of computers to represent a real-life situation. It is not the creation of working models like an actual car, which is sometimes referred to as a three-dimensional model. Many people can visualise a three-dimensional model of a building, a structure or a method of transport, such as cars and planes, but find it difficult to understand the concept of computer modelling.

Models can be quite complex and may require a mainframe computer to run efficiently. They often use purpose-built software for the task, which is expensive but is designed specifically for the task. Spreadsheet software can be used to create a model, but often businesses require a more sophisticated solution. There are many types of model, as we will discover below.

As in most systems, modelling software has inputs, where the user types these in directly or creates a data file for later input. Models have embedded within them a set of rules that are used to manipulate the data in order to provide an output of some form. Care should be taken to understand the difference between the use of a computer model and a calculator. Although several models involve the processing of great quantities of numeric data they are models because the rules can be changed within them. This is not the same as processing great amounts of numeric data to arrive at the answer to a calculation. When creating models, a decision has to be made over the choice of software.

Choice of software

In Chapter **4**, we saw that a choice has to be made about where to get the software to produce the solution. For many modelling applications, software needs to be written specifically for the purpose it is to be used for. Many of the models are so complex that an off-the-shelf solution cannot be found. However, as more and more software houses expand their areas of expertise, this situation is gradually changing. It is now possible, for example, to buy off-the-shelf pilot training simulation software. There have been many types of flight simulators available for a number of years, but these have tended to be rather amateurish and aimed at the hobby market. However, versions of simulators are now available that can be used to train for an air pilot's licence.

There are several types of model, some of which are described here.

Economic

Computer models are often used by governments to predict the future of a nation's economy. Most governments collect money in the form of taxes and then use this money to spend on education and various other public services such as roads and public transport. The more money governments receive in taxation, the better public services will be. Most countries have a form of purchase tax, so that when goods are sold in shops some of the money received has to go the government. Most countries also have some form of income tax whereby when an employee receives their wages they have to pay a proportion of it to the government. Governments can use economic models to see how much money could be raised by increasing these taxes by varying amounts. They can also vary the amount spent on public services and see what effect this would have on the need to raise or decrease the tax rate. Another variable that can be altered is a rise in interest rates. A model can be used to see what effect this may have on how much money

people would have to spend on goods on services. From these results, it would be possible to determine the effect of interest rate rises on the national economy.

Prototype

Prototypes can be physical models built to an exact scale for use in trials and testing. These can be very expensive as they have, by their very nature, to be expendable. It is now possible to use a computer model to test a new car design in crash conditions without having to build and then damage actual cars. Computers are therefore being used more and more to create virtual prototypes, which are obviously cheaper compared with building several physical prototypes. They are created using computer-aided design (CAD) software, which enables the dimensions and the shape to be changed to see the effect of such changes on the performance. Prototypes of integrated circuit boards, aeroplanes and cars are all produced using CAD software. If a physical model of the prototype were required, the CAD system could be connected to a computer-aided manufacturing (CAM) system. This process is more usually referred to as CAD/CAM. The drawings are created on screen and the computer is connected to special machines that are controlled by the CAM software and produce the model.

Climate

In Section **5.2** we saw how the climate is monitored and how records have been kept of the actual values over a number of years. The collected data can also be fed into a spreadsheet model. Models created using spreadsheet software are used to predict trends and also to investigate the effect of increasing and decreasing variables such as greenhouse gas emissions. The results of these changes can be observed using computer models. Where this has happened in the past the predictions can be compared with the actual trends and the model can be refined. The model will contain a number of variables that can be changed to see what effect they will have on the climate.

The level of complexity of the models is such, however, that they tend to be as difficult to interpret as the actual climate itself.

Many scientists are sceptical about the accuracy of global models. Predictions about the future climate of the world are based on factors such as greenhouse

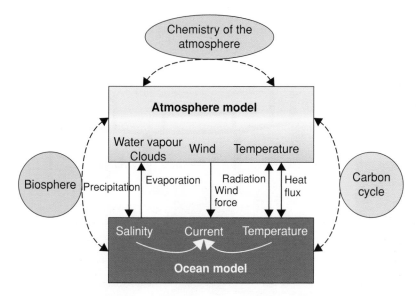

gas emissions. As we cannot be certain about future government policies, developments in technology and economic forces, it is difficult to predict with any accuracy what the future holds. All that can be said is that predictions about future climate change can only be based on particular scenarios. In other words, several IF…THEN situations can be described.

Weather forecasting

Weather forecasting is based on very complex models created using supercomputers. Data from the sensors at the weather stations are fed into the model and calculations are performed. Predictions can be made because similar weather conditions will have been observed over very long periods of time. The computer examines similar patterns of weather from the past and compares them to current conditions and is able to predict the resulting weather.

Variables such as atmospheric pressure, humidity, rainfall, temperature, wind speed and wind direction are recorded all over the earth's surface, usually by automatic, computerised weather stations. These readings are fed into models that analyse the data and combine it with the most recent forecasts to produce a three-dimensional model of the earth's atmosphere. The calculations required to produce this model are so numerous that if it were to be attempted by humans the actual weather for a given day would have occurred before the forecast could be completed!

Using the atmospheric model and by comparing with previous days at similar times of the year with the same or similar conditions a reasonably accurate forecast can

be made. The resulting maps showing isobars and temperatures are produced.

Simulations

Simulations are created to replicate a situation where the user is in control. They are needed because the actual physical components of, for example, an aeroplane are expensive to replace. They are used to teach people to fly aircraft and drive cars, for example (discussed later in this subsection). Without the skills necessary to undertake these tasks in real life the results can be catastrophic: the danger to human life is obvious, particularly if an aeroplane should crash; the cost of building or repairing aircraft or cars can be enormous.

The advantages of such systems are as follows:

◆ It is a safer way of learning.
◆ The same manoeuvre can be repeated several times in quick succession.
◆ Dangerous situations can be simulated at no risk to vehicle or driver.
◆ The costs of running the simulator are much lower that those associated with the actual running of any method of transport in terms of wear on tyres and engine parts as well as the cost of fuel.

There are, however, some disadvantages to using simulators:

◆ They are very expensive to buy and maintain.
◆ It is impossible to replicate all possible difficult situations which a pilot or driver may experience.
◆ Operators may become too overconfident due to the fact that they are not in any physical danger and may make mistakes which would be catastrophic in the real situation.

Air-pilot training

Airlines have always had the need to have some method of training their pilots. This applies to both new pilots and also existing pilots when they have to become familiar with a new type of plane. As discussed above, it is important that this is done as cheaply and as safely as possible.

Flight simulators have been produced that are programmed to react as an actual aircraft would. The system consists of a number of screens that show high-quality animated scenes (for example, this computer-generated image of JFK airport, New York), together with speakers that generate the typical sounds of take-off and engine bursts. Together, these produce typical scenarios that the pilot might face.

The cockpit that the pilots sit in is an exact replica of an actual plane cockpit. In the cockpit will be all the necessary devices needed to fly the plane, such as:

◆ flight yoke
◆ brake pedals or rudders
◆ headsets, including earphones and microphone
◆ transceivers
◆ flight console
◆ screens.

Hydraulic rams are used to cause movement of the 'plane'. An operator controls the whole process and is able to change the computer program in order to create an incident of some sort, such as an engine catching fire. It is possible to create several different types of dangerous incident without causing loss of life or damage to an aircraft. The pilot can be automatically assessed by the system.

Car-driver training
Simulators are also available for car drivers. The same form of graphics and animation software is used to reproduce the situations that car drivers have to negotiate. The rationale for their use is the same: it is safer to allow drivers to learn how to drive without causing damage to the car. In addition to the general advantages of simulators, they are also appealing to car sales companies, as they might attract a visit from

existing customers who then buy cars for young people. Furthermore, some companies could see it as an advertising opportunity to attract news coverage.

Profit forecasts
Companies are in business to make a profit. It is therefore essential that they have the facility to model several potential scenarios. A simple form of profit can be calculated using a model. It calculates the costs involved in producing an item and subtracts these from the income from selling the product. This type of model tends to make use of off-the-shelf spreadsheet software. Details of income and expenditure are entered into the spreadsheet and a formula linking the two used to produce a profit calculation.

However, most companies require more complex models, which can model the rate of selling a product. There is no point on spending money on producing 10 000 items if only 1000 are sold. The company would then be making a loss.

More sophisticated models take into account the current economic climate as well as the effect of taxation when determing the rate of selling. The model can then be used to predict profits based on the rate of selling. The ability to change the variables in a model is what make them most useful in these situations. The effects of changes in taxation, wages, energy prices, rent or mortgage payments can all be observed. One of the most useful features of spreadsheets is the use of the break-even facility. This can be used to produce graphs showing, for example, the number of products that must be sold in a given period for the company to break even.

Architecture
The modelling software used in this case tends to be specially developed CAD software. Architects use

CAD software to design structures such as bridges and buildings. The software has a library of parts of structures built into the software. When designing buildings, for example, architects would have parts such as doors, windows, staircases, roofs and so on available to them. The architect just has to select the parts required and change the dimensions to suit the project being undertaken. They are able to demonstrate the structures in three dimensions and using different viewing angles. Most packages also have the capability to create a three-dimensional walkthrough so that the viewer can actually see inside the building and into individual rooms. Printers can be used to produce hard copy of the design, but due to the size of the drawing that would be produced it is more likely that a graph plotter would be used.

Nuclear research

Scientists looking into nuclear research have always had access to very powerful computer programs. In order that they do not expose themselves to unnecessary radiation they often use computer models to represent nuclear reactions. This enables them to change variables such as temperature and rate of reaction without endangering themselves. These models also allow time to be speeded up so that if the reaction would normally take a long time due to the slow rate of radiation the actual experiment can take place in a much shorter period of time.

Geology / predicting deposits

Geological models are needed so that companies that are exploring for deposits or ores can predict with the greatest accuracy the features of the deposit such as the concentration, distribution and shape of the deposit. In order to do this, they need to create a three-dimensional model. This is not like an expert system that determines the probability of the location of a deposit, but rather depends on a deposit having already been found. The surrounding area is drilled to large depths at different locations of the deposit area. The soil and rock structure is fed into the computer and a three-dimensional model of the geological landscape is then created. This model can be used to model the positioning of the mine tunnels that will be needed.

5.5 Market research

There are many methods by which market research can be carried out, but we are going to concentrate on those that make the greatest use of ICT. Market research involves the collection and analysis of information from sections of the public in order to discover the level of demand for a type of product or service. It is normally carried out by organisations or businesses when a new product is to be launched or when new packaging or development of a product is proposed, although it can be carried out on existing products whose sales might be declining.

There are two levels of research or data gathering. Primary research is when prospective or existing customers are interviewed by the organisation themselves. Secondary research is the examination of existing data that has already been published, usually by another organisation, to determine attitudes and preferences. Obviously, this second method is a lot cheaper but can yield inaccurate results as it may not relate specifically to the company's product.

Businesses, and organisations generally, are not alone in their use of market research. Governments often carry out surveys in order to determine what public reaction would be to tax reforms, say. Two examples of market research are given in the following subsections.

Market research analysts have to design a set of questions and possible responses that will enable them to gain the information they need. The interviews can take place through personal interview, by phone or online – each of these is discussed later in this section.

The use of computers to analyse the data is essential. Using this analysis, the market research analyst makes recommendations to the organisation or business. Decisions on the way a product is launched or whether new packaging will be needed for an existing product is taken at management level.

Research in advertising media

This is the use of market research to judge how effective a particular advertisement is. Whether the advertisement is in a newspaper, on the radio or television, in a cinema or outdoors, data can be collected about it.

There are two ways data can be used. One is specific to a company or product. The other is in a more generalised manner, where the market research company offers the result of its research to any company that is willing to pay for it. The research can be carried out at either of two stages. The first is before the advertising campaign begins. A trial or prototype version is shown to a selected audience and data about their reactions to it are gathered. The campaign is then adapted in the light of these findings. This approach is usually taken when specific products or companies are being advertised. The second stage is to test the reaction after a campaign. This can be done using either phone or online interviews, both of which are described below.

Research in public opinion

Many governments use market research to analyse the reaction to proposed economic changes or legislation that they are planning. There are also public opinion polls, which are carried out on behalf of the media, often to see which political party people are going to vote for in upcoming elections. These are usually carried out by phone. The results used to take days to process, but with the aid of computers they are now normally processed in a matter of hours. More and more companies are carrying out opinion polls online. In order to prevent people 'voting' more than once, a cookie is placed on their computer indicating that they have already voted and to discard any subsequent response.

Interview methods

There are three main ways of using computers to interview people in order to gather data for market research, although the computer system used is very similar for all of them:

- Computer-assisted personal interviewing (CAPI), where the person being interviewed (the interviewee) and the interviewer are together in the same room. The interviewee is asked questions in one of two ways:
  - they sit in front of the computer, normally a laptop (although it can be a handheld portable device with a touch screen and wireless Internet access to communicate with a central computer) and answer the questions put to them by the laptop
  - an interviewer asks them questions as prompted by the computer.

- Computer-assisted telephone interviewing (CATI), where the interviewer is normally to be found in a call centre. The process commences with the computer dialling the phone number of the selected interviewee and then proceeds as for a personal interview, with the interviewer asking the questions and recording the answers.

- Online data capture, or computer-aided web interviewing (CAWI). Market research companies often have a database of people who are willing to take part in market research; or a company may contact some of its customers. These are asked to log on to a particular site and answer a series of questions online by completing a questionnaire or web form. The customers must have access to the Internet and will need to use a web browser.

The questions are of a multiple-choice response type, whereby the interviewee chooses one of usually four alternative responses. The responses to questions are keyed in either by the interviewee or the interviewer, depending on the method being used. The response to one question is used by the computer to identify which question to ask next. Using a series of branching logic statements the computer can change the questions according to the responses received.

Because the responses are typed into the computer, which uses a type of database management software (DBMS), the data can be analysed immediately.

An alternative approach for online data capture is for a company to use pop-ups on its website. However, this method tends not to be as successful as many computer users have pop-up blocking software running.

5.6 Research applications

Most areas of the humanities, sciences and technology require research to be carried out. Private companies tend to spend most on research into developing new products. The power of the computer is essential in any form of research using modern methods. This can be to carry out research using existing data or information available on the Internet or to analyse experimental or collected data using the computational power of a computer. Most research applications require the use of supercomputers. These are computers with over 100 000 dual processors. They are actually a collection of computers that are connected through a high-speed network. In 2007, a supercomputer capable of simulating the brain carried out the simulation of half a mouse brain for ten seconds.

We shall concentrate on a few of the fields which make the greatest use of computers.

Medicine

Medicine requires a great deal of research into the causes of illnesses and diseases, in the hope that this will lead to cures. For example, computer models have been developed to help explain what can go wrong in some pregnancies. Data from ultrasound scanning and blood samples were used to create the models, which were then used to carry out simulated experiments. This led to the discovery of the reasons for the development of a dangerous complication called pre-eclampsia. Developments of computerised brain scanners have led to developments in the study of the human brain. Three-dimensional computer models of human teeth and jawbones have helped in dental research. Two further areas, drug development and genetic analysis, are considered in more detail below.

Developing new drugs

Before a drug is tested it needs to have been 'invented'. This is rarely done by starting right at the beginning. Usually, results of previous research are stored and the computer is used to cross-match the results of this previous research with the results of a new drug that is being developed. As the drug is developed, the computer can be used to monitor the amount of ingredients that are being used. Because the computer is so accurate, the researchers can vary the amounts by very small differences.

Modern drug research also uses the understanding of how the body works at what is called a microbiological level. This means that the chemicals making up a particular drug are studied to see how they affect the cells in the human body. Computer models can be developed to represent these situations. Next, experiments can be carried out using these models to see how changing the structure of the drug affects the way the body reacts. The drug is then trialled using human 'guinea pigs' and if the drug 'works' it can be mass produced.

Another useful aspect of computer models is the way they can be used to predict how poisonous drugs might be, based on their molecular structure. Computer models can also help to predict whether the drugs could possibly cause cancer or even birth abnormalities. They are also able to predict how quickly the chemicals in the drugs can spread through the human body.

Genetic analysis

Finding the genes that make our bodies susceptible to disease has always been a massive task. There are so many genes, and variations of them, that using human beings to perform the calculations required to pinpoint those genes responsible was an impossible task. The

availability of supercomputers and large networks of computers, together with new statistical methods that have been developed, has reduced the size of the task considerably. An analysis of the data that not so long ago would take months to complete can now be performed by the use of parallel networks in a few minutes. The databases used to store the data can be extremely large, as they have to store vast quantities of data.

Cancer patients are benefiting from the analysis of genes. By taking a sample of the cancer, and identifying the genes present, drugs can be prescribed that specifically target the cancers of those patients concerned.

Health records could be kept on databases consisting of information regarding the genetic make-up of patients. As the causes for diseases that are related to genetic make-up are discovered, the patient records could be used to identify those patients at risk, who would then be called for screening and treatment, if necessary.

Science

Science is basically the study of what goes on around us in the world. Scientific research is investigating the causes of these events and how improvements can be made. We will now have a brief look at the way research in scientific applications is affected by the use of ICT and more specifically computers.

Modern day supercomputers have much larger memories and processing power than their predecessors. This has led to the ability to simulate any type of scenario. This facility has been adopted as a major tool by most researchers and is now considered to be a third way of doing science alongside theory and experimentation.

Space research

The use of supercomputers in space research is, amongst other applications, used for:

◆ simulating future space shuttle launches: this is to do with the actual launching of shuttles and many of these simulations relate to improving crew safety and survivability; some involve tests of the systems used to propel the crews to escape; in addition, the effectiveness of the parachutes has been modelled, as well as different arrangements of the shuttle system and methods of landing

◆ predicting the impact of human activity on weather patterns: this involves the modelling of various human activities that affect climate, such as changing use of land (agricultural to urban, deforestisation, etc.), emissions of greenhouse gases (GHGs), the use of substances that deplete the ozone layer and local air pollutants; these can increase the risk of loss of species, reduction in forests, loss of some human settlements, melting of glaciers, etc.; much of the data is retrieved from satellites

- designing safe space exploration vehicles: this is to do with the actual flying of the vehicles as opposed to the safety aspects of launching spacecraft, discussed above; spacecraft are going to have to be larger and able to dock with space stations before allowing astronauts to continue on further journeys from the space stations.

Universities

Universities throughout the world promote research in science; the fields that are studied involve the use of ICT at some level or other. Areas of research in science where computers are used include research in modelling and numerical simulation, which usually make use of spreadsheet software although advanced programming techniques are sometimes used to create purpose-built software. This covers a wide range of topics in probability and statistics, a few of which are given here:

- the modelling and simulation of diseases and medicines: developing statistical models to show how well patients respond in clinical trials compared with their desire to take part
- mathematical biology: immunology (the study of the immune system in humans); epidemiology (the study of factors affecting the health and illness of populations); ecology (the scientific study of the distribution of living organisms); genetics (the science of heredity and variations in living organisms)
- psychology: the application of mathematical models to the areas of memory, reasoning, vision and attention, reading, spelling and speech
- computers: includes numerical analysis and scientific computing
- weather-based simulation models: aims to predict the timing of pest and disease outbreaks, the growth and maturity of crops, the germination and emergence of crop seedlings and how nutrients are absorbed by crops
- chemistry: the calculation of the properties and reactivities of matter; the development and

application of theoretical tools to study chemical systems; simulating metabolic rates in the body

- physics: the modelling of magnetism, radioactivity and other areas
- systems biology: to develop understanding of biological systems through mathematical and computational modelling. It is aimed at identifying how diseases are caused, how to develop new drugs and how to improve horticulture and agriculture
- mathematical sciences: includes statistical methodology and the relationship between mathematics and computer science, as well as operational research.

Research into areas of energy and sustainability are also carried out, including:

- fusion power: the analysis of experimental data combined with high performance computing to study what is required to sustain nuclear fusion
- renewable energy: sources such as wind, water and hydrogen
- sustainable crops: developing approaches to reducing energy usage in producing crops; developing crop varieties that only need a limited amount of water and allow vast reductions in the use of pesticides and fertilizers
- the impact of climate change on the sustainability of agricultural land.

Education

ICT in education

Generally, teachers and students alike are quite positive about the use of ICT to enhance teaching and learning. Research into its effects have shown that it is more effective where there are clear educational objectives linked to its use and where students understand the purpose of using it. Research has also shown that using ICT in lessons allows students to become more independent and to be responsible for their own learning – a development which many teachers have difficulty in coming to terms with.

The uses of ICT in the classroom include:

- online tutorials that can be used to help students to develop their ability to perform basic computer operations such as data entry, saving, copying, formatting disks, etc.; these tutorials help to develop students' basic skills in the use of word processors, spreadsheet packages, database packages, desktop publishers, etc.; other tutorials can be used to develop their skills in touch typing and using presentation software.

- interactive whiteboards, which are used by teachers instead of the more conventional whiteboards, allowing the use of images, video, sound and hyperlinks to enhance subject knowledge
- web design: this can be used to promote schools and provide information for staff, pupils and parents; to show pupils' work to parents and other pupils, particularly across the world; and to communicate information to parents and the community in general, also allowing them to contact the school via e-mail
- digital imaging: digital imaging photography and video can be used to make teaching and learning enjoyable and productive; they are used particularly in areas such as art and media studies
- more recently, podcasting: podcasts are audio broadcasts that can be downloaded from the Internet and listened to using personal media players; there has to be sufficient bandwidth on the school's network to allow downloads and it is only a one-way system: students can listen to but not interact with the recording
- blogging: this is the use of the Internet to enable students to have an area that they can log on to and write what they want; as well as developing ICT skills, it improves student literacy; it is an excellent vehicle for creative writing as well as report writing.

Because ICT is a developing area, much research is carried out into its effectiveness and the gains in learning made by students. Various reports and publications have been produced giving the results of this research.

ICT can also be used effectively by students carrying out their own research in all subjects, whether social sciences and humanities or science. If the research involves interviewing people for their opinions, students can collect information from their own families and neighbours. Research in the natural sciences can be carried out by students conducting experiments and collecting and analysing the resulting data. The software tools at their disposal are very sophisticated, in terms of both modelling and data handling. Comparison with existing research data can be carried out using the Internet.

Teacher education

Research into the use of ICT in teacher education and the training of teachers in the use of ICT has been carried out quite frequently by many Western European organisations. It has, however, only recently been undertaken in the developing world. In 2005, the Digital Education Enhancement Project (DEEP) sought to explore the ways in which ICT can improve access to, and the quality of, teacher education in the global south (sic). It focused on research relating to the impact of the use of ICT teaching styles, student achievement and motivation, and how ICT could be developed to ensure that teachers were able to make effective use of it.

It came to the conclusion that teachers and schools in poor environments can benefit from the use of ICT. It also realised that teachers and students could make use of mobile digital devices, with teachers using them for administration as well as teaching uses. Teachers reported that the use of new technologies had positive effects on attendance, motivation and the quality of student learning, all of which are central to universal basic education (UBE). The study suggested that the use of ICT in some of the poorest parts of the world could also have a significant impact on the self-image, confidence and professionalism of teachers.

5.7 Online applications

We have already looked at online shopping and online banking from the point of view of the customer and also the impact on society. Online booking systems will be described in similar detail in Chapter **6**. This section will focus on the software and hardware that an organisation requires to operate such a service. You will learn about how an organisation uses ICT for these applications, rather than about the impact on society, which is what was discussed in Chapter **3** for shopping and banking.

All organisations that operate online services have to have web servers to handle the transactions from their customers. A web server is the name given, rather confusingly, to both the hardware and software required to facilitate the hosting of websites. Large supermarket chains and banks have their own web servers but smaller-scale operations often use a hosted web server, where they pay a fee at regular intervals to use the server. The website of the shop or supermarket is on the server and their system needs to be linked directly to the database of customer accounts.

They have to employ web designers to design their websites. Web designers need to use a web authoring software package, which allows them to create all aspects of a web page. They can insert sound files, animation files, text files, tables, forms to fill in, and so on. They also need to build security into the website, so that personal details can not be intercepted. There needs to be an interface between the website and the customer database so that data can be accessed by the customer and the organisation's database can be updated at the same time.

Just as the customer needs to have access to a PC and an Internet browser, so too does the designer. The website is created on a PC using the web authoring software and then uploaded onto the organisation's web server ready for live testing. When all the bugs have been removed, the system is implemented.

Online banking

When a customer logs on, their data is transmitted to the bank's web server. When requests for data are made, they are passed on to the bank's Internet banking server, which then accesses the customer information database server. At all stages the connection from the customer's PC to the web server is secure. There are firewalls between the web server and the Internet banking server to prevent direct access from the customer to the customer information database. The web server acts as a 'go-between' between the customer and the personal data on the database.

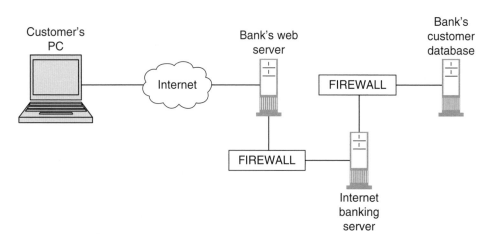

The same sort of set-up is used by other online systems, for example an Internet shopping server, Internet booking server or Internet auction server, depending on the application.

Online shopping

Similar to an online bank, an organisation that operates an online shopping facility needs to have or have access to a web server. Part of the website is a shopping cart system, where the customer places their purchases as described in Chapter **3**. Shopping cart software is readily available, but can be part of the web hosting service and is integral to the web server software used. This software is used by the web designer to create a system whereby the customer selects all the products they wish to purchase; it also handles the payment process.

Online booking systems

As its name suggests, an online booking system is used to book a range of items online, including:

- holidays
- train tickets
- plane tickets
- cinema tickets
- theatre tickets
- appointments.

Chapter **6** discusses how such systems are used in more detail. At this point it is sufficient to know how these systems evolved. Online booking systems are also known as computer reservation systems (CRS). Initially, these were created by airline companies, but were later made available to travel agents. They evolved into global distribution systems (GDS) that are capable of dealing with many airlines at the same time. Most airlines sold their interests in GDS to companies that are specialists in booking or reservation systems and now deal with booking hotels, hire cars and train services as well as plane tickets.

Many customers are using online booking for similar reasons that they use online shopping and banking. Bookings can be made at any time and both time and costs associated with travelling to a travel agent, rail station or hotel are saved. Just as in shopping and banking, security and fraud (considered in some detail in Section **3.5**) are serious concerns.

As with online banks and shopping systems, companies offering online booking services need to own or have access to a web server. In addition, there will be a security/log in server together with a database server, which will contain the details of all the flights, hotels, car hire etc. There will also be a services integrator server, which will deal with the request from the user and search the relevant service(s) required. It is not uncommon for the database server to be some distance from the headquarters of the GDS. For example, Amadeus, which is one of the largest of these organisations, has its headquarters in Spain but its database server is located in Germany. Originally developed by Air France, Iberia, KLM, Lufthansa and SAS, it is now used by 120 airline websites as well as many online travel agents.

5.8 Stock control

In this section we will look at a variety of ways in which ICT is used in stock control. There are automated systems where stock is controlled by the computer with little human input and manual systems where humans use the computer to help them to control stock without actually allowing it to take over the process.

Electronic point of sale

An electronic point of sale (EPOS) terminal is connected directly to the computer and is an integral part of an automated system. These are found at checkouts in nearly all supermarkets and shops. The checkout operator swipes the barcode of the item and the computer uses this to update the stock.

An EPOS terminal in a supermarket consists of a screen (which can be a touch screen), a barcode reader to input the barcode of the product, a number pad to enter the barcode should the barcode label be damaged and a set of scales.

The EPOS system is more than this, however, as each terminal is connected to a computer network. The network server contains the details of each product for sale in the form of a database containing:

- details of the barcode number, which, because of its uniqueness, is the key field
- details of the product such as a description and its price
- for a delicatessen item, the price per kilogram; otherwise the weight or volume of the product
- the number in stock

- the re-order level (the number in stock of that product which when reached means that the product needs to be re-ordered)
- the re-order quantity (the number of the product to be ordered).

There is a related file containing details of the supplier of each product, including their contact details.

When a product's barcode is scanned the system finds this barcode in the file using direct access and reduces the number in stock by one. The computer then compares the number in stock with the re-order level. If the number in stock is equal to the re-order level then the computer creates an automatic order for the re-order quantity using the supplier's contact details.

Benefits to the supermarket

- Goods are re-ordered automatically when the quantity in stock falls to or below the re-order level.
- The processing of customer purchases is faster as there is no need to key in prices.
- The computer system supervises the checkout operators, noting efficiency and time spent at checkout.
- Nobody has to be employed to go round the supermarket marking the prices on goods.
- The computer can identify the bestselling lines.
- It can also identify the busier times of the day, allowing the supermarket to employ more workers at that time and fewer at less busy times.
- Buying trends can be observed easily, in order to identify which products sell best at what time of the year.
- Stock is updated after each transaction, leading to a more accurate idea of stock levels.

Benefits to the customer

- There is less queuing and, when queues do occur, they move more quickly.
- Itemised bills give information to the customer about the price, the size or weight, a general description of each item and also show the total number of items purchased and the total bill price.
- If questions over the bill arise, these can be resolved very quickly as a result of the itemised bill.
- The use of barcodes ensures greater accuracy of data entry as, although there can be a small possibility of

the barcode being misread, there is no danger of human error resulting in the price being mistyped, etc.

Manual systems

Manual stock control systems do not keep track of stock constantly. Stock taking takes place at particular times of the year, if not annually. The use of barcodes can help but even then it can still take a long time to complete the process. Records can be kept on computer, but are only updated periodically.

The database structure is exactly the same as for an EPOS system. The stock control process is still the same as with an automatic system, such that the quantity in stock has to be compared with the re-order level. Because this type of system is not so precise, it is unlikely that the number in stock would be exactly the same as the re-order level so a check needs to be made to see if is below that level. If this is the case, the computer advises the operator that that product needs re-ordering. The details of the supplier together with the re-order quantity are taken from the computer and an order placed manually.

The businesses discussed below usually operate with different timescales. Food wholesalers must move stock before it perishes, whereas manufacturing sometimes has longer time slots.

Manufacturing industry

Stock control here has two aspects. It relates to the product being manufactured and also the raw materials which go toward making it. Let us consider a company that makes gates for the fronts of houses. There would need to be two different stock inventories. One would relate to the raw materials such as the poles and the hinges to make the gate and the other would relate to the completed gates. The raw material inventory would be kept and used just like the systems mentioned above. When the supplies of a raw material fell below the re-order level some more would be ordered. The other stock inventory would be used to determine the value of the stock waiting to be sold. There may in fact be a level in the database above which the manufacturers would not want to go. This level could indicate that they were not selling enough and that there might be a need to temporarily stop production.

Wholesalers and suppliers

These are organisations that sell to retailers. One such wholesaler might be one that bakes bread. The bread is sold to a retailer or supermarket which then sells it on to the general public. Because it is very much aware of its market, it can be certain exactly how many loaves of bread it needs to make each day. For this reason, it cannot afford to be in a position whereby it is failing to produce the requisite amount of bread. Consequently, it must never be in the situation where it runs out of its raw materials, such as flour and yeast.

It probably has a manual system, but must have a stock check at regular intervals, which would be much shorter than a typical manufacturer's. A period of two or three days, if not daily, would be needed to keep a check on the stock.

'Just in time'

It used to be the case that manufacturers would order their raw materials in large numbers and then store them in a warehouse until they were needed in the manufacturing process. This was because of the fear of running out of these materials and not being able to maintain the manufacture of their product. As has already been mentioned, stock control tended to be carried out at periodic intervals, which might only happen annually, so the amount in stock was always bound to be greater than necessary. The result was that companies were paying an unnecessary amount of money on warehouse facilities and the workers necessary to operate them.

The just-in-time system is based on the accuracy of modern computer stock-taking systems. The goods are ordered so that they arrive at their distribution point as required. This removes the need for so many warehouses and also means that the manufacturer does not have unsold stock piling up. It is also used by supermarkets so that they do not end up having lots of unsold stock on their shelves.

In a just-in-time system, the company or supermarket places an order with a supplier when they are on the verge of running out of stock. The order is placed so that the goods will arrive at the company or supermarket when they are required for manufacturing or selling. This system is particularly beneficial to supermarkets as it avoids them having too much stock and means that fewer fresh products are wasted. The disadvantage is that the company or supermarket is unable to cope with sudden rises (or falls) in demand, but it does mean that higher profits are made.

Examination questions

1. Mr George owns a number of garages that sell and service luxury cars. He is looking for ways to use ICT to improve the way the businesses operate and also make a profit.

    Mr George wants to improve the servicing of cars. An expert system can be used to help diagnose a fault in a car during the service.

    Describe how the use of an expert system can have advantages and disadvantages for the company. **[6]**
    You will need to make six points.

2. The car dealers use a driving simulator for customers and teenagers to test cars without going on the roads.

    (a) Describe how this driving simulator could affect both customers and the garage company. **[6]**
    You will need to make six points.

    (b) The software for the simulator will be purpose built. Explain what is meant by this term. **[4]**
    You will need to look at Chapter **4** for part of your answer.
    You will need to make four points.

3. Large supermarkets are being built in countries all over the world.

    (a) Describe how stock control in a supermarket can be processed using a computer system. **[4]**
    You will need to make four points.

    (b) Explain how a 'just-in-time' system could be used by supermarkets for obtaining goods from their suppliers. You should include an evaluation of the effects on the company. **[6]**
    You will need to make six points for this answer.

4. Many companies use the worldwide web in their business. Market research is one area that is being developed.

    Describe two ways that could be used by a company to research the market for a planned product using the worldwide web. **[6]**
    You will need to make six points.

6 The impact of ICT on society 2

You already know about:

➤ online services such as:
  ▷ online transactions
  ▷ online shopping
  ▷ online banking
➤ the effects of the use of online services on society in terms of:
  ▷ employment issues
  ▷ increased leisure time
  ▷ changing working patterns
  ▷ security and privacy of data
  ▷ health and safety issues.

In this chapter, we will consider in some detail the impact of all ICT developments on society, including their effects on:

➤ the digital divide, sometimes called information literacy
➤ catering for disabilities
➤ legal systems
➤ computer fraud
➤ the antisocial use of ICT.

You will also learn about the impact of a wider-ranging set of ICT applications:

➤ home entertainment systems
➤ online auctions
➤ booking systems
➤ information services
➤ government services (at local, regional and central level)
➤ teaching and learning.

6.1 The digital divide or information literacy

The term digital divide relates to the gap between those people who are able to make effective use of ICT and those who are not. It can be defined as the gap between people who use computers and the Internet and those who do not. Initially, it just referred to the use of computers, but more recently it has been extended to include the use of broadband. The lack of use of computers and the Internet can be for any reason, whether lack of access to the hardware and/or software or lack of the necessary skills to use them. The groups of people who do not have such access include the poor, racial minorities, the less educated and those living in a rural setting.

Companies that produce hardware and software solutions are motivated to make further developments since they can sell these to rich people thereby making money. There is no incentive to develop solutions that would be suitable for the poor as this would not involve making the same level of profit. The result is that those developments that are produced for the poorer sections of the community tend to be at a very basic level and rarely cause these people to enhance their ICT skills, thereby widening rather than narrowing the divide.

Some groups would argue that narrowing this digital divide is not as important as providing better health care and more jobs. However, the introduction of such technology by governments in these areas can both generate jobs and provide greater access to better health services.

A major contributor to the digital divide is socio-economic status, with income, educational level and race being among the factors associated with the divide. As highlighted below, many of the effects of the digital divide do not enable the gap to narrow and, in fact, can cause it to widen.

Individuals

At an individual level there are a number of areas where the digital divide has a significant impact.

Health services

There is a vast amount of information on the Internet regarding health and many countries provide online services. The main problem for most countries' health services is how to get this information over to the individual in a clear and easily accessible manner.

Generally, such websites provide individuals with details about medicines and details of common ailments and how to treat them, either recommending a visit to the doctor or hospital or, if it is a minor ailment, how to treat it yourself. Some websites will, depending on the country, list the names and contact details of doctors.

Some websites publish the waiting lists for hospital treatment. This enables patients to compare these and, if choice is available, choose to be treated at the hospital with the shortest waiting list.

Some individual doctor's clinics have their own websites whereby patients can book an appointment, receive consultations by e-mail and order prescriptions.

Patients are able to purchase medicines from private websites, but are advised that as these are not strictly regulated, they cannot be sure exactly what it is they are ordering. There have been a number of cases where an individual has bought medicines on the Internet, only to find the drugs were not what they ordered and were, in some cases, dangerous.

However, these services can only be accessed by individuals with ICT facilities that can receive them, i.e. a PC with broadband access. Services may not be available for a number of reasons, for example cost, remoteness or lack of electricity supply. In these cases, the individuals concerned will not be able to access them.

Not all the benefits to patients have been achieved by the introduction of online services. The general use of ICT in medicine has also helped considerably. For example, many hospitals are now using online portable computer systems. Instead of getting hard copies of X-rays and paper-based versions of patients' health charts, doctors are now receiving electronic versions on trolley-based computers at the patient's bedside. The problem with these developments is that some hospitals can afford the new technology and others cannot.

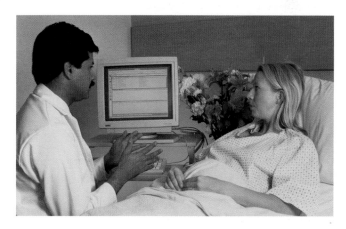

The accessing of patient records can also be done by doctors at home, but if they are in a rural area where broadband connections are poor or non-existent it is the individual patient who can suffer. An 'out of hours'

doctor may not be familiar with a patient and if he or she is unaware of allergies, for example, they can administer the wrong treatment. Patients in a more affluent urban society are likely to benefit more from such a system.

Employment opportunities

Most jobs in the modern world require an understanding of and some skills in ICT. All businesses to some extent and most supermarkets and shops, manufacturing industries and education establishments use ICT in their everyday operations. It is clear, therefore, that aspiring job hunters must have or acquire these skills if they are to be successful in their hopes for a job. Candidates for jobs who do not possess these skills are unlikely to be employed.

Schools and colleges have courses to teach ICT skills to students, but in poor and rural areas often struggle to provide sufficient ICT resources to run the required courses. Richer schools have the facilities and are therefore in a position to provide students with the necessary skills, thus contributing to the digital divide.

Another area affected by the digital divide is that of online recruitment. There are a number of recruitment services offered by job agencies. It is possible for an individual to create a curriculum vitae (CV – a summary of their qualifications, skills and talents) online. Another facility offered by these agencies is to allow individuals to search for job vacancies in a variety of areas. The individual can then browse through the list of available jobs. These jobs will be listed by category and cover the whole spectrum of careers.

However, this assumes that the individual has access to broadband Internet. The poorer, more remote communities will not have access to these jobs and consequently are less likely to be able to advance themselves. This means that they will not be able to earn the money needed to pay for ICT facilities and so the digital divide is perpetuated.

Educational services

These are covered in the final section of this chapter.

Nations

As well as the digital divide at the individual level, there is a divide between nations. This is often referred to as the global digital divide. It has long been known that there is a large gap between Third World nations that perform poorly economically and the so-called First World nations that perform strongly. Unfortunately, the global digital divide accentuates the economic divide. Countries that have widespread access to the Internet and, more specifically, broadband can access worldwide markets far more easily than those who do not.

As has already been mentioned, access to the Internet and ICT in general is a paramount part of education. The result is that people who do not have access to these technologies will remain less educated. It is reasonable to assume that poorly educated nations will be unable to compete effectively in the global economy. Some computer manufacturers, however, are producing very cheap computers that are only available to developing countries.

6.2 Catering for disabilities

The advent of the digital era has provided a number of aids to people with disabilities. Most computers have input devices that make it easier for disabled users to access information on the Internet. In this section we are going to look at the benefits of the use of ICT in a number of fields, with particular reference to shopping, banking, booking systems, health services and employment.

The use of ICT and, more particularly, the Internet has enabled disabled people to carry out many activities taken for granted by able individuals. For example, many disabled people find it difficult to leave their own homes, some have difficulty reading books, newspapers and magazines and some have difficulty communicating.

People who are deaf or hard of hearing can now access and receive information using ICT instead. There are many aspects to the Internet that help people to communicate, for example the use of instant messaging to send text messages and images from one computer to another. This can include using webcams to send video.

People who have sight problems also find the use of ICT beneficial. For example, the size of the fonts can be increased thereby enabling the use of instant messaging, e-mails and chat rooms to communicate with others.

Where a physical disability affects mobility or dexterity, then working from home becomes a possibility through the use of ICT. Other benefits for these people are the ability to carry out online shopping and banking as well as being able to use entertainment services, such as downloading music. All these reduce the need to leave the home. Where the disability affects the movement of the arm, wrist or fingers, then the use of a touch screen or voice recognition systems helps enormously with computer use.

PCs have been developed with many features that benefit disabled people, such as:

- **sticky keys**: instead of having to press two keys together, users can press the Alt, Control or Shift key first, then the character key afterwards (this is activated in *Microsoft Word* by pressing the Shift key five times)
- **filter keys**: this is a tool that allows the computer to ignore brief key presses or where a key is pressed down repeatedly
- mouse keys: the number pad can be configured to control the pointer on the screen
- settings that allow the size and appearance of the pointer, icons, text font size, menus, etc. to be altered
- a mouse that can be configured to have a different type of pointer and/or leave a trail so that people with sight problems can easily pick up where the pointer is
- head pointers: these use a camera positioned on top of the monitor to detect the movement of the head through the use of reflective materials; software then converts these into the movement of the mouse pointer
- **overlay** or **concept keyboards**: the overlay can have much larger characters that can be picked out easily by those people with sight problems and can be selected more easily by those with poor motor control
- purpose-built keyboards: it is possible to have specially manufactured keyboards; for example, Braille keyboards for blind people and keyboards with larger keys for those people who can see but not very well

- predictive word processors: these try to guess what the user is typing in; after one or two letters are typed in, a choice of words appears on the screen and the user can select the correct one; they are often accompanied by voice software that speaks the words to help the user choose the correct one

- **speech recognition software**: this enables the user to speak into a microphone, the speech is converted into text, and word-processing software is used to display the text
- **tracker balls**: these can be used with either hands or feet, and most disabled people find they are easier to use than a mouse to control menus and pointers
- **joysticks**: as with tracker balls, these are easier to control than a mouse, but can often respond to minor involuntary movements
- **touch screens**: the idea is similar to the use of concept keyboards in that characters of the keyboard can be larger or images can be used to replace characters
- **head wand**: this is a wand or rod attached to a headband that enables people with limited or no limb movement to press the keys on a keyboard.

Shopping

We have already looked at online shopping and its benefits in Chapter **3**. However, it has additional benefits for people with disabilities. Disabled people find that shopping online gives the freedom and independence that physical shopping does not. It is convenient as they do not have to travel from their home. This is of particular benefit to those with physical disabilities that make it difficult for them to leave their house. Online shopping also means that their shopping is delivered to their home, eliminating the need to carry heavy shopping bags.

The use of broadband means that the Internet connection can be available twenty-four hours a day, seven days a week. Disabled people who have a condition that makes it difficult for them to sleep at night can therefore access the service at any time. People with eyesight problems may have difficulty reading price labels

and contents labels in shops, but do not need to rush if they are using the Internet in their own home and can also use special features on their computer to make the information easier to read.

Unfortunately, many supermarkets fail to meet the needs of their disabled customers. What they fail to realise is that they are missing out on a market worth millions of pounds. Very few supermarket websites cater for people with disabilities such as sight problems, dyslexia or a physical disability that makes using a mouse difficult. In particular, they tend to include too much text, distracting animations and pop-ups, etc.

Websites that are easier for the disabled to access are also likely to be easier to use by able-bodied individuals. People who use the Internet for online shopping are doing so because it is easier than making the physical journey. If it is found that online shopping takes a long time and that the site has inefficient search engines or complex links then people are going to use a website that makes it quicker and more efficient to shop.

A big criticism of many supermarket websites is that they have too much animation and too many special effects. The focus should be on straightforward text and clear photos. This would particularly help those with sight or reading difficulties. Being consistent in terms of how to navigate through the website is also important. Supermarkets with special websites catering for the visually impaired have inadvertently attracted a wider audience, thereby increasing their profits. Even those individuals with excellent vision are using the website as it is simpler to use.

For example, in 2004 in the UK, the Tesco website was praised by Abilitynet. Abilitynet is a charity organisation whose aims are to help people with disabilities to use computers and the Internet. Although it praised the specially adapted site, it was unable to praise Tesco's normal website. Since then Tesco has incorporated the 'Accessibilty' site into its main website.

One of the biggest problems for the visually impaired is that often it is difficult to enlarge the font size. Text size on most sites is **hard coded**, making it difficult to enlarge – so important for many visitors who have a vision impairment. Another problem for those with eyesight problems is the specialist browser they have to use that is often not produced with these in mind. The result is that specialist features of an online site such as the shopping basket are often incompatible with the browser and cannot be used.

It is not just people with disabilities who are being disadvantaged. The elderly often have problems such as failing eyesight or arthritis, which limits their use of the mouse. They are also the sort of person who finds getting to the supermarket physically difficult.

Banking

Online banking has been a big help to the disabled. Physical disabilities are quite varied in terms of how they prevent people from accessing banking services. People in wheelchairs obviously find it very difficult to travel to the bank, as do individuals with vision difficulties. Other disabled people may find it fairly straightforward to get to the bank but have difficulty when they actually come to use the facilities. People with arthritis are obviously going to find it difficult to grip a pen if they need to sign any documents.

Most banks provide Internet facilities that allow customers to access and amend their accounts online. This is particularly beneficial to those who because of their disabilities would have to resort to phone banking. Those with speech problems, those who are hard of hearing and those who are deaf find it much easier to use the Internet rather than the phone. It also makes it easier to pay bills using online banking rather than writing cheques and then having to leave the house to post the letter.

However, there are similar problems with bank websites as with online stores. Many do not provide accessibility options and those that do sometimes just rely on you changing your browser settings. At least one site has its instructions on how to make the site more accessible in such a small font that somebody with failing eyesight would not be able to read them anyway.

Booking systems

Online booking systems are easier to use for most disabled people than physically going to a railway station or theatre, cinema, and so on, to book in advance. Most booking systems readily identify seating arrangements so that customers can choose an appropriate seat in an appropriate position. Disabled facilities are easier to identify on a website compared with visiting the booking office. As an example let us take a brief look at holiday booking.

The Internet allows users to discover what is on offer in terms of holidays. There are numerous sites available that enable potential customers to find out what particular resorts have to offer. In particular, most sites clearly identify the disabled facilities offered by hotels, aircraft, trains etc. The prices charged by different travel agents can be compared without having to leave the home. This means that a disabled person doesn't have to walk or travel between different travel agents. The other advantage is that people with eyesight problems do not need to read the travel brochures and instead can see the same information on the computer screen, which can be adjusted to increase font size (unless hard coded) and zoom in on images. It is a lot quicker for disabled people to use the Internet in this way rather than visiting travel agents or reading through holiday brochures.

Health services

Moves have been made for disabled people to be able to contact, and gain feedback from, their doctor or other health professionals. An online consultation with their own doctor would save the disabled person the trouble, time and expense of travelling to the doctor's surgery. In particular, it would remove the necessity for those with mobility problems to travel. Those with speech or hearing impediments would also find an online consultation, where they can type in text, easier from a communication point of view.

General health information can be easily found on the Internet through a host of online health websites. However, for disabled people it is not so easy: as with online shopping, few sites cater specifically for the disabled.

Employment

It is accepted that the use of ICT has improved the efficiency of most businesses. The use of ICT is widespread in modern industry and commerce. As industry and the economy become more reliant on the use of ICT, workers are going to find their skills becoming out of date if they do not become more acquainted with the ICT skills needed in the modern workplace.

In general, able-bodied people are at an advantage when competing with disabled people for jobs. If, however, a disabled person has skills which employers need, they will be better placed to take the job on offer. Many re-training centres in countries throughout the world are now offering disabled people the opportunity to acquire skills to place them in a favourable position in the job market. The use of these skills will help people to overcome their disabilities. The opportunity to get a job will also improve their self-esteem and enable them to acquire a certain degree of independence.

The training of the disabled in ICT will help to bridge the digital divide between the disabled and the more able in terms of employment opportunities.

By gaining ICT skills the disabled person will, in a number of job positions, be able to work from home, which will be easier than having to travel to a place of work.

Government

The Labour party – the UK's government party at the time of writing – has been congratulated by a disability group on the accessibility of its website to the disabled, including those with a vision impairment, dyslexia or a physical problem that makes mouse use difficult.

6.3 Legal and political systems
Increased access to legal information

The Internet now allows access to legal information in a form that was not previously available. Many law firms have their own websites, which offer free legal information on a variety of issues in the hope that they can persuade you to employ them if you need more detailed advice.

For example, information is frequently provided on family matters such as divorce, child support and maintenance. Information on house conveyancing is also provided. Conveyancing is the transfer of ownership of a house from the seller to a buyer. A legal contract is drawn up, so legal advice is required, with the process being overseen by solicitors. The second most expensive item that an individual will purchase after a house is usually a car. When purchasing a car, whether from a car company or from a private owner, it is important to read the small print of a contract. A lot of legal advice regarding such contracts is provided by law firms on their websites.

Many people try to plan for the future. They may require legal advice about such things as power of attorney. When you give the power of attorney to somebody you are saying that they can act on your behalf in the event of you being so ill, for example, that you are unable to make rational decisions on your own. This is such a serious document that, again, the process has to be supervised by lawyers. Advice on this is available on most law firm websites. When you make a will, you must get it witnessed and also make sure that the process is carried out within legal requirements. Again, going and discovering what is on legal websites will help you.

Other services, particularly those related to finance, are provided, for example the legal liabilities you have to a bank if you have a dispute. Similarly, insurance companies ensure that their liabilities to individuals, when they have to pay out on a policy, are minimised by using all the legal expertise at their disposal. It is therefore a good idea to find out what the legal implications are with any insurance policy, whether personal, home or car insurance.

Many small businesses are unaware of their legal liabilities when they start up. It is important that they make themselves aware of the insurance implications, tax liabilities and pension rights of their employees as well as the company's rights regarding disputes with customers or suppliers. Guidance is provided on a number of legal advice websites.

On some US websites individuals are asked to fill in an online questionnaire of simple questions about their problem. The website sends this questionnaire to lawyers, who then offer their services.

Increased involvement in focus groups

Focus groups are used in market research. We discussed some aspects of market research in Chapter 5, but did not cover the role of focus groups.

A focus group is a group of people who are invited by a government body, company, business or market research organisation to gather together and discuss the benefits and drawbacks of a product. The word 'product' is used here in its most general sense; for example, it can be a government policy, a person (in the case of politicians), a website, a manufactured item or a service. The members of focus groups are often paid to undertake the work. A moderator is the person employed to guide the discussion and ask questions of the focus group. Observers are sometimes present, able to watch the group from behind a two-way mirror.

Quite often, members of the focus group do not dismiss a product out of hand; instead, as a result of careful questioning by the moderator, changes can be made to make it successful. The key points in using a focus group are selecting appropriate people for the product concerned, asking meaningful questions of them and then acting on the group's recommendations.

Since the advent of the Internet many focus groups have been organised online. One way of doing this is to have the members of the group participating at the same time, using messaging or other teleconferencing techniques to conduct their discussion. The other method is for members to log on at different times and post their contributions to the discussion on a form of message board.

There are a number of benefits of having an online focus group. Members of the group can be drawn from all over the world rather than from a narrow geographical area. The timings of the meetings do not have to take into account the effects of travelling time and amount of traffic. In addition, moderators and observers are no longer required to travel to the meetings. Meals do not have to be paid for. Poor weather conditions are no longer a factor in whether focus group members will turn up.

However, there are also a number of drawbacks in using an online focus group. The interaction between members of the group, and also with the moderator, tends to be reduced. Moderators, who are highly skilled, no longer have much influence over the discussions. Observers are no longer able to watch the reactions of focus group members or the general voice intonations. Focus group members are also less likely to contribute in as much detail as in a face-to-face meeting.

Increased influence with political representatives

The use of the Internet has encouraged political criticism. There are many forms that this takes but the most popular appear to be Internet forums, weblogs (known as blogs) and wikis. Before discussing the impact of these methods of communication we need to define them.

Forums

These are websites used for holding discussions and also allowing postings. Politics and religion are often the basis of forum themes.

Some forums allow anonymous postings or the use of pseudonyms. This can, however, lead to misuse as it is difficult to identify anybody who places a malicious posting. Some sites have registered users, who may be allocated privileges such as being able to edit their own previous postings.

The people in charge of such sites are referred to administrators or moderators. Administrators are more powerful than moderators. Administrators have overall control whereas moderators only have the power to delete, edit and move postings and can also warn members of the forum for misuse.

There are numerous types of software that allow a forum to be created. The forums can be as basic as purely text-based or as complex as the use of multimedia will allow.

Internet forums are not to be confused with chat rooms or instant messaging. Both of these require users to be online at the same time in order to send and receive messages.

Blogs

Application software such as weblog software makes use of features found in Internet forum software. 'Blog' is a shortened form of 'weblog'. These were originally created by individuals to keep a log or record of their daily lives, almost like a diary but written at various points in the day rather than at the end of the day.

A number of blogs are used by individuals to write accounts of issues that they feel are important. Some are written by amateur, or in some cases professional, journalists. Many politicians also have blogs.

They can, in their simplest form, consist purely of text. Other blogs contain all the features of multimedia, including hyperlinks to other blogs.

Blogs have a number of features. The main feature is described as its reverse chronological order. In other words, the first posting or reply you see on a blog will be the latest one. Preceding postings will be in chronological order, with the newest first and the oldest last. A second feature is usually the fact that the blog is unfiltered or uncensored. A third feature is the comments from other users.

Most senior politicians have their own websites but many are now starting to have a blog as well. However, this is more likely to be run by a member of the politician's staff rather than by themselves. One advantage to the politicians is that they perceive that it brings them closer to the voters and the voters, in turn, feel that the politicians are more accessible. Through blogs, voters are able to address the politician directly and, hopefully, get a reply. Contacting politicians has therefore been made easier through the use of the Internet.

Wikis

A wiki is a form of software that allows anybody to create web pages for a site of their own. They use the software to design pages and edit and link them into a format where other users can use and add information to them. The opportunity to create wikis is aimed primarily at websites that are going to be edited and added to by a group of people. This can commonly be a small community. The website Wikipedia is probably the most well known of wikis. It is a site where anybody can come along and edit or add to information already on it. Therein lies its biggest advantage and also disadvantage. It is interactive, in the sense that users can change details, thereby removing errors. However, it does give anybody the chance to give a distorted opinion about something, particularly politics. Wiki was derived, it is believed, from the Hawaiian *wikiwiki* meaning 'quick'. Wikis enable the quick creation of pages and also links to other similar topics. A single page is referred to as a wiki page whereas the collection of pages is called a wiki. A wiki can feature text, images and animation.

Wikis can be thought of as a branch of Internet forums but, unlike forums, they do allow users to edit other users' messages whereas you have to be a moderator or administrator to have that power in a forum.

Political use

The use of blogs, Internet forums and wikis has opened up access to the political debate to anyone who has access to the Internet. Political ideas can be exchanged and the means by which political representatives communicate with their constituents has changed markedly. The use of these features of the Internet has broadened the opportunities for individuals to have free speech. The use of the medium has opened up public participation and does not allow one individual to monopolise discussions.

In much of the world, the media in the form of television and newspapers influence the results of elections, their readers often being persuaded by their political views. The use of the Internet is opening up the debate and broadening the news base on which people base their political views.

Inexperienced people regarding themselves as expert lawyers

'A little knowledge is a dangerous thing' – this popular saying means that when an individual learns a few basic facts about something such as the law, they soon think they are an expert. The ease with which legal information can be found on the Internet can be a drawback. There is so much information readily available to individuals that people can think that they fully understand the workings of the law. This can lead to them believing that in certain situations they have a good case for taking legal action. Good lawyers take many years to become qualified so it is not surprising that people who use the Internet to collect information will not necessarily understand all the implications of what they are reading. This can result in individuals losing lots of money by bringing cases to court that have little chance of success.

6.4   Computer fraud

The increased availability of technologies such as mobile phones, palmtop computers, laptop computers and the Internet has made computer fraud much easier to commit.

There are a number of ways computer fraud can be committed. For example, it has been known for people who are responsible for issuing cheques on behalf of a company to access the relevant software and issue cheques to themselves and friends; they then deposit the cheques into their own bank accounts. Another element of computer fraud is the use of false invoices. The employee of a company can cause a business's computer system to generate invoices for equipment that they do not require. The fraudster has to be in league with employees of the suppliers to arrange delivery of the items to a personal address.

However, in this section we will concentrate on identity theft, which can be carried out using a variety of methods, some ICT based, others not. Identity theft, or identity fraud as it is often called, is to dishonestly take the identity details of another person – name, date of birth, current and/or previous addresses – without their consent. These details are then used in criminal activity, obtaining goods and services by deception. The fraudster needs as many details as possible. There are several ways to get hold of this information:

- Some fraudsters search trash bins for documents of individuals. If they can get bank or credit card statements they can use the bank account details to dishonestly gain access to the person's money.

- Another way is to look over people's shoulders as they are filling in application forms or listening to phone conversations where personal details are discussed in a public place. Alternatively, fraudsters can be on the lookout for people throwing away their credit or debit card receipts on leaving a shop.
- Some fraudsters get jobs in retail outlets or restaurants (or pay somebody who already works

there) in order to use a skimming device. This means that your card can be swiped through a legal device and immediately swiped through another, skimming device that records and stores your card details. It all happens so quickly you hardly notice.

- People's post can be intercepted and credit cards or their statements can be stolen. Some fraudsters have even managed to get the post redirected to an address where they can collect it from.
- Some fraudsters are able to access databases of financial records of companies. First, they get a job in a position of trust with a business that has dealings with a company that keeps financial records. Over a period of time they illegally access that company's database of financial records and download the details of their clients.

As soon as the fraudsters have enough information about the person they are going to defraud they start to use the information to apply for credit cards, loans or mortgages, to take over the individual's bank account and to buy goods over the Internet.

Phishing and pharming, discussed in Chapter 3, are both further examples of identity fraud. In order to limit the ability of the fraudster to access personal details, individuals should install firewall, anti-virus and anti-spyware software. They should always use a password facility to access their computer.

We will examine the implications of identity fraud in later sections.

6.5   Antisocial use of ICT

Antisocial use of ICT can only occur when one person has access to another's machine, either directly or indirectly. Without physically being able to use another person's computer the only way this can be achieved is through the use of a computer network. The Internet is, obviously, the largest network of computers in the world and as such provides the greatest opportunities for antisocial computer users to create most damage. Most people think that hacking is easy but it is not. There are so many methods of protecting your computer that it makes it extremely difficult for anybody to access another computer remotely. However, it is nevertheless possible to achieve if the hacker has the necessary skills. Many PCs lack adequate protection against hacking, viruses and spyware.

Misuse of personal data

With the advent of data protection legislation regarding the security of personal data it has become necessary to define what constitutes personal data. It can be defined as data about a living person such that it identifies that person. Personal data are items such as:

- name
- address
- postcode
- date of birth
- ethnic group
- gender
- occupation.

Data such as the above can be misused in simple terms by deleting it, amending it or passing it on. The first two methods may cause inconvenience, but it is the third method that can cause distress if people do not want others to know any items of that data.

Deleting personal data

This can be achieved in a number of ways. Sometimes hackers use a logic bomb. This is a 'delayed action' piece of malicious code that is designed to go off in one of three ways:

- after a specific period of time or when a pre-defined date has been reached
- when the user fails to respond to a computer command
- when the user carries out a specific task such as amending a file.

Either all data is deleted or only specific records. The action is usually not aimed at an individual but is often carried out by an unhappy IT employee trying to cause inconvenience for their employer. It is usually an IT worker, as they tend to have the necessary skills to commit the action.

Other methods of deleting data can be carried out by hackers who gain access to a computer system. Software exists that can generate passwords very quickly and eventually provide the hacker with the password they need. However, these can be made ineffectual by the computer requiring a password to be given within a specific period of time. Other hackers gain passwords by looking over the shoulders of people whilst they are typing in passwords or by using spyware.

Once into a system it can still be hard to get at the data. It may be protected by access rights, which is when only certain users will be able to view particular files. Also, most files will have passwords on them to prevent access. However, once all this security is bypassed the hacker will be able to delete data. This is an act of vandalism, as there is no financial reward for such action. The hacker just wants to cause inconvenience to individuals and the organisations that hold personal details of people.

Amending personal data

Hackers have to gain access to data, using illegal methods, before they can change the data. When such data is accessed there are items of sensitive data that can be changed and could lead to severe embarrassment of an individual.

Data is kept by a number of organisations, for example:

- hospitals hold information on:
  - ◇ the racial or ethnic origin of individuals
  - ◇ the religious or other beliefs of individuals
  - ◇ the physical or mental condition of individuals
- most businesses hold information on individuals, stating whether they are members of a trade union
- police hold information on:
  - ◇ the committing or alleged committing of a criminal offence by individuals
  - ◇ details about any court cases for an offence committed by or allegedly committed by individuals, including details of any sentences relating to these offences
- government security services hold information on:
  - ◇ the political opinions of individuals
  - ◇ the sexual life of individuals.

If unauthorised people were able to gain access to such information, they could change the details and the resulting harm might be devastating.

Distributing personal data

This is an issue closely related to the privacy of data. The illegal distribution of data for financial gain comes under the heading of computer fraud. Privacy of data refers to the fact that there are organisations that carry information about the individual as listed above. While the data may be accurate and true, the individual concerned may not want their details to be made public.

For example, an ex-criminal may have served a prison sentence but have learned their lesson. They are now attempting to 'go straight'. If their record were made publicly available this could affect their standing in the neighbourhood and cause embarrassment to friends and family.

Other forms of distribution could be regarded as illegal. One organisation might send details of individuals to another organisation without the individual being aware. When organisations collect data from people there must be a box on the form or an address to write to or a phone number to ring which offers the individual the right to prevent this data being distributed to other organisations. A typical paragraph looks like this:

> We may further use Personal Information to contact you about products and services (mainly financial and insurance-related products but, from time to time, with other non-financial products/ services for special campaigns) in which you may be interested, including the products and services of our Group Companies and selected third parties. We may also pass your Personal Information to our Group Companies and selected third party financial service providers to allow them to contact you direct about their financial and insurance-related products and services (and related goods). We, our Group Companies and selected third parties may use different methods of contact such as post, phone (including mobile), fax, e-mail, SMS and other electronic means. If you do not wish to be contacted for the above marketing purposes, you should write to us at any time at xxxxxxxxxxxxxxxxx, phone us on nnnnnnnn or e-mail us at xxxxxxxxxxxxx@ xxxxxxxx.com. Information with account statements will continue to be sent to you even if you ask not to be contacted for the above marketing purposes.

Viruses

Viruses are pieces of malicious program code. They are created to infect computers and move from one computer to another. The effects of viruses are to delete or corrupt data or infect e-mail software so that it can be passed on to everyone in the contacts list on that computer. In its most dangerous form, a virus can erase the whole hard disk of a computer. Viruses are usually attached to e-mails or instant messages. It is important for individuals not to open any e-mail attachment unless they know who the sender is and that they can be trusted. Viruses can also be downloaded from the Internet. It is common for 'free' software to have viruses attached to it so that when unsuspecting users download the software they download the virus at the same time. Any form of file can have a virus, so it is important that users know from where the software originates. This is one reason why nobody should buy pirate copies of software; although, of course, the main reason is that you should not buy any item which has been illegally copied.

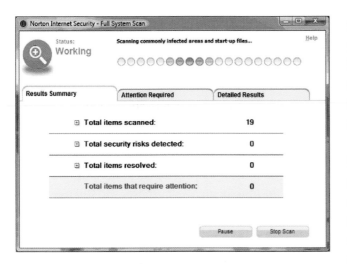

It is important that individuals have anti-virus software installed on their computers, regularly scan their hard disks and regularly update the anti-virus software.

The way that anti-virus software operates is by one of two methods. The most common is that the software contains a list of all known viruses and checks the file extensions on all the storage media in the computer. When it finds one it deletes it. This method, however, only works for viruses that are already known about and is not helpful if a computer is infected with a newly created virus. The way of detecting these is by using anti-virus software that uses rules similar to an expert system and detects any unusual behaviour of the computer system.

One method of protecting against the loss or alteration of data is to create back-up systems on completely different media and keep it separate from the computer system. The virus may attack the hard disk of the system, but there is still a virus-free copy of the data.

Spam

Spam is the use of messaging systems to transfer messages in bulk to a main computer or device. It can be carried out using e-mail (the most common method), instant messaging, blogs, mobile phones, and so on. Several copies of the same message are transmitted in bulk so that it uses up the memory capacity of the device or server concerned. Internet service providers (ISPs) are most affected by these attacks, but are quite powerless to prevent them.

Some calculations have suggested that spam forms 85% of all e-mails in the world. The cost of spam to organisations is extremely high, because of the extra hardware and software that has to be purchased to prevent it. This is without considering the loss of productivity because of the time spent combating the threat of spam.

Spam sometimes gets past the spam filters that people have on their PCs. Usually this is because the spammers use a subject line that does not register a concern. Some business people get a hundred spam messages for every suitable message that arrives. A side effect of using spam filters is that they sometimes delete messages that are not spam.

There is a lot of spam because it is so easy to create. In order to send spam the spammers need e-mail addresses to send it to. There are many companies that are prepared to sell compact disks (CDs) full of e-mail addresses. These can be easily formatted so that they can be copied and pasted into the e-mail address bar of any e-mail software. It costs very little to send spam with broadband.

The companies that gather the e-mail addresses just have to create a search engine to look through websites for the '@' symbol. This signifies an e-mail address and is extracted from the site and saved in a database. The programs which use the search engines are called 'spambots'.

Cyber bullying

Cyber bullying is another form of antisocial use of ICT. It is when people use the Internet or cellphones to send messages to other individuals to intimidate them. It can be just spreading rumours or personal data about one individual to others with the aim of embarassing them or alienating them from their friends.

6.6 Home entertainment systems

The developments in ICT over recent years have led to radical changes in home entertainment systems. A television can be combined with a music centre, and together with a digital video disk (DVD) recorder and player this has become what is now called the home theatre system. In addition, some entertainment systems also incorporate games consoles, although these generally tend to be separate systems. In this section we will be looking at home theatre systems, television, music centres and games consoles in some detail.

Home theatre systems

Home theatre systems are designed to enable viewers to feel that they are watching a movie in a cinema or theatre. There are a number of features that make a home theatre system more absorbing than watching a normal television, in particular surround sound, a large, wide screen, the clarity of the picture and a high definition source.

Surround sound

This is a more realistic sound system than a traditional home system. In a cinema, the sounds you hear are more lifelike, appearing to surround the viewer. This is because there are speakers placed at strategic places around the cinema that allow the sound to come from the direction it appears on the screen, whether it be to the left, in the centre or to the right (and sometimes behind). To recreate this effect in the home, it is necessary to have five or more speakers and a surround sound receiver that can split the sound signal up and redirect it to the appropriate speaker.

Large, wide screen

In a cinema the screen is enormous, quite often as wide as the cinema itself. A standard TV screen is not big enough to recreate this effect so much larger screens are needed. Home theatre systems can have television screens of varying dimensions, but are commonly about 100 centimetres wide and 75 centimetres high. These provide what are called widescreen displays to match the orientation of the cinema screen.

Clarity of picture

The cinema experience is better than watching a standard television because the picture is much clearer and more highly defined. In a cinema, this is through the use of a projector. As it is often too expensive to buy a projector television for home use, the solution is to buy screens that can produce a much sharper picture. Either liquid crystal display (LCD) or plasma screens are considered most suitable for high definition television (HDTV).

A high definition source

In a cinema the movie would be projected onto a screen using celluloid film. Although modern cinemas are moving over to long-playing digital projection systems, copies of the film for archive purposes will still use celluloid. In order to get the best definition in the home, the source will need to be a high definition optical disk such as a blu-ray disk. This means that a blu-ray player will be needed.

Television
Satellite television

Programmes on satellite television are transmitted via communication satellites (see diagram below). The

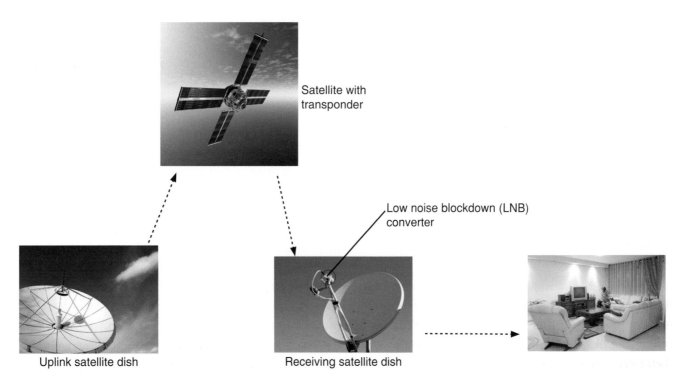

Satellite with transponder

Low noise blockdown (LNB) converter

Uplink satellite dish   Receiving satellite dish

programme signals are sent to an **uplink satellite dish**, which is often over 10 metres in diameter. This dish is pointed at a specific satellite with a **transponder**. The transponder then sends the signal back to earth to the receiving dish, usually that of an individual household.

Because the satellite signal arriving at the receiving dish is quite weak after travelling such a great distance it needs amplifying. The signal is deflected by the shape of the dish to the centre pickup point, which is connected to a low noise blockdown (LNB) converter. This amplifies the signal so that when it finally arrives at the satellite receiver box it can be converted into a form that creates the television pictures. This conversion or decoding enables the signal to be sent on to the television in a form that it can process. The type of satellite dish often means that homes can only receive signals from one satellite.

The receiver box, which is often just referred to as the receiver, also acts as a decryption device. Many satellite television programme providers charge a fee to the viewer. In these cases, the signal is scrambled (i.e. encrypted) so that in order to unscramble or decode the programme signal, the viewer has to buy a viewing card. When the card is inserted into the satellite receiver box, the receiver decodes the signal, enabling the viewer to see the programmes. To continue seeing programmes from the provider the viewer pays a fee every month. The card contains a chip that the programme provider can program to stop the viewer from watching if the fee is not paid.

The provider does not produce the television programmes that it broadcasts on its channels. Instead, it pays the programme producers for the right to broadcast their programmes, which are produced in television studios and then transmitted to the provider. The provider receives these at its broadcast centre and sends them on to the satellite. The signals are radio signals used for transmitting television programmes. In order for the signal to be transmitted to the satellite in a small enough size for the satellite to handle, the signal has to be compressed. This process of compression is called encoding.

Some programme providers have television channels for which the viewer does not pay. These are called free-to-air channels. Even if the viewer does not buy a viewing card, they will still be able to receive some channels using their satellite receiver box.

There are other uses of these satellites. Some cable network companies have arrangements with the programme providers. They are able to use a much bigger receiving dish to capture the signals, so that they can then download the programmes for onward transmission to individual homes via cables under the ground.

Terrestrial television

Although we have called this section terrestrial television, many countries in the world refer to it simply as broadcast television. Programme providers use a powerful aerial or antenna at a broadcast centre to transmit the programme signal. In order that homes that are some distance from the centre can receive the programmes, the signal has to be gathered by transmitters for onward transmission to individual homes. When a programme is being produced the output is split into separate sound and video signals. The transmitter combines the audio and video into one signal for onward transmission. There tend to be numerous transmitters in countries that use terrestrial television. In order for the system to work properly, individual homes must have their aerials pointed in the direction of their nearest transmitter. Televisions have inbuilt receivers to convert the signal into picture and audio.

The broadcast centre and the transmitters all send the programme signals in a straight line. This means that if there are any obstacles in the way the signal will not reach the aerials of some homes. Trees and small buildings are not a problem, but bigger obstacles such as hills or mountains will prevent the signal from reaching its destination. Areas affected like this are often called areas with poor reception.

Broadcast centre   Transmitter   Rooftop television aerial

TV transmitters need a lot of electrical power in order to transmit the signal of a strength suitable enough to cover a very wide area. They generate a lot of heat and need cooling systems in order not to overheat.

Internet television

A number of factors have influenced the development of Internet television:

- the number of people online
- increased Internet connection speed
- decrease in connection costs
- increased bandwidth.

A number of television providers offer their programmes over the Internet. Unfortunately, the quality of reproduction is still not as good as with traditional televisions, with distorted sound and jumpy pictures.

Television programmes

The number of television programmes available to the viewing public has increased unimaginably since the 1980s, as has the number of stations available to the viewer, largely due to the development of satellite television. The picture quality of programmes is improving all the time, due to the development of LCD and plasma screens alongside HDTV.

Films (movies)

There are a number of television channels that show only films and these tend to have 'sister channels', which are HDTV channels, showing the same films but in high definition format.

Films are available for purchase on DVD in all record stores. With the systems that are now available, this is sometimes the best option for viewing film. The developments of blu-ray and DVD-RAM have also led to an increase in quality and show films that are HDTV compatible.

Music centres

Features of a music centre

Music centres can come equipped with the following:

- frequency modulation (FM) tuner
- cassette deck
- CD player
- amplifier
- speakers
- universal serial bus (USB) port

- memory stick
- secure digital memory card
- MP3/*Windows* media audio (WMA).

An **FM tuner** is the radio part of a home entertainment system and is an integral part of a music centre. Many centres have a tuner capable of medium wave (MW) reception and some allow long wave (LW) reception. FM stands for frequency modulated transmission whereas AM is amplitude modulated, equivalent to medium wave radio. Medium wave and long wave refer to the wavelength of the radio signals. The majority of systems come with a digital audio broadcasting (DAB) tuner. Some music centres come with a memory buffer, so that DAB radio programmes can be paused or re-played.

Cassette decks may be becoming out of date as audio cassette tapes become less and less popular, but some music centres still have them. They have, in many countries, been replaced by portable media players of the MP3 type, such as iPods. Commercial production of music to tape is almost non-existent and its other main use, the recording of the narration of books, is decreasing.

A music CD works in exactly the same way as a data CD – it stores data that can be converted into sound. **CD players** make use of laser technology to convert the digital data stored on the CD into electrical signals, which are then converted into sound. There are various types of CD player, some of which are capable of holding many CDs. Although they are more reliable than cassette tapes or vinyl records they are still liable to skip parts of the music if scratched. The software in a CD player is capable of calculating the missing data and so this is less of a problem than a scratched vinyl record or snagged tape. CDs and DVDs are now used to record music from one source for transfer to another, such as from a PC to a home entertainment system.

Speakers are short for loudspeakers. They are the means of output from the music centre. Their job is to convert the electrical signal that they receive from the system into sound. They come in all shapes and sizes, as well as prices. The quality is measured by how well they reproduce the original sound. This can vary from one type of speaker to the next but, contrary to some people's beliefs, it does not depend on the size of the speaker. Often, smaller speakers outperform larger speakers.

Most people are familiar with the **USB port** found in PCs, but these have also become very common in music centres. They are provided so that portable media players or memory sticks can be plugged in. These can then be used either to provide music to be played back or to record to.

Memory sticks, also called USB pen drives, are used to store any form of data, including music. There are portable music players using the name memory stick player, but these are actually just flash memory card based. These flash memory cards are similar to the cards that would be used with a camera or mobile phone as extra memory to store images or video. These music players tend to be about 64 Mb in size, whereas memory sticks that plug directly into the USB port can have a capacity of Gbytes.

You can use an SD memory card to record or playback DAB radio programmes. They are used to store data such as audio. They are also, however, often used in digital cameras, handheld computers and global positioning system (GPS) devices. Radio programmes recorded from DAB radio can also be played back on MP3 players.

MP3 and **WMA** are two formats of storing musical data in a compressed form. Audio data files are very large and normal data compression techniques are weak on two fronts: firstly, the compressed file is normally nearly 90% the size of the original and so not much benefit is derived; secondly, the resulting file is not very good in terms of its sound reproduction. MP3 and WMA are two competing methods of data compression with the same aim – to considerably reduce the size of the music file and maintain sound quality. Both WMA and MP3 players have been produced, with MP3 being the more popular.

Portable or personal stereo systems

Some **digital radios** can only receive radio transmissions served by a DAB transmitter, so not all of them are able to receive FM broadcasts. Some come with an electronic programme guide (EPG) built into the system. This stores all the radio stations and allows you to choose a station by scrolling alphabetically through the stations and then you can see all the upcoming programmes on that station. Some DAB tuners allow you to store stations. The EPG enables you to set yourself reminders and also to record programmes. A pocket radio comes with a set of headphones but the sound quality is not very good, although most are capable of receiving FM broadcasts as well as DAB. The ability to receive AM broadcasts does not seem to be built in to pocket radios. Some of them act as an MP3 player as well. They often have internal

memory and support the use of memory cards, either of which can be used to record radio programmes. A few have inbuilt software that converts the recorded radio programme into MP3 format.

There are two types of **portable media players**. One contains a hard disk while the other uses a solid state form of memory. The hard-disk-based systems tend to have a larger capacity than the solid-state ones. However, the solid-state systems can be very small and are lighter than their hard-disk counterparts. Many of these players are able to play video and have 18-centimetre screens.

Many portable media players have a **clock** and an alarm, so that it is possible to use it as alarm clock.

A **speaker docking station** is a device that is normally placed in a permanent spot. It consists of small speakers with a space between them for the player to fit in. It allows the user to re-charge the player and some docking stations also have an inbuilt radio. This station turns the player into a non-portable micro stereo system.

Interactive games consoles

These, also called video games consoles, started as solo devices but now offer sophisticated graphics requiring powerful processors and graphics engines. This has led to the development of this type of console to cater for a number of competitors playing at the same time. The target group that companies now aim at is older than the original market of younger people. They are quite expensive and so people with large disposable incomes are more likely to purchase them. Now it is possible to play other users all over the world, provided the console has the necessary hardware links to the Internet.

Video-on-demand systems

A video-on-demand (VOD) system allows viewers to watch video over a network. The film is either constantly being transmitted over the network or downloaded in one go to a set-top box, which allows the viewer to watch it at their convenience. Most cable companies that charge for the service offer constant transmission rather than the ability to download.

VOD can be received by devices other than set-top boxes, for example computers with a broadband connection and an Internet browser, mobile phones and portable media players. Whether the film is downloaded or not, it is possible to pause, rewind and replay the film.

The video server that enables the transmission can be placed on a local area network (LAN) or a wide area network (WAN). Such services are available in many countries, including Australia, Taiwan, the UK and the USA.

Projectors

Some households that are able to afford it have projectors that you would normally find in use by organisations to show a presentation. In the home they can be connected to satellite receivers, DVD players and home televisions, as well as computers, and can be used to view television programmes and video recordings as well as VOD. They make use of *Projector* control software, which is built in to the system.

6.7 Internet auctions

An Internet auction is a website that allows people to put an item that they own up for sale. Other users of the site are then allowed to place a bid for that item. The owner can put a reserve price on the item. If this price is not reached in the bidding then the item will be removed from sale. If, however, this price is met, then the user who makes the highest bid is committed to purchasing the item. Sometimes the price an item fetches is considerably below its true value, but on other occasions it is possible for an item to fetch a price which it really isn't worth. This is usually because bidders get carried away in the auction and become obsessed with the desire to own the item and forget all about monetary value. The only equipment that a user needs is a PC together with a modem or broadband Internet connection and an Internet browser.

As with any type of selling online there are potential disadvantages to the system. In particular, these sites often do not have the rigorous security that many large commercial online shopping sites have. As we will see, the payment side is very secure but the actual bidding and delivery side is not so secure.

Before you start using the site you have to register. You have a username and password, just as with an online shopping or banking site. Auction sites have a home page with tabs or menus inviting the user to choose whether they want to buy, sell or go to the user's home page. Other options such as help are provided. When you go to the buy page you will be able to type in a category you are interested in. All the items in that category will be listed, together with information such as the number of people who have bid on it so far, what the current top bid is, and the time and date when the auction is finishing. This is measured down to the last second. You can choose to place a bid or to 'watch' the item. If you choose to watch the item, every time you log on to your own page you can see how the bidding is going on that item. You will also see the items that you are currently bidding on.

When you place your bid the system will tell you if yours is the highest bid. It is not automatic that just because you have bid higher than the current bid that yours will be the highest. Bidders are allowed to type in a price which is the highest they are prepared to bid. The system will not immediately put that bid in but will just lodge a bid that is a few cents higher than the current bid. If, in the meantime, somebody places another bid then the system will look at the highest amount other bidders have placed and use them to find the highest current bid.

If you are successful when the end of the auction is reached, you then pay the owner and give your contact details and wait for the item to arrive. Not all payments are done online. Some sellers ask for a cheque and this means it takes longer for the item to arrive.

An advantage of using these sites is that sellers can sell items they no longer need, which otherwise they would have difficulty in finding a buyer for. An advantage to the purchaser is that they can possibly obtain the goods at a lower price than if they bought them in a shop. There is also a wider market as some goods might not be available in the country where they are being auctioned. Furthermore, there is normally a wider range of products available, partly due to the fact that goods are no longer available elsewhere.

Problems using the system

Generally, people who are buying items at the auction are not buying from the website. They are buying items from individuals so the site cannot be held responsible for the quality of the goods. A good analogy would be the difference between buying an article from a supermarket and buying from a stranger in the street. If the goods are faulty, you can return them to the supermarket and demand your money back or at least get replacement goods. In an online auction sale, you cannot complain to the website as goods are often sold 'as seen'. This means that once you have agreed to purchase the item you have to go through with the transaction.

When a user of the site sees an item they want to purchase they need to decide at the outset whether the seller is trustworthy. Checking the selling history of the seller is quite straightforward. Many online auction sites have a star system and a percentage rating. This indicates the number of satisfied customers the seller has had. Most sites also have a facility enabling you to enquire about the item you wish to purchase. Good sellers give a speedy reply to such queries. You can also benefit from other buyers' questions.

Potential problems for buyers and sellers alike are so common that the UK government, for one, has included these and provided possible solutions on their website www.consumerdirect.gov.uk. Their advice is to check the description of the article and its retail price. Past experience shows that if an item's price seems too good to be true it probably is. The buyer should check the methods of payment the seller will accept. The use of credit cards is the safest method of payment as they offer the greatest likelihood of recompense if the goods do not arrive. Buyers should approach the transaction by deciding the maximum price they are willing to pay and then sticking to it. They should never get carried away in the heat of the moment. They should also check that the price of postage is included and that the seller doesn't suddenly inflate the price the buyer is paying because of this.

In order for somebody to become a buyer or seller they have to register as a member of the site.

Registration normally allows them to be a buyer and/or a seller. Some sites charge a fee for the status of being a buyer or seller. When registering, the person agrees to abide by the rules of that site in terms of honesty. The site usually stipulates that the buyer and seller are operating at their own risk and that the site takes no legal responsibility for the failure of a transaction to be completed satisfactorily. If this situation arises, however, the buyer should try to discover the reason why. The first action should be to contact the seller, as there may be a perfectly satisfactory reason for non-delivery, perhaps a postal problem. If this does not work, the buyer can contact the site and see if they have a system for resolving disputes.

Some countries, for example Australia, have legislation in place to protect both the seller and the buyer. This specifically protects the buyer and the seller if the auction site is not acting on behalf of the seller.

Online transaction services

There are a number of e-commerce businesses that allow payments to be made through auction sites, the most popular of which is Paypal. Such businesses are an intermediary between the buyer and the seller, both of whom need to have accounts with the business. They have to give their bank account/credit card details to the money transfer organisation. When a payment is made by the buyer, the amount is deducted by the organisation from the buyer's credit card account and credited to the seller's account.

The security of the site is enforced by encryption as well as needing a username and password to use the service

Without secure financial services, online auctioning would not have been successful. These services use secure web pages and sites, thus reassuring users that the transaction is safe. There have been very few cases of user data being sold by hackers. The designers of web browsers have gone to some lengths to ensure users recognise when they are on a secure site by the use of a small padlock. The yellow padlock icon found on some websites is meant to show that any information communicated through that website is encrypted. In addition, a certification authority has granted the site validity.

Goods intercepted from online auction details

This is unlikely, but possible. Hackers could get into a computer system and find out the address details of the buyer. They would then have to intercept the delivery person in the act of delivery and provide a plausible reason why they should take the goods on behalf of the buyer. Again, it could only happen on an insecure site and the majority of well-known sites have adequate security to prevent these details being accessed.

Deleting/amending/distributing personal data

The security of these sites is such that the chances of a hacker accessing the data are very slim. The deletion of data would just be an antisocial act but there are such people who would do this. If anyone were to ask the question why a hacker would want to do this they might as well ask why vandals damage property. It happens.

Amending the data would be more profitable. If it were possible to bypass the security of auction sites then fraudsters would be able to amend delivery details and have goods delivered to an address of their own choice.

6.8 Booking systems

This is an area of rapid expansion that is having a significant effect upon travel and concert-, cinema- and theatre-going habits. It is affecting the way that customers buy tickets, particularly when some events can only be booked online. In addition, quite frequently the booking requires the customer to pay an extra fee. Some people regard this as an unnecessary expense but there are those who live in remote areas who would have extra expense in travelling to book a ticket.

Online booking systems usually offer features such as:

- immediate confirmation that the booking has been made
- no double booking of seats
- printing out of **electronic tickets** (e-tickets) or booking confirmation
- a virtual tour, for example of the hotel and its rooms or the plane/theatre/cinema seating arrangements.

This section looks at the impact of these systems on both companies and customers. First, however, we will consider a typical booking system. There are a number of steps which customers go through when booking online. They are fairly similar, regardless of the application. Here we will use booking a flight as an example.

Airlines

All airlines offer online booking. Passengers can book flights and select seats through the use of carefully designed web pages. Online check-in is another service that is offered by some airlines.

Airline reservation systems are able to offer customer services such as e-tickets, hotel room reservations, rental car reservations, frequent flyer programme records and provision for special meal requests.

Airline companies can use the reservation systems to make flight arrangements, view current reservations and check passenger lists. They can issue both paper tickets and e-tickets for a booking made on the system.

Ticketing services include:

- online access for the public to make a booking with the airline
- online access for travel agents to make a booking
- an integrated facility allowing airline companies to make bookings and receive bookings from other airlines.

Below we describe the process involved in booking a flight.

1 Home page

Here is the home page of an international airline.

Notice that you do not have to log on to the site. This is because at this stage there are no personal details to be typed in. Many large airlines require customers to type in their home country so that a choice of departure cities in that country can be offered.

2 Booking details

On the booking details window, it is not unusual to see offers to encourage customers to join a loyalty scheme, whereby points are given to customers for booking a flight. After they have gained a large number of points by using the same airline several times they can exchange these points for free flights. Many airlines use this to encourage customers to book only with them and not with their competitors.

The next page will have spaces for the customer to select the following from a drop-down list:

- departure airport (on this site – 'From')
- destination airport (on this site – 'To')
- departure date
- return date
- departure time
- arrival time
- number of travellers – adults, children and infants
- class of travel, normally economy, business or first.

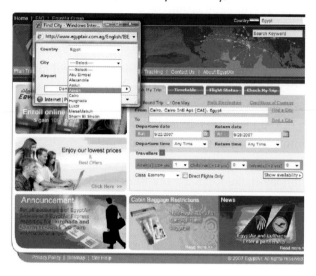

After typing in their requirements, the customer then checks for the availability of seats using a **submit button**. In this example it is the button marked 'Show availability'.

3 Available flights

On this page, the airline lists the available flights. In this example there is only one. If there is more than one, the customer selects the most suitable flight before going to the next page.

4 Cost, customer details and payment options

This page shows you the cost of the flight and the total cost for all the travellers added together.

The customer then clicks on the submit button, which is here labelled 'Customer details'.

The next page asks for the details of every traveller and a subsequent page for the method of payment and details of bank/credit card account. After the credit or debit card details have been accepted by the system some airlines issue a printout of the flight details together with a number, for example: 074 4614 3990077.

5 Checking in

The printout serves as what is called an e-ticket. The customer shows this at the check-in desk and is issued with their boarding pass.

It is also possible to check in online, by logging on to the airline's website, selecting Internet check-in and typing in the e-ticket number. The customer then selects the seat that they wish to occupy on the plane. They print out these details and exchange this printout for their boarding pass at the check-in desk. The advantage of checking in online is that you can choose your seat without having to wait until you get to the check-in desk and find that a seat you would have liked has already been allocated.

Holiday booking systems

These follow much the same process as booking a plane ticket. As with all websites, there is a home page that asks for the type of holiday required. The options tend to be flight only, hotel only or hotel and flight together. The next step is to ask for the country and area of destination, followed by the desired departure date and number of nights for the holiday. The next page normally offers a number of alternative hotels/destinations and prices, from which one needs to be selected. Next, information is requested on the number of rooms required as well as the ages of any children if a flight is being booked. There is normally also the option to buy travel insurance.

Finally, the customer types in their personal details together with credit/debit card details and once payment has been made they will be sent an e-mail confirming the booking. Travel documents will be sent by post or e-mail.

Travel agents

Although a number of people book holidays and flights online, the majority of individuals still use a travel agent. Booking a holiday online can be a long process and there is always the fear that you may not get the cheapest option. Many people put their trust in travel agents as they are more familiar with booking systems.

There are a number of software packages that travel agents can purchase to help them in their search for the appropriate holiday. These packages enable the travel agent to access huge databases containing the details of tens of thousands of flight fares, hundreds of airline companies and thousands of hotels.

In order to operate a booking system the travel agent can purchase either off-the-shelf or purpose-built software. The software chosen will be based on the *Viewdata* system. This is a system that allows travel agents to access the database containing the information they require. It is not part of the worldwide web but is accessed through a telephone connection via a modem or broadband connection on a dedicated network.

Booking plane tickets

Travel agents book plane seats on behalf of a customer. The software that they use enables them to find out about flight destinations, times, dates and availability within a matter of seconds. The records are up to date and the software ensures that updates are maintained constantly. The system looks at both charter and scheduled flights, so that the cheapest option can be determined. This type of system can also include links to other websites, including street maps, currency converters and world weather.

Tickets are booked by the travel agent using the electronic booking systems of airline companies. The travel agent makes the booking and provided it is well in advance of the departure date the booking is free of charge. After the booking is made, the customer will receive full details about the price from the agent. Payment will be expected at a later date.

Booking holidays

The customer goes into a travel agent's office or shop or they telephone them. They discuss possible destinations with the travel agent, who then asks for details of the type of hotel and flight required. The greater expertise of the travel agent means that appropriate hotels and flights can be booked. Travel agents help holiday-makers search through vast amounts of information to make the best possible holiday arrangements. They offer advice on destinations and make arrangements for flights, coach or train journeys. In addition, they advise on hotel accommodation, car rentals and tours.

They are facing stiff competition from online services that holiday-makers can use but most holiday-makers prefer using agents as such sites can be difficult to navigate and use to make quality judgements.

Rail companies

Many rail travellers are now booking their rail tickets online direct with the rail company. Generally, they type in the date of travel together with the departure and destination stations and the website will show the times of the trains that day, together with other information such as the number of changes that are needed and the total time it will take to complete the journey. The customer can select a particular time and the system gives the cost of the ticket and asks how many adults and children are travelling. To proceed with the transaction, the customer chooses the continue option; they will then be asked for personal and credit/debit card details and asked for confirmation that they wish to proceed. Again, once these details have been accepted, an e-mail will be sent confirming the transaction. A number of countries now have the facility that on the day of travel the customer goes to a ticket machine at the station, inserts their credit card and the ticket is issued, thus reducing the time spent queuing to collect tickets.

This method of ticket booking enables the company to make substantial savings compared with the traditional method of going to the station and booking a ticket there. An extra advantage for the rail company is that management of the booking system and the resulting statistics available from it are produced automatically by the system and can be configured to suit the manager's requirements.

Online booking through rail companies is secure, as entry to the sites is password protected and data used in transactions is encrypted.

Cinemas

Computer-based booking systems provide customers with the opportunity to select a cinema in an area of their choice and then to choose the film. They are then offered a choice of different performance times. Having chosen the time, they enter details of the number of tickets required. The website then asks for personal details and credit/debit card details and for confirmation. An e-mail is sent acknowledging the transaction and the customer takes the reference number to the box office to collect the tickets or there may be a ticket machine to collect them from.

Computer-based booking systems allow cinema owners and managers to examine many ways of cutting costs and making profits. As well as giving them many more statistics about how their cinema is performing it means that they can cut costs by reducing the number of staff they need at their box office. Depending on the size of the business, i.e. whether they have just one cinema or a chain of cinemas, the business will have different requirements as to the sort of package they require. Some cinema chains will want a system that allows online booking. In addition they might require automated telephone booking. This is when customers phone up and are automatically given a menu of available films that is read out. Using their telephone keypad and/or voice recognition software, the customer can select the film, type of seats and make payment using a credit or debit card.

For ticketing systems in general, customers can pick up their tickets at the venue using ticket kiosks. There are a number of options available at such a kiosk, but for a ticket that has been booked online the customer would be required to input the credit card that they had used to reserve their seats.

Theatres

These systems are almost identical to cinema booking systems. As there tends to be only one performance on most days of the week, alternative performance times may not be offered. Potential customers can enter their booking request using web forms to select performance and seats and pay using secure payment services.

When a customer wants to make a booking, they are presented with a seating plan of the theatre. They can check the whereabouts of seats in relation to support columns, exits, disabled access, toilets and bars. Some systems allow customers to pre-order interval drinks and programmes.

Additional features are built into some booking systems to prevent an unauthorised person from using your ticket. If you book a ticket through some companies you will be asked for your e-mail address so that the organisers can send you confirmation. They may use this method to send you the actual ticket with a unique bar code, which would be linked to your credit card details. You print this out and take it with you to the venue where the bar code will be scanned.

The booking systems take two forms: a kiosk system operated by theatre employees or an online Internet system. Companies can have both systems operating.

Appointment booking systems

There are systems where you might want to book an appointment with a doctor, a hair dresser, a dentist or your local garage. There are two ways this could be achieved. The first is to log on using a username and password and then there would be a calendar to choose a date from, followed by a list of available times. Depending on who the customer is booking their appointment with, they might be required to give further details. For the doctor or dentist, they might need to give details of their reason for needing an appointment. For the hairdresser, they might say what type of style they want. The garage might require the details of the car such as registration number, make, model and fault with the car.

The second method is a bit more rudimentary in that it might be possible to email the doctor, dentist, hairdresser or garage with the same details, suggesting appointment dates and times and await the response.

Advantages and disadvantages

Many of the following advantages and disadvantages apply equally to all companies, regardless of whether they are travel agents, airlines, train operators, cinemas or theatres.

Advantages of companies using online booking:

- Travel agents and airlines don't have to rent high street premises, which can be very expensive.
- Companies can employ fewer staff and so have a lower total wage bill.
- Travel agents and airlines don't have to pay running costs of a number of their offices for electricity, heating and lighting.
- Companies can attract more customers. The Internet is now used by so many people that companies can advertise to a much wider audience.

Advantages to customers using online booking:

- There is no need to spend money on transport going to and from travel agents, airline offices, stations, and so on.
- People with disabilities find it easier than travelling to the company or organisation.
- Customers can make a booking at any time of day or night.
- They can make bookings quicker than discussing details over the phone.
- There is no risk of double booking.
- They know immediately if their booking has been successful.
- Customers can look at different companies and then choose the best or cheapest option.

Disadvantages to businesses using online booking:

- There is a less personal touch and so it is harder for companies to sell other services that may be available; for example, travel insurance for holidays, flights or meals at hotels.
- There is potential for fraud and interception of account information by hackers, resulting in companies losing money.
- There are other costs involved in running the business; for example, paying website developers.
- There are initial costs such as buying the hardware when starting up.
- They need to retrain staff, which is costly.

Disadvantages to customers using online booking:

- They must have a computer, Internet access and basic computer skills.
- There is a small risk that hackers may intercept data and take money from the customer's account.

- Because customers must use the phone line to carry out online booking, their phone bills can increase.
- If customers don't have broadband, other family members will not be able to use the phone at the same time as one person is using online booking.

Computer fraud

As we have shown above, it is often easier for fraudsters to steal credit card numbers in shops and restaurants than to get them online. However, there are still possible ways it can happen. When credit card information is transmitted using the Internet it may pass through several computers. It is possible to intercept these details, although this is unusual Any payment site will have firewalls and other methods of security including encryption while data is in the process of being transmitted. The likelihood of this data being used for fraudulent purposes is thereby reduced.

Through the use of spyware it is feasible for ticket details to be intercepted. The use of firewalls and anti-spyware software reduces the chance of this happening. Checks at airports, theatres and cinemas can be carried out on credit card details of the owner, so the only person who is likely to lose out would be anybody who has bought the ticket off the fraudster. People who are being sold tickets through a third party should always check their sources.

Deleting/amending/distributing personal data

This is unlikely, but as was explained in the online auction section it is possible. For the same reasons, the security methods employed by companies is such that hackers would find it extremely difficult, if not impossible, to gain access to data.

6.9   Information services

This section discusses a range of sites that provide users with information on topics such as:

- international trading
- governments
- academic institutions
- stocks and shares
- areas of public interest
- educational research.

Trading

Businesses need to be aware of regulations governing trading with other countries. The Internet allows companies to carry out this trading and to take less time to search for information.

Many businesses trade with companies in different countries and the use of the Internet has made this easier. Different trading practices, regulations and standards apply, depending on the country, for example different purchase taxes are charged on sales and purchases in different countries. It is important that companies ensure that accounting for each different value of purchase tax is carried out.

Because of these complexities some people doubt the wisdom of trading overseas. The benefits, however, outweigh the disadvantages. By trading abroad, companies are extending the market they are aiming at, in some cases to include some of the wealthiest and greatest manufacturing countries. It also enables businesses to compare a wider range of suppliers.

Companies need to be fully prepared before trading with other countries. As they are unlikely to know the details of the ways that these countries trade, it is important that they do their research. If companies are importing goods from suppliers it is important that they look into the trading methods employed abroad. Many governments are extremely willing to provide information on their website, offering information and advice.

For exporting companies, it is important that they are aware of the resource implications – it is essential to plan ahead. The target market must be identified and it must be clear that there is a demand for the goods being considered and that their price is at the right level. Consideration will need to be given to language differences. The marketing techniques will need to be considered so that they take account of cultural differences. In addition, the business will need to take account of foreign exchange rates as well as which methods of payment are available. The other consideration is exactly who to contact. There may be government intermediaries and it may be protocol in that country to contact a certain level of management in order to negotiate deals. Again, there are government sites that can help to provide this information.

Governments

Governments have realised the importance of posting their services on the Internet. In the UK, there is a website (http://www.direct.gov.uk/en/index.htm)

where individuals can go to find information about all the services provided by central government. On this site, it puts information about the various services it offers. In Chapter **3**, we had a brief look at some of the services offered, but here we are going to look at a wider range of information services and then in Section 6.10 look at some of these in greater detail.

Here are the services offered:

- education and learning: covers learning at 14–19, educational allowances paid to students, university and higher education and adult learning
- motoring: covers driver licensing, driving tests, advice on buying or selling a vehicle, taxing and roadworthy certificates
- home and community: relates to buying, selling and renting a house, information on what to do in the event of flooding, information about local taxation, repairs and planning and what to do in the event of neighbourhood nuisance
- employment: includes information about looking for a job, working hours and time off, redundancy and allowances for those looking for a job
- money, tax and benefits: covers benefits, tax credits, pensions, taxes, debt, health insurance and managing money
- health and well-being: gives information about medical records, health services, smoking, online health advice, strokes, first aid, emergencies and flu
- travel and transport: gives information about planning journeys, passports, the Highway Code, free travel and concessions
- environment and greener living: gives a quick guide to the environment, recycling, energy and water saving, a greener home, shopping, food and greener travel
- crime, justice and the law: covers crime prevention, becoming a magistrate, victims of crime, prison and antisocial behaviour
- rights and responsibilities: includes information about identity theft, data protection, death, consumer rights, citizenship and how to make a complaint.

Academic institutions

All academic institutions, from schools and colleges through to universities, have to advertise in order to recruit students. It is important that there is local awareness and, for colleges and universities, national awareness of their strengths. It is every institution's aim to increase the recruitment of high-performing students. In order to do this, it is important to advertise to as wide an audience as possible. The most powerful advertising medium in the modern age is the Internet.

The aim is to increase public awareness of the excellence of the institution. To do this, it needs to have a website and well-organised e-mail facilities. Using the Internet, an institution is able to strengthen the relationship it is aiming to build up with prospective students. It will encourage them to join the university by well-targeted e-mails containing information relevant to the specific student.

A website is fundamental to recruitment. It is important that prospective students know everything that the institution has to offer, including courses and extra-curricular activities as well as measurements of success such as job placements at the end of courses. The more exciting the website appears to be, the more interest future students will show.

Below are two such websites:

Notice that although they are laid out differently, there are similarities in the content. Both universities clearly think that job prospects are important. Research opportunities are given prominence on both sites, as are the courses on offer. Notice that Cambridge has a section on sport but Manchester has not – you can decide which is better!

Stocks and shares

The trading of stocks and shares is now communicated worldwide through Internet resources. Some of these are free, but often they are by subscription. Many provide up-to-date figures of prices of stocks and shares to enable businesses and individuals to manage their finances. Many of the sites allow you to create a virtual portfolio, where you go through the process of purchasing shares without actually paying for them. These sites show you how much money you would have made (or lost!) if you had really bought the shares. Many individuals create a portfolio like this as a means of 'testing' the market before they buy shares for real. They can observe trends in the various sectors of the market and when they think they understand how the market is fluctuating they can then buy real shares.

Many of these sites allow investors to buy shares, but they charge a fee. The fee can vary considerably and if an investor buys shares from many different companies this can be quite expensive. It is usually a flat fee per transaction so it is cheaper if a lot of shares are bought. When the investor decides to sell their shares to make a profit or (when share prices are falling) to avoid making an even heavier loss, they are also charged a fee.

Public interest

Many websites have been set up to allow public access to information that is considered to be in their interest. A number of these sites also advise individuals about the 'right to know' laws that are available in certain countries. One popular site is the Friends of the Earth site (www.foe.co.uk). As a result of new information laws in the UK, this website opens up information in the public interest that was previously inaccessible.

The website includes a 'Right to Know' information request generator (at http:/3/community.foe.co.uk/tools/right_to_know/).

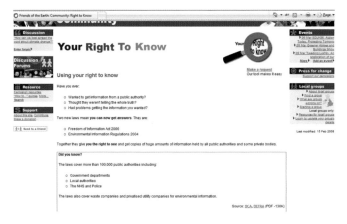

This allows the user to request information from public authorities and guides them through the stages to get to the information they want. It is now possible to request environmental information from companies that previously did not have to disclose such information.

The existence of these types of websites has seriously undermined the role of the newspaper and other media such as television and radio. In addition, the use of blogs to raise public awareness of information that may be of interest to them is now common. Not only are issues raised, but they can also be discussed.

Educational research

In the UK, the National Foundation for Educational Research (NFER) is an organisation that provides teachers with information about educational research. It undertakes around 200 research projects every year, covering all sectors of education, from pre-school to university.

The Foundation is a not-for-profit organisation and as such is independent of outside factors. One of its greatest services is to provide information about the results of research being carried out by other organisations. It offers a link to a free database, which aims to include all recently completed and ongoing post-graduate or equivalent educational research in the UK.

In addition, it manages and updates the International Review of Curriculum and Assessment (INCA) Frameworks Internet Archive. INCA provides

descriptions of government policy on education in 20 countries. It focuses on the curriculum, assessment and initial teacher training frameworks for the education of 3- to 19-year-olds in schools.

Other countries throughout the world have similar sites that allow educationalists to access the latest research both in their own countries and abroad. They are particularly strong in Europe, the USA and Australasia, although such services can also be found in West Asia, Egypt and South Africa.

6.10 Local, regional and central government

In the last section we looked at the type of information services provided by a range of organisations. Now we will consider in more detail those provided by governments, at both national and local level. As well as providing information, most governments also have departmental websites that allow individuals to apply for various services. We will focus on examples in the UK, but many other governments worldwide offer similar services.

Central government – Inland Revenue

In various countries, the Inland Revenue allows individuals to complete their tax forms online and then make payments. The login window to the UK site looks like this:

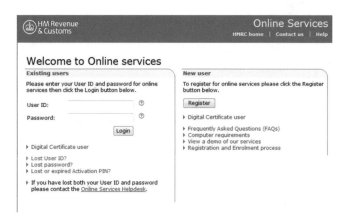

Income tax records

With individuals being allowed to file their tax claims online, there is now a wealth of information held by the government on its citizens. For example, an online tax return in India consists of a *Microsoft Excel* file. The first two worksheets of the spreadsheet look like this:

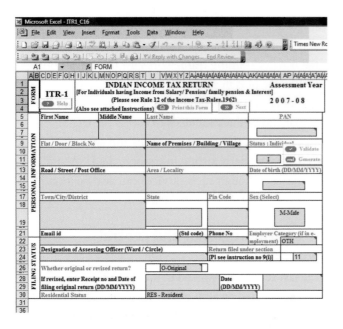

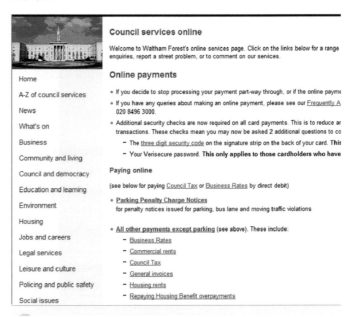

The system will store login details. As you can see from the sheets above, data such as names, addresses, phone numbers, e-mail addresses, dates of birth, salaries and tax owed are all stored on the system.

Tax collection and payment

Governments throughout the world collect taxes online. For example, in India tax payers can make electronic payment of taxes through the Internet banking facility offered by the authorised banks. They are also provided with an option to make electronic payment of taxes via the Internet using credit or debit cards. These facilities are available on most systems worldwide.

Budget calculations

Most governments use computer models of spending and income to calculate their budgets. These models include the projected amount of money to be spent on defence, welfare services, health, transport, roads and government employee salaries. It also includes projected income from taxation such as income tax, purchase taxes, company taxes, capital gains taxes, taxes on alcohol, smoking etc. The difference is be the surplus or loss that they will be left with. Using the model, several 'what if' scenarios can be investigated to determine the effect of increasing or reducing certain variables. In this way, they will be able to balance the books.

Local government

Websites

Local governments usually have their own websites. They hold information about the services they offer and often include online services for individuals to use. Below is a typical local council website for a district of England in the UK.

You can see the range of services that are offered online. For example, it is possible to pay several bills online, including business rates (a local tax on business premises), council tax (a form of local taxation that every household has to pay) and housing rents (the rent that is payable to the council for those people who live in council-owned housing). The index on the left of the page lists many more services that are available, giving information on each of them.

Electoral register

In order for citizens to vote in an election they have to be on what is called in many countries the electoral register. Usually, any individual has the right to inspect the electoral register, which is publicly available. In the UK, there are two registers: the public or full register and the edited register.

The full register contains the names and addresses of everyone registered to vote and is kept up to date on a monthly basis. Although anyone can look at it, hard copies can only be issued for specific reasons such as use in elections and law enforcement. Credit reference agencies can use the register to confirm the name and address of an individual applying for a credit card. Anyone who has committed a crime and maybe refuses to give their address can be traced on the electoral register.

The edited register is available for general sale but individuals can choose not to be on this version when they apply to register. In Australia, by contrast, no details on the electoral register are available for sale.

In the UK, when registering an individual must supply their:

- title (Mr, Mrs, Miss, etc.)
- surname (last or family name)
- other names (Christian or first name and any middle names)
- previous surname (if applicable, e.g. name changed as a result of marriage)
- current address (full postal address where the applicant resides at the time of application)
- previous address (full postal address where the applicant was previously resident)
- previous local government region (only needed if applicant has moved from another area)
- date of move (if applicable, the date the applicant moved to the new address)
- nationality (only if not British, Commonwealth or Irish citizen)
- edited register (whether the applicant wants their name to be included on the edited register or not).

Local tax records

Individuals can log on to the local government website to pay their local tax online. In the UK, this is called council tax and you can pay online, as the screen below shows.

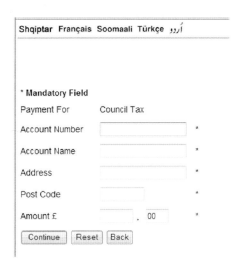

A record of the amount of tax that each household has paid is kept on a large secure database and the data can be cross referenced with the electoral register to ensure that each household is paying the correct amount.

Budget calculations

Just as with central or national government, budget decisions have to be made at local government level as well. Local governments will also use computer models of spending and income to calculate their budgets. These models will include the projected amount of money to be spent on local roads, street lighting, council house building, local transport, cleaning services and local government employee salaries. It will also include projected income from taxation such as council tax or local income tax, council house rents and other local government services that are charged for, such as planning applications and market trading fees. The difference will be the surplus or loss that they will be left with. Just as with central government, local officials will use the model to perform a number of 'what if' scenarios so that they can determine the effect of increasing or reducing certain variables.

Issuing of documents

Many governments now provide facilities to apply for documents such as passports, identity cards and driving licences online.

Passports

Individuals can apply for a passport online. Below are two sample screens showing the process. As you can see from just two parts of the application, the amount of personal information held on an individual could, if stolen, provide enough data for identity fraud.

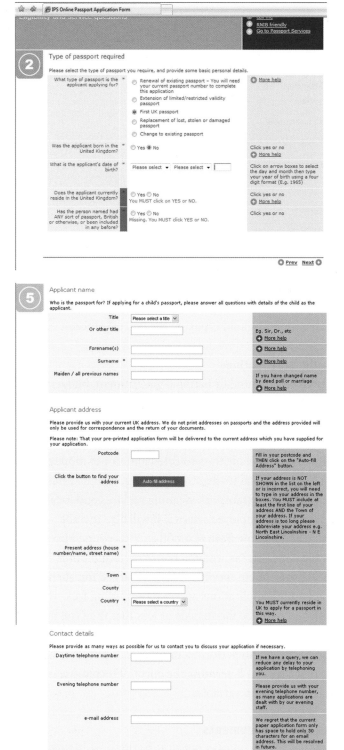

Identity cards

As is already done in many countries worldwide, the UK intends to introduce identity cards. The plan (at the time of writing) is that certain sectors of the community, such as airport and other workers in security-sensitive jobs, will have an identity card by 2009. The applicant will need to provide biographical information covering basic personal details (e.g. name, address, date of birth). In addition, biometric information (e.g. facial image, fingerprints) will be recorded. This will allow an individual's identity to be checked and will help to prevent people attempting to defraud the system. Each person will need to re-enrol once every ten years, in much the same way as passports are currently renewed every ten years.

The National Identity Register (NIR) will be used to store all identity data and the government has assured people that the NIR will be securely recorded and maintained. However, it will have links with other government systems to share identity data, and will support identity-checking services.

Many countries throughout the world already have identity card systems but often, in order to prove they are who they say they are, applicants have to attend a short interview to obtain the card. The application forms, however, are available online. One country where one aspect of an application to get an identity is online is in Pakistan. Pakistanis who either work abroad or hold dual nationality can obtain a National Identity Card for Overseas Pakistanis (NICOP).

The data contained in a computerised passport is basically the data that would be found on a non-electronic passport. Information such as passport type, a code identifying the country of issue, the passport number, the name of the passport holder, their date of birth, their gender, the date of expiry, countries visited and visas issued.

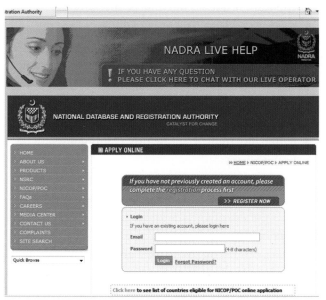

In order to apply they need to be able to scan various documents to be transmitted online. Some of these are outlined below.

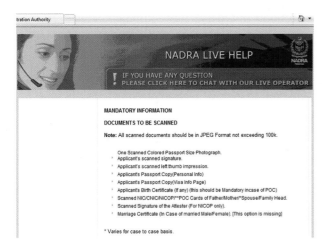

Driving licences

It is also possible to apply for a UK provisional driving licence online, as well as other services associated with driving licences (e.g. a new style licence or a replacement licence).

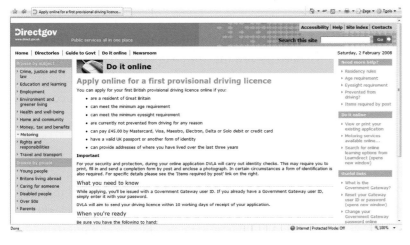

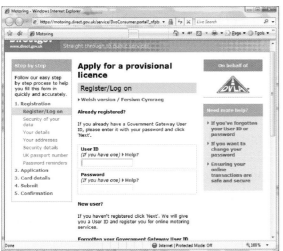

Governments prefer this process to take place online for a number of reasons. It reduces the number of staff needed to process applications as a greater number of applications can be processed in a shorter period of time and fewer staff are required to actually input the data to the system.

Governments and Internet security

Governments employ as much security as is possible on their websites. When users log on to the website, all information that is sent and received tends to be transferred through a secure socket layer (SSL) connection. SSL creates a secure link between the user's browser and the government's server. SSL with 128-bit encryption is popularly adopted.

The aim is to ensure that data is not altered between the user's computer and the government server and that unauthorised users cannot read it. The sign that the connection is secure is the padlock icon that is displayed at the bottom of the screen.

Another level of security is that if the user forgets to log off or their computer remains inactive for a period of time then the system automatically logs them off.

Governments must also ensure that their operating systems always have the latest security measures (i.e. anti-virus software) installed. They should also incorporate firewalls to prevent unauthorised access. The government also allocates user IDs and passwords, in addition to usually blocking access after a number of incorrect attempts to log in.

The concern is that despite all this security there is still sufficient data about individuals on these sites to facilitate identity theft, as well as opportunities for antisocial use of ICT. No system is infallible but governments do tend to take the utmost precautions to keep hackers out. In addition, when data is transmitted to external agencies or even between government departments that are sharing data the data should always be encrypted. Furthermore, these departments should be connected on a network of computers that would probably not be connected externally to the Internet.

Passports, identity cards and driving licences are now computerised to such an extent that they can have data in the form of biometric details, barcoded data or data held on a magnetic strip. This makes them machine readable at points such as airports or police stations and makes it easier to verify if it is genuine. The data, particularly biometric data, can be used to make sure that the person who is carrying the document has not stolen it or had it withdrawn. A number of individuals are concerned about the fact that they are no longer free to go where they choose without being checked on and the extra cost of producing these electronic documents is being paid for by the owner.

6.11   Use of ICT in teaching and learning

ICT systems are being used more and more for teaching and learning, as we saw in Chapter 2. Whilst it is obviously important that students should have knowledge and understanding of all aspects of the use of ICT in education, it is equally important that they are aware of the social impact of these developments, particularly the impact on individuals with disabilities as well as the impact of the digital divide, computer fraud and the antisocial use of ICT.

Schools, universities and colleges
CAL, CBL, CAI and CBT
The main issue of the use of computers in the learning process is how they affect the learning of the disabled and how effective they are, given the existence of the digital divide.

Students with disabilities tend to progress at a slower pace than their more able counterparts. The benefits of using CAL for such students are many. One of the greatest benefits is that the computer never criticises the student, being ever-patient regardless of the rate of progress. Another is that all approaches to the use of computers in learning involve using the computer interactively. Computers can be programmed to vary the speed at which students go through materials and also alter the level of difficulty based on previous responses. When using computer-aided instruction (CAI) software, the student can also be involved in structuring their own learning experience by choosing different pathways. Students can learn at their own pace and can repeat sections over and over again which would not be otherwise be possible except with the most patient of teachers!

In the early days of computers in education, the digital divide was felt to be between the richer schools that could afford to provide hardware and software to their students and the poorer ones that could not. The divide was further extended between those schools that had acquired access to the Internet and those that

had not. More recently, the acquisition of broadband services seems to divide the haves and the have-nots.

The digital divide between rich and poor schools has been reduced by governments providing money to the poorer schools in order to buy equipment. However, discussions of the education-related digital divide moved on from only being concerned with students having regular access to computers and the Internet. They have now widened to include technology-related skills and training.

On the other hand, it is worth mentioning that the use of ICT has led to the narrowing of the digital divide in certain circumstances. For example, students in remote areas are actually benefiting from the use of ICT to improve their educational experiences.

Computer-aided assessment
Teachers are able to monitor the progress of each student using computer-aided assessment. As well as providing students with feedback, progress can also be recorded for the teacher to examine whenever they want. A more accurate breakdown of a student's progress can be made in terms of marks for each aspect of an activity and this can happen immediately.

Students with disabilities, in particular, often have a high need for reward. The computer can be programmed to provide formative assessment, providing comments particularly on what the student has achieved successfully and informing on what the next stage could be.

Record keeping
This was discussed briefly in Chapter 2. The impact of this on society is now measured by the fact that the data can be transferred from school to college to university and between different schools, colleges and universities.

Antisocial use of ICT
This applies equally to computer-aided assessment and record keeping. There is a risk of students hacking into systems and amending results or question papers, so precautions are essential. This is particularly the case if students answer using computers.

There are a number of actions a hacker could attempt if they get into the system. For example, they may choose to delete data. Prior to a test, if the hacker feels under-prepared, they could go as far as to delete the upcoming paper so that it cannot be used. Encrypting the paper will not prevent deletion, but adequate password security and the use of firewalls should. Backup copies of the paper or copies of an alternative paper should always be kept. If the hacker chooses, instead, to pass copies of the paper around to fellow students and the teachers find out, then the paper might need to be withdrawn. A backup will not help in this case but an alternative paper would. Alternatively, the hacker may enter the system with the intention of changing some of the questions, but if the paper is encrypted this becomes impossible.

Once papers have been completed, hackers could attempt to delete responses if they feel they have done poorly. Backups would remove the danger of the effect of this and encryption should prevent it. The hacker may access the test results after the paper has been marked. Again, deleting the results will not be fatal if there are backups. Changing the results would also not be fatal provided backups are compared to the results on the system periodically to ensure they are the same. Distributing the results might be embarrassing for students with poor grades, but again encryption should prevent this happening.

With regard to record keeping, the advent of whole databases of student test results being accessed by different institutes across network connections has caused much concern in countries such as the USA. In the UK, there is a plan to integrate these results across the country. However, there is the possibility felt by many concerned individuals that hackers could intercept the data and make it public. They could even possibly access the main database and change students' results or delete them.

Examination boards
Computer-aided assessment
As was described in Chapter 2, examination boards now use online marking systems to mark examination papers. The papers are scanned by workers at the examination board and then put onto a server. This is accessed by the examiner using special marking software, for which they need broadband access. The paper is marked by the examiner in the usual manner by allocating marks for each part question. The computer adds the marks together to arrive at the total. This method has helped examination boards produce a variety of statistics indicating student strengths and weaknesses over a whole cohort of students.

Antisocial use of ICT
It is feasible that a hacker could get into such a system and access student records. However, all marks are encrypted and the systems are equipped with firewalls. It should be impossible to gain access to the marks in anything other than an unintelligible form.

Examination questions

1   Mr George owns a number of garages that sell and service luxury cars. He is looking for ways to use ICT to improve the way the businesses operate and also make a profit.
    Mr George wants to improve the servicing of cars. Describe how a customer could use the Internet to book their car into a garage for servicing.   [2]
    You will need to make two points.

2   A bank is required to employ more disabled computer operators. This requires a new computer system for the processing of transactions.
    (a) Discuss the implications of the use of ICT in an antisocial manner for disabled and other people who work from home.   [6]
        You will need to make six points.
    (b) Staff will need training before they can use the new system. Describe the benefits of computer-based systems that can be used for this training.   [4]
        You will need to look at Chapter 2 for part of your answer.
        You will need to make four points.

3   There are divides between various groups in the world. There are those who have access to ICT and those who do not – this is called the digital divide.
    (a) Describe a range of reasons to show how ICT can enable a physically disabled person to live a fuller life and join society.   [4]
        You will need to make four points.
    (b) Local governments can use the worldwide web to interact with its clients such as disabled citizens. Explain how local government could use ICT with its stakeholders.   [4]
        You will need to make four points.

4   Many people buy items using the worldwide web. They can buy from shops or auction sites. Discuss the advantages and disadvantages for someone shopping in this way.   [6]
    You will need to look at Chapter 3 to help with some of your answer.
    You will need to make six points.

7 Computer networks

You should already have some basic knowledge of computer networks such as:

➤ local area networks
➤ wide area networks
➤ intranets
➤ the Internet
➤ topologies such as ring, bus, star and hybrid.

In this chapter you will learn about how computers are connected together to form networks. In particular, you will learn in more detail about:

➤ network protocols
➤ types of network
➤ what applications networks are used in
➤ different types of network security
➤ types of electronic conferencing.

For this chapter we will be looking at the different types of computer network, local area network, wireless local area network and wide area network. Before we do we will need to look at the different types of protocols that are used in the Internet and the hardware components that make up a network.

7.1 Internet protocols and network hardware

Internet protocols

Protocols are basically sets of rules. The protocols when humans communicate with each other are based on certain rules. Visual guides to these rules are provided by hand gestures and facial expressions. There are rules to do with speaking – who speaks first, how to respond and how to maintain a conversation. There are special rules or conventions about listening, i.e. not interrupting the other person. Finally, there is the matter of understanding. People are unable to maintain a conversation if they cannot understand what the other is saying. All these rules, also called

protocols of conversation, represent different layers of communication. They work together to help people successfully communicate.

The need for protocols also applies to network devices. However, while a child can learn protocols, computers are unable to do so. Network engineers therefore write the rules for computers to follow in order to communicate with each other. These must always be followed in exactly the same way; although humans sometimes break their own protocols, if computers did so the network would crash. These rules apply to different layers of communication and involve making decisions as to which physical connections are used, how to listen, how to interrupt, how to say goodbye. These are the important elements of communication and involve the decision as to which language to use. This process is called handshaking, which we will look at later in this section.

A network communication protocol is a standard method for transmitting data from one computer to another across a network. There are many different types of protocol to allow for the different types of data that might be transmitted, the most important of which are discussed below.

There are a number of models representing the Internet group of protocols. One has seven layers, another has five and the original model had four. Here we will look at a very much simplified five-layer model, only concerning ourselves with one or two examples per layer.

Protocol/Services	Layer
modems	1 Physical
WiFi, Ethernet	2 Data link
Internet protocol (IP)	3 Network/Internet
transmission control protocol (TCP) user datagram protocol (UDP)	4 Transport
file transfer protocol (FTP) hypertext transfer protocol (HTTP) **tel**ecommunication **net**work (Telnet) secure shell (SSH)	5 Application

- The physical layer is the layer at which basic communication takes place – in very simplified terms, data is transmitted bit by bit from device to device.
- The data link layer can be considered to be the go-between from the network layer to the physical layer. It acts upon requests for services from the network layer and requests services from the physical layer devices.
- The network layer is known as the Internet layer when dealing with TCP/IP protocols. It is responsible for forwarding packets, i.e. making sure that data gets from its source to its destination. It is also responsible for routing, i.e. choosing the path that the data is going to take from source to destination.
- The transport layer is responsible for dividing the data to be transmitted into smaller packets and also adds the address of the source device and that of the destination device to the header details of each packet.
- The application layer consists of protocols that use the transport layer to deliver services to the network or Internet layer.

Ethernet

Ethernet is the name given to a basic set of protocols that are used to operate a local area network (LAN). An Ethernet LAN is made up of:

- devices that send or receive data, such as PCs, printers and the various types of server
- network devices that receive and forward data packets, such as hubs, switches and routers
- the medium connecting the device, which is usually one of twisted pair, fibre optic or coaxial cable.

TCP/IP

TCP ensures that data is transmitted accurately, while IP makes sure that it is delivered to the correct address. Every device on a network (including the Internet) has an individual IP address, which consists of four bytes of data. (A byte is eight binary digits or bits.) The bytes are given in decimal integer form; examples are 193.156.17.8 and 194.78.25.134. The maximum address is 255.255.255.255. If all the combinations were to be used, there would be 4 294 967 296 IP addresses or computers catered for. In practice, these are not enough for all the possible computers, so other techniques are used, such as local addressing and sub-netting. However, these are beyond the scope of this textbook.

Suppose you had to send a long document, say 32 pages, through the post, but only had small envelopes. You might have to send four pages at a time using a total of eight envelopes. To ensure that the whole document had arrived, you would have to number each envelope and make sure the correct address was put on each one. This way you could check with the recipient that they had received all eight envelopes. This is how TCP/IP works. Data is divided into packets, with each packet having the destination and source IP addresses attached to it. IP makes sure that it gets to the correct address and TCP ensures that all eight packets arrive at the recipient computer. Because the packets might go by different routes it is possible that data might get lost in transmission. If a packet has not arrived within a certain time, the TCP handshake sends another copy of that packet. Because there may be delays this could lead to two identical packets eventually arriving at the address. TCP ensures that any duplicates are removed. As well as the IP destination address the packet will have a sequence number attached. This will tell the destination device what number packet it is. If there were just eight packets, each packet would be assigned a sequence number from 1 to 8. The destination device could then receive these in any order but would be able to put them back into the correct sequence using the sequence numbers. The common uses of TCP are the worldwide web, e-mail and the transfer of files, whether securely or otherwise. The major strength of TCP is that it ensures that data is transmitted without error and in the correct order.

Handshaking

With many protocols, though not all, before devices can communicate with each other they have to recognise each other and agree that communication can take place. With human communication the initiation of a conversation often starts with a handshake. The equivalent exchange between computers is also called handshaking. Firstly, the physical means of communication is set up. The handshake that then takes place establishes the protocol to be followed, i.e. the rate of transfer of data that will be used, the parity check to be employed, how interrupts will be carried out, the alphabetic code to be used etc.

Parity checking is a means of verifying that data has been transmitted accurately. For example, each packet of data might consist of a number of bytes, such as:

1 10010101
2 10110111
3 00011110

The bit at the left-hand (the start) of the byte is called the parity bit, whilst the remaining seven bits are used to represent the data being transmitted. The most common form of parity checking is called even parity, which means that there must be an even number of ones in each byte. In the examples above, we can see that in Example 1 the data is represented by 0010101. This is an odd number of ones (three) and so the parity bit is set to 1 to give us an even number of bits (i.e. there are four ones in 10010101). Example 2 has a data representation of 0110111, which has five ones so again we need to set the parity bit to 1 to give us 10110111 (six ones). Finally, Example 3 shows 0011110 as the data part of the byte; as this contains four ones, which is even, the parity bit stays at 0.

Errors in transmission may well affect individual bits of data and will therefore be detected when parity is checked, indicating that an error has occurred

UDP

UDP is a very basic protocol, but it does have its uses. TCP is said to be a connection-oriented service, as it requires handshaking to take place before any data can be exchanged. TCP also has a congestion control

mechanism, which means that it limits the speed of data transfer so that bandwidth is reduced. This reduces the potential for congestion and loss of data. However, the lack of speed of transmission and the delays encountered in ensuring accuracy of data transmission mean that TCP is generally considered to be unsuitable for real-time applications.

UDP is considered to be a connectionless service, as no handshaking is required prior to the transmission of data. Data packets are simply sent, with the address of the computer to which they are to be transmitted attached to each packet. It has no congestion control mechanism and thereby enables data to be transmitted at very fast speeds. Unfortunately, it is possible that packets of data fail to arrive at their destination and UDP has no means of checking whether they have arrived or not or even in the correct order. A destination and source address are attached, but not a sequence number. Even so, UDP is much more suitable than TCP for real-time applications such as Internet telephony and video-on-demand systems. These types of application can put up with slight errors in transmission, but any delays in transmission or interruptions would be catastrophic. Imagine a movie that is being played across the Internet being interrupted because a packet of data had not been sent and the server was having to re-send it.

FTP

The most common use of the Internet other than searching web pages for information is the download. For example, many people use the Internet to download music files to their portable media players; data files are also downloaded, as are videos. All these downloading exercises make use of just one protocol, the FTP. In the hierarchy of protocols, it is one layer above TCP/IP and UDP, although it uses TCP/IP to transmit data. As its name suggests, it is used to transfer data from one computer to another. In order to do this there has to be a logging-on process. As this is a client–server system, the client might have to log on to the server by identifying the server and then typing in a correct user name and password. After a successful log on, the client computer is able to download files from, as well as uploading files to, the server. The drawback with FTP is that there is no security, as data is not encrypted prior to its transmission. Passwords and user ids, as well as the data itself, are transmitted as normal data and, if intercepted, can be easily used. In order to overcome this, secure sockets layer (SSL) or secure shell (SSH) protocols are used in conjunction with FTP, so that data can be encrypted.

HTTP

HTTP is the protocol for transferring data across the Internet. It is the set of rules used to transfer data between computers and servers within intranets or using the worldwide web. It generally uses TCP/IP to transmit the data and messages. HTTP is based on a client–server relationship. The client computer makes a request to the server using HTTP, generally through the use of a browser. The request can be made either by typing in a uniform resource locator (URL) to the web browser or by clicking on a hyperlink within a page being viewed. An example of a URL is www.bbc.co.uk. The URL is then converted into an IP address, which is used to locate the server. This server will store resources such as text, images and numbers either in those formats or as hypertext mark-up language (HTML) pages, portable document formats (PDFs), etc. It will also hold an HTTP daemon, a program whose sole purpose is to wait for requests from clients and deal with them when they arrive, causing the requested files to be sent back to the client.

Telnet

Telnet is a network protocol used on the Internet or within local area networks (LANs). The main purpose is for the user of a computer to gain access to another computer and use software and data on that machine. The user's computer emulates the other computer, which is usually a server, and whatever commands are typed in are executed by the remote server. The resulting actions appear on the user's computer screen. Telnet works at the same layer as FTP and can be used to access and transfer data. Telnet is a protocol that allows computers to connect to each other. Most remote computers or servers, though not all, will require the user to have an account with it and there will need to be a login procedure. The user's computer has Telnet client software and the remote computer has Telnet server software to facilitate the connection.

As with FTP, there have been a number of security issues raised with Telnet. It was originally designed for, and used by, organisations where data security was not even thought of as being a problem. However, as the use of the Internet has increased so has the number of people who want to gain access to other peoples' servers. Telnet as a protocol for accessing the worldwide web has lost popularity because of its security problems. As with FTP, attempts have been made to add security to Telnet, but most existing Telnet protocols do not support this additional security.

Telnet is still, however, considered to be a very useful tool in helping to diagnose server and network faults in LANs. For example, network administrators use it to send instructions remotely to a server, router or switch to make changes to them and carry out tests.

SSH

SSH is a network protocol that allows data to be exchanged securely between two computers. It is on the same level as Telnet and FTP but has greater security. In order to use SSH, the user logs on to the remote computer in a similar way to Telnet. SSH provides many of the features of Telnet, but in addition it uses encryption so that if data such as passwords are intercepted they will not be understood. It is a client-server protocol, where the client is a receiver of services and a server is a provider of services, and it uses public key authentication (see Section **3.5**), so that it can identify that the remote computer is genuine. As with Telnet, its main use is to log into a remote machine and execute commands and so it is used by network administrators to communicate remotely with all types of server.

Network hardware

Having looked at the protocols involved in using the Internet, it is now time to have a look at the hardware that is required so that computers can be connected together to form a network. Most of the devices listed below can be used in local area networks or wide area networks (WANs).

Network hub

A hub is a device that can have a number of other devices or computers connected to it. It usually has eight or sixteen ports, each of which can have a network lead connected to it, so allowing up to sixteen computers to form a network. It does not read any of the data in the packets which arrive from a computer, but just sends them on to all the computers on the network, including the one that sent it. The hub may amplify the signal before sending it on. A hub that does not amplify the signal of the data packets but merely sends the data on its way is called a passive hub and is sometimes referred to as a concentrator. They are often used in small LANs. Active hubs do amplify the signal to prevent the signal from deteriorating over long distances and tend to be used in much larger networks.

Switches

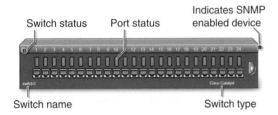

A switch (abbreviated from switched hub) is a more advanced piece of network hardware than a hub. If a hub has eight computers transmitting data through it then the data can get very congested; this congestion can be even worse with 16- and 24-port hubs. Congestion happens because the data is sent from the originating port to all other ports on the hub, so only one packet of data can pass through the hub at any one time. It is possible that a computer on such a network would have to wait for the other seven to transmit their data through the hub before it could transmit its data. With a switch, the data from any computer is transmitted to its destination without congesting the other ports.

A fully operational switch (i.e. one that has been used on a network for some time) will know the addresses of each device attached to it as it has them stored in the form of an internal table. When it is installed for the first time, or new devices are connected to it, the switch is capable of learning the addresses from the data packets it is sent. When it is sent a packet from one device, it notes the address of the device that sent it and forwards the packet on to all the other computers and switches/hubs it is connected to, except for the device it received it from. At this point it does not know the location of the address of the computer that it is sending it to. When the packet arrives at its destination, that computer will send back an acknowledgement packet. When this packet arrives at the switch it can be sent directly to the original computer as the switch already knows its location. In addition, the switch will store the address of the recipient computer that has sent the acknowledgement. In future it will be able to send packets directly to that computer as it now knows its location. The addresses it stores are what are called

media access control (MAC) addresses. A MAC address is not the IP address, but is the physical address given to the device by the manufacturer. It will usually be written on a label on the NIC or device and consists of twelve characters, the first six of which are a code representing the manufacturer. A data packet contains the MAC addresses of the source device and the receiving device.

Routers

A router enables data to be 'routed' between different networks, for example between an Ethernet LAN and a WAN of any description. By contrast, a switch would be used to connect local PCs or other devices. It provides any necessary conversion of protocols, from Ethernet to TCP/IP, for example. It can incorporate a firewall to provide network security. Its function is to transport TCP/IP protocols between two networks and to allow private networks to be connected to other networks such as the Internet. All this is done by the router software. The hardware is just the physical device that is used to connect networks, and includes the necessary hubs and cabling.

In a LAN using Ethernet, each packet of data sent from a computer is seen by all the other computers connected to the network. Each computer checks to see if they were meant to receive it. This sort of network is very simple to run and control. However, as networks increase in size and the traffic on the network increases there is likely to be a reduction in efficiency of the network. Most large companies have more than one network in order to keep the traffic within each network at a manageable level. However, there will be times when the computers of one network will want to talk to each other. A router is therefore used to connect LANs together and to connect them to the Internet, if needed. It stores information about which computer is connected to which network. The router will inspect every packet of data being sent by any computer on the networks connected to it. It is also able to translate protocols to the one being used by the recipient network. It is usually connected to one port on one switch on the LAN. Each device on the same network will have the first part of the IP address in common. The router will send the packet to the switch, which will then deliver it using the MAC destination address given in the packet. If the MAC address does not match any device on its immediate network it will pass it on to another switch on the same network. As the router has identified the network as being the correct one, the device must be somewhere on that network so the process will be repeated until the device is found.

Dedicated cabling

There are three types of cable used in computer networks:

- twisted pair: two conducting wires twisted around each other; this reduces the magnetic interference and hence data loss in such a system
- coaxial cable: a conducting wire surrounded by a plastic non-conducting layer, which is in turn covered by a cylinder of conducting material and finally surrounded by a PVC jacket; they are no longer used in computer networking although they used to be the main type used in Ethernet networks
- fibre optic cable: optical fibres that are individually coated with a plastic resin and then sheathed in a plastic layer.

The use of a particular type of cable depends on the topology of the network. Slow Ethernet, which has a bandwidth of 10 Mbit/s, can use any of the three types. Fast Ethernet, which has speeds at or in excess of 100Mbit/s, uses twisted pair or fibre optic cable. Local Talk networks, which are specific to Apple computers, use only twisted pair cable.

Fibre optic   Coaxial cable   Twisted pair

Servers

There are many types of server involved in the running of the various aspects of a computer network, as well as being part of the Internet. File servers are normally used to store user data, for example documents, presentations, videos, spreadsheets and database files. A file server allows users to save and load data using the network rather than having to have physical storage within their computer or without the need for any secondary storage device. Most networks allow users to log on and use the server's hard disk as if it were there in their own computer.

There are application servers, which deal solely with distributing applications software to each network computer. Applications that work individually or stand alone can be installed on the local workstation's hard disk, but larger or multi-user applications such as school administration systems or commercial applications will operate from a dedicated application server.

There are also web servers, proxy servers, e-mail servers, printer servers, fax servers etc. (Proxy servers are described later, in the section on WANs in Section **7.2**.) This implies that you need a physical box to hold each server. It is possible, however, that organisations may buy servers that have a number of services running in the same box. Experience has shown, however, that there are circumstances where, over time, the load on the server may increase to a point where the server is unable to cope. The organisation may then need to revert to spreading the services out between different boxes and, at the same time, invest in back-up strategies.

The use of the term 'server' implies a physical entity, but it can equally be applied to the software that runs the sharing of files. To communicate over the Internet, for example, this server software often uses FTP. The hard disks in a file server (there are usually more than one) are treated as a unit, with several working together as one medium. Normally there are separate disk units, with one set being a mirror image of the other. Thus, if one set is corrupted the second set can be brought into use.

File servers tend to offer limited levels of security, only allowing access to particular files to specific users or groups. The use of user ids and passwords enables the server to identify the level of access available to a user. There should only be one user with administrator privileges. A second administrator login is provided by most systems but this is usually held under lock and key in a safe and would only be used in the event of illness or other circumstances preventing the administrator from undertaking their duties.

Network cards

A network interface card (NIC) is a card that fits into a slot on the computer motherboard. It enables the computer processor to connect to the server or other computers. It is this card that is allocated the IP address of the computer or workstation. Through this card the computer is able to communicate with the other computers or server so that features such as file transfer can take place. The card is normally fitted with a connection point so that network leads can be plugged into it, although many now allow wireless connection.

7.2 Network types
LANs

As its name implies, a local area network serves a local area. It is usually housed within a building or a number of buildings within a small geographical area, for example a school normally has a LAN. A small LAN typically consists of a number of computers and other devices connected to hubs or switches, which are connected in turn to each other. One of the hubs or switches is normally connected to a router, cable modem or a broadband modem, in order to connect to the Internet, thus becoming part of a WAN. A LAN is used to share software, hardware and files of data.

We will look at the four common LAN topologies – ring, star, bus and hybrid (sometimes called a tree network) – before moving on to consider the uses of LANs.

Ring networks

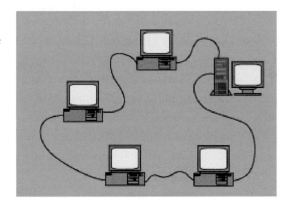

Ring networks are falling out of favour and are now rarely found. Each computer (including the server) is connected to each of its neighbours and data is transmitted around the network. As it passes from one computer to the next, each computer removes any data relevant to itself and adds any data it wishes to send. Data therefore goes around the whole network continuously.

Advantages:

◆ It performs better than a star network when traffic is very heavy.

Disadvantages:

◆ A faulty connection between two computers results in the whole network crashing.
◆ Adding a new device to the network can cause difficulties as it has to go in between two existing devices.

Bus networks

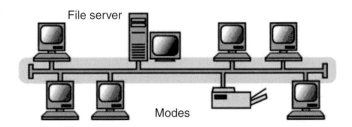

A bus network has each computer or device connected to a common spine. The spine consists of cabling with network leads attached to it and each computer. When a computer or device sends data it travels along the spine until it reaches the computer that requires it. Each end of the spine has a terminator so that data does not disappear into thin air.

Advantages:

◆ It is easy to connect a new device to the network. There is no need to upset or rewire any of the other devices unlike with a ring network.

◆ If one of the devices fails then the rest of the network can carry on as normal.

◆ It does not have to rely on a hub or switch and there is less cable and therefore costs are lower compared with a star network.

Disadvantages:

◆ It can be difficult to identify the cause of the problem if the whole network breaks down.

◆ If there is a fault in the spine all computers are shut down.

◆ The technology being employed is considered to be increasingly old-fashioned and star or tree/hybrid networks are the topologies being employed when creating new networks.

Star networks

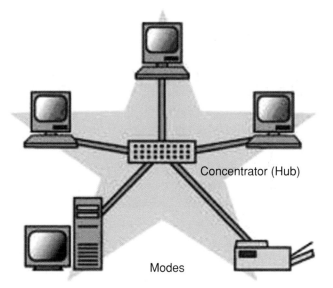

Concentrator (Hub)

Modes

A star network has each computer or device connected to a central hub or switch. If it is a hub, each computer or device sends its data along a cable to the hub. The data is then sent from the hub along the cables to all the computers and other devices in the network. The hub does not perform any routing of the data and consequently the data is sent to all other computers and devices on the network, regardless of whether they should be receiving it or not.

Advantages:

◆ If one computer or device fails, the rest of the network can carry on.

◆ If there are problems with the network, each device or computer can be inspected without disturbing the others.

Disadvantages:

◆ If the concentrator breaks down the whole network will crash.

Hybrid/tree networks

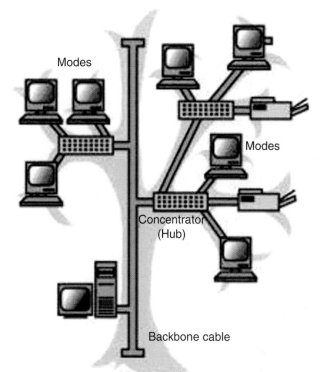

Modes

Modes

Concentrator (Hub)

Backbone cable

A hybrid network is made up of star networks where each hub and the server are connected to a common bus-type backbone. This type of network topology is one where the hubs at the centre of star networks are linked to a common spine. This spine is the bus part of the network, where some computers and other devices will be connected as well as the hubs from the star networks. There is often no need for terminators in this type of network as the hubs perform that function, providing there are at least two of them. Quite often the hubs will link to each other so that you get stars within stars forming part of the hybrid network (see the right-hand side of the above diagram). This type of network is proving to be very popular with network managers.

Advantages:

◆ It employs star network advantages with those of the bus network.

Disadvantages:

- It can be difficult to wire the sections together.
- It has the same limitations of a star network in that individual sections can be put out of action if a hub or switch breaks down, or the whole network will not work if there is a fault in the spine.

Intranets

The most common use of a LAN is to create an intranet. An intranet is a website located on a private network within an organisation. It is only for the use of members of that organisation. It operates very much like the Internet, using a web browser as the mechanism for accessing information, but only members of the organisation can access information from the site and they are the only ones who can send information to it. In order to access the intranet, users may have to log on with a user id and password, so people outside the organisation are unable to access it.

An intranet can be made up of a number of LANs and it is possible to gain access to a WAN through dedicated fibre optic or telephone connections. It is also possible for users of the intranet to be connected to the Internet through a computer set up for that purpose. Firewalls, however, prevent people outside the organisation from accessing the intranet. Intranets can also be run completely independently of the Internet and there is no need for access to be provided unless the organisation requires it.

The major difference between the Internet and an intranet is one of size. The Internet is global and can be accessed by anyone with access to a computer and web browser. An intranet tends to be much smaller although there are some that belong to multi-national organisations and so cross national boundaries. The data transfer using an intranet is faster than over the Internet, meaning that page downloads are quicker to perform. There is far greater security within an intranet when compared with the Internet.

An intranet has a major advantage over a traditional LAN. It is based on Internet protocols and is independent of the type of workstation or the software being used on the network. If each computer has a web browser then any member of the organisation can obtain the information they need from any computer.

In an intranet there is a client–server relationship set up between computers, devices and the server. Each computer and device, just as it would be on the Internet, is allocated an IP address and, similarly, files of data are identified using a URL. The data being transmitted uses HTTP. Other protocols used within an intranet are those you would expect on the Internet, such as TCP/IP and FTP, with HTML being used to format the data.

Intranets are useful to organisations in several ways:

- providing e-mail, although it is only local e-mail and can only be used for sending messages within the organisation
- getting members or employees more in contact with each other through the use of e-mails and even videoconferences
- making it easier to share information across an intranet rather than sending memos
- providing faster access to documents and statistics
- sharing diaries and organising meeting times
- providing discussion forums
- bringing members and employees up to date with the organisation's policies.

Local e-mail and business networks

Most businesses recognise that an intranet or LAN is a very powerful use of computers, for many of the reasons given above. An intranet offers faster communication and access to information than the Internet, and these private networks provide security and protection by using firewalls as well as log-in access and secure servers. The business can put information on the intranet that they feel their employees need to access to, such as company newsletters, job listings, stock exchange reports, catalogues and price lists.

For businesses, there are many advantages. It reduces day-to-day expenses such as paper costs: many forms that are completed in a traditional office setting can be replaced by filling in the form online. Furthermore, there may be company manuals that are very bulky and difficult to use to find information. These could be put online instead and search engines implemented to make it easier to locate information. Telephone directories could also be put on to the intranet, which would not just save paper but would also save time when looking for an internal number for a colleague, particularly in larger organisations.

Other uses could include discussion forums, whereby employees could discuss progress with projects or share information. It would also be possible to have instant messaging software so that internal memos could be sent from colleague to colleague, thereby reducing the costs of the internal post system that many companies have.

The easiest way of communicating through a business network, however, is by use of LAN-based or local e-mail. It allows the employees of the business to communicate quickly and easily. There are two ways of doing this. There is the use of an Internet service provider (ISP), which allows access to Internet e-mail services. Managers make use of the e-mail software provided and use it for internal e-mails but close the access off to employees whilst still using the normal e-mail software facilities. The other way is to buy purpose-built LAN-based e-mail software. In this case, the server does not act as a mail server, but is used as a database for storing the messages which can be accessed as and when needed. Either way, the service works just like an Internet e-mail service, with every user having their own e-mail address.

WLANs

A wireless local area network (WLAN) is so-called because it behaves like a LAN but has no wires or cables, other than the wiring that connects the WLAN access points together. A WLAN uses either spread spectrum radio waves or infrared signals to enable devices to communicate with each other over a network. Spread spectrum simply means that the original data signal, which could have quite a narrow bandwidth, is converted to be spread out over a wider bandwidth. In effect, this makes the signal louder and makes it detectable at greater distances than would normally be possible. These distances are, however, still quite small, generally a few tens of metres. Those devices that constitute a WLAN can only communicate over a small area within range of the nearest wireless access point.

Provided the user has a laptop or other portable communication device fitted with a network card, then the connection to the network becomes mobile. They must not, however, move too far away from the nearest available wireless access point. As well as business use, WLANs have become the network of choice in the home. Because the distances in a normal home are relatively small and the cost of cabling from one room to another is expensive, most homeowners with more than one computer choose to have a WLAN.

WLANs mean that all the computers can access the same services, for example printers and Internet access, from any place the user chooses to work. It also means that new computers or other devices can be added to the network without the added expense and inconvenience of extra cabling.

However, there are some drawbacks with using a WLAN. One is security, or lack of it. It is possible for anybody with a laptop with network connectivity to log on to a network just by being in the vicinity of the WLAN. This is not such a problem for businesses, as most network administrators are sensible enough to employ complex data encryption techniques. These are available with home-based systems as well, but unfortunately, a number of home WLAN users do not secure their network. There are also interference problems, as you would expect with any radio frequency transmission. This can cause interruption of data transmission and loss of connectivity. Computers and other devices connected to a WLAN do tend to transmit and receive data at a slower rate than cable based LANs. In order to create a WLAN, there may be need for additional hardware to add to the network needed for a LAN.

Wi-Fi

Wi-Fi is short for 'wireless fidelity'. The term 'Wi-Fi' refers to the technology used in most WLANs. PDAs and other handheld devices or laptops with wireless cards can connect to the Internet via Wi-Fi.

Wi-Fi is wireless networking – the ability to connect to a network or PC using radio waves instead of cabling. Data transmission rates are faster and there is a greater range than with Bluetooth. It is perfectly suited to setting up small networks in the home or office.

A wireless network uses radio waves. Data is translated into a radio signal and then transmitted. A wireless router receives the signal and decodes it. The router then sends the data via cable using Ethernet protocols to the Internet. When data comes from the Internet to the WLAN the router translates the data into a radio signal for transmission to a network device.

Although it is possible to connect networks wirelessly over long distances, we will concentrate on the more reliable short-distance Wi-Fi technology in this book.

We will now look at the principal hardware that is required or can be used with a WLAN, before discussing the two key means of data transmission.

Laptops

These are an optional element of a WLAN, but in order to gain the full benefit of having the mobility afforded by such a network a laptop is desirable. A laptop as a stand-alone computer allows the user flexibility as to where they use it. It normally weighs between one and eight kilograms. It has a battery so users don't have to be near a power socket to use it, although the battery life is limited, usually to between two and four hours of constant use, and then they have to be re-charged. They are designed to conserve power, so that the battery does not run out too quickly. The standby and hibernate modes use very little power. It is still possible to use a laptop as the battery is being re-charged although this tends, on average, to double the amount of time needed to re-charge it.

You can use a laptop computer for the same types of work as desktop computer, but they tend to be more expensive than a comparable PC. As well as having a keyboard, laptops come equipped with a touchpad instead of a mouse and these can be irksome to use, particularly if you are not used to them. A mouse can be attached if required and many users take advantage of this.

There may also health and safety implications when laptops are used in schools, particularly for young people who use the laptop 'on their laps', because they are much closer to a source of radiation. Schools should ensure that laptops are placed on a desk or similar flat surface.

Wireless network cards

A wireless network interface controller (WNIC) performs exactly the same functions as an ordinary NIC but communicates by transmitting data in the form of radio waves rather than using cables. In order to use a laptop in a WLAN, it does have to have network connectivity. This is provided by a network card that can be plugged in to a socket in the laptop. Most modern laptops, however, come pre-fitted with a mini network card, which is substantially smaller than a PC network card, for example. All the user has to do is to switch it on or off using a small switch at the side of the laptop.

Obviously, desktop computers also have to have wireless network cards fitted if they are to be used on a WLAN. These can be fitted internally. They can be set up to communicate with either a router or a wireless access point.

Wireless routers

A wireless router tends to look just like a normal router. The only visible signs of it being different are its antenna and the lack of cables connecting it to the various computers on the network. It has a power supply and usually one cable that connects it to the Internet broadband connection. There are a number of features built into a wireless router because of the possible breaches of security:

◆ Wi-Fi protected access (WPA), a complex encryption system
◆ wireless MAC address filtering, which only allows access to the network by devices with certain MAC addresses, which the user can specify; any user trying to access the network with a computer or other device which has a MAC address not stipulated by the network administrator will have access blocked; IP address filtering can also be employed, whereby only devices with specific IP addresses are allowed to connect to the network
◆ 'invisible mode' configuration, so that the wireless network cannot be scanned by outside wireless clients; in order to connect to the network they have to type in the wireless network name – if they can't, they will be unable to communicate with the router.

Wireless access points

A wireless access point (WAP) is a means of connecting wireless devices to a wired network. It plugs into the network via a cable, which then provides all the facilities of that network to

the wireless devices. They are limited in the area that they can cover and can only handle traffic from a maximum of about 30 devices. A WAP is not a router as it cannot perform those functions; it is more like a hub. However, many modern wireless routers do contain WAPs. This is the reason that most home users buy a router which has a

Laptop externally fitted WNIC

Laptop internally connected WNIC

PC WNIC

WAP built in rather than buying a separate router and access point. In business, where the cost implications are probably higher due to the greater number of computers and devices, it is usual to see routers and separate WAPs. Furthermore, the type they use is likely to be more powerful than those used in a domestic situation.

Devices that can be used in a WLAN

There are many different devices that can communicate with other devices on a WLAN. We have already mentioned laptops, PCs and routers. Others include:

- mobile phones: many mobile phones have Bluetooth and infrared features for connecting with individual computers, but some are now fitted with WNICs that allow them to communicate with a wireless router and enable them to access the Internet
- printers: some printers now come equipped with built-in network cards, which allow laptop users to communicate with them directly
- personal digital assistants (PDAs): many of these have Bluetooth, infrared connectivity and WNICs, which allow them to connect to a WLAN
- portable media players: some of these are fitted with WNICs, which allow them to connect to a WLAN for Internet access.

Each of these has a varying amount of connectivity depending on the size and power of the device. Most have a small area over which they can communicate.

Methods of data transmission

There are two major methods of data transmission over a wireless network. The vast majority of networks now use spread spectrum radio wave transmission, but there is a case to be made for the use of infrared.

- Spread spectrum radio wave transmission is the transmission of data through radio waves, but by increasing the bandwidth of the original data. It is meant to increase the security of the data and prevent it from being intercepted. It is achieved usually by randomly switching frequencies during the transmission of data. Random number generators are used to generate random frequencies within a given band and the data switches between these. The receiver and transmitter stay synchronised by the use of the same random number generators. It allows computers and other

devices to communicate through walls, thereby increasing the network area.

- The use of infrared in WLANs is not common. The principle is that an infrared light source pulses on and off to transmit data in bits. The advantage of an infrared system is that it cannot be used to communicate through walls so it is impossible for somebody outside the building or room to 'eavesdrop' a network conversation. Because of the wavelength it uses, it does not get interference from other radio sources, which is a common problem with radio-based WLANs. The disadvantages are the lack of range of the system. As data cannot be transmitted through walls this means that the user has to be in the same room as the printer, for example, if the user wants to print. This means that more access points are needed and this in turn increases the cost.

WPANs

A wireless personal area network (WPAN) is one which is of very limited size and used by just one person. The preferred method of connection is via Bluetooth. Bluetooth is used for connection between devices over very short distances and is based on spread spectrum transmission. The idea is that a person within a building, usually their home, can create such a network to enable communication between any of their PDA, mobile phone, laptop computer, desktop computer, portable media player and printer. Because Bluetooth is the preferred standard, the distance over which such a network can extend is very small, up to a maximum of about 10 metres. It enables users to transfer photos from the camera on a mobile phone, as well as contact details to their PC or laptop. It allows them to carry out the functions they would normally do using a LAN.

MANs

A metropolitan area network (MAN) is similar to a LAN in that it can be owned by one organisation, but it covers a much larger area than a conventional LAN and is often owned by a consortium of users. A MAN can extend across a whole city but is still only accessible by the users as defined by the organisation or consortium. It does have a connection point to WANs, allowing access by individuals using the shared access to this and other resources. An example of a MAN would commonly be found in university campuses to enable the sharing of facilities such as libraries, research findings, videoconferencing and local e-mail.

WANs

A wide area network (WAN) is formed by connecting a number of LANs through a router or a modem. It covers a much larger geographical area than a LAN or a MAN. Private WANs can be set up by organisations to connect their LANs by the means of leasing telephone lines or private fibre optic cable purely for their own use. This can, however, be expensive and so many organisations prefer to pay an ISP for a connection to the Internet and communicate that way instead. If it is deemed necessary to increase security, virtual private networks (VPNs) can be set up. Firewalls are used to provide extra security at the connection point of the LAN to the WAN, within either the modem or the router. The use of an existing telecommunications network causes data transmission rates to be slower in a WAN than a LAN.

A WAN needs some additional hardware that isn't necessarily required with a LAN: routers (with modem-type functions included) and proxy servers. These are described below, followed by a discussion of the main uses of WANs.

Modems

Modems used to be the key gateway connecting LANs to a WAN. A gateway is an interface between a LAN and a WAN. Routers, modems and firewalls are all considered to be gateways.

The role of the modem was to convert the digital data from a computer into analogue data for transmission through telephone lines. With the introduction of broadband, however, there is little need for analogue-to-digital conversion in networks so they have been replaced by routers. A specially configured computer could also act as a gateway but this is rarely used.

HTTP proxy servers

A proxy server is a special type of server that acts as a buffer between a WAN (usually the Internet) and a LAN. It is able to pass on service requests to the Internet and pass back the pages requested. It retrieves web pages sent by an Internet server and then passes them on to the computer which requested them, having first filtered out any information as requested by the organisation. It also passes on to the server requests for pages from the original computer. Any pages it receives back it stores and this means that when another computer requests that page, instead of sending a request to the server it has it available on hand. This speeds up browsing considerably.

The Internet

The Internet is a special type of WAN. It is a network of computer networks. It is worldwide and, unlike many other types of network, is publicly accessible to anybody with an Internet connection. The most common way of connecting is through a broadband modem or router, which connects to the public telephone line and via this an ISP is contacted. All the computers on the Internet can be classified as either clients or servers. The servers are those that provide services, for example mail servers or webservers. The client computer is able to access the worldwide web and ask for information, which the webserver provides.

Extranets

An extranet is a means of extending an organisation's intranet for use by selected people outside the organisation. It is particularly useful to companies who wish to enable customers, sales people or suppliers, for example, to use the facilities of their intranet.

In order to maintain security and confidentiality of data, firewalls, VPNs and authentication techniques are used, together with complex data encryption techniques. Extranets have many uses. Customers and an externally based sales force can be provided with up-to-the-minute catalogues. Training facilities and courses can be shared with other companies. Projects can be set up and operated with business partners. They are also used so that employees can work from home and have access to all the facilities that they would have from the intranet at work.

E-mail

This is the main means of communication over the Internet. It is simply a method of sending mail, whether in the form of messages, documents, photos etc. It is now more popular than traditional postal services for sending letters because of the possibility of immediate response to the mail. It works through the use of ISPs. Mail is sent from the user to their ISP and they then send the mail on to the addressee's ISP, which puts it in the recipient's mail box. When the recipient next logs on to their ISP and accesses their mailbox, the mail will be there. An e-mail address always has a domain name as part of it, for example hotmail.com. Each person or ISP has an IP address that is decoded from the domain name part of the e-mail address. This is how the various routers in the chain of computers can know where to forward the mail.

Business networks

WANs are used by businesses that need to connect their existing LANs together and also need access to the Internet. It might be that their LANs are remote from each other and in order to streamline their operations they want to have all their offices able to communicate. As we have already seen, the speed of data transfer across a WAN is somewhat slower than that of a LAN. This is tolerated by businesses because the volume of data between branches is far less than within their internal offices. In order to do this, businesses often make use of VPNs.

Virtual private networks

A VPN is not a physically private network, as it uses the Internet or another WAN to transmit data. The data remains encrypted throughout its journey and is only decrypted at the destination computer. This process is called tunnelling, as it is using a secure means to tunnel through a publicly accessible network. A VPN normally consists of LANs that may be remote from each other, such as different branches of an organisation, but need to be connected together. Rather than using dedicated lines, a public access network is used but tunnelled through to provide security. It enables organisations to communicate over a large area but is cheaper than creating a conventional WAN. The security employed consists of firewalls, encryption, the use of IP security (IPsec) and an authentication, authorisation and accounting (AAA) server.

Videoconferencing

A videoconference is a means of communication between two or more different locations in real time. For a videoconference to take place, hardware such as small video cameras or webcams, computers, monitors or projectors, microphones and loudspeakers or headphones are needed.

The communication can take place using a LAN for internal conferences, but the main use of videoconferencing occurs through a WAN such as the Internet. It enables users to communicate by a method that allows all the participants to hear and see all the other participants. Videoconferencing is covered in more detail in Section **7.4**.

Telephone call centres

WANs are used with telephone call centres, particularly virtual call centres. We have seen how large scale call centres operate in Chapter 2, but more and more companies are moving away from large call centres and are employing their call operators to work from home.

A call server distributes a call to an available operator connected to the WAN. Voice over IP (VOIP) is employed to transfer calls from the server to the operator. The software used in any type of call centre is called computer telephony integration (CTI) software. It has features such as the operator being able to see who is calling. In addition, the server can identify the number being dialled by the caller and direct it towards the relevant operator together with any data held on the system about the caller, for example account details in the case of a bank's call centre.

Online booking, shopping and banking systems

Each of these systems, as we have seen in earlier chapters, requires the use of the Internet, which is, as previously discussed, a WAN. Each user accesses the Internet from their own PC or laptop and can then connect with the main server. In each of these applications, it is unlikely that the browser being used is based in their computer. It is more likely that the browser is to be found on the server and when the user accesses the application they are actually using the bank's, booking system's or shop's own browser to log on to. When details are transmitted through the network from the customer's PC to the server, each data packet is heavily encrypted whilst in transit. The server will also have a firewall to provide extra security.

7.3 Network security

In Section **7.1** we have seen numerous references to security. This is needed simply because once users can log on to a server they are then able to find information on that server that other users have placed there. Data in transit can also be intercepted. There is a need for security to prevent users from accessing data they are not supposed to view and, in addition, if they do manage to access the data these unauthorised users must be prevented from reading it. In short, we either prevent access or, if that is not possible, prevent users from being able to understand any data they might access. Most networks employ both of these software-based techniques to be doubly sure of keeping data private and confidential. Before we look at these, let us consider the physical security methods that can be employed to safeguard access to data.

Physical security

This is where procedures are put in place to prevent the user from gaining physical access to computers or the rooms where they are kept.

Securing computer rooms

If an unauthorised user gains access to a computer or network all the data stored there is vulnerable to being accessed and misused. This is of great concern to major organisations

In any computer room, all the doors and windows should be locked when not in use. Computers should be screwed to the tables or benches. A burglar alarm should be fitted. Doors between rooms should also remain locked when not in use. Servers are particularly vulnerable as they hold all the data. Most servers are lockable and should be locked when not in use. They should also be in a separate room with restricted access, possibly with a number pad lock fitted to the door or a pass card with a magnetic stripe. These could be programmed to prevent access to specific groups of users outside certain time periods.

Although closed-circuit television (CCTV) surveillance systems do not prevent entrance, they can deter would-be computer thieves or potential unauthorised users.

Security guards

Security guards are normally provided by a security firm that has been contracted to carry out the security services for an organisation's computer facility. They wear uniforms, thereby making themselves visible to visitors, whether invited or uninvited. Security guards can be used in a number of ways. They can patrol the building and intercept any unauthorised visitors. They can be used to respond to alarms going off. They could also be used to monitor the CCTV footage to keep a look out for intruders. Although they do not have the power of arrest like a police officer, they are able, in many countries, to make 'citizen's arrests' and keep a suspect under control until a police officer arrives.

Software security

Although physical security is important, this does not tend to be the major source of intrusions into networked computer systems. Most threats come from hackers or fraudsters who gain access to networks remotely and do their business from home or Internet cafes. Here we will look at the major methods of preventing access to personal and private data.

Firewalls

Firewalls are designed purely to prevent unauthorised access. A firewall can come in two forms – either hardware or software – but is often combined into one device. Many organisations have hundreds of computers that form networks and many of these are connected to the Internet. If an organisation does not have a firewall in place then all these computers become accessible to unauthorised users via the Internet. Organisations therefore place firewalls at the points of access to the Internet. The way firewalls work is to filter out information from a message and see if it is allowable traffic. It will examine the data packets which come to it and filter out the parts of the packet to see what they are. It can look at the IP address and if it is not part of its 'allowed' addresses it will prevent the packet from continuing. It can do the same for domain names. It can also be programmed with certain words or phrases that are not acceptable and prevent packets with that text in them from proceeding.

Encryption

Encryption is the name given to the converting of data into a code by scrambling or encoding it. The resulting symbols appear all jumbled up. This means that even if a hacker or fraudster gains access to the data they will not be able to understand it. It is used to prevent unauthorised users from being able to read other people's messages. The codes used are so complicated that even the most dedicated hacker with plenty of time to spare and with hacking software to help them would be extremely unlikely to crack the meaning of the data.

The way that encryption works is that the computer that is sending the message uses an encryption key to encode the data. The receiving computer has a decryption key that can translate it. The encryption key is the way the information is encoded. In simple terms, the computer might change every letter in the alphabet to a letter five further on in the alphabet. For example, A would become F, B would become G, C would become H and so on. (Incidentally, this is too easy a code to decipher and would never be contemplated as an encryption system.) The receiving computer would have a corresponding decryption key, which would know that 5 has to be taken off each letter. The process of decryption here is basically reversing the encryption. In real life it is not that easy.

In a real situation, public key/private key encryption is used. Let us consider a computer belonging to Ali. Any computer that wants to send a message to Ali's computer knows the public key and can encrypt a message going to that computer. To decode the message a separate key is used called the private key. Only Ali's computer knows that key. This process is based on the fact that although an encryption key may be discovered, the key is so complex that just knowing it doesn't mean that the message can be decrypted.

Digital certification

Digital certificates are issued by a certificate authority, which must be a body that both computers trust. These are needed so that public key encryption can be verified. The digital certificate serves to confirm that both the receiving and sending computer are who they say they are. It is essential for secure servers to have such a certificate as evidence of authenticity.

Once the certificate authority has issued the certificate to both computers, it can then give each one the public key of the other.

Authentication techniques

There are many ways in which a computer user can prove that they are who they say they are. This process is called authentication. This can be done, for example, by using a password which only you know, through digital certificates or by the use of biometric data. These three

types are examples of something you know, something you have which only belongs to you and something about you. It is generally accepted that to use only one of these methods is insufficient evidence of authenticity. At least two are required. In banking, for example, to withdraw money from an ATM you need to present something you own (your bank card) and something only you know (your PIN or password). That is why online banking requires you to type in your password (something only you know) and have a digital certificate (something you own). Eventually, the third feature may well be brought into play by having maybe a fingerprint reader attached to your PC.

Anti-virus software

Anti-virus software is used to find viruses and then remove them from the host computer. There are two main ways of doing this. One is to scan a disk looking for filenames that match those in a database the anti-virus software has access to. The other is to scan the disk and monitor ports to the computer looking for suspicious behaviour. When the software discovers a virus, it does one of three things: try to repair the file; quarantine the file by not allowing any other software to access it; or delete the file.

In order to be effective, anti-virus software has to be updated on a regular basis with the names and definitions of any new threats.

There are some disadvantages with using anti-virus software. It does slow down the running of the computer. Anti-virus definition files are becoming very long as new viruses and variants of existing viruses appear. Scanning files takes longer as each virus pattern has to be searched for. A number of users who have become disenchanted with the performance of their PC, have uninstalled the anti-virus software and are prepared to run the risk of becoming infected rather than have their work slowed down. They are reassured by their use of firewalls but may be unaware that these may not pick up viruses that are attached to e-mails and programs.

Apart from viruses, anti-virus software also deals with and tries to eliminate Trojan horses and worms. A Trojan horse doesn't replicate like a virus; rather, it is a program that claims to be something it isn't, usually a piece of useful software. When executed it causes damage such as deleting files. A worm replicates like a virus but does not need human intervention to move to another computer. It uses information about the method of communication a computer uses (FTP etc.) to cause itself to be transported to another computer.

User ID

This is the first piece of information that a user has to type in when logging on to a network system. It identifies the user to the system. For each group of user IDs, the system allocates certain privileges. Some users will be able to access nearly all the facilities of the network (only the administrator has access to all of them), while others will only have access to some of them. Every server has a database of user IDs together with the personal details and passwords of each registered user. If the server can't find the user ID on its database, it rejects the log in. The user id or user name is often chosen by the user themselves although some systems prefer to give each user an ID as an extra layer of security, preventing the user from using an easily guessable user ID. When the system allows a user to choose it will tell them if that ID is already in use, particularly likely if it is a common name. The system often provides the user with available alternatives that are very close to the chosen name.

Passwords

Having got a user ID the user will be given a password that they are able to change as and when they want. The password enables the user to complete the log-in process. The database will check the password that is typed in with the one stored in the database. If it is incorrect the system asks the user to re-type it. On many systems, if there are three unsuccessful attempts at logging on the user is thrown out of the system and no subsequent log in is allowed for that user ID. In such circumstances, the user will not be allowed to log in until they have spoken with the administrator of the network and explained why they have forgotten their password.

When choosing a password it is important to choose one which you will not forget, but also you must never choose a password which somebody else might guess, for example your favourite football team, your favourite singer, your date of birth. You must change your password regularly.

Chip and PIN cards

Systems are now in place in some organisations where chip and PIN card readers are slotted into keyboards. Before users can log on to the system they have to insert their card and key in a PIN. The software checks the PIN entered against that on the chip of the card. This could also be considered as a level of physical security, as without possession of a card the user cannot access the computer.

Anti-spam

Spam is the term used for unwanted e-mail messages. It is unsolicited, in other words it has not been asked for. A number of senders do it with malicious intent. If sufficient are sent in enough bulk they can soon fill up the available disk space on a server, causing delays in data transmission and taking up valuable time in deleting all the unwanted mail.

Anti-spam software is installed on the e-mail server, just like any other software package. You then configure it to filter out unwanted e-mails. It can be configured to reject e-mails with certain phrases in the subject line or in the body of the message. It can reject e-mails if there are suspicious attachments or the sender is not in your address book. Good anti-spam software will be automatically updated regularly.

Anti-pop-up software

Anti-pop-up software is often referred to as **pop-up** blocking software. Pop-up adverts can at best be annoying as they interfere with your view of a website or can be malicious, containing viruses and spyware. The HTML code that causes the pop-up is embedded within the page being loaded by your browser.

Pop-up blockers are usually free and are often incorporated into the web browser. They are actually programs that read the HTML code of the web page and identify any part of the code that would open another window. It removes that part of the code, thereby preventing the pop-up from appearing.

There are blockers written in **Java code** but these will not work with *Flash*-activated pop-ups. However, good pop-up blocking software is able to detect these codes and deactivate them as well. But many of these are targeted by spyware writers and so you should be wary when downloading and implementing them.

Anti-spyware software

Spyware is software put on your computer with malicious intent. It allows people to access your machine and control its functions. Some spyware is just inconvenient. It can cause pop-ups enticing you to visit certain sites you would not normally visit. It can take over your web browser, changing your home page and menus. In its most malicious form it can search your hard disk for personal information like credit card numbers and passwords. Often this will run as a background operation so you won't even notice it is happening.

Anti-spyware software operates in a similar manner to anti-virus software. It scans the disk for any named spyware programs that it has stored in its database. When it finds them it removes them. To be effective, it needs to be continually updated with the names of any new threats.

Key logging is the use of hardware to register what the user is typing in. The keys that are pressed on the keyboard are detected. Most anti-spyware software will detect the presence of a key logger.

Wired equivalent privacy of information

Wired equivalent privacy of information (WEP) was the original standard of wireless network security when WLANs were first developed, but it has since been superseded by WPA. It is still used in routers, but is fairly basic and would only deter users stumbling across a network by accident. It can be easily cracked by a determined hacker. The greatest drawback is the short length of the encryption key, which limits the number of possible codes.

Wi-Fi protected access

WPA built on the WEP standard, but had greater complexity in its encryption, with longer keys. It also incorporated user authentication, which wasn't present in WEP. It can be installed on all devices enabled with WEP.

7.4   Electronic conferencing
Hardware

Electronic conferencing requires additional hardware to that found in a standard desktop system: phone handsets (landline or mobile), for telephone conferencing; webcams, microphones and speakers for videoconferencing.

Webcams, microphones and speakers have all been described in Chapter 1.

Software

There are three types of software that can be used to hold a conference, each with their own applications.

Conference software

Conferencing software compresses the audio and video elements produced by the microphones and webcams into packets of data for transmission through the computer network. The compression is carried out using a codec, which is a circuit capable of converting the audio and/or video input to the computer into a digital stream of bits and then compressing them. A large number of bits are discarded in the process as the compression ratio can be many hundreds to one. The skill in the programming of the software is to reduce the amount of data so that it is transmitted quickly enough to be real time, but to maintain the quality of the video and audio at the same time. Echo cancellation software, which allows talking in real time and keeps communications synchronised, is also required. The only software required for phone conferencing is that required on the telephony server, although voice over IP (VOIP) software (described below) can be used to conduct phone conferences through PCs.

VOIP software

VOIP is a way of having phone conversations using the Internet as the vehicle of communication. The advantage of this system is that to most users international or long-distance calls are at the very least the same price as a local call or at best are free. The drawback is that you can only make these phone calls for this level of cost if the recipient uses the same ISP as you do. The other disadvantage if you rely on VOIP for all your phone services is that many ISPs do not make emergency services available.

Again, the software converts the speech into digital data and then compresses the audio stream of bits into small packets of data to enable faster transmission of the data.

Skype is a type of VOIP software that uses its own VOIP network but has a fixed scale of charges. It runs on a peer-to-peer model rather than the usual VOIP client–server model. This means it stores phone numbers on each user computer rather than on a central server.

Instant messaging

Instant messaging is the exchange of text messages across the Internet in real time between two or more people logged into a particular instant messaging service. It is an interactive service, as people can reply immediately to others logged into the same system. It requires a user name (often an e-mail address) and a password. When someone logs on for the first time they have to make a list of people they want to contact – these individuals need to agree to be contacts, as you can only send messages to people who give you permission to do so. Then they select the individual they want to talk to and send a message. If the contact happens to be online at the same time they can reply, leading to a conversation. When a buddy (somebody you allow to communicate with you) logs on, you are automatically notified. Similarly, when they log off you are told. Some more advanced systems allow voice calling and video phone calls but these are not common.

There is instant messaging software available to businesses for use on their LAN. These run over TCP/IP and do not need to be installed on a server but can operate over a network without needing to address the server. They often provide facilities for recording conversations.

Types of electronic conferencing

Videoconferencing

How a videoconference operates has already been discussed in Chapter **2**. We have also seen, above, how videoconferencing software works. Here we will look at some of the advantages and disadvantages of video conferencing.

Advantages when compared with conventional conferences:

- Meetings can be called at short notice.
- No time is spent on travelling.
- No money is spent on travelling.
- No money is spent on booking conference facilities.
- It is more economical to have short meetings.
- It is more environmentally friendly as less car/plane movement is needed.
- It is safer, as large multi-national companies no longer have to send their representatives by air to meetings.
- It saves companies money in wages, as while their workers are travelling they still have to be paid.

Disadvantages:

- Confidential or legal documents may need to be seen in their original form.
- Signatures to these documents may be needed.
- There is no direct eye contact, which plays a large part in group conversation – videoconferencing

sometimes gives the impression that the person speaking is avoiding eye contact.

- Delegates may be put off by the camera, as many people are self-conscious when being videoed, especially if the conference is being recorded.
- The quality of the video/audio can be low, depending on the bandwidth.
- Interruption to, or breakdowns of, the transmission can occur.
- Power cuts may prevent the conference from continuing or taking place in the first instance.

Overall, the quality of communication is lower than either a face-to-face or phone conference (discussed in the next subsection).

Phone conferencing

We looked at how phone conferencing operates in Chapter **2**. A phone conference is very similar to a videoconference, but without the video. It has some of the advantages of videoconferencing, but has disadvantages too.

Advantages:

- There is less cost than a videoconference as there is no need for webcams or large screens.
- There is less cost than a videoconference as there is no need for wide bandwidth, which can be expensive to obtain.
- The quality of sound reproduction is much better than in a videoconference.
- There is no worry about how you look.
- It has all the advantages of a videoconference when compared with face-to-face conferences other than being able to call conferences at short notice, since the time and date have to be arranged in advance with the service provider.

Disadvantages:

- You cannot see facial expressions.
- Documents cannot be seen.
- Conferences may be interrupted by power cuts.
- The number of participants is limited.

Instant messaging

As we have already seen in Chapter **2**, instant messaging can be used by two or more people logged onto the instant messaging service at the same time.

Advantages:

- The service is instantaneous – unlike e-mail.
- This can save time and money for businesses, as problems can be resolved immediately.
- The service is easy to use. After logging on, the user just clicks the name of the person they want to chat to and starts the conversation.

Disadvantages:

- A young person could easily have their e-mail address added on to the instant messaging contact list of a stranger who could turn out to be a not very nice person.
- Some children would rather sit at home on the computer then go out, so instant messaging could be a contributing factor to childhood obesity.
- It is distracting and addictive to students and workers, getting in the way of more important activities and tasks.
- Sending files through instant messaging file transfer poses security risks on many systems.

Uses of electronic conferencing

Businesses

Videoconferencing, in particular, has not had much of a takeup. Despite a sudden upsurge in the USA after 9/11, it is still not proving a popular method of convening meetings. Nevertheless, those companies that do use them have experienced benefits in time saving, as employees are not having to have whole days out of the office just flying to a conference. However, some resistance has been met from employees whose work requires them to sit at a computer all day and they like to wear casual clothes for work. They feel that for a videoconference they have to wear suits and dress smartly. Another problem that faces company executives is that when they are close to making a deal with another company they tend to feel more secure if the deal is carried out face to face.

Teleconferencing is a useful tool for companies or employees to call impromptu meetings. They are easier to arrange than a videoconference and you don't have to move to a special room. You can make the call from your desk. However, while it is beneficial for small groups of employees who are spread apart geographically it is very difficult to engage larger groups of workers fully into conversations. Audio-only conferences are also less

appealing to a number of workers as communication can only be carried out verbally. Workers either need visual aids or feel they can write down their thoughts more clearly than replying to questions immediately they are asked.

Instant messaging is used throughout businesses for mini-conferences and liaising with colleagues.

Schools

Videoconferencing between schools across international borders has particular benefits. It brings students together from different cultures and helps them understand these cultures in a way that they could not achieve unless they were to physically visit the country. They can share information and ideas with each other. The linking of schools through videoconferencing can also facilitate the exchange of teachers, particularly if the schools have strengths in different subjects.

It also enables students to experience different environments in terms of geographical area. Similarly, it gives children from a rural background the opportunity to experience life in the city and vice versa.

The use of teleconferencing in schools has had a major impact on educating children who are unable to come to school for health or other reasons, as they can receive tuition by means of a telephone conference.

Unfortunately, due to misuse of the service most schools do not allow the use of instant messaging in class. Students tend to get distracted by it and do not use it for the purpose it could be used for in lessons.

Research meetings

Many higher education institutions are using videoconferencing for research meetings. They are finding it particularly useful for courses where class sizes are very small and opportunities for discussion are limited. By creating a conference with larger institutions at some distance from their own site they can encourage students to partake in high-level conversations about their research projects and common research interests.

Telephone conferencing is used at some higher education institutions for researchers to stay in touch with their supervisors. Such a scenario exists at Oxford and Cambridge Universities where a special course in biomedicine operates on a shared basis between the two universities. It is a requirement of the course that students report on their research periodically with their two mentors.

Examination questions

1 Local government offices are to have their LANs linked to form a WAN. Explain what is meant by these terms and discuss the hardware and software that would be required. [6]
   You will need to make six points.

2 Because the data they deal with is mainly personal and confidential, they will need to consider employing security methods to prevent unauthorised users from accessing the data.

(a) Discuss the physical methods that they could use. [5]
   You will need to make five points.

(b) Discuss the software methods that they could use. [6]
   You will need to make six points.

8 Software selection

You already know how to:

- ➤ open and use a variety of software packages.

In this chapter you will learn how to:

- ➤ select the most appropriate software for a task.

For this chapter you will need:

- ➤ no additional materials.

8.1 Software uses

Different software packages are used to perform different tasks on a computer. Sometimes it is easy to decide which program (applications software) is the most appropriate for a given task. At other times some tasks could be completed using two different pieces of software. Both will do the job and making the right choice can be difficult. In order to make the right choices you need to understand the strengths and limitations of each type of software. To help you, here is a list of the most common software types:

- text editor
- word processor
- desktop publisher
- database package
- spreadsheet package
- charting package
- presentation authoring package
- web browser
- e-mail editor
- graphics package
- programming languages.

You will already be familiar with some of these types of software, but the following section will help you to decide between one type of software and another for any given task.

Text editor

A text editor allows you to type and edit plain text. It has few or no features that allow you to format a document. Text editors can be used to write some programming code (like HTML) and to edit system files within the computer and are often supplied with the computer's operating system. Examples of text editors are *Notepad* and *WordPad* within *Microsoft Windows*.

Word processor

A word processor allows you to create, edit and format documents. This can include defining page layout and document formatting. Many current word processors have additional features including file management and the ability to integrate data from a data file into a document using a process called mail merge. Further details of mail merge can be found in Chapter **15**. One example of a word processor is *Microsoft Word*, which has many additional features that are not found in all word-processing software. Further details of this can be found in Chapter **10**.

Desktop publisher

A desktop publisher has most of the features of a word-processing system, although it may not always include mail merge. A desktop publisher has the ability to manipulate images and text (as have many current word processors), but often offers more features and flexibility when dealing with images. It usually has greater control over the layout of a document and prepares a document for the production (commercial printing) process, using features like full-colour processing, spot colour, frames and colour separations. One example of a desktop publisher is *Microsoft Publisher*. Further details of this can be found in Chapter **10**.

Database package

A database is a collection of data items and the links between them. The database gives structure to (organises) the data items and gives you the tools that you can use to search (interrogate) the data. This is managed by a database management system (often called a DBMS). The majority of databases are very large and contain millions of data items (you may have studied some of these in earlier chapters). Databases can be flat file (using a simple two-dimensional table) or relational, which is more complex, where data items are linked together within the database (see Chapter **11** for more details). Data in a database can be searched (interrogated) and the results presented as information for the user. Databases can often be accessed and edited by more than one person at a time. One example of a database package is *Microsoft Access*. Further details of this can be found in Chapter **11**.

Spreadsheet package

A spreadsheet is a grid of information often used to display financial or statistical information. Data is arranged in rows and columns. Spreadsheets are very good at performing calculations and modelling situations. This involves changing data and examining the effect that this has on other data. One of the most common types of modelling is financial modelling, where you can try out options using 'what-if scenarios'. Spreadsheets can only be accessed and edited by one person at one time. One example of a spreadsheet package is *Microsoft Excel*, which has many of the features of a flat file database. Further details of this can be found in Chapter **14**.

Charting package

A charting package allows you to create a variety of different graphs and charts. These are sometimes separate packages or can be included in spreadsheets or databases. Within this book we will use the charting facilities offered within *Microsoft Excel*. Further details of this can be found in Chapter **11**.

Presentation authoring package

A presentation authoring package allows you to create multimedia presentations and displays. Text, images, animations, sound and video clips can be included. This software is often used to support a speech or presentation of information to an audience. One example of a presentation authoring package is *Microsoft PowerPoint*. Further details of this can be found in Chapter **10**.

Web browser

A web browser allows you to display web pages from an intranet (within an organisation or a local area network) or the Internet (on the worldwide web). Text, images, animations, sound and video clips can be included on these web pages. One example of a web browser is *Microsoft Internet Explorer*. Further details of this can be found in Chapter **9**.

E-mail editor

An e-mail editor allows you to prepare, create, edit and send messages and to read e-mail messages from other users. It enables you to access your mailbox using your e-mail address. E-mail messages can be sent to many people at the same time and can be used to send files attached to the e-mail from one location to another almost instantly. Some e-mail editors operate within a web browser (e.g. *Hotmail*) and can be accessed from almost anywhere. Others are dedicated programs (e.g. *Microsoft Outlook*) and can only be accessed from a computer on which it is installed and configured. Further details can be found in Chapter **9**.

Graphics package

A graphics package allows you to create and manipulate images. There are two types of graphics package. A vector graphics package draws points, lines, curves and polygons using mathematical equations. This means that when an image is enlarged there is little loss of quality. The second type of graphics package uses bitmap graphics, which stores the details of each pixel (or dot) of a drawing, so if an image is enlarged or reduced the image can appear pixelated (it looks like a series of blocks, often with jagged edges).

Programming languages

A programming language is used to write code that will perform a task within the computer. A computer program follows a sequence of instructions to perform a pre-defined function. Specific details of programming languages are outside the scope of this book, although they could be used to fulfil several of the tasks in the practical section at A2 level. Small elements of some programming languages can be used within many of the applications packages listed above (e.g. macros within a word processor, spreadsheet or database package) or as underlying code (e.g. *Visual Basic for Applications* within *Microsoft Word*, *Excel* or *Access*).

Activity 8.1

Identify software names

For each of the following software types, name the applications package that you will use:

- text editor
- word processor
- desktop publisher
- database package
- spreadsheet package
- charting package
- presentation authoring package
- web browser
- e-mail editor
- graphics package
- programming languages.

Research and write a paragraph about the features of each of these packages. If you wish to produce this electronically, you can use the file ACTIVITY 8.1 TEMPLATE.DOC from the CD to help you.

Activity 8.2

Describe the most appropriate software package for a task

For each of the following tasks, select the most appropriate application package(s) for the task and justify your choice.

Task 1

Produce a full-colour booklet for a local company using web offset-printing machines.

Task 2

Present sales figures to the company directors, showing the changes in sales of a number of products and the profit margins over the last five years.

Task 3

A local shop sells televisions. It needs to store the information and search for different makes, models and prices. Using the information stored about the televisions sold and its customers, the company wants to automatically write letters to some of these customers.

Task 4

A local shop sells fridges and freezers. The owner needs to store the information about each fridge in stock and those they have recently sold. She also needs to store records of the customers who have bought the fridges.

Task 5

A new company designs commercial artwork. It needs to be able to create and edit the artwork on a computer, and send copies of it electronically to clients.

T **Teacher's note**

This activity is suitable for small group discussion rather than as an individual exercise. This would enable the students to give detailed justification of their choices.

T **Teacher's note**

Extend this activity by including tasks that are relevant to the students, for example tasks within the school or college, or other areas where the students have background knowledge.

The following chapters demonstrate the skills required for the practical examinations using a PC platform, with *Microsoft Windows XP* and *Microsoft* *Office 2003*. Different versions of these packages may have minor variations, but they operate in similar ways and generally have the same functionality.

9 Communication

You already know how to:

➤ send an e-mail
➤ receive an e-mail
➤ locate and download information from the Internet.

In this chapter you will learn how to:

➤ send an e-mail attachment
➤ receive and save an e-mail attachment
➤ reply to an e-mail
➤ forward an e-mail
➤ copy an e-mail to another mail recipient
➤ use the Internet to locate information on a specified website
➤ use the Internet to search for information using a search engine
➤ evaluate Internet sources
➤ evaluate whether information is relevant and fit for purpose.

For this chapter you will need:

➤ no additional materials.

9.1 Using e-mail

Before you can use e-mail you must have an e-mail address and mailbox. There are different ways of obtaining these: your school or college may have an internally hosted mailbox which you can use, you may be given mailbox facilities when you subscribe to other Internet services, or you can subscribe to web-based mailboxes through the Internet. In this chapter you will use an Internet subscription mailbox. To demonstrate these skills a new e-mail account has been set up with *MSN Hotmail*; although this will be used for the exercises in this chapter, the vast majority of the skills are transferable to other e-mail editors and the underlying structures are the same. All mailboxes have a storage limit. It can be very easy to fill your mailbox – if this happens,

you will not be able to receive e-mail messages sent to you.

 Hint It is sensible to organise saved e-mails in folders and regularly delete e-mail messages that are no longer required.

E-mail etiquette

When using e-mail, try to use the following basic rules. Following these should help you to gain respect within the online community:

♦ Do not type using all capital letters. This is more difficult to read than lower case, and is also regarded by many as shouting in an e-mail.
♦ Do not leave the subject line blank.

- Do not use coloured text and backgrounds. These are more difficult to read and can take up valuable space in an e-mail inbox. Also, not all e-mail editors can interpret the codes.
- When sending a number of people the same e-mail use 'bcc' rather than 'cc' (see the next section) as it protects their e-mail addresses from being passed on and reduces the risks of them receiving junk mail.
- Do not forward chain letters and similar types of e-mail as these can take up valuable space in an e-mail inbox.
- Do not give out phone numbers, personal details, bank account details, etc. in e-mails.
- E-mail communication is private. In most countries you are likely to be breaking the law if you post the content of an e-mail to you in a public place without the sender's permission.
- Compress or **zip** e-mail attachments where possible before sending them.

Send an e-mail

Task 9.1

Send an e-mail message to Brian Sargent letting him know that Chapter 8 of the book is almost complete. Copy this message to a user called ictcorex@cie.org.uk and send a blind carbon copy to design.h@cie.org.uk.

Make the subject line for the e-mail '9713 A level text book'.

1 Open your web browser and access your e-mail account, using your e-mail address and password.

2 Click on the Mail 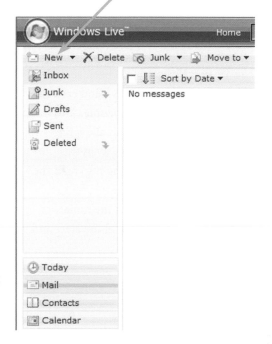 button, followed by New.

This opens the New Message area.

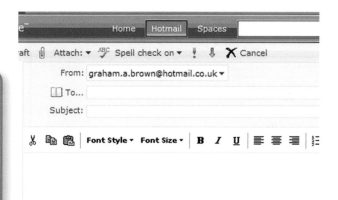

3 Enter the recipient's e-mail address in the To: box. Make sure that you type the address correctly, including any punctuation marks. One small error in this data entry means that the message does not get sent to the correct person. This person is not aware that you have ever sent them a message. If you have contacts that you e-mail regularly, add them to your contacts list (sometimes called an address book) and select them from the contact list. This reduces the chance of errors when typing e-mail addresses.

4 If you wish to send a copy of the message (with any attached files) to another person add their name to the Cc: (carbon copy) box. This is not initially visible in *Windows Live Hotmail*, and needs to be selected by

pressing the left mouse button on the hyperlink for

Show Cc & Bcc ·

5 Names added to the Bcc: (blind carbon copy) box are sent a copy of the message (with any attached files), but the recipient and people in the carbon copy box are not aware that this copy has been sent. This prevents the e-mail address that was blind carbon copied from being passed to other people.

6 Add a Subject: line to the message to allow the person receiving the e-mail to know what the message is about. This will enable them to read the most urgent e-mail messages first.

7 Enter the content of the message in the main message box. Always use a greeting at the start and a salutation at the end.

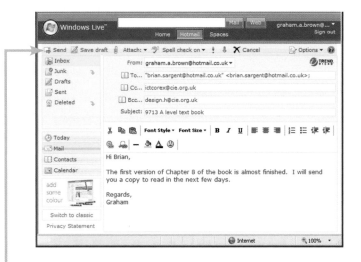

8 When you have checked your e-mail to make sure that it is error free, click on Send. The e-mail will then be sent to the recipient's mailbox.

Activity 9.1

Send an e-mail

Send an e-mail to your teacher with the subject line 'e-mail'. Copy this to two other people in your class, informing them that you can now communicate with them via e-mail. Your teacher will send you a reply.

T Teacher's note

Supply all students with your work e-mail address.
When they e-mail you, reply individually, asking them to send you a document on e-mail etiquette.

Receive an e-mail

1 Click on Inbox. Any e-mails received will appear in this window. In this example a new e-mail message, displayed in bold, has been received.

2 To open this message, click the left mouse button on the sender's name.

3 The message will look similar to this.

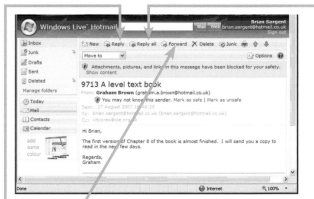

4 Use the Forward option if the message has been sent to the wrong person, or you wish someone else to reply to the message. This sends the entire message to a third person. You can still add a comment to the main message box using this feature if you wish to do so.

5 To reply to this message, use the Reply button. If you want to reply to the sender and anyone copied into the original message using the Cc: feature, use **Reply all**.

Note that this feature does not add the person who was added to the original message using the **Bcc:** box. You can write your response and keep the original message with it.

Send an e-mail attachment

Task 9.2

Send an e-mail message to Brian Sargent with Chapter 8 of the book attached to the message. Make the subject line '9713 A level text book'.

1 After opening the e-mail, reply to the earlier message. You need to use **Reply** to send this message back. Prepare your e-mail for sending as you did for Task **9.1**.
2 Enter the e-mail address, subject line and body of the message. The completed message should look similar to this.

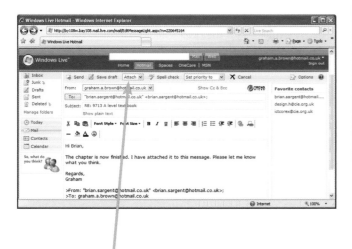

3 Click on **Attach** to start the process of attaching the document to the message.
4 A small drop-down menu appears. For this task you need to select the **File** option.
5 If you do not know the path (storage location) of the file, click on **Browse...**. This will allow you to select the file using the **Choose file** window. Select the file that you want to attach, followed by **Open**. This process can be repeated to attach multiple files to a message. Depending upon the file size and the speed of your Internet connection

this may take a long time. When the final file has been selected click on the **Attach** button. This attaches the message to the file.

6 When the file has been attached to the message it should be visible. In this case, it can be seen here.

7 When you have checked the message and it is ready to be sent, click on the **Send** button.

Activity 9.2

Receive and reply to an e-mail with an attachment

Read the e-mail reply from your teacher. Reply to this e-mail, sending them the document that they have requested. The document must be complete and ready to send before you start to attach it.

Receive and save an e-mail attachment

1 Click on **Mail**. All e-mails received will appear in this window. In this example a new e-mail message has been received. The paper clip shows that the message has an attachment.

2 Open this message by clicking the left mouse button on the sender's name. The message will look similar to this.

3 Make sure that the message is from a user that you know and trust. If so, click the left mouse button on the **Mark as safe** hyperlink.

4 To open the attachment, click the left mouse button on the attachment name, within the attachment section of the message.

5 The **File Download** window will appear. It will look similar to this.

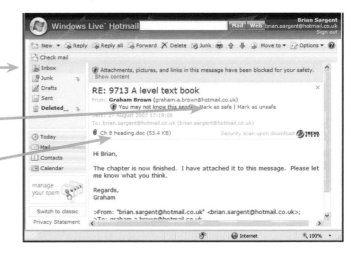

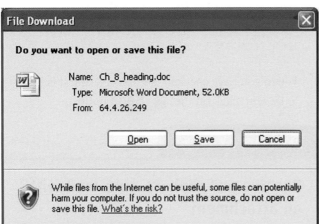

> **Hint**
> - E-mail attachments can be used to transmit viruses.
> - Do not open an attachment unless you are expecting it and know and trust the sender.
> - If you send an attachment to someone, let them know that you are sending it before you do so. If you receive an attachment from someone that you don't know, delete it.
> - Scan all file attachments for viruses or choose an e-mail editor that scans all attachments for you automatically.

6 Click on **Save** to save the file.

7 Specify the filename and the storage location for the file. When the file has been saved, you will be asked whether you wish to **Open** the file, **Open Folder** (if you have downloaded a folder containing files) or to **Close** the window. The window will look similar to this.

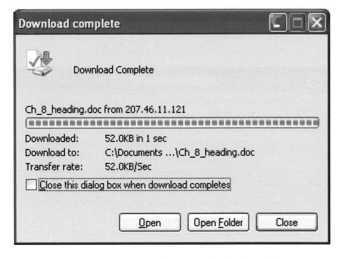

9.2 Compress files

In order to reduce transmission time (and storage space) for file attachments, it is often useful to compress data files before sending them. This can be done for a single file, or a number of files can be 'zipped' into a folder.

Compress a file or files for transmission

Compression of files can be done within the *Microsoft Windows* environment if you are using a later version of this product. In older versions of *Windows* you will need to use an additional program (e.g. *WinZip*) to perform this function. In later versions of *Windows* this can be done by opening **My Computer** and selecting the file or files to be compressed. Using the <Shift> key allows you to select consecutive files. Using the <Ctrl> key whilst selecting files allows you to make multiple selections from within the folder. This includes selecting files that are not listed in consecutive order.

1 Select the file or files to be compressed. Press the right mouse button and select **Send To** from the available options.

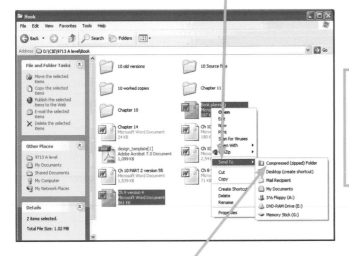

2 Select **Compressed (zipped) Folder** from the drop-down menu.

3 The two files will be compressed and added to a new folder, which may look similar to this, or this:

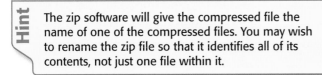

Book planning
Compressed (zipped) Folder
56 KB

Book planning
1,644 KB

4 This single zipped file is smaller in size than the two original files and can be sent as a single file attachment to an e-mail recipient.

> **Hint**
> The zip software will give the compressed file the name of one of the compressed files. You may wish to rename the zip file so that it identifies all of its contents, not just one file within it.

Decompress all files after transmission

Earlier in this chapter you learned how to send an e-mail attachment to another e-mail user. If a user sends you an e-mail attachment which contains a zipped folder, you can open or save the folder in the same way as you did earlier in the chapter. If you open the folder it appears in a similar way to other folders, the only difference being that the folder displays the symbol to show that it is zipped.

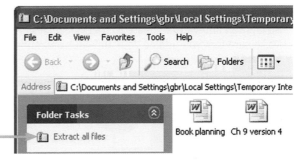

1 To extract all compressed files from a zipped folder, go to the **Folder Tasks** area and click on the **Extract all files** icon. This opens the **Extraction Wizard**.

> **Hint**
> In some versions of *Windows* it may be necessary to right mouse click on the filename and select the menu option for Extract All….

2 Select the directory to extract the files into – the wizard will suggest one, but this may not be the one that you require. Use the browse option to help if you are not sure of the pathway. When you have selected the correct directory or folder, click on `Next >`.

3 Use the tick box if you wish to see the extracted files and click on `Finish`.

9.3 Virus detection within e-mail attachments

> **Hint**
> Compressed (zipped) e-mail attachments can be used to hide virus files, as these are more difficult for anti-virus software to detect than a single file containing a virus. You will therefore need to be more careful checking for a virus with this type of file.

Viruses can hide within a number of file types. As a simple rule, a virus is a computer program, so if a file sent to you can contain a program, it may hold a virus. Examples are programs with file extensions such as .exe, .bat and .com. Other file types known to contain viruses include .pif and .scr. Some applications packages can also be used to carry or hide viruses, for example programs such as *Microsoft Word*, *Excel* and *Access* which allow macros that can be written and saved. Other programs which can easily carry a virus are those which contain an underlying programming language, like *Access* and *Excel* (which both use *Visual Basic for Applications*). Folders (and sub-folders) can also be used to try to hide virus files from anti-virus checking software, so make sure that you virus scan all files within a compressed folder. Sometimes your file compression software will do this for you.

If you were to search for a single word like 'snowboarding', you would get almost 23 million results.

Results **1 - 10** of about **22,900,000** for **snowboarding**

So, before starting to search the Internet, think very carefully about the topic to be searched for and the sort of information that you want. Identify the information on this topic that you do want and the information that you do not require.

Activity 9.3

T Teacher's note

Assign each student two others to whom they can send the compressed file.

Send a compressed file as an e-mail attachment

Use the same document that you sent in Activity **9.2**. Send it in a compressed format to your teacher and two other students in your class. Your teacher will tell you who these should be.

Open the compressed files sent to you by the two people in your class. These should each contain a document on e-mail etiquette. Save these documents in your user area (using different filenames) in both compressed and uncompressed formats.

T Teacher's note

Each student has two other copies of the document on e-mail etiquette as well as their own. These could be used for peer marking, evaluation and discussion.

You want information about:	You do not want information about:
Learn to snowboard ✓	Snowboarding games ✗
Getting started ✓	Snowboarding holidays ✗
Beginner ✓	Snowboarding discussion groups ✗
	Snowboarding equipment sales ✗

This list gives you the starting point for your search. For the first search, you can use the Google search engine. First formulate the search string and then use this to perform the search.

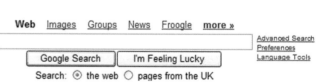

You always start with the most important elements of the search. Because learn to snowboard is not a single word you must place this in speech marks. This means that the complete string is searched for, rather than each of the three words individually. The start of my search string will be "learn to snowboard". The next phrases needed are getting started and beginner so you need to place "getting started" in speech marks and, as either one of these options would be acceptable, use OR between them. You add this to the first string like this: "learn to snowboard" "getting started" OR beginner. To remove the things that you do not want in the search from the results you use the - sign. In this case you do not want games, holidays, discussion groups or equipment sales. When the whole string is complete it will look like this:

"learn to snowboard" "getting started" OR beginner -games -holiday -"discussion group" -sales

9.4 Using the Internet

You will already be familiar with using the Internet, simple searching, downloading and saving information from the Internet. When you search, the search engine will often give you several hundreds, thousands, or even millions of responses that match your search. The results from your search can often give you many that you do not want. Using advanced search techniques can help you to avoid many of these unwanted responses.

Advanced Internet search techniques

Task 9.3

Search the Internet for information on 'learn to snowboard'. This information must be suitable for a complete beginner with little knowledge of the sport.

When this string is entered into the search engine it gives results like this.

As you can see this has reduced the number of results from almost 23 million to 736. Not all of these will be suitable. The next stage of the process is to identify from the results of the search which sites might be suitable for you to open and investigate. It is clear from this screenshot that even though you tried to remove holidays from the search, some websites have still been shown. In this instance you can dismiss these manually (many of the sponsored links will be included in this category). Looking at the results you may decide that the first website may be the most suitable. Using the hyperlinks will allow you to investigate these sites. Further tips on evaluating Internet sources are given in Section **9.5**.

>
> Spelling errors in search strings are the most common reason for problems with Internet searches. To help solve these problems, enter the search string into your word processor, check the spelling, then cut and paste the search string into your web browser.

Activity 9.4

Advanced Internet-search techniques

Search the Internet for information on 'learn to scuba dive'. This information must be suitable for a complete beginner with little knowledge of the sport.

Boolean operators for Internet searching

There are three Boolean operators. They are AND, OR and NOT. These are sometimes used in Internet searching. In recent years the AND operator has not been used as fully; searching for **snowboard and lessons** has been replaced by just **snowboard lessons** in current web browsers (i.e. the web browser assumes that the AND operator is required between words). Many current web browsers cut out small and commonly used words in their search. If you are looking for a specific small word within a phrase, use either the speech marks around the whole phrase or use the plus sign (+) before the word. For example, if you have been given part of a website address for a good site like 'Snowboarding [something] air', you can search with **snowboarding +air**. The use of the OR operator as demonstrated in the previous section with; **"getting started" OR beginner** would find either of these search strings. The NOT operator is, as seen earlier, the use of the minus sign, so **-games** should rule out sites with a reference to games within them.

Locating information from a given URL

Searching within a restricted environment (e.g. within a single website) can be useful for educational purposes. It allows you to obtain a set of pre-determined results without fear of obtaining the type of inaccurate or inappropriate material that can be obtained through normal searches on the Internet. Examination boards and other educational institutions use these to give particular responses to searches. They can be used in practical examinations to test your ability to search and to give you material in a secure environment that may be relevant to your course and to your examinations. If you are required to search on one of these websites, there are two methods that may help you. The first is using the internal search engine, which works in the same way as an Internet search engine. These usually accept Boolean operators and simple search strings and generally give you a restricted number of documents or sources. This is very useful if you have to identify the most appropriate source and use that for a particular task. The second method of searching is using a site index. There is usually a reference to this from the home page (although it is often in small text and not always obvious). This should take you to an index page listing the contents of the website. This method may take longer to search but is always worth investigating if your initial searches do not find the document, file or page that you are searching for.

9.5　Evaluating Internet sources

You have already learned the skills needed to download a variety of file types from the Internet and store these locally. In the previous sections you have studied how to import (and in some cases manipulate) these files. You have already taken into account issues of copyright and the legality of these actions. Now you will look at information given on a website and make decisions on how valuable this information is.

Evaluate the available information

Before looking for information on the Internet, decide on the purpose of the information that you are gathering. Work out the answers to these questions before you start:

- What information do I want? For example: Do you want facts about an activity or information on how to do the activity?
- Who is this information going to be presented to? For example: Do you wish to present the information to children aged between five and seven or to the parents of these children?
- When will the information be presented? For example: Is the presentation next week or at the end of next month (when some of the information could be out of date)?
- What will be the method of delivery? For example: Do you intend to give a *PowerPoint* presentation, create a website or provide a written report?

Select only the information that matches your answers to the questions above. When you have selected a range of information that looks as though it may be suitable, check whether the information presented is fact or opinion, biased or valid.

Fact or opinion

Sometimes it is very difficult to distinguish between the two. Facts are often written as a simple statement, for example 'Fiji lies in the Pacific Ocean'. Opinions are often supported by evidence. When a fact is debatable, words and phrases like 'possibly', 'maybe', 'it is probable', etc. may be used. Opinions are sometimes easily recognised because words like 'believe', 'opinion', 'think', 'could', 'might' and 'would' are used. However, sometimes opinions are presented as if they are facts.

Sometimes, the information given by experts as a 'fact' is really an opinion, where these 'facts' are based upon the knowledge available at the time. Sometimes it is only discoveries and advances made in science or technology that proves that these opinions are not facts. For example, in 1959 IBM stated, 'The world potential market for copying machines is 5000 at most.' At the time this statement was thought to be a fact, we now know that this was an opinion that was presented as a fact.

Bias

Bias is a lack of objectivity or fairness in the treatment of topics. For example, a loyal football fan may offer an opinion of their team which they believe is fact, yet when looked at objectively (with no favour to one side or another) contains a biased view. On websites the bias can sometimes be identified when information keeps directing you to purchase a product or products.

Validity of information

For information to be valid, it must be both accurate and reliable.

- For reliability you must check the source of the data. Check the publisher of the data. Is it from a trusted source? Try to find out how the information was collected. Check if other reliable sites have links to it. Check if the site contains lots of advertising (sites supported wholly by advertising are less likely to be reliable than those funded in other ways). Look at the URL for the website to check what sort of organisation hosts the site. Sites with a URL containing .ed, .ac or even .gov are more likely to be more reliable than a commercial organisation.

> **Hint**
>
> .ac is an academic website
> .co is usually a commercial website
> .com is usually a commercial website
> .ed is an educational website
> .gov is a government website
> .org is a charity or organisation
> .sch is a school website

- Another measure of reliability is how up to date the website is. The most recent update of a site can usually be found in the site information or from clues in the text, such as news items which contain dates. Another clue can be the number of hyperlinks that no longer work – websites with current information usually check to make sure that the links to other sites work.

- ◆ Sometimes the validity of the information can be discovered by the types of phraseology used within the site. Does the information appear to be factual, or has the author used rhetoric or irony in their language? Check the references to printed materials or other documents which may be online. These references often verify the author's assertions and use of supporting evidence.
- ◆ Another indicator of a site's validity is the use of endorsements from reputable organisations. Some websites are created with URLs that are very similar to genuine sites, so pretending to be the genuine site but giving biased, false or inaccurate information.

Look at the content of the website, not the features used to produce it. It is often worth copying the text and pasting it into a word processor to avoid the distractions of website features.

Readability of information

The information must be in a format that will be easily read by the proposed target audience. There is no point in extracting information on science for a group of eight-year-old children by looking at a website containing research articles on nuclear particle science.

Activity 9.5

Evaluate information downloaded from the Internet

Search the Internet for information on 'healthy eating'. The information will be used to teach a class of children aged ten or eleven. Produce a document containing at least four different pieces of the information found. For each item of information, identify:

- the source of the information (including the URL)
- whether it is fact or opinion
- whether it is biased
- how reliable the source is
- how accurate the source is
- how current the material is
- whether it is suitable (including readability) for your audience.

10 Document and presentation production

You already know how to:

- open and close documents and presentations
- download and save information from the Internet
- create and edit documents in a word processor
- create and edit presentations
- enter and edit text
- evaluate information found on the Internet
- evaluate whether information is relevant and fit for purpose
- proofread and spell check your work.

In this chapter you will learn how to:

- enter and edit data from a variety of sources
- understand the importance of accurate data entry
- check and correct data entry using appropriate software tools
- manually proofread and correct data entry
- place and manipulate images and other objects into documents and presentations
- create a link from a document or slide
- control a document to be edited by multiple users
- create and edit a master document/slide
- create styles to be used in documents and presentations
- create and edit headers and footers
- set breaks and amend document sections
- understand the need for corporate house styles and apply them consistently
- create and edit tables within documents and presentations.

For this chapter you will need these source files from the accompanying CD:

- BOARDER.JPG
- CLIENT.CSV
- ENTER.TXT
- EVALUATE.RTF
- IMAGE.RTF
- NURSE.RTF
- SHARKS.RTF
- SILOGO.JPG
- SIMC.RTF
- SLOGAN.JPG

In this chapter you will learn how to create and develop word-processed documents in *Microsoft Word*, desktop-published documents in *Microsoft Publisher* and presentations in *Microsoft PowerPoint*. Many of the features of the three packages used within this chapter: *Word*, *Publisher* and *PowerPoint* are identical; many others have only minor differences between them. The major difference is that the **word processor** does not need a text box in order to add text, while in the **desktop publisher** and presentation authoring software a text box is needed. However, within the word processor text boxes are useful for the placing and arranging of images.

10.1 Entering and editing data from different sources

Generic file types

You are already familiar with adding and editing text, and opening and closing documents within the word processor. At this level you must be able to open documents from generic file types and understand their features and limitations. There are a number of common file types that are generic and can be used in the majority of applications packages on different hardware platforms. Common generic files include the following:

◆ Text: these files have a .txt file extension. A text file is an unformatted ASCII file that can be opened in any word processor. There is not a single format: text files can cover a vast number of different variations, including operating system specific formats (like MS-DOS and *Windows*) and a multitude of regional settings. It is important that you experiment with the regional text settings for your local region when using this format. Some software vendors use text files as data sources for other applications. They contain data fields that are separated by tabs, commas etc. and data records that are separated by carriage returns.

◆ Rich text format: these files have a .rtf file extension. This is a file type that saves formatting within the document, so allowing some formatting to be passed from one applications package to another.

◆ Comma separated values: these files have a .csv file extension. This file type takes tabular data (e.g. from a spreadsheet) and saves it in text format, separating data items with commas.

Import a text file into *Word*

The following method will allow you to import a variety of text and document formats and include them as part of your document. These include .doc (*Word* documents), .rtf and .txt formats. There are many forms of .txt file: they may be typed text similar to this, or could be text files exported from databases and spreadsheets to be used as data sources for mail merging or databases. These formats are imported into a word-processed document like this:

1 Position the cursor where you wish to place the file.

2 Select the Insert menu (an alternative method is to press the <Alt> and <I> keys together), then File…. The Insert File window will appear.

3 Select the file type in the Files of Type: box; if you do not know the file type, select All Files (*.*), which will show all available files in the current folder.

4 Select the required file by clicking on the filename followed by 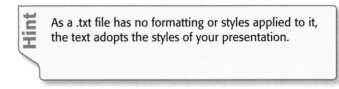.

Import a .csv file into *Word*

To import a .csv file into a word-processed document, follow Steps 1 to 4 above. Note that .csv is not shown as a file type in the initial list box, so ensure that the file type is set to All Files (*.*). When you insert the file, it will not be in tabular format, as it was originally saved. If you wish to do this you should highlight all of the inserted data, then select the Table menu, followed by Convert, then Text to Table…. Use the Convert Text to Table window to change the settings if needed.

Import a .txt file into *PowerPoint*

1 To place a .txt file into an existing *PowerPoint* presentation select the Outline tab.

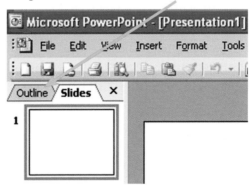

2 If this tab is not visible click on the Normal View (Restore panes) button in the bottom left corner.

3 Select the slide that you wish to place the text in, then the Insert menu, followed by Slides from Outline..., followed by the filename. This will place the text into a number of new slides. Each paragraph with no initial tab becomes a slide title. Tabs at the beginning of a paragraph determine the structure: one tab creates Level 1 body text, two tabs Level 2, and so on.

> **Hint**
> As a .txt file has no formatting or styles applied to it, the text adopts the styles of your presentation.

Import a .rtf file into *PowerPoint*

This uses a similar method to .txt format, with **Insert**, then **Slides from Outline…**, before selecting the filename. With rich text format, the styles saved within the document apply to the presentation. For example, style Heading 1 becomes the slide title; style Heading 2 creates Level 1 body text, and so on.

Import a .txt. .rtf or .doc file into *Publisher*

1   To insert a .txt, .rtf or .doc file into *Publisher*, create a text box using the 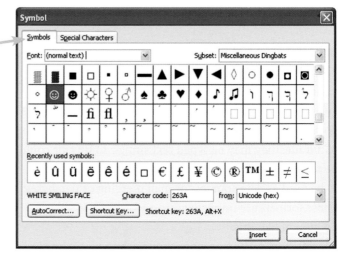 button (on the left side of the window) and place the cursor inside the text box.

2   From the **Insert** menu, select the **Text File…** option, before selecting the correct file type and filename and clicking on **OK**.

Import a .csv file into *Publisher*

To import a .csv file into the desktop publisher, import it as an object (see Section **10.3**).

10.2   Using special characters and editing text

You are already familiar with keying in text, numbers and dates. In this section you will examine other features that can be entered as text, such as special characters (including mathematical symbols and accents), superscripts, subscripts and automated text, as well as looking at efficient ways of editing text that has already been entered.

Use special characters in *Word*

1   To insert a special character, move the cursor to where the character is to be placed and select the **Insert** menu, then **Symbol…**. The **Symbol** window appears. This gives a wide array of commonly used symbols. These will vary from machine to machine, depending upon the software installation and regional settings. It looks similar to this.

2   If the symbol that you are looking for is not visible select a new option from the **Subset:** box. This is where commonly used symbols are grouped together, for example mathematical symbols and arrows. Some fonts contain only symbols. Browse the **Font:** list to identify these (e.g. Wingdings and Zapf Dingbats).

3   You will sometimes need to use special characters with accents that are needed for specific languages (e.g. è é ê ë ü û). You can select these by clicking on the symbol then **Insert**. If the symbol that you want is not readily visible use the scroll bar to view the other characters in the selected font set.

4   Other special characters can be found by selecting the **Special Characters** tab. This is useful for characters like the ellipsis (three dots used to show that there was text before or after the current text) and copyright symbols. This **Special Characters** tab also holds the accented characters found in some languages.

Use special characters in *PowerPoint*

This is identical to using special characters in the word processor (using **Insert**, then **Symbol…**), but the **Symbol** window does not contain the **Special Characters** tab.

Use special characters in *Publisher*

If your cursor is in a text box, then the process is identical to using special characters in the word processor (using **Insert**, then **Symbol…**).

Use superscript and subscript characters in *Word*

Superscript characters are those that sit above the baseline (e.g. m^2), and subscript characters are those that sit below the baseline (e.g. x_1). These are often used in dates as well as mathematical and scientific formulae. In recent versions of *Word*, dates are automatically superscripted for you. If you enter a date like this, 18th December, as you enter the text, the 'th' is automatically reduced in size and superscripted to produce 18th December. If you wanted to enter text like

16 metres^2, you need to manually superscript the '2' like this:

1 Type in the text for the whole line, for example: '… if the volume was 16 metres2, what …' .

2 Highlight only the character(s) to be superscripted, in this case the number '2'.

3 Select the **Format** menu, then **Font…**, and select the **Superscript** tick box before clicking on OK. This will superscript the highlighted section.

> **Hint**
>
> It is easier to superscript or subscript characters after all the text has been entered, rather than as it is typed it. If you set subscript or superscript and then type in the character(s), you have to remember to unset it again before entering the next portion of text.

To type in chemical formulae like H_2O and CO_2 you will need to enter the '2' as a subscript. To do this, you use the same method as for superscripts but instead select the **Subscript** tick box.

> **Hint**
>
> Superscript and subscript are types of formatting. You can save time if you need to create more than one superscript or subscript character using the format painter. This copies the formatting from one part of a document and applies it to another. To use the format painter, select a character that already has the correct format (superscript or subscript) then select the button. Next use the mouse to highlight the character(s) to be formatted and the original format will be applied to the new character(s).

Use superscript and subscript characters in *PowerPoint*

This is identical to inserting superscript and subscript characters in the word processor (by highlighting them, then using **Format**, then **Font…**).

Use superscript and subscript characters in *Publisher*

If your cursor is in a text box, then the process is identical to inserting superscript and subscript characters in the word processor (by highlighting them, then using **Format**, then **Font…**).

Use AutoText in *Word*

AutoText is a collection of pre-defined text of commonly used phrases that can be inserted into a document to save

time repeatedly typing them. Standard AutoText phrases like 'Dear Sir or Madam:' and 'In regards to:' are stored within the document template and are simply entered by selecting the **Insert** menu, then **AutoText**, and then selecting from the sub-menu the phrase that you want to insert. (You can add your own personal choices by setting up or editing an existing document template using **Tools**, then **Templates and Add-Ins…**. You can apply different document templates to your documents, but for the purposes of this course the standard AutoText features are the only ones required.) Within the standard features, there are settings for a document's header and footer, as shown here.

- PAGE -

Author, Page #, Date

Confidential, Page #, Date

Created by

Created on

Filename

Filename and path

Last printed

Last saved by

Page X of Y

> **Hint**
>
> AutoText is also available for the header and footer using the View menu, Header and Footer, then Insert AutoText. Additional options for the header and footer are also available using this method, like inserting the date and time.

Use automated date and time values in *Word*

Automated date and time values can be added to your documents. These can show the date and time whenever a document is created, edited or printed. It is useful for helping to identify which is the latest version of a document. To insert a date or time variable:

1   Place the cursor where you wish to place the date and/or time.
2   Select the Insert menu, then Date and Time....
3   There are options in the Date and Time window to select the format that you require by clicking on it.
4   Setting the Update automatically tick box will ensure that this information is updated every time the document is opened or printed.

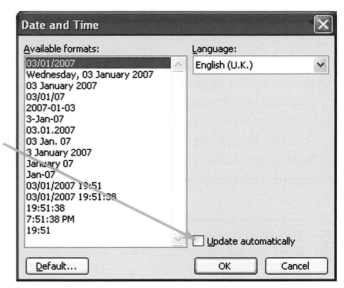

Use automated date and time values in *PowerPoint*

This is similar to inserting the date and time in the word processor. Make sure that you have placed the cursor within a text box, in order for the Insert, then Date and Time... to function correctly. If you require the date and/or time on every slide, make sure that you place this text box on the master slide.

Use automated date and time values in *Publisher*

This is similar to inserting the date and time in the word processor. Make sure that you have placed the cursor within a text box or table, in order for Insert, then Date and Time... to function correctly. If you require the date and/or time on every page, make sure that you place this on the master page.

Tips for editing text in *Word*

You are already familiar with how to highlight areas of the text using the mouse, but within *Word* there are several shortcuts that make editing easier. The table below gives some of the most useful.

Action	How?
Highlight	
Highlight a single word	Double click the left mouse button on the word.
Highlight a sentence	Hold down <Ctrl> and single click with the left mouse button on any word in the sentence.
Highlight a paragraph	Triple click the left mouse button anywhere within the paragraph.
Highlight a larger segment of text	Click the left mouse button once at the start of the area to be highlighted, hold down the <Shift> key and then click the left mouse button at the end of the area to be highlighted.
Delete	
Delete an area of text	Highlight an area of text and press the <Delete> key.
Move	
Move text using **drag and drop**	Highlight an area of text, left mouse click once on the highlighted area, holding down the left mouse button as you do so. Drag the highlighted text, which appears as a rectangle or single vertical bar rather like the text cursor until you reach the required place. Release the left mouse button to drop the text into this place.
Move text using **cut and paste**	Highlight an area of text. Use the Edit menu, then Cut to place the text on the clipboard. Move the cursor to the required place. Use the Edit menu, then Paste to insert the text. A copy of the text remains in the clipboard for immediate re-use, should you wish to paste it again.

Cut	
Cut an area of text	Highlight an area of text. Use the Edit menu, then Cut to remove the original text and place it in the clipboard.
Copy	
Copy an area of text	Highlight an area of text. Use the Edit menu, then Copy to leave the original text in place, as well as placing copy of the text in the clipboard.
Copy text using drag and drop	Hold down <Ctrl> whilst you drag the text to the required place. '**+**' will be displayed next to the cursor while you move it.
Paste	
Paste text from the clipboard	Move the cursor until you reach the required place. Use the Edit menu, then Paste to place a copy of the text (or other object) last placed in the *Windows* clipboard.

Hint

Keyboard shortcuts:

Cut	<Ctrl> X
Copy	<Ctrl> C
Paste	<Ctrl> V

Toolbar shortcuts:

Cut ✂

Copy 📋

Paste 📋

Hint

When performing any editing ensure that the document remains consistent in terms of styles, line spacing, etc.

Activity 10.1

Enter and edit text

(i) Open the file ENTER.TXT from the CD in your word processor. Replace the text '[table goes here]' with a table created from the file CLIENT.CSV.

(ii) All of the chemical formulae mol·kg^{-1} should have the -1 superscripted.

(iii) The chemical formula SO_4 should have the 4 subscripted.

(iv) Move the text 'Tasks to Perform:' so that it becomes the top line of the document.

(v) Replace the text '[place French phrase here]' with 'Activités de proximité'.

(vi) Make sure that this phrase has the correct accents.

(vii) Replace the word 'Copyright' with © (the copyright symbol).

Tips for editing text in *PowerPoint*

All of the tips given for *Word* work equally well with *PowerPoint* (including all of the keyboard shortcuts).

Tips for editing text in *Publisher*

All of the tips (except those for highlighting a sentence) that are given for *Word* work equally well with *Publisher* (including all of the keyboard shortcuts).

10.3 Importing an image or other object from an external source
Import files and link and embed objects

Remember that the majority of files (including images, sound files and other objects) that you may wish to use are copyright protected. As such you must obtain permission from the owner to use them before proceeding. To import a file means to take a file that has been created in a different piece of software, and to accept it (read it) in the current software. To embed an object is to take data about a file – such as the source software, its location and format – and store this within the current application. An example would be to take information from a spreadsheet (in this case the object) and place it within a word-processed document. There are different methods of storing such information in your document:

- ◆ **Embedded files**: these are created by inserting them into a document or presentation. It takes the contents of the file at that moment in time and adds it to the document or presentation. Later changes made to the original file do not appear in the document or presentation. However, the data in the document or presentation can be changed by double clicking on the embedded object to open the original application.
- ◆ **Linked objects**: these are stored separately and loaded only when they are needed. They require less memory as only the file details (e.g. the filename) are stored within the document or presentation. Changes made to the original data are automatically made to the corresponding data in the document or presentation. If the document or presentation is not open when the changes are made, you will be requested to update this data as soon as you re-open the file.
- ◆ **Object linking and embedding**: this is where a file is embedded and linked at the same time. The following section describes how to do this.

Embed a stored file as an object into *Word* or *Publisher*

Stored files can be in almost any format: they may include text, images, tables, spreadsheets, database extracts, graphs, charts, sound files and video clips. Embedding works with all of these file types, except for text and images. If a file is stored on storage media like a hard drive, network drive or external storage media (like a CD, floppy disk, etc.), then it is imported into a word-processed document like this:

1 Position the cursor where you wish to place the file. If you wish to wrap text around the image, you must open a text box first (using **Insert**, then **Text Box** and drawing the text box onto the page before placing the cursor inside the text box).
2 Select the **Insert** menu, then **Object…**. The **Object** window will appear.
3 Select the **Create from File** tab.
4 Either type in the filename and its path or use the Browse… button to help you find the object to embed.

5 Select the required file by clicking on the filename followed by Insert . In this example, the file D:\test.xls has been selected. The **Object** window will now look similar to this.

6 Click on OK if you only require the object to be embedded but not linked, or select the **Link to file** tick box if you wish to have the file object link embedded into the document.

Import an image from a file into *Word*

1 Position the cursor where you wish to place the image.
2 Select the **Insert** menu, **Picture**, then **From File…**. This opens the **Insert Picture** window.
3 Click on the required image, before pressing the Insert button.

> **Hint**
> You can use the button from the Drawing toolbar in place of Step 2.

Import an image into *PowerPoint*

In *PowerPoint*, importing images from file, clip art, scanner or digital camera is all completed using options from the **Insert** menu, then **Picture**, before selecting the method of importing. For each type of import, follow similar processes to those that you used in the word processor.

Import an image from file into *Publisher*

Follow Steps 2 and 3 from 'Import an image into a word processor' (using **Insert**, **Picture** and **From File…**).

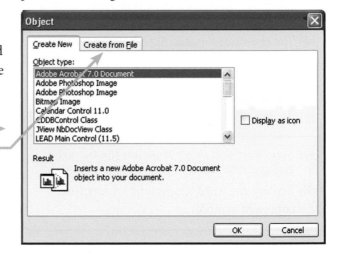

Import an image from clip art into *Word, PowerPoint* or *Publisher*

Clip art is a collection of professionally drawn pictures that can be edited to suit your needs. Many word-processing and desktop-publishing packages are sold with a range of clip art included. To import clip art into a document:

1   Position the cursor where you wish to place the image.
2   Select the Insert menu, Picture, then **Clip Art…**. This opens the **Insert Clip Art** pane within the window.
3   Use the search engine to locate the required image, and click once on the image to place it into the document.

Import an image file from a digital source into *Word, PowerPoint* or *Publisher*

In the context of this syllabus a digital source is a scanner or digital camera.

1   To use either of these peripherals, select the **Insert** menu, then **Picture and From Scanner or Camera…**.
2   Select the device that you wish to use from the drop-down list. The options available will vary depending upon the hardware installed in your computer.

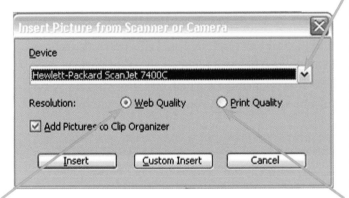

3   To scan or import low-resolution images with a small file size, perhaps to use on a web page, select the **Web Quality** radio button. If the image is to be higher quality, select the **Print Quality** button.
4   Make sure that the image is placed on the scanner before you click on Insert. The image will be placed within your document.

Import an image file from a web page into *Word*

First check with the owner of the image that you have permission to use it. To import a web-based image into a document:

1   Position the cursor where you wish to place the image. If you wish to wrap text around the image, you must open a text box first.
2   Open your web browser, select the image that you wish to use and right mouse click on the image. There are two alternative methods:
   ◇ Select **Copy** and then **Paste** the image into the word-processed document.
   ◇ Use **Save Picture As…**, then save the file in a storage location before using the **Insert** menu, **Picture**, then **From File** from within the word processor.

Import an image file from a web page into *PowerPoint* or *Publisher*

This is similar to inserting an image file from a web page into the word processor. Open your web browser; select the image that you wish to use and right mouse click on the image. You can use **Copy** and then **Paste**, or use **Save Picture As…**, to save the file; then **Insert, Picture, From File** within *PowerPoint* or *Publisher*.

Insert a table into *PowerPoint*

A new table can be created using **Insert**, then **Table** and specifying the number of rows and columns to be used in its construction. To insert an existing table – including those created in a word processor, spreadsheet or a data table (this can include queries) from a database – it is easier to **Copy** the required data from an open application and **Paste** it onto the slide. An alternative is to save an object like a table as a separate file. To embed this file into the presentation select **Insert, Object…** and click in the **Create from file** radio button. Either type in the filename (and path) or use the Browse… button to select the file. If the table is a working document and you wish to update the original data from within the presentation, click on the **Link** tick box.

Import a chart into *PowerPoint*

A new chart can be created using **Insert**, then **Chart** and specifying the data to be used for the chart in the datasheet provided. Several of the chart features available in *Microsoft Excel* can be used. By right mouse clicking on the chart, the chart type and data series can be amended (see Section **11.11** for further details). An *Excel* chart can be created by selecting **Insert**, then **Object** and **Microsoft Excel Chart**. This will allow all of the charting features within *Excel* to be used and embedded within the *PowerPoint* presentation. This requires the creation of a new chart, but has features like the chart wizard available to help you (see Section **11.11**). To insert an existing chart Copy the chart from an open application and Paste it onto the slide. An alternative is to use an existing chart and embed this file into the presentation. To do this select Insert, Object and the Create from file radio button. Select the required file and use the Link tick box if you wish to object link embed the chart.

Import a media file into *PowerPoint*

Both sound clips and video clips can be inserted into a presentation. There are two methods of performing this operation. The first is identical to that used in embedding a stored file as an object into a word-processed document, using Insert, Object and Create from file, before selecting the required file. Alternatively:

1 Position the cursor where you want to place media file.
2 Select the Insert menu, then Movies and Sounds, which gives these options.

> Movie from Clip Organizer...
>
> Movie from File...
>
> Sound from Clip Organizer...
>
> Sound from File...
>
> Play CD Audio Track...
>
> Record Sound

3 If you have used Clip Organizer to group a number of media files together then you can use the 'from Clip Organizer' options on this menu. Selecting either Movie from File… or Sound from File… allows you to select the file that you would like to embed into the presentation.
4 Select the required file, then click on

> OK .

10.4 Manipulating an image

Earlier in the chapter you looked at placing an image file within an applications package. If you are using a word-processing package, make sure that you have placed your image in a text box. This allows you to easily move and place an image with precision. It also allows text to be wrapped around the text box.

Use a text box with an image in *Word*

To create a new text box select Insert, then Text Box and use the cursor to position the approximate size and position of the text box on the page. Insert the image into the text box (as described in the previous sections). With the text box still highlighted, select Format, then Text Box to open the Format Text Box window. Select the line colour in the Colors and Lines tab: selecting a

line the same colour as the background (it may show 'No Line' in the box) will make the text box invisible. Go to the **Layout** tab for *text wrapping*. To make the text wrap around the text box use tight or square (depending upon the shape of the image files). There are other options for text wrap. The text can be wrapped above and below an image but not alongside it or the image can be placed in front of the text, or behind the text.

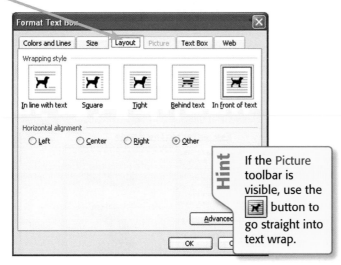

It is vital that you place the image with absolute precision in relation to the page or column margins and other objects upon the page. This process is called *precision framing*. If you are asked to place an object within a column or at the top of a page, there is an expectation that the image will be within one or two millimetres of the margin settings. This is an example of precision framing, with the right text margin and the edge of the image perfectly aligned. To move an image, select the text box (positioned just outside the image) and drag the text box to the required place.

If an image has been placed inside a text box, to resize the image select the image (not the text box) and drag the handles in the corners of the image to stretch or shrink the image. Using the corners will maintain the *aspect ratio* of the image (its proportion), whereas using the handles in the centre of any side will distort the image. If you wish to *crop an image* (cut off part of it), click on the image, then select the **Crop** button from the **Picture** toolbar. (If the **Picture** toolbar is not visible, right click on the image and select **Show Picture Toolbar**.) Place the cursor over one of the handles of the image. When you drag the handle, it will crop that part of the image.

To change the contrast or brightness of the image, right mouse click on the image, select **Format Picture…**, then the **Picture** tab. The colour can also be changed into black

and white or greyscale, which is a useful way of saving storage space when only black-and-white printers are available. Another useful way of saving space is to compress the images. This is particularly useful when creating very long documents containing a number of images (or other large objects). To do this click on Compress… to open the **Compress Pictures** window. If you wish to compress all of the images in a document at once select **All pictures in document**. You can select the resolution that you wish to use (those displayed may vary depending upon the printer that you are using) and click on OK to compress the image or images. If you have already cropped an image, the **Compress Pictures** window also gives you an option to delete the cropped areas of images.

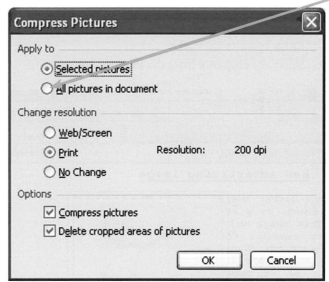

Place and manipulate an image in *Word*

Task 10.1

Place and manipulate an image in *Word*

Open the document IMAGE.RTF from the CD. Place the image BOARDER.JPG into the document so that it is aligned with the top right of the text. Crop the image along the red dotted line. Resize the image so that it fills about a quarter of the page.

1. Open the file in the word processor using the **File** menu, then **Open**.
2. Select the file IMAGE.RTF, then click on [Open ▾].
3. Save the file as a *Word* document.
4. Insert a text box in which to place the image using **Insert**, then **Text Box**.
5. Place the text box by holding the left mouse button and dragging the box until it is the correct size (or even taller than needed).
6. Click the left mouse button inside the text box to place the cursor.
7. Place the image with **Insert**, then **Picture, From File…** and select the file BOARDER.JPG followed by [Insert]. The text box will shrink itself vertically, to fit the aspect ratio of the image.
8. Click the left mouse button on the image so that the image handles are visible.
9. Select the crop tool from the **Picture** toolbar.

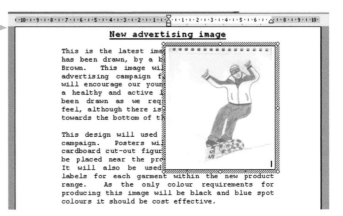

10. Move the cursor to the handles of the picture, hold down the left mouse button and drag the handle(s) to crop the image.

Hint
The crop tool will probably snap to a pre-set grid within the page. To gain fine control over the cropping or placing of an image or text box hold down the <Alt> key at the same time as dragging the handle.

11. The image will now look similar to this.
12. Resize the text box, then resize the image. Make sure that you do not have the crop tool selected whilst resizing.

13. To make the text wrap around the text box, right mouse click on the text box and select **Format Text**

Box from the drop-down menu. Select the **Layout** tab, followed by the style of wrapping required. For this example, you can select **Square**.

14 Use the handles to move the text box so that it aligns with the top of the text and the right margin of the page.

15 An alternative is to select the **Layout** tab, followed clicking on ⌈ **Advanced...** ⌋, then the **Picture Position** tab. For this task we can align the text box to match the top of the first line of text and the right margin. Set the picture positions as shown here for this. Use the radio buttons and drop-down lists to help you.

16 When you are sure that the image is correct, you can remove the excess that has been cropped from the file, in order to reduce the file size. This is important if you are working on documents containing a number of images. To do this, right mouse click to select the image (not the text box), then select **Format Picture**. Select the **Picture** tab followed by clicking on ⌈ **Compress...** ⌋. The **Compress Pictures** window appears.

17 Click on the **Delete cropped areas of pictures** tick box to remove the excess areas cropped from the pictures from the file.

18 Click on the **Compress pictures** tick box to reduce the file size. This does mean that images do not appear as high quality when printed.

19 If you have multiple images in a document you can apply these operations to all of them at once by selecting **All pictures in document**, before clicking on ⌈ **OK** ⌋. The finished document should look similar to this.

Activity 10.3

Manipulate an image

Select an appropriate package. Open the file IMAGE.RTF from the CD. Place the image BOARDER.JPG into the document so that it is aligned with the top left of the text. Crop the image along the red dotted line.

Resize the image so that it fills about a quarter of the width of the page margins. Place the image SLOGAN.JPG at the bottom of the document so that it is resized to fill the full width of the text area. Crop this so that only the top two lines of the slogan are visible and this sits below the text.

10.5 Including and evaluating information downloaded from the Internet

You have already learned the skills needed to download a variety of file types from the Internet and store these locally. In the previous sections you have covered how to import (and in some cases manipulate) these files. You have already taken into account issues of copyright and the legality of these actions. In Chapter **9** you studied how to evaluate information found on the Internet. In this section you must apply all of this knowledge and these skills and techniques to search the Internet, locate suitable information, evaluate whether it is fit for purpose and, if so, incorporate it into your work. You will need to focus on relevant copyright laws, which vary from country to country, but all have the same principles:

◆ You may not copy, adapt or distribute text or images without permission from the owner.
◆ You may not communicate these to the public by electronic transmission without permission from the owner.
◆ You may not rent out or lend copies without permission.
◆ You may not perform them in public without the owner's permission.

In many cases, authors also have the right to be identified on their works and to object if their work is changed. Authors can charge you to use their material, although some authors will not do so if it is being used for educational purposes. If an author will not allow you to use material, it is illegal to do so.

Activity 10.4

Evaluate information downloaded from the Internet

Search the Internet for information on sharks. Your audience will be your class; you can choose the method of delivery, but it must be appropriate to the audience. Using the information that you have found, insert extracts of the information and annotate them with comments on their sources (including the URLs): are they fact or opinion; are they biased; how reliable is the source; how accurate is the source; how current is the material; and is it suitable (including readability) for your audience? Ensure that all images used within your delivery are suitably placed, resized and cropped if necessary.

10.6 Creating a link from a document or slide

What is a hyperlink?

A hyperlink is a reference within an electronic document to another place in the same document (often to a heading or a bookmark) or to a different document. A hyperlink is often referred to simply as a link. To follow a link you usually click the left mouse button on the link. Hyperlinks are the foundation of any hypertext system, including the Internet. Hyperlinks can be used to open links within different applications packages.

What type of hyperlink do you require?

Before you start, you must decide upon the type of link that is required. There are a number of possible links. You can:

◆ open an existing word-processing document
◆ open an existing file of a different type, for example a spreadsheet, database or web page
◆ move to another place in the existing document
◆ create a new document
◆ send an e-mail message to another person.

Create a hyperlink in *Word* or *Publisher*

1   Open an existing word-processing document.
2   Enter the text or place the image that you will use to set the hyperlink. Select this text or image by highlighting it. Make sure that you are precise when selecting a word or small portion of text for the hyperlink.
3   Select the Insert menu, then click on Hyperlink…. This opens the Insert Hyperlink window.

4   The text displayed for the hyperlink is shown in the **Text to display:** area. If an image is selected for the link, this will show '<<Selection in document>>' in a greyed-out box. In this example, the actual word 'hyperlink' has been typed into the document and highlighted.

5   Select from the **Link to:** box on the left side of the window the type of link that you wish to create:

◇ **Link to an existing file or web page**: this will allow you to open an existing document, external file or web page. To select a document or other file type, browse using the **Look in:** window, select the file to open, then click on [OK]. If the file to link to is a web page, enter the web address (URL) in the **Address:** box, then click on [OK].

◇ **Link to a place in the existing document**: this will allow you to jump to a section of the current document. In the case of a word-processed document, this could be to the top of the document, any headings within the document (in this example there is only a single heading called 'New heading') or any bookmarks that you have placed within the document (in this case there is a single bookmark called 'Comment'). Select the place to link to from the available list, then click on [OK].

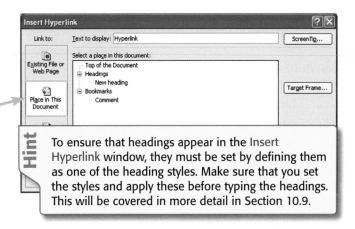

> **Hint**
> To ensure that headings appear in the Insert Hyperlink window, they must be set by defining them as one of the heading styles. Make sure that you set the styles and apply these before typing the headings. This will be covered in more detail in Section 10.9.

◇ **Link to create a new document**: this will allow you to type in the pathway and filename for the document that you wish to create, with options to create the document now or later. Name the file before clicking on [OK].

◇ **Link to send an e-mail**: this will allow you to define an e-mail address for the recipient and the subject line for the e-mail. If you use this option repeatedly it will show you the recently used e-mail addresses, to enable you to select from the list rather than typing an e-mail address. Enter the required data before clicking on [OK].

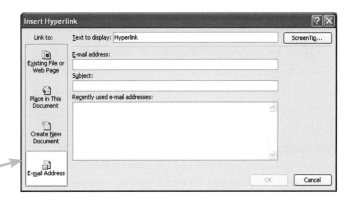

Test a hyperlink in *Word* or *Publisher*

To use an existing hyperlink hold down the <Ctrl> key and press the left mouse button on the text or image containing the hyperlink. Text containing a hyperlink looks like this. Hold the cursor over the hyperlink to give you brief details of the link and how to operate it.

Hide a hyperlink in *Word*

Highlight the hyperlinked text and then select the **Underline** [U] button which will remove the underlining from the link. Change the font colour back to the same colour as the body text (usually black) using the **Font Color** [A▼] button. The link still exists and can be used (it is still visible if you hover the cursor over it), but is otherwise invisible to the user.

Use bookmarks

A **bookmark** is a point in a document that has been given a name, so that you can identify it for future reference. As well as marking a place for you to jump to a new part of an existing document using a hyperlink, a common use of bookmarks is to identify text that you may wish to update in the future.

Add a bookmark in *Word*

To insert a bookmark, place the cursor where the bookmark is required, press the left mouse button, then from the **Insert** menu select **Bookmark…**. This will open the **Bookmark** window. Type in a name for the bookmark in the **Bookmark name:** box then click on [**Add**]. The bookmark name can contain numbers (but not start with a number) and spaces are not allowed.

Move to a bookmark in *Word*

To move the cursor to a bookmark, select the **Insert** menu, followed by **Bookmark…**. Click the left mouse button on the bookmark that you wish to go to and click on [**Go To**]. This is much quicker than searching through a multi-page document for the section that you need.

♦ link to a place in this document: this will allow you to link to any individual slide within the presentation. Select the required slide from the list and then click on [**OK**]. This will build the link so that when the text or image which has been selected is clicked on, it will jump to the appropriate slide.

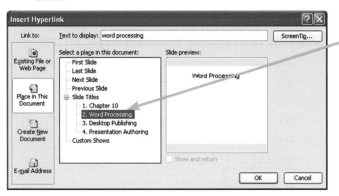

Hint

Creating links within a presentation means that you can create alternative paths through a presentation for different audiences.

Activity 10.5

Create hyperlinks in a document

Open the document SHARKS.RTF from the CD. Use the text 'nurse shark' to create a hyperlink to the file NURSE.RTF. Add a little more information about sharks and the sources you have used to the end of the document and create three more hyperlinks to web pages containing the original information. You may use the information that you gathered in Activity **10.4** to help you. Create a new hyperlink from the word 'hyperlink' that will allow the user to send you an e-mail about sharks. Save this document as a *Word* (.doc) file for later use.

Activity 10.6

Create a multi-path presentation

Create a new presentation which contains hyperlinks, including at least two different hyperlink options on the front page. Use these options to run different paths through the presentation. Make sure that at least one other slide is common to both paths, and each path has at least one slide that cannot be seen unless that path is selected.

10.7 Controlling a document to be edited by multiple users
Document control

There are times in the creation of a large document when more than one user will work on the same document at the same time. This can lead to a lot of potential problems, especially if two people working at the same time make different changes to the same document. If they then save their amended version with the same filename, the first file is overwritten by the second and the first person's work will be lost. To avoid this, **version**

Create a hyperlink in *PowerPoint*

This works in a similar way to inserting a hyperlink in Word or Publisher. Open an existing presentation and highlight the text or image to be used for the hyperlink. Select **Insert**, then **Hyperlink…**. The **Link to:** box has four options. Three of these – linking to an existing file or web page, linking to create a new document, and linking to send an e-mail – are identical to the procedures used in *Word* or *Publisher*. The option that is slightly different is:

control is needed. The simplest type of version control involves using a systematic numbering system, with the files held in a single storage area called a file **repository**. The first person would save the file as 'file1', the second as 'file2' and the number is incremented each time it is revised. Some users number the files incrementally and add their initials to the filename, for example 'file3gb' so that file 3 can not be saved twice. There are other, more complex forms of version control involving locking and file merging.

It is usual for a document to have a person called the editor who is responsible for it. This person is sometimes one of the original authors of the document. A number of people usually revise the document. These revisions could be made to the content. Proofreaders make revisions when they check the spelling, grammar and accuracy of the work. The editor collates all the revisers' comments and proofreader's notes, in order to make final decisions that will produce the finished document. Most revisers make their suggested changes and comments electronically on the document using tracked changes. One person (usually the editor) will be responsible for ensuring that version numbering is maintained and that deadlines are met. This chapter uses the example of a single document that will be reviewed and edited electronically by more than one person, with a systematic numbering system for revisions.

Protect a document for editing in *Word*

Note that some earlier versions of *Word* have a window rather than a task pane for setting document protection and are unable to provide the same detailed level of protection.

1 To protect all of the document, select the **Tools** menu, then **Protect Document**…. This will open the **Protect Document** task pane.

2 Select **Editing restrictions**, and tick the box for **Allow only this type of editing in the document**.

3 There are times when you wish to ensure that the document is protected as either 'read only', 'track all the changes made' or 'for comments'. Select from the drop-down list box for **Editing restrictions** the type of editing that you wish to allow for this document. Possible options are:

◇ **Tracked changes**: this allows another user to edit the document and to make changes. Each change is recorded within the document for approval or deletion by the original author or by the

person assigned to perform the final editing on a document. This allows several authors to reword sections or to suggest other improvements, and a final decision can be made by a single author. See the next section for further details.

◇ **Read only**: this allows another user to read the document but not to make changes to it.

◇ **Comments** only: this allows another user to add comments to the document but not change the text or layout.

4 If you wish to protect the whole document from all users move to Step 4 in the next section.

> **Hint**
>
> To protect part of a document, first protect the entire document, as shown here, then remove the restrictions from the parts that you will allow to be changed.

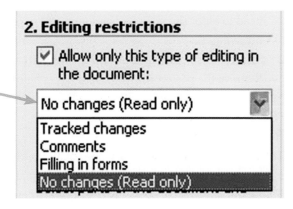

Remove restrictions in a protected document in *Word*

There are times when some parts of a document need to have the restrictions removed. In this case the restrictions are removed before protection can start. There are two methods of removing these restrictions. They are for all users or for selected individuals. Selected individuals can be added using the **More users…** option as shown here.

This will allow specified users to be given access to certain areas of the document. A new user is entered using an e-mail address or a *Windows* user account; semi-colons are used to separate users if more than one is added.

1   Add the users first if these are required.
2   Highlight the area that you wish to be unrestricted.
3   Select the user, or choose **Everyone**, then choose the option from the drop-down menu.
4   When you are ready to apply the protection to the document click on [Yes, Start Enforcing Protection]. This lets you allow access to others, either by using a password or by allowing some user accounts to change the document. Select the required option using the radio buttons and enter either the password or the user account details. If you select the user authentication method, those users that you specify will be able to remove or change the document protection.

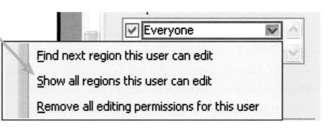

Protect a document from opening or editing in *PowerPoint* or *Word*

1   To protect all of the document, select the **Tools** menu, then **Options**. Select the **Security** tab.
2   You need to enter a password to open the file in the **Password to open:** box and/or a password to edit the file in the **Password to modify:** box.
3   Click on [OK].

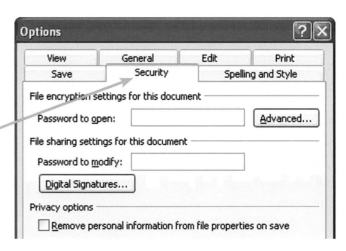

Remove the protection from a *Word* document or a *PowerPoint* presentation

1   Open the presentation. In order to do this you will need to enter the passwords to open and to edit the presentation.
2   Select **Tools**, then **Options** and the **Security** tab. Remove the passwords from both boxes before clicking on [OK].

Track changes

Tracking changes is keeping a record of all the changes made to a document during its revision and final editing. Before the most recent word processors were developed,

this was done by a number of revisers handwriting their suggested changes onto a printout. The editor made a final decision about the changes before these were edited into the original document. More recent developments in word processors like *Word* can record all of the changes made to a document by any user. This is very useful when a single document needs to be revised by more than one person. The changes can be reviewed by the editor of the document, who makes the final decisions on whether to keep or discard the changes made by each of the revisers. This person maintains an overview of the document to make sure that it is consistent and coherent.

Identify changes in *Word*

Track Changes needs to be turned on before you can see this feature. To turn on Tracking go to the Tools menu and select Track Changes.

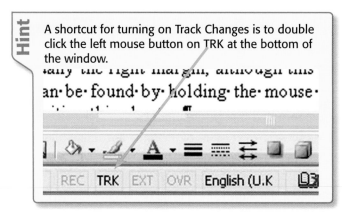

> **Hint**
>
> A shortcut for turning on Track Changes is to double click the left mouse button on TRK at the bottom of the window.

There is also a Reviewing toolbar which makes the revising and editing easier. If this is visible it will look similar to this.

If it is not selected, it can be opened using the View menu, then Toolbars and selecting Reviewing. The Display for Review box on the left allows you to select from a drop-down menu what is visible on the screen whilst you are working. Select Final Showing Markup from this drop-down list so that the finished document with all changes can be viewed.

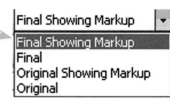

If Final Showing Markup has been selected, the visible annotation includes any comments that have been inserted and revisions of the text. With each comment or revision is a note as to who made the changes and the date and time that they were made. An outline of some of the revisions are visible in the margin (usually the right margin, although this can be changed). Further details of this can be found by holding the mouse over the revision. This sample mark-up was created whilst writing this chapter.

There are two mark-ups in this text. The first is noted in the mark-up box on the right. This shows that the word 'when' has been deleted from the text. The second mark-up is shown by the red underlined area. This shows the content of the revision, in this case a new section inserted into the text. By holding the mouse over this mark-up the details of the insertion, the name of the reviser, the date and time are visible. The black vertical line in the text also indicates to the editor that there is a revision in this section.

Accept or reject revision changes in *Word*

Whilst writing this section of the chapter, two changes have been made to the text: a hyphen has been marked into 'Markup' and added the text 'the option for' has been added. Track Changes has been selected and the Final Showing Markup option has been selected. The section of text now looks like this.

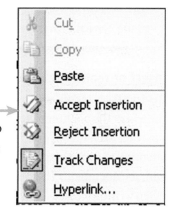

The mouse is held over the first revision to show the details of the revision. If the right mouse button is clicked on the revision, a drop-down menu appears.

Select Accept Insertion to allow this or Reject Insertion to remove the insertion. In this case these three words were not needed so Reject Insertion was selected, which removed the three words from the sentence. The hyphen was required, so using the same method this insertion was accepted into the document and the reviewing notes were removed from the file.

There is an alternative method for accepting and rejecting changes made during revision. This uses the navigation, accept and reject change buttons on the

Reviewing toolbar. If a number of revisions have been made to a document they can be edited by clicking on the **Previous** ⊡ or **Next** ⊡ button to find the correct revision, then using the Accept Change ⊡▾ or Reject Change/Delete Comment ⊡▾ button. Notice the drop-down menu options on these buttons. These will allow you to select the single revision, a group of revisions (if they are highlighted together) or all of the revisions to be accepted or deleted.

Activity 10.7

Edit and revise a document with multiple users

Open the document that you saved in Activity **10.5**. Set Track Changes to on and open the reviewing pane. Save the document and pass this to three other members of your class, one after the other, so that they all work on the same file, rather than multiple copies being created. Their task is to revise your work electronically, adding their ideas and notes about sharks. Collect the revised document and edit this, accepting and rejecting the suggested changes made. Save this document for later use.

Insert or remove revision comments in *Word*

Revision comments are notes added to but not included in the text of the document and are used where a reviser does not want to change the text but wishes to draw an editor's attention to something within the text. They can be printed with the document. They are also useful for leaving notes when writing long documents. For example:

> **Insert or remove revision comments in *Word***
>
> Revision comments are notes added to but not included in the text of the document and are used where a reviser does not want to change the text but wishes to draw an editor's attention to something within the [text] ┈┈┈ **Comment [GB1]:** Add to this section

To insert a comment, place the cursor where the comment is required, or highlight a section of text. In the example above, the highlighted text has been shown within the blue brackets. Click on the **Insert Comment** ⊡ button. Type the comment within the text box in the margin (shown in blue above) and click the cursor back onto the text of the document when you have finished. To delete a comment, click the left mouse button on the text box containing the comment, then click on the **Reject Change/Delete Comment** ⊡▾ button.

Activity 10.8

Add comments to a document

Open the document that you saved in Activity **10.7**. Add suitable revision comments to the document. Save this document for later use.

Compare and merge documents

This allows two versions of the same document to be compared, and merged together. It is especially useful when a document has been revised by a number of people at the same time, and all of the changes need to be placed in the same document for editing. Each difference between the files is identified, and noted in the final document as tracked changes. Comments from the two files are also merged into a single document. In order to keep the original documents intact, it is recommended that when 'compare and merge' features are used they are merged to a new document, rather than into an existing one.

Compare and merge documents in *Word*

1   Save your document and select the Tools menu, then **Compare and Merge Documents**. The Compare and Merge Documents window will open.

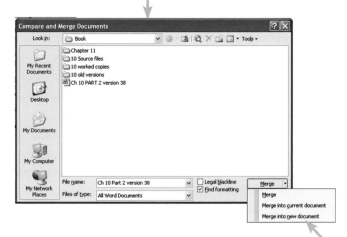

2   Select from the list the document that you wish to merge with your open file and select the drop-down menu for the ⊡ Merge ▾ button by using the ▾ symbol.

3   From the drop-down menu select the **Merge into new document** option. The formatting style of one document can be kept during the merge. Select

the document that you wish to use as the master document for this formatting using the radio button, then click on [Continue with Merge]. The merge will take place and the word processor will allocate the new document a name. Save this document with your own filename before making further changes.

10.8 Setting up the format for a document, page or slide

What is a master document or master slide?

These are referred to by different names in different software packages, but the idea is to design the layout of your document or slides before you start. The page or slide you do this on is called a master document or master slide. The page layout and document structure are set up in a master page or master slide. This can include the page layout, paper (or display) size and orientation, margin settings, gutter settings, column settings, corporate logos and colour schemes. For presentations, you also need to consider whether you need audience or presenter notes. The formatting of the document is also organised at this stage and is defined as a series of styles (see Section **10.9**). It is worth remembering that few low- to medium-cost printers

can print right to the edge of a page. The majority of documents require margins to be set so that there is white space between the edge of the text, (and often) images and the edge of the page. Where a document is to be bound into a book or booklet, additional white space is allowed on one side of the page to allow for the binding. This is called a gutter. This will usually be on the left side of odd-numbered pages and on the right side of even-numbered pages.

Set up the page layout in *Word*

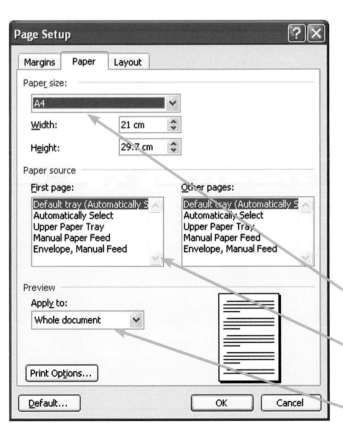

Word does not use a master document, instead using a template and outlines. These can be edited, but the page setup can be amended without the use of the template. There are a number of pre-defined templates that can be used, but for this task we will set the page layout details manually. *Word* is versatile enough to allow you to have different page setups for different sections of a document, but this task requires the whole document to be the same.

1 Create a new document. Select the File menu followed by Page Setup.

2 The Page Setup window has three tabs. To select the paper size for the document, select the Paper tab.

3 Select the Paper Size: using the drop-down menu; for this task you need to set this to A4. As you select A4, the width and height of the paper changes automatically.

4 The Paper source section may not look like this; it depends on the printer assigned to your computer.

5 Make sure that the settings are applied to the Whole document. This is found in the Preview area.

6 Select the Margins tab, which looks similar to this.

7 Use the Orientation area to set the page orientation to landscape by pressing the left mouse button on the image. Make sure that you change the page orientation before changing the margin settings.

8 In the Margins area, change the top margin to 5 centimetres, the bottom margin to 3 centimetres, and the left and right margins to 2 centimetres. Change the Gutter setting to 2 centimetres.

9 Use the Multiple pages: box to select Mirror margins. This makes sure that the gutter is in the correct place on facing pages. Check that it looks like this before clicking on OK.

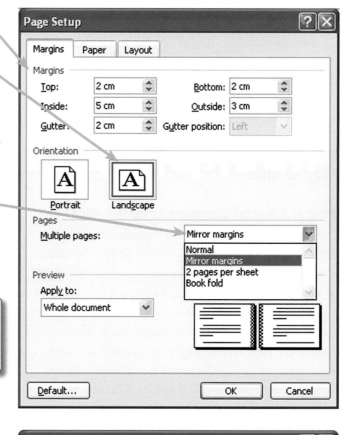

> **Hint**
>
> In the Pages area, use Book fold to produce facing pages printed on the same sheet of paper.

10 To set the document into three columns select the Format menu, then Columns… to open the Columns window.

11 Select Three columns as shown.

12 Change the spacing between the columns to 1 centimetre.

13 Column widths can be adjusted here if you wish. These columns can apply to the whole document (as shown here) or to a section of the document.

14 Click on OK.

15 Make sure that you save the page layout before starting any other work on this document.

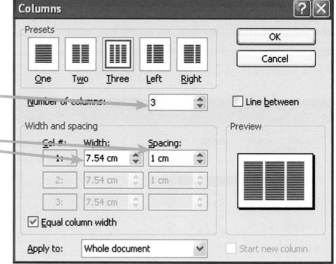

Activity 10.9

Set up a word-processed document

Create a new document in your word processor with an A4 page size, landscape orientation and set into a booklet fold. Set the top, bottom, left and right margins to 2 centimetres and the gutter to 2 centimetres, placed on the inside of the page. The booklet can be set up with four pages. Set the document into a single column. Import the file EVALUATE.RTF from the CD into your document and apply the page settings to this document. Save this document for future use.

Set up a master document in *Publisher*

Set up the page layout in a desktop publishing package

Create a new document with an A4 page size and landscape orientation. Set the top margin to 5 centimetres, the bottom margin to 3 centimetres and the left and right margins to 2 centimetres. Set a gutter of 2 centimetres, to the right on the even pages and to the left on the odd pages. Set the document into three columns with a 1-centimetre space between the columns.

1 Create a New publication.
2 Select from the task pane the option for **Blank Publications** and then select **Full Page**.
3 Select the File menu, followed by **Page Setup**….
4 The **Page Setup** window has two tabs. To select the paper sizes for the document select the **Printer and Paper** tab.
5 Select the **Paper Size:** for the document using the drop-down menu. For this task, you need to set this to be A4.

6 Use the **Orientation** area to set the page orientation to landscape, using the radio button for landscape, then click on OK.

7 To change the margin settings, use the **Arrange** menu, and then select **Layout Guides**…. This opens the **Layout Guides** window. Make sure that you select the **Margin Guides** tab.

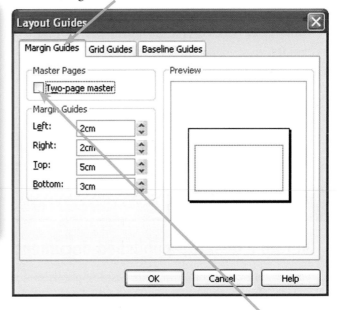

8 For this task you need to set a gutter, so select **Two-page master**. The margin guides will then change from left and right to inside and outside margin guides, as shown.
9 To work out the value so that you can set the inside margin, add the gutter width to the width of the side margin. Enter this value into this window as shown.

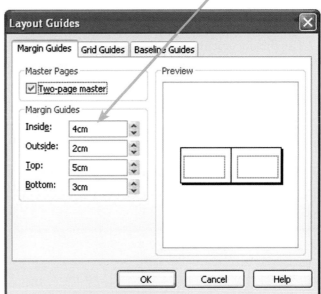

10 To set the three columns, first select the **Grid Guides** tab. Select three columns and a 1-centimetre space between the columns in the **Column Guides** section.

11 It is often useful to add a centre guide between the rows and columns before clicking on OK. This allows you to see the centre of the space between columns and can be very useful if you want to overlap images into this area of white space. Click on the tick box to add the centre guides.

12 Save your document settings to use in the next task.

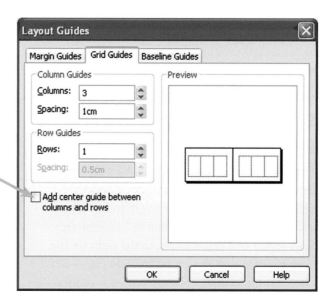

Activity 10.10

Set up a desktop-published document

Create a new document in your desktop publishing package with an A4 page size and portrait orientation. Set the top margin to 6 centimetres and the bottom, left and right margins to 3-centimetres. Place a 3-centimetre gutter to the right of the even pages and to the left of the odd pages. Set the document into 2 columns with a 1-centimetre space between them. Import the file SIMC.RTF from the CD into your document. Save this document for future use.

Set up a master page in *Publisher*

Task 10.4

Set up a master page in a desktop publishing package

Use the document layout that you saved in Task **10.3**. Set up a master document to be used by the South India Motor Company. It should have the company name in a 32-point sans-serif font across the top on the inside of the page and a small logo (the same height as the text) to the right of the company name, using the file SILOGO.JPG from the CD, on the outside of the page. The top of this text should be exactly 3 centimetres from the top of the page. It should look similar to this.

South India Motor Company   S^{IM}C

 Hint A serif font contains short strokes at the end of individual letters, these can be found in fonts like Times New. A sans-serif font is one without these serifs, such as Arial.

 Hint In *Publisher*, hold down the <Ctrl> key and press M as a keyboard shortcut to select and deselect the master page (instead of using Step 2).

1 Open the publication that you saved in Task **10.3**.

2 You need to access the master page, so that the company name and logo appear the same on every page of the document. Select the View menu, then Master Page.

3 To add a text box to the page, find the Objects toolbar, then select the text box using the ▣ button.

4   Drag out the text box onto the right-hand page only; make sure that the text box is large enough to add the text in a large font. Also, the width of the text box needs to match the width of the text area of the page (fits to the margins), so that if you decide to centre align the text, it is correctly aligned within the margins. Select the font style that you wish to use from the **Formatting** toolbar. Make sure that you have chosen a sans-serif font. Enter a font size of 32 points and enter the company name in the text box. You will need to resize the text box so that it fits the height of the text, but do not adjust the width.

5   You need to move the top of the text box so that it lines up 3 centimetres from the top of the page. Use the drag handles to line up the top of the text box with the 3-centimetre mark on the ruler to the left of the window.

6   Insert the logo using **Insert**, then **Picture**, then **From File…**. This will place the logo on the page.

7   The logo will need to be moved and resized. Use the drag handles on the corners of the image to do this. Using a handle in the centre of the edge will distort the aspect ratio of the image, whereas corner handles will keep the aspect ratio. Drag the image into the correct place on the page. You will notice that in this example the company name and logo have been placed in an area outside the page margins. This is so that these will not overlap any other items placed within the margins on any page of the document.

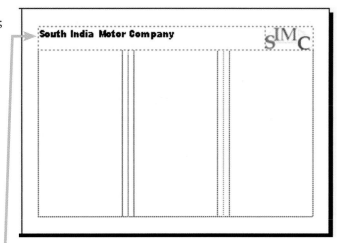

8   The right-hand page is now complete. You need to mirror this page on the left. Copy the company name, paste it and place it on the left page so that the text box is right aligned with the margin. Format the text so that it is right aligned within the text box by selecting the text and clicking on the right align icon 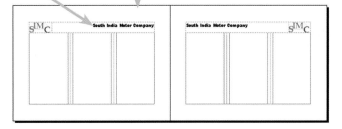.

9   Copy and paste the image and place this to the left of the company name, again aligned to the margin. It should look like this.

10 Exit the master page using **View** and **Master Page**.

Activity 10.11

Set up the page layout in a desktop publishing package

Use the document layout that you saved in Activity **10.10**. Set up a master document to be used by the South India Motor Company. It should have the company name in a 22-point bold, sans-serif font across the top on the page. The top of this text should be exactly 3 centimetres from the top of the page. The company name must not extend beyond the left and right margins. Use the file SILOGO.JPG from the CD to place a small logo, 1-centimetre high in the centre of the page. The top of this image should be exactly 4.5 centimetres from the top of the page. It should look similar to this.

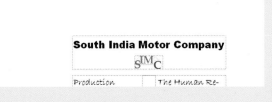

Set up a master slide in *PowerPoint*

Task 10.5

Set up the slide layout

Create a new presentation to be delivered on-screen using a multimedia projector. The presentation will have presenter notes and audience notes, both to be printed on A4 paper with a landscape orientation. The master slide should have 'South India Motor Company' in the bottom right corner, an automated slide number in the bottom left corner and a small logo containing the image in SILOGO.JPG from the CD in the top right corner.

1 Create a new presentation. Set up the method of delivery by using the **File** menu, then **Page Setup…**. For this task, go to the **Slides sized for:** box and select **On-screen Show**. This will automatically select the width and height of the slides to match the settings for a monitor or multimedia projector.

2 The choice of an on-screen show will change the slide orientation to its default landscape setting. Should you need portrait (e.g. for an on-screen presentation using a vertical monitor), change this using the radio button.

3 The task tells you that the orientation for the notes pages needs to be landscape. Use the **Notes, handouts & outline** section on the right-hand side of the **Page Setup** window to select landscape orientation, before clicking on OK.

4 To set up the master slide, select the View menu, then **Master**, then **Slide Master**.

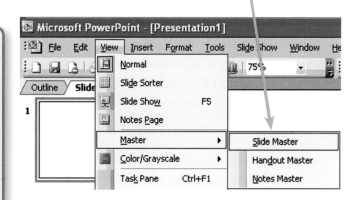

5 You can resize and move any of the text boxes on the master slide. For this task you need to put the slide number in the bottom left corner. Drag the **Number Area** from the bottom right to bottom left. You will need to delete the **Date/Time Area** first.

6 Format the **Number Area** so that the slide numbering is left aligned, using the **Align Left** button.

7 To add the text you can either add a text box or place the text in the footer:
   ◇ Add a text box in the bottom right corner of the slide using **Insert**, then **Text Box**. Drag out the text box and enter the text 'South India Motor Company'. Resize the text box if necessary.
   ◇ Enter the text 'South India Motor Company' in the footer, right align the text and move the footer to the right-hand side of the slide.

8 Insert the logo using **Insert**, then **Picture**, then **From File…**, selecting the logo file. This will place the logo on the master slide.

9 Move and resize the logo before selecting **Close Master View** from the **Slide Master View** toolbar.

10 Although the number area has been placed in the correct area of the master slide, it has not yet been activated. To activate the slide number, select the Insert menu, then Slide Number. The Header and Footer window will appear.

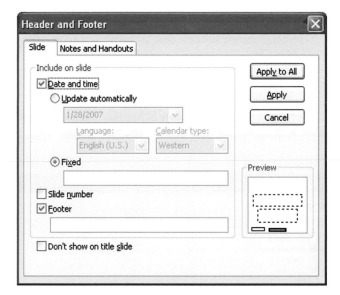

11 You can add the Slide number by clicking on the tick box, and remove the Date and time and Footer (unless you entered the text in the footer in Step 7) by deselecting the tick boxes for these options. When you have selected the items that you require, click on **Apply to All**, which will apply the slide numbering to all slides in the presentation.

12 Save your presentation settings to use in the next task.

Activity 10.12

Set up the slide layout

Create a new presentation to be delivered on-screen using a multimedia projector. The presentation will have presenter notes and audience notes, both to be printed on A4 paper with a portrait orientation. The master slide should have 'South India Motor Company' in the top left corner, an automated slide number in the top right corner and a small logo containing the image in SILOGO.JPG from the CD in the centre at the bottom of the slide.

Set up the slide colour scheme in *PowerPoint*

Task 10.6

Set up the slide colour scheme

Use the presentation settings that you saved in Task **10.5**. Set up the presentation with a pale blue background, dark blue titles and black body text.

1 Open the presentation that you saved in Task **10.5**.

2 Select the Slide Design Design... button, which is found on the Formatting toolbar. This will open the Slide Design task pane which will look similar to this.

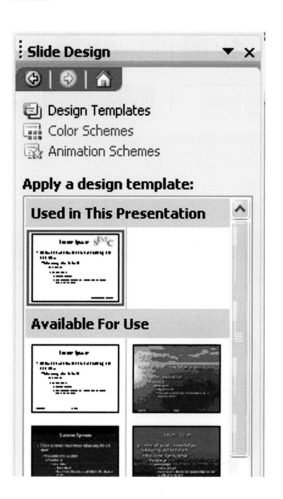

3 Check the design templates that are available for use. You may find a pre-designed template that will be suitable for the task. In this example, none of the design templates have a pale blue background.

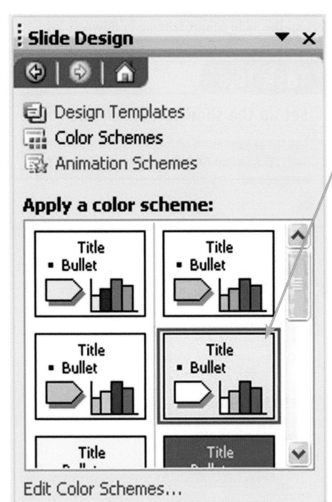

4 To design the style manually, select **Color Schemes** from the **Slide Design** pane. This will list available designs, as shown to the left.

5 Check the colour schemes to see if one matches the requirements. This colour scheme appears to have a light-grey background and black text but does not have dark blue titles.

6 Select the colour scheme that is the closest to meeting your needs by clicking on the image. This applies the style to your slide.

7 As the style does not meet all of the requirements of the task, select **Edit Color Schemes…** at the bottom of the pane. The window should look similar to this.

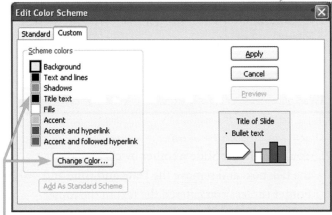

8 Select the title text by clicking the left mouse button on the **Title text** colour, then | Change Color… |.

9 This will open the **Title Text Color** window. Select the colour that you require for the title text by clicking the left mouse button on the colour palette; check that you have selected the right shade, and then click on | OK |.

10 Click on | Apply | to apply the new colour to the current colour scheme. This new colour scheme has been added to the list of colour schemes in the slide design pane. You will find it at the bottom of the list. You may need to use the scroll bar in order to see it.

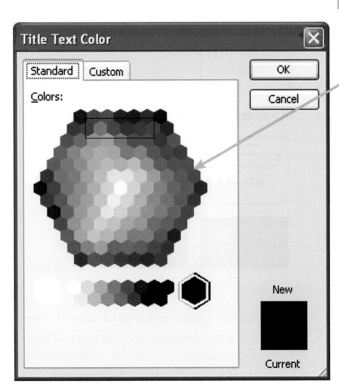

11 To apply this scheme to all the slides in your presentation, move the mouse over the style in the **Slide Design** pane. You will see the handle for a drop-down menu which will look similar to this.

12 Select **Apply to All Slides** from this menu.

13 Save your presentation for future use.

Activity 10.13

Set up the slide colour scheme

Use the presentation settings that you saved in Activity **10.12**. Set up the presentation with a pale green background, dark green titles and dark blue body text.

10.9 Using and applying styles

You have already used many different features in your documents, for example different fonts, point sizes, enhancements (like bold, italic and underline), paragraph settings and line spacing. It can be a slow process, setting all of these features repeatedly when creating text. To ensure consistency of presentation and to save you time it is recommended that you define a number of pre-set styles for the text and apply them consistently throughout a document.

Define styles in *Word*

Task 10.7

Set up the styles for a document

Use the document that you saved in Task **10.3**. Define the styles for the document so that it has a:

(i) **body text style** with:
- a size of 10 points
- single line spacing
- a sans-serif font
- fully justified text.

(ii) **heading style** with:
- a size of 18 points
- single line spacing
- a serif font
- centre aligned text
- spacing before of 9 points
- spacing after of 3 points
- underlining.

1 To define a style, select the **Format** menu, then **Styles and Formatting**…. This will open the **Styles and Formatting** pane. You can identify information about each style by holding the cursor over the style name. Be careful not to press the left mouse button, or this will overwrite your current style with the style that you are looking at. The details of the style will look similar to this.

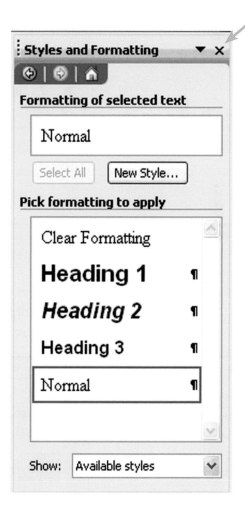

2 *Word* has several default styles that are saved in the template file that is used by your word-processed document. Each style is easy to recognise, as the styles show some of the features included within them. Here is an example of some of the available styles.

3 To create a new style, click on New Style….

4 This opens the New Style window. The style definitions include the font details, paragraph settings, line spacing, the format of the text including bullets, numbering and text enhancements like bold, underline and italic.

5 Enter the style name in the Name: box. For this task you can call the style 'Body'.

6 The style type will be paragraph, and you can base it on the style Normal, which is an existing body style.

7 Go to the Formatting section and select a sans-serif font using the drop-down menu.

8 Set the text alignment to fully justified.

9 Change the point size to 10.

10 Set the line spacing to single. The new style should look similar to this.

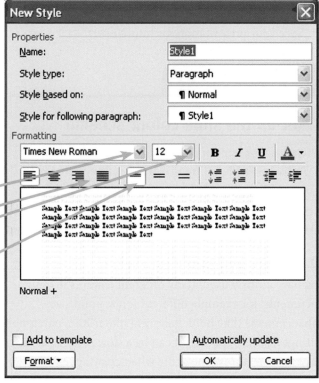

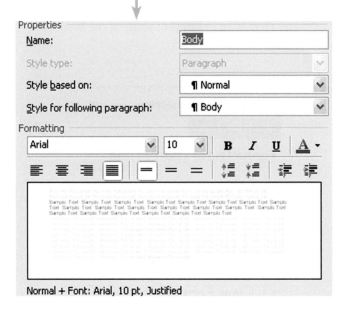

11 Click on OK.

12 The heading style is created in a similar way. Call the style 'Own Heading'. The font, point size, alignment and line spacing are all set as outlined above. The underline is set using the **U** button.

13 You will need to edit the formatting of the style by clicking on Format ▾. This will show you a drop-down list. This drop-down list allows you to change all of the formatting details for this style, including features like tabulation, borders, shading, text wrapping around frames, bullets and numbering.

14 Select Paragraph… from the list. This will open the Paragraph window. Using the Indents and Spacing tab, change the spacing before to 9 point and the spacing after to 3 point. Click on OK to return to the New Style window.

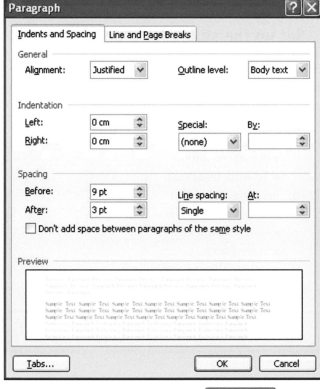

15 To create the new style, click on OK.

Apply styles in *Word*

1 Move the cursor into the text to be formatted.
2 Go to the style box in the **Formatting** toolbar and select the correct style from the drop-down list.

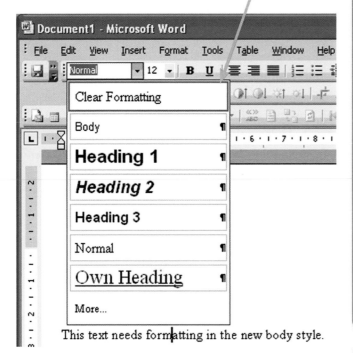

Hyphenation in *Word*

1 *Word* will automatically hyphenate words for you. If you wish to set hyphenation to manual, in order to have more control over the process, select **Tools**, then **Language**, then **Hyphenation**….
2 Click on **Manual…** and this will automatically run through a manual hyphenation check in your current document.

Tabulation in *Word*

1 Tab stops appear on the ruler in *Word*. To place a tab stop select the type of tab stop required. They are **L** left tab, **⊥** centre tab, **⌐** right tab, **⊥** decimal tab (where numbers are aligned on the decimal point) and **I** bar tab (which places a vertical bar at that point rather than placing text). Click the left mouse button on the left tab icon to the left of the ruler to change the type of tab stop; this cycles through all the available options.
2 When you have selected the correct type of tab stop, click the left mouse button on the ruler to set the tabulation. This tab stop can be dragged within the ruler. For precision placing of the tab stops use the **Format** menu, then **Tabs**….

Activity 10.14

Set up the styles for a word-processed document

Use the document that you saved in Activity **10.9**. Define the styles for the document so that it has a:

(i) **body text style** with:
- a size of 12 points
- single line spacing
- serif font
- fully justified text.

(ii) **heading style** with:
- a size of 14 points
- single line spacing
- a sans-serif font
- centre aligned text
- spacing before of 6 points
- no spacing after
- bold and italic.

Apply these styles to the document.

Define styles in *Publisher*

1 This process is almost identical to the one used in *Word* with **Format**, then **Styles and Formatting**… to open the **Styles and Formatting** pane. To create a new style, click on **New Style…** . The **New Style** window in *Publisher* looks like this.

2 If you work through Task **10.7** again, the new style name 'Body' goes in here.

3 Click on [Font ...] to choose the sans-serif font and set the point size to 10, before returning with [OK].

4 Click on [Paragraph ...] and use the **Alignment** drop-down list to set fully justified text. In the **Line spacing** section use the drop-down list for **Between lines** to set the line spacing to 1sp (double line spacing is 2sp and so on). Return to the New Style window with [OK].

5 Click on [OK] to create the new style.

6 To create the style for your new heading, repeat Steps 1 to 4, entering a style name of 'Own Heading', with an 18-point serif font, centre aligned and single line spaced.

7 To underline the text within this style, click on [Font ...] and the **Underline:** box. Use the drop-down list for this box to select the style of underlining required, before returning with [OK].

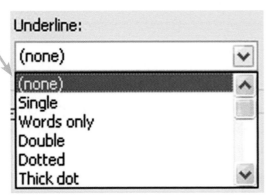

8 To amend the spacing before and after the heading, click on [Paragraph ...], then the **Line spacing** section. Change the settings for **Before paragraphs:** and **After paragraphs:** to those shown here.

9 Click on [OK] to return to the New Style window and [OK] again to set the style.

Apply styles in *Publisher*

This is identical to applying styles in *Word*. See the section above for further details.

Hyphenation in *Publisher*

This is identical to hyphenation in *Word*. See the section above for further details.

Tabulation in *Publisher*

This is very similar to setting tab stops in *Word*, with tab stops placed on the ruler. To select the type of tab stop, hold down the <Shift> key and select from the left end of the ruler. The tab stops available in *Publisher* are . [L] left tab, [⊥] centre tab, [⌐] right tab and [⊥] decimal tab. These are placed and edited using the same methods as *Word*. See the section above for further details.

Activity 10.15

Set up the styles in a desktop publishing package

Use the document that you saved in Activity **10.11**. Define and apply these styles to the document, so that it has a:

(i) **body text style** with:
- a size of 12 points
- single line spacing
- a sans-serif font
- fully justified text.

(ii) **heading style** with:
- a size of 16 points
- single line spacing
- a serif font
- right aligned text
- spacing before of 6 points
- spacing after of 2 points
- bold and italic.

Define styles in *PowerPoint*

The first part of defining styles is to set the slide colour scheme, as shown earlier in this chapter. All other elements that make up a style can be found in the slide master section within *PowerPoint*.

1. To change the master slide details, select the **View** menu, then **Master**, then **Slide Master**. This will look similar to this.

2. To change any of the styles, click on the style, then select the font, point size and text colour from the **Formatting** toolbar. The text colours available will show the pre-defined colours selected in your colour scheme (from the earlier section), as well as offering you the option of adding new colours. This can be done for the title style and for each level of the bulleted lists.

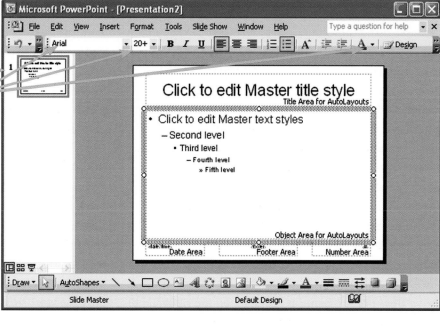

3. To edit the type of bullet point for each level, click on the text for that level then select the **Format** menu, followed by **Bullets and Numbering....** Select the bullet style that you require, followed by OK.

4. To exit from the master slide, click on **Close Master View** from the **Slide Master View** toolbar.

10.10 Headers and footers

A **header** is the area of a document between the top of the page and the top margin. A **footer** is the area of a document between the bottom of the page and the bottom margin. You can insert text or graphics into headers and footers. This might include the author's name, the document's filename, page numbering or even a company logo. Headers and footers can be found in many printed documents, including those that have been word processed or desktop published, and in presentations, web pages and reports from spreadsheets and databases.

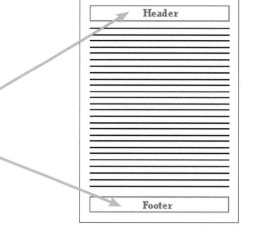

Use headers and footers in *Word*

To access the header and/or footer in a *Word* document, select the **View** menu, then **Header and Footer**. This will move the cursor into the header and open the **Header and Footer** toolbar. This toolbar contains many useful features; each of these features can be added to the header or footer by clicking on the button, as shown below.

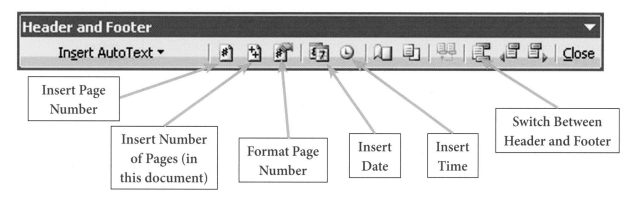

Some of the features available using these buttons can be found using the Insert AutoText drop-down menu. This contains other forms of automated text which can also be inserted. The Insert AutoText drop-down menu will look similar to this.

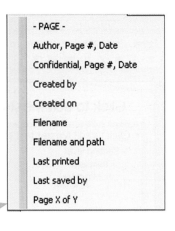

If a document is split into separate sections using a section break (see the next section), the headers and footers of each section can be linked together. If they are linked together they will be the same. If the header or footer does not say 'Same as Previous' on the right-hand side and you wish to keep the header or footer the same as the previous section click on the Link to Previous button. This will link the two sections together. Similarly, if the two sections are already linked together and you want to remove the link, click on the Link to Previous button. This button acts as a toggle to turn this feature on and off. If this feature is turned off, then any changes that you make to the header or footer will not be made to the other sections of the document. This is very useful if you need to have a split page orientation within a document, as you will discover later in the chapter. To navigate between the headers or footers of different sections of a document, use the Show Previous and Show Next buttons from the Header and Footer toolbar.

Use headers and footers in *Publisher*

To access the header and/or footer in a *Publisher* document select the View menu, then Header and Footer. This will move the cursor into the header and open the Header and Footer toolbar. This toolbar contains fewer features than the toolbar in *Word*. The available options are Insert Page Number, Insert Date, Insert Time and Show Header/Footer (which is the same as Switch Between Header and Footer in *Word*).

Use headers and footers in *PowerPoint*

The header and footer in *PowerPoint* are located in the set-up of the master slide from the presentation. You have already looked at this earlier in this chapter.

10.11 Footnotes

A footnote is text added to a document and is used to make a comment or to provide a reference source. Footnotes can be seen in the printed document, unlike comments. A footnote contains two parts. The first is the reference mark, which looks like this.[1] The second part is the text which is placed at the bottom of the page (see below).

Add a footnote in *Word*

To insert a footnote, place the cursor where the reference mark is required. Select the Insert menu, followed by Reference, then Footnote…. This will open the Footnote and Endnote window. An endnote will place all of the references at the end of the section or the end of the document. A footnote will place them at the bottom of the page you are working on. Footnotes and endnotes can be numbered or lettered in a variety of styles.

Move or duplicate a footnote in *Word*

To move a footnote or endnote, highlight the reference mark in the text, then use drag and drop or cut and paste. Use copy and paste to duplicate a footnote.

10.12 Sections

A section is the area of a document which has common page formatting. Examples of this would be a document where one section is in portrait orientation, then another section in landscape orientation, or a change of layout within a page from one column to three columns.

A break is a split between two pages, sections or columns, or it can be inserted to force text wrapping. Breaks are usually used to separate two areas of a document with different formatting.

Use breaks and sections in *Word*

To insert a break in *Word*, select the Insert menu, then Break…. This will open the Break window. The three options under Break types will insert a break without creating a new section of the document. You can use the Page break option to move

---

[1] This is the text for the footnote in the section above. It usually contains comments or references to other sources.

to the start of a new page; this is much easier than trying to arrange page breaks by repeatedly pressing the <Enter> key. The **Column break** option allows you to move to the top of the next column, which is useful for documents with multiple columns. The **Text wrapping break** is used to force a line break (like a carriage return), but if used with fully justified text will keep the left and right alignment and add additional spaces in the centre of the text.

The section breaks allow a document to have different margin settings and/or split page orientation using the **Next page** option. The **Continuous** option allows you to have different sections on the same page and is useful for having different column layouts on the same page.

To remove a break in *Word*, click on the **Show/Hide** ¶ button; this will make the break (and its type) visible on the page. Highlight the break and use the <Delete> key.

Task 10.8

Set up a document with split page orientation, a section break, headers and footers

Create a page size of A4 and portrait orientation. Set all of the page margins to 4 centimetres, but with no gutter. Import the document EVALUATE.RTF from the CD. Define the styles for the document so that it has a:

(i) body text style with:
- a size of 11 points
- 1.5 line spacing
- serif font
- fully justified text
- no spacing before or after the text.

(ii) heading style with:
- a size of 16 points
- single line spacing
- a serif font
- left-aligned text
- spacing of 8 points before and after the text.

Change the page orientation to landscape immediately before the heading 'Perspective and Bias'. Format all of the text from this point onwards into two columns with a 1-centimetre gap between the columns.

Set a header that contains your name left aligned, the date centre aligned and the time right aligned to the page margins. Set a footer that contains the page number left aligned and the filename right aligned to the page margins. These need to be applied throughout the document.

1. Using the skills practised so far in this chapter, set up a page size of A4, portrait orientation and page margins. Import the file and set up the two styles, applying these to all of the text.
2. Move the cursor to the start of the heading 'Perspective and Bias' and click the left mouse button.
3. Select a section break for the next page with **Insert, Break…**, then a section break with the **Next page** type.
4. Highlight all the text from this point onwards and select **Format, Columns…** and choose Two columns.
5. Change the size of the gap between the columns to 1 centimetre, before clicking on [OK].
6. Move back to the start of the document (to the portrait page) and click the left mouse button in the text.
7. Select **View**, then **Header and Footer**. Check that the tab stops are in the correct place. Ensure that the

centre tab stop is placed 6.5 centimetres from the left margin (this is half of the 13-centimetre line length) and that the right tab stop is set to 13 centimetres.

8 Add your name to the left of the header, either by using Insert Autotext and then the Created by option, or by typing your name.

9 Move to the centre of the header by pressing the <Tab> key. Then enter the date using the automated date 🔲 button. Use <Tab> again to move to the right of the header and enter the automated time using the 🕓 button.

10 Use the Switch Between Header and Footer 🔲 button to move to the footer. Check that the tab stops are in the correct place, again with the centre tab stop 6.5 centimetres in and the right tab stop 13 centimetres from the left.

1 Enter the page number, left aligned, using the 🔲 button, press the <Tab> key twice to move to the right of the footer and enter the filename using Insert Autotext, then the Filename option.

2 Move to the next page using the Show Next 🔲 button.

3 Make sure that you use the Link to Previous 🔲 button so that the 'Same as Previous' text to the top right of the header is removed before changing any of the settings.

4 Drag the right tab stop to 21.7 centimetres (to match the page margins) and the centre tab stop to 10.85 centimetres.

5 Move down to the footer for this section, then repeat Steps 13 and 14.

> **Hint**
> Hold down the <Alt> key to get precision measurements when dragging the tab stops.

Activity 10.16

Set up a document with split page orientation, a section break, headers and footers

Create a page size of A4 and landscape orientation. Set all of the page margins to 3 centimetres, but with no gutter. Import the document SIMC.RTF from the CD. Define the styles for the document so that it has a:

(i) body text style with:
- a size of 14 points
- single line spacing
- a serif font
- fully justified text
- no spacing before the text
- 14 point spacing after the text.

(ii) heading style with:
- a size of 18 points
- single line spacing
- a sans-serif font
- centre aligned text
- no spacing before or after the text.

Remove any extra carriage returns between paragraphs. Insert the title 'South India Motor Company' in heading style immediately before 'Production'. Insert a break immediately before 'Production' and format all of the text from this point onwards into three columns with a 2-centimetre gap between the columns.

Change the page orientation to landscape immediately before the heading 'Needs'. Format all of the text from this point onwards into two columns with a 2-centimetre gap between the columns.

Set a header that contains automated page numbering left aligned, your name centre aligned and the date right aligned to the page margins. Set a footer that contains the filename and path centre aligned to the page margins.

Insert a section break in *Publisher*

In *Publisher* you can only have a section break between pages, unlike *Word* where you can have a section break within a page. To insert a section break between pages in *Publisher*, select the page where you want to start a new section by pressing the right mouse button on the page in the page sorter (at the bottom left of the window). This may look similar to this.

Select Insert, then Section… from the drop-down menu to open the Section window. Choose the options that you require before clicking on OK. The section break will be shown in the page sorter like this.

In earlier versions of *Publisher*, the position of the section break is shown using an asterisk (*).

Insert a column break in *Publisher*

To insert a column break within a text box in *Publisher*, move the cursor to the point where you want to insert the column break and click the left mouse button. Hold down the <Ctrl> and <Shift> keys and press <Enter>.

10.13 Widows and orphans

If you start a paragraph of text on one page but there isn't enough room on the page to fit the last line, the single line of text which appears at the top of the next page is called a widow. Similarly, sometimes you start a paragraph at the bottom of a page but you can only type in one line before the rest of the text goes onto the next page. The first line of the paragraph at the bottom of the page is called an orphan. These lines should be avoided when producing a document and you are likely to be penalised if you include these in any submission for the practical examinations. These can be manually avoided by inserting a Page Break or a Text Wrapping Break, which does not show the reader that you have forced the page break at this point. For more information on breaks, refer to Section **10.12**.

Automatically avoid widows and orphans in *Word* and *Publisher*

In both *Word* and *Publisher*, you can automatically avoid widows and orphans using paragraph options. Select the paragraph or paragraphs that you wish to set this feature for. Go to the Format menu, followed by Paragraph…, then select the Line and Page Breaks tab. Select the Widow/Orphan control tick box.

10.14 Applying house styles

Most organisations have a corporate house style. This can be seen on letter heads, business cards, advertising, websites, company vehicles and, of course, their products. House style can range from company logos to recognised colour schemes, fonts, point sizes, etc. You will probably recognise many international companies' advertising by the colour scheme or other stylistic features that they use, long before you can read the company name on the material. In ICT terms you should always adopt a specific style for the work that you produce. Anything produced for a company will usually have a logo, colour scheme, font style, paragraph style, page layout (particularly if using headed notepaper), page formatting and pre-defined styles for bullets and numbering.

If you are required to produce work in your practical examinations, it is important that you apply these to every element that you produce, whether it relates to a document, presentation or any other form of communication, especially when it is for customers or clients. In previous sections of this chapter you have set up styles within both documents and presentations.

10.15 Tables

Tables are particularly useful for laying out elements of a page in documents, presentations and even websites. It is sometimes helpful to use a table to structure all or part of a document or presentation, then to remove some or all of the gridlines so that the structure can not be seen by the reader.

Insert a table in *Word*

1   Select the Table menu, followed by Insert, then Table…. This opens the Insert Table window.

2   Enter the number of rows and columns required for the table.

3   If you want to select from a range of pre-defined table formats including colour schemes, gridlines and three-dimensional effects you can use 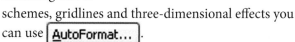.

4   When you have selected the sizes and formatting that you want, click on OK.

Insert a row or column into a table in *Word*

1 Move the cursor into the table and left mouse click. The cursor must be placed in a cell where the row or column is to be inserted.
2 Select the Table menu, followed by Insert. This opens this sub-menu.
3 A row or column can be added to the left, to the right, above or below the currently selected cell.

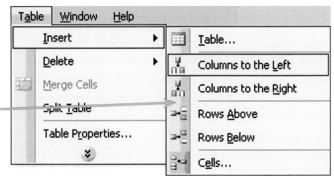

Delete a row or column from a table in *Word*

1 Move the cursor into the table and left mouse click. The cursor must be placed in a cell where the row or column is to be deleted. If a number of rows or columns are to be deleted at the same time highlight one cell in each of the sections to be deleted.
2 Select the Table menu, followed by Delete. This opens this sub-menu.
3 The entire table can be deleted, or one or more rows or columns. If you select Rows or Columns this will delete those currently selected within the table. Note that selecting a single cell in a row and using this method will delete the entire row containing that cell.

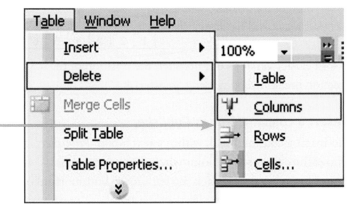

Delete cells from a table in *Word*

1 Move the cursor into the table and left mouse click. The cursor must be placed in the cell to be deleted. If a number of cells are to be deleted at the same time highlight all of the cells.
2 Select the Table menu, followed by Delete. From the sub-menu select Cells…. This will open the Delete Cells window.
3 This will allow you to delete rows or columns or to shift all the cells in that row or column (with their contents) either up or left (depending upon your choice) to replace the cell or cells that you have removed. It will however change the shape of the resulting table. For example, in the left-hand table below, selecting the cells containing the letters L and M and selecting Shift cells left from the Delete Cells window will result in the right-hand table.

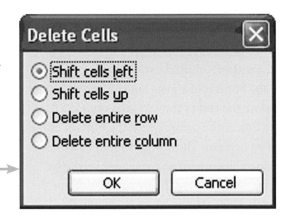

A	B	C	D	E
F	G	H	I	J
K	L	M	N	O
P	Q	R	S	T

A	B	C	D	E
F	G	H	I	J
K	N	O		
P	Q	R	S	T

Using gridlines and borders within a table in *Word*

Gridlines within a table can be visible or hidden. These can only be viewed on the screen and are never visible when a document is printed. They can be made visible or invisible using the Hide Gridlines and Show Gridlines options from the table toolbar. If you wish to make the gridlines visible when printed you must use borders.

1 Move the cursor into the table and left mouse click.
2 Select the Format menu, followed by Borders and Shading… to open the Borders and Shading window.

3 Select the **Borders** tab.

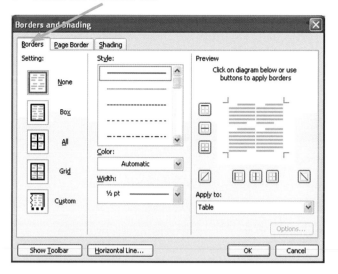

4 To place borders on all of the gridlines select either **All** or **Grid**. The option for **All** will place identical thickness borders on the gridlines, while the option for **Grid** will emphasise the outer border. You can change the style, colour or width of the lines using the relevant sections. Individual settings can be applied to individual cells or the entire table using the **Preview** area in the window. Unless specifically asked to change any of these settings in the practical examination, use the **All** or **Grid** options and do not spend valuable examination time adjusting the settings.

Merging cells within a table in *Word*

1 Highlight the cells to be merged together. These cells must be next to each other.

2 Select the **Table** menu, then **Merge Cells**. This action will change a table from:

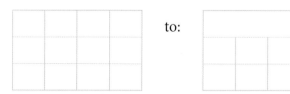

to:

Insert a table in *Publisher*

1 Select the **Table** menu, followed by **Insert**, then **Table**…. This opens the **Create Table** window.

2 Enter the number of rows and columns required for the table.

3 If you want to select from a range of pre-defined table formats including colour schemes, gridlines and three-dimensional effects, you can use **Table format:**.

4 When you have selected the sizes and formatting that you want, click on ☐ **OK** ☐.

Edit an existing table in *Publisher*

1 Move the cursor into the table and left mouse click. If you wish to insert or delete rows and/or columns the position of the cursor will be vital.

2 Select the **Table** menu and use **Insert** or **Delete** to perform these actions on the whole table, individual rows, columns or cells. This operates in a similar way to editing rows, columns and cells within a table in *Word*. The option to merge cells is available in *Publisher* and works in a similar way to *Word*, but the option to hide gridlines is not available.

3 Selecting the **Table** menu, then **Select** will allow you to select all or part of the table, so that you can format the cells, in the same way that you would format text outside the table.

Insert a table in *PowerPoint*

1 Select the **Insert** menu, followed by **Table**…. This opens the **Insert Table** window.

2 Enter the number of rows and columns required for the table, then click on ☐ **OK** ☐.

3 Use the **Tables and Borders** toolbar to change the sizes and formatting.

Edit an existing table in *PowerPoint*

Double click the left mouse button on one of the outside gridlines of the table and the **Format Table** window will appear. This can be used to adjust the lines, shading, vertical cell alignment and internal margins for the table. When you have made the changes, click on ☐ **OK** ☐ to return to the slide.

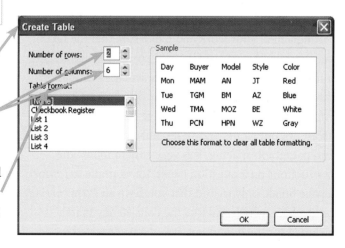

Create and edit tables

In each of your software packages, create a 5-by-6 table like this:

Department	Location	Contact	Hours	e-mail
Head Office	Chennai	Sukrit Suresh	9–5	ssuresh@simc.co.in
Production	Bangalore	Vishna Pitroda	6.30–5.30	vp@simc.co.in
Payroll	Bangalore	Suraj Yadav	8–4	s.yadav@simc.co.in
Research and Development	Bangalore	Joshi Patel	10–6	jpatel@simc.co.in
Main Showroom	Vellore	Arwan Singh	9–5	arwansingh@simc.co.in

Make sure that all the text fits within the table without text wrap. Delete the 'Hours' column and the row containing 'Payroll'. Make the column headings and row headings bold. Include gridlines within the table like this:

Department	**Location**	**Contact**	**e-mail**
Head Office	Chennai	Sukrit Suresh	ssuresh@simc.co.in
Production	Bangalore	Vishna Pitroda	vp@simc.co.in
Research and Development	Bangalore	Joshi Patel	jpatel@simc.co.in
Main Showroom	Vellore	Arwan Singh	arwansingh@simc.co.in

10.16 Proofreading and error correction

Before starting this course you will have used the automated spell check features of the software. Use this and an automated grammar checker to help you to remove some errors that you might have made in your work. Do not worry about the differences in spelling that can occur with dictionaries from different regions, for example centre and center; these should not be penalised in the examinations. It is important that you also read through all of your work and make sure that the text or data that you have typed is 100% correct. A significant number of marks can be lost in practical examinations through careless checking of your data entry. Check that your documents or slides also have consistency in all areas, not only fonts and styles, but also in line spacing and paragraph spacing. It is very easy to follow the instructions on a question paper, for example to remove a page break, only to find that you have an extra carriage return later, which will lose the consistency marks awarded for the document. If you have inserted section breaks or page breaks, make sure that there are no blank pages (or those containing just the header and footer) unless you are told in the question paper to do so.

Part of the proofreading and error correction will be to check for widows and orphans. Even though you may have applied automatic widow and orphan control, it is always good practice to check that these have been removed – it is possible that you did not apply it to every paragraph. Make sure that other objects, like bulleted or numbered lists, tables, graphs and database or spreadsheet extracts are not split over two pages. Again, inserting appropriate breaks should avoid these problems. Make sure that you have set the correct page orientation for each section of the document, or the correct slide format for your target audience and type of delivery. Make sure that the text that you enter is suitable for your target audience. If you are producing a presentation for young children, keep the words (and sentences) short and easy to read. Try to get your document 100% correct.

11 Databases and charts

You already know how to:

- define database record structures
- enter data into a database
- select subsets of data within a database
- sort data within a database
- produce and export reports for use within another package
- produce and label graphs and charts from a charting package
- create, rename and delete files using an operating system
- access folders/directories within the operating system.

In this chapter you will learn how to:

- design and create the most efficient database structure to solve a problem
- link data tables by creating and using relationships
- understand the importance of accurate data entry
- check data entry using validation and verification
- select subsets of data using multiple criteria
- sort data in a database using multiple criteria
- enter formulae to calculate results
- use the display features of the database to produce a report
- group data
- summarise data
- export data using different file formats
- produce an appropriate type of graph or chart with suitable labels
- add and edit data series and axes in a graph or chart.

For this chapter you will need these source files from the accompanying CD:

- BOAT.CSV
- CARS.CSV
- CLIENT.CSV
- CUSTOMER.CSV
- SALES.CSV

11.1 Introduction and terminology

Data storage

A single data item is known as a **field**. Each field has a specified type (e.g. it may contain numbers, text, a date, etc.). A **record** is a collection of fields (which may be of different data types) containing information about one person or one object. In terms of a database, a **file** is a logically organised collection of records, usually where all the records are organised so that they can be stored together.

You will be using *Access*, which is part of the *Microsoft Office* suite. *Access* stores its data in the form of tables, which are organised by rows and columns. Each row of the table contains a record. Each column in the table represents a field and each cell in that column has the same (pre-defined) field type. Within *Access* several tables can be stored in a single database. Here is an example of a small data table containing three records and five fields:

Field name

Records

Customer ID	Forename	Surname	Date	Order number
TX00343	Sukrit	Patel	14 March 2008	453450
TX00345	Jenna	Smith	5 January 2007	000142
TX00346	Juan	Ramirez	16 July 2008	453987

Fields

11.2 Designing a database structure

Before you consider creating a database structure you must first design it. Before you can do this, you must answer the following questions:

- Which data items do you need to store?
- What field names should you use?
- Do you need one or more tables?
- Which field(s) should be primary key field(s)?
- What relationships will be needed?
- What data type should you use for each field?
- What field length should be used for each field?
- Which validation rules will help reduce data entry errors?

The answer to each question will help you to structure the database in the most efficient way.

Task 11.1

The South India Motor Company is designing a new database to store information on its employees, their job details and information about the branches in which they work. For each employee, it needs to hold information on the employee's name, their payroll number (which is unique to them and has two letters followed by four digits, the first letter is always M or C), the branch that they work at and the job that they perform. For each employee, the job code and description needs to be stored along with the rate of pay for that job. For each branch of the company, it needs to record the branch number, the branch name, the address and a weighting which is used to calculate salaries. This weighting ensures that employees living in areas where housing and other costs are high receive more pay than workers in areas where housing costs are lower. The weighting is a decimal value between 0 and 2.

Design the structure of the database you would build to hold this data.

Which data items do you need to store?

From the task you are told that the following data should be stored:

- employee name
- employee payroll number
- job code
- job description
- job rate of pay
- branch number

- branch name
- branch address
- branch weighting.

You must look carefully at this data and ensure that each of these sections will be suitable for a single

Hint The use of a bulleted or numbered list for recording the data to be stored will save you time and effort.

field. In this case the employee name will be better split into forename and surname. The branch address should be split into a number of lines (for this example you can select three fields).

What field names should you use?

The field names must be short enough to ensure that printouts fit on a page without wasted space and long enough to be meaningful. In some database packages you cannot have a field name longer than eight characters. Check if this is the case with the software you are using. A good convention is to avoid using spaces within field names as some databases do not accept these (*Access* does accept them).

Looking at the data items which need to be stored, you will create a field name for each:

		Hint
Employee name	Forename	Field names may change if more than one table is used.
	Surname	
Employee payroll number	PayNumber	
Job code	JobCode	
Job description	JobDescription	
Job rate of pay	RateOfPay	
Branch number	BranchCode	
Branch name	BranchName	
Branch address	BranchAdd1	
	BranchAdd2	
	BranchAdd3	
Branch weighting	Weighting	

Do you need one or more tables?

Having selected the field names (these may change), you need to decide upon the number of tables to be used. This task could be completed using a single table. However, this will be very inefficient as some data items (e.g. the branch address, name, weighting, job description and rate of pay) will need to be stored for each employee, leading to the repeated storage of some data. There will also be other disadvantages to a single table. If a rate of pay for a particular job were changed it would need updating for every employee's record. The data that needs to be stored falls into three categories, data about the employee, the branch and the job. As each of these is related to the employee it is logical to store the data as three tables. This means that the field names will need to be set out like this:

Branch table	
Branch number	Code
Branch name	Branch
Branch address	Address1
	Address2
	Address3
Branch weighting	Weighting

Employees table	
Employee name	Forename
	Surname
Employee payroll number	PayNumber
Job code	JobCode
Branch number	BranchCode

Job table	
Job code	Job
Job description	Description
Job rate of pay	RateOfPay

Which fields should be primary key fields?

As you have chosen to use three tables for this task, you need three key fields. The primary key field for each table will be the field that contains unique information. In the case of the Employees table, you were told in the task that the employee's payroll number was 'unique to them' so this will be an obvious choice for primary key field. For the job table, the job code field will contain unique values and will be suitable to use as a primary key. For the branch table, the branch code will also contain unique values and should become the primary key field for this table. It makes the database easier to organise if you list the primary key field as the first field in the table, as shown here.

> **Hint**
> If a field holds unique numeric values, do not assume that it will need to be an Autonumber field type. If this field is not used for calculations, it will often be better to use a Text format for the field.

Our data structure will now look like this:

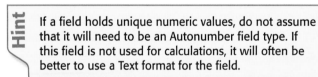

Branch table	
🔑	Code
	Branch
	Address1
	Address2
	Address3
	Weighting

Employees table	
🔑	PayNumber
	Forename
	Surname
	JobCode
	BranchCode

Job table	
🔑	Job
	Description
	RateOfPay

What relationships will be needed?

Relationships are only needed if tables need to be linked together. There are different types of relationships between fields in different tables. The relationship can be a one-to-one (1–1) relationship, where each record in one table relates to only one record in another table; or it can be a one-to-many (1–∞) relationship, where one record in one table can relate to many records in another table.

The relationship between the Employees table and the Job table will need to be created between the JobCode field in the Employees table and the Job field in the Job table. This will need to be a one-to-many relationship as one record in the Job table could match many employees within the company who have the same job.

The relationship between the Employees table and the Branch table will need to be created between the BranchCode field in the Employees table and the Code field in the Branch table. This will also need to be a one-to-many relationship as one record in the Branch table (which gives the details of one branch of the company) could match many employees within the company who work in that branch.

The relationships should be mapped onto a relationship diagram like this:

What data type should you use for each field?

There are a variety of field types that could be selected. Depending upon the package used they can have different names. There are three main types of field:

◆ **Alphanumeric**
Alphanumeric data can store alpha characters (text) or numeric data that will not be used for calculations.

◆ **Numeric**
A numeric field type (as the name suggests) is used to store numeric values that may be used for calculations. This does not include numeric data like telephone numbers, which should be stored in an alphanumeric field type. There are different types of numeric field including:

◇ integer (and in some packages long integer) fields, which will store numeric data where only whole numbers are required

◇ decimal formats, which will allow a large number of decimal places, or a specified restricted number, if this is set in the creation of the field properties when the database is set up

◇ currency values, which allow currency formatting to be added to the display. These include currency symbols and regional symbols. The database does not store these as this would use up valuable storage space.

◆ **Boolean**
A Boolean (sometimes called logical) field type is used where a Yes/No (or True/False, 0/1) response is required.

There are other field types as well, like memo, date and time. These may not be available in all packages.

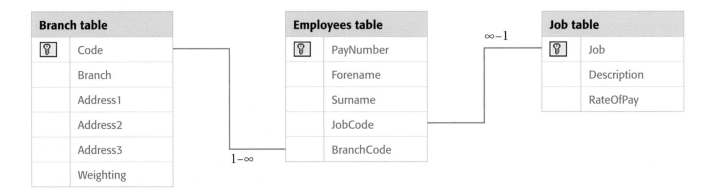

In order to select the correct field type you will have to look carefully at the data which will be stored. For the Employees table, the payroll number contains alpha characters as well as numeric characters so must be set as an alphanumeric field. In *Access* this has been called a 'text' field. Both **Forename** and **Surname** are text values so they should also be alphanumeric fields. The **JobCode** and **BranchCode** fields both contain numeric data, but none of the data within these fields is used for any calculation, so both fields will also be alphanumeric.

Employees table

Key	Field name	Field type
🔑	PayNumber	Alphanumeric
	Forename	Alphanumeric
	Surname	Alphanumeric
	JobCode	Alphanumeric
	BranchCode	Alphanumeric

The same process must be carried out for the Job table. The **Job** field does not have any calculations that could be performed upon it, so will be alphanumeric. It must also be the same field type as the **JobCode** field in the Employees table. This will make sure that the relationship will work. The **Description** will contain a description of the job in words, like 'Mechanic' or 'Sales adviser' so this field will be alphanumeric. The **RateOfPay** will be a currency value in Indian Rupees, so this field will be designed as a currency field type. For some packages you will need to set it as a numeric field. You will then choose the currency from the different types of numeric field.

Job table

Key	Field name	Field type
🔑	Job	Alphanumeric
	Description	Alphanumeric
	RateOfPay	Numeric : Currency

For the Branch table, the **Code** field will not require calculations, so will be designed as alphanumeric (which also matches the **BranchCode** field in the Employees table). The **Branch** name and address fields all contain text data, so will be alphanumeric fields. The weighting will be numeric and contain values between 0 and 2 which are set to a maximum of two decimal places.

This will be designed as a numeric field. You will then choose decimal from the different types of numeric field and set it to two decimal places.

Hint Only use a numeric field type if the data may be used for a calculation.

Branch table

Key	Field name	Field type
🔑	Code	Alphanumeric
	Branch	Alphanumeric
	Address1	Alphanumeric
	Address2	Alphanumeric
	Address3	Alphanumeric
	Weighting	Numeric : Decimal 2 decimal places

What field length should be used for each field?

Access uses a 'text' field type to hold alphanumeric data. In *Access*, only text fields require their lengths to be set. The field will be set with the shortest possible length, so that valuable storage capacity is not wasted. The most efficient method of calculating the length of any field is to look at the data, find the longest data item and count the number of characters. This count must include spaces. Note down the field lengths that you will require for each field. Some field lengths can be obtained from the information given, for example in Task **11.1** the **PayNumber** needs to be set to six characters in length, as you are told in the task that the payroll number 'is unique to them and has two letters followed by four digits'. If the data for the **JobDescription** field is analysed for this company and the longest data item is 'Systems Analyst and Programmer', the field length would need to be set to 30 characters. This was found by counting all the characters (including the spaces).

Which validation rules will help reduce data entry errors?

Look at each field and see if there are validation rules that could be applied to reduce data entry errors. These validation rules could include a range check, which checks that data fits within a specified range. A good example of this will be the weighting field in the branch table. The weighting must be between 0 and 2 (but cannot be equal to either of these values) so a rule could be applied to this field such that $0 < weighting < 2$. A length check may be used to make sure that a field has the correct number of characters, for example the **PayNumber** field in the Employees table must be two letters, followed by four digits. This could be done by setting a validation rule to check that six characters only are entered and that the first character is M or C. The rule for this will be 'Like "M?????"' or 'Like "C?????"'. In order to restrict the last four characters to numbers an input mask can be used; this will be "LL0000". See Section **11.3** for further details. Some fields like **Forename** and **Surname** cannot be validated as there are too many possible names.

When you have the answers to these questions, you can start to create the database structure.

Examples of validation rules include:

Rule	Allows
<>0	Not zero
>3 and <9	Numbers between 4 and 8 inclusive
<#1/1/2009#	Dates before 2009
>#31/12/2007# and <#1/1/2009#	Dates in the year 2008

Examples of input mask characters include:

0	Must enter a digit
9	May enter a digit or space
L	Must enter a letter
?	May enter a letter
A	Must enter a letter or digit
a	May enter a letter or digit
&	Must enter any character or a space
C	May enter any character or a space

Activity 11.1

Design a database structure

The Cubanacan Tourist Organisation in Cuba is designing a new database to store information on its hotels and employees (both past and present). For each hotel, it needs to hold information on the hotel's reference number (which is unique to it, is eight characters long and starts with CU followed by six numbers), the hotel name, the resort name, the distance from the nearest airport in whole kilometres, the telephone number and basic double room cost. For each employee, it needs to hold information on the employee's name, their employee number (which is a six-digit number), the reference number of the hotel that they work in, their job description and whether they are currently employed there.

Design a database structure to solve this problem.

T Teacher's note

This activity is suitable for peer marking and for paired, group or class discussion.

11.3 Creating a database structure
Create a new database

Task 11.2

Create the database for the structure that you designed for the South India Motor Company in Task **11.1**.

1 Select the File menu, then New.
2 Select Blank Database from the New File window pane.
3 Enter a filename like SIMC (short for South India Motor Company), then click on [Create].

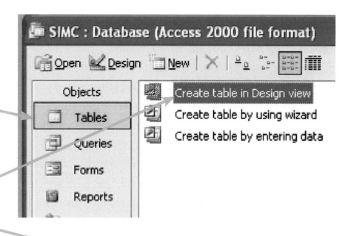

Create the Employees table

4 Select Tables from the available options (this may appear as a list or as a tab depending on the version of *Access* being used).

5 Double click the left mouse button on the option to Create table in Design view.

6 Type the field names in the field name column.

7 Select the data types from the drop-down list.

> **Hint**
>
> In *Access* use a 'text' field type for alphanumeric data.

8 Highlight the PayNumber field by putting the mouse pointer over it and clicking on it using the left mouse button.

9 Add the primary key to this field by clicking on the 🔑 symbol on the toolbar. This should add the primary key symbol to the left of the PayNumber field name.

10 Add the field sizes to all text fields by selecting each field in turn and editing the field size in the Field Properties box. In this case the field size has been changed from the default 50 characters to 6 characters.

11 Enter the Input Mask. In this case the input mask has been set to restrict data entry to two alphanumeric characters followed by four numeric digits.

12 Enter the Validation Rule. This is the rule that the package will use to stop some data entry errors. In this case the rule will only allow M or C as the first character of this field.

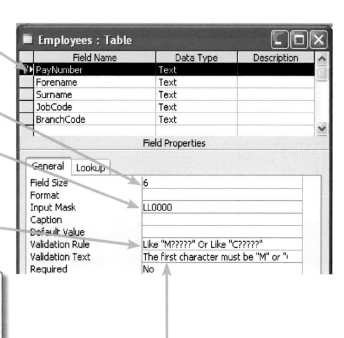

> **Hint**
>
> Here are some quick tips for setting other field types in *Access*:
> - To set a percentage value select a Currency data type, then in the Format section select Percent.
> - To store a date or time, select a Date/Time data type, then select the Format.
> - For a Boolean or logical field type select a Yes/No data type, then Format to choose from Yes/No, True/False or On/Off.

13 Enter the Validation Text. This text is the error message that is given to the user of the system, if data is entered that does not meet the validation rule.

14 Save the table as 'Employees'.

Create the Branch table

Repeat Steps 4 to 14 for the Branch table.

A brief description of each field can be entered into the **Description** area. This will help the user of the database with data entry. Give the user helpful instructions telling them what is required in this field. This is not used by the database to check the data. Instead, it gives the user a little help when using the form to enter data. An example for the **Code** field is: 'Enter the branch code for this branch of the company. This will be a numeric value between 1 and 999.'

> **Hint**
> For Integer field types in *Access*, use Integer for a whole number between 0 and 255 and Long Integer if a larger whole number is required.

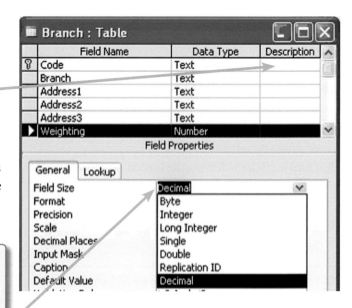

For numeric fields, the **Field Size** box is used to display the type of numeric field. This is selected from the drop-down list. The number of decimal places can be set using the **Decimal Places** section of the table. In this case, set the **Weighting** field to 2 decimal places. Add the validation rule and text as shown.

Create the Job table

Create the Job table using the design for the database structure Steps 4 to 14 above. The completed Job table should look similar to this.

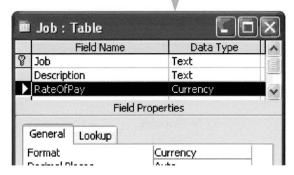

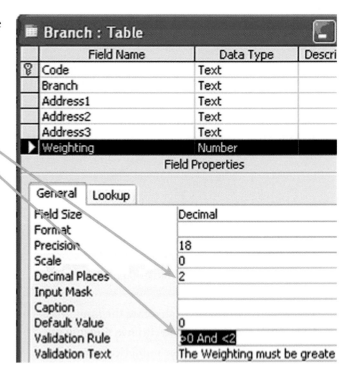

Now that all three tables are complete, the relationships between the tables can be built.

Create a relationship

1 Select the Tools menu, then **Relationships…**. This will open the **Relationships** window in *Access*. All of the tables that have been created are visible in the Show Table window.

2 Select each table in turn and click on **Add** to add each table to the **Relationships** window. When all of the tables have been added, close the Show Table window.

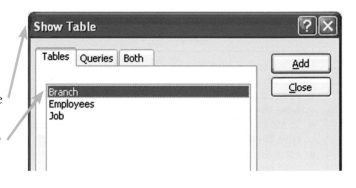

3 The first relationship needs to be created between the fields **Job.Job** and **Employees.JobCode**. This will be a one-to-many relationship. In the **Relationships** window click on the **Job** field in the Job table, then drag and drop this field onto the **JobCode** field in the Employees table.

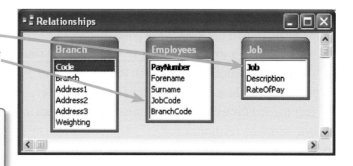

> **Hint**
>
> When table names and field names are referred to together they are often shortened. This is done using notation in the form of TableName.FieldName. Examples of this notation are:
> - Employees.JobCode, which means the field JobCode within the Employees table
> - Branch.Address1, which is the Address1 field within the Branch table.
>
> This notation is used in the rest of this chapter.

4 The **Edit Relationships** window will now appear. Check that the correct fields are present within this window before proceeding.

5 Click on Join Type.. to check that the correct type of relationship is going to be created. The relationship type can be seen in the **Relationship Type** box.

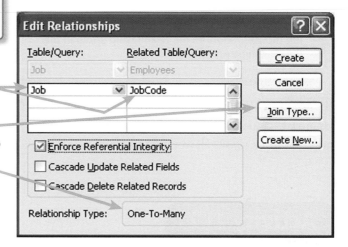

6 This will open the **Join Properties** window. Check carefully that the option that you choose is relevant to the task you are doing. In this task you need to have a list of different jobs and their codes held in the Job table. The employees must have a **JobCode** in the Employees table that matches this job. There may be some jobs in the job table that have no employees doing them. There can be no employees without a job. In order to keep this structure you must click on the radio button for option 2, then the OK button.

7 Check that the **Relationship Type** is showing one-to-many, and then click on Create to create the relationship. The relationship that you have just created can now be seen as the arrow in the Relationships window.

8 The second relationship necessary for this database needs to be created between the fields **Employees. BranchCode** and **Branch.Code**. This will again be a one-to-many relationship. Drag and drop the **BranchCode** field in the Employees table onto the **Code** field in the Branch table. Click on Join Type.. to check the relationship in the **Join Properties** window.

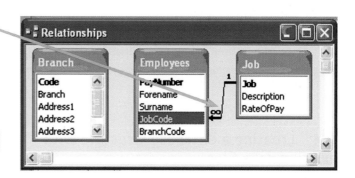

9 In this task you need to have a list of branches and their codes held in the Branch table. Each employee must be attached to a branch by having a **BranchCode** in the Employees table. There can be no employees without a branch. In order to keep this structure you must again click on the radio button for option 2, then the [OK] button. Check that the **Relationship Type** is showing that this is a one-to-many relationship.

10 Click on [Create] to create the relationship. The relationship that you have just created can also be seen in the **Relationships** window.

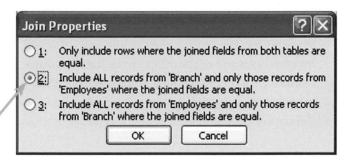

> **Hint**
>
> To edit an existing relationship, double click the left mouse button on the relationship arrow in the Relationships window.

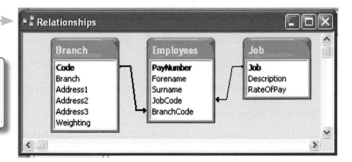

The structure for this database has been created and data can now be added to test that the structure, validation rules and input masks all work as intended.

Activity 11.2

Create a database structure

In Activity **11.1** you designed a database structure for the Cubanacan Tourist Organisation in Cuba. Now create this structure in your database package.

(i) Collect evidence of all the tables showing all of the field types. You may use screenshots to help you. Make sure that the primary keys are clearly visible on your printout. Place your name and school/college name in the header of your page(s). Save and print this evidence.

(ii) Collect evidence of all the validation rules and input masks used in the creation of tables. You may use screenshots to help you. Place your name and school/college name in the header of your page(s). Save and print this evidence.

(iii) Prepare a relationship diagram showing the relationships between these tables. Make sure that the relationship types are clearly visible on your printouts. You may use screenshots to help you. Place your name and school/college name in the header of your relationship diagram. Save and print this diagram.

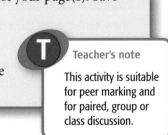

T Teacher's note

This activity is suitable for peer marking and for paired, group or class discussion.

11.4 Creating a database structure with existing data files

Sometimes you may have to set up a database structure from given data files. In this case the database structure will usually been designed for you.

Create a new database

1 Select the **File** menu, then **New**.

2 Select **Blank Database**.

3 Enter a filename like HC (the name of the garage in Task **11.3** opposite), then click on [Create].

Task 11.3

You work for a small garage called HC, selling used cars. You have designed and are going to test a small database to record the cars in stock and customers' details when they buy a car. Using a suitable software package, create a new database. Import the files CARS.CSV and CUSTOMER.CSV from the CD. You will need to use the following information to create the tables:

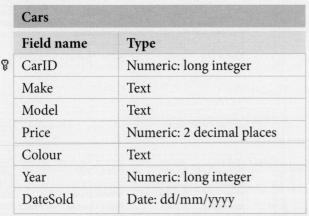

Cars	
Field name	**Type**
🔑 CarID	Numeric: long integer
Make	Text
Model	Text
Price	Numeric: 2 decimal places
Colour	Text
Year	Numeric: long integer
DateSold	Date: dd/mm/yyyy

Customer	
Field name	**Type**
🔑 CarID	Numeric: integer
Forename	Text
Surname	Text
Address1	Text
Address2	Text
Postcode	Text

🔑 denotes primary key

Print evidence of the tables showing all of the field types. Make sure that the primary keys are clearly visible on your printout. Save and print this diagram. Establish a one-to-one relationship between the CARS.CarID and CUSTOMER.CarID fields.

Prepare a relationship diagram showing the relationship between these tables. Make sure that the relationship type is clearly visible on your printout. Save and print this diagram.

Create the Cars table

4 Select the File menu, then Get External Data, then Import….

5 Find the file that you are going to import, in this case CARS.CSV.

6 If the file is not visible, check that you are looking for the right file type. You may need to change the file type to Text Files before the file name that you are looking for is visible.

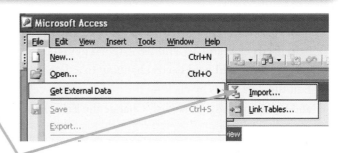

> **Hint**
> Files saved as comma separated variable files (in .csv format) are text files.

7 Select CARS, then click on **Import**.

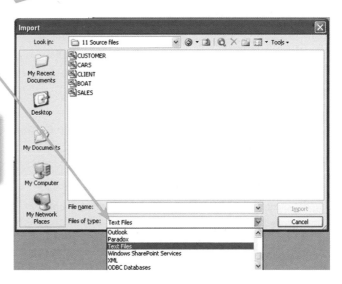

8 The **Import Text Wizard** helps you with the importing of the data file. The majority of file types (including .csv and .txt formats) will need a **Delimited** format (i.e. fields separated by characters such as commas or tabs). The wizard should detect this and suggest that you select this file format. Then click on Next > .

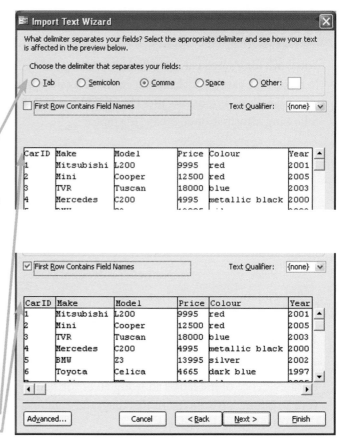

9 Choose the type of delimiter that will separate the fields. This will depend upon the regional settings of your software. This may be tabs, commas, semicolons or other characters. Also, if you are importing from some formats of .txt files you may need to select the type of text qualifier (usually speech marks) used in the data file.

10 Examine the first row of the sample data shown in the **Import Text Wizard** window. Decide whether this row contains the field names that you require or contains the first row of data. If the first row contains the field names click on the **First Row Contains Field Names** tick box. As you tick this box the first row changes from this ————— to this. ———————

11 Click on Advanced... . The **Import Specification** window will appear.

12 Check that all the field names and data types match those specified in the design. In this case the **Price** and **DateSold** fields are not correct. They do not match the field types specified in the task. The **Price** field needs changing to a numeric (currency) field and the **DateSold** field needs changing to a date field.

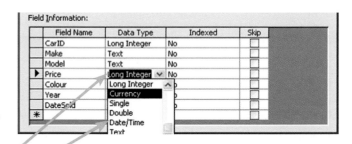

13 Edit the data types by clicking the mouse on the cell and using the drop-down list. Change the **Price** to a currency data type.

14 Change the **DateSold** field to a Date/Time data type using the drop-down list.

15 The format of the date can be set here, as can other structural formats like regional settings for decimals.

16 Click on OK , then Next > .

17 As you are creating a new table rather than appending an existing table, click on the radio button for **In a** New Table then Next > .

18 Use the next window of the wizard if you wish to omit fields from the importing process. If this is the case highlight the field and then select **Do not import field (Skip)**.

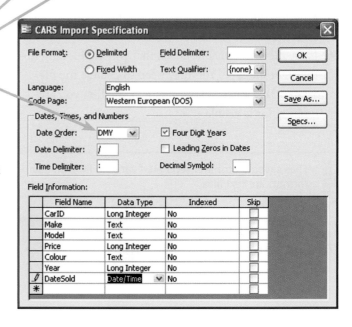

19 As this task requires the CarID to be the key field, this field needs to be the indexed field (used by *Access* to internally organise data), but duplicate entries should not be allowed for this field. To ensure this, select the CarID field, then the Yes (No Duplicates) option from the Indexed: box so that each car will have a unique ID. When you have selected these, click on Next >.

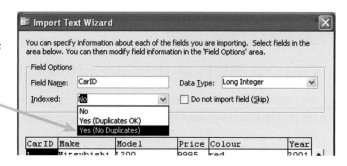

20 Check that the correct field is set as the index field. In this case it will be the CarID field as this is the primary key field identified in the task. To do this, click on the **Choose my own primary key** radio button, then choose the CarID field from the drop-down list. When you have finished these choices, click on Next >.

21 When asked for the table name for the **Import to Table:** enter CARS (it may already appear in the text box for you), then click on **Finish.**

Your first table is now imported. If there are any errors during the import these will appear in a separate table with a filename indicating that there were import errors. If you have selected all of the correct data types for each field this is unlikely to occur.

Create the Customer table

Repeat Steps 4 to 21 to create the Customer table. Ensure that the CarID field is set as the primary key field. Before creating the relationship between the tables, select the **View** menu, then **Design View** to go into the design view of each table and check that all of the field types are correct. Check that the CARS.Price field has the correct number of decimal places and is set to the correct type of currency for your regional settings.

Create the relationship

To create the relationship between the CARS and CUSTOMER tables, you can assume that each customer only buys one car. That means that once a car has been sold the customer details are added to the CUSTOMER table and the date sold is added to the CARS table. By creating a one-to-one relationship that links the tables, data can be drawn from both tables at the same time to be used within a query. This can also help you with the production of mail-merged letters or other automation (see Chapters **15** and **16**). Create the relationship between the two tables, as outlined earlier in this chapter. The finished relationship should look like this.

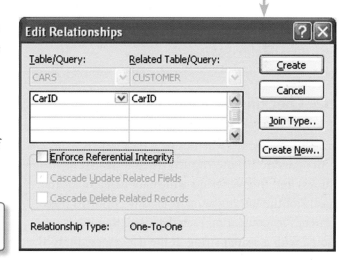

Create a database structure with existing files

You work for a firm called Jimmy Lee that sells small pleasure boats. You have designed and are going to test a small database to record the boats in stock and those sold to clients. You need to record a client's details when they buy a boat.

(i) Using a suitable software package, create a new database. Import the files BOAT.CSV and CLIENT.CSV from the CD. You will need to use the following information to create the tables:

Boat	
Field name	**Type**
🔑 BoatID	Numeric: long integer
Make	Text
Type	Text
Price	Numeric: 2 decimal places
Length	Numeric: integer
Year	Numeric: long integer
Sold	Boolean

Client	
Field name	**Type**
🔑 BoatID	Numeric: long integer
Forename	Text
Surname	Text
Telephone	Text
Email	Text

🔑 denotes primary key

(ii) Add validation to ensure that Boat.Type field only allows 'Yacht', 'Power' or 'Jet Ski' to be entered.

(iii) Add an input mask to Client.Telephone to ensure that the telephone number is stored as five digits, a space then six digits.

(iv) Print evidence of the tables, showing all of the field types. Make sure that the validation rule for Boat.Type and the primary keys are clearly visible on your printouts. Establish a one-to-one relationship between the Boat.BoatID and Client.BoatID fields.

(v) Prepare a relationship diagram showing the relationship between these tables. Make sure that the relationship type is clearly visible on your printout. Save and print this diagram.

T Teacher's note

This activity is suitable for peer marking and for paired, group or class discussion.

11.5 Checking data entry

It is vital that you understand the importance of accurate data entry when using a database. A database is designed to be interrogated (used to search for things) and to give results which are based upon the results of the interrogation. It usually performs these searches by comparing each data item that it has stored with a search string. If the data entered into the database or the search string contains an error (e.g. there is a spelling mistake), then the interrogation will not find that data item and the search would give incorrect results. Data entered into a database is usually checked using processes called validation and verification.

Validation

Validation is a process where the software checks that the data entered into it is *reasonable*. This does *not* mean that the data entered is the correct data. Validation checks include the following:

◆ **Range check**: checks that the data is within a given range. For example, in Activity **11.3**, if the company only sold boats made after the year 1989, a range check could ensure that the value in the Year field was between 1990 and the present day.

◆ **Look-up check**: makes sure that the data matches one of a limited number of valid entries. For example, the type of boat may be Yacht, Power or Jet Ski. When there are a large number of valid entries to check against, this can be done using a data file. This is known as a file look-up check. An example of this could be used for the Make field in Activity **11.3**, if there was a table which held all the valid makes of boat sold by the company. As new data is entered it would be checked to ensure it matched an entry within this data file.

◆ **Format check**: ensures that the data matches a pre-determined pattern of letters and/or numbers. For example, the Telephone field in Activity **11.3** could have a format check to ensure that there are five numbers followed by a space then six more numbers. Some database packages use an input mask to perform this function.

◆ **Length check**: ensures that the data is a reasonable length. For example, the Forename field in Activity **11.3** could have between 2 and 25 letters.

◆ **Type check**: ensures that the data is of a particular data type. For example, only numbers should be entered in the Price field in Activity **11.3**. This is not needed in many modern databases, as the software performs the type check for you.

You have already seen earlier in this chapter how validation routines can be added to fields within the database to help reduce the number of data entry errors.

Verification

Verification is a process used to check that the data has been entered accurately, is consistent and has not been corrupted. There are two types of verification. One type is used to check the integrity of data as it is passed between one part of a computer system and another, or between two computer systems. This looks for errors in the transmission of data. The other is used to check that data has been entered accurately into a computer system. This type of verification is relevant to data entry in databases. Verification of data includes the following:

◆ **Double entry verification**: data is entered twice, usually by different users, and the entries are compared by the system. If the two entries are identical the data is accepted; if the two entries are different an error is flagged and the incorrect entry is corrected by the user.

◆ **Visual verification**: data is entered and the original data is compared to the data entered into the system; for example, by comparing the data on the data capture form with a printout of the database, or with the entered data on the screen.

 Hint
It is very easy to drop a large number of marks on practical database questions by failing to check and correct data entry errors.

Activity 11.4

Add data to an existing file and verify data entry

(i) Make a copy of the database that you used in Activity **11.3** in *Windows Explorer*. Rename this file for use with this activity.

(ii) Add this data to the Boat table within this database.

BoatID	Make	Type	Price	Length	Year	Sold
51	Orkney Orkadian 20	Power	16995	19	2004	No
52	Matelot	Power	6995	20	1982	No
53	Hardy Fishing 24	Power	39950	24	2002	No
54	Seahog Sealord Fast Fisher	Power	6350	17	1985	No

(iii) Print out the table as a report and verify that the data you have entered is 100% accurate.

(iv) The boat with the ID number 10 has just been sold. Change the Sold value for this boat and add the following customer details to the Client table:

BoatID	Forename	Surname	Telephone	Email
10	Kimji	Damji	09909 909090	bigKD@website.com

(v) View this record on the screen and verify that the data you have entered is 100% accurate.

(vi) Save your new database and print copies of both of the amended tables.

11.6 Performing searches

At this level you are required to perform searches on multiple criteria and produce high-quality output to certain specifications. Performing searches in *Access* is carried out using queries and the high-quality output is done using reports. You are going to use the database that you saved in Activity **11.4** to perform Task **11.4**.

Task 11.4

Use the database you saved in Activity **11.4**.
(i)   Find all the yachts with a length of between 30 and 40 feet that were made during or after the year 1995 by Bavaria. Print out the results of this search.
(ii) Find and print the details of only the boats that have been sold and the clients who bought them.

Create a new query using the wizard
Task 11.4(i)

1 Open the database that you saved in Activity **11.4**.
2 Select **Queries** in the **Objects** box and then **Create query by using wizard** from the options.

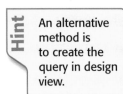

> **Hint**
> An alternative method is to create the query in design view.

3 Select the Boat table as the source of data.
4 Select all the fields (using the 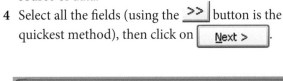 button is the quickest method), then click on **Next >** .

5 Click on the **Detail** radio button, then **Next >** .
6 Type in the name for the query, click on the **Modify the query design** radio button, then click on **Finish** .
7 Check that you are in **Design View**. To select the yachts, enter ' "Yacht" ' in the **Criteria:** line for the **Type** field.

> **Hint**
> Using the and buttons allows you to switch between the Design View and Datasheet View of a query at any time. This allows you to check that each stage of a query gives the correct results.

8 To select the length between 30 and 40 feet, enter '>30 AND <40' in the **Criteria:** line for the **Length** field.
9 To select all the boats made in or after 1995, enter '>=1995' in the **Criteria:** line for the **Year** field.

> **Hint**
> An alternative for Step 9 would be to use >1994 in the Criteria: line for the Year field.

10 To select the boats made by Bavaria, you have to use a wildcard search. This means searching for part of a string within a field. Within queries in *Access* the * is used to show a wildcard, so enter 'Like "*Bavaria*" ' in the **Criteria:** line for the **Make** field. This will search for the word Bavaria anywhere within this field. If the search string was entered as *2 it would locate any data item with 2 at the end; for example it would find the records for 'Bavaria 32', 'Contessa 32' etc., but would not find a record like 'Bavaria BMB 29' as the 2 is not at the end of the string. Likewise, if the search string Sea* was entered; all the boats with 'Sea' at the start would be located like 'Searay 245 Weekender' and 'Seadoo RX DI'. The entries for all of these stages should look like this.

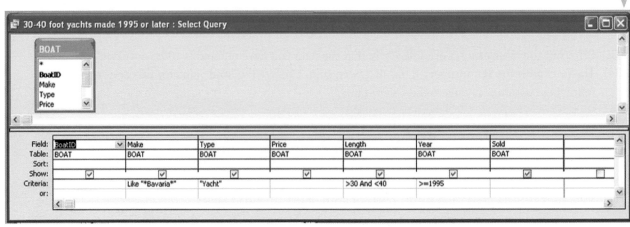

11 Save the query and use the Datasheet View button to view the selected data. Check that the results match the criteria that were given to you in the task. The results should look similar to this.

30-40 foot yachts made in 1995 or later						
Boat ID	Make	Type	Price	Length	Year	Sold
13	Bavaria 350 Sportline	Yacht	£82,500.00	36	2004	No
31	Bavaria 32	Yacht	£49,950.00	34	2006	No
43	Bavaria 32	Yacht	£52,125.00	34	2006	No
45	Bavaria 31	Yacht	£40,350.00	31	2004	No
47	Bavaria 350 Sportline	Yacht	£52,000.00	36	1997	No

Hint

To exclude data items from a search, use NOT followed by the item to be excluded, or use <> for is not equal to: for example, to find all the boats in the database which do not have Jet Ski as a type use <>"Jet Ski" in the Criteria: line for the Type field.

Task 11.4(ii)

This question requires you to extract data from both the Boat and the Client tables together.

1 Click on **Create a new query by using the wizard**.

2 Select the Boat table as the first source of data by selecting it from the drop-down menu under **Tables/Queries** and select all the fields, using the >> button.

3 Select the Client table as the second source of data and select from this the **Forename**, **Surname** and **Telephone** fields. Use the > button, then click on **Next >**.

4 Click on the **Detail** radio button, then **Next >**

5 Name the query. Click on the **Modify the query design** radio button, then click on **Finish**.

6 To select the sold items, enter "Yes" in the criteria line for the **Sold** field. This should look similar to this.

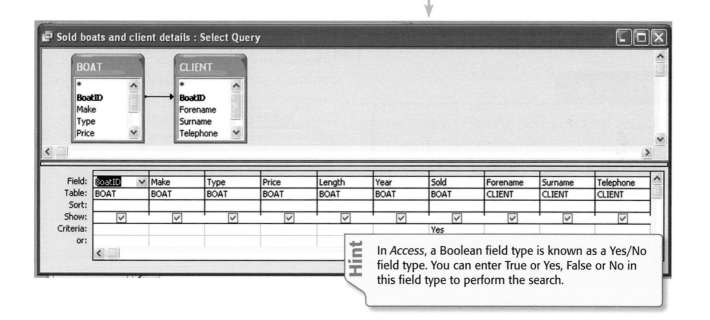

Hint

In *Access*, a Boolean field type is known as a Yes/No field type. You can enter True or Yes, False or No in this field type to perform the search.

7 Save the query and use the Datasheet button to view the selected data. Check that the results match the criteria that were given to you in the task. The results should look similar to this.

Sold boats and client details									
BoatID	Make	Type	Price	Length	Year	Sold	Forename	Surname	Telephone
2	Sealine 218	Power	£21,500.00	21	2005	Yes	Shahad	Sharreif	01223 553311
7	Kawasaki Zxi 1100	Jet Ski	£2,995.00		1996	Yes	Li	Kwong	01223 100001
10	Crusader 18	Power	£2,995.00	17	1995	Yes	Kimji	Damji	09909 909090
42	Contessa 32	Yacht	£27,000.00	32	1983	Yes	Jeremy	Smith	08888 888888

Performing searches

Use the database saved in Activity **11.4** and perform the following searches:

(i) Find and print the details of all the power boats under 25 feet long which cost between £10 000 and £30 000.

(ii) Find and print the details of all the yachts under 30 feet in length that were made after 1980.

(iii) Select from the database the details of those boats that have been sold. Print only the Forename, Surname, Make and Year for each of these boats.

11.7 Sorting data

The easiest method of sorting data using multiple criteria within *Access* is to sort while you are using the report wizard. You are going to use the database that you saved in Activity **11.4** to perform Task **11.5**.

Task 11.5

Using the database saved in Activity **11.4**, print the Boat table sorted into descending order of Type, then ascending order of Length.

Sort within the report wizard

1 Open the file if it is not already open.

2 Select the Reports tab, then Create report by using wizard.

> **Hint**
> If an examination question asks you to 'produce a report' it does not necessarily mean use *Access*. The word 'report' will be used in a generic sense to mean a document that is prepared ready to be presented to someone else.

3 From the drop-down menu under Tables/Queries, select the Boat table as the source of data.

4 Select all the fields required in the report then Next >.

5 If grouping is required, select this before clicking on Next >. Grouping is collecting all like data

together (like sorting), but rather than repeatedly printing the same data the repeated item is printed once as a header for the group. This is covered in Section **11.9**.

6 The sorting is assigned in this window.

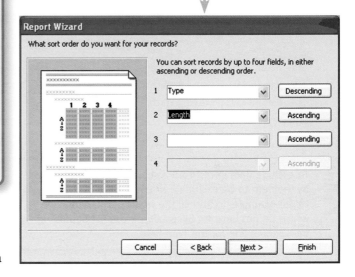

7 Select the fields for the sort as shown. The sort is prioritised so that the top row is the primary sort, in this case Type. Within each Type the data is sorted into Length order. The buttons for Descending and Ascending toggle between the two. When you have selected the correct sort, click on Next >.

8 Complete the final steps of the wizard to obtain the sorted report which will look similar to this (the report will be more than one page long).

Boat table sorted descending on Type then ascending on Length

Type	Length	BoatID	Make	Price	Year	Sold
Yacht	22	37	Minstral 680	£16,500.00	1984	☐
Yacht	24	15	Macwester Rowan Crown	£5,500.00	1985	☐
Yacht	25	23	Jaguar 25	£9,995.00	1984	☐
Yacht	26	19	Contessa 26	£12,500.00	1980	☐
Yacht	26	22	Contessa 26	£19,400.00	1992	☐
Yacht	26	25	Contessa 26	£12,950.00	1981	☐
Yacht	28	35	North Beach 24	£32,500.00	2006	☐
Yacht	30	33	Etap 30i	£44,950.00	2001	☐
Yacht	31	30	Ta Yang	£45,500.00	1995	☐
Yacht	31	14	Seeker 31	£21,950.00	1982	☐
Yacht	31	1	Ta Yang	£22,950.00	1982	☐
Yacht	31	45	Bavaria 31	£40,350.00	2004	☐
Yacht	32	40	Sadler 32	£24,950.00	1981	☐
Yacht	32	42	Contessa 32	£27,000.00	1983	☑

To change the sort order of an existing report, open the report in design view and select the [≡] button. This will open the Sorting and Grouping window for editing.

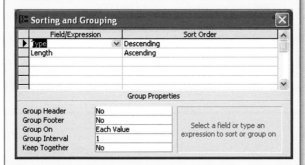

Activity 11.6

Sort data

Using the database saved in Activity **11.5**, print the details of all the power boats under 25 feet long which cost between £10 000 and £30 000, sorted into ascending order of Length then descending order of Year.

11.8 Performing calculations on numeric data

Calculations are used in *Access* instead of having additional fields, as an additional field would take up valuable storage space on your system. There are two main types of calculations that occur within *Access*:

♦ A calculated field is used to display the result of a calculation on each record selected within a query, rather than displaying stored data. The result is recalculated each time a value within the formula changes.

♦ A calculated control is used to display within a report the result of a calculation using the results of a query for the calculations. Some pre-defined functions are built into *Access* to calculate summaries of data, as a whole or within groups of data (see Section **11.9**). In this section, however, you will add a calculated control manually to a report.

A number of functions can be used in both calculated fields and calculated controls, including Sum, Avg, Count, Min, Max, StDev and Var.

Create a calculated field

Task 11.6

Using the results of the search saved in Task **11.4** (for all the yachts with a length of between 30 and 40 feet which were made during or after the year 1995 by Bavaria), add a new field which calculates the cost per foot of each boat. The formula that you will need is the Price divided by the Length. Save the result of this task.

1 In Design View, open the query that you saved in Task **11.4(i)**.

2 Move the cursor to an empty cell in the Field: row.

3 Enter the formula **PricePerFoot: [Price]/[Length]** into this cell. This names the calculated field PricePerFoot and stores within it the Price divided by the Length. Note that you must place square brackets around each field name.

You can use all the normal mathematical operators within a calculated query.

4 Examine the results in Datasheet View using the Datasheet [▥][▾] button. Although the calculation has been performed, the temporary PricePerFoot field does not use any of the formatting from the underlying table. Return to Design View using the [◩][▾] button to add this formatting.

5 Highlight the calculated field by clicking the mouse on it. Click the right mouse button over the field to select a drop-down menu. Choose Properties from the drop-down menu to open the Field Properties window.

6   Select the **Format** row in the window, and choose the appropriate format, in this case **Currency**.
7   Select the number of **Decimal Places** required for this field, in this case 2.
8   Close the window and again check the **Datasheet View** to ensure that you have obtained the expected results.

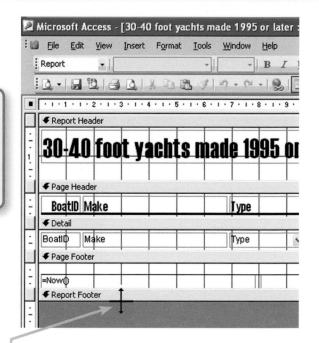

Activity 11.7

Perform calculations on numeric data

Using the results of the search saved in Activity **11.5** (power boats under 25 feet long between £10 000 and £30 000), add a new field which calculates the cost per foot of each boat. The formula that you will need is the price divided by the length. Ensure that this field has the most appropriate format. Save and print the results of this activity.

Create a calculated control

Task 11.7

Using the results of the search saved in Task **11.6** (for all the yachts with a length of between 30 and 40 feet which were made during or after the year 1995 by Bavaria), calculate the average price per foot for these boats.

1   Create a new report, using the **Report Wizard**, showing the results of the query amended in Task **11.6**. Make sure that all fields are visible (including the calculated field), and that you select landscape orientation so that it fits on the page without changing the design of the report.
2   View this report in **Design View**. You are going to place the calculated control which will calculate the average in the report footer, so that it will appear once at the end of the document. When you look, the report footer does not appear to exist, so place the cursor as shown, left mouse click and drag down about 1 centimetre to make the report footer visible.
3   The report should look similar to this.

4 Select the toolbox using the  button. The toolbox looks like this.

5 Use the ab| button to select a text box.

6 Place the cursor on the report footer, directly below the **PricePerFoot** control, click and hold the left mouse button, to drag a new text box the same size as the **PricePerFoot** control in the **Detail** section above. The new control should look similar to this.

7 Click the right mouse button on the control and select **Properties** from the drop-down menu.

8 You can change the name of the control from the *Access* defaults (in this case it is called Text23).

9 In the **Control Source** cell for the **Text Box**, add the formula or function which will perform the calculation. In this example you will enter **=Avg([PricePerFoot])**. Note the square brackets to show a field name and the round brackets as part of the function.

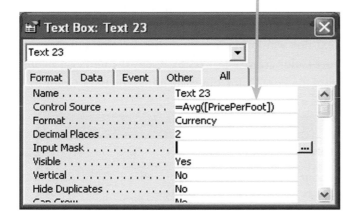

10 Set the format of the control, as you did in the previous section for calculated fields. Again, this does not take the formatting from the underlying table.

11 Add the required decimal places if necessary.

12 Left mouse click on the label (this is the box with Text23 in it). As you click here the properties

window changes to show the properties of this label. This label is called 'Label24'. A label is a control that gives information to the user; it is often used as a prompt for data entry on a form, or for telling a user what the information being displayed is in terms of a report.

13 Change the label **Caption** to the text that you wish to appear in the report. In this case change the label caption to Average price per foot.

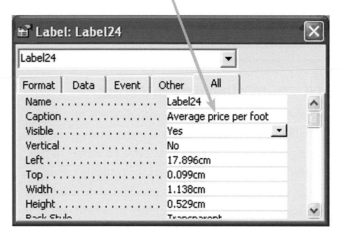

14 Make sure that the entire label caption is visible within the label in the report footer. If it is not, enlarge the label box using the handles at each corner, so that the text is fully visible. See Section **11.9** for further details. The completed controls should look similar to this.

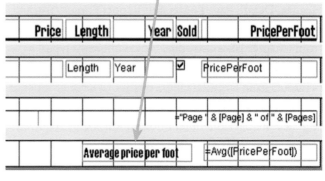

15 Select the Print Preview of the report by clicking on the 🔍▾ button.

16 Check that the calculated control is correct.

> **Hint**
> To print out evidence of formulae or functions used, produce a screenshot of the design view of the query or the calculated control, as has been done here.

Activity 11.8

Perform calculations on numeric data

Using the results of the search saved in Activity **11.7** (power boats under 25 feet long between £10 000 and £30 000), calculate the average price, the maximum price per foot and the minimum price per foot for these boats. Ensure that each of these calculations has the most appropriate format. Save and print the results of this activity.

11.9 Outputting data in *Access*

The ability to generate reports within *Access* means that there is a wide range of display features that can be used. Some of these have already been covered earlier in this chapter such as selecting formats for controls within the design view of the reports. It is good practice to ensure that, where possible, the correct format is held within the structure of the underlying table(s). You started to look at the structure of *Access* reports in Section **11.8** when you added a calculated control to a report. However, we did not cover the structures of these reports in depth. This section will give more detail to this area.

Access report structure

When you look at the design view of an *Access* report, you can see that it has five sections: **Report Header**, **Page Header**, **Detail**, **Page Footer** and **Report Footer**. You are already familiar with the function of headers and footers from Chapter **10**, so why does *Access* offer two types of header and footer? The answer to this is that many printouts from large data files consist of a large number of pages. Some information needs to appear on every page (e.g. field names) and other information is only required at the start or end of the entire document. The items that are only required at the start of the document are placed in the **Report Header**. Those required only once at the end of the document (like the calculated control in Section **11.8**) are placed in the **Report Footer**. Items that are needed on every page are placed in the **Page Header** or **Page Footer**. The **Detail** section of the report is used for the individual records within the report. Controls can be moved from one section of the report to another by dragging and dropping them. It is sensible to do this by moving the control and its label at the same time. These are selected

together by holding down the <Shift> key whilst selecting the second item. To select multiple items drag the cursor (which becomes a rectangular lasso) over all the items.

As you have seen in Section **11.8**, the features of each calculated control can be changed using the properties window. Many of these features will be required for the practical examinations, including changing many font features like the font style, enhancements, size and alignment. These are amended here.

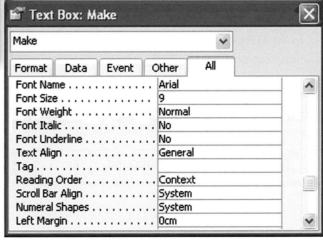

The properties window can also be used to hide objects. Setting the **Visible** property to **No** will make the control invisible. Another method of hiding objects is to change either the font colour or the background colour of the control so that they match each other. This is useful for using the same report template for printing an invoice and a delivery note. By changing the background colour of the controls for the financial sections of the invoice, the printout can be used for checking the delivery quantities and products for an order. Scroll down the **Text Box** window until both the **Back Color** and the **Fore Color** are visible, like this. Copy the numeric value from the **Fore Color** and paste it into the **Back Color** to replace the original colour.

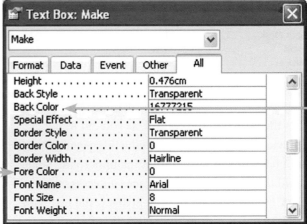

Ensure that all data and labels are visible when creating reports in *Access*. The report wizard will produce a framework for the report but it is essential that you look at the finished report and manually edit the controls so that every label and data is fully visible when printed. Each control has a series of drag handles that can be used to move or resize the control. The slightly larger handle in the top left corner is used to move the control around the report. The other seven handles are used to resize the control in various directions. When resizing a control like this it is useful to select both the label in the **Page Header** and the text box in the **Detail** row and manipulate them together. Do this by selecting both using the <Shift> key and holding this down whilst you stretch, shrink or move both controls at the same time, as has been done in this example.

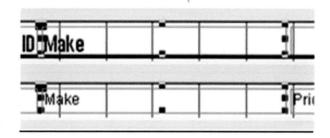

In practical examinations you will need to use these skills to produce a variety of outputs, for example to produce labels, personalised tickets etc. This is covered in more detail in Chapters **15** to **17**.

Produce alternative output formats, like labels and tickets

Task 11.7

Using the results that you saved in Activity **11.5**, produce labels to place on folders containing the details of each boat that has not yet been sold. Each label should look like this:

		BoatID	BoatID
Make	Make	**Length**	Length
Type	Power	**Price**	Price
Sold	☐	**Year**	Year

1 Perform a new query (as shown in Section **11.6**).
2 Select all the fields from the Boat table. In the **Boat. Sold** field, set the search criteria to False.
3 Create a new report using the report wizard and select a **Columnar Layout**.
4 Enter the **Design View** of the report and delete the report header and footer and all of the controls within them. To do this, select the View menu, followed by **Report Header/Footer**.
5 You are warned with a window like this.

Microsoft Access

⚠ **Deleting these sections will also delete all controls in them. You will not be able to undo this action.**

Do you want to delete these sections anyway?

Yes   No

The warning shows that this will delete the contents from both report header and footer with one action. To proceed, click on [Yes].

6 Follow a similar procedure using **View**, then **Page Header/Footer**, to delete these areas as well.

7 Manipulate the controls within the **Design view** of the report so that they are arranged like this.

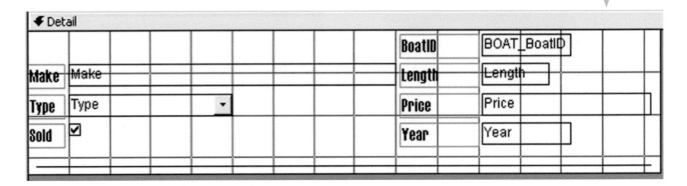

8 This will require some resizing and movement of the controls as well as changing the size of the controls using their handles. The first few records of the finished result will look like this.

		BOAT_BoatID	51
Make	Orkney Orkadian 20	Length	19
Type	Power	Price	£16,995.00
Sold	☐	Year	2004

		BOAT_BoatID	52
Make	Matelot	Length	20
Type	Power	Price	£6,995.00
Sold	☐	Year	1982

		BOAT_BoatID	53
Make	Hardy Fishing 24	Length	24
Type	Power	Price	£39,950.00
Sold	☐	Year	2002

		BOAT_BoatID	54
Make	Seahog Sealord Fast Fisher	Length	17
Type	Power	Price	£6,350.00
Sold	☐	Year	1985

Output the selected data

Using the results that you saved in Activity **11.5(iii)** to help you, produce tickets to a boat show to give to each client who has bought a boat. The ticket should look like this:

This ticket allows:

Forename	Surname

free entry to the boat show. They have recently bought this boat:

Year	Make

Produce a grouped report using the wizard

Access has the facility to group data. This is a process of collecting groups of similar data together for display purposes. There is a hierarchy of groups, with one field having higher priority than others, rather like the priorities when data is sorted by more than one field. Each group has the group header displayed only once, rather than viewing multiple occurrences of the same data item.

Using the database saved in Activity **11.4**, print the Boat table grouped by Year then by Length. Sort the data in descending order of Year and Length.

1 Create a new report using the report wizard.
2 Select all the fields from the Boat table, followed by Next >.
3 Select the fields to group by in priority order, with the highest priority first. Select the first field (in this case Year), then click on Next >. Repeat for the second field, and so on. The grouping window will look similar to this.
4 Step through the rest of the wizard, clicking on Next >, the sort order required for fields not included in the grouping, Next >, then the layout style for the grouped data. For this task, select Stepped and click on Next >.

5 Complete the rest of the report wizard as shown earlier in this section. The start of the resulting printout should look similar to this.

Task 11_8

Year	Length	BoatID	Make	Type	Price	Sold
1980						
	26					
		19	Contessa 26	Yacht	£12,500.00	☐
1981						
	26					
		25	Contessa 26	Yacht	£12,950.00	☐
	32					
		17	Tayana	Yacht	£13,000.00	☐
		40	Sadler 32	Yacht	£24,950.00	☐
1982						
	20					
		52	Matelot	Power	£6,995.00	☐

6 Grouping the data adds extra headers in the design view of the report. In this report, the wizard has added a **Year Header** and a **Length Header**. These headers and their controls are manipulated in the same way as any other report control (covered earlier in this section). This report is grouped correctly,

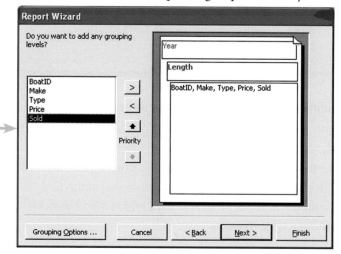

but the grouped data has not been sorted into descending order as specified in the task. Use the ![button] button to select the design view and click on ![button] for sorting and grouping. Select each field in turn before changing the sort order from **Ascending** to **Descending**. The start of the amended printout should look similar to this.

Task 11_8

Year	Length	BoatID	Make	Type	Price	Sold
2007						
		49	Seadoo RXP	Jet Ski	£7,500.00	☐
		8	Premium 3D	Jet Ski	£5,495.00	☐
		20	Seadoo RX DI	Jet Ski	£5,300.00	☐
		26	Seadoo RX DI	Jet Ski	£5,200.00	☐
	31					
		48	Bavaria BMB 29	Power	£85,000.00	☐
2006						
		5	Seadoo RX DI	Jet Ski	£4,699.00	☐
	21					
		44	Searay 215	Power	£24,995.00	☐

It is easy to identify specific groups within the printouts. For example, the group of two boats built in 1981 that are 32 feet in length can be clearly seen. Selecting groups of data is also very useful for producing summaries of the data within each group. You will look at summarising data in the next section.

Activity 11.10

Grouping data

Using the database saved in Activity **11.4**, print the Boat table grouped by **Type**, then **Length**, then **Year**. Sort the data in descending order of **Type**, ascending order of **Length** and descending order of **Year**.

Summarise data using the simple query wizard

You can use a simple query to make it easier to analyse the data. This is achieved by using simple functions to perform calculations on the data. A simple query can calculate a sum, average, minimum or maximum and count the number of records for a selected field or fields within a table or query.

Task 11.9

Using the database saved in Activity **11.4**, calculate the average price of a second-hand yacht for each year.

1 Select **Queries** from the available options.

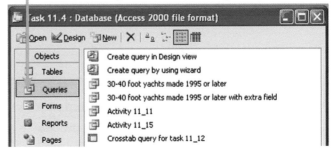

2 Click on ![New] to allow you to select the type of query that the wizard will perform.

3 Select the **Simple Query Wizard**, then click on ![OK].

> **Hint**
> Selecting **Create query by using wizard** is an alternative for Steps 2 and 3.

4 Select the table (or other query) that you wish to use for the search. In this example, the data will come from just the Boat table.

5 The fields required must be selected – in this case **Price** (for the calculation), **Type** (to select only the yachts) and **Year** – followed by ![Next >].

6 Click on the **Summary** radio button followed by ![Summary Options ...].

7 The Summary Options window is where the calculations are performed. Click on the tick box for the function that you require for each field. In this case you want the average price.

8 When you have selected all of the required options, click on ![OK], then ![Next >].

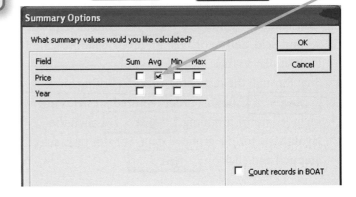

9 Name the query, ensure that the radio button for **Modify the query design** is chosen, then click on Einish .

10 Set the criteria line for the **Type** field to "Yacht" to select only the yachts. Remove the tick from the **Show** tick box for the **Type** field. This will ensure that the **Type** field does not appear in the displayed results even though it has been used to perform the search. Save the query and view the results using the Datasheet [icon] ▼ button. The resulting summary query should look similar to this.

Year	Avg Of Price
1980	£12,500.00
1981	£16,966.67
1982	£23,283.33
1983	£27,000.00
1984	£13,247.50
1985	£5,500.00
1991	£34,000.00
1992	£19,400.00
1995	£45,500.00
1997	£52,000.00
2001	£44,950.00
2004	£61,425.00
2006	£44,858.33

Activity 11.11

Summary queries

Using the database saved in Activity **11.4**, calculate the average age of a second-hand boat in each type.

Summarise data using crosstab queries

You use a crosstab query to make it easier to analyse the data in two dimensions, by restructuring and calculating the data. A crosstab query can calculate a sum, average, count or other type of total for data that is grouped by two types of information. This produces a two-dimensional grid which has one type of information down the left-hand side of a datasheet and another across the top, with summary data between.

Before starting to attempt any question using a crosstab query it is important to identify the row headings, column headings and data to be summarised (this is the data that the calculation will be performed upon).

Task 11.10

Using the database saved in Activity **11.4**, create a crosstab to count the number of boats of each type built in each year after 1996.

Before you start using the computer, it is often easier to sketch a planning diagram for the layout of the crosstab. In this task you are asked to produce a result similar to this:

> _Year_
> | | 1997 | 1998 | 1999 | 2000 | ... |
> _Type_ | Jet Ski | | | | | |
> | Power | Count the number of boats |
> | ... | | | | | |

> **Hint**
> A hand-drawn diagram similar to this is sometimes given in practical examination questions.

The row headings will be **Types** of boats and the column headings will be the **Years**. The calculation to be performed will be the counting of the boats. In this case, because you require the count summary it does not matter which field you select for the calculation. However, if a question requires a calculation on, or summary of, a particular field, that field must be selected.

Summarise data using the crosstab query wizard

1 Select **Queries** from the available options.

2 Click on [New] to allow you to select the type of query that the wizard will perform.

3 Select the **Crosstab Query Wizard** then OK .

4 Select the source from which to extract the fields for the crosstab query. In this case all of the data will be extracted from the Boat table, so this table should be selected followed by Next > .

5 Select the field to be used for the row headings (use the planning diagram that you sketched to help you). In this case it is **Type**. Then click on Next > .

6 Using the planning diagram, select the field for the column headings, in this case **Year**, then click on [**Next >**].

7 Select the field to be used for the calculation. In this case it does not matter which field is selected as you are going to count the number of items.

8 Select **Count** from the list of available functions. In this case you do not need a subtotal for each row, so the tick box **Yes, include row sums** can be left blank. Then click on [**Next >**].

9 Name the crosstab query, ensure that the radio button for **Modify the design** is chosen, then click on [**Finish**].

3 Set the **Criteria:** line for the **Year** field to >1996 to select only the boats built after 1996. Save the query and view the results using the Datasheet [▦][▾] button. The resulting crosstab query should look similar to this.

Type	1997	1998	2000	2001	2002	2003	2004	2005	2006	2007
Jet Ski								1	1	4
Power		2	1	1	2	3	5	4	4	1
Yacht	1			1			2		3	

Activity 11.12

Crosstab queries

Using the database saved in Activity **11.4** to help you, create a crosstab to summarise the average price for each length of boat, for each boat type, selecting only the boats with a length between 24 feet and 30 feet inclusive. Use the **Type** as the row labels and the **Length** as column headings. Save your database.

11.10 Exporting data into different packages

Sometimes it is necessary to export data into a different database or into a different format. This is so that it can be read by a different package (which may even be on an alternative hardware platform). Fortunately, this is very easy to do using *Access*. Before you start you must make sure that you know the format needed.

Task 11.11

Export the results of the summary data extracted in Task **11.9**. Export this data in a format that can be used by another software package to produce a graph.

Before you start the process you must decide which format you want to use to export the data. This will depend on the software packages that you have. Many people who have a standard installation of the *Microsoft Office Professional* package do not have the facilities to produce graphs and charts within *Access*. The solution to this is to export the data in a format that can be read by *Microsoft Excel*. The exact choice of file types for the export will depend on the export filters that have been installed on your machine when the software was installed. Changes to these settings are beyond the scope of this course, but you must be flexible enough to be able to export into a range of formats that could be used by the charting package. If you have selected *Excel* as your charting package, a suitable export format for the data would be an *Excel* file. There may be a number of these to choose from. Always select the latest version where possible, but if these are not installed, then saving the data as a text file would provide you with an alternative that can be opened in most software packages.

Export data into *Excel*

1 From the main database window select the data to be exported. This may be in the form of a table, query or even a report.

2 Select the **File** menu, then **Export...**.

3 For this task you need to export the summary data that you extracted in Task **11.9**. You will export this data into a format that you can use within our chosen

charting package. Scroll down the list until the latest version of *Excel* is found. Select this option and *Access* will offer you the same filename as the query. Change this if you wish to, before clicking on [Export]. The data has now been exported and can be seen in the location that you selected for the save. This data is now in a format that can be opened in *Excel*.

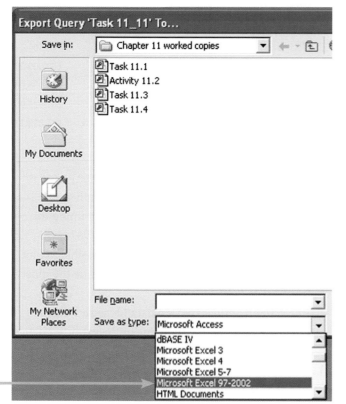

Activity 11.13

Exporting data

Export the results of the summary data extracted in Activity **11.11** in a format that can be used by another software package to produce a graph.

Publish a report from *Access* in *Microsoft Word*

Reports in *Access* can be exported using the **Publish to Word** [W] [▼] option from the **Database** toolbar. This exports the file to your storage area in rich text format (.rtf), then opens *Word*. It automatically imports the file into *Word* ready for you to use.

11.11   Producing graphs and charts in *Excel*

Selecting the most appropriate type of chart for any application is perhaps the most difficult area for many students. When you open any computer-based charting package there are a number of different options, many of which appear different but perform the same basic function. It is often better to use a limited number of chart types. The most useful are:

- ◆ **pie charts**: used to compare parts of a whole; these are often used to show comparisons using percentage values; pie charts are most effective if there are a small number of segments
- ◆ **bar charts**: used to emphasise the contrast between different quantities; these can be vertical (called 'column charts' in *Excel*) or horizontal; vertical bar charts should be used where time is to be plotted (this includes plotting months or comparing years)

- ◆ **line graphs**: used to show the relationship between one variable and another; they can be created using straight lines or curves (often to plot trends between the variables).

Other types of chart are used to compare two or more sets of data; these include comparative bar charts and comparative graphs with more than one type (e.g. a combination of bar chart and line graph).

Create a chart

Task 11.12

Use the data that you exported in Task **11.11** to help you:

(i) create a graph or chart to display the average price of second-hand yachts for each year

(ii) create a graph or chart comparing the average prices in 1981, 1991 and 2001.

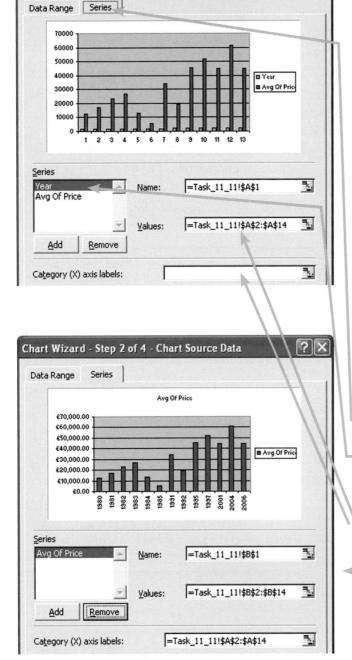

Task 11.12(i)

Year	Avg Of Price
1980	£12,500.00
1981	£16,966.67
1982	£23,283.33
1983	£27,000.00
1984	£13,247.50
1985	£5,500.00
1991	£34,000.00
1992	£19,400.00
1995	£45,500.00
1997	£52,000.00
2001	£44,950.00
2004	£61,425.00
2006	£44,858.33

1 Look at the data and decide which type of chart is most appropriate. For this task, you are comparing the average prices of yachts for sale each year.

Because you are not looking at parts of a whole object (the lack of percentage values is normally a good clue to this) it will not require a pie chart. You are plotting the years and comparing values (in this case the average price) so a bar chart would be suitable. A line graph would not be suitable as the category axis (containing the dates) does not fit a linear scale (1986, 1987, 1988, etc. are missing) and it would not be possible to plot trends. In conclusion, a bar chart would be the most appropriate type.

2 In *Excel*, open the exported data file with File, then Open…, selecting the filename of the exported data file from Task **11.11**, then click on Open .

3 Highlight all of the data before selecting the Chart Wizard . You have already decided that the bar chart would be the most suitable chart type, so select the vertical bar chart from the available options (called a column graph in *Excel*), then click on Next > .

4 The wizard attempts to create the chart, but in this case (as sometimes happens) it assumes that the dates (because they are numeric) are a second data series rather than the category axis labels. To adjust this select the Series tab.

5 Make sure that the Year series is highlighted in the Series box.

6 The values of the Year series should be used as the category axis labels. Highlight and copy the contents of the Values: box.

7 Paste this into the box for the Category (X) axis labels:.

8 Then click on Remove to remove this data series. The new source data window should now look like this.

9 Check that you have the correct data series visible and that the dates are fully visible as labels on the category axis, then click on Next >.

10 Add an appropriate title.

11 Add axis labels to the chart before clicking on Next >.

12 Place the chart as either a new chart, or alternatively as an object in an existing chart. Either option is suitable in this case. Select the required option and then click on Finish.

The completed chart should look similar to this.

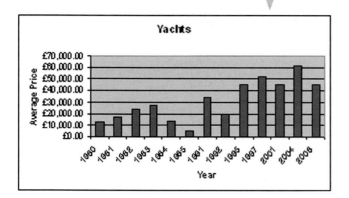

Task 11.12(ii)

1 Repeat Step 1 of Task **11.12(i)**. Again, a pie chart would not be suitable. A bar chart would be suitable. A line graph would also be suitable as the category axis (containing the dates) has regular intervals (1981, 1991 and 2001), so it will be possible to plot the trends. Either a bar chart or a line graph could be used, but as dates will be used for the category axis, you will again select a bar chart.

2 Open *Excel*.

3 Open the exported data file with **File**, then **Open…**, select the filename of the exported data file from Task **11.11**, then click on Open.

4 Data that cannot be highlighted in one block is known as non-contiguous data. To select this data to create the chart you must hold down the <Ctrl> key and select each cell in turn using the left mouse button. The spreadsheet with the data selected should look like this.

5 Select the chart wizard and the vertical bar chart from the available options, then click on Next >.

6 The wizard attempts to create the chart, but again, because the dates are numeric and the

data is non-contiguous, the data series and labels need redefining. In this case it is easier to delete all of the data series after selecting the **Series** tab. This is done by repeatedly clicking on Remove. Click on Add to add a new data series, then click on the button for the **Name:** box. To select the name for this series, click the cursor in cell B1 on the worksheet once. This will enter this cell address in the **Source Data – Name:** window. Pressing <Enter> will take you back to the **Source Data** window with the cell address in the **Name:** box.

7 To select the values for this series, move the cursor to the **Values:** box before clicking on the button. Hold down the <Ctrl> key and select cells B3, B8 and B12 before pressing the <Enter> key.

8 To select the category axis labels, move the cursor to the **Category (X) axis labels:** box before clicking on the button. Hold down the <Ctrl> key and select cells A3, A8 and A12 before pressing the <Enter> key. Click on Next >.

9 Enter appropriate titles and labels. The completed chart should look similar to this.

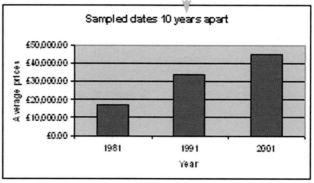

	A	B
1	Year	Avg Of Price
2	1980	£12,500.00
3	1981	£16,966.67
4	1982	£23,283.33
5	1983	£27,000.00
6	1984	£13,247.50
7	1985	£5,500.00
8	1991	£34,000.00
9	1992	£19,400.00
10	1995	£45,500.00
11	1997	£52,000.00
12	2001	£44,950.00
13	2004	£61,425.00
14	2006	£44,858.33

10 Click on [Next >] and then on [Finish].

11 Save the spreadsheet as you will use this again in the next section.

Hint Take great care when placing or manipulating (e.g. resizing) charts to ensure that all of the chart and all of the titles, labels and legend (if used) are fully visible.

Activity 11.14

Creating a chart

Using the data that you exported in Activity **11.13** to help you, create a graph or chart to display the average age of each type of boat in stock.

Add data to an existing graph or chart

It may be necessary for you to add a second data series, or to amend any of the settings to an existing chart.

Task 11.13

(i) Import the file SALES.CSV from the CD and create a chart to compare the value of the sales for the company.

(ii) Add a second data series to this chart to show the number of items sold, using the following data:

Month	Number of sales
January	136
February	75
March	277
April	158
May	290
June	949
July	1151
August	1024
September	286
October	78
November	531
December	261

(iii) Add a secondary axis for this data series and rescale this axis to have a minimum value of 50 and a maximum value of 1200.

(iv) Ensure all labels are fully visible.

Create a chart
Task 11.13(i)

1 Examine the data and decide which type of chart is most appropriate. For this task, you are comparing the sales figures from the boatyard for each month. Because you are not looking at parts of a whole object (percentage values are normally a good clue to this) it will not require a pie chart. You are plotting the months and comparing values (in this case the average of price) so a bar chart would be suitable. A line graph would also be suitable as the category axis (containing the dates) has regular intervals (each month with none omitted), and the chart will be showing sales trends. The conclusion, looking at each of these options, is that either a bar chart or a line graph would be appropriate. Either option could be used but, as sales trends will plotted, you will select a line graph.

2 Create the chart using the skills that you have already developed earlier in this chapter. The chart should look similar to this.

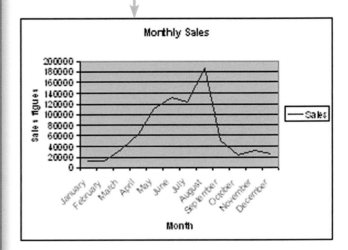

Add a second data series
Task 11.13(ii)

1 Before adding data to the chart, the data must first be added to the spreadsheet. Take care with the data entry – a significant number of marks are dropped in practical examinations through careless data entry and lack of careful verification of the data when it has been entered. Enter the name for the data series ('Number of sales') in cell C1 and the data values in cells C2 to C13.

2 In order to add a second data series you need to click the right mouse button on the existing chart, but not on any particular feature of the chart (e.g. an axis, a data series, etc.). This will display a small drop-down menu. If the whole chart has been selected the menu will look similar to this.

3 Select Source Data..., to return you to the Source Data window within the wizard.

4 Add a new data series using the skills that you have learnt earlier in this section. Use cell C1 for the name and cells C2 to C13 inclusive for the values.

Add and rescale the secondary axis
Task 11.13(iii)

1 If the legend is not present, use the same drop-down menu as in part (ii) to select the Chart Options....
Select the Legend tab, click on the required position for the menu and click on [OK].

2 You need to select the second data series on the chart by clicking on the line within the chart. When this is successful the plotted points can be seen.

3 Right mouse click on the new series but avoid clicking on one of the data points.

4 Choose Format Data Series... from the drop-down menu.

5 Select the Axis tab, then click on the radio button for Secondary axis, followed by [OK]. This will add the secondary axis to the chart.

6 In the question you are asked to rescale the secondary axis. To do this, you must select the secondary axis by right clicking on it, then selecting Format Axis... from the drop-down menu. The Format Axis window will appear.

Select the Scale tab, then add the new minimum value by entering 50 into the Minimum: box and the maximum value by entering 1200 into the Maximum: box, followed by [OK]. The chart should now look similar to this.

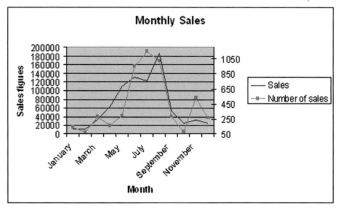

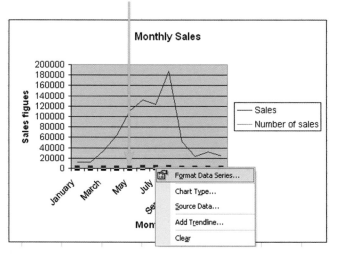

Manipulate a chart
Task 11.13(iv)

1 This chart still needs editing and improving before it is complete. The title needs changing to reflect the second data series. This is done by right mouse clicking on the chart, selecting **Chart Options…**, then the **Titles** tab, and amending the title.

2 Add the label for the second value axis whilst you are in this tab.

3 It may be that all of the labels for the months are no longer fully visible, as a result of the extended legend. If so, move the legend to a more suitable position using **Chart Options…**, selecting the **Legend** tab, and changing the **Placement**.

4 The sales figures on the primary axis are not formatted as currency values. To change this, right mouse click on the primary (left) axis, select **Format Axis…** from the drop-down menu, select the **Number** tab and click on the format that you require. The completed chart should now look similar to this.

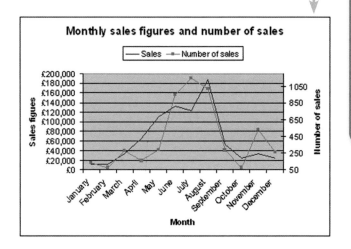

Activity 11.15

Adding data to an existing chart or graph

(i) Import the file SALES.CSV from the CD and create a chart to compare the sales figures.

(ii) Add a second data series to this chart using the following data:

Month	Website hits
January	1030
February	1974
March	1067
April	7389
May	6396
June	5840
July	8992
August	7136
September	2772
October	3005
November	6962
December	2385

(iii) Add a secondary axis for this data series and rescale this axis to have a minimum value of 1000 and a maximum value of 9000.

(iv) Ensure all labels are fully visible.

Integration

12.1 What is an integrated document, presentation or report?

In the examination you may be asked to create a document, presentation or report which contains text, images, data, charts, etc. If you are asked to create a document, select either a word processor or desktop publishing package (see Chapter **8** for more information on which of these packages to choose). A presentation would require a presentation authoring package.

A report in terms of the examination is 'a written document describing the findings of some individual or group'. In terms of the examination, the word 'report' is always used in this context, it does *not* mean a report created in *Microsoft Access*, although there are times when it might be appropriate to use this. Choose your software package carefully, using Chapter **8** to guide you.

This chapter covers selecting the data and placing it into a document or presentation.

12.2 Integrating data from several sources
Create an integrated document, presentation or report

Identify the type of data that you wish to place into your final document. In the examination you may be asked to produce evidence of your method (or the structure of the database that you have been asked to create or amend) or to produce extracts of the data. It is vital that you decide on whether you are collecting evidence of how you created or edited something, or are producing extracts of data. Each of these will require a different range of skills.

Produce evidence of your method

This will always require you to produce a screenshot of the computer or current window in order to prove how you have produced something. There are many excellent packages available that will produce screenshots (or screen capture), many of which are available as freeware. If you are already familiar with one of these packages using them may save time in the practical examination. Because each of these packages operates in a different way, they are beyond the scope of this book. Instead you can use the basic tools provided within the *Windows* environment. Sometimes in the practical examination you may be asked to show evidence both before and after you have changed something. In that case, produce screenshots before and after and include both in your final document.

Taking screenshots within *Windows*

1 To capture the current screen display showing everything except the mouse pointer, press the <Prt Scr> (or <Print Screen>) key on your keyboard at any time.

2 If you wish to show only the current window select <Alt> and <Prt Scr>. This takes the screen contents into the windows clipboard. If you want the entire screen or window, go to Step 4.

3 If you only need to use part of the screen, paste the screenshot into *Microsoft Paint*. Use the rectangular select tool to select the area that you wish to use. Select the **Edit** menu, then **Copy** to store this in the clipboard.

4 The screenshot can then be pasted into your document or presentation using the **Edit** menu and **Paste** (or <Ctrl> and V on the keyboard).

Produce evidence of the data in *Access*

You have already produced queries, reports and calculated controls in *Access* in Chapter **11**, but it is not always easy to produce the evidence of this for the practical examinations. Tables and queries can be copied and pasted into a document, but they do not always appear in the document as they are viewed on the screen. An example of this would be to copy and paste the Boat table from Task **11.4** into a document. In the database the **Sold** field appears as a tick box with a tick for yes, yet when this field is pasted into a document it is shown as either 'Yes' or 'No' and looks like a text field. The only clue to the field being Boolean is the right alignment of the data, rather than the usual left alignment that can be seen in the other text fields. In this case, if it was necessary to show the tick boxes then a screenshot would be needed.

Task 12.1

Print evidence of the report created for Task **11.8** in rich text format.

In examination questions you might need to show formatting, headers, footers, calculated controls or grouping from an *Access* report. If this is the case, create the report in *Access* as described in Chapter **11**. This can be printed from *Access* if it needs to be submitted in printed form. If this prepared report needs to be included in another document, or submitted electronically, the best method is to export the report in rich text format, which contains the text formatting from the report. However, this would not display the tick boxes that are shown here.

Task 11_8

Year	Length	BoatID	Make	Type	Price	Sold
2007						
		49	Seadoo RXP	Jet Ski	£7,500.00	☐
		8	Premium 3D	Jet Ski	£5,495.00	☐
		20	Seadoo RX DI	Jet Ski	£5,300.00	☐
		26	Seadoo RX DI	Jet Ski	£5,200.00	☐
	31					
		48	Bavaria BMB 29	Power	£85,000.00	☐
2006						

To display the contents of the **Sold** field you must change the display properties of this field in the original table.

1 Open the Boat table in **Design View**.

2 Select the **Sold** field.

3 Select the Lookup tab at the bottom left of the window.

4 Use the drop-down menu in the Display Control box to select Text Box.

5 Save the changes to this table.

6 Delete the original report (or rename it so that you know that this is an old version).

7 Recreate a new report using the report wizard. The report should look similar to this. Note that the tick boxes have been replaced by text boxes.

8 This can now be exported into rich text format by right mouse clicking on the report and selecting **Export…** as shown in Section **11.10**.

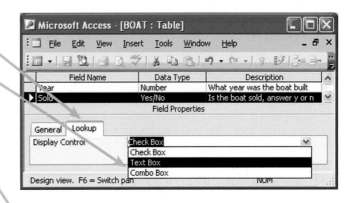

Task_11_8

Year	Length	BoatID	Make	Type	Price	Sold
2007						
		20	Seadoo RX DI	Jet Ski	£5,300.00	No
		49	Seadoo RXP	Jet Ski	£7,500.00	No
		8	Premium 3D	Jet Ski	£5,495.00	No
		26	Seadoo RX DI	Jet Ski	£5,200.00	No
	31					
		48	Baveria BMB 29	Power	£85,000.00	No
2006						

Activity 12.1

Submit evidence of a report created in *Access*

Print evidence of the report created for Activity **11.10** in rich text format.

12.3 Ensuring consistency of display

It is very easy to forget about the consistency of a document's display when you are importing objects into an integrated document. It is worth noting the corporate house styles before creating objects like graphs, charts, tables and database extracts. By doing this you can create these objects to match the style of the completed document or presentation. An example of this is to use the same font style for the title and labels when creating a graph or chart to insert into a final document. Every part of a finished document should look identical in terms of font style, line and paragraph spacing, paragraph settings, margin settings and headers and footers. Even where page orientation has been changed within a document, the new sections should still appear the same distance from each page margin. If you include tables or database extracts in the document these should have the same margin setting and font styles as the body text. For example, in a document with two lists, make sure that the formatting for the lists is identical (bullets, numbering or lettering) and that other formatting like line spacing before and after the list is consistent.

It can be time consuming to keep editing a document to make sure that it is consistent, but it is essential when presenting documents to managers or clients. In the business world the quality of your work reflects directly on you, your colleagues and the whole business. In the practical examination, if you are not very careful about this you are likely to lose a significant number of marks. This can be relevant in a question that is assessing your knowledge and understanding, if the question paper asks you to prepare a report, document or presentation on a topic; you are likely to be marked on both the subject content and on the quality of the document that you produce.

Repagination

In Chapter **10** you developed skills using breaks for pages, columns and sections. It is important that when inserting breaks into documents that you always check that you have:

◆ no widows or orphans (as shown in Section **10.13**)

◆ no lists are split over more than one page (this can include bulleted, numbered or lettered lists)

◆ no tables or charts are split over more than one column or page.

Good example:

Accuracy

How accurate is the information? How detailed is the information, does it have the depth required from an author with expertise? Is the website just superficial with little real substance? How much care has been used to set up the website? It is often easy to spot spelling and grammar errors if the text is copied and pasted into a word processor. If the website contains a number of errors it is unlikely to be genuine.

Sources

What sources are referred to? Take a look at the hyperlinks and printed sources that are referred to. These can provide further information, often supporting the author's arguments. You can also check the author's research to view how valid their conclusions are. The references are vital if the document is from an academic organisation, a full listing of reputable sources in this field are important in validating a document.

Currency

How up to date is the information? Find out when the page was set up or last modified. A document without that information is unlikely to be updated regularly. If the website has many links that do not work, it is unlikely to be a reliable source of information in terms of currency.

Poor example:

Accuracy

How accurate is the information? How detailed is the information, does it have the depth required from an author with expertise? Is the website just superficial with little real substance? How much care has been used to set up the website? It is often easy to spot spelling and grammar errors if the text is copied and pasted into a word processor. If the website contains a number of errors it is unlikely to be genuine.

Sources

What sources are referred to? Take a look at the hyperlinks and printed sources that are referred to. These can provide further information, often supporting the author's arguments. You can also check the author's research to view how valid their conclusions are. The references are vital if the document is from an academic organisation, a full listing of reputable sources in this field are important in validating a document.

Currency

How up to date is the information? Find out when the page was set up or last modified. A document without that information is unlikely to be updated regularly. If the website has many links that do not work, it is unlikely to be a reliable source of information in terms of currency.

Precision framing

Make sure that objects like tables and charts always fit precisely into the column or page margins, unless you are told in the question to do something different. Examiners are unlikely to give much tolerance if images or other objects invade the margin. Sometimes this tolerance can be as small as 1 or 2 millimetres.

Activity 12.2

Check consistency, pagination and precision framing

Open each activity that you completed in Chapter **10**. Check the consistency of presentation, the pagination and check that all objects placed within each document fit precisely in the margins. Save each completed document with a new version number.

13 Output data 1

You already know how to:

➤ print a document
➤ print a presentation.

In this chapter you will learn how to:

➤ print a draft copy of the final version of a document
➤ print e-mails with a file attachment
➤ print a table, query or report in a database
➤ print a database relationship diagram
➤ print slides, presenter notes and audience notes in a presentation
➤ print file structures
➤ print a graph or chart
➤ change chart colours to print in black and white
➤ change a presentation to print in black and white.

For this chapter you will need these source files from the accompanying CD:

➤ BOATSALE.XLS
➤ SALES2.XLS

13.1 Printing a draft copy or final version of a document

You have already developed many of the skills needed for this chapter. There is often no difference between a draft copy and a final copy of a document in terms of the way that it looks. In some cases draft documents may be produced to a lower quality than final copies, in order to save on expensive printer consumables. In the practical examinations there will be no need to change your printer settings or include watermarks on your documents, unless you are asked to do so in the question paper.

13.2 Printing e-mails with a file attachment

Open your e-mail browser or editor. Enter the address or addresses and the subject line and attach the file to the e-mail. The details of the file attachment should be visible within the window, along with the other items entered. The examiners will check very carefully that each of these items is present and correct. In this example the address, subject and attachment are all clearly visible.

If you need to send evidence of this as part of the practical examination, copy the screen using <Alt> and <Prt Scr>, before pasting this into a document.

As you can see from these diagrams, different e-mail editors each have a different appearance. You must examine your e-mail editor and make sure that the address or addresses, subject line, attachments and body of the message can be seen on the screen at the same time.

The two examples shown on the previous page and here are *Hotmail*, a web-based e-mail editor, and *Microsoft Office Outlook*. When you choose your e-mail editor, make sure that all of these elements can be seen.

13.3 Printing from *Microsoft Access*

You have already covered many of the skills required for this in Chapter **12**. Although the sections below show you how to produce printouts of each area, remember that screenshots can be one of the most effective forms of evidence, although documents containing a number of screenshots can soon become extremely large. This can give problems such as not having enough memory to work on the file; not having enough space to store the file; it taking a long time transfer the file when it is sent; and the file slowing down (or even crashing) a printer if it does not have enough memory installed.

Print a table or query

Open the table or query, and copy and paste the data into an evidence document. This document can be saved, transmitted or printed. A table or query can be printed directly from *Access* by right mouse clicking on the table name or query name and selecting **Print** from the drop-down menu. Printing from both of these produces the raw data with no formatting. If improved presentation, grouping or other features are required, then you need to create a report from the query and use one of the following methods.

Print a report

This can be completed in a similar way to tables and queries. The report can be opened and printed using **File**, then **Print…**, or printed by right mouse clicking on the report name and selecting the **Print** option from the drop-down menu. Reports can be exported for inclusion in an evidence document as outlined in Chapter **11**.

Print a database relationship diagram

Open the **Relationships** window from within *Access* using the **Tools** menu, **Relationships…**. The relationships that you have created will be visible as a line linking two fields, one from each table. To show the type of relationship, right mouse click on the line and select **Edit Relationship**. This opens the **Edit Relationships** window. Taking screenshots of this will show the examiner that you have selected the right join types from the correct fields. If there is more than one relationship in the database, you will need to screenshot each relationship separately.

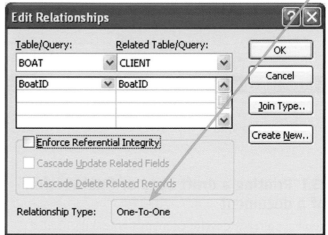

Hint

Do *not* use **File**, then **Print Relationships…**, as this only shows that the relationship exists. It will allow you to print the diagram, but this does not give details of the join types, which will be needed for the practical examinations.

13.4 Printing from *Microsoft PowerPoint*

You have already covered many of the skills required for this in Chapter **10**. Although the sections below will show you how to produce printouts of each area, remember that screenshots are often the most effective method of providing the examiner with evidence in the practical examinations. For all of the printing options from *PowerPoint* select the File menu, then Print….

Print slides

In the **Print what:** section, select **Slides**. This will print only the slide(s) content with no additional notes or space.

Print presenter notes

In the **Print what:** section, select **Notes Pages**. This will print the slide(s) content together with the presenter notes that you have inserted in the Notes section for each slide.

Print audience notes

In the **Print what:** section, select **Handouts**. This will give you several options to select from in the handouts section. Decide upon the format for your notes pages. Select **6 Slides per page:** if you wish to maximise the number of slides on a page that can be read easily, without the space for notes.

If you wish to give your audience the chance to write notes about your presentation, select **3 Slides per page:**. This will show three slides and give space alongside each one for note taking, like this.

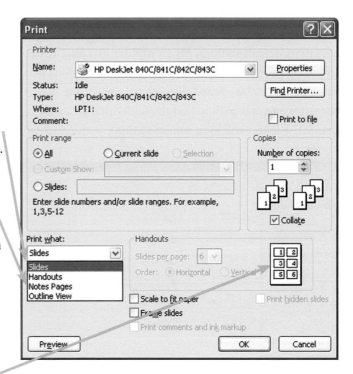

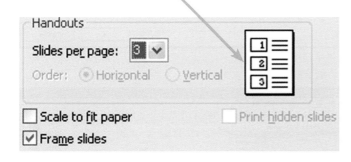

Using Pure Black and White settings can reduce printer consumable costs.

Change a presentation to black and white in *PowerPoint*

To change a presentation from colour into black and white, open an existing presentation. Select the View menu, then **Color/Grayscale**. There are two variations that may be used, both of which allow you to set objects like bitmaps, images, clipart and charts into greyscale. The **Grayscale** option shows features like text shadows, embossing, pattern fills and object shadows in greyscale, whereas the **Pure Black and White** option does not show shadows, embossing and pattern fills but does show object shadows as black. Select the required type from the list.

13.5 Printing file structures

The best place to examine and print file structures is using **My Computer** within the *Windows* environment. **My Computer** is more versatile than using an applications package because it automatically shows all file types, whereas an applications package like

Microsoft Word would only show text files or document files in its default settings. **My Computer** can usually be found on the **Start** menu, although in some versions of *Windows* it can be opened through a desktop icon. Select the drive and sub-path to find the folder that you wish to print. The folder will look similar to this.

Take a screenshot of the window using the <Alt> and <Prt Scr> keys. Paste this screenshot into your evidence document. If you need to show the file details, like the file type or date and time stamp, right mouse click on the background of the window. This will give you a drop-down menu like this.

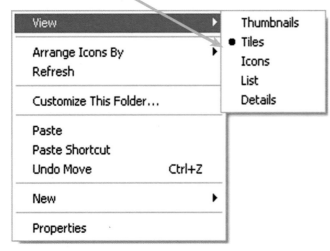

Select **View**, then **Details**. The window will now display all of the file details like this. ─────

This type of file evidence can also be used to show evidence of your file naming and file structure. The path for each of these folders is shown in the address bar.

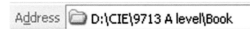

13.6 Printing a graph or chart from Microsoft Excel

To print any chart stored within an *Excel* spreadsheet click the left mouse button on the chart to select it, then select the **File** menu, then **Print…**. This will print the chart as shown on the page. If you have not placed your name, centre number and candidate number on the chart this is unlikely to gain you any marks in the practical examination. These details must be included. If you have not included these select **File**, then **Print Preview…**. Select the **Setup…** button at the top of the window, and within the **Page Setup** window select the **Header/Footer** tab. This will look like this.

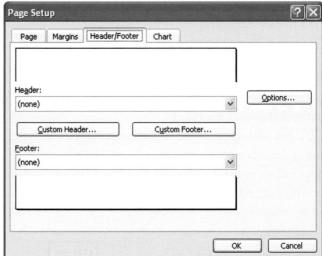

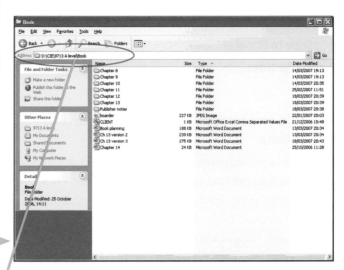

Hint

This is useful if you are required to produce evidence that you have made suitable backup files during a practical examination.

Click on [Custom Header...] or [Custom Footer...], then enter your name, centre number and candidate number in one of the three section boxes, and click on [OK]. Click on [OK] to close the Page Setup window, before clicking on [Print...] to print the chart.

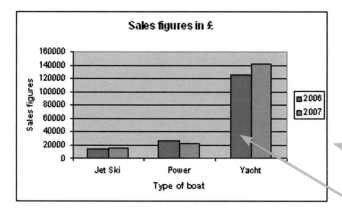

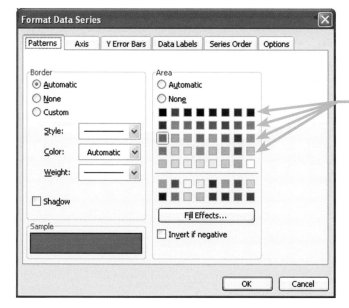

Print in black and white

Printing any document created in colour on a black-and-white printer can cause problems. This book has sections of coloured text designed to outline key elements, like keywords are annotated in red, instructions to follow are in blue and field names are in green. If a page containing these three colours was printed on a black-and-white printer each of the three colours would appear as a shade of grey. It would be impossible to identify which words were keywords, instructions or field names. The use of colour in images is equally important; some colours appear identical in greyscale, particularly colours like red and green. You must be able to change the colour settings within your documents, diagrams and charts to enable the different sections to be distinctive when they are printed in black and white.

Change chart colours in *Excel*

Task 13.1

Open the file BOATSALE.XLS on the CD. Change the chart colours so that each data series is distinctive when printed on a black-and-white printer.

1 Open the spreadsheet BOATSALE.XLS. The chart should look similar to this.
2 Select the data series that you wish to change by double clicking the left mouse button on the data series in the chart.
    In this case you have selected the 2006 sales figures. This opens the Format Data Series window.
3 Make sure that you are in the Patterns tab.
4 You can select from contrasting shades of greyscale, as shown here.
5 Or you can select from the range of fill effects by clicking on [Fill Effects...] to open the Fill Effects window. Select the Pattern tab.

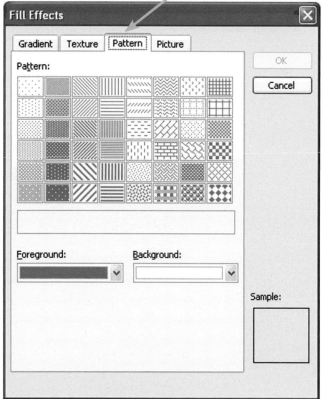

6   Choose a black **Foreground:** colour and select
    the pattern that you want to use for the fill, before
    clicking on [OK].

7   Repeat Steps 2 to 6 for the second data series to see
    this.

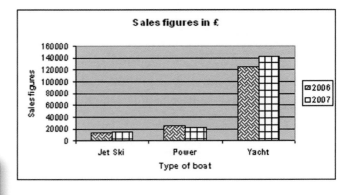

Activity 13.1

Change the chart colours in *Excel*

Open the file SALES2.XLS on the CD. Change the
chart colours so that each data series is distinctive
when printed on a black-and-white printer.

Using spreadsheets

14.1 What is spreadsheet modelling?

A spreadsheet model uses a spreadsheet to explore different possible answers. These models are usually financial, mathematical or scientific. This is sometimes called 'what if' modelling and shows what will happen to the results if you change some of the data within a spreadsheet. It can also be used to discover simple rules within the model. In the context of the examination, you may be asked to build a simple spreadsheet model and change data within the model, or even the model itself, to produce different results.

14.2 Creating a spreadsheet model
Create a model using *Microsoft Excel*

As you have already seen in Chapter 11, *Excel* has the ability to produce a range of graphs and charts. It also has other functions and features which we will explore in this chapter. These include:

- the ability to perform calculations
- the ability to manipulate data
- multiple worksheets
- a wide range of functions allowing you to perform complex calculations
- database-like facilities for searching and sorting
- the ability to produce high-quality output.

When you are asked to create a data model that 'looks like this' it is important that you copy the model in the question paper exactly as shown. Do not move cells around to 'make it look better' and do not add enhancements (like colour and formatting) unless asked to do so. This is very important. It is easy to lose marks by trying to 'improve' the spreadsheet, for example by trying to centre align a column of figures showing prices to two decimal places. *Excel*, quite correctly, should automatically right align this data, so by centre aligning this data it is now in a form which is more difficult to read – although it may 'look better' it is incorrect and you will lose marks. Do not insert rows or columns, or remove rows or columns containing blank spaces, unless instructed to do so.

Import a .csv file into *Excel*

Task 14.1

Open the file EMPLOY.CSV from the CD in a new workbook and place the file RATES.CSV on a new sheet within the workbook called Rates. Save this spreadsheet.

Comma separated values (csv) is the file format that will probably be used for any source files supplied with the practical examination (see Section **10.1** for further details of .csv files). This file type can be imported into almost all spreadsheet packages on any platform, although the delimiters (usually commas) may be different for your regional settings. You are going to attempt Task **14.1** using *Excel*. To open a .csv file:

1 Select the File menu, then Open….
2 Using the Files of type: drop-down menu, select Text Files.

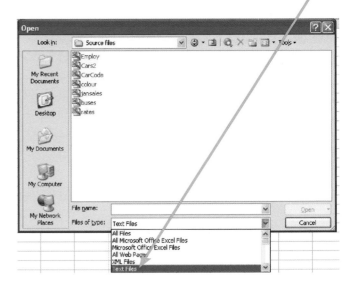

3 Select the file 'Employ' from the list and click on Open.

Use a multi-layered workbook

The file RATES.CSV needs importing into a new worksheet within the current workbook.

4 You must first insert a blank worksheet. Select the Insert menu, then **Worksheet**. This will add a new worksheet which is given a name by *Excel*, in this case 'Sheet1'.

5 To rename this sheet move the mouse over the sheet name – 'Sheet 1' – and press the right mouse button to open the drop-down menu. It will look like this.

6 Select Rename from this menu. The text 'Sheet 1' will be highlighted.

7 Overtype the highlighted text with 'Rates' and press <Enter> to make this change.

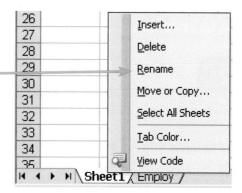

Import a .csv file into *Excel*

8 Data can be imported into a sheet using the Data menu. From this menu select Import External Data and then Import Data... from the sub-menu. This opens the Select Data Source window.

9 Use the Look in section to find the source file (note that *Excel* will probably default to My Data Sources). You may need to change the drive name and select the path to the file that you wish to import. Click on OK and the Text Import Wizard window will appear, looking similar to this.

10 Make sure that the Delimited radio button is selected before clicking on Next >.

11 Click on the Tab box to remove the tick. Place a tick in the Comma box to make commas the correct delimiter.

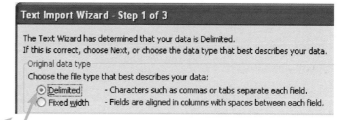

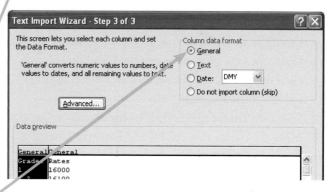

Hint
If you use regional settings that use semicolons as the delimiters, select the semicolon box instead.

Hint
If you use regional settings that use commas as decimal places, change the settings using the Advanced... options.

12 Press Next > to move to Step 3 of the wizard.

13 Select each column in turn and select the correct formatting for that column. In the Column data format section of the window select a General format type for each of the three columns. Then click on the Finish button. The Import Data window will appear.

14 In this window, click on the radio button for Existing worksheet. You should place the data in the top left cell. The easiest way to do this is click the left mouse button in cell A1, then click on OK. Save this as an *Excel* workbook to use in the next task.

Activity 14.1

Create a spreadsheet model using external files

Open the file CARS2.CSV from the CD in a new workbook and place the file COLOUR.CSV on a new sheet within the workbook. Name this sheet 'Colour'. Place the file CARCODE.CSV on a new sheet within the workbook, naming this sheet 'Code'. Save your spreadsheet.

Insert a column

Task 14.2

Using the spreadsheet that you saved in
Task **14.1**:
(i)   insert a new column with the heading 'Code'
      between the Surname and Location columns
      in the Employ sheet
(ii) delete the Pension column
(iii) delete the row for the employee Gourank
      Sughandi
(iv) insert a new row 59 between the entries for
      Nripesh Ravi and Yamila Sharma.

Save this spreadsheet.

1 Open the spreadsheet that you saved in Task **14.1**. To
   insert the new column before the Location column,
   click the left mouse button in any cell in column D
   (which contains Location).
2 Select the Insert menu, then **Columns**.
3 Move the cursor into cell D7 and enter the label
   'Code'.

Delete a column

4 Click the left mouse button in any cell in column G
   (which contains 'Pension').
5 Select the Edit menu, then **Delete**.
6 Click on the radio button for **Entire column** and
   then [OK].

Delete a row

7 Click the left mouse button in any cell in row 65
   (which contains Gourank Sughandi).
8 Select the Edit menu, then **Delete….**
9 Click on the radio button for **Entire row** and then
   click the left mouse button on [OK].

Insert a row

10 To insert the new row 59, click the left mouse button
    in any cell in row 59.
11 Select the Insert menu, then **Rows**.

Activity 14.2

Insert and delete rows and columns

Using the workbook that you saved in Activity
14.1:
(i)   insert a new column between the CarCode
      and Model columns in the sheet Cars2 with
      the heading 'Make'
(ii) delete the row containing CarID 31
(iii) insert a new row between CarID 9
      and 11.

Save your spreadsheet.

14.3   Checking data entry

The most common reason for losing marks on this type
of practical question is the lack of care taken with data
entry. Although it may seem obvious, each label should be
carefully checked to make sure that there are no spelling
errors or errors in the spacing or case (capitals and small
letters) of the labels entered. This is often overlooked, but
can lead to errors when the data is searched on or sorted at
a later stage. Check each item of data very carefully, make
sure that the decimal point (or comma) is in the correct
place and that there are no spaces. The data entered into
the spreadsheet may be used for a variety of searches
and sorts. Each error in data entry may mean that it is
impossible to complete all other sections of this question.

Data entry

Task 14.3

Using the spreadsheet that you saved in Task **14.2**, enter the following data into the new row 59:

Payroll	Forename	Surname	Code	Location	Grade	Rate
MOT1722A13756	Sukan	Sellan			2	

Prepare the cells E2, E3 and E4 so that only a number between 0.8 and 2.5 can be entered. In cell E2, enter the value 0.9. In cell E3, enter the value 1.05. In cell E4, enter the value 1.2. Check all of your data entry. Save this spreadsheet.

1 Move the cursor into cell A59 and enter the data 'MOT1722A13756'.

2 Move the cursor into cell B59 and enter the data 'Sukan'.

3 Move the cursor into cell C59 and enter the data 'Sellan'.

4 Move the cursor into cell F59 and enter the data '2'.

> **Hint**
>
> Remember to resize the column widths so that all data and labels are fully visible.

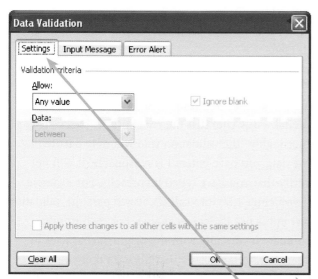

Verify your data entry

5 You have just entered new data into the spreadsheet model. It is vital that the data entry is checked thoroughly. Compare carefully each of the four data items, character by character, to make sure that the data that you entered into the spreadsheet is an exact duplicate of the data given in the question, in this case Task **14.3**, and is in the correct cells. See Section **11.5** for more details.

Use validation rules in *Excel*

For Task **14.3** you are going to set up a validation rule for cells E2, E3 and E4.

6 Highlight all three cells at the same time. This will allow you to set the rule once and it will be applied to all three cells.

7 Select the Data menu, then **Validation**…. This will open the **Data Validation** window, which will look similar to this.

8 The rule is set in the **Settings** tab.

9 Use the drop-down menu in the **Allow:** box to select the type of data to allow. Because you are going to enter numbers between 0.8 and 2.5 select **Decimal** from this menu. As you select **Decimal**, the window changes to show these boxes.

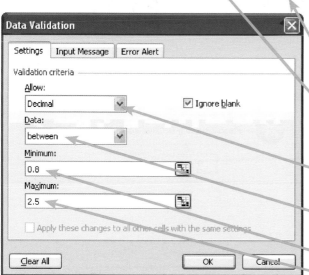

10 Select **between** from the Data: drop-down menu, if it is not already visible.

11 Set the **Minimum:** value to 0.8 by typing this value.

12 Set the **Maximum:** value to 2.5 by typing this value.

13 If you wish to give the user information about the data to be entered in this cell, use the Input Message tab. For this task you do not need to do this.

14 To enter an Error alert if a user enters the wrong data, select the Error Alert tab.

15 Enter Stop as the validation Style: using the drop-down menu. This will prevent invalid data being entered into these cells.

16 Enter a Title: for the error message. Make sure that this gives the user meaningful information about what has caused the error message.

17 Enter the contents of the Error Message:. Make sure that this gives the user meaningful information that will let them enter valid data into the cell.

18 Click on OK to enter these settings for the validation rule.

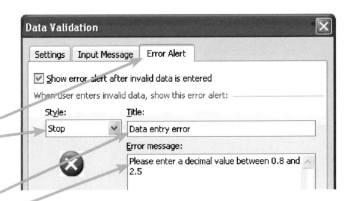

Test validation rules

Test each of the three cells with the data shown in this table. This has been selected so that it tests normal data (that should work), abnormal data (that should not work) and extreme data (that should work but test the boundaries of what is acceptable). See Section **11.5** for more details on types of validation checks.

Data	Type of data	Expected outcome	Actual outcome
−56	Abnormal	Error message	
0.79	Abnormal	Error message	
0.8	Extreme	Works	
1.8	Normal	Works	
2.5	Extreme	Works	
2.51	Abnormal	Error message	
42	Abnormal	Error message	
Test	Abnormal	Error message	

If the data is abnormal, this error message should appear. The title text appears here.

The error message text appears here.

Perform all of the tests and make sure that the expected results and actual results are the same. If not, then there is likely to be an error in the validation rule.

This needs correcting before all of the tests are done again. Do not start entering real data until you have fully tested your validation rules.

Enter additional data

1 Move the cursor into cell E2 and enter the data '0.9'.

2 Move the cursor into cell E3 and enter the data '1.05'.

3 Move the cursor into cell E4 and enter the data '1.2'.

Verify the additional data entry

You have just entered new data into the spreadsheet model – it is vital that the data entry is checked thoroughly. The validation rule will only ensure that the data you have entered is reasonable. It will not verify that you have typed it correctly. For example, if you enter 1.50 into cell E3, it will pass the validation test but is not the correct value. For each number compare it carefully with the original, character by character, to make sure that the data that you entered into the spreadsheet is an exact duplicate of the data given in the question. Save your spreadsheet to use in the next task.

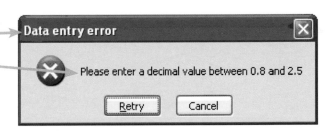

Activity 14.3

Data entry, validation and verification

Using the workbook that you saved in Activity **14.2**, enter the following data into a new row 13 in the sheet Cars2:

CarID	Code	CarCode	Make	Model	Cost	Sale	Ccode	Colour	Year
10	W1b			Clio	3995				2003

Prepare the cells B1, C1 and D1 so that only a number between 1.2 and 2 can be entered. In cell B1, enter the value 1.6. In cell C1, enter the value 1.45. In cell D1, enter the value 1.4. Check your data entry for errors.

Show evidence of your validation rule and the test data that you selected and used to make sure that they function correctly. Show evidence of the error message. Save your spreadsheet.

Name a cell

Task 14.4

Using the spreadsheet that you saved in Task **14.3**, name cell E2 'One', cell E3 'Two' and cell E4 'Three'. Name the cells from A2 to B5 'Pay'. These cells will be used to perform calculations. Save this spreadsheet with a new filename.

1 Click the cursor in cell E2.
2 Use the Insert menu, followed by Name, then Define… from the sub-menu. The Define Name window will appear.
3 In the Names in workbook: box enter the name 'One'.
4 Click in the Refers to: box, then on cell E2. This will place the reference to this cell into the Refers to: box. Ensure that you delete the existing contents of the box before entering your cell reference.

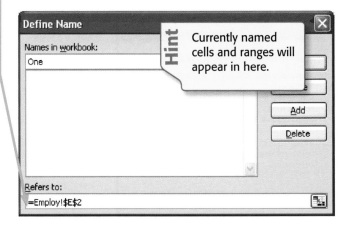

5 Click on **Add** to add this name to the cell.
6 Repeat this process, naming cell E3 'Two' and cell E4 'Three'.
7 Click on OK .

Name a range

8 Highlight the range A2 to E5.
9 Select the Insert menu, followed by Name, then Define… from the sub-menu. In the Names in workbook: box enter the name 'Pay'.
10 The Refers to: box should already contain the reference to the range from the original highlighting: =Employ!$A$2:$B$5. Click on **Add**, then OK to close the Define Name window.

Resize and hide rows and columns

Rows and columns can be resized by dragging the column width using this handle.

Row heights and column widths can also be resized from the Format menu. To resize a row height, select the rows to be changed (or click here to select the entire worksheet), select

Format, then Row. The options available from the sub-menu are **Height** (which allows you to specify the row height in pixels), **Autofit** (which fits the rows to the font size of the data within the row), **Hide** (which will remove the row from view but not delete it) and **Unhide**. If you wish to make a hidden row visible, select the rows either side of the hidden row, before using the **Unhide** option. You can amend column widths in a similar way to row heights, using the Format menu, then **Columns**.

Activity 14.4

Using named cells and ranges

Open the workbook that you saved in
Activity **14.3**. In the worksheet Cars2, name cell
B1 'Normal', cell C1 'Ford' and cell D1 'VW'.
These cells will be used to perform calculations.
Save your spreadsheet.

Protect parts of the spreadsheet

You can protect parts of the spreadsheet to stop anyone
from changing, deleting or moving important data within
the sheet. This can involve protecting a worksheet within
a multi-layered workbook or cells within a worksheet.
For the purposes of the practical examinations you will
only need to protect individual cells, rows or columns.

There are two stages to protecting cells. The first stage
is to identify the cells that do not require protecting:

1 Highlight these cells.
2 Select the Format menu, then Cells… This opens the
  Format Cells window, which will look similar to this.
3 Select the Protection tab.
4 To remove the protection from the selected cells,
  remove the tick from the tick box for Locked.

This stage can be completed many times to unprotect
cells, rows or columns in different parts of the
spreadsheet.

The second stage of the process is to protect the
worksheet:

5 Select the Tools menu, followed by Protection, then
  Protect Sheet…. This will open the Protect Sheet
  window, which will look similar to this.
6 You have the option to use a password to stop other
  users removing the protection from the sheet, and
  there are a variety of options that can be selected
  using the tick boxes.

> **Hint**
> Passwords can be removed by selecting File, then
> Save As…. From the Tools menu within the Save As
> window, select General Options. Select the password
> (by double clicking on the asterisks '******') and then
> press the <Delete> key, followed by [OK].
> Save the file, replacing the existing workbook.

Manipulate windows

Sometimes it is important for you to be able to see two
different parts of a spreadsheet on the screen at the same
time. This can present a problem if the spreadsheet is
very large and the two parts are in different places on the
sheet. There are two methods that can be used to see
different areas of the sheet at the same time:

◆ split the window
◆ freeze panes within the window.

Use split windows

For the practical examination you will need to know how
to split a window into two areas.

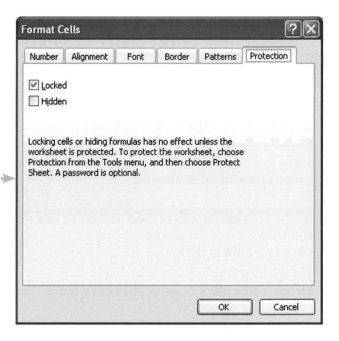

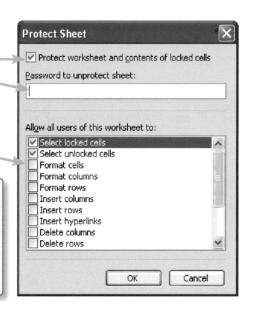

1. Select the small handle at the top of the right-hand scroll bar.
2. Drag this grey handle down to split the window into two parts; the scroll bars in each part can be used to navigate independently. This example shows splitting the window horizontally.

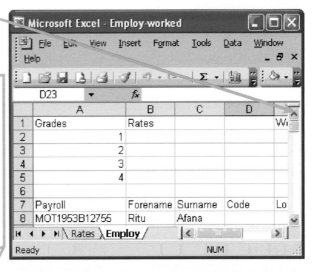

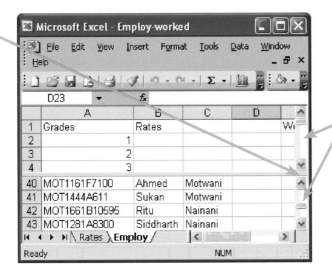

3. Split windows can also be used with a vertical split. To do this select the grey handle on the bottom scroll bar and drag this to the left. The new split window will look similar to this.
4. To restore the windows, grab the grey drag handle and drag it back to the original starting position.

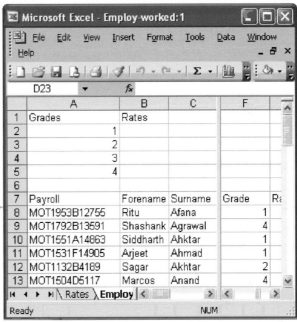

Freeze and unfreeze panes

Freezing a pane within a window will stop part of the sheet from scrolling. For example, in the spreadsheet shown, if you want to make sure that the data in rows 1 to 7 and in column A are always visible and do not scroll off the screen, then freezing the frames is the best method.

1. Move the cursor to cell B8, which is the first cell that will be allowed to scroll.
2. Select the Window menu, followed by Freeze Panes. The new window will show the frozen panes with a darker line like this.
3. To unfreeze the panes select Window menu, followed by Unfreeze Panes.

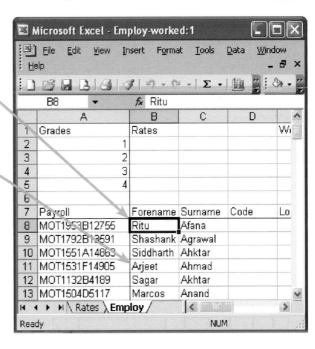

14.4 Manipulating strings
Join and concatenate strings

If you need to join two strings together, this can be done using the & (ampersand) command or the concatenate function.

Task 14.5

Copy this data into a new spreadsheet. Place the full name of Ritu Afana into cell D2.

	A	B	C	D
1	Payroll	Forename	Surname	
2	MOT1953B12755	Ritu	Afana	

1 Move the cursor into D2.
2 Enter the first formula in the table into this cell followed by the <Enter> key.

3 Repeat for each formula in turn.

This table shows a number of formulae that could be used, together with their results.

Formula in cell D2	Result	Comment
=B2&C2	RituAfana	Name returned with no space between
=CONCATENATE(B2,C2)		
=B2&" "&C2	Ritu Afana	Add a space between the two strings
=CONCATENATE(B2," ",C2)		
=C2&", "&B2	Afana, Ritu	Add a space and comma between the two strings – this result has been reversed into Surname, Forename format
=CONCATENATE(C2,", ",B2)		

Extract data from strings and find the string length

If you need to split a string into different parts, there are a number of functions within *Excel* to help you do this. You can extract characters from the left, right or middle of the string. You can identify the length of the string and extract number values from a text string (where it contains some values). The following table shows examples where data has been extracted from the string in cell A2 using a number of these functions.

Formula in cell D2	Result	Comment
=LEFT(A2,1)	M	Extracts the leftmost character from the string
=LEFT(A2,2)	MO	Extracts the left two characters from the string
=LEFT(A2,4)	MOT1	Extracts the left four characters from the string
=RIGHT(A2,1)	5	Extracts the rightmost character from the string
=RIGHT(A2,2)	55	Extracts the right two characters from the string
=RIGHT(A2,4)	2755	Extracts the right four characters from the string
=MID(A2,3,1)	T	Extracts the third character from the string
=MID(A2,3,4)	T195	Extracts four characters starting at the third character
=MID(A2,7,2)	3B	Extracts two characters starting at the seventh character
=LEN(A2)	13	Counts the number of characters in the string
=LEN(B2)	4	Counts the number of characters in the forename

To extract numbers from a string, use the functions shown above to extract only the numbers part. For example, Mid(A2,4,3) would give you the number 195, and extract number values from a text string (where it contains some values). The following table shows examples where data has been extracted from the string in cell A2 using a number of these functions.

There are more complex formulae using a number of functions that will do this, but these are less likely to appear in the practical papers.

Task 14.6

Using the spreadsheet that you saved in Task **14.4**, enter a function in the Code column to extract the eighth character of the Payroll number. Replicate this function for all employees. Save your spreadsheet.

1   Click the cursor in cell D8.
2   Enter the formula =**MID(A8,8,1)**
3   Replicate this formula for cells D9 to D67.
4   Save this spreadsheet.

Activity 14.5

Extract data from strings

Open the workbook that you saved in Activity **14.4**. In the worksheet Cars2, enter a function in the CarCode column to extract the left two characters of the Code. Enter a function in the CCode column to extract the third character of the Code. Replicate these functions for all cars. Save your spreadsheet.

Transpose cells using paste special

When you transpose a block of cells in a spreadsheet the rows become columns and the columns become rows. You may need to transpose cells from a row in one area of a spreadsheet to a column in another area or a column

to a row. For example, to change the column of names to a row of names, starting at cell C1, using this example:

	A	B	C	D	E	F
1	Ritu Afana					
2	Shashank Agrawal					
3	Siddharth Ahktar					
4	Arjeet Ahmad					
5	Sagar Akhtar					

1   Highlight the cells in A1 to A9 and copy these into the clipboard.
2   Move the cursor to cell C1 and press the right mouse button in this cell to obtain the drop-down menu.
3   Select Paste Special… from this menu to open the Paste Special window, which will look similar to this.

4   To transpose the cells when you paste them, tick the **Transpose** box before clicking on **OK** . The results will look like this.

	A	B	C	D	E	F
1	Ritu Afana		Ritu Afana	Shashank Agrawal	Siddharth Ahktar	Arjeet Ahmad
2	Shashank Agrawal					
3	Siddharth Ahktar					

14.5   Using formulae

Formulae can be used for a variety of mathematical calculations. In this section, you will use some simple mathematical formulae.

It is good practice to use cell references in formulae rather than to use actual values. This means that if

that value were to change, in a future version of the spreadsheet, only a single cell needs to be amended, rather than the numbers in each formula in the spreadsheet. As well as cell references, it is acceptable to include named cells and named ranges within formulae. In this example you are going to perform some simple calculations using formulae.

Task 14.7

Copy this spreadsheet model into a new worksheet, naming cell B1 'pay' and cell E1 'tax'. Calculate the Gross pay, Tax, Net pay and Percentage of the time taken by each person.

	A	B	C	D	E	F
1	Rate of Pay	£5.60		Tax Rate	22%	
2						
3	Name	Hours	Gross	Tax	Net	% Time
4	Brian Sargent	14				
5	Graham Brown	9				
6	Total					

1 Name cell B1 'pay' and cell E1 'tax' (see Section **11.4** on naming cells).

2 Click in cell B6 and the formulae shown in the table.

Cell reference	Formula in cell	Comment
B6	=B4+B5	Adds the contents of the two cells together

3 Repeat for cells C4 to F4.

Cell reference	Formula in cell	Comment
C4	=B4*B1	Multiplies the contents of B4 by the contents of cell B1
	=B4*$B$1	Multiplies the contents of B4 by the contents of cell B1, using an absolute reference (see following subsection for further details on absolute referencing)
	=B4*pay	Multiplies the contents of B4 by the contents of the named cell pay (B1)
D4	=C4*E1	Multiplies the contents of C4 by the contents of cell E1
	=C4*$E$1	Multiplies the contents of C4 by the contents of cell E1, using an absolute reference
	=C4*tax	Multiplies the contents of B4 by the contents of the named cell tax (E1)
E4	=C4-D4	Subtracts the contents of D4 from the contents of C4
F4	=B4/B6	Divides the hours worked in B4 by the total hours worked in B6
	=B4/$B$6	Divides the hours worked in B4 by the total hours worked in B6, using an absolute reference

4 Replicate cells C4 to F4 in cells C5 to F5. The results you get, and whether they are correct or not, will depend on which formulae you used, as discussed below.

Absolute and relative referencing

Absolute referencing fixes a cell reference so that when the formula is copied this cell reference never changes. To set an absolute reference place a $ sign before the part of the cell reference that you wish to fix. For example in the formula =B4*$B$1 the reference to the cell B1 is fixed so that when the formula is replicated, this reference will always remain the same.

Relative referencing allows the cell reference of a cell to be changed during the replication process. For example in the formula =B4*$B$1 the reference to the cell B4 is a relative reference so that if this is replicated down the next formula is =B5*$B$1 and if =B4*$B$1 is replicated to the right the next formula is =C4*$B$1

In Task **14.7**, you entered formulae into cells C4 to F4 and copied them to the row below – replicated them. The results you got depended on which version of the formula in cells C4 to F4 that you used. The following table shows each formula and the result when it is replicated.

Original	Formula	Copied to	Result	Works	Comment
C4	=B4*B1	C5	=B5*B2	✗	The reference to B5 is correct but it will not find the rate of pay because it is looking in B2 rather than B1.
	=B4*$B$1		=B5*$B$1	✔	This multiplies the rate of pay by the hours worked for this person.
	=B4*pay		=B5*pay	✔	This multiplies the rate of pay by the hours worked for this person.
D4	=C4*E1	D5	=C5*E2	✗	The reference to C5 is correct but it will not find the tax rate because it is looking in E2 rather than E1.
	=C4*$E$1		=C5*$E$1	✔	This multiplies the gross pay for this person by the tax rate.
	=C4*tax		=C5*tax	✔	This multiplies the gross pay for this person by the tax rate.
E4	=C4-D4	E5	=C5-D5	✔	This subtracts the tax to be paid from the gross pay for this person.
F4	=B4/B6	F5	=B5/B7	✗	This divides the hours this person has worked by the contents of the cell below the total hours worked. This will probably give a division by zero error.
	=B4/$B$6		=B5/$B$6	✔	This divides the hours this person has worked by the total hours worked.

If necessary, change your formulae to use absolute references and again replicate them in row 5. Your results should look like this.

	A	B	C	D	E	F
1	Rate of Pay	£5.60		Tax Rate	22%	
2						
3	Name	Hours	Gross	Tax	Net	% Time
4	Brian Sargent	14	£78.40	£17.25	£61.15	61%
5	Graham Brown	9	£50.40	£11.09	£39.31	39%
6	Total	23				

Activity 14.6

Using formulae with absolute and relative referencing

Open the workbook that you saved in Activity 14.5. In the worksheet Cars2, enter a formula in cell G4 (in the Sale column) to calculate the Cost of the car multiplied by the contents of the cell named 'Normal'. Replicate this formula for all the cars. Save your spreadsheet.

Indices

Task 14.8

Create a spreadsheet model to calculate x^y for any given values, for example 3^4, x^2 where $x = 3.14$, and 4.12^{-2}.

Indices are sometimes called powers. They are commonly used in mathematical and scientific formulae. To calculate values like 3^4 or x^2, a spreadsheet provides you with the ideal tool. You could calculate 3^4 by multiplying (=3*3*3*3) or with the formula =3^4. However, this will not allow these figures to be changed without changing the formula. A better solution is to create a small spreadsheet model like this.

	A	B
1	Index	4
2	Number to multiply	3
3	Answer	=B2^B1

1 Copy the spreadsheet model shown.

By changing the values in B1 and B2, we can get different answers that will be shown in cell B3:

2 Place 4 in B1 and 3 in B2 to calculate 3^4.

3 Place 2 in B1 and 3.14 in B2 to calculate x^2 where $x = 3.14$.

4 Place −2 in B1 and 4.12 in B2 to calculate 4.12^{-2}.

Using indices

Create a spreadsheet model to calculate x^y for any given values. Use this to calculate:

(i) 4^5
(ii) x^4 where $x = 2.9$
(iii) 0.7^{-3}
(iv) 24^6
(v) x^y where $x = 5$ and $y = 3$.

14.6 Using functions

There are a large number of built-in functions within *Excel*. In this section you will learn how to use several of the functions that are used most widely in the practical examinations. This section does not contain all of the functions available or all those that may be used in the examinations.

Task 14.9

Create a new spreadsheet model to calculate:

(i) the whole number part of 84.56453
(ii) 84.56453 rounded to two decimal places
(iii) 84.56453 rounded to the nearest whole number.

Use the INTeger function

INT takes the whole number (integer) part of a number and ignores all digits after the decimal point.

1 Click in cell A1 and enter the number 84.56453.
2 Click in cell B1 and enter the formula =INT(A1) The result should look like this.

Use the ROUND function

ROUND will round a number up to a specified number of decimal places. There are different ways in which the ROUND function can be used. The first is to round a number to a specified number of decimal places.

To round the number in cell A1 to two decimal places and store the result in cell B2:

3 Click in cell B2.
4 Enter the function =ROUND(A1,2) The '2' specifies the two decimal places and will give the result 84.56.

To round the number in cell A1 to the nearest whole number and store the result in cell C2:

5 Click in cell B2.
6 Enter the function =ROUND(A1,0) The 0 specifies zero decimal places and so will round to the nearest whole number, giving the result 85.

The table below gives further examples of using ROUND function.

Function	Result	What it does
=ROUND(A1,2)	84.56	Rounds the contents of A1 to two decimal places
=ROUND(A1,1)	84.6	Rounds the contents of A1 to one decimal place. Note that the figure 84.56453 has been rounded *up* to 84.6
=ROUND(A1,0)	85	Rounds the contents of A1 to the integer value. Note that the figure 84.56453 has been rounded *up* to 85
=ROUND(A1,-1)	80	Rounds the contents of A1 to the nearest 10. The negative value for decimal places allows this function to round whole numbers
=ROUND(A1,-2)	100	Rounds the contents of A1 to the nearest 100

Use the SUM function

Task 14.10

Copy this spreadsheet model and calculate:

(i) the Total number of hours worked by Brian, Graham and Stuart

(ii) the Average number of hours worked per person

(iii) the Maximum number of hours worked by any of these three people

(iv) the Minimum number of hours worked.

	A	B
1	Rate of Pay	£5.60
2		
3	Name	Hours
4	Brian Sargent	14
5	Graham Brown	9
6	Stuart Morris	6
7	Total	
8	Average	
9	Maximum	
10	Minimum	

SUM adds up a list of numbers. This is often used to find column totals or row totals.

1 Click in cell B7.
2 Enter the formula =SUM(B4:B6) This should give the value 29.

There are other ways of using the SUM function, some of which are shown in the table below. As you can see, the range of cells selected within these functions can include individual cells (or even values), ranges of cells, named ranges, named cells or a combination of these. The average, maximum, minimum and count functions also work in this way.

Function	Equivalent formula	What it does
=SUM(B4:B6)	=B4+B5+B6	Adds up the contents of all the cells within the range B4 to B6
=SUM(D4,D8,D9)	=D4+D8+D9	Adds up the contents of the cells D4, D8 and D9
=SUM(D4:D8,F2)	=D4+D5+D6+D7+D8+F2	Adds up the contents of the cells within the range D4 to D8 and the contents of cell F2
=SUM(HRS)	none	Adds up the contents of all the cells within a named range called HRS; this could be used with any named range

Use the AVERAGE function

AVERAGE calculates the mean (average) of a list of numbers.

3 Click in cell B8.
4 Enter the formula =AVERAGE(B4:B6). This should give the value 9.666667.

There are other ways of using the AVERAGE function, some of which are shown in the table below.

Function	Equivalent formula	What it does
=AVERAGE(B2:B4)	=(B2+B3+B4)/3	Calculates the mean of the cells within the range B2 to B4
=AVERAGE(D2,D4,D8,D9)	=(D2+D4+D8+D9)/4	Calculates the mean of the cells D2, D4, D8 and D9
=AVERAGE(D4:D7,F2)	=(D4+D5+D6+D7+F2)/5	Calculates the mean of the cells within the range D4 to D7 and cell F2
=AVERAGE(HRS)	none	Calculates the mean of all the cells within a named range called HRS; this could be used with any named range

Use the MAXimum function

MAX calculates the maximum value in a list of numbers.

5 Click in cell B9.
6 Enter the formula =MAX(B4:B6). This should give the value 14.

Use the MINimum function

MIN calculates the minimum value in a list of numbers.

7 Click in cell B10.
8 Enter the formula =MIN(B4:B6). This should give the value 6.

The completed spreadsheet should look similar to this.

	A	B
1	Rate of Pay	£5.60
2		
3	Name	Hours
4	Brian Sargent	14
5	Graham Brown	9
6	Stuart Morris	6
7	Total	29
8	Average	9.666667
9	Maximum	14
10	Minimum	6

Use the COUNT function

COUNT looks at the cells within a given range and counts the number of these cells containing numbers. Using the spreadsheet from Task **14.10**, if you wanted to count the number of numeric (number) values in the range A1 to B6 enter the formula =COUNT(A1:B6). This will return the answer 4.

Use the COUNTA function

COUNTA looks at the cells within a given range and counts the number of these cells that are not empty. Using the spreadsheet from Task **14.10**, if you wanted to count the number of non-blank (not empty) cells in the range A1 to B6 then enter the formula =COUNTA(A1:B6). This will return the answer 10.

Use the COUNTIF function

COUNTIF looks at the cells within a given range and counts the number of these cells that meet a given condition. The condition is placed in the function and can be a number, a string, an inequality or a cell reference. There are a number of ways the COUNTIF function can be used.

Task 14.11

Open the file BOAT3.XLS from the CD in a new workbook. Name the cells B2 to B13 'Type' and the cells D2 to D13 'Sold'.

(i) Enter formulae in cells G2 to G4 to calculate how many boats there are of each Type.
(ii) Enter formulae in cells G7 to G8 to calculate how many boats have been sold or not.
(iii) Enter formulae in cells G11 to G12 to show how many boats cost less than £20 000 and how many cost £20 000 or more.

Save your spreadsheet with a new filename.

1 Open the file.
2 Name the ranges B2 and B13 and D2 to D13 (as shown in Section **14.3**).
3 Click in cell G2 and enter one of the formulae from the table below.

> **Hint**
> Check the examination question – if it asks you to use both absolute and relative referencing then the third option is required. The last option is the most efficient.

Cell	Function	What it does
G2	=COUNTIF($B$2:$B$13,"Yacht")	Counts the number of cells in the range B2 to B13 that contain the word 'Yacht'
	=COUNTIF(Type,"Yacht")	Counts the number of cells in the named range Type (B2 to B13) that contain the word 'Yacht'
	=COUNTIF($B$2:$B$13,F2)	Counts the number of cells in the range B2 to B13 that contain the same text as the contents of cell F2
	=COUNTIF(Type,F2)	Counts the number of cells in the named range Type (B2 to B13) that contain the same text as the contents of cell F2

4 Enter similar functions in cells G3 and G4.

5 Click in cell G7 and enter one of the following formulae.

G7	=COUNTIF($D$2:$D$13,"Y")	Counts the number of cells in the range D2 to D13 that contain the character 'Y'
	=COUNTIF(Sold,"Y")	Counts the number of cells in the named range Sold (D2 to D13) that contain the character 'Y'

6 Enter a similar function in cell G8 using the character 'N'.

7 Click in cell G11 and enter the following formula.

Hint

If the question paper asks you to use both absolute and relative referencing, this cannot be done without using nested functions, which are covered later in this chapter.

G11	=COUNTIF($C$2:$C$13,"<20000")	Counts the number of cells in the range C2 to C13 that contain a value less than 20 000

8 Click in cell G12 and enter the following formula.

Hint

Always use speech marks around the inequalities, as shown in these examples.

G12	=COUNTIF($C$2:$C$13,">=20000")	Counts the number of cells in the range C2 to C13 that contain a value greater than or equal to 20 000

The completed spreadsheet should look similar to this.

	A	B	C	D	E	F	G
1	Make	Type	Price	Sold		Type	Count
2	Ta Yang	Yacht	£22,950.00	N		Yacht	2
3	Sealine 218	Power	£21,500.00	Y		Power	7
4	Searay 215	Power	£17,995.00	N		Jet Ski	3
5	Norman 20	Power	£3,650.00	Y			Count
6	Seadoo RX DI	Jet Ski	£4,699.00	N		Sold	
7	Sadler 32	Yacht	£24,950.00	N		Yes	3
8	Kawasaki Zxi 1100	Jet Ski	£2,995.00	Y		No	9
9	Premium 3D	Jet Ski	£5,495.00	N			Count
10	Jeanneau Leader	Power	£13,795.00	N		Price	
11	Crusader 18	Power	£2,995.00	N		<20000	9
12	Cleopatra 850	Power	£12,995.00	N		>=20000	3
13	Maxum 2400SCR	Power	£18,950.00	N			

Hint

Note that when you have currency values, these should always be formatted in your local currency (unless specified otherwise in the examination question), using Format, then Cells…, then Currency from the Number tab.

9 Save the file with a new filename.

Use the SUMIF function

SUMIF looks at the cells within a given range and adds the total from those cells that meet a given condition. The condition is placed in the function and can be a number, a string, an inequality or a cell reference. Like the COUNTIF function, there are a number of ways SUMIF can be used. This task will demonstrate one way of using SUMIF.

Task 14.12

Use the spreadsheet that you saved in Task **14.11**. Enter 'Total Price' in cell H1. Enter formulae in cells H2 to H4 to calculate the total of all the prices for each boat type. Save your spreadsheet.

1　Click in cell H1 and enter the data 'Total Price'.

2　Click in cell H2 and enter the formula:

=SUMIF($B$2:$B$13,F2,C$2:$C$13)

Hint You could use named ranges rather than absolute referencing for cells B2 to B13 and C2 to C13.

This will check the contents of the cells in the range B2 to B13. Each time that the contents of a cell matches the value held in cell F2 (which contains 'Yacht'), it adds the price from the cell in the same row (within the

	A	B	C	D	E	F	G	H
1	**Make**	**Type**	**Price**	**Sold**		**Type**	**Count**	**Total Price**
2	Ta Yang	Yacht	£22,950.00	N		Yacht	2	£47,900.00
3	Sealine 218	Power	£21,500.00	Y		Power	7	£91,880.00
4	Searay 215	Power	£17,995.00	N		Jet Ski	3	£13,189.00
5	Norman 20	Power	£3,650.00	Y		**Count**		
6	Seadoo RX DI	Jet Ski	£4,699.00	N		**Sold**		
7	Sadler 32	Yacht	£24,950.00	N		Yes	3	
8	Kawasaki Zxi 1100	Jet Ski	£2,995.00	Y		No	9	
9	Premium 3D	Jet Ski	£5,495.00	N		**Count**		
10	Jeanneau Leader	Power	£13,795.00	N		**Price**		
11	Crusader 18	Power	£2,995.00	N		<20000	9	
12	Cleopatra 850	Power	£12,995.00	N		>=20000	3	
13	Maxum 2400 SCR	Power	£18,950.00	N				

range C2 to C13) to the total. When it has checked all of the cells in the range, it displays the total for this item.

3　Replicate this formula in cells H3 and H4. The completed spreadsheet should look similar to this.

4　Save your spreadsheet.

This function has the same flexibility as the COUNTIF function, in that it can be used with named ranges, named cells or values

Use the IF function

IF looks at a given condition and performs an operation if the condition is met, or a different operation if the condition is not met. The operations could be simply placing a number or label in the cell, it could involve a reference to another cell or it could involve a more complex calculation.

Task 14.13

Open the file BOAT4.XLS from the CD in a new workbook. The Wind column needs to contain 'Yes' if the type of boat is a yacht and 'No' if it is a power boat or a jet ski.

The most appropriate function for doing this is the IF function.

1　Open the file.

2　In cell E2 enter the formula:

=IF(B2="Yacht","Yes","No")

The format within the brackets for this function is: the condition, followed by a comma, then the operation if the condition is true (in this case it enters the text 'Yes' in this cell), then another comma, and then the operation if the condition is false (in this case it enters the text 'No' in this cell).

3　Replicate this formula from E2 down to E13. The completed spreadsheet should look similar to this.

	A	B	C	D	E
1	**Make**	**Type**	**Price**	**Sold**	**Wind**
2	Ta Yang	Yacht	£22,950.00	N	Yes
3	Sealine 218	Power	£21,500.00	Y	No
4	Searay 215	Power	£17,995.00	N	No
5	Norman 20	Power	£3,650.00	Y	No
6	Seadoo RX DI	Jet Ski	£4,699.00	N	No
7	Sadler 32	Yacht	£24,950.00	N	Yes
8	Kawasaki Zxi 1100	Jet Ski	£2,995.00	Y	No
9	Premium 3D	Jet Ski	£5,495.00	N	No
10	Jeanneau Leader	Power	£13,795.00	N	No
11	Crusader 18	Power	£2,995.00	N	No
12	Cleopatra 850	Power	£12,995.00	N	No
13	Maxum 2400 SCR	Power	£18,950.00	N	No

Use the SUBTOTAL function

SUBTOTAL is a function that can be used in place of a number of others. The first variable passed to this function tells it the type of subtotal to calculate. For example if the function =SUBTOTAL(1,A2:A4) is used, it will calculate the AVERAGE of the range A2 to A4. If this function was changed to =SUBTOTAL(9,A2:A4) it would calculate the SUM of this range. This table shows the some of the codes and their use.

Code	Function
1	AVERAGE
2	COUNT
3	COUNTA
4	MAX
5	MIN
6	PRODUCT
7	STDEV
8	STDEVP
9	SUM
10	VAR

Use the LOOKUP functions

There are three variations of the LOOKUP function that can be used within *Excel*: LOOKUP, VLOOKUP and HLOOKUP.

The LOOKUP function is used to look up information using data in the first row or the first column of a range of cells and returns a relative value. For the purpose of the practical examinations, this is probably the least useful of the three formulae.

VLOOKUP is a function that performs a vertical look-up of data. This should be used rather than HLOOKUP when the values that you wish to compare your data with are in a column to the left of the data that you want to retrieve. In this spreadsheet example, the Type column needs to contain the TypeName that has been looked up from the vertical list in cells E1 to F4.

	A	B	C	D	E	F
1	Make	Tcode	Type		Code	TypeName
2	Ta Yang	1			1	Yacht
3	Sealine 218	2			2	Power
4	Searay 215	2			3	Cruiser
5	Norman 20	2			4	Jet Ski
6	Seadoo RX DI	4				
7	Sadler 32	1				
8	Kawasaki Zxi 1100	4				

The Tcode will be used to look up the TypeName. Cell C2 needs to contain the formula:

=VLOOKUP(B2,$E$2:$F$5,2,FALSE)

In this formula, the contents of the cell B2 (the number 1), are looked for in the range from E2 to F5 (a named range could have been used here).

When it matches this answer in the left column of this range (column E), it looks up the result from column number 2 (column F) of this range. The final comma followed by False is optional. If this value is set to False then the function will only look up the exact value (in this case 1), if this was set to TRUE the function would find the next largest value in the left column of the range of cells and use this value to give the result. This lookup can be used for values on the same sheet, from different worksheets in the same workbook and even from external files. Note that the reference to cell B2 has not got absolute referencing so that it will look up each different Tcode as the formula is replicated.

HLOOKUP is a function that performs a horizontal look-up of data. This should be used rather than VLOOKUP when the values that you wish to compare your data with are in the top row of the data that you want to retrieve. The values to be looked up are stored in the rows below this cell in the same column. In this spreadsheet example, the Type column needs to contain the TypeName that has been looked up from the horizontal list in cells B1 to E2.

	A	B	C	D	E
1	Code	1	2	3	4
2	TypeName	Yacht	Power	Cruiser	Jet Ski
3					
4	Make	Tcode	Type		
5	Ta Yang	1			
6	Sealine 218	2			
7	Searay 215	2			
8	Norman 20	2			
9	Seadoo RX DI	4			
10	Sadler 32	1			
11	Kawasaki Zxi 1100	4			

Cell C5 needs to contain the formula:

=HLOOKUP(B5,$B$1:$E$2,2,FALSE)

This looks up the contents of the cell B5 (the number 1) in the range from B1 to E2 (a named range could have been used here). When it matches this answer in the top row of this range, it retrieves the result from row 2 of this range. Again the final comma followed by False allows you to have an exact match or not depending on your requirements. This lookup can also be used for values on the same sheet, from different worksheets in the same workbook and even from external files.

Task 14.14

Using the spreadsheet that you saved in Task **14.6**, enter a formula in the Rates column to look up the Rate, using the Grade for the lookup value and the file RATES.CSV. Make sure that you use both absolute and relative referencing within your function. Replicate this function so that the rate of pay is shown for each Grade. Save your spreadsheet.

1 Open the spreadsheet file that you saved in Task **14.6**.

2 Open the file RATES.CSV.

3 In the file that you saved in Task **14.6** move the cursor to cell B2.

4 Enter the function:

=VLOOKUP(A2,rates.csv!$A$2:$B$22,2)

This function is easily entered as follows:
◇ Type =VLOOKUP(
◇ Click the left mouse button in cell A2.
◇ Type a comma.
◇ Go to the RATES.CSV spreadsheet and highlight all of the cells in the range A2 to B22.
◇ Type a comma.
◇ Enter a 2 (to indicate that the return value should be the second column).
◇ Close the brackets.
◇ Press <Enter>.
◇ Check that the spreadsheet has added the $ signs in all four places in the range to fix this as an absolute reference. If these are not present, they can be added manually.

5 By using absolute and relative referencing this cell can now be copied down using the drag handle and the formula will replicate correctly. The completed functions will look like this.

	A	B
1	Grades	Rates
2	1	=VLOOKUP(A2,rates.csv!$A$2:$B$22,2)
3	2	=VLOOKUP(A3,rates.csv!$A$2:$B$22,2)
4	3	=VLOOKUP(A4,rates.csv!$A$2:$B$22,2)
5	4	=VLOOKUP(A5,rates.csv!$A$2:$B$22,2)

Hint

Make sure that the format of the cells used within a lookup function are always the same. If you try to compare numeric and text values an error will occur.

Activity 14.8

Using functions

Open the workbook that you saved in Activity **14.6**.

(i) Enter a function in the Make column to look up the Make, using the CarCode for the lookup value and the sheet Code which contains the file CARCODE.CSV. Make sure that you use both absolute and relative referencing within your function.

Hint

In part **(i)**, make sure that you sort the data (but not the top row) in CARCODE.CSV into CarCode order for the VLOOKUP function to work correctly. (See Section **14.10** for information on how to sort data.)

(ii) Enter a function in the Colour column to look up the Colour of the car, using the CCode for the lookup value and the sheet Colour. Make sure that you use both absolute and relative referencing within your function.

(iii) Replicate these functions so that the Make and Colour of each CarID is shown.

(iv) Save your spreadsheet.

Use nested formulae and functions

Most of the formulae and functions that you have used so far can be used as part of a nested formula. This is when one formula or function is placed inside another one. An example of this can be seen using this spreadsheet.

	A	B	C	D	E
1	Make	Type	Price	Sold	Ski sale
2	Ta Yang	Yacht	£22,950.00	N	
3	Sealine 218	Power	£21,500.00	Y	
4	Searay 215	Power	£17,995.00	N	
5	Norman 20	Power	£3,650.00	Y	
6	Seadoo RX DI	Jet Ski	£4,699.00	N	
7	Sadler 32	Yacht	£24,950.00	N	
8	Kawasaki Zxi 1100	Jet Ski	£2,995.00	Y	
9	Premium 3D	Jet Ski	£5,495.00	N	

The Ski sale column should show the price of the boat if the Type is jet ski and Sold is N. If the item is not a jet ski or is sold it should show 'n/a' for not available. In order to do this you must use a nested IF statement. The formula is going to be placed in cell E2. The nested IF statement for this cell will be:

$$=IF(B2=\text{“Jet Ski”},IF(D2=\text{“N”},C2,\text{“n/a”}),\text{“n/a”})$$

To create this, you have used an outside formula to test if the contents of cell B2 matches 'Jet Ski'; if not, it returns the 'n/a' message. This part of the formula looks like this:

$$=IF(B2=\text{“Jet Ski”}, \{\textbf{second formula in here}\} ,\text{“n/a”})$$

The second formula checks cell D2 to see if the item is sold. If it is sold it returns the message 'n/a'. The second formula is IF(D2=“N”,C2,“n/a”). If cell D2 contains 'N' this means that it is not sold. As this second formula is placed in the Yes section of the first formula (which means both of the conditions have been met), the contents of cell C2 (which is the price of the jet ski) are displayed.

For some parts of the practical examination you may need to have several functions or formulae nested inside each other. They may not always be the same type of function.

Task 14.15

(i) Using the spreadsheet that you saved in Task **14.14**, enter a function in the Location column to calculate the location weighting for each employee. Use the Code value. If the code is:

- A – use the weighting held in the named cell One
- B – use the weighting held in named cell Two
- E – use the weighting held in named cell Three
- none of these – return the number 1.

(ii) In the Rate column use a function that will use the Grade to look up the Rate in the named range Pay and multiply this by the contents of the location column.

(iii) Replicate these functions for each person.

Save your spreadsheet.

1 In cell E8 enter the nested IF function:

=IF(D8=“A”,One,IF(D8=“B”,Two,IF(D8=“E”,Three,1)))

As you can see, there are three functions, nested inside each other. You can use the same shortcuts shown in Task **14.14** rather than typing this into the cell.

2 In cell G8, enter the function:

=VLOOKUP(F8,Pay,2)*E8

3 Replicate both functions using drag down, then save your spreadsheet.

Using nested functions

(i) Using the workbook that you saved in Activity **14.14**, change the formulae in the Sale column so that it becomes a function that will calculate the selling price of the car, using the Make of the car. If this is:

- Ford – multiply the Cost by the named cell Ford
- VW – multiply the Cost by the named cell VW
- neither of these – multiply the Cost by the named cell Normal.

(ii) Replicate this function for each car. Save your spreadsheet.

Use date and time functions in *Excel*

In this section you will learn how to use several of the date and time functions that may occur in the practical examinations. This section does not contain all of the functions available, or all those that may be used in the examinations. Date values are stored in *Excel* as numbers: 1 January 1900 is stored as 1, 2 January 1900 as 2 and so on. Times are stored as decimal parts of the days, so the value 1.5 would refer to 12 noon on 1 January 1900, and 6am on 1 January 2008 would be stored as 39448.25 because this is 39 448 days after 1 January 1900 and 6am is exactly a quarter of the way through the day. These values are formatted so that they appear as dates and/or times.

> **Hint**
> Note that the dates shown in this chapter are in UK dd/mm/yyyy format. If you use the US format of mm/dd/yyyy you will need to adjust your formulae accordingly.

Use the WEEKDAY function

Task 14.16

Open the file JANSALES.CSV from the CD in a new workbook. For each order, show the day that the order was placed. Save your spreadsheet.

WEEKDAY is used to return a number between 1 and 7 from a given date. If the day is a Sunday, 1 is returned, Monday is 2 and so on. For this question you need to find the code for the day and then look up the name of the day.

1 Open the file JANSALES.CSV.
2 Create a new heading in cell E1 by typing the label 'Weekday'.
3 In Cell E2 enter the function:

=WEEKDAY(C2)

4 In Cell F2 enter the function:

=VLOOKUP(E2,$H$2:$I$8,2)

5 Replicate these functions for all orders and save your spreadsheet.

Use the DAY function

Task 14.17

Create this spreadsheet in a new workbook. Use functions to put the day, month and year parts of the date into cells B2, B3 and B4, respectively.

	A	B
1	Date	14/08/2008
2	Day	
3	Month	
4	Year	

DAY is a function that is used to return a number between 1 and 31 from a given date.

1 Create the spreadsheet.
2 In cell B2, enter the function =DAY(B1)
3 This will return the value 14, as this is the day part of the date.

	A	B
1	Date	14/08/2008
2	Day	14
3	Month	
4	Year	

Use the MONTH function

MONTH is a function that is used to return a number between 1 and 12 from a given date.

4 In cell B3, enter the function =MONTH(B1)
5 This will return the value 8, as this is the month part of the date.

	A	B
1	Date	14/08/2008
2	Day	14
3	Month	8
4	Year	

Use the YEAR function

YEAR is a function that is used to return the year from a given date.

6 In cell B4, enter the function =YEAR(B1)

7 This will return the value 2008 as this is the year part of the date.

	A	B
1	Date	14/08/2008
2	Day	14
3	Month	8
4	Year	2008

Calculate the number of days between two dates

Task 14.18

Create this spreadsheet in a new workbook.

(i) Calculate the number of days between the Start and End dates.

	A	B
1	Start date	30/01/2008
2	End date	15/07/2008
3		
4	Days	
5	Months	

(ii) Calculate the number of months between the Start and End dates.

(iii) Change the End date to 15/07/2010, and again calculate the number of months between the Start and End dates.

(iv) Enter the text 'Years' in cell B6 and calculate the number of years between the Start and End dates.

To calculate the number of days between two dates, you need to subtract the first date from the second.

1 Create the spreadsheet.

2 In cell B4, enter the formula =B2-B1

3 When you press the <Enter> key, the answer is given in date format and appears as '15/06/1900'. To show the number of days, you need to reformat this cell as a number. Select the Format menu, then Cells....

4 On the Number tab select Number in the category box and set the number of Decimal places: to 0.

This will change the contents of this cell to display the correct answer.

	A	B
1	Start date	30/01/2008
2	End date	15/07/2008
3		
4	Days	167
5	Months	

Calculate the number of months between two dates

To calculate the number of months between two dates, you need subtract the month function for the first date from the month function for the second.

5 In cell B5, enter the formula =MONTH(B2)-MONTH(B1)

6 Make sure that this cell is formatted as a number, as shown in Steps 3 and 4 above.

	A	B
1	Start date	30/01/2008
2	End date	15/07/2008
3		
4	Days	167
5	Months	6

Calculate the number of months between two dates over a year apart

To calculate the number of months between two dates over a year apart two functions have to be used. These are the YEAR and the MONTH functions.

1 Enter the data 15/07/2010 in cell B2.

2 In cell B4, enter the formula:

=(YEAR(B2)-YEAR(B1))*12+MONTH(B2)-MONTH(B1)

This formula multiplies the difference between the year values by 12, to turn this part of the answer into months. It then calculates the remaining month values and adds these.

3 Make sure that the cell is formatted as a number rather than as a date.

	A	B
1	Start date	30/01/2008
2	End date	15/07/2010
3		
4	Days	897
5	Months	30

Calculate the number of years between two dates

To calculate the number of years between two dates, you need to subtract the year function for the first date from the year function for the second.

1 In cell A6, enter the data 'Years'.

2 In cell B6, enter the formula:

=YEAR(B2)-YEAR(B1)

3 Make sure that this cell is formatted as a number.

	A	B
1	Start date	30/01/2008
2	End date	15/07/2010
3		
4	Days	897
5	Months	30
6	Years	2

If the date in cell B1 was more recent than the date in B2, as shown here, the formula in cell B6 would need to be changed to:

	A	B
1	Start date	15/07/2010
2	End date	30/01/2008

=YEAR(B1)-YEAR(B2)

This will avoid getting a negative answer. To make sure that the formula would work for either date being the most recent, the formula in cell B6 would need to be changed into a conditional function with both options possible like this:

=IF(B1>B2,YEAR(B1)-YEAR(B2),YEAR(B2)-YEAR(B1))

> **Hint**
>
> The ABS function can be used in place of this formula. ABS calculates the absolute value (with no positive or negative values), so this cell can instead contain:
>
> =ABS(YEAR(B1)-YEAR(B2))

Use the HOUR function

> **Task 14.19**
>
> Create this spreadsheet in a new workbook. Use functions to put the hour, minute and second parts of the time into cells B2, B3 and B4, respectively.
>
> | | A | B |
> |---|---|---|
> | 1 | Time | 15:13:27 |
> | 2 | Hours | |
> | 3 | Minutes | |
> | 4 | Seconds | |

HOUR is a function that is used to return a number between 0 and 23 from a given time.

1 Create the spreadsheet.

2 In cell B2, enter the function =HOUR(B1)

3 This will return the value 15, as this is the number of hours in the time using the 24-hour clock.

	A	B
1	Time	15:13:27
2	Hours	15
3	Minutes	
4	Seconds	

Use the MINUTE function

MINUTE is a function that is used to return a number between 0 and 59 from a given time.

1 In cell B3, enter the function =MINUTE(B1)

2 This will return the value 13, as this is the minute part of this time.

	A	B
1	Time	15:13:27
2	Hours	15
3	Minutes	13
4	Seconds	

Use the SECOND function

SECOND is a function that is used to return a number between 0 and 59 from a given time.

1 In cell B4, enter the function =SECOND(B1)

2 This will return the value 27, as this is the number of seconds within this time.

	A	B
1	Time	15:13:27
2	Hours	15
3	Minutes	13
4	Seconds	27

Calculate the difference between two times

> **Task 14.20**
>
> Create this spreadsheet in a new workbook. Calculate the difference between the Start time and End time, presenting the results:
>
> | | A | B |
> |---|---|---|
> | 1 | Start time | 11:45 |
> | 2 | End time | 14:07 |
> | 3 | | |
> | 4 | Difference | |
>
> **(i)** in hours in cell B4
> **(ii)** in hours and minutes in cell B5
> **(iii)** in hours, minutes and seconds in cell B6.

To calculate the difference between two times, subtract the first time from the second. The format of the resulting answer can be specified using the TEXT function, depending whether the result is required in hours, hours and minutes, or hours, minutes and seconds. The calculation is the same, but the presentation of the results is different.

1 Create the spreadsheet.
2 In cell B4, enter the function:

=TEXT((B2-B1),"h")

This formats the result to hours only with a one- or two-digit answer depending upon the number of hours.

3 In cell B5, enter the function:

=TEXT((B2-B1),"hh:mm")

This formats the result to hours and minutes, but forces two digits for the hours.

4 In cell B6, enter the function:

=TEXT((B2-B1),"h:mm:ss")

This formats the result to hours, minutes and seconds.

	A	B
1	Start time	11:45
2	End time	14:07
3		
4	Difference	2
5		02:22
6		2:22:00

3 In cell E2, enter the function:

=RIGHT(D2,2)

This extracts the two right-hand characters from the time late (the minute values). If the cell contains a zero, this will extract that zero.

4 In cell G2, enter the function:

=E2*F2

5 Replicate these functions for all journeys
6 Save the spreadsheet for later use.

Task 14.21

Open the file BUSES.CSV from the CD in a new workbook. For each journey, if the bus was late, calculate the number of minutes it was late and the total number of passenger minutes late for that journey. The number of passenger minutes is the number of passengers on the journey multiplied by the number of minutes that the bus was late. Save your spreadsheet.

This problem is a little more difficult than it would appear. Calculating the number of minutes late if the bus was late involves using a time manipulation within an IF function. The result of this calculation (because it will be in text format) will need either converting into a numeric value or extracting as a number (this method is shown below). If a number value for the minutes is not extracted it is not possible to multiply this by the number of passengers to obtain the total number of passenger minutes for the journey. Note that this is not the only way of solving this question.

1 Open the file BUSES.CSV.
2 In cell D2, enter the function:

=IF(C2>B2,TEXT(C2-B2,"h:mm"),0)

This calculates the number of minutes late if the bus was late. For journeys that were on time or were early a zero is returned.

Test the data model

To thoroughly test a data model you must select appropriate test data. Refer back to the section on testing validation rules (see Section 14.3) and use the same methods to test the spreadsheet model. Select normal data that you would expect to work with your formulae, select extreme data to test the boundaries and select abnormal data that you would not expect to be accepted. Carefully check that each formula and function works as you expect it to by using simple test data. Work out the expected results first and try the test data in the spreadsheet. You can then check the actual results and see if they match the expected results. Check that the ranges cover all of the data that you wish to use. Many marks are lost in practical examinations by careless use of ranges within formulae and functions. Check that everything works before using real data in your model.

14.7 Adjusting page layout
Adjust the page settings

Most of the features for page layout in *Excel* can be found using the **File** menu followed by **Page Setup...**. This opens the **Page Setup** window, which has many functions within four tabs. Changing the page orientation can be done using the radio buttons on the **Page** tab.

The scaling section of the **Page** tab allows you to manipulate the way the document is printed. It is sometimes necessary to force your printouts to fit on a single page or onto a particular number of pages wide or tall. This can be changed by clicking on this radio button. The number of pages wide and tall can then be specified, either by typing the numbers in the boxes or by using the up and down arrows to increase or decrease the value in the box by one for each click of the left mouse button.

The paper size and print quality can also be selected from this window before moving to a different tab or clicking on **OK**.

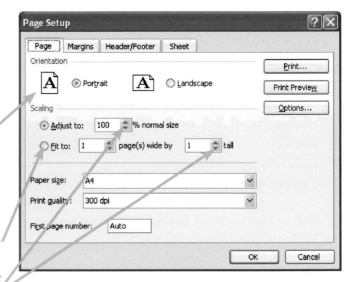

Adjust the margins

Select the **Margins** tab from the **Page Setup** window. The margin settings for all four margins can be entered in the boxes or by using the up and down arrows to increase or decrease the value in each box by 1 millimetre. The spreadsheet can be centre aligned on the page, both horizontally and vertically, using the two tick boxes. When you have made the changes to the margin settings, move to a different tab or click on **OK**.

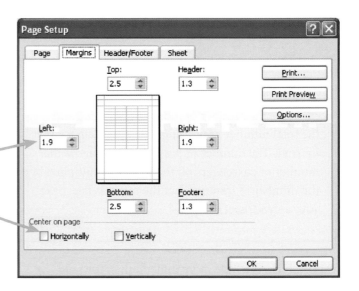

Use headers and footers

In the practical examination papers you will probably need to place your name, centre number and candidate number in either the header or footer of each page. Select the **Header/Footer** tab from the **Page Setup** window. To use the standard header and footer options, such as automated page numbering, your name, etc., select from the drop-down list for either the header or the footer.

To personalise the header or footer click on either the **Custom Header...** or the **Custom Footer...** button. For this example, you can click on the **Custom Header...** button. This will allow you to enter your own text or to add one of the features from the buttons in the **Header** window. (see next page)

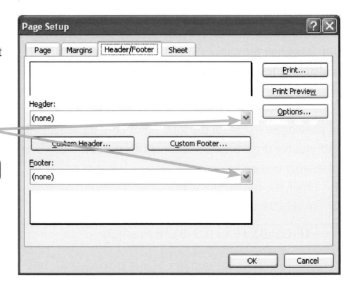

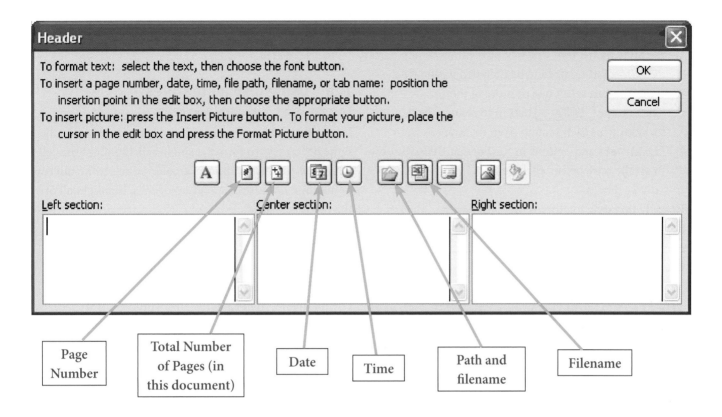

Page Number

Total Number of Pages (in this document)

Date

Time

Path and filename

Filename

Add the required information to the header and move to a different tab or click on OK.

Display row and column headings

Select the Sheet tab from the Page Setup window. Place a tick in the box for Row and column headings to display these when the spreadsheet is printed.

To hide these, remove the tick from the Row and column headings box.

Display gridlines

Using the Sheet tab, place a tick in the box for Gridlines to display these when the spreadsheet is printed:

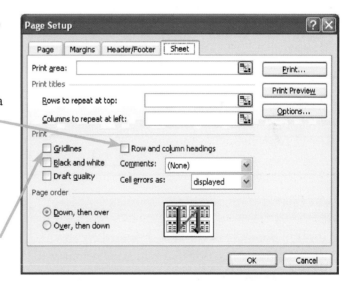

Apply corporate house styles

In a business situation, you may have to produce your spreadsheet model to match the house style of the company that you are working for. In an examination question you may be given a set of styles that need to be applied to the spreadsheet model. These could include font styles, borders, backgrounds, point size or number formatting. If these are used a number of times within the spreadsheet it will be easier to create a style and apply it to the required cells. To create a new style:

1 Select the Format menu, then Style.... This will open the Style window, which will look similar to this.

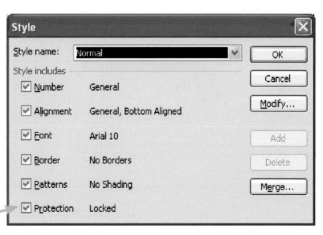

2 Replace the name **Normal** with a new style name in the **Style name:** box. The tick boxes show which parts of the formatting need to be included within this style. You can select one or more of these.

3 Click on the Modify... button to change the formatting of each section from the tick boxes.

4 Use the tabs and options in the **Format Cells** window to set the style before clicking on OK .

To apply this style to other cells:

1 Select the cells and then select **Format**, then **Style**.

2 Select the name of the style from the drop-down list.

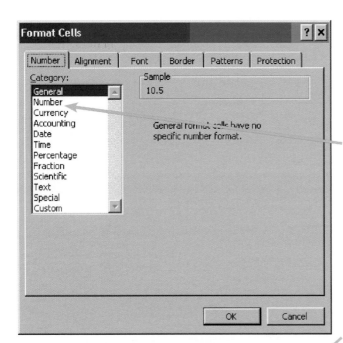

3 Click on OK to apply this style to the cell or cells selected.

14.8 Using display features
Format rows, columns and cells

Formatting cells, rows and columns all involve using the same processes. To format a single cell, highlight the cell before formatting; for a row or column, select the full row or column; or to format a group of cells, highlight all of the required cells.

Format cells

Most formatting can be completed using the **Format Cells** window, which can be located by selecting the Format menu, then **Cells…**. This window has six tabs, with a range of formatting options. The **Number** tab will change the way that numeric values are displayed.

Format numbers

To change the number of decimal places displayed (this does not change the number stored), select **Number** from the **Category:** list. In this case you can try this using a small spreadsheet that contains one number and one formula and looks like this:

Values

	A
1	10.5
2	21

Formulae

	A
1	10.5
2	=2*A1

When you change the formatting of cell A1 to no **Decimal places:** using **Number** the result looks like this:

	A
1	11
2	21

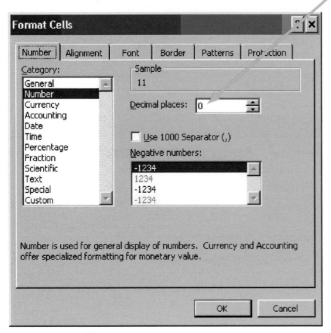

As you can see, the figure displayed in A1 is not the one used for the calculation. It is important for you to use functions like ROUND and INT, rather than just formatting for some spreadsheet work.

Format currency

The **Category:** options in the **Number** tab will also allow you to set **Currency** values for cells. This is used to display monetary values for a number of countries. You may find different options to those shown depending upon the regional settings of your software. Using the same example as above, you will now format both of the cells into US dollars.

1 Highlight both cells and select **Format**, then **Cells…**, then **Currency** in the **Category:** box.

2 Select the required number of **Decimal places:** from the list (make sure that you understand the number of decimal places expected for the country that you will be using). In this case, US dollars have two decimal places.

3 Select the correct currency, in this case US dollars and click on [OK].

4 The two cells that you have formatted should look like this.

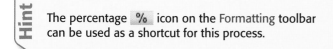

	A
1	$10.50
2	$21.00

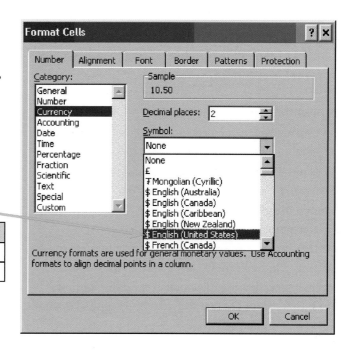

Some currencies like Japanese Yen have no decimal places and so will need to be formatted to zero decimal places. If the currency symbol that you are looking for (e.g. ¥) does not appear in the drop-down list, there are a number of text options available – JPY is the international standard code for Japanese Yen.

Format percentages

In the **Category:** options in the **Number** tab you can set cells into **Percentage** format. It is important to remember that if you want to display 15% in a cell, you must enter 0.15 before formatting the cell as a percentage value. Before using this feature, you should make sure that you understand the maths needed to change decimals to percentages.

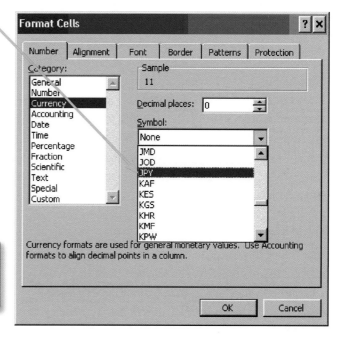

> **Hint**
> The percentage % icon on the Formatting toolbar can be used as a shortcut for this process.

Format fractions

You can also set cells into **Fraction** format in the **Category:** box. This feature is adequate for displaying simple fractions but it does have its limitations. After selecting **Fraction**, specify the number of digits for the parts of the fraction and the type of fraction required, including equivalent fractions when using simple fractions like quarters and eighths.

Format numbers as text

There may be times when you need to format a number as text. When you do this it appears in the cell like a number but it will be left aligned. This should only be

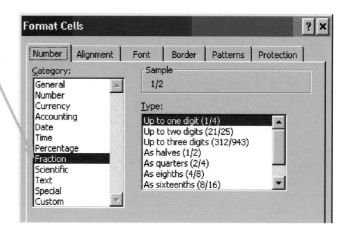

used if the number in the cell is not needed for any calculation. Select the **Number** tab and then select **Text** from the **Category:** list.

Format dates

Date formatting is required for cells containing date values. One of these formats was applied to the cells used in the earlier section on date functions. The date formatting is also selected using **Format**, then **Cells…**, then the **Number** tab, followed by selecting **Date** from the **Category:** list.

There are a number of types available for date formatting. Although these can be seen in the **Type:** list, you may find that your list looks very different to this. These differences are due to the settings applied to your software, both to the *Windows* operating system and to the set-up within *Excel*. Different regional settings will offer different format options, for example in the United Kingdom the date for 25 March 2008 may be formatted as '25/03/2008', yet on a machine in the United States it may be formatted as '03/25/2008'. The regional variations of these settings can be changed using the drop-down list for **Locale (location):**. This will also allow dates with a text component, like '25 March 2008', to be formatted into different languages, such as '25 de marzo de 2008' in Spanish. As part of the practical examinations you may be required to produce different versions of a spreadsheet formatted for audiences in different parts of the world.

Format times

Time values can be formatted in a similar way to the date. Different format types can be selected from the **Type:** list and regional variations to time formatting can also be adjusted using the **Locale (location):** list.

Change text orientation

It is often difficult to get a spreadsheet to fit onto a single screen or page. One reason for this is that the labels across the top of the sheet need too much room. A solution to this problem is to rotate the text within those cells by ninety degrees so that it is vertical within the cell rather than horizontal.

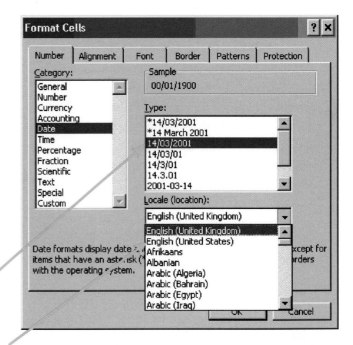

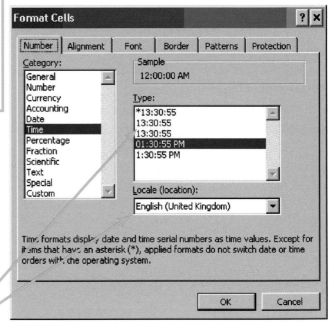

Task 14.22

Open the file BOAT2.XLS from the CD in a new workbook. Change the text orientation of the headings to make the printout fit on a single page width.

1 Open the file BOAT2.XLS.
2 Highlight cells A1 to F1 inclusive.
3 Select the **Format** menu, then **Cells…**.
4 Select the **Alignment** tab.

5 To rotate the text within the cells, click and hold the left mouse button on the red drag handle within the orientation window.

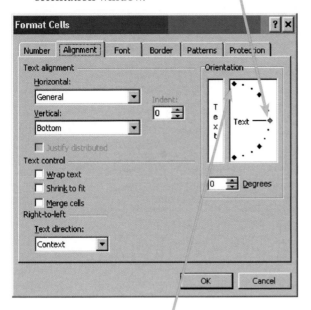

Drag this handle into the top left corner of the box and click on [OK]. This will rotate the headings so that they appear like this:

Boat Name	Boat Identification Number	Cost Price	Sale Price	Profit	Profit Margin
Ta Yang	1	£16,150.00	£22,950.00	£6,800.00	30%
Sealine 218	2	£15,100.00	£21,500.00	£6,400.00	30%

Change cell alignment

The contents can be aligned both horizontally and vertically within each cell. There are a variety of options for changing these settings which can be found using the drop-down menus for **Horizontal:** and **Vertical:** within the **Text Alignment** section of the **Alignment** tab. Some of the available options are illustrated here:

Horizontal alignment

Option:	General	Left (Indent)	Center	Right (Indent)	Justify
Text example	Boat for hire	Boat for hire	Boat for hire	Boat for hire	Boat for hire
Numeric example	74	74	74	74	74
Comment	Left aligns text but right aligns numbers	Text and numbers left aligned			

With the **General** option the text aligns to the left and the numbers align to the right. **Left (Indent)** forces all text and numbers to be left aligned, with a small indent between the cell border and the left of the text or number. The **Center** option centre aligns the cell contents. **Right (Indent)** forces all text and numbers to be right aligned, with a small indent between the cell border and the right of the text or number. **Justify** fully justifies the contents of the cell.

Vertical alignment

Option:	Top	Center	Bottom	Justify
Text example	Boat for hire	Boat for hire	Boat for hire	Boat for hire
Numeric example	74	74	74	74

The **Top** option aligns the cell contents to the top of the cell; **Center** vertically aligns to the centre of the cell; and **Bottom** aligns the contents to the bottom of the cell. The **Justify** option forces the text to align vertically to both the top and bottom of the cell.

Text wrap

Where there is too much text to fit within the available column width of a cell and you want the text to appear on more than one line in the cell, you can format the cell with text wrapping. To turn on text wrapping in part of the spreadsheet, highlight the cell or cells, then open the **Alignment** tab in the **Format Cells** window. In the **Text control** section of the window, use the left mouse button to tick the **Wrap text** box. An example of this is 'Boat for hire' in the spreadsheet above.

Conditional formatting

Conditional formatting is when the cell formatting depends upon the value held within that cell. This is very useful if you wish to highlight or emphasise data within a cell automatically. For example, here is a column containing numbers between 1 and 10. If you want to emphasise those cells that contain more than 6, this could be done easily with conditional formatting. To do this:

Before:

	A
1	6
2	4
3	7
4	9
5	1
6	10
7	8

After:

	A
1	6
2	4
3	7
4	9
5	1
6	**10**
7	8

1 Highlight all cells in the range A1 to A7.

2 Select the Format menu, then Conditional formatting…. The Conditional Formatting window will appear.

3 Select **greater than** from the second drop-down list and enter the number 6 in the third box.

4 Click on ⎢ **Format…** ⎥, which opens the Format Cells window. In this case the formatting selected has been to make the text bold and apply a yellow background colour (see the next subsection for further details).

5 Click on ⎢ **OK** ⎥.

4 Click on ⎢ **OK** ⎥.

Change font styles

Font styles can be changed using the Font tab within the Format Cells window.

1 To change the typeface of the font, use the drop-down list in the Font: section.

2 The point size can be changed in the Size: section.

3 Use the Font style: section if you wish to make the font bold, italic or both of these.

4 You can select different underline options like single underline or double underline using the drop-down list in the Underline: section.

5 The font colour can be selected using the drop-down list for Color:, which allows you to select a pre-defined colour from the palette.

6 Select the Normal font tick box to remove all the features like bold, italic and underline from the cell.

7 Use the Preview section to view the settings for the cell, before clicking on ⎢ **OK** ⎥.

Enhance and emphasise cells

The Format Cells window can be used to apply a variety of enhancements or other features that will emphasise the contents of cells, as described below.

Fill cells with colour or patterns

There are a variety of options for providing cells with coloured or shaded backgrounds. These can be used for fixed formatting of cells or for conditional formatting. They can be used in a variety of ways to highlight cells or provide enhanced boxes or borders for different areas of the worksheet. To change the colour or shading patterns:

1 Highlight the cells to select them.

2 Select the Format menu, then Cells… and select the Patterns tab.

3 Select a colour from the available colours in the Cell shading section or use the drop-down list to select a black-and-white Pattern: for the cell shading.

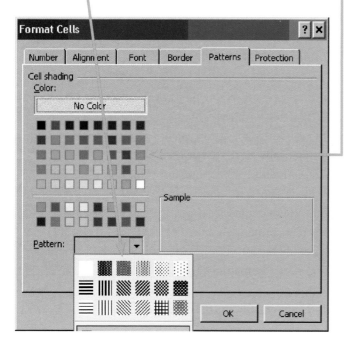

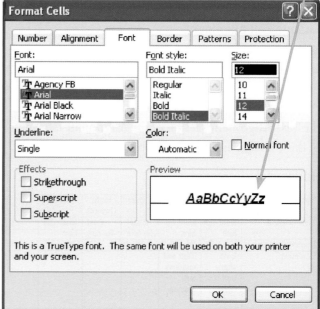

Change borders

Cell borders can be changed for all or part of the spreadsheet using the **Border** tab. Highlight the areas that you wish to change and choose the style and weight (thickness) of the line from the **Line** section of the window. Click on the **Outline** button to apply this style to the outline of the cells, or **Inside** to apply this style to the inner gridlines within the highlighted area. If you wish to apply colour to these lines, this can be selected using the drop-down palette in the **Color:** section. In the example shown here, the outside of the highlighted area will be set to a thick red line and all internal gridlines will be set to a dark blue dashed line. These changes will only take place when you click on [OK].

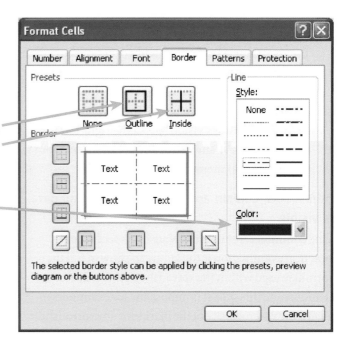

Merge cells

Cells can be merged together to improve the layout of the worksheet. This technique is often used for headings at the top of the worksheet, or sections within the worksheet. In this example, cells in the range A1 to C1 are to be merged into a single cell. This will reduce the width of the three columns and still allow the heading to be large and easy to read.

1   Highlight the three cells A1, B1 and C1.
2   Click on the **Merge and Center** ⊞ button from the **Formatting** toolbar. This will merge the cells and centre align the contents of the cell.

	A	B	C
1	**Monthly Sales**		
2	**Month**	**Sold**	**Income**
3	January	3	£29,500
4	February	5	£122,950

	A	B	C
1	**Monthly Sales**		
2	**Month**	**Sold**	**Income**
3	January	3	£29,500
4	February	5	£122,950

Add a comment to a cell

Task 14.23

Open the file BOAT2.XLS from the CD.
Add a comment to the boat in cell A4, the Searay 215, to say that it is awaiting a repair to its hull.

Comments can be added to cells in a similar way to the use of comments with a word-processed document.
To insert a comment:

1   Select cell A4.
2   Select the **Insert** menu, then **Comment**.
3   Type the text for your comment in the box, in this example information about the Searay 215.

To hide the comment:

1   Move your cursor into cell A4 and press the right mouse button.

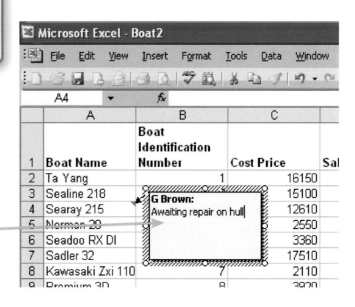

2 Select Hide Comment– the cell will appear like this. The red triangle in the top right corner of the cell indicates that there is a comment present in this cell. When you move the cursor and hover it over cell A4 the comment is displayed. To make sure that the comment is always visible, press the right mouse button in cell A4 and select Show Comment from the drop-down menu.

Adjust row, column and cell sizes so that all data is visible

One common error in the spreadsheets section of a practical examination is the failure to show in full the formulae used within the spreadsheet. If you do not demonstrate this skill, it is impossible for examiners to award the vast majority of the marks for any spreadsheet question. To solve this you will need to show the formulae used and to make sure that the widths of the columns are adjusted so that all of the data and formulae can be seen.

Display formulae

To display the formulae used within a spreadsheet:
1 Select the Tools menu, then Options….
2 Click on the View tab.
3 Click in the Formulas box to place a tick there
4 Click on ☐ OK ☐.

If you wish to return the spreadsheet to displaying the values, follow the same process but remove the tick from the Formulas box.

Adjust column width and row height

It is very important that the cells in your spreadsheet are wide enough to show all of the labels, data and formulae. To adjust the column widths and make all of the columns fit the data and labels held within them at the same time:
1 Highlight all of the spreadsheet by clicking the left mouse button in the top left corner of the spreadsheet.

	A
1	3
2	6

2 Select the Format menu, then Column, followed by AutoFit Selection.

Use a similar process to adjust the row heights using Format, Row then AutoFit Selection.

To adjust an individual column width:
1 Hold the cursor over the column boundary. The cursor will change to look like this.

	A	B	C
1	Number	Sales Pr	Cost
2	6		

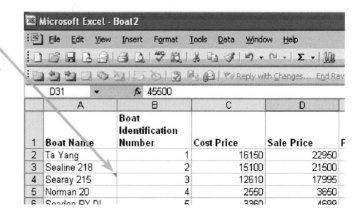

2 Click and hold the left mouse button, dragging the column width to the required size.

Adjusting the row height is a similar process, select the drag handle for the row height at the row boundary and move this as necessary.

It is also possible to adjust the row height to a pre-determined height using the Format menu.
1 Select the cells that need to be adjusted, or the entire sheet as shown above.
2 Select Format, then Row.
3 Select Height… to open the Row Height window, which will be similar to this.
4 Enter the Row height: and click on ☐ OK ☐.

Adjust the column width by a similar process, using Format, Column and Width… in the same way.

14.9 Perform searches
Search using AutoFilter

Task 14.24

Open the file BOAT2.XLS from the CD in a new workbook. Select from all the data:
(i) all the boats with a Sale Price of less than £9995
(ii) all the boats with a Cost Price of between £5000 and £10 000
(iii) all the boats containing the word Seadoo in the Boat Name.

Before starting any search it is important to select all of the data to be searched upon. If the data has a row containing headings the search will be performed more efficiently. If not, insert a blank row above the data and use this in place of the heading row for the following tasks and activities.

Task 14.24(i)

To select all boats with a Sale Price of less than £9995:

1 Open the file BOAT2.XLS.
2 Highlight the cells in the range A1 to F51 (i.e. all of the data).
3 Select the Data menu, then Filter.
4 Choose AutoFilter from the sub-menu. This will show an arrow next to each heading.
5 For the first question, the column needed for the search is the Sale Price. Press the left mouse button on the arrow for this column.
6 The drop-down list will allow you to choose one of the values. To use any other operator, select the (Custom…) option from the list to open the Custom AutoFilter window, which will look similar to this.
7 Select from the first drop-down list the operator to be used in the search, in this case is less than.
8 In the top right box select 9995 from the drop-down list. If it is not available, type the value into the box. In this case, the value will be available from the list if you highlighted all of the data in Step 2.
9 Click on **OK** to perform the search. The results should look like this.

Task 14.24(ii)

To select all boats with a Cost Price of between £5000 and £10 000:

1 Remove the previous search by selecting (All) from the drop-down list for the Sale Price column. This must be done each time you wish to start a new search or Excel will perform the search on only the results of the previous search.
2 Follow Steps 1 to 5 above.
3 Press the left mouse button on the arrow for the Cost Price column.
4 Select the (Custom…) option from the list to open the Custom AutoFilter window, which will look similar to this.
5 Select from the top left drop-down list the first operator to be used in the search, in this case is greater than.

6 Type 5000 in the top right box. This value is not available from the list as there is no boat with a Cost Price of exactly £5000.
7 Click on the radio button for And.
8 Select from the bottom left drop-down list the second operator to be used in the search, in this case is less than.

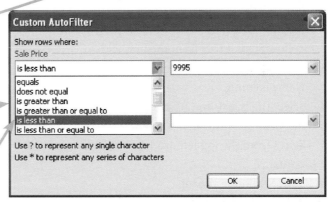

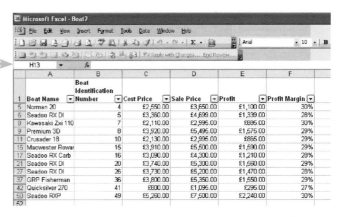

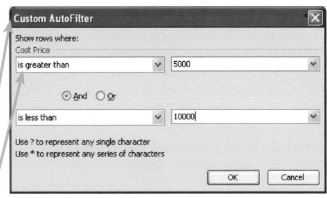

9 Type 10000 in the top right box.

10 Click on [OK] to get results similar to this. ➔

Boat Name	Boat Identification Number	Cost Price	Sale Price	Profit	Profit Margin
Jeanneau Leader 545	9	£9,740.00	£13,795.00	£4,055.00	29%
Cleopatra 850	11	£9,150.00	£12,995.00	£3,845.00	30%
Tayana	17	£9,190.00	£13,000.00	£3,810.00	29%
Contessa 26	19	£8,780.00	£12,500.00	£3,720.00	30%
Jaguar 25	23	£7,030.00	£9,995.00	£2,965.00	30%
Contessa 26	25	£9,080.00	£12,950.00	£3,870.00	30%
Seadoo RXP	49	£5,260.00	£7,500.00	£2,240.00	30%

Task 14.24(iii)

To select all boats containing the word 'Seadoo' in the Boat Name:

1 Remove the previous search by selecting (All) from the drop-down list for the Sale Price column.

2 Follow Steps 1 to 5 from the first search.

3 Press the left mouse button on the arrow for the Boat Name column.

4 Select the (Custom…) option from the list to open the Custom AutoFilter window.

5 Select from the top left drop-down list the operator 'contains'.

6 Type Seadoo in the top right box and click on [OK] to get results similar to this. ➔

> **Hint**
>
> Searching using AutoFilter is very quick and easy but has its limitations. As we have seen, you can search for two criteria in a single column, and you can apply other filters to other columns to further refine searches. If you need to search on three or more criteria in a single column, then a database package is likely to be more suitable.

Boat Name	Boat Identification Number	Cost Price	Sale Price	Profit	Profit Margin
Seadoo RX DI	5	£3,360.00	£4,699.00	£1,339.00	28%
Seadoo RX Carb	16	£3,090.00	£4,300.00	£1,210.00	28%
Seadoo RX DI	20	£3,740.00	£5,300.00	£1,560.00	29%
Seadoo RX DI	26	£3,730.00	£5,200.00	£1,470.00	28%
Seadoo RXP	49	£5,260.00	£7,500.00	£2,240.00	30%

Activity 14.10

Performing searches

Open the file BOAT2.XLS from the CD in a new workbook. Select from all the data:

(i) all the boats with a Sale Price of less than or equal to £5350

(ii) all the boats with a Sale Price of between £30 000 and £50 000

(iii) all the boats containing the word SeaRay or Bavaria in the Boat Name.

Search on two columns

Task 14.25

Open the file that you saved in Task **14.16**. Select from all the data all the orders on 10 or 14 January with an order number ending in 4.

1 Open the file that you saved in Task **14.16**.

2 Highlight the cells in the range A1 to F101.

3 Select the Data menu, then Filter, followed by AutoFilter.
4 Press the left mouse button on the arrow for the Date column.
5 Select the (Custom…) option from the list.
6 Select equals from the drop-down list of operators.
7 Select 10 January 2008 from the drop-down list of values.
8 Make sure that the radio button for Or is selected.
9 Select equals for the second operator.
10 Select the second date, 14 January 2008, from the drop-down list of values.
11 Click on [OK] to perform the first part of the search. 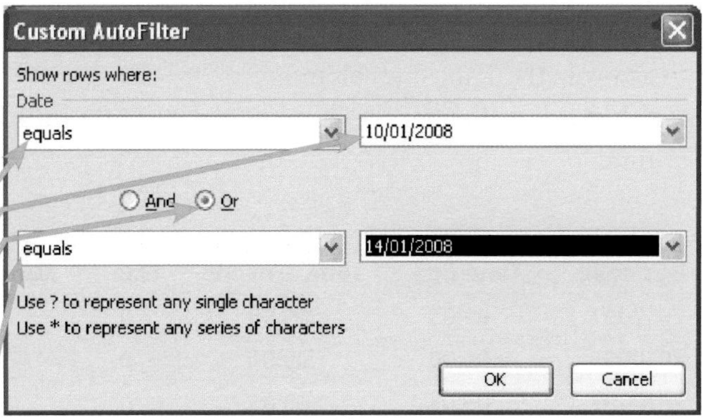
12 The second part of the search involves the Order number, so select the (Custom…) option from the AutoFilter arrow in this column.
13 Because the Order number is a text string even though it contains numbers, you can select the ends with operator from the drop-down list.
14 Place a 4 in the top right box, either by typing or using the drop-down list.
15 Click on [OK] to complete the search. The results should look like this.

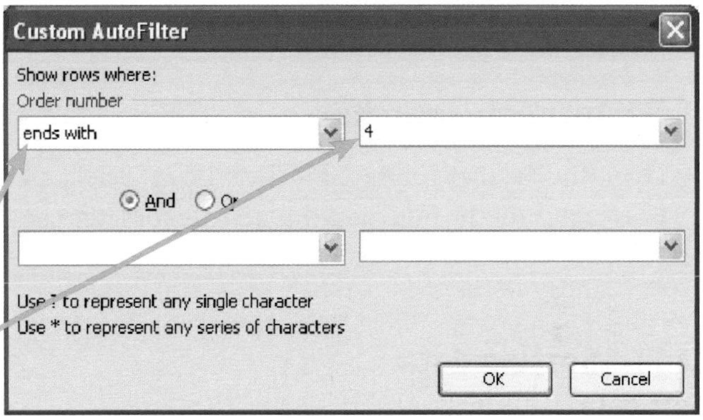

Order number	Customer	Date	Product Code	Weekday	Day
201G524	528	10/01/2008	43202	5	Thursday
201E544	768	14/01/2008	43108	2	Monday

Custom AutoFilter

Show rows where:
Date
equals — 10/01/2008
○ And ● Or
equals — 14/01/2008
Use ? to represent any single character
Use * to represent any series of characters
[OK] [Cancel]

Custom AutoFilter

Show rows where:
Order number
ends with — 4
● And ○ Or
Use ? to represent any single character
Use * to represent any series of characters
[OK] [Cancel]

Activity 14.11

Performing searches on two columns

Open the file that you saved in Task **14.16**.
Select from all the data:
(i) all the orders on 9 or 22 January with an order number ending in 9
(ii) all the orders on 16, 17 or 18 January with a customer number between 299 and 400.

Search on a text value appearing as a number

Task 14.26

Open the file that you saved in Task **14.21**. Select all the buses where the Time due was before 9:15 and where the Minutes was less than 1.

In this question the Minutes field appears to be a number value but is a string extracted from the time. For this question you must identify that the only value less than 1 is a text '0' and use equals 0 in the search. If the search was more complex, you would need to turn the text into numbers using the VALUE function then search on the numeric value.

1 Open the file that you saved in Task **14.21**.
2 Highlight the cells in the range A1 to G118.
3 Select the Data menu, then Filter followed by AutoFilter.

4 Select the (Custom...) option from the AutoFilter arrow in the Time due column.

5 Select is less than for the operator and 09:15 for the time.

6 Click on [OK] to perform the first part of the search.

7 Select the AutoFilter arrow in the Minutes column and select 0 from the resulting drop-down menu. The results should look like this.

Bus code	Time due	Time arrived	Late	Minutes	Passengers	Passenger minutes
2630097	09:05	09:05	0	0	39	0
2660095	09:00	09:00	0	0	32	0
2670098	09:07	09:06	0	0	5	0
2670100	09:11	09:11	0	0	16	0

Activity 14.12

Performing searches

Open the file that you saved in Task **14.21**. Select all the buses that were 5 minutes late with 40 or more passengers on the bus. Save this activity for later use.

14.10 Sorting data

Sort data

Before sorting any data it is important to select all of the data for each item. One of the most common errors in practical examinations is to select only a single column, or only a few columns and perform the sort. If you were to do this the integrity of the data would be lost. Here is an example showing correct and incorrect sorts on employees pay grades and rates of pay. Note how the data for each person has been changed.

In this example, this simple error could have disastrous consequences, as each employee would receive the wrong rate of pay. The areas show the areas selected for the sort.

Original data		
Name	**Grade**	**Rate**
Sagar	2	Rp18375
Marcos	4	Rp34000
Vikram	1	Rp14400
Kratika	2	Rp17500

Sorted correctly with all data selected		
Name	**Grade**	**Rate**
Kratika	2	Rp17500
Marcos	4	Rp34000
Sagar	2	Rp18375
Vikram	1	Rp14400

Sorted with only the name column selected		
Name	**Grade**	**Rate**
Kratika	2	Rp18375
Marcos	4	Rp34000
Sagar	1	Rp14400
Vikram	2	Rp17500

Task 14.27

Open the file RATES.CSV on the CD in a new workbook. Sort the data into descending order of status, then descending order of rate.

1 Open the file RATES.CSV in a new workbook.

2 Highlight the cells in the range A1 to C22.

3 Select the Data menu, then Sort... to open the Sort window, which will look similar to the one on the right.

4 Make sure that the radio button for Header row is selected. If not, press the left mouse button on this. If this is not selected the Grade, Rate and Status labels will be included in the sort.

5 The primary sort is on the Status column. Select this field from the drop-down list in the top box and select Descending.

6 The secondary sort is on the Rate column. Select this field from the drop-down list in the second box and select Descending.

7 Click on [OK] to perform the sort. The results should look similar to this. ———→

Grade	Rate	Status
5	Rp50000	F
4.8	Rp45000	E
4.6	Rp40000	D
4.4	Rp38000	D
4.2	Rp36000	D
3.8	Rp30000	D
4	Rp34000	C
3.6	Rp28000	C
3.4	Rp26000	C
3.2	Rp24000	C
2.8	Rp19000	C
3	Rp22000	B
2.6	Rp18500	B
2.4	Rp18000	B
1.8	Rp17000	B
1.6	Rp16500	B
2.2	Rp17700	A
2	Rp17500	A
1.4	Rp16200	A
1.2	Rp16100	A
1	Rp16000	A

Activity 14.13

Sorting data

Open the file that you saved in Activity **14.12**. Select all of the buses, then sort the data into ascending order of the minutes late and then descending order of the number of passengers.

14.11   Output selected data

Provide evidence for the examiner

Make sure that all printouts or submissions for the practical examinations show all of the labels, data or formulae in full. Make sure that all column widths and row heights are set so that all the data, labels or formulae are fully visible. Remember that the examiner can only mark what can be seen. If you don't show that you have done it, it won't get you any marks.

Remember that if you are asked for a report, that could be a printout from a spreadsheet with titles, name, centre number and candidate number etc. in the header or footer. You may be asked to display extracts of your work. It is acceptable to produce screenshots for evidence of extracts, validation rules and comments and to place these into documents to provide evidence of the skills that you have been asked to show. Make sure that in the practical examination the examiner has evidence of all of your work. Doing the work is not enough – you must give evidence that you have the required knowledge and skills.

Hint
Note that the Rate has been formatted as a currency, Rupees.

Export data

You may be required to export your spreadsheet data into different formats for a variety of purposes. In *Excel* this is done using the Save As… command from the File menu. This will allow you to export the data into common text formats like rtf (rich text format), txt (text format) and csv (comma separated values) and into web page format. It will also allow you to export the data into a variety of other software packages, but these are dependent upon the options chosen when your *Microsoft Office* package was set up. To use any of these features, select the Filename: for the export and select the file type required in the Save as type: box.

Mail merge

In this chapter you will learn how to:

➤ create the structure of the master document
➤ use a source file to merge with the master document
➤ set up fields for automatic completion
➤ set up fields and prompts for manual completion
➤ set up fields to control record selection/omission at mail merge run time
➤ automatically select the required records
➤ manually proofread and correct documents and source files
➤ use appropriate software tools to ensure documents and files are error free
➤ generate form letters and labels.

For this chapter you will need these source files from the accompanying CD:

➤ BOATCLEAN.CSV
➤ BOATCLEAN.RTF
➤ BOATEXTRA.RTF
➤ BOATOFFER.RTF
➤ BOATSALES.RTF
➤ BOATSALES.TXT
➤ CARJAN.CSV
➤ CARLAUNCH.RTF

➤ CARMODEL.RTF
➤ CARSALES.RTF
➤ DINNER.RTF
➤ JETSKI.JPG
➤ JETSKI.RTF
➤ LARGE.JPG
➤ LARGE.RTF
➤ PINKCAR.RTF

➤ POWER.JPG
➤ POWER.RTF
➤ SMALL.JPG
➤ SMALL.RTF
➤ YACHT.JPG
➤ YACHT.RTF

15.1 What is a mail-merged document?

A mail-merged document is created using a master document and a source file containing data. The two are combined to create copies of the document containing data taken from the source file. The most common use of mail-merged documents is to produce personalised letters to a number of people. The contents of the letter have parts that are the same for all people and parts that are personal to the reader. When using the mail merge, the parts that are the same for all people only need to be typed once, even if hundreds of letters are to be created. The personal part of this letter is added using a placeholder, which will hold the individual information taken from the data source. The placeholders can hold information from a data source and/or instructions called merge codes (sometimes called field codes). The information from the data source is often a person's name and address, but may also include information about products that they have bought from a company. For the practical examinations you may be given a copy of a document that will become your master document (and contains the parts for all people) and a source file (which may need you to use a database, spreadsheet or word processor). You will need to merge the files into a number of personalised documents.

15.2 Creating a master document

Create a master document in the word processor

A master document will usually be supplied to you as a source file. However, if a document to be used as a master document is only small you may be asked to create this document. The source document may be provided in a format suitable for use with any word processor. For example, it might be in a .rtf (rich text format) or a .txt (text format) file. This may need importing or opening into your word processor and you will need to save it as a word-processor file. You will need to import or create the document, carefully spell check and proofread the document and check that it has a consistent layout. You must then save two copies of this document as word-processed files, making sure that you have a back-up copy before you start to add the placeholders. You may need to go back to this backed-up copy if you experience any problems.

Add an automated date to the master document

> ## Task 15.1
>
> Open the file BOATCLEAN.RTF from the CD and use this to prepare a master document for a mail merge. Replace the text 'Date here' with an automated date field. Save this file for later use.

1 Open the file BOATCLEAN.RTF. You will notice that this document contains highlighted sections that will need replacing with merge codes.

2 Spell check and proofread the document. Correct any errors found (there are two).

3 Highlight the section Date here and replace this with an automated date. To do this select the Insert menu, then Field…. This opens the Field window which looks similar to this.

4 Using the drop-down menu from the Categories: section, select Date and Time.

5 Select the date from the Field names: drop-down list. This can be the date that the mail merge was created, the date it was saved, the current date or the date the document was printed. For this example, you can select the Date field name.

6 Select the date format that you want to use from those available in the Date formats list. Click on OK to insert the date.

7 You may need to remove the highlighting from the date section. This part of the letter should now look similar to this.

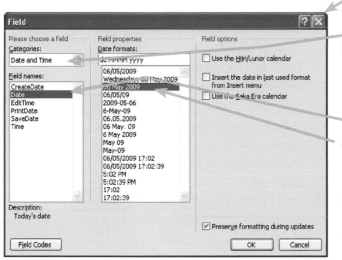

8   Save the document as a *Word* document, BOATMASTER.DOC. Save a back-up copy of this file as it will be used several times in future exercises.

15.3   Creating a source file

There are many types of source file that can be used with *Word*. These can include your *Microsoft Outlook* Contact List, tables in *Word*, *Microsoft Excel* spreadsheets, data within *Microsoft Access*, external databases using OLE-DB or Open Database Connectivity (ODC), SQL databases, tables from HTML documents or web pages and many more. Many of these are beyond the scope of this book. For the purposes of the practical examinations, you will need to learn about only three of these: tables in *Word*, *Excel* spreadsheets and data within *Access*. *Access* is the most powerful of these three data sources as you can take data from either tables or queries. The option of using queries allows you to perform and save complex searches on your data and then use the saved query for the mail merge.

Create a source file

Task 15.2

Use the file saved in Task **15.1** as the master document for a mail merge. Add to the letter the customer's name, address and a personalised greeting from the source file BOATCLEAN.CSV from the CD. The letter will specify the make of boat that the customer purchased. The letter is to be sent to customers who bought a yacht, to offer them a keel-cleaning service. However, it does not need to be sent to Mr McGregor, as he has already booked his yacht for cleaning.

The source file should have been prepared using the data needed for the letter, although source files often contain other data as well. In the case of Task **15.2**, the source file must contain data for the customer's name and address, which must include all parts of the customer's address including the postcode or zip code, the customer name for the greeting and the type of boat purchased by the customer. The price to be charged for cleaning the keel and the contact name for this person are to be entered

at run time, so these do not have to be included in the source file.

The rest of this task is completed in Section **15.4**.

15.4   Running a mail merge using the task pane

In *Word* the easiest way of linking the source file and the master document is using the Mail Merge task pane. Although the task pane contains some features that may be needed for the practical examinations, it also contains a lot of features that will not be used.

1   Open the master document, for this task BOATMASTER.DOC.

2   Select the Tools menu.

3   Choose the option for Letters and Mailings and select Mail Merge from the sub-menu. This will open the Mail Merge task pane. There are six steps to using this task pane; the first is shown here.

4   As the master document for this task is a letter, click on the radio button for Letters.

5   To move to the next step, select the Next option.

6   The open document, BOATMASTER.DOC, will be the master document, so click on the top radio button to Use the current document.

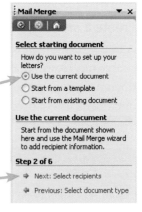

7   To move to the next step and select the recipients, click the left mouse button on Next option.

8   The Select recipients area can now be seen in the task pane. Click on the radio button for Use an existing list if you intend to use an existing file as a data source.

9   Select Browse... to view the records in the source file. This opens the Select Data Source window.

10 Change the pathway of the file until you locate the source file, for this task BOATCLEAN.CSV.

11 When you have selected the data source and clicked on [Open], the **Mail Merge Recipients** window will appear and will look similar to this.

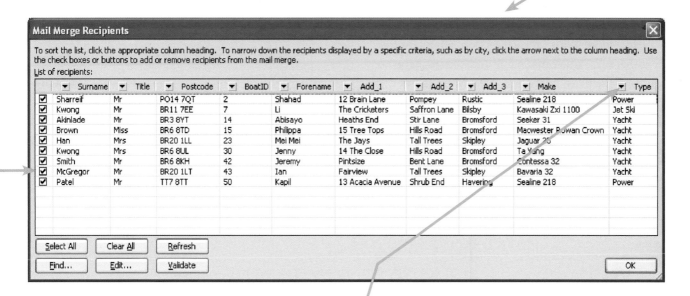

12 One of the criteria for this mail merge is to produce letters for customers who bought a yacht. The search feature within the task pane is used through the selection button, rather like the AutoFilter feature in *Excel*. To select all the yachts, select **Yacht** from the drop-down list for the **Type** field.

13 To sort the data by a field press the left mouse button on the column heading and all of the data will be sorted for you. Clicking once will sort the data into ascending order and a second time into descending

order. Each time you click on the heading of a field it will toggle the sort order for that field.

14 If you wish to manually remove a record from the mail merge press the left mouse button on the tick box on the left hand side to remove the tick. In this example, you need to remove Mr McGregor from the list as he has already booked his yacht in for cleaning. The **Mail Merge Recipients** window will now look similar to this.

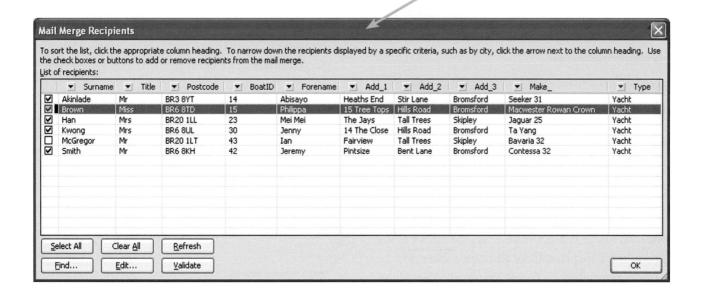

15 Click on [OK] to return to the task pane and select **Next** to move onto the next step.

16 You now need to replace each of the highlighted areas of text in the master document with a placeholder for the correct fields from the source file. Although *Word* has pre-defined settings for the Address Block and the Greeting line, you will probably find it easier to select more items for each section. Highlight the text that says Customer name and address here to position the placeholder and select **More Items….** This opens the **Insert Merge Field** window, which looks similar to this.

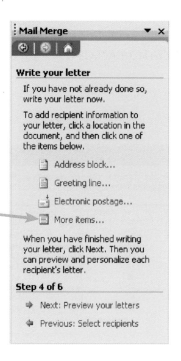

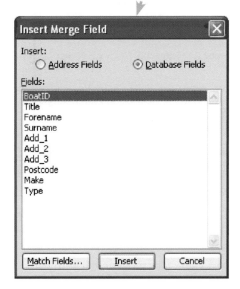

17 Click on the radio button for **Database Fields**.

18 For each of the required fields, highlight the field and then click on the [**Insert**] button to add the placeholder at this point.

19 When all of the field placeholders for the address block have been added, click on [**Close**]. This will leave the address block looking like this.

Wednesday, 26 September 2007

«Title»«Forename»«Surname»«Add_1»«Add_2»«Add_3»«Postcode»

Ref: Keel cleaning service

20 Remove the highlighting from this section.

21 Each placeholder has a double bracket (called a chevron) around it to show that it is a placeholder. Note that these symbols can only be added using the mail merge pane. If you try and type them in, the mail merge will not work. Place the cursor at the end of the Title placeholder and type a space. Do the same at the end of the Forename placeholder. At the end of the Surname placeholder, press the <Enter>

key to force a carriage return, which will move the next placeholder down onto the line below. Do the same at the end of the Add_1, Add_2 and Add_3 fields. The address block should now look like this.

Wednesday, 26 September 2007

«Title» «Forename» «Surname»
«Add_1»
«Add_2»
«Add_3»
«Postcode»

22 Highlight the text that says Customer name here and select **More Items…** to open the **Insert Merge Field** window again.

23 Select the Title and Surname fields from the available database fields before clicking on [**Close**]. Remove the highlighting from these placeholders and insert a single space between them. Place a comma after the Surname merge code.

24 Highlight the text that says boat make in here and replace this with the placeholder for the Make field. Click on [**Close**] to return to the task pane.

25 Make sure that there is a single space before and after the placeholder and that the highlighting is removed.

> **Hint**
> When running a mail merge, check carefully the spacing before and after any automated text.

26 Select **Next** to move onto the next step.

27 This stage will allow you to look at the letters in turn and to reselect the letters to be merged. Use the arrow keys to look at the previous or next letter. When you are happy with the mail merge, select **Next**.

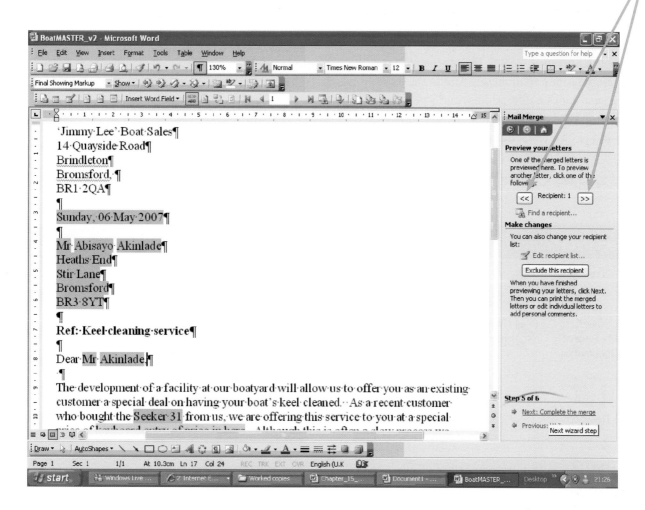

28 Step 6 allows you to print all of the letters during the merge using the **Print…** option. The option to **Edit individual letters…** gives you the flexibility to check the letters before sending them to the printer. Before using either of these options, make sure that you save the master document.

29 When you select one of these options it will run the mail merge for you. Selecting **Edit individual letters…** will open the **Merge to a New Document** window, which looks like this.

Selecting **Print…** gives a similar window called **Merge to Printer**.

30 Click on the radio button for **All**, then click on ▢ **OK** ▢. This will run the mail merge. In this case, it will create a five-page document, with a different letter on each page. Save the letters with a new filename.

15.5 Running a mail merge without the task pane

Although the next task is very similar to Task **15.2** a different approach is required. The task pane will not give us all of the required features so we are going to create the mail merge manually. Before you start, you must make sure that the **Mail Merge** toolbar is visible on the screen. If this toolbar is not shown, select the **View** menu, then **Toolbars** and the **Mail Merge** toolbar. The majority of this toolbar will be inactive (appear greyed out) until you start to use it.

Insert fields using the Mail Merge toolbar

Task 15.3

Use the file saved in Task **15.1** as the master document for a mail merge. Add to the letter the customer's name, address and a personalised greeting from the source file BOATCLEAN.CSV from the CD. The letter will specify the make of boat that the customer purchased.

As you may have noticed, this is the same as Task **15.2**. You will now use a different method to solve this problem.

1 Open the file BOATMASTER.DOC that you saved in Task **15.1**. Make sure that you have a back-up copy of this file.

2 Click on the Open Data Source [icon] button from the Mail Merge toolbar. This opens the Select Data Source window, which will look similar to this.

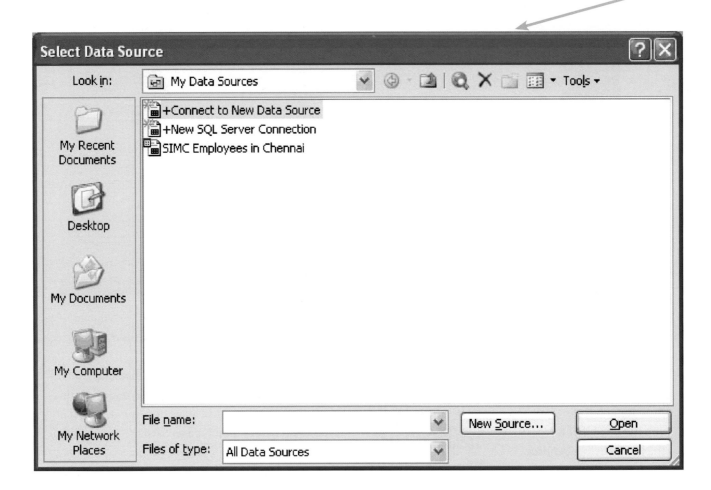

3 Find the pathway to the data file that you intend to use as the source, for this task the file BOATCLEAN.CSV. When you have selected the data source, it becomes linked to the master document. The

Select Data Source window will close and the Mail Merge toolbar will show most of its buttons as being available for use.

4 To insert the address block, highlight the text Customer name and address here and click on the Insert Merge Fields ▤ button.

5 Select the Title, Forename, Surname, Add_1, Add_2, Add_3 and Postcode fields from the list in the **Insert Merge Fields** window, using the same method as you used with the task pane in Task **15.2** (Steps 16 to 19). Reformat these placeholders by adding spaces and carriage returns and removing the highlighting.

6 Replace Customer name here with the Title and Surname fields. Reformat to add a space between the fields, remove the highlighting and add a comma at the end of the line.

7 Replace boat make in here with the Make field. Again, tidy up the formatting and remove the highlighting.

Create mail-merged letters with Fill-in and Skip-if

Task 15.4

Open the file BOATSALES.RTF from the CD and use this to prepare a master document for a mail merge. Replace the text 'Date here' with an automated date field. The customer's name, address and a personalised greeting will be added to the letter from the source file BOATSALES.TXT. The letter will specify the make of boat that the customer purchased. When the letters are produced, the price of the engine overhaul will be inserted manually at run time and the name of the contact at the boatyard will be given – it will usually be Christopher Moon, but may be one of the other mechanics. Letters will only be sent to all customers who bought power boats or jet skis, except Mr Shahad Sharreif, who has already booked his boat in for an overhaul.

1 Open the file BOATSALES.RTF. Save the document as a *Word* document and make a back-up copy of this file.

2 Click on the **Open Data Source** ▦ button from the Mail Merge toolbar and find the file

BOATSALES.TXT. When you have selected the data source, it will be linked to the master document. The **Select Data Source** window will close and the **Mail Merge** toolbar will show most of its buttons available for use.

3 To select the mail merge recipients you can use the **Mail Merge Recipients** ▨ button. This will allow you to use the AutoFilter function and select the recipients manually. You can use this option to filter out the customers who bought power boats or jet skis and you can filter out Mr Shahad Sharreif. In this example you are going to select these records using a method involving conditional variables.

4 Replace the date with the automated date field using **Insert**, then **Field**…. Select **Date and Time** and choose the format for the date. Remove the highlighting.

5 To insert the address block, highlight the text Customer name and address here and click on the Insert Merge Fields ▤ button.

6 Select the Title, Forename, Surname, Add_1, Add_2, Add_3 and Postcode fields from the list in the **Insert Merge Fields** window. Use the same method as used with the task pane in Task **15.2** (Steps 16 to 19). Reformat these placeholders by adding spaces and carriage returns and removing the highlighting.

7 Replace Customer name here with the Title and Surname fields. Reformat to add a space between the fields, remove the highlighting and add a comma at the end of the line.

8 Replace boat make in here with the Make field. Again, tidy up the formatting and remove the highlighting.

Use FILLIN

9 The price of the service needs to be filled in with a price when the mail merge is run. Select the text enter price here by highlighting it. You will now replace this text with a **FILLIN** command. This command can be found by using the Insert Word Field ▾ button on the Mail Merge toolbar. Select the drop-down list, which gives these options.

9   Select **Fill-in…** from this list. This opens the **Insert Word Field: Fill-in** window, which looks similar to this.

10 This window allows you to enter text to ask the user for the information you would like them to type. This is called the prompt. It will also allow you to enter default text, which is useful if many (but not all) letters have to have the same text, as you do not have to retype it each time. Enter the **Prompt:** for the user of the mail merge. Note that the instructions for the user must be clear and concise – this may be assessed in the practical examination. In this example you can enter 'Type in the price for servicing the engine of this boat. Enter it in this format: £320.00 and do not press the return key.'

11 Make sure that the **Ask once** tick box is not ticked, as this question will need to be asked for each letter. Click on [OK] to close this window. A new window will appear that will allow you to see the Fill-in box in the document. Enter a short but meaningful name for this; in this example, enter 'Price' followed by [OK]. The prompt will appear when the mail merge is run and individual prices can be entered for individual boats.

12 This places the FILLIN command into the text and looks similar to this.

13 Check that the spacing around this field is correct. Note that this variable will appear in the letter as the text that you entered.

14 Click the right mouse button on the command that you have just created. This opens a menu which looks similar to this.

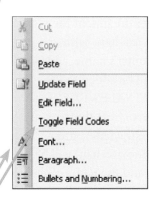

15 Select the option for **Toggle Field Codes**, which will show the underlying code for this merge field. The letter will now look similar to this.

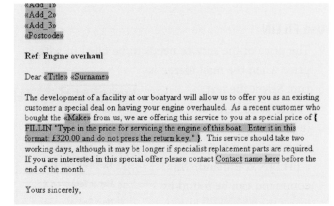

16 Edit the text that says 'this boat' so that it says 'the '.

17 You can now amend the Fill-in prompt to insert the make of the boat when it prompts for the price for servicing each boat. Place the cursor after 'the' and use the **Insert Merge Fields** 🔲 button to insert the Make field into the Fill-in prompt. The letter will show the make of the first boat in the data file and will look similar to this.

«Add_1»
«Add_2»
«Add_3»
«Postcode»

Ref Engine overhaul

Dear «Title» «Surname»

The development of a facility at our boatyard will allow us to offer you as an existing customer a special deal on having your engine overhauled. As a recent customer who bought the «Make» from us, we are offering this service to you at a special price of { FILLIN "Type in the price for servicing the engine of the Kawasaki Zxi 1100. Enter it in this format: £320.00 and do not press the return key." }. This service should take two working days, although it may be longer if specialist replacement parts are required. If you are interested in this special offer please contact Contact name here before the end of the month.

Yours sincerely,

18 Use the same method to create a FILLIN variable to replace the text Contact name here. Select the Fill-in option from the Insert Word Field menu and enter suitable text for the Prompt:, giving the user enough information to let them fill in the details in the letter correctly. In this example, most of the letters will have the name of the chief mechanic Christopher Moon in the placeholder for this field. Add this name to the Default fill-in text: box like this.

19 Make sure that the Ask once box is not ticked and click on ⟨ OK ⟩. Remove the highlighting and check the formatting.

20 Repeat Steps 15 to 18 within this field so that the user can see which boat they are entering the details for. The letter should now look similar to this.

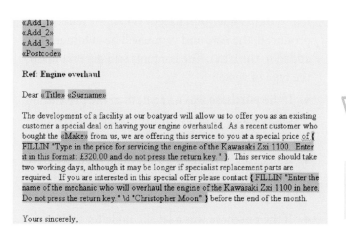

«Add_1»
«Add_2»
«Add_3»
«Postcode»

Ref: Engine overhaul

Dear «Title» «Surname»

The development of a facility at our boatyard will allow us to offer you as an existing customer a special deal on having your engine overhauled. As a recent customer who bought the «Make» from us, we are offering this service to you at a special price of { FILLIN "Type in the price for servicing the engine of the Kawasaki Zxi 1100. Enter it in this format: £320.00 and do not press the return key." }. This service should take two working days, although it may be longer if specialist replacement parts are required. If you are interested in this special offer please contact { FILLIN "Enter the name of the mechanic who will overhaul the engine of the Kawasaki Zxi 1100 in here. Do not press the return key." \d "Christopher Moon" } before the end of the month.

Yours sincerely,

Use SKIPIF

If you were to run the mail merge now, all the letters would be produced. However, letters do not need to be produced for customers who bought a yacht. The SKIPIF command will allow the mail merge to miss out any letters to people who have bought a yacht.

1 Place the cursor at the start of your document.

2 Click on the ⟨ Insert Word Field ▾ ⟩ button from the Mail Merge toolbar and then select the Skip Record If… option from the drop-down menu. This opens the Insert Word Field: Skip If window.

3 Select Type from the Field name: drop-down menu, select Equal to from the Comparison: drop-down

menu, and then type in the word 'Yacht' in the Compare to: box. The window should look like this. ——

4 Click on ⟨ OK ⟩ to insert the SKIPIF.

5 To remove the record for Mr Shahad Sharreif there are a number of ways of creating the SKIPIF command. In this example, you can search and miss out the letter using the Forename or Surname, but the only unique field is the BoatID. It is therefore a better option to use that field for the command. Again, click on the Insert Word Field button from the Mail Merge toolbar and select Skip Record If… from the drop-down menu.

6 Select BoatID from the Field name: drop-down menu, select Equal to from the Comparison: drop-down menu and type in the number 2 in the Compare to: box. The number 2 is the ID number of the boat. The window should look similar to this. ——

7 The merge commands for the two SKIPIF functions will appear like this in the document. These merge commands always appear at the start of the document.

«Skip Record If...»«Skip Record If...» 'Jimmy Lee' Boat Sales
14 Quayside Road
Brindleton

8 Save the master document with a new filename.

9 To run the mail merge, click on the Merge to New Document button from the toolbar.

10 Enter the variables required by both FILLIN commands and when the mail merge has been completed you should have only three letters, two to Mr Kwong and one to Mr Patel.

> **Hint**
> Using this method rather than selecting from the recipients list means that you will have to enter the price and name of the mechanic for each record, even if they are omitted by the SKIPIF function.

11 Save the letters with a new filename.

Create mail-merged letters

Open the file CARSALES.RTF from the CD and use this to prepare a master document for a mail merge. Replace the text 'Date here' with an automated date field. The customer's name, address and a personalised greeting from the source file CARJAN.CSV will be added to the letter. The letter will specify the year, make and model of the car that the customer purchased. Do not send the letter to customers whose car was made in or after 2005. Do not send the letter to Mrs Natsumi Tang.

> **Hint**
>
> Use the Mail Merge Recipients button to filter out Mrs Natsumi Tang.

15.6 Using field codes

Now that you have tried setting up a mail merge, you can consider the types of commands that can be used within the merge. These commands are called field codes. They allow you set up fields so that they can be completed manually (by hand), or to set up fields to automatically select (or omit) records from the mail merge at run time. You have already used one of the fields to be completed manually in Section **15.5**, where the FILLIN command (field code) was used to enter a price for the letter. Also in Section **15.5**, you used the SKIPIF field code to omit records at run time. The following sections will cover other field codes that may be useful.

15.7 Setting up fields for manual completion

You have already used the FILLIN command to add different prices to individual letters and to add the names of different mechanics for the engine overhauls. If the merge requires a single variable for all of the selected letters use the **Ask once** tick box within the FILLIN command, which will reduce the amount of data entry at run time. This could save you valuable time in the practical examination. The FILLIN command is versatile

enough to enable you to complete almost all automated tasks where data needs to be added at run time.

15.8 Setting up fields for automatic completion

The most useful command for automatically changing text within a mail-merged letter is the conditional IF… Then…Else… field code. Different responses can be used within a single document, depending on the person to whom the letter is being sent.

Task 15.5

Open the file BOATOFFER.RTF from the CD and use this to prepare a master document for a mail merge. Replace the text 'Date here' with an automated date field. The customer's name, address and a personalised greeting from the source file BOATSALES.TXT will be added to the letter. The letter will specify the make of boat that the customer purchased. When the letters are produced, the date and venue will be automatically added to the letter. The contents will depend upon the type of vessel:

- If the purchase was a yacht, then the prize draw event will take place on 14th August at 8:00pm at the Bromsford Yacht Club.

- If the purchase was a power boat, then the prize draw event will take place on 7th August at 7:00pm at Maudsley Marina.

- If the purchase was a jet ski, no letter will be created.

1 Open the file BOATOFFER.RTF. Save the document as a *Word* document and make a back-up copy of this file.

2 Click on the **Open Data Source** button from the **Mail Merge** toolbar. This opens the **Select Data Source** window.

3 Find the pathway to the data file that you intend to use as the source, in this example BOATSALES.TXT. When you have selected the data source, it becomes attached to the master document. The **Select Data Source** window will close and the **Mail Merge** toolbar will show most of its buttons as being accessible.

4 Replace the date with the automated date field using **Insert**, then **Field….** Select **Date and Time** and choose the format for the date. Remove the highlighting.

5 To insert the address block, highlight the text Customer name and address here and click on the **Insert Merge Fields** button.

6 Select the Title, Forename, Surname, Add_1, Add_2, Add_3 and Postcode fields from the list in the **Insert Merge Fields** window, using the same method as used with the task pane in Task **15.2** (Steps 16 to 19). Reformat these placeholders by adding spaces and carriage returns and removing the highlighting.

7 Replace Customer name here with the Title and Surname fields. Reformat the text to add a space between the fields, remove the highlighting and add a comma at the end of the line.

Use If…Then…Else…

8 The text date and venue needs to be replaced with the conditional data described in Task **15.5**. In order to do this we have to replace the text with an If…Then…Else… command. Highlight the text to be replaced and click on the Insert Word Field button on the **Mail Merge** toolbar to obtain this drop-down list.

9 Select If…Then…Else… from the list. This opens the **Insert Word Field: IF** window, which will look similar to this.

10 Select the **Field name:** from the drop-down list in the top left box, in this case Type.

11 Select the **Comparison:** type as **Equal to**, using the drop-down list.

12 In the **Compare to:** box, enter the text 'Yacht'.

13 Using the information from Task 15.5, in the **Insert this text:** box, type in the text '14th August at 8:00 at the Bromsford Yacht Club'. This text will be displayed only if the Type field is Yacht.

14 Enter into the **Otherwise insert this text:** box the text '7th August at 7:00 at Maudsley Marina'. This text will be displayed only if the Type field is not Yacht. The completed window should look like this.

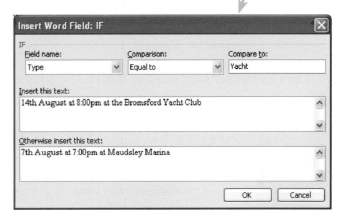

15 Click on **OK** to create the merge field code.

16 Use the SKIPIF merge code to miss out the letter if the Type is Jet Ski, using the same method as for Task **15.4**.

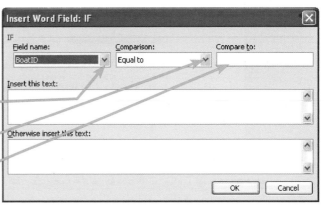

17 As in all previous examples, tidy up the formatting and remove the highlighting. Save your master document. Make sure that you have only a single full stop at the end of the merged sections. Run the mail merge as shown in previous sections. You should get eight letters. Save the letters.

Hint

Look at the source file BOATSALES.TXT to check the case (use of capitals) of the data in the Type field (you will need this for Task **15.6**). Make sure that you match the case in the merge codes to the case in the data file for these mail merge features to work as expected.

Use multiple If...Then...Else... field codes

Task 15.6

After preparing all of the letters in Task **15.5**, the manager wishes to change the letters so that they have the following contents, depending on the type of vessel:

- If the purchase was a yacht, the prize draw event will take place on 14th August at 8:00 at the Bromsford Yacht Club.
- If the purchase was a power boat, the prize draw event will take place on 7th August at 7:00 at Maudsley Marina.
- If the purchase was a jet ski, the prize draw event will take place on 7th August at 9:00 at Maudsley Marina.

1 Open the merged letter saved in Task **15.5**, which should look similar to this.

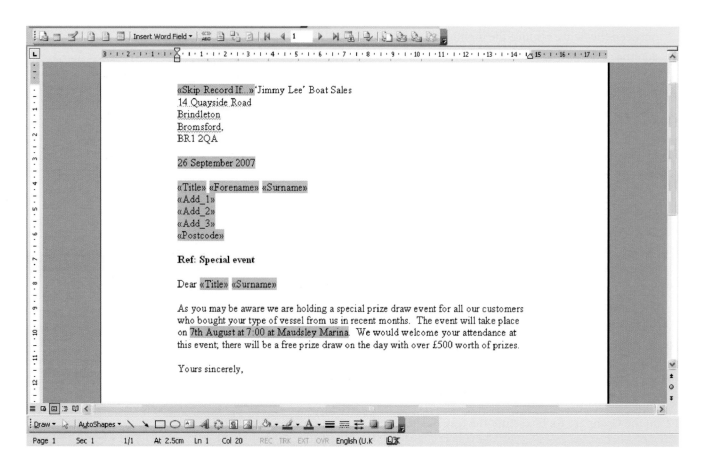

2 Right mouse click within the field code (the grey area) to obtain this menu.

3 Select **Toggle Field Codes**, which will show the underlying code for this merge field and will look similar to this.

As you may be aware we are holding a special prize draw event for all our customers who bought your type of vessel from us in recent months. The event will take place on { IF Power = "Yacht" "14th August at 8:00pm at the Bromsford Yacht Club" "7th August at 7:00pm at Maudsley Marina" }. We would welcome your attendance at this event; there will be a free prize draw on the day with over £500 worth of prizes.

> **Hint**
>
> Note that *Word* may show the value of the first data item in the source data as part of the merge field code, rather than the merge field name. In this example, the Type field was selected and rather than viewing the code {IF Type = "Yacht" … *Word* has displayed the contents of the Type field for the first record, which is Power.

> **Hint**
>
> Note that sometimes the Type field is replaced by the word 'Power' in each of the If…Then… Else… statements. To change these in order to show the full merge codes, click the right mouse button on the word 'Power' for each IF statement, then select Toggle Field Codes.

4 Delete the current field code and in its place insert the three letters 'abc'. You are going to replace each of these letters in turn with a merge field. As these merge fields are not visible when you have inserted them, you need to use the three letters to get the correct position, without accidentally deleting the codes that you have just added. Carefully highlight each of these letters in turn and replace each with a merge field for one of the required items. This involves selecting **Insert Word Field** from the **Mail Merge** toolbar and adding the If…Then… Else… command as shown in the previous section. When this has been completed for all three sections, if you right click on the position of the field code (although the field code will not be visible) and select **Toggle Field Codes** this will show the code. This needs to be repeated three times, once for each field code. The final result (which can be checked for errors) should look like this.

As you may be aware we are holding a special prize draw event for all our customers who bought your type of vessel from us in recent months. The event will take place on { IF { MERGEFIELD Type } = "Yacht" "14th August at 8:00pm at the Bromsford Yacht Club" "7th August at 7:00pm at Maudsley Marina" }{ IF { MERGEFIELD Type } = "Power" "7th August at 7:00pm at Maudsley Marina" "" }{ IF { MERGEFIELD Type } = "Jet Ski" "7th August at 9:00pm at Maudsley Marina" "" }. We would welcome your attendance at this event; there will be a free prize draw on the day with over £500 worth of prizes.

5 Delete the SKIPIF placemarker at the start of the file, to allow the mail merge to also produce the letters to customers who bought a jet ski. Carefully check through the master document for errors. Save your master document so that it can be used later in this chapter before running the mail merge.

Activity 15.2

Create mail-merged letters

Open the file CARLAUNCH.RTF from the CD and use this to prepare a master document for a mail merge. Replace the text 'Date here' with an automated date field. The customer's name, address and a personalised greeting from the source file CARJAN.CSV will be added to the letter. The letter will specify the make and model of the car that the customer purchased. When the letters are produced the date and venue will be automatically added to the letter:

- If the Address2 field contains Cambridge, the presentation will take place on 1st August at 7:00pm at the Grand Cambridge Hotel.
- If the Address2 field contains Histon, Coton or Girton, the presentation will take place on 7th August at 7:30pm at the Palace Hotel in Histon.

Do not send the letter to Mr Graham Brown.

Use pre-defined text with If…Then…Else…

Task 15.7

Open the file BOATEXTRA.RTF from the CD and use this to prepare a master document for a mail merge. Replace the text 'Date here' with an automated date field. The customer's name, address and a personalised greeting from the source file BOATSALES.TXT will be added to the letter. Replace the text 'Place new paragraph here.' with a new section of text using the following rules:

- If the type of boat is a yacht, insert the text from the file on the CD, YACHT.RTF.
- If the type of boat is a power boat, insert the text from the file on the CD, POWER.RTF.
- If the type of boat is a jet ski, insert the text from the file on the CD, JETSKI.RTF.

1 Open the file BOATEXTRA.RTF. Save the document as a *Word* document and make a back-up copy of this file.
2 Click on the Open Data Source 🔲 button from the Mail Merge toolbar. This opens the Select Data Source window.
3 Find the pathway to the data file and select the file BOATSALES.TXT as your data source.
4 Replace the date with the automated date field using Insert, then Field. Select Date and Time and choose the format for the date. Remove the highlighting.
5 To insert the address block, highlight the text Customer name and address here and click on the Insert Merge Fields 📄 button.
6 Select the Title, Forename, Surname, Add_1, Add_2, Add_3 and Postcode fields from the list in the Insert Merge Fields window, using the same method as used with the task pane in Task **15.2** (Steps 16 to 19). Reformat these placeholders by adding spaces and carriage returns and removing the highlighting.

7 Replace Customer name here with the Title and Surname fields. Reformat to add a space between the fields, remove the highlighting and add a comma at the end of the line.

To produce the different text for each type of boat from the three external files, you need to include nested merge codes. A single placeholder will be used to hold an If…Then…Else… command and within this command will be a command to include text from an external file.

8 Highlight the text Place new paragraph here. and click on the Insert Word Field ▾ button from the Mail Merge toolbar.
9 Select If…Then…Else… from the drop-down list. This opens the Insert Word Field: IF window.
10 Select the Field name: from the drop-down list in the top left box, in this case select the Type field.
11 Select the Comparison: type as Equal to using the drop-down list.
12 In the Compare to: box enter the text 'Yacht'.
13 Do not include any text in either of the boxes; we will add the external file details later. The completed window should look like this.

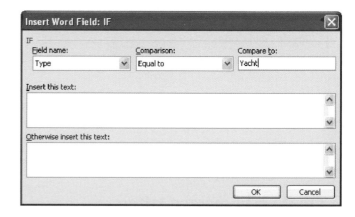

14 Click on OK to create the merge field code.
15 Right mouse click on the current position of your cursor. If you are in the correct place, the menu will look similar to this.

16 Select the **Toggle Field Codes** option. This will show the underlying code for this merge field and will look similar to this.

> Dear «Title» «Surname»
> As a valued customer we would like to invite you to the launch of a new range of product. { IF Power = "Yacht" "" "" }
>
> We can do a special deal on this product, call into the shop to discuss this with us, and

17 Place the cursor between the second pair of speech marks and press the left mouse button.

18 Select the Insert menu, then **Field** to open the **Field** window.

19 Select (All) from the **Categories:** drop-down list.

20 Scroll down the list in the **Field names:** box and click on IncludeText.

21 You must type in the pathway of the data file containing the correct text for yachts. This text is stored in the file YACHT.RTF. The pathway that you type will be different from the one shown here.

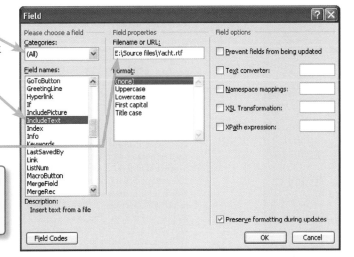

> **Hint**
> You must know the full pathname for the file, as there is no browse option for locating this file.

22 Click on [OK] to create the merge field code. The document will look similar to this.

> «Postcode»
>
> **Ref**: View the latest in marine technology
>
> Dear «Title» «Surname»
> As a valued customer we would like to invite you to the launch of a new range of product. { IF Power = "Yacht" " Try the latest in ocean-based satellite navigation. The latest Dygitell range of satellite navigation systems brings affordable solutions to traditional marine navigation. Switch on to find your exact GPS position, plan your course avoiding all known hazards, including sand banks, underwater obstructions and, of course, busy commercial shipping lanes. There are three models to view, starting from only £99." "" }
>
> We can do a special deal on this product. Call into the shop to discuss this with us and we will offer you, as an existing customer, excelle[...]
>
> Yours sincerely,

> **Hint**
> In this example, the Type field has been replaced by the word Power, and the reference to the external source document has been replaced by the text from that document.

23 Repeat Steps 9 to 22 twice more to add the nested commands for power boats and jet skis. The finished letter showing the merge codes should look similar to this.

24 As in all previous examples, tidy up the formatting and remove the highlighting. Save your master document. Make sure that you have only a single full stop at the end of the merged sections and no extra carriage returns. Run the mail merge as shown in previous sections. Save the letters.

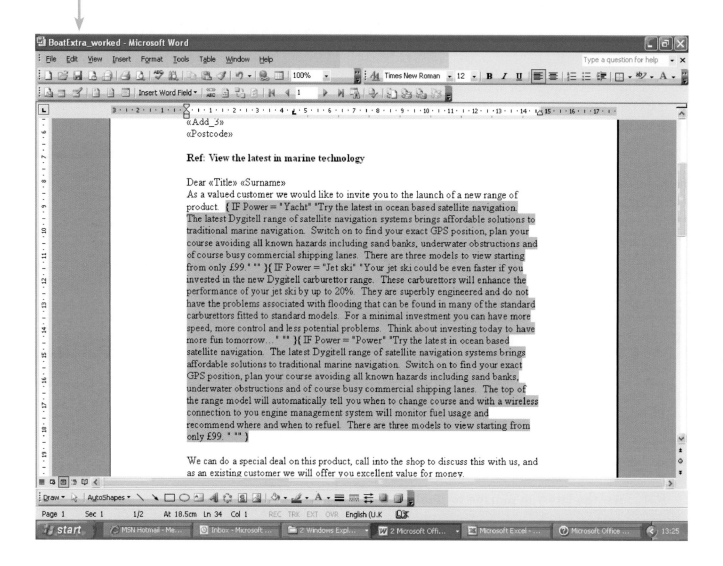

Activity 15.3

Create mail-merged letters using external text

Open the file CARMODEL.RTF from the CD and use this to prepare a master document for a mail merge. Replace the text 'Date here' with an automated date field. The customer's name, address and a personalised greeting from the source file CARJAN.CSV will be added to the letter. Replace the text 'Place new paragraph here.' with a new section of text using the following rules:

- If the price of the previous car was under £7000, insert the text from the file SMALL.RTF.
- If the price of the previous car was £7000 or more, insert the text from the file LARGE.RTF.

Use images with If…Then…Else…

Task 15.8

Use the file saved in Task **15.7** as the master document for a mail merge. Add an image to the top right corner of the letter. The image will be selected from the CD at run time using the following rules:

- If the type of boat is a power boat, insert the image file POWER.JPG.
- If the type of boat is a jet ski, insert the image file JETSKI.JPG.

1 Open the master document that you saved in Task **15.7**. Save the document with a new filename and make a back-up copy of this file. Because the master document has been set up previously and links to an external source, you will be shown a window to check that you wish to open the document and the attached data source. This warning is to show you that the document contains data linked to another file (which could have a potential virus risk). The window will look similar to this.

2 Click on [Yes] to open the document.

3 The best way of ensuring that the image is in the correct place in the letter is to insert a text box. To do this, select the **Insert** menu, then **Text box**.

4 A large text box appears asking you to 'Create your drawing here'. Ignore this box. Press and hold the left mouse button to draw the text box in the correct place by dragging the text-box lasso so that it looks like this.

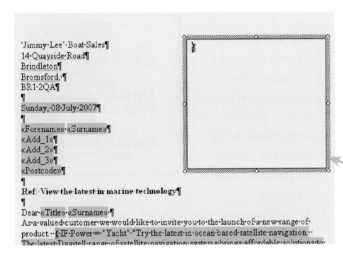

5 Type a single character into the text box. Text boxes which have no contents tend to disappear.

6 Right mouse click on the border of the text box to get this drop-down menu.

7 Select **Format Text Box…** from this menu. This will open the **Format Text Box** window, which will look similar to this.

8 You are going to hide the text box from view. Select the **Colors and Lines** tab in the **Format Text Box** window (if it is not already visible).

9 In the **Line** section, select the drop-down menu for the **Color:** and select **No Line** from the options.

10 For this task it is unlikely that the text will need to wrap around the text box, but it is always worth setting up text wrapping in case the name of a customer, or the address line for a customer is very long. To set the text wrapping, select the **Layout** tab and choose **Square**.

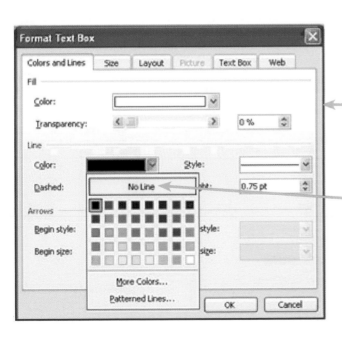

11 The text box is now set up, so click on [OK] to close the **Format Text Box** window.

To produce the different image for each type of boat from the three external files, you need to include nested merge codes using a similar method to that shown above. A single placeholder will be used to hold an If…Then… Else… command and within this command will be a command to include the image file.

12 Highlight the character typed in during Step 5.
13 Click on the [Insert Word Field ▾] button from the **Mail Merge** toolbar.
14 Select If…Then…Else… from this list. This opens the **Insert Word Field: IF** window.
15 Select the **Type** field from the drop-down list for the **Field:**.
16 Select the **Comparison:** type as **Equal to** using the drop-down list.
17 In the **Compare to** box enter the text 'Yacht'.
18 Do not include any text in either of the boxes; you will add the image file details later. Click on [OK] to create the merge field code.
19 Right mouse click on the current position of your cursor. If you are in the correct place the menu will look similar to this. ──────▶

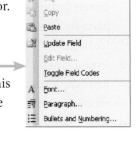

20 Select **Toggle Field Codes**. This will show the underlying code for this merge field and will look similar to this. ↘

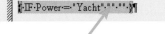

21 Place the cursor between the second pair of speech marks and press the left mouse button.
22 Select **Insert**, then **Field** to open the **Field** window.
23 Scroll down the list in the **Field names:** box and select **IncludePicture**. ──────
24 Enter the pathway of the data file containing the image of a yacht. This image is stored in the file YACHT.JPG. The pathway that you type will be different from the one shown here. ──────
25 Click on [OK] to create the merge field code.
26 The text box may look similar to this, or it may include the image in place of the pathway. If this

includes an image you may need to resize the text box so that you can see the end of the merge code. This can then be reduced again when you have finished entering the merge code.

27 Click at the end of the merge field code and repeat Steps 13 to 25 twice more to add the nested commands for power boats and jet skis. The finished text box showing the merge codes may look similar to this, ──────▶ or may include the images in place of the pathways and filenames.

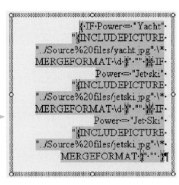

28 As in all previous examples, tidy up the formatting and remove the highlighting. Save your master document. Make sure that you have only a single full stop at the end of the merged sections and no extra carriage returns. Run the mail merge as shown in previous sections. Save the form letters.

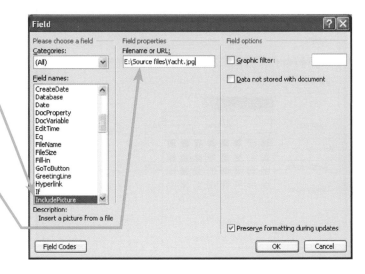

Create mail-merged letters using external images

Use the file saved in Activity **15.3** as the master document for a mail merge. Add an image to the top right corner of the letter. The image will be selected from the CD at run time using the following rules:

- If the price of the previous car was under £7000, insert the image file SMALL.JPG.
- If the price of the previous car was £7000 or more, insert the image file LARGE.JPG.

15.9 Setting up fields to control record selection

There is a variety of methods to select records for the mail merge. When you worked through Section **15.4**, there were facilities to select individual records from the source data within the task pane. In Section **15.5** you used the SkipIf command to omit records at run time. This is likely to be one of the most useful tools. There are other options available like NextIf which will extract the data for the merge from the next record rather than from the current record. To use the NextIf command, follow the instructions for Section **15.5** and replace SkipIf with NextIf.

Select records using the Mail Merge Recipients window

The most recent versions of *Word* have made the selection of records much easier, using the Mail Merge Recipients window. You have already used this feature in Section **15.4** when creating the master document using the task pane. This feature is available on the Mail Merge toolbar by clicking on the Mail Merge Recipients button. This allows you to select using an auto-filter similar to searching within *Excel*.

Open the file DINNER.RTF from the CD and use this to prepare a master document for a mail merge. Replace the text 'Date here' with an automated date field. The customer's name, address and a personalised greeting from the source file BOATSALES.TXT will be added to the letter. Produce this letter for ladies who do not live in Skipley.

1 Open the file DINNER.RTF and prepare this as a master document using BOATSALES.TXT as a source file. Add the relevant merge codes for the date, customer details and greeting. Refer to earlier sections of this chapter for help on this.
2 Click on the Mail Merge Recipients button from the Mail Merge toolbar.
3 The Mail Merge Recipients window will open and look similar to this.
4 To select only the ladies, select the drop-down list in the title field which will offer these options. We need to select the Miss and Mrs categories, or not select the Mr category. To do either of these searches, select the (Advanced...) option. This opens the Query Options window (see next page).

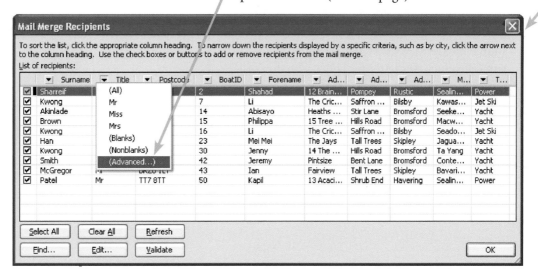

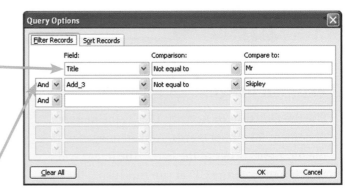

5 In the Field: section, use the drop-down menu to select the Title field.

6 In the Comparison: section, use the drop-down menu to select Not equal to.

7 In the Compare to: section, enter the text 'Mr'. This will filter out all of the men from the available records.

8 To remove the people who live in Skipley, select the And option from the available logical operators.

9 In the Field: section, use the drop-down menu to select the Add_3 field.

10 In the Comparison: section, use the drop-down menu to select Not equal to.

11 In the Compare to: section, enter the text 'Skipley'.

12 When you have checked that all of the search criteria are correct, click on [OK] to create the query. This selects the records fitting these criteria.

13 Run the mail merge as shown in previous sections and save the form letters.

Activity 15.5

Record selection

Open the file PINKCAR.RTF from the CD and use this to prepare a master document for a mail merge. Replace the text 'Date here' with an automated date field. The customer's name, address and a personalised greeting from the source file CARJAN.CSV will be added to the letter. Produce this letter for ladies who do not live in Kings Lynn or Trumpington.

Select records from a *Access* query

If you need to select records from a relational database (see Chapter **11** for more details), create a single query containing all of the required fields. Use this query as your single data source for the mail merge. The *Access* query can be used to select the data for the mail merge rather than this selection being performed in the word processor. This is likely to be more complex in the database and should only be used where the selection criteria are too complicated to be used in the **Mail Merge Recipients** window in *Word*.

15.10 Creating mail merge labels

Task 15.10

Produce mail-merged address labels for the letters created in Task **15.9**. These labels must be 6 centimetres wide and 4 centimetres high and fit 3 across the page and 5 down the page. There must be a 1-centimetre gap between each label.

1 The easiest method of creating address labels is using the **Mail Merge** task pane. Open a new document and save it as 'Task 15 labels'.

2 Select the **Tools** menu.

3 Choose the option for **Letters and Mailings** and select **Mail Merge** from the sub-menu. This will open the **Mail Merge** task pane. As you are going to create mail merge labels, click on the radio button for **Labels**.

4 To move to the next step, select the **Next** option.

5 You need to create the template for the labels on the page. In the **Select starting document** section, choose the second radio button, to **Change document layout**.

6 To set up the size layout of the labels on the page, select **Label options…** from the **Change document layout** section. This opens the **Label Options** window, which will look similar to this.

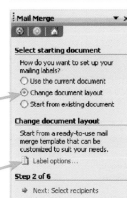

7 In the **Label information** section of this window there are a vast number of different companies who manufacturer the labels and an even wider range of products to choose from. For the purposes of the practical examinations you will be required to produce labels of a specific size. Unless you already know of a manufacturer and a product that is the right size, go to the **Label products:** section and use the drop-down menu to select **Other/Custom**.

8 To create a new label with the sizes specified in the task you need to click on the [New Label…] button. This opens the **New Custom** window, which will look similar to this. The window layout may vary, depending on the type of printer selected (e.g. laser, inkjet or dot matrix) and the size of the paper to be used for the labels. In this case, the window title bar shows that this is for a laser printer.

9 In the **Label name:** box, enter the name for your new custom designed label.

10 Set the **Label height:** to 4 centimetres.

11 Set the **Label width:** to 6 centimetres.

12 To achieve the gap of 1 centimetre between each label the **Vertical pitch:** must be set to 5 centimetres, which is the 4 centimetres for the label height plus the 1-centimetre gap.

13 The **Horizontal pitch:** must be set to 7 centimetres, which is the 6 centimetres for the label width plus the 1-centimetre gap.

14 Set the **Number across:** to 3 as specified in the task.

15 Set the **Number down:** to 5.

16 To work out the side margin you need to add together the width of three labels and the two gaps between them. This gives a width that is used of 6+1+6+1+6 centimetres. This total of 20 centimetres is taken from the page width (21 centimetres) to leave 1 centimetre. This 1 centimetre is the space left for both left and right side margins, so each side margin is half of this: 0.5 centimetres. Set the **Side margin:** to 0.5 centimetres.

> **Hint**
> The top margin is set by the printer settings – you should not change this.

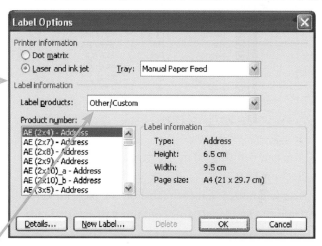

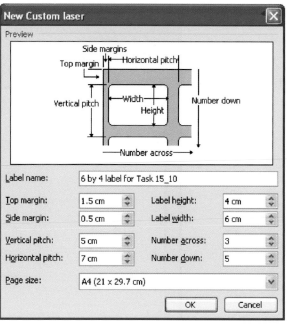

17 Click on [OK] to return to the Label Options window.

18 Click on [OK] again to create the page formatting.

19 To move to the next step and select the recipients, select the Next option.

20 The Select recipients area can now be seen in the task pane. Click on the radio button for Use an existing list if you intend to use an existing file as a data source.

21 Select Browse… to view the records in the source file. This opens the Select Data Source window.

22 Change the pathway of the file until you locate the source file, for this task BOATSALES.TXT.

23 When you have selected the data source and clicked on [Open], the Mail Merge Recipients window will be opened and will look similar to this.

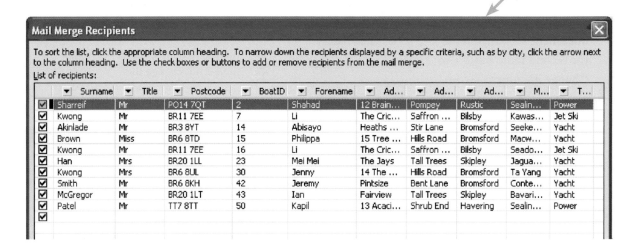

24 You can edit this list as required, as shown in Section **15.9**.

25 You will notice that each label on the page (apart from the first label) now contains a merge code for the next record.

26 To move to the next step so that you can arrange the labels, select the Next option.

27 To insert the merge fields from your data source, select More items… from the task pane.

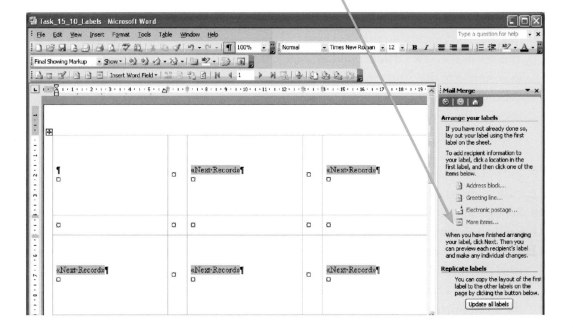

28 Use the **Insert Merge Field** window to add the correct fields to the first label. Select the Title, Forename, Surname, Add_1, Add_2, Add_3 and Postcode, clicking on ⟨Insert⟩ after each one.

29 Close the **Insert Merge Field** window and then format the address details, using the same methods that you used earlier in the chapter. The finished address block should look similar to this.

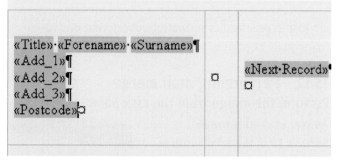

30 You can copy the layout of the first label to the other labels by clicking on the ⟨Update all labels⟩ button in the task pane.

31 Select Next to preview the labels. This shows the first few labels with the data included.

32 Select Next to complete the merge and select **Edit the labels**. The edit option will run the mail merge and allow you to save the labels, enabling you to check for errors in the practical examination.

Activity 15.6

Mail merge labels

Produce mail-merged address labels for the letters created in Activity **15.5**. These labels must be 4.5 centimetres wide and 3.5 centimetres high and fit four across the page and six down the page. There must be a 0.5-centimetre gap between each label.

15.11 Using manual methods and software tools to ensure error-free accuracy

Use techniques described in earlier chapters (e.g. proofreading and error correction from Section **10.16**) to help you create accurate documents. Use the techniques for validation and verification that you studied in Chapters **11** and **14**.

Check the source data

Check the source data thoroughly before you attach the data source to your master document. Use validation and verification techniques to try and ensure that the data is as accurate and error free as possible. The type of checking will depend upon the format of the source data, for example validation rules can be applied to database and spreadsheet files, but not as easily to text-based sources.

Check the master document

Check the master document thoroughly, using automated features like spelling and grammar checks as well as proofreading the document. Check for careless errors, as these can cost a significant number of marks in the practical examinations. Avoid the use of page breaks and section breaks for aesthetic reasons, as these will rarely fall in the same place when additional text, images or other objects are added to the document during the mail merge. To avoid widows and orphans, use the automated settings within the word processor rather than manually inserting breaks (see Section **10.13**).

Test the merge

When conditional text is entered into the master document at run time, it does not always appear within the body of the document as you intended. Take particular care with punctuation and grammar, especially if the conditional text forms part of a sentence. The best way of testing this is to use one example of each piece of conditional text. For example, if you want to test the merge for Task **15.5**, there are two options to be tested.

One piece of conditional text is used when the Type is Yacht, and a different piece when the Type is Power.

Open the **Mail Merge Recipients** window and select one recipient for each type, as shown here.

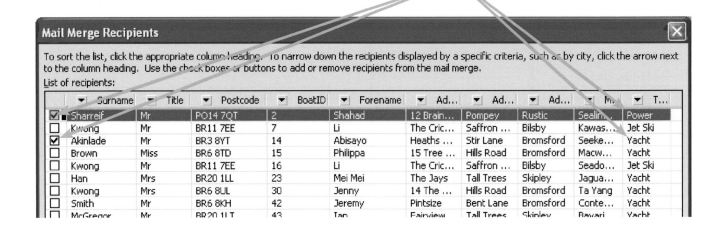

This will allow the merge to run with only two letters produced. These letters can be proofread to check for errors both in the conditional text and in the way the conditional text merges with the body text.

The check for errors tool

If you are using the **Mail Merge** toolbar there is a **Check for Errors**  button which will help you to find mistakes in the mail merge process. When you use this option the **Checking and Reporting Errors** window opens and looks similar to this.

Select the option which suits you. The first option saves memory by not having an open form letters file – instead it reports the errors in a new document. Options 2 and 3 run the merge, with or without a report document. Click on [OK] to test the merge. This will report a number of errors that may occur in the merge codes and calculations.

Final check

When all of the mail-merged letters are generated, proofread each letter manually. This final stage may seem unnecessary, but a very significant number of marks are lost in practical examinations every year due to inadequate checking.

15.12 Performing mail merge
Perform the merge from the task pane

As you worked through Section **15.4**, the final window of the task pane allowed you to select **Print...** or **Edit individual letters...**. Both of these options are useful. If you wish to test the mail merge (as described in the Section **15.11**) then the option to **Edit individual letters...** is better than printing. If all of the testing has been completed and you know that the mail merge will work correctly, then use the **Print...** option to save time. For the practical examination you should always use the **Edit individual letters...** option as it allows you to carefully check your work before it is submitted.

Perform the merge from the toolbar

The **Mail Merge** toolbar has four buttons on the right-hand side that perform various types of merge.

The first button is **Merge to New Document** [icon]. This performs the same function as **Edit Individual letters...** in the previous subsection. It allows the merged letters or documents to be checked prior to printing. It also allows you to select an individual record for the merge, or a consecutive selection of records. When you select this option it opens the **Merge to New Document** window, which looks similar to this.

The second button is **Merge to Printer**. A similar window opens to allow simple record selection at run time, but this option sends the form letters or documents to the printer, in the same way as **Print...** in the previous subsection.

The third button is **Merge to E-mail**, which opens the **Merge to E-mail** window. The will send the letter or document to the e-mail address specified for each record. Select the **To:** drop-down menu to select the field containing the e-mail address and run the merge in the same way as before. This only works if you have an e-mail field within your data source.

The fourth button is **Merge to Fax**. To use this option your computer must have fax software and a fax modem installed. The data source must hold a field (or column) containing the fax number of each person that the merged document is to be sent to. This works in a similar way to the e-mail option but is less likely to be tested in the practical examinations, although you may still be asked questions relating to it.

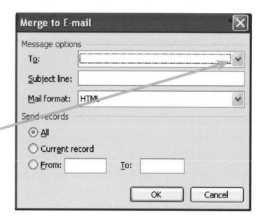

16 Automation

16.1 Selecting suitable software

The software selected for each automation task will depend upon the resources available to you and the requirements of the examination question. It is quite likely that in the practical examination papers you will be asked to use a particular method to create a solution to a problem. For example, you may be asked to create a menu to select different documents from a range of standard letters using hyperlinks; or you may be asked to select a document from a range of documents using macros. For these questions, you need to be familiar with all of the methods outlined in this chapter to enable you to answer the range of questions that may be given for the A2 practical paper.

However, in some questions you may be given a free choice of methods. You will need to look carefully at the question being asked. If the question asks for calculated data embedded within a document (perhaps for an invoice), then consider embedding a section of a spreadsheet into a word-processed document using paste linking. If you are required to select data from a database and place this into a standard document, consider mail merging from a pre-defined query in the database rather than from a table. If this selection involves choosing the document and the data, there are two possible alternatives. One is to create the selection process in *Microsoft Access*. The other is to link a query in a database to the selection of a document using a hyperlink. Each question will require you to consider carefully your choice of software. It is vital that you spend a little time at the start of the examination identifying the correct software and planning your approach. To do this you need to read through the question paper fully before starting to answer any of the questions.

16.2 Creating a menu system in *Microsoft Word*
Select a document using a hyperlink in the word processor

Task 16.1

Create a menu system for a company called Jimmy Lee Boats to select from the CD one of the following letters to customers:

- keel cleaning using the file BOATCLEAN.RTF
- prize draw offer using the file BOATOFFER.RTF
- engine overhaul using the file BOATSALES.RTF
- latest products using the file BOATEXTRA.RTF
- ladies evening using the file DINNER.RTF

1 Open a new document in *Word*.
2 Enter the text 'Jimmy Lee Boats' and 'Menu for standard letters' as a title at the top of the document.
3 Add the instructions for selecting the hyperlinks.
4 Enter the five pieces of text that will be used to create the links. These are: 'Keel cleaning', 'Prize draw offer', 'Engine overhaul', 'Latest products' and 'Ladies evening'. Your page may look similar to this.

5 Highlight the text to be used for the first hyperlink, in this case 'Keel cleaning', and press the right mouse button to obtain this drop-down menu.

> **Jimmy Lee Boats**
> **Menu for standard letters**
>
> To select the required letter, hold down the CTRL key and click the left mouse button on the hyperlink.
>
> **Keel cleaning**
> **Prize draw offer**
> **Engine overhaul**
> **Latest products**
> **Ladies evening**

> **Hint**
> Hyperlinks can also be added by highlighting the text, then selecting the Insert menu, followed by Hyperlink....

6 Select Hyperlink…. This will open the Insert Hyperlink window, which looks similar to this.

7 In the **Link to:** section of the window, select **Existing File or Web Page.**

8 Use the **Look in:** section to select the file that you wish the hyperlink to open, in this case BOATCLEAN. RTF, and click on OK .

9 The text <u>Keel cleaning</u> will now appear as a hyperlink, in a blue underlined font.

10 To activate this hyperlink hold down the <Ctrl> key and click the left mouse button on the link. This will open the document BOATCLEAN.RTF automatically.

11 Create similar hyperlinks from the other four items of text to open the relevant files. Check that each hyperlink works using <Ctrl> and click.

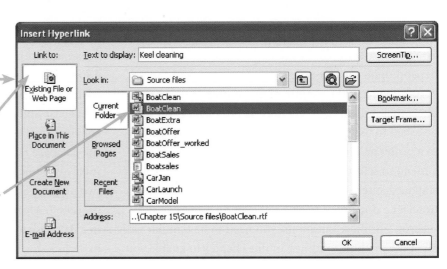

Edit a hyperlink in the word processor

1 Press the right mouse button anywhere within the hyperlink to be edited. This drop-down menu will appear.

2 Select **Edit Hyperlink…** and the **Edit Hyperlink** window will open. This can be used to change any of the hyperlink settings.

3 An alternative to this is to remove the hyperlink and create a new one. This is particularly useful if you did not highlight all of the correct text to create the link.

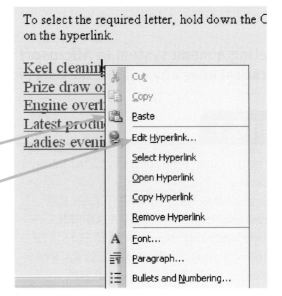

Activity 16.1

Using hyperlinks for a simple menu

Create a menu system for a garage called HC to select from the CD one of the following letters:

■ discount servicing using the file CARSALES.RTF
■ new dealership using the file CARLAUNCH.RTF
■ eco-cars using the file CARMODEL.RTF
■ pink Ecomini using the file PINKCAR.RTF

16.3 Creating a macro in *Microsoft Word*

T **Teacher's note**

Note that in some network and stand-alone computer systems the facility to record and use macros will be disabled due to the security requirements of your school or college. This section will give a brief insight into the use of macros to create a menu option system, but be advised that the use of macros can affect the use of your word processor and, in extreme cases, can mean that *Word* will need to be re-installed. It is important that macros are used only if allowed by your school or college.

Select a document using a macro in the word processor

Task 16.2

Create a menu system for Jimmy Lee Boats to select from the CD one of the following letters to customers:

- keel cleaning using the file BOATCLEAN.RTF
- prize draw offer using the file BOATOFFER.RTF
- engine overhaul using the file BOATSALES.RTF
- latest products using the file BOATEXTRA.RTF
- ladies evening using the file DINNER.RTF

Hint

Before you start recording, it is a good idea to be in a different directory from the one containing the files that you want your macro to open. This will mean that your macro will open the file, even if you are not already in that directory.

Create a new toolbar in *Word*

As mentioned in the warning above, you need to be very careful when using macros. It is sensible to create a new toolbar in which to place your macros. If there are problems, it is easier to remove the toolbar rather than try to remove individual macros from existing toolbars.

1 Select the Tools menu, then Customize.... This opens the Customize window.

2 Select the Toolbars tab, which looks similar to this.

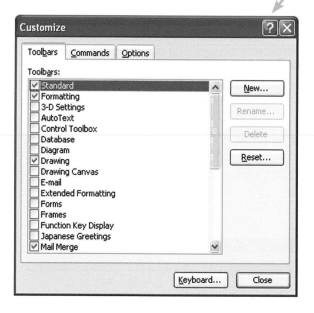

3 Click on New... to create a new toolbar. This opens the New Toolbar window, which looks similar to this.

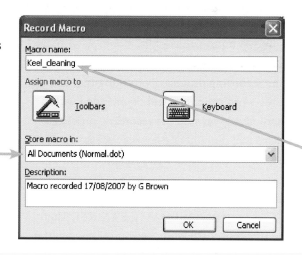

4 Enter the Toolbar name:, in this case 'My macros'.

5 In the Make toolbar available to: box select either the current document name, in this case Practice document, or the template Normal.dot. If you leave this as the default template name (Normal.dot), the new toolbar will appear whenever the word processor creates a new file or uses an existing file with that template. To avoid this, select the current document name from the list.

6 The new toolbar will be shown on the screen but will contain no buttons.

7 Close the Customize window.

Record a macro in *Word*

8 Select the Tools menu, then Macro. From the Macro sub-menu, select the option to Record New Macro.... This opens the Record Macro window, which looks similar to this.

9 Enter the Macro name: in the box; in this case the macro is to open the letter for keel cleaning. You must ensure that there are no spaces in the macro name, so the macro name will be Keel_cleaning (Keel underscore cleaning).

10 Select where you wish to store the macro from the drop-down list in the Store macro in: box. If you select All documents, the macro will probably be

available to all users of the machine in all of their documents (again dependent upon local security settings and provision). If it is just for the practical examination, select the current document name from this list.

11 Add a brief description of the purpose of this macro. It is a good idea to include your name, centre number and candidate number in the description. The completed window should look similar to this.

12 Click on [OK] to start recording the macro.

13 A small **Stop Recording** toolbar will appear on the screen and looks similar to this.

14 The right ◫ button pauses the recording of the macro and the left ◻ button stops the recording process. Everything that you do within the word processor will be included within the macro, until you stop the recording process. The macro will remember every key press you make so that it can repeat that sequence when you run it.

15 Select the **File** menu, followed by **Open**….

16 Locate and open the file BOATCLEAN.RTF. Then click on the **Stop Recording** ◻ button to stop the recording.

17 Close the file BOATCLEAN.RTF so that you can test that the macro works properly in the next section.

Add a macro to the toolbar in *Word*

18 Select the **Tools** menu, then **Customize**…. This opens the **Customize** window.

19 Select the **Commands** tab at the top of the window.

20 Scroll down the **Categories:** list until you find the **Macros** option. Select this option with the left mouse button.

21 The **Commands:** box will show the recorded macro as a *Visual Basic for Applications (VBA)* project.

22 Press and hold the left mouse button on the project name. Drag this project and drop it into the empty toolbar, which looks like this.

23 The toolbar will now contain the macro and will appear similar to this.

24 Repeat this process to create another four macros and place them on the toolbar. The finished toolbar should look similar to this.

My macros ▼ ✕

Project.NewMacros.Keel_cleaning Project.NewMacros.Engine_overhaul Project.NewMacros.Prize_draw Project.NewMacros.Latest_products Project.NewMacros.Ladies_evening

25 This is very difficult to read and therefore use, so you are going to rename each of the macros. Leave the Customize window open. Press the right mouse button on the first macro name; this gives a drop-down menu similar to this.

26 Rename the macro as 'Keel_cleaning', using the text box within the Name: option of this menu.

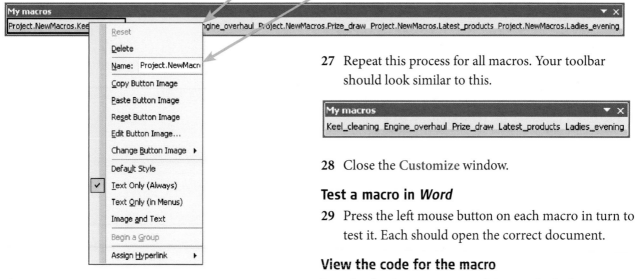

27 Repeat this process for all macros. Your toolbar should look similar to this.

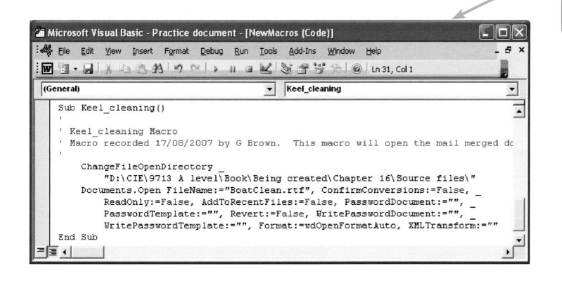

28 Close the Customize window.

Test a macro in *Word*

29 Press the left mouse button on each macro in turn to test it. Each should open the correct document.

View the code for the macro

In order for the macro to work it records the key presses in the form of a code. This code is recorded in *Visual Basic for Applications* (*VBA*), the programming language that underpins all of the *Microsoft Office* application packages. This code may be required by the examiners as evidence that the macro that you have recorded works correctly. To view this evidence, you must:

1 Select the Tools menu, then Macro. From the Macro sub-menu, select the option for Macros…. This opens the Macros window, which looks similar to this.

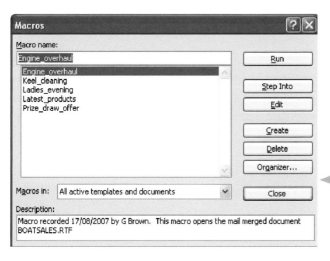

2 To view the code, click on [Edit]. This will open the *Visual Basic* editor and allow the evidence of the macro to be viewed, used for screenshot evidence or printed. The code for the Keel _cleaning macro looks similar to this.

```
Microsoft Visual Basic - Practice document - [NewMacros (Code)]
File  Edit  View  Insert  Format  Debug  Run  Tools  Add-Ins  Window  Help

(General)                                    Keel_cleaning

Sub Keel_cleaning()
'
'  Keel_cleaning Macro
'  Macro recorded 17/08/2007 by G Brown.  This macro will open the mail merged do
'
    ChangeFileOpenDirectory _
        "D:\CIE\9713 A level\Book\Being created\Chapter 16\Source files\"
    Documents.Open FileName:="BoatClean.rtf", ConfirmConversions:=False, _
        ReadOnly:=False, AddToRecentFiles:=False, PasswordDocument:="", _
        PasswordTemplate:="", Revert:=False, WritePasswordDocument:="", _
        WritePasswordTemplate:="", Format:=wdOpenFormatAuto, XMLTransform:=""
End Sub
```

Notice how the information that you added as a description (which should include your name, centre number and candidate number) has been placed within the code as comments.

Activity 16.2

Using macros for a simple menu

Create a menu system for a garage called HC to select from the CD one of the following letters to customers:
- discount servicing using the file CARSALES.RTF
- new dealership using the file CARLAUNCH.RTF
- eco-cars using the file CARMODEL.RTF
- pink Ecomini using the file PINKCAR.RTF

16.4 Creating a macro in *Microsoft Excel*

> **T** Teacher's note
>
> Note that in some network and stand-alone computer systems the facility to record and use macros will be disabled due to the security requirements of your school or college. This section will give a brief insight into the use of macros to automate some commonly performed tasks within a spreadsheet. Be advised that the use of macros can affect the use of your spreadsheet, including the keyboard shortcuts.

Task 16.3

A teacher in an International school gets data exported from a database. This data is to be used in a spreadsheet as part of an electronic mark book. Create a macro to manipulate data automatically, in a number of different data files with a similar structure. The macro must:
- insert a new row at the top of the worksheet
- add the heading 'Tutor' to column B and the heading 'Option subjects' to column C
- split the first column into three columns with the headings 'Forename', 'Surname' and 'Set'.

Perform these operations on the files CLASS1.CSV, CLASS2.CSV, CLASS3.CSV, CLASS4.CSV, CLASS5.CSV and CLASS6.CSV from the CD. Save these files.

Manipulate data using a macro in a spreadsheet
Create a new toolbar in *Excel*

1 Open the file CLASS1.CSV.
2 Select the Tools menu, then Customize…. This opens the Customize window.
3 Select the Toolbars tab and click on New… . This opens the New Toolbar window, which looks similar to this.

4 Enter the Toolbar name: – in this case My Macros – and then click on OK . The new toolbar will be shown on the screen but will contain no buttons.
5 Close the Customize window.

Record a macro in *Excel*

6 Make sure that the security level in *Excel* is set to medium (or low) before attempting to create or use macros. To set the security levels, select the Tools menu, then Options…. Select the Security tab and click on Macro Security… . Click on the radio button for medium (or low) followed by OK. Close the Options window by clicking on OK .

7 Select the Tools menu, then Macro. From the Macro sub-menu, select the option to Record New Macro…. This opens the Record Macro window, which looks similar to this.

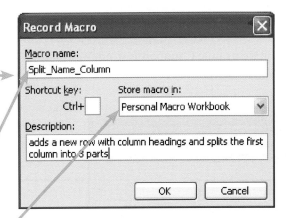

8 Enter the Macro name: in the box; in this case the macro will insert a row and heading names and split the Name column. You must ensure that there are no spaces in the macro name, so it will be Split_Name_Column (Split underscore Name underscore Column).

9 Select where you wish to store the macro from the drop-down list in the Store macro in: box. Select Personal Macro Workbook, so that this macro will appear whenever you open *Excel*.

> **Hint**
> If you store a macro in your Personal Macro Workbook and want to edit this macro (you may need to do this if you are asked to print out the *VBA* code for the examiner), you will need to unhide the Personal Macro Workbook window. This can be done using the Unhide… option from the Window menu.

10 Add a brief Description: of the purpose of this macro by editing the default text as you did when you recorded a macro in *Word* (in Section **16.2**). Include your name, centre number and candidate number in the description. Click on [OK] to start recording the macro.

11 A small Stop Recording toolbar will appear on the screen that looks similar to this.

12 Record all of the actions in the following sequence in the macro:
  ◇ Highlight row 1 of the spreadsheet.
  ◇ Insert a new row using the Insert menu followed by Rows.
  ◇ In cell B1 enter the label 'Tutor'.
  ◇ In cell C1 enter the label 'Option subjects'.
  ◇ Highlight column B and insert two new columns by selecting Insert followed by Columns twice.

> **Hint**
> An alternative method of inserting these columns would be to highlight columns B and C, then select the Insert menu followed by Column.

◇ Highlight column A. Select the Data menu, followed by Text to Columns…. This opens the Convert Text to Columns Wizard. Click on the radio button for Delimited and click on [Next >]. This column uses spaces as a delimiter, so click on the Space tick box in the Delimiter section, and remove the tick from the Tab delimiter tick box before clicking on [Next >], then [Finish] to close the wizard.
◇ In cell A1, enter the label 'Forename'.
◇ In cell B1, enter the label 'Surname'.
◇ In cell C1, enter the label 'Set'.
◇ Highlight cells A1 to E1 and make these cells bold.

> **Hint**
> It is good practice to make the column headings stand out from the rest of the spreadsheet – making these cells bold will do this.

13 Click on the button to stop the recording process.

Add a macro to the toolbar in *Excel*

14 Select the Tools menu, then Customize…. This opens the Customize window. Select the Toolbars tab. Ensure that you tick the option for the My Macros toolbar.

15 Select the Commands tab at the top of the window.

16 Scroll down the Categories: list until you find the Macros option. Select this option with the left mouse button.

17 In the Commands: box, select the Custom Button option, then click on [Rearrange Commands...]. This opens the Rearrange Commands window, which looks similar to this.

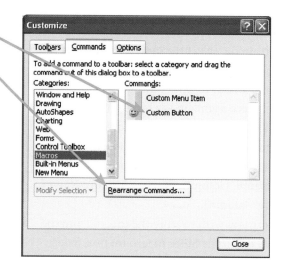

18 Click on the radio button for Toolbar:.

19 Use the drop-down list in the Toolbar section to select the My Macros toolbar.

20 Click on [Add...]. This will open the Add Command window.

21 Scroll down the Categories: list until you find the Macros option. Select this option with the left mouse button.

22 In the Commands: box, select the option for a Custom Button. Click on [OK] to add this command to the toolbar. The Add Command window will close and the new button will have been added to the My Macros toolbar.

23 Click on [Close] to close the Rearrange Commands window, and then on [Close] to close the Customize window. The toolbar will now contain a button and will appear similar to this. ────────→

24 Click on the New Macro button in the My Macros toolbar. The first time that this is selected, the Assign Macro window opens and looks similar to this.

25 Press the left mouse button on the appropriate macro; this places the macro name into the Macro name: box. Click on [OK] to assign this macro to the button.

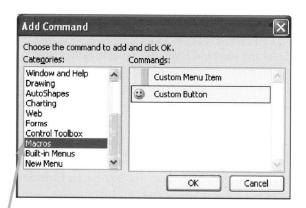

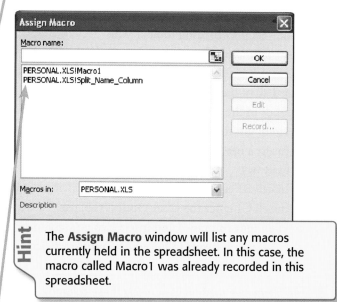

Hint The **Assign Macro** window will list any macros currently held in the spreadsheet. In this case, the macro called Macro1 was already recorded in this spreadsheet.

Test a macro in *Excel*

1 Press the left mouse button on the button for the macro to test it. Note that you will need to reload the original source data file. This is because the current file was changed during the recording of the macro. The macro should perform the correct functions. If not, you need to record a new macro. This is quicker and easier than trying to edit the *VBA* code.

2 Make sure that this macro performs the same function on all the other class lists, using the files CLASS2.CSV, CLASS3.CSV, CLASS4.CSV, CLASS5.CSV and CLASS6.CSV. Open each of these files in turn and press the macro button once. Each file can then be saved as an *Excel* workbook.

View the code for the macro

The macro code may be required by the examiners as evidence that the macro that you have recorded works correctly. The macro details are stored in a hidden workbook called PERSONAL.XLS. You must make sure that the Personal Macro Workbook is not hidden before starting these instructions. To view this evidence you must:

1 Select the Tools menu, then Macro. From the Macro sub-menu, select the option for Macros. This opens the Macros window.

2 To view the code, select the macro name and click on [Edit]. This will open the *Visual Basic* editor and allow the evidence of the macro to be seen, printed or used for screenshot evidence. The code for the Split_Name_Column macro looks similar to this.

> Activity 16.3
>
> ## Using macros to manipulate columns
>
> Using all six of the class list files saved in Task **16.3**, create a macro to automatically split the Option Subjects column into four columns with the headings 'Option A', 'Option B', 'Option C' and 'Option D'.

16.5 Using paste-linked spreadsheets

The advantage of using linked spreadsheets is that one or more small spreadsheets can hold important data that you may change. Other spreadsheets can be linked to this so that they automatically update the important data from this sheet whenever those spreadsheets are opened. Paste linking two spreadsheets is an alternative to entering external referencing to a cell, or range of cells, from another sheet. Paste-linked spreadsheets are ideally suited to producing invoices for companies, where the range of products or their prices can change on a daily basis.

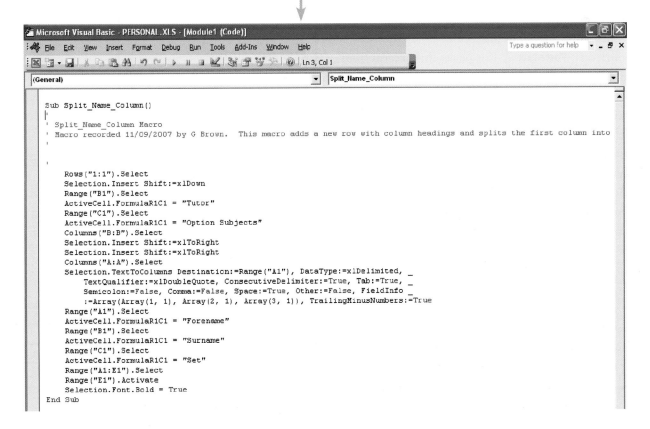

Create an invoice in *Excel*

Task 16.4

The Global Hire Car Company hires out cars from the Belo Horizonte international airport in Brazil. It uses spreadsheets to help it to produce invoices for customers. The file ITEMS.CSV from the CD contains details of the daily hire charges for each type of vehicle; the rates can be changed on a daily basis. The file INVOICE.XLS contains a partly created template for the invoice and this links to the file CUSTOMERS.CSV which contains the customer details.

(i) Paste link the contents of ITEMS.CSV into cells A12 to C21.

(ii) Enter this booking into the INVOICE spreadsheet:

Customer id	Date	sm2	sm4	f4	f5	e4	e5	sp2	pc7	pc10	lim
12	23/03/2009					1	1			3	

Extract only the items that have been ordered. Print the invoice.

(iii) Change the daily rate for a ten-person people carrier in the file ITEMS.CSV to 35. Amend the number of executive five-door cars to three and reprint the invoice.

---

1 Open the files ITEMS.CSV and INVOICE.XLS in *Excel*.

2 Copy the data from cells A2 to C11 in ITEMS.CSV by highlighting these cells and using the **Edit** menu, followed by **Copy**.

3 Go to INVOICE.XLS and click the cursor in cell A12.

4 Select from the **Edit** menu the option for **Paste Special…**. This opens the **Paste Special** window, which looks similar to this.

5 Click on **Paste Link**. This places this excerpt from the ITEMS spreadsheet into the invoice. If any of the figures in the ITEMS spreadsheet change, the relevant cells in this invoice will also change.

6 To insert the booking into the INVOICE spreadsheet, move the cursor into cell B2 and press the left mouse button. Enter the customer number 12 into this cell. Because much of the invoice has been created for you, the customer details and discount rates will appear in the spreadsheet automatically.

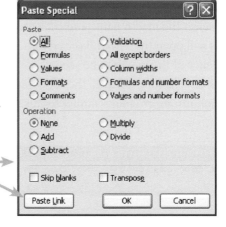

Hint

Look at the functions and formulae used to create this invoice. These are types of functions and formulae that you will be expected to create in the practical examinations. Notice that there are several variations on the lookup formulae and that each one is designed so that if there is no data the cell does not show an error message.

7 In cell D10, enter the date 23/03/2009.

8 Enter the number 1 in both cells D16 and D17.

9 Enter the number 3 into cell D19 as the bookings for the ten-seat people carriers.

10 To extract only the items that have been ordered you must use the auto-filter function. The filter must apply to only the bottom area of the invoice so you need to highlight cells A10 to E24.

11 Select the **Data** menu, then **Filter** followed by **AutoFilter**.

12 To select the items ordered, select the AutoFilter arrow in cell D10.

13 From the drop-down menu, select (**NonBlanks**). This will select only the rows containing data or labels. The finished invoice should look similar to this.

14 To change the daily rate for the ten-seat people carrier, go into the ITEMS spreadsheet. Change the value in cell C10 from 33 to 35.

Customer Details	
Customer id	12
Name	Julio Gomez Travel
Add1	Calle 4 Mz. 3 Lote 17 Parque Industrial
Add2	Deit R/A Anacleto Canabal 1ra. Seccion Villahermosa
Add3	Tabasco CP 86280
Country	Mexico

Customer Requirements				
Hire cost		**Date**	23/03/2009	
Code	Vehicle	Daily charge	Number of days	Cost
e4	4 seat executive	BRL 28.50	1	BRL 28.50
e5	5 seat executive	BRL 32.50	1	BRL 32.50
pc10	10 seat people carrier	BRL 33.00	3	BRL 99.00
			Subtotal	BRL 160.00
		Discount Code	b	BRL 16.00
			Total	BRL 144.00

15 Move back to the INVOICE spreadsheet and notice how the Daily charge for this type of vehicle (as well as the Cost, Subtotal, discount amount and Total) has automatically updated in this invoice.

16 Place the cursor in cell D17 in the ITEMS spreadsheet and change the number of these cars booked from 1 to 3. The invoice will update and look similar to this.

Customer Details	
Customer id	12
Name	Julio Gomez Travel
Add1	Calle 4 Mz. 3 Lote 17 Parque Industrial
Add2	Deit R/A Anacleto Canabal 1ra. Seccion Villahermosa
Add3	Tabasco CP 86280
Country	Mexico

Customer Requirements				
Hire cost		**Date**	23/03/2009	
Code	Vehicle	Daily charge	Number of days	Cost
e4	4 seat executive	BRL 28.50	1	BRL 28.50
e5	5 seat executive	BRL 32.50	3	BRL 97.50
pc10	10 seat people carrier	BRL 35.00	3	BRL 105.00
			Subtotal	BRL 231.00
		Discount Code	b	BRL 23.10
			Total	BRL 207.90

The Global Hire Car Company hires out cars from the Belo Horizonte international airport in Brazil. It uses spreadsheets to help it to produce invoices for customers. The file VEHICLE.CSV from the CD contains details of the hire charges for each type of vehicle; the rates for these can change on a daily basis. The file INVOICE.XLS contains a partly created template for the invoice and this links to the file CUSTOMERS.CSV, which contains the customer details.

(i) Paste link the contents of VEHICLE.CSV into cells A12 to C21.

(ii) Enter each of these bookings into the spreadsheet:

Customer ID	Date	sm2	sm4	f4	f5	e4	e5	pc7	pc10	satnav	fridge
16	27/02/2009						1			1	1
5	1/3/2009	2	1							3	

For each invoice, extract only the items that have been ordered. Save and print the invoice.

(iii) Change the daily rate for the hire of satellite navigation in the file VEHICLE.CSV to 8. For the customer with ID number 5, change the booking of the small four-door car to a four-door family car and reprint this invoice.

16.6 Creating a menu system in *Microsoft Access*

In *Access* a form can be used to create a menu (this can also be called a splash screen). A variety of buttons and other features like drop-down boxes can be added to the form and these can be used for a variety of uses, such as opening other forms (to allow data entry), running queries or producing reports.

Create command buttons on an *Access* form

Task 16.5

Open the database SIMC2.MDB from the CD. This database contains reports showing the employees in Goa, the employees in Chennai and a salary analysis for all employees. Create a menu system that allows the user to open each of these three reports.

1 Open the database file SIMC2.MDB in *Access*.
2 Select **Forms** in the **Objects** box and then **Create form in Design view** from the options.

This opens a new blank form, which looks similar to this.

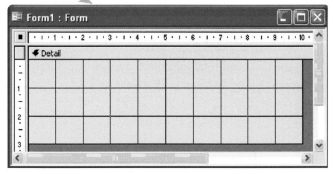

It also opens a copy of the Toolbox toolbar, which looks similar to this. The Toolbox toolbar may appear anywhere on the screen or it may be with the other toolbars at the top of the screen. If it is not present, you will need to select the View menu, followed by Toolbox.

3 Click on the **Command Button** button from the **Toolbox** and move the cursor onto the blank form. Press the left mouse button and drag the lasso to create a command button on the form. As you release the left mouse button, the rectangular shape that you have just dragged

will become the button and the **Command Button Wizard** will run. This looks similar to this. ↓

4 For this question, we want to make the button open the report called Employees in Goa. In the **Categories:** section, select **Report Operations**.

5 In the **Actions:** section, select **Preview Report**. When both of these selections have been made click on Next >. The wizard should now look similar to this.

6 Select the report **Employees in Goa** from the list before clicking on Next >.

7 The next stage of the **Command Button Wizard** is to choose how the button will appear. Buttons can have text or images on them to show their function. For the purpose of the examination it is recommended that simple text statements are used. These will save you valuable time. Click on the top radio button for Text and enter the text 'Employees in Goa' in the text box alongside the radio button. This is the text that will be displayed in the button.

8 Click on Next > to move on to the final stage of the wizard.

9 *Access* will assign the command button a name. If you wish to rename the command button (this makes it easier if you wish to edit the *VBA* code at a later date), you can enter the name for this button.

Enter the text 'Employees in Goa' into the box before clicking on Finish. The button should now be visible and appear similar to this.

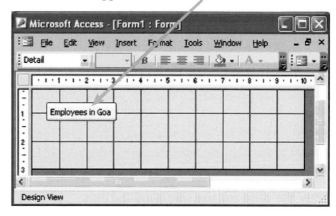

10 Repeat this process to create command buttons for 'Employees in Chennai' and 'Salary analysis'.

11 The form and its buttons can be resized or moved by selecting the button and using the drag handles.

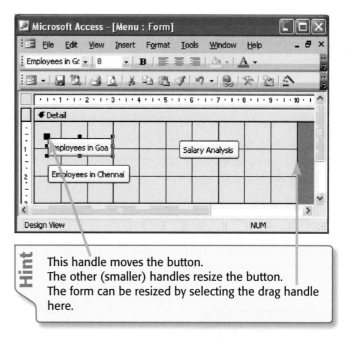

Hint

This handle moves the button.
The other (smaller) handles resize the button.
The form can be resized by selecting the drag handle here.

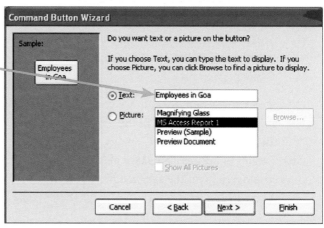

12 When all three buttons have been created, close the form. You will be asked if you wish to save the design of the form. Click on | Yes |.

13 Enter a name for the form; in this case call the form 'Menu' or 'SplashScreen'. The form has now been created and can be tested.

Test a command button in *Access*

14 Open the form called Menu that you saved in the previous step.

15 Press the left mouse button on each button in turn to test it. Each should open the correct document. To return to the menu, close the report.

View the code for the command buttons

1 Select the Design View of the form by clicking on the Design ⬐ button.

2 Select the Form Design toolbar (you may need to open this using View and Toolbars), and then click on the Code 🖼 button from this toolbar.

This will open the *Visual Basic* editor and allow the evidence of the code to be viewed. The code for the Employees in Goa command button looks similar to this.

```
Private Sub Employees_in_Goa_Click()
On Error GoTo Err_Employees_in_Goa_Click

    Dim stDocName As String

    stDocName = "Employees in Goa"

    DoCmd.OpenReport stDocName, acPreview

Exit_Employees_in_Goa_Click:
    Exit Sub

Err_Employees_in_Goa_Click:
    MsgBox Err.Description
    Resume Exit_Employees_in_Goa_Click

End Sub
```

Activity 16.5

Using a form for a simple menu

Open the database BOATS.MDB from the CD. This database contains reports showing a full printout of the Boat table, a sorted printout of the Boat table, the 30–40-foot yachts made in 1995 or later, and all the power boats under 25 feet costing between £10 000 and £30 000. Create a menu system that allows the user to open each of these four reports.

16.7 Creating a menu system in *Access* to select user defined data

Task 16.6

Open the database SIMC2.MDB from the CD.
(i) Create a menu system to enable selection of one of the branches of the company.

Create a menu system that allows you to select:
(ii) a report that shows all of the employees from the selected branch
(iii) a series of address labels for all of the employees from the selected branch using Avery L7263 labels.

Features of *Access* forms can be used to select specified data within a query. A command button can be used to open a report based upon the selection criteria from the form. This involves adding a method of selection to a form. For the purposes of this section we will use the same form, although in some questions it may be useful to use more than one form. The principles involved when using more than one form are identical to those shown in this section.

Create a list box on an *Access* form (Task 16.6(i))

1 Open the database file SIMC2.MDB in *Access*.

2 Select Forms in the Objects box and then Create form in Design view from the options to open a new blank form and the Toolbox toolbar.

3 Click on the List Box 🖳 button from the Toolbox and move the cursor onto the blank form. Press the left mouse button and drag the lasso to create a list box on the form. As you release the left mouse button the rectangular shape that you have just dragged will become the list box and the **List Box Wizard** will run. This looks similar to this.

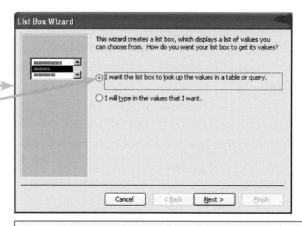

4 Click on the radio button for **I want the list box to look up the values in a table or query**. Then click on [Next >].

5 Task **16.6** asks you to select one of the branches from the database. This information is held in the field **Branch.Branch** (which is the Branch field within the Branch table). In the **View** area of the **List Box Wizard** select the radio button for **Tables**.

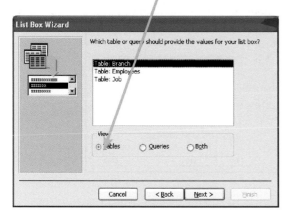

6 Select the **Table: Branch** from those available and click on [Next >]. The wizard will now look similar to this.

7 Select the **Branch** field from the **Available Fields:** and click on > to place this in the **Selected Fields:** box.

8 Select the **Code** field in the same way. This field is needed as it is the primary key field within this table. If you forget to select this field, *Access* will select it for you. When both fields have been selected, click on [Next >].

9 In the next window, select the order that you wish to sort this list into. In this case, it is sensible for you to list the branches in alphabetical order of the branch

name, so select the **Branch** field and make sure that the button shows [**Ascending**]. Then click on [Next >].

10 The next stage of the wizard shows you how the list box will appear on the form. It should show only the **Branch** names. If it also shows the **Code** for each branch, tick the **Hide key column (recommended)** box. Click on [Next >].

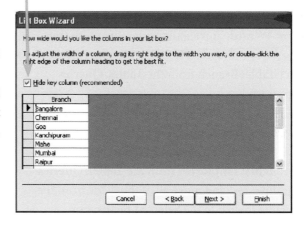

11 In the final window, in the box that asks **What label would you like for your list box?** enter the text 'Branch Name'. To complete the wizard, click on [Finish].

12 The form needs to be saved using the **File** menu, followed by **Save**. Use a short but meaningful fieldname; in this case, enter 'frmMenu' followed by clicking on [OK].

13 You need to know the name of the list box that you have created. Press the right mouse button on the list box, not on the label. From the drop-down menu select the **Properties** option (it is at the bottom of the menu). The **List Box** properties window should appear and look similar to this.

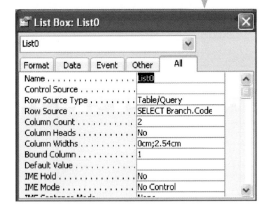

14 Change the **Name** of the list box by overtyping the default name (in this case List0) with a new name like 'BranchList'.

15 Save and close the form.

The list box has now been set up. It is stored in the form frmMenu and has a list box name of BranchList. You will need this information to help you to create the query that will be used to select the data for both reports.

Create a query to select data from the list box

16 Select **Queries** in the **Objects** box and then **Create query by using wizard**. This will open the **Simple Query Wizard**. You should be familiar with this wizard from Chapter **11**.

17 Select **Table: Branch** from the **Tables/Queries** drop-down list.

18 Select from the **Available Fields:** box the **Code, Branch, Address 1, Address 2** and **Address 3** and move these into the **Selected Fields:** box.

19 Select **Table: Employees** from the **Tables/Queries** drop-down list and move all of the fields from the **Available Fields:** to the **Selected Fields:** box.

20 Select **Table: Job** from the **Tables/Queries** drop-down list and move all of the fields from the **Available Fields:** to the **Selected Fields:** box. Click on [Next >] to move to the next page of the wizard.

21 Make sure that the radio button for **Detail** is selected before clicking on [Next >].

22 Enter the name for the query. You can call this query 'qryBranchSelection'.

23 Click on the radio button for **Modify the query design** before clicking on [Finish].

24 To complete the query the selection criterion from the list box on the form must be entered. Press the left mouse button in the **Criteria:** box for the **Branch. Code** field.

Field:	Code	Branch	A
Table:	Branch	Branch	B
Sort:			
Show:	☑	☑	
Criteria:			

25 Enter 'Forms!frmMenu!BranchList' into this box. This is the criterion that points to the list box on the form. This asks the query to compare the value from the form called frmMenu in the list box called BranchList with the data items held in this field within the database. When you have entered this and pressed the <Return> key the text will change to show square brackets around each *Access* element. It should look similar to this.

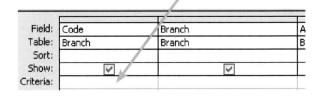

Field:	Code	Branch	Address1
Table:	Branch	Branch	Branch
Sort:			
Show:	☑	☑	
Criteria:	[Forms]![frmMenu]![BranchList]		

26 Save the changes that you have made to the query and close the query.

Create a report to show only the employees selected in the query (Task 16.6(ii))

1 Select Reports in the Objects box and then Create report by using wizard. This will open the Report Wizard. You should be familiar with this wizard from Chapter **11**.

2 Select Query: qryBranchSelection from the Tables/Queries drop-down list.

3 Select from the Available Fields: box the Code, Branch, Forename, Surname, Description and RateOfPay and move these into the Selected Fields: box. Click on Next > to move to the next page of the wizard.

4 The wizard will attempt to arrange the report layout for you, suggesting that the code and branch name should only appear once on the printout. In this case it is a sensible option. Click on Next > to continue.

5 No grouping is required on the data, so click on Next >.

6 Sort the data as required, for example into ascending order of Surname, then Forename. Click on Next >.

7 Arrange the report so that it will fit onto the page. The fields selected for this report contain a large number of characters, so selecting a page Orientation of Landscape will help to ensure that all the data fits without truncation.

8 In the Layout section of the wizard, choose the format for the presentation of the report. There are a number of suitable options for this question. In the practical examinations you may be asked to produce a particular layout for your report. If the layout that you require is not available, select the closest layout and when the report has been created go into the Design View of the report and edit the layout. See Section **11.9** for more details. When you have selected the required layout, click on Next >.

9 Select the style for the report followed by clicking on Next >.

10 Enter the title for your report. This becomes the report name and is produced as the title on the report. For this example enter Branch Employees and then click on Finish.

11 Save and close the report. At this stage ignore any error messages like this. This message occurs ⟶

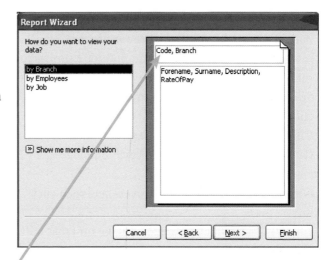

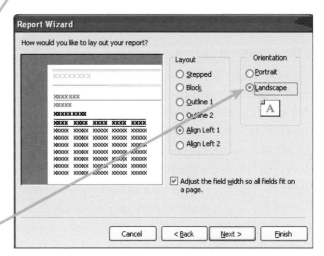

because the report cannot be generated until the form is used.

Create a command button to run the report

12 Select Forms in the Objects box and then open the form frmMenu in Design View.

13 Click on the Command Button ▣ button from the Toolbox. Press the left mouse button and drag the lasso to create the button on the form and run the Command Button Wizard.

14 For this question we want to make the button open the report called Branch Employees. In the Categories: section, select Report Operations.

Report Wizard ⓘ The wizard is unable to preview your report, possibly because another user has a source table open in exclusive mode. Your report will be opened in design view.

OK

15 In the **Actions:** section, select **Preview Report.** When both of these selections have been made click on ![Next >]. The wizard should now look similar to this. ──────────────────────→

16 Select the report **Branch Employees** from the list and click on ![Next >].

17 Click on the radio button for **Text**, and enter the text for this button as 'Report for Branch Employees'. Click on ![Next >].

18 Name the button 'BranchEmployees' and then click on ![Finish].

19 Check the layout of your form to make sure that no controls or labels overlap and that the form will be easy for other people to use.

20 Save the form.

Test the command button

21 Make sure that the form is open in form view. Select a branch name from the list box on the form. For this example, select the city of Chennai from the list box. When it has been selected it will appear like this. ──────────────────

22 Press the left mouse button on the command button to test it. This should open the correct report, and within the report show only the employees where the branch is, for example Chennai. You may need

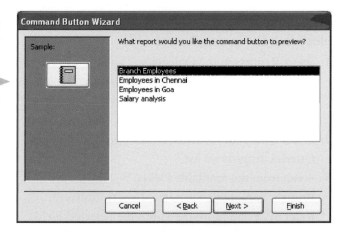

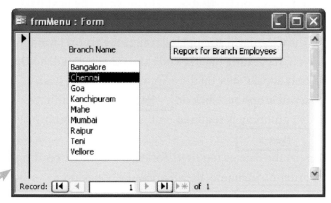

to adjust the controls within the design view of the report to ensure that all of the data is visible (see Section **11.9**). The report should look similar to this.

23 To return to the menu, close the report.

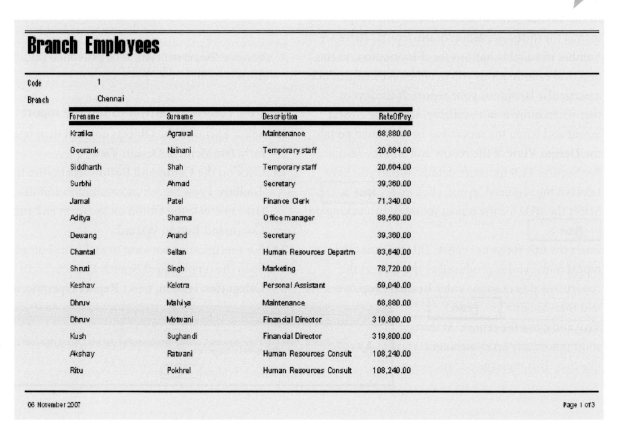

Create a report to produce address labels for the employees selected in the query (Task 16.6(iii))

1 Select Reports in the Objects box and then New.

> **Hint**
>
> In this case you do not select the option for Create report by using wizard as this would not allow you access to the label wizard.

2 From the New Report window select the option for the Label Wizard.

3 Use the drop-down menu to select the automated query that you designed in Task **16.6(i)**: qryBranchSelection. Click on [OK].

4 In this question the manufacturer and type of label have been specified as Avery L7263 labels. Select the name of the manufacturer from the drop-down list in the **Filter by manufacturer:** section, in this case Avery.

5 Locate and select the product number using the **Product number:** from the list box. This will select the correct product and show the size of each label on the sheet. In this case the product number is L7263. If the product does not appear within this list, change the **Unit of Measure** from **Metric** to **English**, then search again for the product. When you have made the selection click on [Next >].

6 Set the font styles in the next stage of the wizard. Remember that address labels need to be produced using a reasonably large, easy-to-read font. When you have selected the styles, click on [Next >].

7 Select the Forename, Surname, Address1, Address2, Branch and Address3 from the **Available Fields:** and place them into the **Prototype label:** area. Arrange the fields in an appropriate layout for an address label:

◇ Notice that Forename and Surname have been placed on the same line with a single space between them.

◇ Where you want a new line you will need to select the field and enter a carriage return before entering the next field.

◇ In this database the field Branch is the name of the town so this makes up part of the address of each branch of the company.

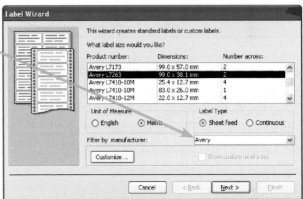

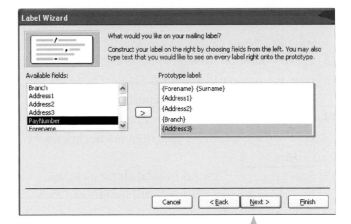

The window should look similar to this.

8 When you are satisfied with the label layout, click on [Next >].

9 If you wish to sort the labels into order this can be done in the next window. Select the fields to sort by and move them from the **Available fields:** box

to the Sort by: box using the $>$ button. Click on Next > for the final stage of the Label Wizard.

10 Enter a suitable name for the labels, in this example 'Address labels for a chosen branch on Avery L7263'. Click on Finish . At this stage, ignore any error messages that may occur. This is because the report cannot be generated until an item from the list box in the form has been selected.

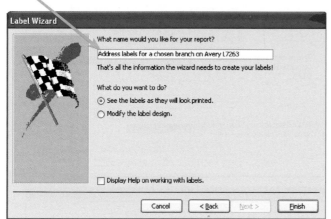

Create a command button to produce the labels

11 Select Forms in the Objects box and then open the form frmMenu in Design View.

12 Click on the Command Button button from the Toolbox. Press the left mouse button and drag the lasso to create the button on the form. Place this button just below the command button to open the 'Report for Branch Employees'. When the mouse button is released, the Command Button Wizard will run.

13 For this question we want to make the button open the report called Branch Employees. In the Categories: section, select Report Operations.

14 In the Actions: section, select Preview Report. When both of these selections have been made, click on Next > .

15 Select the option for Address labels for a chosen branch on Avery L7263 from the list box and click on Next > .

16 Select the radio button for Text, and enter the text for this button as 'Labels for Branch Employees'. Click on Next > .

17 Name the button 'BranchLabels' and then click on Finish .

18 Save the form and switch to form view using the button on the Form Design toolbar.

Test the command button

19 Select a branch name from the list box on the form. For this example, select the city of Teni. When it has been selected it will appear like this.

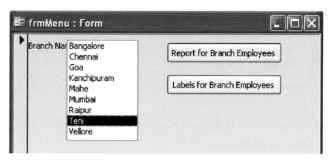

20 Press the left mouse button on the command button for Labels for Branch Employees to test it. This should open the correct report showing all the labels for only the employees where the branch is Teni. The labels should look similar to this.

Uttara Jain	Keshav Khuznetsov
Manduri House	Manduri House
456 Katpadi Road	456 Katpadi Road
Teni	Teni
India	India
Teng Liu	Kratika Menon
Manduri House	Manduri House
456 Katpadi Road	456 Katpadi Road
Teni	Teni
India	India
Mohammed Morzaria	
Manduri House	
456 Katpadi Road	
Teni	
India	

Activity 16.6

Using a form for a simple menu

Open the database BOATS.MDB from the CD.

(i) Create a menu system to enable selection of the type of boat.

Then select:

(ii) a report that shows all of the boats for sale from the selected type

(iii) a series of labels to be used to advertise the boats for sale of a particular type using RankXerox 926L90404 labels. Each label should include the Make, Year, Type and Length of the boat.

Create reports to produce address labels for different-sized labels

Task 16.7

Open the database SIMC2.MDB from the CD. From your menu select one of the branches of the company. Create a menu system that allows you to select a report that shows all of the employees from the selected branch, or to select a series of address labels for all of the employees from the selected branch using either Avery L7263, HP 92996 P, Inmac 6099 or Unistat 38933 labels. The Avery L7263 labels are the most commonly used type within the company.

An option group is a series of linked buttons. They can be option buttons, tick boxes or toggle buttons. Each of these is used to select a value that will be used to select the correct data from within the query. When you select a button or tick the box, the value given to that button or box will be given to the option group. This value is then used to select the data from within the query in the same way as the method shown earlier in this section using the list box.

Before attempting to create an option group for Task **16.7** you need to create address labels for each of the four different sizes and makes of label. Steps 1 to 10 for Task **16.6(iii)** have created the layout for labels to be printed on Avery L7293 stationery. Copy these steps three more times, changing the **Manufacturer:** and **Product Number:** required in Steps 4 and 5. These must be for **HP 92996 P**, **Inmac 6099** and **Unistat 38933** labels. Each time you follow these steps, ensure that at Step 10, you use an appropriate name for each report. This name will identify the purpose of the report, the name of the label's manufacturer and the product number.

> **Hint**
> If the manufacturer that you are searching for is not visible in your list, try looking under Other/Custom to find the label that you want.

Create an option group on an *Access* form

1 Select **Forms** in the **Objects** box and then open the form **frmMenu** in **Design View** by selecting the form name and clicking on ✎ Design .

2 Select the **Option Group** button from the **Toolbox** and move the cursor onto the form **frmMenu**. Press the left mouse button and drag the lasso to create an option group on the form. Do not overlap existing objects on the form. This lasso needs to be reasonably large, as it will need to contain one button or tick box for each of the four label types. As you release the left mouse button the rectangular shape that you have just dragged will become the option group and the **Option Group Wizard** will run. This looks similar to this.

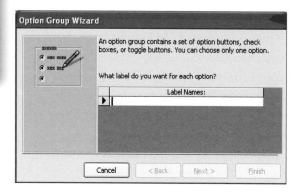

3 In the **Label Names:** box enter the product name for each of the four labels. When you have entered one Product name, click the cursor in the empty box below to start the next one. Do not press the <Enter> key or click on Next > until you have entered all four of the names. (Pressing the <Enter> key has the same effect as clicking on Next > .)

4 The next stage in the wizard asks if one of the options that you have just entered is to be the default choice. For this task, you are told that the Avery L7263 labels are the most commonly used type within the company, so click on the Yes radio button, followed by the option for Avery L7263 labels

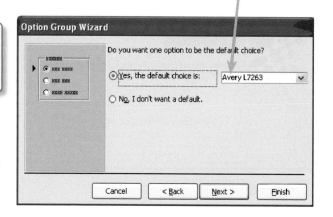

from the drop-down list box. When these have been selected click on 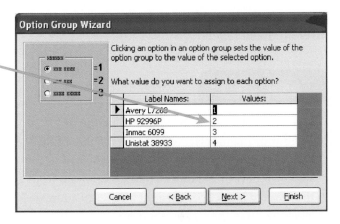 Next > .

5   The wizard will assign each **Label Name:** a value. In this example the exact value given is not very important, but it is important that each label name has a different value. Select the values that you want and click on Next > .

6   Either save a screenshot or write down each name and the value assigned to it. You will need this information later on in the chapter.

7   The wizard allows you to select how the option group will appear on the form. Choose the type of control that you wish to be displayed. There are three choices.

   ◇ In this example, **Option buttons** (radio buttons) have been selected. As you change the different type of control the **Sample** display will give you an idea what the finished control will look like.

   ◇ In this example, the option for **Check boxes** has been selected. The **Sample** shows these.

   ◇ The option group will look similar to this if **Toggle buttons** are selected.

8   There are a number of options to change how the option group will appear on the form. These can be selected from the **What style would you like to use?** section of the wizard, but it is unlikely that layout style will be required in the practical examinations. For this task, select **Option buttons** and **Sunken** style for the **Option Group** then click on Next > .

9   Enter the caption for the option group – this will be displayed on the form with the buttons/tick boxes. Enter a caption like 'Select the label type'. When the caption is complete, click on Finish .

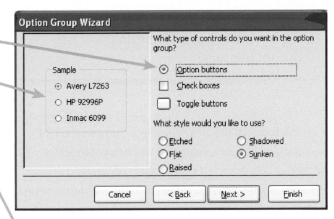

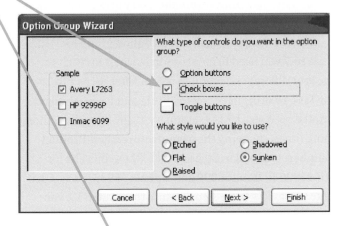

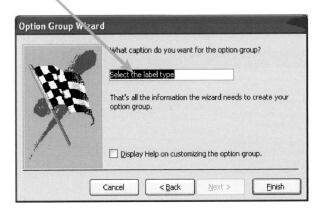

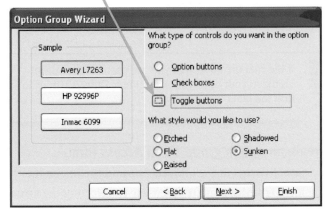

10 The details of the option group can now be seen on the form and will look similar to this. ────────

11 Save the form.

12 Select the **Properties** for the option group by clicking the right mouse button on the **Option Group** drag handle and then selecting **Properties** from the drop-down menu.

13 Select the **All** tab so that the properties window looks similar to this. ────────

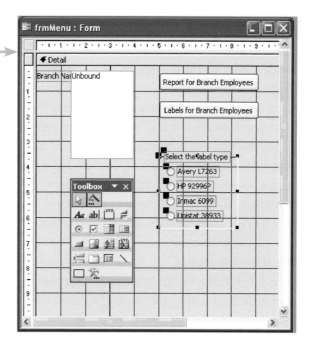

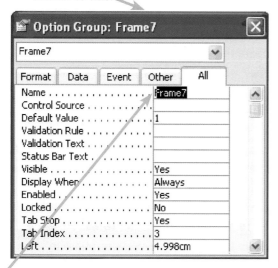

14 Identify the name that *Access* has given to the option group from the name box. You will need this name later on. In this case the option group has been called Frame7.

The rest of this task is completed in Section **16.8**

16.8 Using *Visual Basic for Applications*

VBA is the programming language behind *Access*. You have created the option group, but this does not yet have

an effect upon the labels that are printed. To do this you must go into the code which has been written in *VBA* and change this code so that it selects different reports depending upon the option selected within the option group.

Task 16.7 (cont.) Edit the *VBA* code

1 Select the **Code** 📖 button from the **Form Design** toolbar. This opens the *Visual Basic* editor for the frmMenu form. It shows all of the code (programming language) that makes the form operate. Find the section of code that relates to the command button **Labels for Branch Employees**. This code should look similar to this – but will need to be changed.

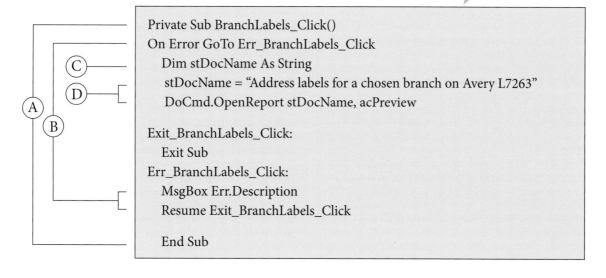

```
Private Sub BranchLabels_Click()
On Error GoTo Err_BranchLabels_Click
    Dim stDocName As String
    stDocName = "Address labels for a chosen branch on Avery L7263"
    DoCmd.OpenReport stDocName, acPreview

Exit_BranchLabels_Click:
    Exit Sub
Err_BranchLabels_Click:
    MsgBox Err.Description
    Resume Exit_BranchLabels_Click

End Sub
```

What does the code do?

First we have to understand what the code does.

A The code shown on the previous page is called a subroutine. This is because it is a subset of the whole program code. It starts with the Private Sub statement and contains all the code upto and including the End Sub command. The name of this subroutine is called BranchLabels_Click(). The name BranchLabels is the name of the control to print the branch name. You gave this name to the control in Step 17 in Task **16.6(iii)**. The _Click() shows that this command will operate when the mouse button is clicked on this control.

B The first line starting On Error instructs the program what to do if there is any problem whilst this section of code is running. In this case, if there is an error it jumps to the section called Err_BranchLabels_Click. Within this section it opens a messagebox (using the MsgBox command) to tell the user what the error is. This message is the code Err.Description. This information would tell the user (or programmer) what has gone wrong. After the error message has been displayed it resumes (continues) by jumping to the label Exit_BranchLabels_Click. This then exits from the subroutine.

C The stDocName part of this statement is the name of the document/query/report/etc. that will be used. *Access* does not know what sort of information this will be, or how much storage space to allocate it. The code tells the program what data type it is (there are different types of information: Byte, Boolean, Integer, Long, Currency, Single, Double, Decimal, Date, String (text) or Array, to name just a few of the available types). This statement tells *Access* to save storage space (dimensions) for string data type (in this case it will hold alphanumeric data) and allows *Access* to set aside the correct amount of storage space for the data.

D The first of these two lines tell *Access* the name of the string that it will use. The string is called stDocName and contains the text 'Address labels for a chosen branch on Avery L7263', which is the name of the report to produce the Avery labels. The second line instructs *Access* to DoCmd (do the command) OpenReport with the name given earlier. The report is to be opened in Preview mode (rather than Design View).

What do you want the code to do?

2 At the moment, this code prints the addresses onto Avery labels. You want the code to print on the chosen label type. To do this, you will need to:

◇ look in the form **frmMenu** at the contents of the **OptionGroup** called **Frame7**

◇ compare the value of the user's response in Frame7 with the value 1 (the value for the Avery L7263 labels)

◇ if the value is 1, open the report called **Address labels for a chosen branch on Avery L7263**

◇ compare the value of the user's response in Frame7 with the value 2 (the value for the HP 92996 P labels)

◇ if the value is 2, open the report called **Address labels for a chosen branch on HP 92996 P**

◇ compare the value of the user's response in Frame7 with the value 3 (the value for the Inmac 6099 labels)

◇ if the value is 3, open the report called **Address labels for a chosen branch on Inmac 6099**

◇ compare the value of the user's response in Frame7 with the value 4 (the value for the Unistat 38933 labels)

◇ if the value is 4, open the report called **Address labels for a chosen branch on Unistat 38933.**

Change this into *VBA* code

3 The only section of the code that needs amending is this:

```
stDocName = "Address labels for a chosen branch on
Avery L7263"
```

Rather than assigning the string name for this single report, you need to have four different report names, one for each type of label. A different report name will be used for each of the numbers in the option group. The code looks in the option group called Frame7 in the form frmMenu and finds the value assigned to the button that has been pressed. The code to do this is:

```
Forms.frmMenu.Frame7.value
```

This is embedded into a series of IF statements, so that if the value on the form is 1, then it loads the first report and so on. The completed code for this section looks like this:

```
Private Sub BranchLabels_Click( )
On Error GoTo Err_BranchLabels_Click
    Dim stDocName As String

    If Forms.frmMenu.Frame7.value = "1" Then stDocName = "Address labels for a chosen branch on Avery L7263"
    If Forms.frmMenu.Frame7.value = "2" Then stDocName = "Address labels for a chosen branch on HP 92996P"
    If Forms.frmMenu.Frame7.value = "3" Then stDocName = "Address labels for a chosen branch on Inmac 6099"
    If Forms.frmMenu.Frame7.value = "4" Then stDocName = "Address labels for a chosen branch on Unistat 38933"
    DoCmd.OpenReport stDocName, acPreview
Exit_BranchLabels_Click:
    Exit Sub
Err_BranchLabels_Click:
    MsgBox Err.Description
    Resume Exit_BranchLabels_Click

End Sub
```

4 Save the code using the File menu, then Save.
5 Close the *Visual Basic* editor, which will return you to the Design View of the form.
6 Save the form and switch to View the form using the ▣▾ button. The finished form should look similar to this. ────────▶

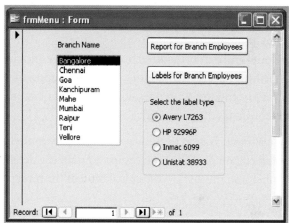

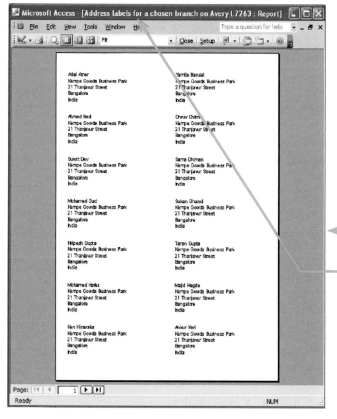

Test the code

It may be difficult to see which labels are which when the form is tested. To check that the option group buttons (or tick boxes) assign the correct values and therefore open the correct reports we need to check each button in turn.

7 Select a Branch Name from the list box.
8 Click on the Avery L7263 button in the option group.
9 Click the left mouse button on the Labels for Branch Employees command button. This will open the label report and will look similar to this.
10 Check that this has opened the expected report, by looking at the name given to the report.
11 Close the report when you have checked that it is correct.
12 Repeat Steps 8 to 11 for each of the other options within the option group. If there is a problem with any of these reports, you can open the form in Design View, select the code and edit it until the form works as expected.

Using a form for a simple menu

Open the database BOATS.MDB from the CD. Using the menu that you created in Activity **16.6** to select a type of boat, create a menu system that allows you to select a series of labels to be used to advertise the boats for sale of a particular type using RankXerox 926L90404, May + Spies 000203, Avery C2244 or Avery C2414 labels.

Each label should include the Make, Year, Type and Length of the boat. The RankXerox 926L90404 labels are the most commonly used type within the company.

16.9 Performing calculations in *Access* using data selected from a form

Task 16.8

Open the database ORDERS.MDB from the CD. This database contains orders for new cars for the South India Motor Company from the Mumbai showroom. There are three tables holding information on the customer, the model and extras required by the customer and the cost of each of these extras. The company has a policy of offering a variety of discounts, depending upon the time customers have to wait for their new car and on the discount negotiated with the salesperson. This discount could be 0%, 5%, 10%, 15% or 20% and is calculated when the invoice is produced.

Create a menu system to allow you to select by model or by customer, enter the discount and produce an invoice for each customer. The invoice must contain the details of the customer, the car and the extras chosen by the customer and must show the calculation of the total price, including the discount selected from the menu.

Use this menu to produce invoices for:
- customers buying Barracuda cars with a 15% discount
- customers buying Cobra cars with a 20% discount
- car(s) for Sukrit Suresh with a 5% discount
- car(s) for Vishwan Singh with a 10% discount.

Create the form in *Access*

1 Select Forms in the Objects box, then select Create form in Design view.
2 Select the File menu, then Save As… and save the new form with the name frmMenu.
3 Enlarge the form by dragging the handle in the bottom right corner of the grey area, so that it is large enough to create the menu, which will include two drop-down list boxes, an option group and command buttons.
4 This menu form is a little more complex than those produced earlier in this chapter, so it is a good idea to design the layout of the menu on paper before developing the form. The menu will require a layout similar to this.

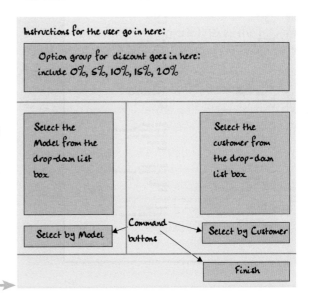

This layout has all the key elements. Each button for 'Select by Model' and 'Select by Customer' should be close to (preferably just below) the drop-down lists for each of these sections. The option group needs to be selected for both of these processes, so it has been placed at the top of the screen. Instructions have been provided for the user and a button to quit has been included.

5 Click on the Label **Aa** button from the **Toolbox** and move the cursor onto the form **frmMenu**. Press the left mouse button and drag the lasso to create space to enter the instructions on the form. This needs to be reasonably large and the font chosen will need to be a clear, easily read font. Enter suitable instructions for the user. It should look similar to this.

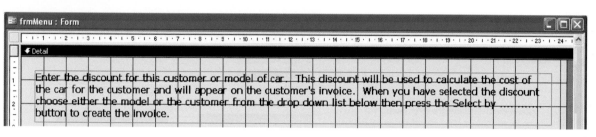

Hint

In the practical examinations you will be expected to give clear instructions to users, and may be awarded marks for this without being told to do so in the question paper.

Create the option group to select the discount percentage

6 Click on the **Option Group** button from the **Toolbox** and move the cursor onto the form **frmMenu**, just below the instructions. Press the left mouse button and drag the lasso to create an option group on the form. Do not overlap the instructions on the form. This needs to contain five buttons or tick boxes. As you release the left mouse button, the **Option Group Wizard** will run.

7 In the **Label Names:** box enter the discount rates. Do not press the <Enter> key or click on Next > until you have entered all five of the names.

8 The next stage in the wizard asks if one of the options that you have just entered is to be the default choice. For this task, the default choice will be No discount. Select this option, followed by clicking on Next >.

9 Change the values for each option button/tick box. These should be the percentage values of the discount. These figures will be used in the calculations used to produce the final invoice for the customer. Enter these values, as shown here, then click on Next >.

10 Choose how the option group will appear on the form. For this task it is better to select either **Option buttons** or **Check boxes** (tick boxes) so that these buttons look different from the command buttons. Then click on Next >.

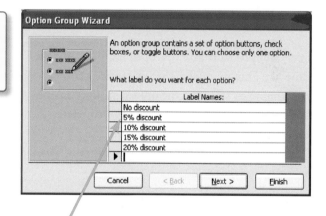

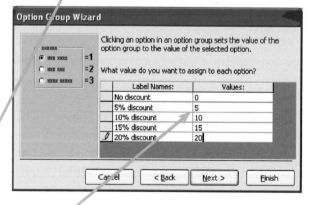

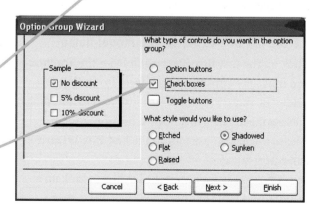

11 In the final stage of the wizard, enter the text (caption) for this option group, giving further instructions to the user. Click on | Finish | to complete the wizard.

12 *Access* will probably give this option group a default name like Frame1. Check that this is the option group name by selecting the option group, clicking the right mouse button and selecting **Properties**. You can change this to a more meaningful name like 'Discount_Percent' in the **Properties** window. Save the form.

> **Hint**
>
> Do not use spaces in the control name. If you wish to show spaces, replace them with an underscore character. For example, 'Discount Percent' should be 'Discount_Percent'.

Create the lines

13 In the hand-drawn design of the form shown earlier in this section, parts of the form were separated using lines. Draw these onto the form using the **Line** ╲ button from the **Toolbox** toolbar. Like all *Access* controls, the format of the line can be changed using the **Properties** window.

Create the list box to select the model name

14 Click on the List Box ▦ button from the **Toolbox** and move the cursor onto the form, to the left just below the line. Press the left mouse button and drag the lasso to create a drop-down list box. As you release the left mouse button the **List Box Wizard** will run.

15 Select the option for **I want the list box to look up a value from a table or query** and click on | Next > |.

16 Click on the radio button for **Tables** and select the **Table: Model** option from the list box, followed by clicking on | Next > |.

17 Select the **ModelName** field from the **Available fields:** box and click on | > | to move this into the **Selected fields:** box. Then click on | Next > |.

18 Sort the order into ascending order on the **ModelName** field, then click on | Next > |.

19 There is no need to adjust the columns in this task, so click on | Next > | again.

20 Enter the label for this control – this will provide instructions for the user. You could enter 'Choose the model of the car then press Select by Model'. Click on | Next > | to complete the wizard.

21 *Access* will probably have given this List box a default name like List1. Check this name by selecting the list box, clicking the right mouse button and selecting **Properties** to open the **Properties** window. You can change this to a more meaningful name like 'ModelList'. Save the form.

Create the list box to select the customer

22 Click on the List Box ▦ button from the **Toolbox**, and press the left mouse button and drag the lasso to create a drop-down list box to the right of the previous list box. The **List Box Wizard** will run.

23 Select the option for **I want the list box to look up a value from a table or query**, then click on | Next > |.

24 Click on the radio button for **Tables** and select the **Table: Customer** option from the list box, followed by clicking on | Next > |.

25 Select the **CustomerRef**, **Forename** and **Surname** fields from the **Available fields:** box and click on ⟦ **>** ⟧ to move these into the **Selected fields:** box. Then click on ⟦ **Next >** ⟧.

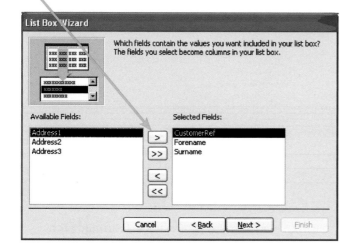

26 Sort the order into ascending order on the **Surname** field, then into ascending order on the **Forename** field before clicking on ⟦ **Next >** ⟧.

27 Make sure that the tick box for **Hide key column** is selected before clicking on ⟦ **Next >** ⟧.

28 Enter the label for this control – this will provide instructions for the user. You could enter 'Select the customer from the list then press Select by Customer'. Click on ⟦ **Finish** ⟧ to complete the wizard.

29 Change the default name for this list box to **CustomerList** in the **Properties** window. Save the form.

Create the query to select by model name

30 Select **Queries** in the **Objects** box and then **Create query by using wizard**. This will open the **Simple Query Wizard**. You should be familiar with this wizard from Chapter **11**.

31 Select each of the tables in turn from the **Tables/Queries** drop-down list. Select all of the fields from each table. When you have finished, the **Selected Fields:** box should contain all of the fields in the database. Click on ⟦ **Next >** ⟧.

32 Make sure that the radio button for **Detail** is selected before clicking on ⟦ **Next >** ⟧.

33 Enter the name for the query. You can call this query 'qryModelSelection'.

34 Click on the radio button for **Modify the query design** before clicking on ⟦ **Finish** ⟧.

35 To complete the query, you need to enter the selection criterion from the list box on the form. Press the left mouse button in the **Criteria** box for the field **Model.ModelName**.

Address3	ModelName	BasicPrice
Customer	Model	Model
☑	☑	☑

36 Enter the criterion that points to the list box on the form – 'Forms!frmMenu!ModelList' – into this box. When you have entered this and pressed the <Return> key the text will change to show square brackets around each *Access* element. It will look similar to this.

dress3	ModelName	BasicPr
:tomer	Model	Model
☑	☑	
	[Forms]![frmMenu]![ModelList]	

37 You now need to calculate the cost of the extras to be added to the price. The easiest method is to perform new calculations within the query. Add a new field called **SatNavCalc**. This field will contain either 0 if the customer did not order satellite navigation, or the charge for the satellite navigation system for the model of car chosen. As the field **Sales.SatNav** is a Yes/No field, the data is stored in *Access* as either 0 for No or −1 for Yes. If we apply basic mathematics and multiply the value in **Sales.SatNav** by the price in **Model.SatNav** we get 0 if the item was not ordered or 'minus the price' if it was ordered. By multiplying this by −1 we can get the correct value. The formula for this is:

Sales_ClimateControl: ClimateControl	SatNavCalc: [Sales_SatNav]*-1*[Model_SatNav]	⌐
Sales		
☑		

Hint When entering a field for use in a calculation, use an underscore rather than a full stop in the fieldname, i.e. enter Sales_SatNav rather than Sales.SatNav.

For example:

◇ If the field Sales.SatNav is Yes and Model.SatNav contains 230 the calculation would be:

−1 (for the Yes)*−1*230

This calculation gives 230, which is the correct value.

◇ If the field Sales.SatNav is No and Model.SatNav contains 230 the calculation would be:

0 (for the No)*−1*230

This calculation gives 0, which is again the correct value.

38 Two more fields and similar formulae need adding to the query, one for leather seats and one for climate control. The same principles apply as shown in Step 37. The completed formulae will look like this.

Field:	LeatherCalc: [Sales_Leather]*-1*[Model_Leather]	ClimateControlCalc: [Sales_ClimateControl]*-1*[Model_ClimateControl]
Table:		
Sort:		
Show:	✓	✓
Criteria:		

39 Save the changes that you have made to the query and close the query.

Create the query to select by customer

40 Rather than duplicating Steps 30 to 39 for the customer query, it will be far quicker and much easier to copy the query **qryModelSelection** and change the copy for the customer selection. Select **Queries** from the available **Objects** and click the right mouse button box on **qryModelSelection**. Select **Copy** from the drop-down menu.

41 Right mouse click the cursor on the background in the same window and select **Paste** from the drop-down menu.

42 In the **Paste As** window, enter the **Query Name:** 'qryCustomerSelection' and click on **OK**.

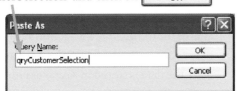

43 Open the query **qryCustomerSelection** in **Design View** by selecting the query name and clicking on **Design**.

44 Highlight the text entered in Step 36 and delete it from the **Criteria** row.

45 Move the cursor to the **Criteria** box for the field **Customer.CustomerRef** and press the left mouse button.

46 Enter the criterion that points to the customer list box on the form – 'Forms!frmMenu!CustomerList' – into this box and press the <Return> key. The text

will change to show square brackets around each *Access* element. It will look similar to this.

Field:	CustomerRef	Forename
Table:	Customer	Customer
Sort:		
Show:	✓	✓
Criteria:	[Forms]![frmMenu]![CustomerList]	
or:		

47 Save the changes that you have made to the query and close the query.

Create the invoice when selecting by model name

48 Select **Reports** in the **Objects** box and then **Create report by using wizard**. This will open the **Report Wizard**. You should be familiar with this wizard from Chapter **11**.

49 From the **Tables/Queries** drop-down list select the **Query: qryModelSelection**. Use the > button to select the following fields and place them in the report: **Forename, Surname, Address1, Address2, Address3, ModelName, BasicPrice, SatNavCalc, LeatherCalc** and **ClimateControlCalc**. Click on **Next >**.

50 For the invoice there is no need to group or sort the data, so click on **Next >** twice.

51 Select the required layout from the options. This will be changed when you lay out the invoice in design view, but choosing **Columnar** will make it slightly easier than the other options. Make sure that the radio button for **Portrait** is selected. When you have made your choice, click on **Next >**.

52 Select the font style for the report and click on **Next >**.

53 Enter the name to be given to the report – 'InvoiceSelectbyModel' – choose the radio button for **Modify the report's design** and click on [Finish]. The report design will look similar to this. →

54 Edit the label in the **Report Header** to say 'South India Motor Company – Invoice'.

55 You are going to place the label entered in Step 54 in the **Detail** section, so that it appears with every car. First enlarge the space in the **Detail section** by dragging the grey bar entitled **Page Footer** down another five centimetres.

56 Highlight all of the controls in this section with the lasso tool and drag them down about 4 centimetres, within the same section.

57 Drag the label from the **Report Header** into the top of the **Detail** section.

58 Close the **Report Header** by dragging the grey bar entitled **Page Header** up to the top.

59 Add a new label containing the text 'To' and place this at the top of the **Detail** section.

60 Move the text boxes for **Forename, Surname, Address1, Address2** and **Address3** to the top of the **Detail** section. Delete the labels from each of these text boxes. If you accidentally delete the text box, use **Edit** and **Undo** to recover the controls. Move and resize these controls and place them as shown here.

61 Move the label and the text box containing **ModelName** up slightly. Change the caption (text) in this label to 'Model Ordered'.

62 Select all the remaining eight controls, the labels and text boxes and move these below and to the right of the label containing **Model Ordered**.

63 Change the label containing the text **BasicPrice**, so that it has a space between the words Basic and Price.

64 Change the label for **SatNavCalc** so that it reads 'Satellite Navigation'. Change the label containing **LeatherCalc** to 'Leather Seats' and change the label **ClimateControlCalc** to 'Climate Control'. The new report will look similar to this.

65 Click on the **Text box** [abl] button from the **Toolbox** toolbar. In the **Detail** section, add a new text box directly below all the other text boxes. Edit the text in the label for this text box so that it contains 'Total Price'.

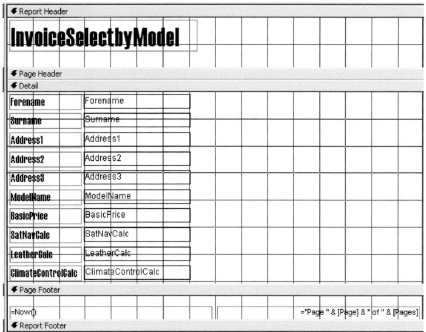

Hint Use cut and paste if you find this easier.

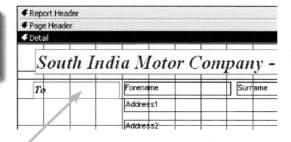

66 Right mouse click on the **Text Box** for **Total Price** and select **Properties** from the drop-down menu to open the **Properties** window for this control. Change the **Name** of this **Text Box** to 'TotalPrice'.

67 Select the **Expression Builder** from the **Control Source** section by clicking in the **Control Source** box and then on the ⟨ ... ⟩ button to the right of the box.

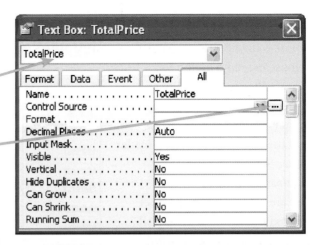

68 The **Expression Builder** helps you to create formulae without having to remember the range of notation used by *Access*. In the left window of the **Expression Builder** is a list of all of the places where data can be gathered. You are going to use the four controls already on the report which hold the data from the underlying query. These are: **BasicPrice**, **SatNavCalc**, **LeatherCalc** and **ClimateControlCalc**. Start by double clicking the left mouse button on the **Reports** folder to expand it.

69 Double click the left mouse button on the **Loaded Reports** sub-folder, and again on the report name for this report. This will ensure that the fields in the current report are visible in the centre window.

70 In the centre window, select each of the controls containing the data that you need to add. Start by selecting the **BasicPrice** text box. This is done by double clicking the left mouse button on the control name. Then click the left mouse button on the ⟨+⟩ button, followed by the next control, and so on. The completed expression appears at the top of the window and should look similar to this. Click on ⟨ OK ⟩ to place this expression into the control.

71 Use the **Properties** window and the **Format** section to format the **TotalPrice** text box as **Currency**.

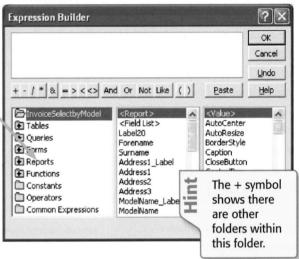

> **Hint** The + symbol shows there are other folders within this folder.

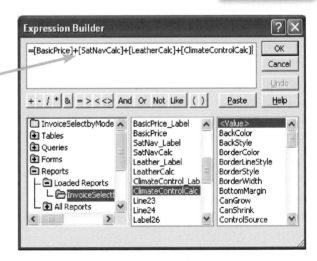

72 Create another new text box in the **Detail** section, directly below the **Total Price** box. Change the label of this text box so that it displays 'Discount'.

73 Using the text box **Properties**, select the **Expression Builder** from the **Control Source** section. Select in the left window of the **Expression Builder** the form **frmMenu** and select in the middle window the control containing the **Discount_Percent** taken from this form.

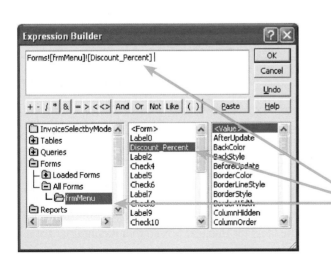

74 Multiply this by the value in the **Total Price** control of the current report (calculated in Steps 66 to 70) and then divide the answer by 100 to get the percentage. Use the 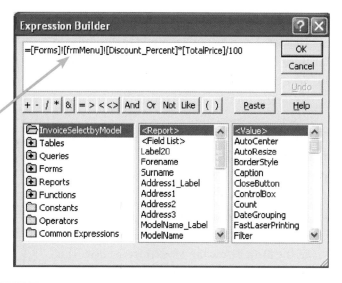 button to multiply and the two left windows to select the controls. Use the button to divide. The completed expression should look similar to this.

75 Click on [OK] to place this expression into the control.

76 Use the **Properties** window and the **Format** section to format the **Discount Text Box** as **Currency**.

77 Create a third new text box in the **Detail** section, directly below the Discount box. Change the label of this text box so that it displays 'Amount Due'.

78 Use the **Expression Builder** to calculate the amount due. This is the value from the **Total Price** text box minus the value from the **Discount** text box. Format this text box as **Currency**. The completed report should look similar to this.

79 Save the changes that you have made to the report and close this report.

Create the invoice when selecting by customer

80 Rather than duplicating Steps 48 to 79 for this invoice, repeat the process from Steps 40 to 42 to copy the report InvoiceSelectbyModel and paste it as 'InvoiceSelectbyCustomer'.

81 Open the report InvoiceSelectbyCustomer in Design View by selecting the report name then clicking on Design.

82 Right click the mouse button on the report control (in the top left corner) and select **Properties** from the drop-down menu.

83 Move the cursor into the box for **Record Source** and select the drop-down menu. Select qryCustomerSelection from this list.

84 Use the **Properties** window to change the caption to 'InvoiceSelectbyCustomer'.

85 Because a customer may have ordered more than one new car, you need to move the title and customer details into the **Page Header**. This will allow these details to be displayed only once. Enlarge the **Page Header** section (as described earlier) and drag these

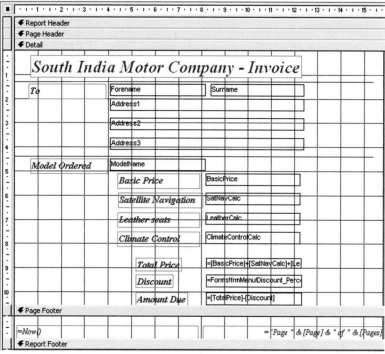

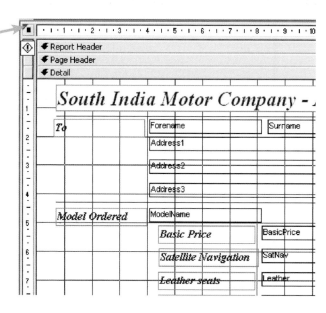

controls from the Detail row into the Page Header. The new report should look similar to this.

86 Save the changes that you have made to the report and close the report.

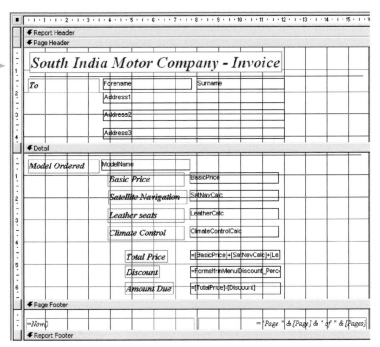

Create the command button to select by model

87 Select the form frmMenu so that it is open in Design View.

88 Use the Command Button ▣ tool to add a new command button. Place this on the left of the form below the ModelList list box. This will open the Command Button wizard.

89 In the Categories: section select Report Operations and in the Actions: section select Preview Report. Then click on ⟨ Next > ⟩.

90 Select the report InvoiceSelectbyModel for this button and click on ⟨ Next > ⟩.

91 Ensure that the radio button for Text is selected and add the text 'Select by Model' to the button, then click on ⟨ Next > ⟩.

92 Give the command button a meaningful name like 'SelectByModel' before clicking on ⟨ Finish ⟩.

Create the command button to select by customer

93 Use Steps 87 to 92 to help you create a new command button below the CustomerList list box. Make this

button preview the report InvoiceSelectbyCustomer. Label this button 'Select by Customer' and name the control 'SelectByCustomer'.

Create the command button to quit the menu

94 Use Steps 87 to 92 to help you create a new command button at the bottom of the form. Make this button perform a Form operation and complete the action to Close form. Save the finished form, which should look similar to this.

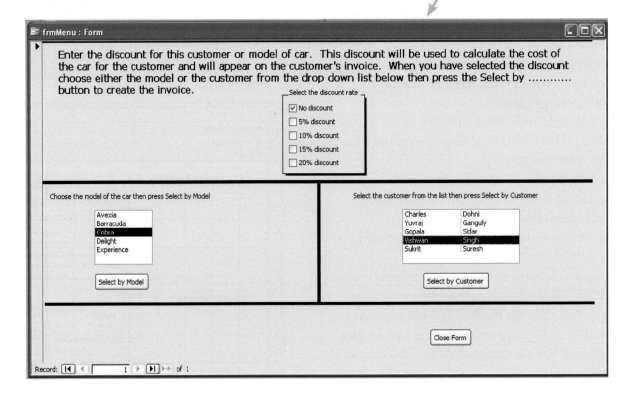

Test the form

The process of testing a form like this involves creating a test plan. Writing in detail about this process would require a book on its own. This section however, just gives the bare outline of this topic, sufficient for the practical examinations.

The test plan will include the tests that you wish to perform, the input required and the expected output. It is often easier to split the testing into two parts: testing the selection and testing the calculations.

1   Start by testing the selection. This can be produced on the computer or as a quick handwritten test plan like this.

Test	Input	Expected Output	Actual Output
Command Button			
Select by Model	Select by Model Button Pressed	Opens Invoice Select By Model	
Select by Customer	Select by Customer Button Pressed	Opens Invoice Select By Customer	
Close Form	Close Form Command Button Pressed	Closes form frmMenu	
List Box			
Select by Model	Avexia	One car for Vishwan Singh	
	Barracuda	Cars for Vishwan Singh and Charles Dohni	
	Cobra	Cars for Gopala Sidar and Yuvraj Ganguly	
	Delight	One car for Sukrit Suresh	
	Experience	No cars	
Select by Customer	Charles Dohni	Barracuda with leather seats & climate control	
	Yuvraj Ganguly	Cobra with climate control	
	Gopala Sidar	Cobra with all three extras	
	Vishwan Singh	Barracuda with all three extras	
		Avexia with leather seats & climate control	
	Sukrit Suresh	Delight with leather seats	

The expected output is worked out by looking at the data stored in the tables. *Do not* use the form to gather the expected results. Try each of the tests in turn, and write the results in the Actual output box. The results in the expected and actual output boxes should be the same. If they are not, correct the command button, list box, query or report and repeat the test until you get the required result.

2   Test all of the calculations. For each car, calculate by hand what the expected results should be and write these down. Here is an example of the calculations done by hand.

Cobra	Expected Results				
Basic price	19600				
Satellite navigation	210				
Leather seats	600				
Climate control	260				
	19600 + 210 + 600 + 260				
Total price	10670				
Discount %	0%	5%	10%	15%	20%
		0.05 × 10670	0.1 × 10670	0.15 × 10670	0.1 × 10670
Discount	£0.00	£1,033.50	£2,067.00	£3,100.50	£4,134.00
Amount due	£10,670	£19,636.50	£18,603.00	£17,570	£16,536.00

3 Perform the test twice, by selecting this car using each command button. This is because each command button opens a different report and these are not identical. Check that the expected results match the actual results on each test. Test this car with each of the percentage values on the form to make sure that the values assigned to each tick box within the option group are correct and that the calculations give the correct results. Repeat this process for each model of car and combination of extras.

It is unlikely that in the practical examinations you will have time to thoroughly test all possibilities, so try to test all of the selection and a sample of the calculations.

Use the form

Use the database to produce the invoices outlined in Task **16.8**.

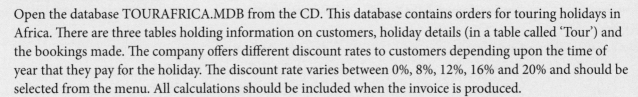

Activity 16.8

Open the database TOURAFRICA.MDB from the CD. This database contains orders for touring holidays in Africa. There are three tables holding information on customers, holiday details (in a table called 'Tour') and the bookings made. The company offers different discount rates to customers depending upon the time of year that they pay for the holiday. The discount rate varies between 0%, 8%, 12%, 16% and 20% and should be selected from the menu. All calculations should be included when the invoice is produced.

Create a menu system to allow you to select by tour name or by customer and produce an invoice for each customer. The invoice must contain the details of the customer and all of the holiday details from the Tour table. The cost of flights must be added to this (if a flight has been booked) to give a total price. The total price and the discount rate (from the menu) should be used to calculate the discount amount. The actual price that the customer must pay will be the total price minus both the discount and the deposit paid. Ensure that there is an exit button on the form.

Use this menu to produce invoices for:
- customers booking Across Africa with a 12% discount
- customers booking a City Break with a 16% discount
- tours booked by Cama Masakadza with a 20% discount
- tours booked by Mbongeni Mupariwa with an 8% discount.

16.10 Be flexible

It is impossible within the scope of this book to cover all of the possible methods that can be used to solve practical questions at this level, or to show all possible question types and scenarios. Use the skills that you have developed to meet the question requirements. Be flexible in your approach – if one application does not offer

all of the features that you need to answer a question, integrate the data between packages. For example, if a text document is presented to you, and you are required to place information from a spreadsheet into it so that it could be constantly updated, copy the data from the spreadsheet and use paste link to place the data into the document.

17 Output data 2

Hint

This chapter will provide you with useful examination techniques that will allow you to prove to the examiners your range of practical skills.

17.1 Printing a mail-merged document

You have already developed many of the skills needed for this chapter. Printing mail-merged documents is identical to printing any other word-processed document. The skills that you have learned in previous chapters can be used to help you produce documents such as letters,

labels, cards, invitations, quotations, orders, invoices, statements and passes. The only time that this requires additional work is when you need to provide to the examiner the evidence of the merge codes that you have used. These can be shown by printing the master document.

If there are any conditional operators used within the master document ensure that the underlying merge code is visible. To do this click the right mouse button on the merge code and select **Toggle Field Codes** from the drop-down menu, so that the full field code within this placeholder is visible. Repeat this for each placeholder on the page. The code should look similar to this.

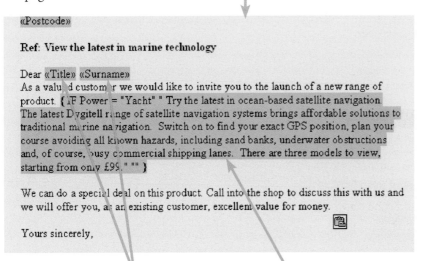

In this example, two fields are visible without the selection of **Toggle Field Codes** and for the third field (containing the conditional code) the **Toggle Field Codes** option has been selected.

If you use the **Mail Merge Recipients** window (see Section **15.4**) to select the records for the mail merge, you will need to produce screenshot evidence of your selection, similar to this.

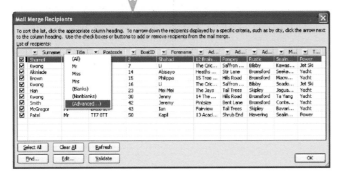

You may also need to include evidence of the **Query Options** window.

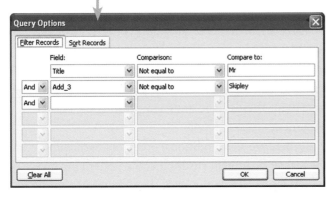

Hint

Remember that using the Print Screen <Prt Scr> button on the keyboard, then pasting the screenshot into a word processor can also provide evidence for the practical examinations. If you use screenshots in a document to provide evidence, ensure that your name, centre number and candidate number are printed in the header or footer of the document.

17.2 Printing evidence of hyperlinks

1   To print evidence of a hyperlink, click the right mouse button on the hyperlink. This will give a drop-down menu, which looks similar to this. →

2   Select **Edit Hyperlink…** to display the **Edit Hyperlink** window, which looks similar to this.

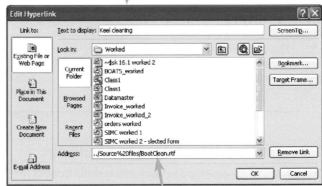

3   The pathway of the hyperlink is visible here. You can produce a screenshot of this window and use it to present the evidence to the examiner.

17.3 Printing macros

Although this book covers recording macros rather than creating them in *Visual Basic for Applications* (*VBA*) code, macros still need to be printed from the *Visual Basic* editor.

1 This can be found by selecting the **Tools** menu, followed by **Macro**. From the **Macro** sub-menu choose the option for **Macros...**. This will open the Macros window, which looks similar to this.

2 Select the macro that you wish to print and click on [**Edit**]. This will open the *Visual Basic* editor.

3 All macros attached to the document will be shown within the editor. In this case only the first macro is visible in the window.

4 Ensure that your name, centre number and candidate number are visible within the code (these should have been added when you created the macro) and select **File**, then **Print...**.

5 This will open the **Print** window, which looks similar to this.

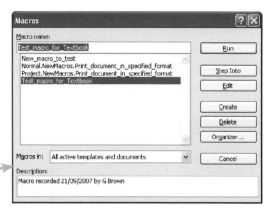

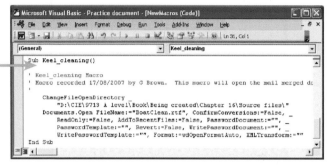

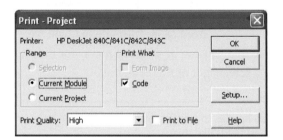

In this example (and for all questions within the practical examinations), you are only concerned with a single module of code so click on [**OK**]. This will print the code showing evidence of all the macros that you have created.

17.4 Printing forms in Access

The *VBA* code underlying *Access* forms (similar to macros in Section **17.3**) will provide the examiners with evidence of many of the methods that you have used.

1 To access the underlying code for the form, open the form in **Design View** by selecting the form name and clicking on the Design **Design** button.

2 Open the **Form Design** toolbar, and then select the **Code** button from this toolbar. This will open the Visual Basic editor and allow the evidence of the code to be viewed. Then follow Steps 4 and 5 in Section **17.3**.

If you have used option groups with assigned values for each button (or tick box) within your *Access* forms, then evidence of the values assigned will also need to be shown.

3 To show the default value for the option group, click the right mouse button on the option group and select **Properties** from the drop-down menu. Ensure that you select the whole option group and no individual control within the group. The **Properties** window for the group will appear, showing the default value for this group, and looks similar to this.

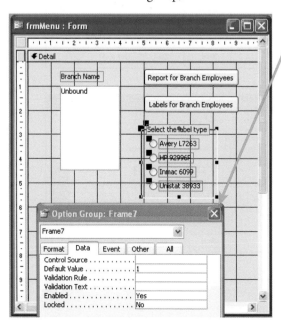

4 Produce and save a screenshot of this window.

5 To show the values assigned to each button (or tick box), select each button in turn and produce and save a screenshot of the **Properties** window for the button. Your screenshots should look similar to this.

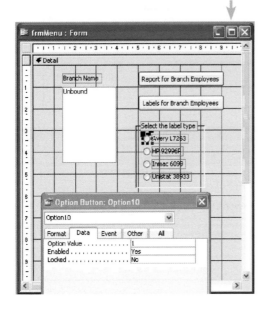

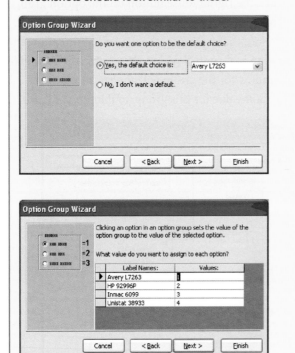

17.5 Printing linked queries in Access

Where queries are linked to forms (or select data based upon run-time data entry within the query), print out the evidence of the links from the query. In order to do this:

1 Open the query in **Design View** by clicking on the Design ![Design] button after selecting the query name.

2 Make sure that all of the fields containing the references to a form (or run-time data entry) are fully visible.

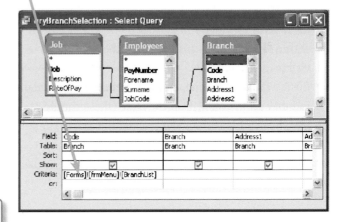

3 The examiner will need to see the code that you have entered so that you can be awarded marks for this. Produce a screenshot of this evidence.

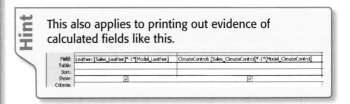

4 To open the form that this reference points to in **Design View**, select the form name and click on the Design ![Design] button.

5 Click the right mouse button on the control used for the reference, and display the **Properties** window like this. In this example, the **Properties** window has been enlarged so that all of the details in the Row Source are visible.

6 Make sure that you also produce and print a screenshot of the list box as it is being used, so that the examiner can see that you have created it correctly. It should look similar to this.

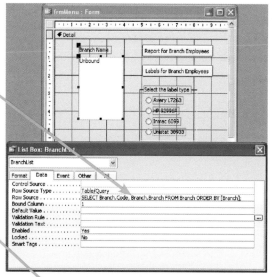

17.6 Printing calculated controls in Access reports

Where reports contain calculated controls, evidence of the calculation can be shown using two different methods:

◆ enlarging the calculated control
◆ producing a screenshot of the **Properties** window.

Both methods require you to open the report in **Design View**, by selecting the report name and then clicking on the **Design** button.

Enlarge the calculated control

Make sure that all of the calculated controls are fully visible. This may require you to stretch the drag handles on the control so a section of a report like this will become this.
Produce screenshot evidence of these controls.

Produce a screenshot of the Properties window

If it is not possible to enlarge the control, due to the layout of the report, you will need to select each control in turn and produce a screenshot of the Properties window, enlarging it to show the **Control Source**.
Produce a screenshot of this evidence.

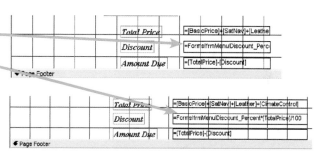

Hint

Remember, all that the examiner sees in the practical examination is the evidence that you produce. Make sure that you illustrate all of the knowledge, skills and techniques that you have applied in the examination by printing all of the evidence.

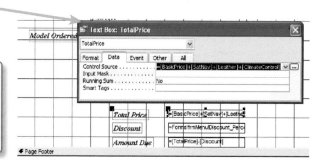

Glossary

*Please note that terms within a definition that appear in **bold type** are also defined in the glossary.*

.csv	*See* **comma separated values.**
.rtf	*See* **rich text format.**
.txt	*See* **text file.**
abnormal data	Data that is of the wrong type (e.g. text in a numeric **field**) or is outside the accepted range (e.g. an exam mark percentage of 110).
absolute referencing	Fixes a cell reference within a spreadsheet so that when the formula is copied this cell reference never changes.
active hubs	**Hubs** that amplify the data signal when a data **packet** passes through it.
actual results	Results obtained as a result of live testing.
administrator	The person who is in control of a computer network.
administrator privileges	The privileges that only one person, the **administrator**, possesses, such as allocating user names and passwords as well as access rights.
aggregated information	Personal details of individuals combined to provide information without naming those individuals.
alphanumeric	A field type where any character is acceptable input – sometimes called text.
amplifier	A part of a sound system that makes the sound louder so that it can be easily heard.
AND	Used to search with two (or more) conditions, where both (or all) conditions must be true for the result to be true.
anonymised information	Personal details of an individual where the name or other identifying information is left out.
aspect ratio	The proportion of length to width of an image. Maintaining the aspect ratio means to keep the original proportion of the image (without distortion) and is usually needed when images are resized.
autotext	A collection of pre-defined, commonly used phrases that can be inserted into a document in order to save time repeatedly typing them.
AVERAGE	Function within *Microsoft Excel* that calculates the mean (average) of a list of numbers.
backward chaining	A form of reasoning in expert systems where the conclusion has been put forward by the user. The expert system produces a list of reasons why that may be so and the user has to verify that those reasons do apply to the situation.
bar chart	Chart that uses blocks or bars to graphically represent a comparison between different quantities.
baseline	A line on which the text rests, used in **word processors** and **desktop publishers.**

batch process control	Microprocessor control of a **process** where specific amounts of raw materials are combined together and mixed for a certain length of time.
bitmap graphics	A graphics format that stores the position and colour of each pixel (or dot) of a drawing, so that if an image is enlarged or reduced the image can appear **pixelated.**
blog	An abbreviation of weblog. Blogs were originally used by individuals to keep a diary but were written at various points in the day rather than at the end of the day. They are now used by people to enable others to contribute to discussions.
Bluetooth	A technology-enabling **device** for communicating as part of a network over very short distances.
blu-ray disk	An optical disk with very large capacity using a short wavelength for its laser beam close to the blue/violet spectra (hence its name).
bookmark_	A named reference point in an electronic document, frequently used to **hyperlink** to within the document or to identify text that may need to be updated in the future.
Boolean	A logical thought process developed by the English mathematician and computer pioneer, George Boole. *See* **Boolean operator.**
Boolean operator	The logical operators **AND, OR** and **NOT**, which are used in searches (queries) within data handling applications and return the value True or False.
break	A split between two pages, sections or columns, or inserted to force text wrapping at the end of a line of text.
broadband	A high-speed method of transmitting data using a number of data channels through one cable, giving users faster access to the **Internet** together with shorter download times.
browse	To read and navigate through a series of web pages received from the **Internet.**
browser	A piece of application software that allows users to look at and interact with all the information on the worldwide web.
bus network	A network that has each computer or **device** connected to a common spine. The spine consists of cabling with network leads attached to it and each computer.
byte	A binary number consisting of eight binary digits, often used as a measure of storage e.g. 1MB (one million bytes).
CAA	*See* **computer-aided assessment.**
CAD software	*See* **computer-aided design software.**
CAI	*See* **computer-aided instruction.**
CAL	*See* **computer-aided learning.**
calculated control	A control within a **database** report, the effect of which is re-applied at run-time. It is often used to display the result of a calculation using the selected data.
calculated field	A **field** within a **database** query that is recalculated each time the query is opened. It is used to hold the results of calculations on the data held in each record (selected within a query), rather than displaying stored data.
call centre	A large open-plan office space that organisations use to house their operators so that they can receive and answer customer phone calls. It involves computer networks and several operators to handle a large volume of calls.
CAPI	*See* **computer-assisted personal interviewing.**
card payment gateway system	An online service used by auction, booking and shopping **websites** to allow customers to pay over the **Internet**. It involves the encryption of personal data so that data is transmitted securely. It is the interface between the organisation's website and the bank's computer.

carpal tunnel syndrome	A medical condition causing pain in the forearm and wrist that can be caused by repetitive use of the keyboard.
CATI	*See* **computer-assisted personal interviewing**.
CAWI	*See* **computer-assisted personal interviewing**.
CBL	*See* **computer-based learning**.
CBT	*See* **computer-based training**.
charting package	Software that allows the creation of a variety of different graphs and charts. These are sometimes separate packages or can be included in **spreadsheets** or **databases**. Within this book we will use the charting facilities offered within *Microsoft Excel* (further details can be found in Chapter **11**).
chat room	A form of conference **website** where like-minded people can get together to communicate in real time using text messages.
chip and PIN	A technology that is used in debit and credit cards for payment in stores or use with ATMS. The chip is read by a card reader machine and is compared with the number typed in by the customer. It helps to ensure security of transactions.
client–server system	A system within networks where computers act as clients to a main server. The client computers make requests of a server, which then services these requests.
CMC	*See* **computer-mediated communications**.
coaxial	A type of cable that was once predominant in connecting computers within a network. The conducting wire was surrounded by a plastic tube, then another wire and then an outer plastic tube.
codec	A circuit capable of converting audio and video data into a digital form and then compressing it for transmission across a network.
comma separated values	A file format (.csv) used to hold tabular data, e.g. from a **spreadsheet** or **database** table. It stores it as a text-based file using commas (or semi-colons in some locations) to separate the data items.
comments	Allows a user to add non-printing comments to a document without changing the content of the document. Comments are also used within a script or programming language to explain declarations or subroutines.
communication satellite	A man-made satellite that stays in space for telecommunications purposes. They are used for phone communications as well as television and radio broadcasting.
compression ratio	The amount by which a file of data can be compressed into a smaller file, e.g. A 100:1 compression ratio would reduce a file to one hundredth of its size.
computer programmer	A person who writes software routines for use in various applications. They usually work in conjunction with a **systems analyst** who directs the requirements of a program.
computer telephony integration software	The software used in a call centre, which brings together all aspects of a telephone centre and controls the handling of phone calls.
computer-aided assessment	Any aspect of assessing student's work using a computer.
computer-aided design software	Software that allows the user to draw objects in two or three dimensions. Engineers and architects are the main users of CAD in construction projects.
computer-aided instruction	The process where a computer takes charge of the learning process and acts independently of any teacher input.

computer-aided learning	The use of computers and ICT to support the teacher in the learning process. The teacher is in control and uses ICT as a resource around which a lesson might be planned.
computer-assisted personal interviewing	Used in **market research**; the interviewer either asks the interviewee questions as prompted by the computer or allows the interviewee to respond to questions using the computer.
computer-assisted personal interviewing	Used in **market research**; the interviewer is normally to be found in a call centre. The computer dials the phone number of the selected interviewee and then proceeds as for **computer-aided personal interviewing**, with the interviewer recording the responses.
computer-assisted personal interviewing	Used in **market research**, interviewees log on to a **website** and complete a **questionnaire** or web form online.
computer-based learning	A term used interchangeably with **computer-aided learning**. *See* **computer-aided learning**.
computer-based training	A term used interchangeably with **computer-aided instruction**. *See* **computer-aided instruction**.
computer-mediated communications	The collective term given to communication services such as e-mail, instant messaging and chat rooms.
concept keyboards	Used by people who may have disabilities, usually an A4-sized tray that can have an overlay sheet in it. The overlay sheet can consist of boxes with phrases in, letters of the alphabet, numbers or other symbols.
congestion control mechanism	A mechanism used by the **TCP protocol** to reduce the speed of data in order to reduce the transmission speed of data packets, thereby reducing the congestion in networks.
connectionless service	A service offered in a network that requires no **handshaking** to take place, typically found in the **UDP** protocol.
connection-oriented service	A service that requires **handshaking** to take place before any data can be exchanged, typically found in the **TCP protocol.**
continuous process control	Microprocessor control of a process whereby variables do not tend to fluctuate by a great deal but the conditions must be continuously maintained, e.g. the temperature in a refrigeration process.
control software	Computer programs that allow computers or microprocessors to automatically control a system.
control system	An automated system that is controlled by a computer or microprocessor.
cookie	A text file sent to a user's web browser by a web server. They can be used by web servers and organisations to monitor the behaviour of users.
copy	To take a **highlighted** object and place a copy of it into the clipboard, leaving the original object intact.
COUNT	Function within *Microsoft Excel* that looks at the cells within a given range and counts the number of these cells containing numbers.
COUNTA	Function within *Microsoft Excel* that looks at the cells within a given range and counts the number of non-blank (not empty) cells.
COUNTIF	Function within *Microsoft Excel* that looks at the cells within a given range and counts the number of these cells that meet a given condition.
crop	To remove unwanted areas of an image – this may change the aspect ratio but will not distort the image.

CTI software	*See* **computer telephony integration software.**
cubital tunnel syndrome	A medical condition similar to **carpal tunnel syndrome**, but which occurs in the elbow and is most commonly caused by regularly making lengthy mobile phone calls.
currency	The unit of money used by countries, e.g. Egyptian pounds, Kenyan shillings and rupees in India and Pakistan.
cut and paste	To move a **highlighted** object by cutting the object and pasting the object into a new location. This holds another copy of the object in the clipboard for if it needs to be pasted again into another location.
cut	To take a **highlighted** object and place it into the clipboard, removing it from its original location.
data capture form	*See* **data collection form.**
data collection form	A form used for collecting data for input to a system, which can be hard copy or screen based.
data flow	The flow of data through a system in terms of input, processing and output.
data flow diagram	A diagram used to represent the way data flows through a system. It is used to show where data comes from in an organisation, how it is processed and where it goes to.
data logging system	The hardware and software used in the collection of data, usually by means of **sensors**. It is often an enclosed system.
database	A collection of data items and the links between them that is organised and stored so that it can be interrogated.
database management system	A complex software system used to control, maintain and manage a **database.**
DAY	Function within *Microsoft Excel* that returns a number between 1 and 31 as the day value from a given date.
DBMS	*See* **database management system.**
decrypt	To remove encryption from received data, thus enabling the user to understand what would otherwise be unintelligible. *See also* **encryption.**
delete	To remove or erase a **highlighted** object.
design	A stage in the **systems life cycle** occurring after an existing system has been analysed and before a new system is created.
desktop publisher	Software that allows text and graphics to be imported from other applications and then arranged and laid out for the production of a printed document.
device	Normally a piece of computer hardware that is used to provide input, output or data storage by reading from or writing to a data medium.
digital divide	The gap between those people who are able to make effective use of ICT, computers and the **Internet** and those who are not.
digital imaging	The use of specialised computer software to make drawings.
direct changeover	A method of **implementation** that involves the replacement of an old system with the new system without time delay.
discrete process control	Microprocessor control of a process whereby several items are produced one at a time, with measured time gaps in between each item.
double entry verification	A type of **verification** where data is entered twice, usually by different users, and the entries compared by the system.
download	To receive a file of data from another computer or network, e.g. the **Internet**.

drag and drop	To move a **highlighted** object by selecting a drag handle and, whilst holding down the left mouse button, dragging the object to a new location.
duty of confidence	The responsibility of an employee to the company they work for and the customers whose personal details they are dealing with to maintain the confidentiality of the data.
duty of fidelity	The responsibility of an employee to remain loyal to the company they work for as long as they are employed there. They should not pass on company secrets to other organisations.
electronic ticket	Replacement for paper tickets that customers normally receive when booking a plane ticket. The electronic ticket (e-ticket) number is stored on the airline computer system and the customer picks up the paper ticket on arrival at the airport.
e-mail editor	Software that allows users to read, create and send e-mail messages.
embedded file	One data file embedded within another file of a different type. Clicking on the embedded file will open the original application and allow editing of the embedded file.
encrypted data	Data that has been changed into a meaningless collection of characters so that it can be transmitted securely.
encryption key	The code that is used to change normal data into **encrypted data.**
encryption	The process of creating **encrypted data.**
end effector	A **device** used in computer **control systems** that is attached to the end of a robot arm so that the arm can perform tasks such as tightening bolts, spray painting and welding.
endnote	Text added to the end of a section or the end of a document, used to make a comment or to provide a reference source.
Ethernet	The basic set of **protocols** that are used to operate a **local area network** .
event chain diagram	A diagram showing the relationship between events and tasks in project management. Many of these can be incorporated in a **Gantt chart.**
examination of documents	One of the four methods used to research how an existing system operates. All documents, input and output, are examined so that the way a system works can be determined.
expected results	The list of expected results of tests that are going to be performed on a new system.
expert system	A computer-based system that makes use of human knowledge to solve problems. It has a **user interface,** a **knowledge base** (consisting of a **rules base** and **database** *of facts*) and an **inference engine.** It is used to determine probabilities of outcomes in a certain scenario such as oil prospecting, car fault diagnosis or medical diagnosis.
extreme data	A type of data used to test a system. Where data must be within a certain range, extreme data is the data on either boundary of the range.
feasibility study	The examination of a situation to see whether a new system is viable or not. If it is, then the project carries on and the new system is created.
fibre optic	A type of cabling used in computer networks, consisting of optical fibres that are individually coated with a plastic resin and then sheathed in a plastic layer.
field	A place used to hold a single data item within a **database.**
field code	Individual item of information taken from the data source in a mail-merged document.
file compression	*See* **zip.**
file look-up check	A **validation** check that makes sure that the data entered matches one of a limited number of valid entries, where these valid entries are stored in an external data file, table or query.
file server	A type of server used to store user data, e.g. documents, presentations, videos, **spreadsheets** and **database** files for access by other computers on the network.

file	A logically organised collection of records, usually where all the records are organised so that they can be stored together within a **database.**
FILLIN	Function used when mail merging in *Microsoft Word* that asks the user to enter text to be placed within the document when the mail merge is run.
filter keys	A facility that causes the computer to ignore brief key presses or where a key is pressed down repeatedly.
firewall	An interface between two networks that prevents access to one from the other by unauthorised computers.
Flash	Software that allows animation and user interaction in web pages – it is sometimes used to create **pop-ups.**
flash memory card	A form of electrically erasable programmable read-only memory (EEPROM), which is solid state memory. It can be used as removable storage.
flat file database	A **database** structure using a simple two-dimensional table.
FM tuner	The radio part of a home entertainment system.
footer	The area at the bottom of a document between the bottom of the page and the bottom margin.
footnote	Text added to the bottom of a page within a document, used to make a comment or to provide a reference source.
format check	A **validation** check that makes sure that the data matches a pre-determined pattern of letters and/or numbers.
format painter	A tool used in many packages to copy the formatting from one part of a document and apply it to another.
forums	A term used to describe **websites** that are used for holding discussions and that allow postings.
forward chaining	A form of reasoning in **expert systems** that produces a number of possible outcomes. It is usually used in diagnosis applications. It allows an expert system to add facts to its **knowledge base.**
Frequently Asked Questions	Typical questions that users of a system ask, together with the answers to such questions, when they don't understand aspects of a system.
Gantt chart	A graphical representation of progress being made in projects, where each task in the project can be represented.
global digital divide	The gap between countries whose economies make effective use of ICT, computers and the **Internet** and those who do not.
graphics package	Software that allows the creation and manipulation of images (pictures) on the computer.
gutter	The part of a document, usually white space outside the page margin, where the document will be bound together.
hacker	An unauthorised user of computer systems.
hacking	The use of illegal methods to gain access to another user's computer.
handshaking	The initial communication between two **devices** that enables exchange of data to take place.
hard coded	Data that is embedded within the program code, e.g. in HTML the setting of font sizes and types, preventing the user from changing them.
head wand	A rod attached to a headband that a person with limited or no limb movement wears, allowing them to press the keys on a keyboard or choose options from a touch screen.

header	The area at the top of a document between the top of the page and the top margin.
help desk	Usually a telephone service, where the operators help people with their problems. It is used frequently to help with technical problems related to computers.
highlight	To select an object, e.g. a piece of text, image, file, cell, etc., so that it can be edited or manipulated.
HLOOKUP	Function within *Microsoft Excel* that looks up data using data organised in horizontal rows.
HOUR	Function within *Microsoft Excel* that returns a number between 0 and 23 as the number of hours shown on a 24-hour clock from a given time.
hub	A **device** that connects computers together in a network and distributes data from one device to the others on the network.
hybrid network	A network made up of star networks where each hub is connected to a common backbone of the type used in **bus networks.**
hyperlink	A reference within an electronic document to another place in the same document or to a different document. Hyperlinks are the foundation of any hypertext system, including the worldwide web. Hyperlinks can be used to open links within different applications packages.
identity theft	The copying of the details of a person for illegal use by another. Copying details of a credit card onto another card is a common method.
IF	Function within *Microsoft Excel* that looks at a given condition and performs an operation if the condition is met, or a different operation if the condition is not met.
If … Then … Else …	Function within mail merge that looks at a given condition and performs an operation if the condition is met, or else performs a different operation if the condition is not met.
implementation	The installing of a new ICT system to replace an existing system.
inference engine	The reasoning part of an expert system, which is used to infer results from the user's inputs.
input device	A **device** that is used to input data to a computer.
input mask	The name given to a format check in some packages such as *Microsoft Access*.
input screen	The screen display that is used to input data, usually consisting of input forms.
instant messaging	The exchange of text messages across the **Internet** in real time between two or more people logged into a particular instant messaging service.
INT	Function within *Microsoft Excel* that calculates the **integer** (whole number) part of a number and ignores all digits after the decimal point.
integer	A whole number with no decimal places.
Internet	A **wide area network** consisting of an international network of computer networks.
Internet protocol	A connectionless **protocol** used for transmitting data across a computer network.
Internet service provider	An enterprise that provides individuals and organisations with access to and the associated services of the **Internet.**
interrupts	A signal from a hardware **device** telling a processor that it needs attention, e.g. used with **TCP** to indicate the non-arrival of a data packet.
interview	A conversation between a person asking questions of a person and the person giving answers.
intranet	A **website** located on a private network within an organisation that is only for the use of members of that organisation. **Internet protocols** are used in the transmission of data.
IP	See **Internet protocol**.

IP address	An address assigned to each **device** connected in an **IP** network that allows the identification of the device for communicating data and usually consists of four bytes of data.
ISP	*See* **Internet service provider.**
Java code	Programming code used to develop web-based applications.
joystick	An input **device** that consists of a stick that is gripped by the hand and moved around, controlling the cursor, pointer or other objects on the screen, and buttons that can be used to select options from menus.
just-in-time system	A method of stock control whereby supplies are ordered just before stock runs out.
knowledge base	Part of an **expert system** consisting of the **database** of facts and the **rules base.**
knowledge engineer	The person responsible for the creation and maintenance of an **expert system.**
LAN	*See* **local area network.**
LCD	*See* **liquid crystal display.**
length check	A **validation** check that makes sure that the data contains no more than a pre-defined number of characters.
line graph	Charts used to graphically represent the relationship between one variable and another.
link	Commonly used abbreviation for **hyperlink.**
linked object	Data placed into the current document/presentation/web page etc. that is updated whenever the original data is changed.
liquid crystal display	A technology used in producing the flat, thin screens used in laptop computers and large screen televisions. It uses very small amounts of electric power.
local area network	A number of computers connected together to share software and hardware either within a small geographical area or within a single building.
look-up check	A **validation** check that makes sure that the data entered matches one of a limited number of valid entries.
lookup	A generic term for looking up specified results from a table of data.
LOOKUP	Function within *Microsoft Excel* which looks up data using the first row or the first column of a range of cells and returns a relative value.
MAC address	*See* **media access control address.**
media access control address	The physical address given to a **device** by the manufacturer – not to be confused with an **IP address** that can be allocated on starting up a network. Each MAC address is unique to its device.
MAC address filtering	A method of security used in wireless networks whereby the **router** prevents access to the network by **devices** with specific **MAC addresses** stipulated by the user.
mainframe computer	A large computer that is accessible from many computer terminals and has extremely large processing power.
MAN	*See* **metropolitan area network.**
market research	The collection and analysis by organisations of information from sections of the public in order to discover the level of demand for a type of product or service.
master file	A file that holds all fixed data but can be updated periodically using a **transaction file.**
MAX	Function within *Microsoft Excel* that calculates the maximum value in a list of numbers.

medium	A material used for holding data which is used by a **device**, e.g. a disk is a storage medium and a disk drive the associated device; paper is an output medium and the printer the output device, etc.
merge codes	Instructions coded (programmed) into a mail merge document that control the format of the merged document and may produce different results (e.g. text or images) depending upon other conditions.
message board	A form of **Internet forum** where members post messages for other users to see.
metropolitan area network	A network similar to a LAN, but one that usually extends over a much larger area such as a whole city. It is often owned by a consortium of users.
MIN	Function within *Microsoft Excel* that calculates the minimum value in a list of numbers.
MINUTE	Function within *Microsoft Excel* that returns a number between 0 and 59 as the number of minutes shown on a clock from a given time.
model	A computer representation of a real-life process.
modelling	Creating a programmed simulation of a situation or process that will allow data to be changed and examining the effect that this has on other data. This is often done with a **spreadsheet** and can be used to predict future trends.
moderator	Person in charge of an Internet forum. They have the power to delete, edit and move postings and can also give warnings to members of the forum if they misuse it.
MONTH	Function within *Microsoft Excel* that returns a number between 1 and 12 as the month value from a given date.
move	To remove a **highlighted** object from one location and place it in a new location.
network interface card	A card that fits into a slot on the **device's** motherboard and is needed for the device to connect to a network and be recognised. It is this card that is allocated the **IP address**.
NIC	*See* **network interface card.**
normal data	Data that is within an acceptable range and is usual for the situation.
NOT	Used to search with two (or more) conditions, where if the condition is True the result is False and if the condition is False the result is True.
numeric	Consisting of numbers: real, integer or fixed decimal.
object linking and embedding	A technology that allows a file to be embedded and linked at the same time to other documents/files and objects. Data that is available in other applications can be accessed and manipulated from the current document/file.
observation	A method of collecting data in the analysis phase of the **systems life cycle**. The **systems analyst** watches and records all the activities going on in the existing system, enabling them to see the process as a whole.
off-the-shelf software	Existing software that a **systems analyst** may recommend for the **implementation** of a new system.
online service	A service provided via the **Internet** that allows users to access the service by using their PC and a **router** or modem, e.g. online shopping and banking.
OR	Used to search with two (or more) conditions, where one (or more) of the conditions must be true for the result to be true.
ordered	The arranging of data in a specific order such as alphabetical or numerical order.
orphan	The first line of the paragraph at the bottom of the page, with the rest of the paragraph appearing on the next page.

overlay	*See* **concept keyboard.**
packet	A block of data grouped together only for transmission across a network.
parallel running	A method of systems **implementation** that has the new system and the old system running side by side until the new system is relatively error free and can be left to run on its own.
parity check	A check performed on transmitted data where one of the bits in a byte of data is used to check that the data has been transmitted correctly.
passive hub	A **hub** that allows the transmission of data without affecting the strength of the data signal. *See also* **active hub.**
password	An authentication technique used to access a computer system. The user types in their username followed by their password which only they know. This method of security relies on the user never revealing their password to other users.
paste	To take a copy of an object from the clipboard and place it in a new location.
PDA	See **personal digital assistant.**
personal digital assistant	A handheld computer fitted with a touch screen that is activated by using a detachable stylus. Text is entered by pressing a keyboard that appears on the screen.
personal identification number	Usually typed in to a PIN reader when using a **chip and PIN** card.
Pert chart	Short for 'project evaluation and review technique', a tool used to evaluate progress in project management with a graphical representation of each task that is needed to bring a project to completion.
pharming	A process whereby the user, typically a bank customer using online banking, of what appears to be a genuine **website** is redirected to a bogus website. The customer thinks they are dealing with their bank but are actually sending their details to a fraudster's website.
phased implementation	A method of systems **implementation** that involves the introduction of the new system one part at a time. This method continues until all aspects of the existing system have been transferred to the new system.
phishing	A method of fraud where the user or customer is sent an e-mail purporting to be from the bank asking for their account details and passwords. On receipt of this information the fraudster is able to access the customer's account online and defraud that person.
physical variable	Usually an analogue form of data found in the physical world that is continually varying, such as temperature, pressure, humidity, etc.
picture check	Another name for **format check.** *See* **format check.**
PID	*See* **proportional-integral-derivative.**
pie chart	Chart used to graphically represent parts of a whole, often with percentage values.
pilot running	A method of systems **implementation** that is implemented in one branch of an organisation whilst the other branches continue with their existing system. The new system is introduced gradually to one branch at a time.
PIN	See **personal identification number.**
pixelated	An effect causing individual pixels in a bitmap image to be enlarged so that each small single-coloured square that makes up the bitmap is visible to the eye.
placeholder	A control placed within a mail merge document that is used to hold **field codes** or **merge codes.**

plasma screen	A type of flat panel screen that is used with high definition television, allowing much larger screens than those associated with cathode ray tube televisions to be used.
PLC	*See* **programmable logic controller.**
podcasting	Audio broadcasts that can be downloaded from the **Internet** and listened to using personal media players.
pop-up	Usually a small separate window that appears when browsing the Internet. It is often used for advertising purposes.
precision framing	The accurate placing of an image (or other object) to align to the page, column margins or other objects upon the page.
presentation authoring package	Software that allows you to create multimedia presentations and displays using a series of linked slides.
price comparison service	A **website** that gives a comparison of prices from different retailers together with a link to the retailer's website.
primary research	A method of data gathering used in **market research** whereby prospective or existing customers are interviewed by the organisation themselves. *See also* **secondary research.**
process control	The use of computers or microprocessors to control a process, usually industrial, such as the maintaining of a production line.
processing	The manipulation of input data to produce a required output from an ICT system.
program (verb)	To create a set of instructions that will produce a required output from an ICT system.
program documentation	The written documents that accompany a program upon **implementation**. It advises on how the program works, what the instructions mean and how to make future amendments.
programmable logic controller	A type of computer or microcomputer that is used for a single purpose. It is able to accept analogue and digital inputs, and a set of logic statements is used to compare the input with a pre-set value. Depending on the result, it activates the output **devices**. *See also* **proportional-integral-derivative.**
programmer	Somebody who writes programs. *See also* **computer programmer.**
programming language	A computer-based language that is used to write code that will use a sequence of instructions to perform a task within the computer.
project management	A method of ensuring that a project is completed within the timescale and monetary budget allowed by a business.
prompt	Text used to instruct the user what information they are required to enter when a mail merge is run.
proportional-integral-derivative	An algorithm that is an integral part of closed loop computer controlled systems. It calculates the difference between the input value and the pre-set value, and then causes the **programmable logic controller** (PLC) to make proportional changes to the output so that the pre-set value is eventually reached.
protocol	A set of rules that governs how communication between two **devices** will occur.
public key authentication	A feature of **encryption** that allows one computer to know that a computer trying to communicate with it is genuine.
public-key	A type of **encryption key** that is given out by a computer to enable other computers to encrypt data to send to it.
purpose-built software	Software that is especially created by **programmers** for a particular situation.

questionnaire	A collection of questions written down on a form that enables collection of data. The answers to the questions are normally completed on the form itself.
range check	Checks that the data is within a given range.
RAS	*See* **remote access services.**
read only	Allows a user to view the document/file but not to make changes to it.
record	A collection of fields containing information about one data subject (usually a person) or one object within a **database.**
relational database	A **database** structure where data items are linked together with relational tables. It maintains a set of separate, related files (tables), but combines data elements from the files for queries and reports when required.
relative referencing	Automatically adjusts a cell reference within a **spreadsheet** to refer to different cells relative to the position of the formula during the replication process.
remote access services	Services that allow people working away from home to access the desktop on their own PC remotely.
remote control	An input **device** that allows the user to control other devices from a distance. It is most frequently used with home entertainment systems.
report layout	How a report (an output form) is set out in terms of, for example, headings and the output from the system.
repository	Single storage area for files edited by multiple users, usually managed by a single user with files saved using version control.
requirements specification	An element of the analysis phase of the **systems life cycle.** It is a list of the features of a system that is required, including general user requirements and specific requirements.
rich text format	A file format (.rtf) used for text-based files that saves the formatting within the document, so allowing some formatting to be passed from one applications package to another.
ring network	An increasingly rare type of network topology. Each computer is connected to each of its neighbours and data is transmitted around the network.
robot	A **device** often used in industrial applications to act independently, having been programmed to carry out a specific task or tasks.
ROUND	Function within *Microsoft Excel* that rounds a number up to a specified number of decimal places.
router	A network device used to connect a **local area network** (LAN) to a **wide area network** (WAN). It handles any differences in the protocols being used by the WAN and LAN, and directs data packets to the correct network.
rules base	In an **expert system**, a set of rules that an **inference engine** uses, together with the data or facts in the **knowledge base**, to reason through a problem.
scenario	A description of a set of circumstances. It is used to set the scene for some examination questions.
screen display	Sometimes used interchangeably with **screen layout**, but usually refers to output as displayed on a computer monitor.
screen layout	The layout of the data on a screen to aid input.
SD memory card	*See* **secure digital memory card.**
SECOND	Function within *Microsoft Excel* that returns a number between 0 and 59 as the number of seconds shown on a clock from a given time.

secondary research	A method of **market research** that involves the examination of research that either the organisation concerned or another organisation has carried out before. *See also* **primary research.**
section	The area of a document that has page formatting that applies throughout that section.
secure digital memory card	A type of memory card used to record digital audio broadcast (DAB) radio programmes and used in digital cameras, handheld computers and global positioning system (GPS) devices.
secure shell	A network **protocol** that is used for remotely accessing a computer or server using **encryption** security.
secure sockets layer	A network **protocol** that uses **encryption** to allow online web transactions.
sensor	A **device** used to monitor physical variables such as temperature and pressure. They are used in monitoring and **control systems.**
shell	Software that provides the **user interface, knowledge base** editor, **inference engine** and explanation system in an **expert system.** The **knowledge engineer** uses it to build a system to solve a particular set of problems.
shopping cart software	Software used to create the representation of a shopping cart for customers to buy goods online.
single stepping	A type of testing after a system has been developed. The system is run one step at a time so that the exact point where the any differences between actual results and expected results occurred can be clearly seen in the programming code.
skimming	A type of identity fraud where a card that is swiped legitimately in a retail outlet is swiped again on another machine that reads all the details from the card. This data is then transferred to a blank card for further use.
SKIPIF	Function within mail merge that allows the mail merge to omit documents if certain conditions are met when the mail merge is run.
speech recognition software	Software that is able to convert input speech to text for use with text-based applications.
spreadsheet	Software used for performing calculations and for modelling situations using data arranged in a grid consisting of rows and columns.
spyware	Software put on a computer with malicious intent that allows people to access that computer and control its functions.
SSH	*See* **secure shell.**
SSL	*See* **secure sockets layer.**
star network	A network topology where each computer or **device** is connected to a central **hub** or **switch**
sticky keys	A feature used in many types of software that allows the user to press combination keys such as <Ctrl> C consecutively rather than simultaneously. It is very helpful for people with poor motor coordination.
storage medium	A medium used for storing data, e.g. magnetic disk, tape or optical disk.
style	Pre-defined settings relating to the formatting of text, such as font size, typeface, font alignment, etc. that can be applied to text to ensure the consistency of display.
submit button	A button or icon found in many input forms that when pressed causes the data on the screen to be stored.
subscript	Characters that sit below the **baseline** in a piece of text and usually have a reduced point size, e.g. the number 2 in H_2O.

SUBTOTAL	Function within *Microsoft Excel* that calculates the function for a range of value or cells. The parameters passed to this function determine how it will work, e.g. it could be used to calculate the SUM, the AVERAGE, etc.
SUM	Function within *Microsoft Excel* that adds up a list of numbers or specified cells.
SUMIF	Function within *Microsoft Excel* that looks at the cells within a given range and adds the total from those cells that meet a given condition.
supercomputer	A computer that has hundreds of thousands of dual processors. It is a collection of computers that are connected through a high-speed network.
superscript	Characters that sit above the **baseline** in a piece of text and usually have a reduced point size, e.g. the number 2 in $7\,m^2$.
switch	A **device** that can have a number of other devices or computers connected to it. It is able to direct network traffic using the **MAC address** of a data **packet.**
systems analysis	A phase in the **systems life cycle**. When an existing system is to be replaced by a new system, this phase involves examining the existing system in detail using some or all of **interviewing** users, giving **questionnaires** to users, **observation** of people using the existing system and **examination of documents** used in the existing system.
systems analyst	An individual who is responsible for the phases of the **systems life cycle** being carried out.
systems documentation	A detailed overview of the whole system, including test plans, test results, the results of the analysis of the existing system, what is expected of the system and decisions that were made at the **design** stage.
systems flowchart	Used in the design of a new system, a diagrammatical representation of how data will flow through the new system. It includes programming requirements, although not the detail of programming required.
systems life cycle	The stages in the creation or modification of a new information system.
table	A two-dimensional grid of data organised by rows and columns within a **database**. Each row of the table contains a record. Each column in the table represents a **field** and each cell in that column has the same (pre-defined) field type.
TAN	*See* **transaction number.**
TCP	*See* **transmission control protocol.**
technical documentation	Documentation that accompanies a new or modified information system. It is developed to help any **systems analyst** or **programmer** understand the technical aspects of the system.
teleworking	A method of working that involves employees spending all or some of their working week at home, using their home as an office and making use of ICT to do so.
terminator	The endpoint at either end of the spine in a **bus network.**
text editor	Software that allows you to type and edit plain text. It contains few or no features that allow formatting of documents.
text file	A file format (.txt) used for text-based files that contains an unformatted ASCII file, although there are file format variations depending upon the operating system. These files can be opened in any **word processor.**
text wrapping	A feature to make the text automatically wrap around any object (e.g. a text box or frame) in a document.
TEXT	Function within *Microsoft Excel* that changes the formatting of the current cell from a numeric or date/time value into text format.

touch screen	An input **device** that allows the user to choose from options on the screen by pressing the option on the screen with a finger.
tracked changes	An electronic record of all changes made to a document during editing. This shows the changes made and usually includes the editor's name and when the changes were made.
tracker ball	A **device** that looks like an upside-down mouse and is designed for users who have limited ability regarding movement of their fingers or hand. The key feature is the large ball in the middle of the device that is controlled by using the palm of the hand and enables the user to control the pointer on a screen. There are also a number of buttons, depending on the application.
transaction file	A working file used in **database management systems** that contains transactions that, when used together with a **master file**, produce the required output and an updated master file.
transaction number	A password that is used once only as a security method in online banking.
transmission control protocol	A network **protocol** for the transmission of data that ensures that data is delivered accurately.
transponder	A **device** used for transmitting television programmes. It is attached to a communications satellite, which receives signals from the **uplink satellite dish** and transmits them back to earth to receiving satellite dishes.
Trojan horse	A program similar in effect to a **virus** except that it does not replicate itself. It appears to be a useful piece of software, but when executed deletes files on the hard disk.
troubleshooting guide	Part of user documentation that comes with a new ICT system. It advises users on how to overcome commonly occurring problems.
tunnelling	The use of a publicly accessible network to carry **encrypted data** from source to destination computers.
twisted pair	Type of network cable used to transmit data between **devices** on a network. It consists of two conducting wires twisted around each other. This reduces the magnetic interference and hence data loss during transmission.
type check	A **validation** check that makes sure that the data is of a particular data type.
UDP	See **user datagram protocol**.
uniform resource locator	The unique address of any document found on the **Internet**. Typically the address is divided into parts. The first part of the address gives the **protocol**, commonly HTTP, the second part gives the name of the computer (e.g. www.cie.org.uk). There is sometimes a third part which gives the directory on the computer where the document file name can be found.
universal serial bus port	A type of port that allows a variety of **devices** to connect to computers or microprocessors so that data can be received from or sent to the devices.
unordered	An unordered file of data is one wherein the data is not in any particular order. It is not sorted on any particular field.
Uplink satellite dish	A very large satellite dish used by television broadcasters to transmit programme signals to a communications satellite for onward transmission to satellite receivers.
URL	*See* **uniform resource locator**.
USB port	*See* **universal serial bus port**.
user datagram protocol	A very basic network protocol offering a connectionless service i.e. no handshaking takes place.

user documentation	Documentation that is provided to the user of a new ICT system to enable the user to understand how to operate the new system.
username	The identifier a user types into an ICT system in order to gain access to the system. Every user has a unique username so that authentication can be carried out.
user interface	The method by which a computer interacts with a user. It normally consists of a specially designed screen that allows the user to input information as well as providing output to the user.
validation	A process where the software checks that the data entered into it is reasonable, often in a **database** or **spreadsheet.**
vector graphics	A graphics format that draws and controls the properties of points, lines, curves and polygons using mathematical equations, ensuring that when an image is enlarged there is little loss of quality.
verification	A process that checks the accuracy of data entry or that data has not been corrupted during transmission, often using **double entry** or **visual verification.**
version control	A filenaming convention used to manage files edited by multiple users, where each saved version of a file is given a managed naming convention, often identifying sequential version numbers and sometimes authors' initials.
video-on-demand	A system that allows viewers to watch video over a network. The film is either constantly being transmitted over the network or downloaded in one go to a set-top box, allowing the viewer to watch it at their convenience.
virtual private network	The use of publicly accessible networks to communicate private information. It is not physically private but involves the use of security methods that make it practically impenetrable.
virus	A software program that can replicate itself over and over again on a hard disk. It also transfers from one computer to another and may modify or delete files from a hard disk.
visual verification	A type of **verification** where data is entered and the original data is compared visually to the data entered into the system.
VLOOKUP	Function within *Microsoft Excel* that looks up data using data organised in vertical columns.
VOD	*See* **video-on-demand.**
voice over IP	The use of the **Internet** to send voice data in the form of digital data packets using **Internet protocols.**
VOIP	*See* **voice over IP.**
VPN	*See* **virtual private network.**
web authoring package	Software used for creating web pages.
web browser	Software that allows you to display web pages from an **intranet** or the **Internet.**
web server	The name given to both the hardware and software required for the hosting of websites. Large organisations often have their own web servers but small organisations tend to use a hosted web server.
webcams	Miniature video cameras that are connected to computers to transmit video across a network. Their main use is in videoconferencing.
weblog	*See* **blog.**
website	A collection of interrelated web pages that relate to one topic or organisation and are usually accessible via the **Internet.**

WEEKDAY	Function within *Microsoft Excel* that returns a number between 1 and 7 from a given date. If the day is a Sunday, 1 is returned, Monday is 2 and so on.
wide area networks	A network formed by connecting several **local area networks** together using **routers** or modems.
widow	A last line of text of a paragraph that appears at the top of a page, with the rest of the paragraph on the previous page.
Wi-Fi protected access	A method of wireless network security that has very complex encryption, with long keys, and that also incorporates user authentication.
wiki	A **website** created for the purpose of any user who has access to it being able to edit it.
wireless access point	A means of connecting wireless **devices** to a wired network.
wireless local area network	A **local area network** with no wires or cables, other than the wiring that connects the WLAN access points together. A WLAN uses either spread spectrum radio waves or infrared signals to enable **devices** to communicate with each other.
wireless network interface controller	A **device** that acts like a network card but communicates by transmitting data in the form of radio waves rather than by using cables.
wireless personal area network	A small communications network usually created for use by just one person using **Bluetooth** technology.
WLAN	*See* **wireless local area network.**
WNIC	*See* **wireless network interface controller.**
word processor	Software that allows you to create, edit and format documents.
worldwide web	A system of connected HTML documents accessed via the **Internet** using a **web browser.**
worm	A piece of destructive software that replicates like a **virus** but uses information about the method of communication a networked computer uses to cause itself to be transported to another computer.
WPA	*See* **Wi-Fi protected access.**
WPAN	*See* **wireless personal area network.**
YEAR	Function within *Microsoft Excel* that returns the year from a given date.
zip	To reduce the number of bytes needed to save a file, either to save storage space or to reduce transmission time.

Index